D1567941

Pearson
ECONOMICS

Marcel Lewinski • Grant Wiggins

PEARSON

Upper Saddle River, New Jersey • Boston, Massachusetts • Chandler, Arizona • Glenview, Illinois

For Student Edition with Online Student Center 6-year access, order ISBN: 0-7854-6996-6
ISBN-13: 978-0-78-5468578
ISBN-10:   0-78-546857-9
5 6 7 8 9 10 V011 15 14 13 12 11

PEARSON

About the Author

Marcel Lewinski

Marcel Lewinski is currently Adjunct Professor of History Education at Illinois State University. Previously, he was an award-winning high school social studies teacher. He has taught a wide range of subjects, including economics, world history, United States history, geography, political science, sociology, and contemporary problems. Lewinski is professionally active in many organizations and has given presentations at many state, regional, and national conferences. He has conducted numerous workshops for social studies teachers and has traveled all over the world. As author of several books on social studies, Lewinski acts as a consultant to school systems and has served as a contributor to various educational publications.

Program Reviewers

Consulting Author

Grant Wiggins

Grant Wiggins is the President of Authentic Education in Hopewell, New Jersey. He earned his Ed.D. from Harvard University and his B.A. from St. John's College in Annapolis. Wiggins consults with schools, districts, and state education departments on a variety of reform matters; organizes conferences and workshops; and develops print materials and Web resources on curricular change. He is the co-author of award-winning and highly successful materials on curriculum published by the Association for Supervision of Curriculum Development (ASCD). His work has been supported by the Pew Charitable Trusts, the Geraldine R. Dodge Foundation, and the National Science Foundation.

Over the past twenty years, Wiggins has worked on some of the most influential reform initiatives in the country, including Vermont's portfolio system and Ted Sizer's Coalition of Essential Schools. He has established statewide consortia devoted to assessment reform for the states of North Carolina and New Jersey. Wiggins is the author of *Educative Assessment* and *Assessing Student Performance,* both published by Jossey-Bass. His many articles have appeared in such journals as *Educational Leadership* and *Phi Delta Kappan.*

v

Contents in Brief

UNIT 1 Introduction to Economics

INTRODUCTION

Essential Question, Unit 1

How does economics affect everyone?

Chapter 1
How can we make the best economic choices?

Chapter 2
How does society decide who gets what goods and services?

Chapter 3
What role should government play in a free market economy?

Go online with Unit 1
Find these interactive resources at PearsonSuccessNet.com

Visual Glossary online
- Opportunity Cost
- Incentives
- Free Enterprise

How the Economy Works online
- What does an entrepreneur do?
- How can innovation lead to economic growth?
- How are public goods created?

Video News Update Online
Powered by *The Wall Street Journal* Classroom Edition
- Watch video clips of current economic issues in the news.

Economics on the go
- Action Graphs
- Content Review Audio
- Economic Dictionary Audio

WebQuest online
- The Economics WebQuest challenges students to use 21st century skills to answer the Essential Question.

MICROECONOMICS

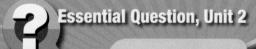

Essential Question, Unit 2

Who benefits from the free market economy?

Chapter 4
How do we decide what to buy?

Chapter 5
How do suppliers decide what goods and services to offer?

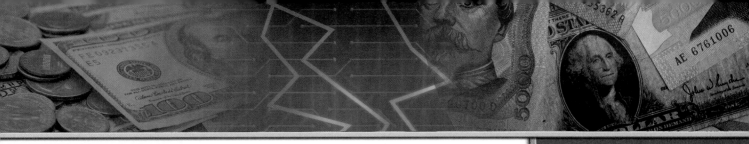

Go online with Unit 2
Find these interactive resources at PearsonSuccessNet.com

Visual Glossary online

- Law of Demand
- Law of Supply
- Equilibrium
- Perfect Competition

How the Economy Works online

- How does elasticity affect consumer demand?
- What are production costs?
- How does a market react to a shortage?
- How is broadcasting regulated?

Video News Update Online
Powered by
The Wall Street Journal Classroom Edition

- Watch video clips of current economic issues in the news.

Economics *on the go*

- Action Graphs
- Content Review Audio
- Economic Dictionary Audio

WebQuest online

- The Economics WebQuest challenges students to use 21st century skills to answer the Essential Question.

Chapter 6
What is the right price?

Chapter 7
How does competition affect your choices?

MICROECONOMICS

Go online with Unit 3
Find these interactive resources at PearsonSuccessNet.com

Visual Glossary online

• Corporation
• Productivity of Labor

How the Economy Works online

• How can a small business grow?
• How can collective bargaining settle differences?

Video News Update Online
Powered by
The Wall Street Journal
Classroom Edition

• Watch video clips of current economic issues in the news.

Economics on the go

• Action Graphs
• Content Review Audio
• Economic Dictionary Audio

WebQuest online

• The Economics WebQuest challenges students to use 21st century skills to answer the Essential Question.

Essential Question, Unit 3

How can businesses and labor best achieve their goals?

Chapter 8
Why do some businesses succeed and others fail?

Chapter 9
How can workers best meet the challenges of a changing economy?

UNIT 4 Money, Banking, and Finance

MACROECONOMICS

Go online with Unit 4
Find these interactive resources at PearsonSuccessNet.com

Visual Glossary online
- Money
- Capital Gains

How the Economy Works online
- How does the fractional reserve system work?
- What is the function of a municipal bond?

Video News Update Online
Powered by
The Wall Street Journal
Classroom Edition
- Watch video clips of current economic issues in the news.

Economics on the go
- Action Graphs
- Content Review Audio
- Economic Dictionary Audio

WebQuest online
- The Economics WebQuest challenges students to use 21st century skills to answer the Essential Question.

Essential Question, Unit 4

How can you make the most of your money?

Chapter 10
How well do financial institutions serve our needs?

Chapter 11
How do your saving and investment choices affect your future?

MACROECONOMICS

Go online with Unit 5
Find these interactive resources at PearsonSuccessNet.com

Visual Glossary online
- Gross Domestic Product
- Inflation

How the Economy Works online
- What causes a recession?
- How do workers deal with structural unemployment?

Video News Update Online
Powered by
The Wall Street Journal
Classroom Edition
- Watch video clips of current economic issues in the news.

Economics on the go
- Action Graphs
- Content Review Audio
- Economic Dictionary Audio

WebQuest online
- The Economics WebQuest challenges students to use 21st century skills to answer the Essential Question.

Essential Question, Unit 5

Why does it matter how the economy is doing?

Chapter 12
How do we know if the economy is healthy?

Chapter 13
How much can we reduce unemployment, inflation, and poverty?

UNIT 6 Government and the Economy

MACROECONOMICS

Essential Question, Unit 6

What is the proper role of government in the economy?

Chapter 14
How can taxation meet the needs of government and the people?

Chapter 15
How effective is fiscal policy as an economic tool?

Chapter 16
How effective is monetary policy as an economic tool?

Go online with Unit 6
Find these interactive resources at PearsonSuccessNet.com

Visual Glossary online
- Progressive Income Taxes
- Fiscal Policy
- Monetary Policy

How the Economy Works online
- Where do your federal taxes go?
- What causes the national debt to spiral?
- How does the Fed make monetary policy?

Video News Update Online
Powered by
The Wall Street Journal Classroom Edition
- Watch video clips of current economic issues in the news.

Economics on the go
- Action Graphs
- Content Review Audio
- Economic Dictionary Audio

WebQuest online
- The Economics WebQuest challenges students to use 21st century skills to answer the Essential Question.

UNIT 7 The Global Economy

MACROECONOMICS

Go online with Unit 7
Find these interactive resources at PearsonSuccessNet.com

Visual Glossary online

- Free Trade
- Globalization

How the Economy Works online

- How do specialization and trade benefit nations?
- What are the stages of economic development?

Video News Update Online
Powered by
The Wall Street Journal Classroom Edition

- Watch video clips of current economic issues in the news.

Economics on the go

- Action Graphs
- Content Review Audio
- Economic Dictionary Audio

WebQuest online

- The Economics WebQuest challenges students to use 21st century skills to answer the Essential Question.

Essential Question, Unit 7

How might scarcity divide our world or bring it together?

Chapter 17
Should free trade be encouraged?

Chapter 18
Do the benefits of economic development outweigh the costs?

Personal Finance Handbook

Special Features

Graphs, Charts, and Tables

Many graphs, charts, and tables help you visualize key economic concepts.

Action Graph
online

Graphs and charts labeled with the **Action Graph** icon have been specially enhanced online. To view these animated charts, visit **PearsonSuccessNet.com** The online label indicates an Action Graph.

▶ Economics & YOU

Read and view illustrations to understand how economic principles can affect high school students.

Economics & YOU

The Substitution Effect

When the price of one good increases, people have an incentive to buy substitutes. *Your decision to purchase a less expensive lunch is the substitution effect in action.*

Roast Beef sandwich $4.50 $5.25

Chili $1.99

REDUCED

The substitution effect also applies when a drop in price creates a cheaper alternative. *Your purchase of the reduced-price car is another example of the substitution effect.*

Complex and difficult content is visually displayed to explain how economic principles can affect you.

How the Economy Works

View the illustrated diagrams to understand the processes by which our economy operates.

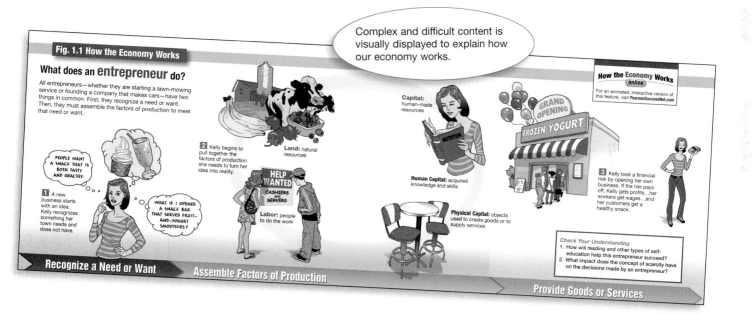

▶ Innovators

See how creative entrepreneurs and other individuals have affected our economy and daily life.

▲ Melinda and Bill Gates

Career Center

Look into the future—explore your different career paths and opportunities.

Complex and difficult content is visually displayed to explain different career opportunities.

Career Center
Computer Science

Careers in Computer Science
- Computer applications engineer
- Internet Web designer
- Computer programmer
- Database administrator
- Systems administrator

Profile: Internet Web designer

Duties
- connect people, businesses, and organizations to the Internet by designing Web sites
- design, construct, test, and maintain Web sites based on analysis of user needs

Education
- bachelor's degree in computer science

Skills
- strong problem-solving skills
- ability to communicate well with team members and customers

Median Annual Salary
- $108,070 (2007)

Outlook
- Expected to experience 28 percent growth

How to Use This Program

Economics is all around you. Developing an understanding of the impact of economic principles on your day-to-day life will help you to make better economic choices. It will prepare you to live in a global economy. It is money in your pocket.

Economics is organized around Essential Questions. An Essential Question is a launching pad for exploring ideas. It doesn't have just one right answer. The answer to an Essential Question changes as you learn more or as circumstances change.

WebQuest online

To complete the Chapter Essential Question WebQuest, visit **PearsonSuccessNet.com**

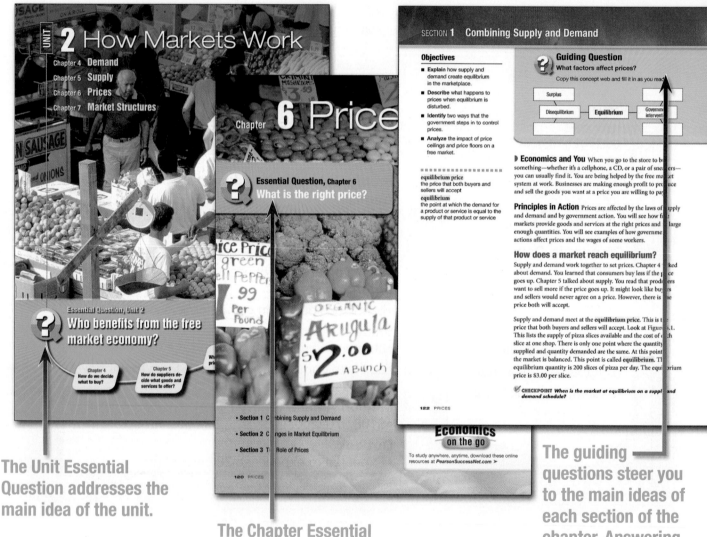

The Unit Essential Question addresses the main idea of the unit.

The Chapter Essential Question addresses the main idea of each chapter. Answering the Chapter Essential Question helps you answer the Unit Essential Question.

The guiding questions steer you to the main ideas of each section of the chapter. Answering the Section Guiding Questions helps you think about the Chapter Essential Question.

"Once you have learned to question and to persist in your questioning, nothing can stop you. That's why a curriculum framed around Essential Questions is so important.**"**
—Grant Wiggins, coauthor of *Understanding by Design*

Essential Questions Journal

Use your Essential Questions Journal to build answers to Essential Questions.

Also available online at PearsonSuccessNet.com

How to Use This Program

In your textbook

Every chapter has a How the Economy Works feature that helps you visualize economic principles in action.

1 Follow the numbered steps.

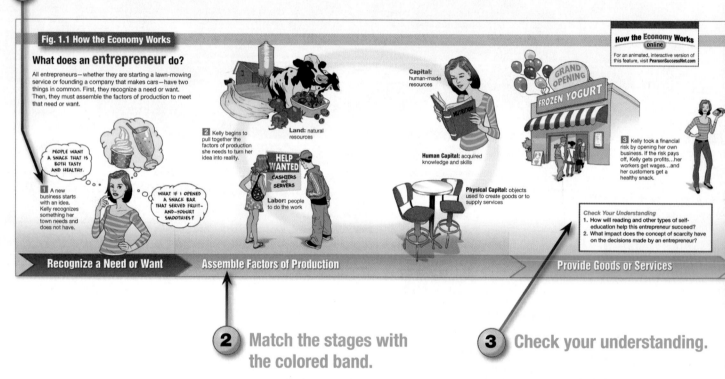

Fig. 1.1 How the Economy Works

How the Economy Works online
For an animated, interactive version of this feature, visit PearsonSuccessNet.com

What does an **entrepreneur** do?

All entrepreneurs—whether they are starting a lawn-mowing service or founding a company that makes cars—have two things in common. First, they recognize a need or want. Then, they must assemble the factors of production to meet that need or want.

PEOPLE WANT A SNACK THAT IS BOTH TASTY AND HEALTHY.

1 A new business starts with an idea. Kelly recognizes something her town needs and does not have.

WHAT IF I OPENED A SNACK BAR THAT SERVED FRUIT-AND-YOGURT SMOOTHIES?

2 Kelly begins to pull together the factors of production she needs to turn her idea into reality.

Land: natural resources

HELP WANTED CASHIERS and SERVERS

Labor: people to do the work

Capital: human-made resources

Human Capital: acquired knowledge and skills

Physical Capital: objects used to create goods or to supply services

3 Kelly took a financial risk by opening her own business. If the risk pays off, Kelly gets profits...her workers get wages...and her customers get a healthy snack.

Check Your Understanding
1. How will reading and other types of self-education help this entrepreneur succeed?
2. What impact does the concept of scarcity have on the decisions made by an entrepreneur?

Recognize a Need or Want | Assemble Factors of Production | Provide Goods or Services

2 Match the stages with the colored band.

3 Check your understanding.

Go online at PearsonSuccessNet.com

Use an interactive version of How the Economy Works to help you learn. ▼

Fig. 6.5 How the Economy Works

How does a market react to a shortage?

◀ Download the Visual Glossary or animated versions of How the Economy Works and Action Graphs to your MP3 player. Study anytime, anywhere.

online

VISUAL GLOSSARY

Use the Visual Glossary online to learn the meaning of key economic terms.

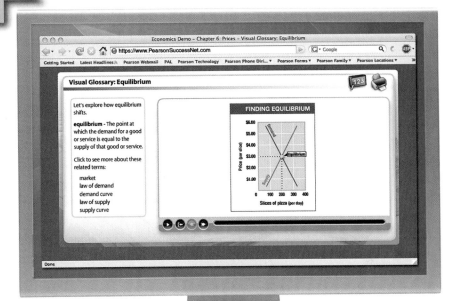

Visual Glossary: Equilibrium

Let's explore how equilibrium shifts.

equilibrium - The point at which the demand for a good or service is equal to the supply of that good or service.

Click to see more about these related terms:

market
law of demand
demand curve
law of supply
supply curve

FINDING EQUILIBRIUM

Why do governments track business cycles?

There are two branches of economics. In **macroeconomics,** economists look at the big picture. They study the overall economy using information such as unemployment, inflation, production, and price levels. One way of looking at an economy as a whole is to figure out the **gross domestic product** (GDP). The GDP is the total value of all final goods and services produced in a country in one year. It is an important measure of an economy. It allows us to make comparisons among different countries. It also allows us ~~to see how one economy is doing compared~~

Action Graph
online

Follow the references on the text page to the Action Graph. Action Graphs present economic principles in a graphic format.

Fig. 3.1
Gross Domestic Product 1900–2006

SOURCE: Louis D. Johnston and Samuel H. Williamson, "What Was the U.S. GDP Then?" MeasuringWorth.Com, 2007.

GRAPH SKILLS

A growing GDP is one sign of a healthy economy.

1. How much did GDP grow between 1990 and 2006?
2. Which periods in this graph may represent downturns in the business cycle?

Action Graph
online

For an animated version of this graph, visit **PearsonSuccessNet.com**

How to Use This Program

Before long, you will be out on your own and managing your own household. In order to be successful, you will have to manage your money, no matter how much or how little you have. The Personal Finance Handbook on pages PF1–PF49 gives you useful guidelines for making the most of your money and avoiding consumer errors.

WebQuest online

Go online for a hands-on experience. Take what you have learned and put it into action. Prepare yourself for navigating the real world of money and finance.

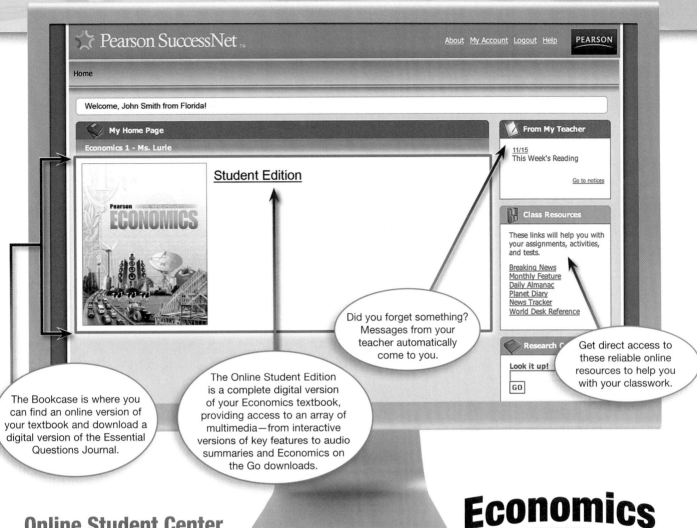

Online Student Center

Visit Economics Online at
PearsonSuccessNet.com to access your
assignments, review key concepts, and
download Economics on the Go.

Economics *online*

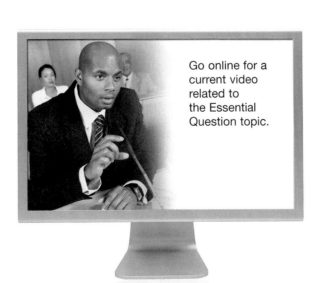

Video News Update Online
Powered by
The Wall Street Journal
Classroom Edition

Graph Preview

Economists collect and evaluate data to develop and test their ideas. They display their ideas and the data that support them in charts and graphs to make their ideas easier to understand. As you study economics, you will see many graphs. Graphs in this book that include the Action Graph logo have an animated version online. You can download them to your MP3 player.

▶ Interpreting Line Graphs

Economists track trends in the economy. Graphs are useful to present large amounts of data visually. Line graphs show changes over time. To interpret a graph, you have to identify the type of data presented.

If you analyze the graph below, you can see a trend. The tax rate went up sharply during the 1930s and 1940s. Since then, it has slowly gone back down.

The title of the graph tells you the topic of the graph.

Fig. 15.4 Top Marginal Tax Rate, 1925–2007

The label on the y-axis tells you what the numbers on the vertical axis represent.

On this graph, it is the percentage of income paid in taxes each year.

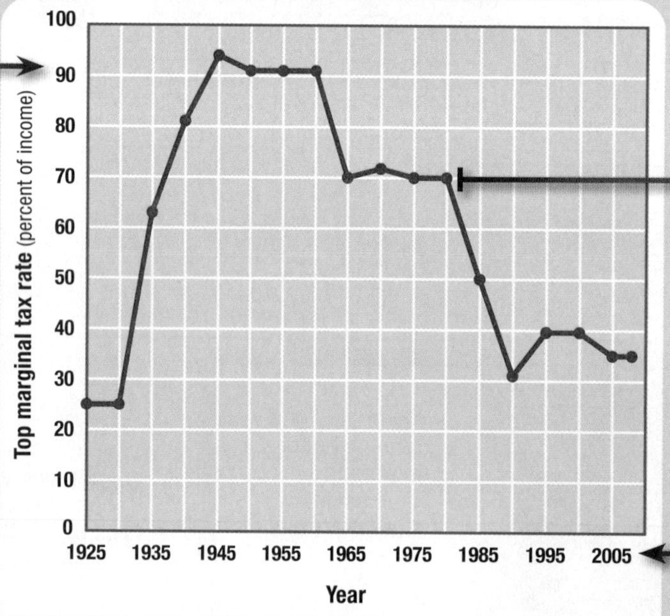

Each point on the graph represents a value of the data. This chart shows that between 1930 and 1945, the tax rate increased from 25 percent to 95 percent. In general, tax rates have dropped since then. The lowest rate since 1930 occurred in 1990.

SOURCE: Tax Policy Center: Urban Institute and Brookings Institute

The label on the x-axis tells you what the numbers on the horizontal axis represent.

The source line tells you where the data come from.

On this graph, it is the span of years over which the changes occurred.

▶ Interpreting Bar Graphs

Bar graphs show the relationships between two or more sets of data. They also illustrate trends. In the bar graph below, the relationship is between level of education and the mean, or average, income for men and women. You can use the data on this graph to make two generalizations about levels of income: on average, men earn more money than women, and the more education a person has, the more money the person is likely to earn.

Follow the same steps used to interpret a line graph.

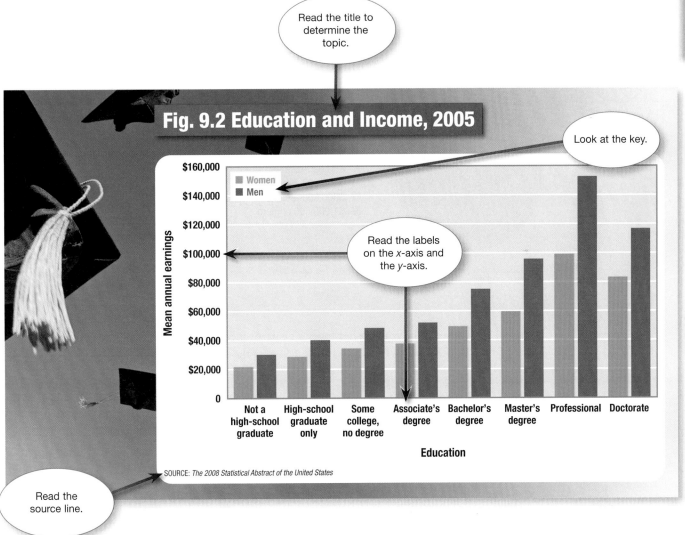

Read the title to determine the topic.

Fig. 9.2 Education and Income, 2005

Look at the key.

Read the labels on the *x*-axis and the *y*-axis.

Mean annual earnings

- Women
- Men

$160,000
$140,000
$120,000
$100,000
$80,000
$60,000
$40,000
$20,000
0

Not a high-school graduate | High-school graduate only | Some college, no degree | Associate's degree | Bachelor's degree | Master's degree | Professional | Doctorate

Education

SOURCE: *The 2008 Statistical Abstract of the United States*

Read the source line.

▶ Using Circle Graphs

Circle graphs show how individual parts relate to a whole. Circle graphs are also known as pie charts, because they look like a pie cut in wedges. Circle graphs represent 100 percent of a given field. The circle graph below shows income information about businesses run by a single owner, or proprietor. Use the key to identify what each wedge represents.

Match the blue color, which occupies 67 percent of the circle, with the information on the key. You see that 67 percent of businesses run by a single owner show income of less than $25,000 per year. Only 1 percent of businesses with a single owner earn $1,000,000 or more per year.

Fig. 8.1 Characteristics of Proprietorships

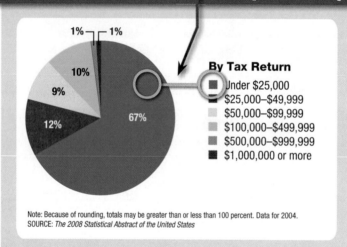

By Tax Return
- Under $25,000
- $25,000–$49,999
- $50,000–$99,999
- $100,000–$499,999
- $500,000–$999,999
- $1,000,000 or more

Note: Because of rounding, totals may be greater than or less than 100 percent. Data for 2004.
SOURCE: *The 2008 Statistical Abstract of the United States*

NOTE Because of rounding, the totals on a circle graph may be greater than or less than 100 percent.

For example: 5.8 rounds up to 6 percent, and 4.4 rounds down to 4 percent. When you add 5.8 and 4.4, the total is 10.2 percent. On a circle graph, these amounts would be displayed as 6 percent and 4 percent, adding up to a total of 10 percent.

Data can be transferred from a chart or table to a graph. The data in the chart below provide the same information as the circle graph above.

Income	Percentage
Under $25,000	67
$25,000–$49,999	12
$50,000–$99,999	9
$100,000–$499,999	10
$500,000–$999,999	1
$1,000,000 or more	1

▶ Understanding Population Pyramids

Population pyramids, or age structures, show the distribution of population by age and gender. They are called pyramids because in many instances they are wider at the bottom and narrower at the top.

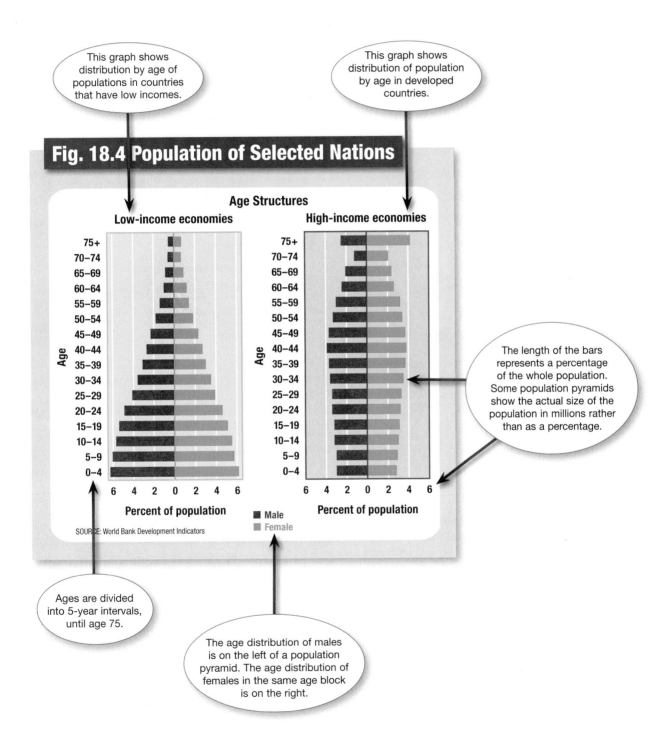

This graph shows distribution by age of populations in countries that have low incomes.

This graph shows distribution of population by age in developed countries.

Fig. 18.4 Population of Selected Nations

Age Structures

Low-income economies

High-income economies

The length of the bars represents a percentage of the whole population. Some population pyramids show the actual size of the population in millions rather than as a percentage.

SOURCE: World Bank Development Indicators

■ Male
■ Female

Ages are divided into 5-year intervals, until age 75.

The age distribution of males is on the left of a population pyramid. The age distribution of females in the same age block is on the right.

▶ Reading Circular Flow Models

Some charts used in economics do not present data. Instead they illustrate an economic process. The circular flow model shows how two basic parts of an economy work together. In this illustration of the macroeconomy at work, the two elements are households or consumers and firms or businesses.

Everything on this simplified chart is happening at the same time. The movement of the economy never stops.

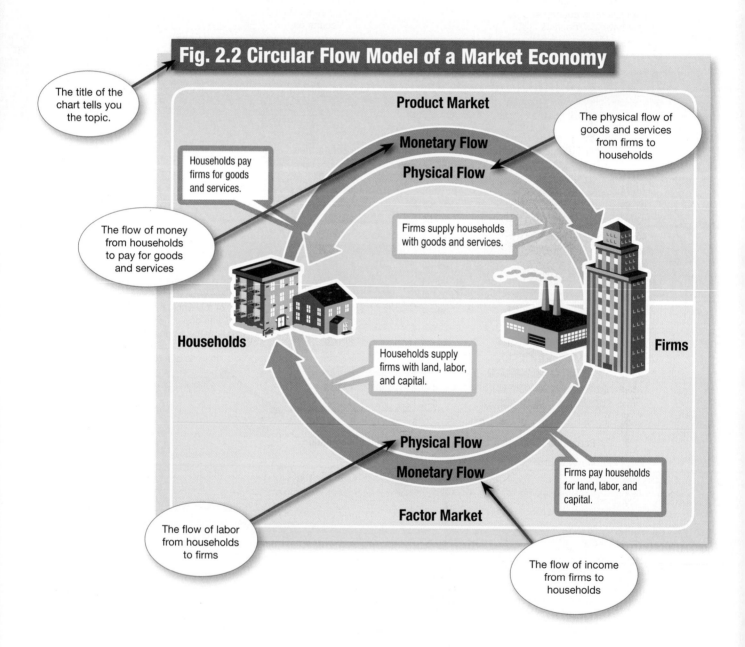

Fig. 2.2 Circular Flow Model of a Market Economy

The title of the chart tells you the topic.

Product Market

Monetary Flow

Physical Flow

The physical flow of goods and services from firms to households

Households pay firms for goods and services.

Firms supply households with goods and services.

The flow of money from households to pay for goods and services

Households

Households supply firms with land, labor, and capital.

Firms

Physical Flow

Monetary Flow

Firms pay households for land, labor, and capital.

Factor Market

The flow of labor from households to firms

The flow of income from firms to households

UNIT

1 Introduction to Economics

Essential Question, Unit 1

How does economics affect everyone?

Chapter 3
What role should government play in a free market economy?

Chapter 1
How can we make the best economic choices?

Chapter 2
How does a society decide who gets what goods and services?

Chapter 1 What Is Economics?

- **Section 1** Scarcity and the Factors of Production

- **Section 2** Opportunity Cost

- **Section 3** Production Possibilities Curves

Economics on the go

To study anywhere, anytime, download these online resources at *PearsonSuccessNet.com* ➤

▶ **Which CD to buy?** How many hours to study? Which movie to see? If you are like most people, you constantly face decisions like these. That is because you do not have enough time and money to do everything. You have probably taken part in economics without even knowing it. All you need to do is make a purchase. When you buy something, you become part of a larger system. Businesses, government, and people like you are all part of this system.

Economics is the study of how people make choices when they face a limited supply of resources. In this chapter you will begin your study of economics. You will start by learning about two basic economic ideas: scarcity and trade-offs.

■ ■

Reading Strategy: Summarizing
When you summarize something you are reading, you restate the information in your own words. As you read the text in this chapter, ask yourself the following questions:

• Who or what is this chapter about?

• What is the main thing being said about this topic?

• What details are important to understanding this chapter?

Visual Glossary
online

Go to the Visual Glossary Online for an interactive review of **opportunity cost.**

How the Economy Works
online

Go to How the Economy Works Online for an interactive lesson on **entrepreneur.**

Action Graph
online

Go to Action Graph Online for animated versions of key charts and graphs.

Objectives

- **Explain** why scarcity and choice are the basis of economics.
- **Describe** what entrepreneurs do.
- **Define** the three factors of production and the differences between physical and human capital.
- **Explain** how scarcity affects the factors of production.

economics
the study of how people seek to satisfy their needs and wants by making choices

scarcity
the principle that limited amounts of goods and services are available to meet unlimited wants

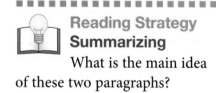

Reading Strategy
Summarizing
    What is the main idea of these two paragraphs?

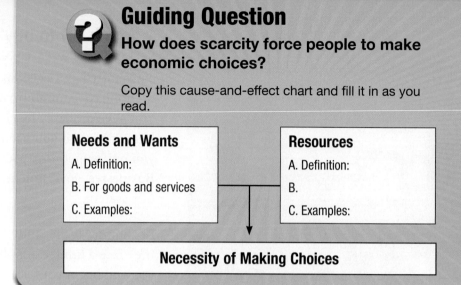

Guiding Question

How does scarcity force people to make economic choices?

Copy this cause-and-effect chart and fill it in as you read.

Needs and Wants
A. Definition:
B. For goods and services
C. Examples:

Resources
A. Definition:
B.
C. Examples:

Necessity of Making Choices

▶ **Economics and You** Decisions are not easy. There are so many ways you could spend your money. You really want that new video game that just hit the stores. You also want to see a concert that is coming. Yet, at the same time, you need to pay your car insurance. You only have a limited amount of money. You cannot have it all. How will you choose?

Principles in Action Scarcity forces us all to make choices. It makes us decide which choices are most important to us. In this section, you will examine the problem of scarcity. You will see how scarcity relates to resources such as water.

How does scarcity force us to make choices?

Economics is the study of how we make choices when faced with a limited supply of resources. Individuals, businesses, and governments all need to make choices because of scarcity. **Scarcity** is the most basic economic problem. Our wants are greater than what is available. Scarcity forces us to decide what is most important to us.

We cannot have everything we need or want. We all have to make choices. We have to choose whether we want to spend our time playing basketball, surfing the Internet, or doing homework. Businesses have to choose whether to hire more workers and how much of a product to make. The local government has to choose between repairing roads and building a new school.

What is the difference between needs and wants?

All people share certain **needs.** A need is something that is necessary to remain alive. To survive, we all need food, water, clothing, and a place to live. Governments also have needs. Many people think that a strong military defense, good schools, and a safe environment are needs. Most of us want more than just the basic needs. Our **wants** are things that we do not need to survive but that make our lives better.

What are goods and services?

Goods are the things that people, businesses, and governments buy. Cars, televisions, and beds are examples of goods. Goods are manufactured. Manufacturing is the process of turning materials into products we use. Some everyday products are soap, radios, TVs, eyeglasses, school buses, and even textbooks. **Services** are the work done for other people for a fee. The action can be performed by another person or business or by the government. Most of the jobs in the United States and Canada are service jobs. For example, your teacher provides a service. Doctors, store clerks, soldiers, and postal workers all provide a service.

Why are our resources limited?

As you have learned, scarcity forces us to make choices. Every country and person has **resources** they use to get the things they need and want. A resource is anything that people use to make things or to do work. Resources are limited. Our wants and needs are always greater than the resources we have to meet them. People, businesses, and governments all have choices to make.

Is scarcity the same thing as shortage?

Scarcity is not the same thing as a **shortage.** Shortages can be renewed or replaced. For example, let's say you want a popular new electronic game, but the stores are out of them. This is a shortage, not scarcity. The game maker can make more games. How about fresh water? There seems to be plenty of water, but no more can be made. This is scarcity.

For something to be considered scarce, it must meet three requirements:
  1. It must be something we really desire.
  2. It must have more than one use.
  3. It must be something that exists only in limited amounts.
We all have had scarcity in our own lives. For example, when you want to go see a concert that is sold out, you experience scarcity.

need
something essential for survival such as food or clothing

want
something that people desire but that is not necessary for survival

goods
the physical objects that people, businesses, or governments buy

services
the actions or activities that one person performs for another

resources
anything that people use to make things or do work

shortage
a situation in which people want more of a good or service than producers are willing to supply at a particular price

Fig. 1.1 How the Economy Works

What does an **entrepreneur** do?

All entrepreneurs—whether they are starting a lawn-mowing service or founding a company that makes cars—have two things in common. First, they recognize a need or want. Then, they must assemble the factors of production to meet that need or want.

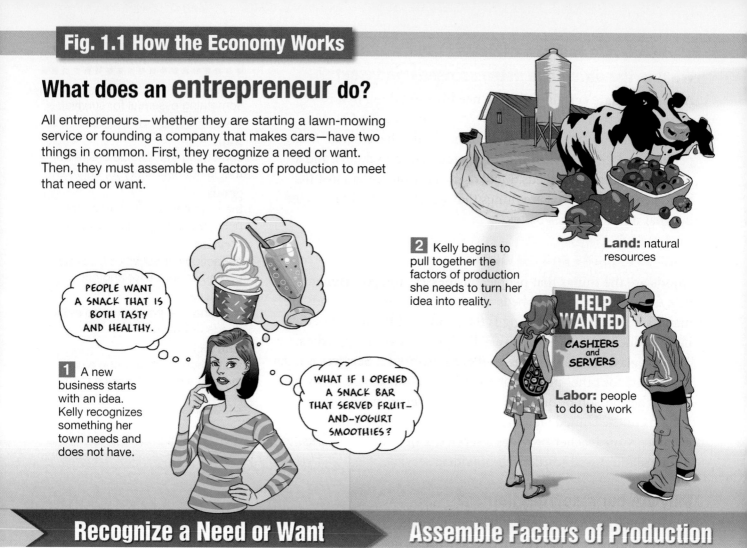

1 A new business starts with an idea. Kelly recognizes something her town needs and does not have.

PEOPLE WANT A SNACK THAT IS BOTH TASTY AND HEALTHY.

WHAT IF I OPENED A SNACK BAR THAT SERVED FRUIT-AND-YOGURT SMOOTHIES?

2 Kelly begins to pull together the factors of production she needs to turn her idea into reality.

Land: natural resources

HELP WANTED
CASHIERS and SERVERS

Labor: people to do the work

Recognize a Need or Want

Assemble Factors of Production

You probably also have experienced scarcity of time when you have too little time to do everything you want or need to do. Countries have scarcity because their wants are greater than their resources. A country may want to spend more on education and health. But it also has to pay for roads and defense.

Scarcity also is a problem for business. Business owners always have to make decisions about which goods and services to provide. They have to decide how much of a product to make. They do not have the resources to do everything they want. For example, maybe a toy business chooses to make more of a popular doll than of a board game. If fewer people buy dolls or if too many of them are made, the business loses money. On the other hand, if many people buy the dolls, the business makes money.

✔ **CHECKPOINT** *Why are goods and services scarce?*

Capital: human-made resources

Human Capital: acquired knowledge and skills

Physical Capital: objects used to create goods or to supply services

3 Kelly took a financial risk by opening her own business. If the risk pays off, Kelly gets profits…her workers get wages…and her customers get a healthy snack.

Check Your Understanding
1. How will reading and other types of self-education help this entrepreneur succeed?
2. What impact does the concept of scarcity have on the decisions made by an entrepreneur?

Provide Goods or Services

What are entrepreneurs?

How are scarce resources turned into goods and services? **Entrepreneurs** play a key role. These are people who decide how to combine resources to make new and better products. They hope to make money. They take risks to make new ideas happen. **Figure 1.1** shows how one person became an entrepreneur.

What are the factors of production?

The first task faced by any entrepreneur is to assemble the **factors of production.** The three main factors of production are **land, labor,** and **capital.**

What is land?

Land refers to all natural resources used to make goods and services. Natural resources refer to materials found on Earth. These include oil, water, minerals, land for farming, and forests.

entrepreneur
a person who decides how to combine resources to create goods and services

factors of production
the resources that are used to make goods and services

land
all natural resources used to produce goods and services

labor
the effort people devote to tasks for which they are paid

capital
any human-made resource used to produce goods and services

What is labor?

Labor is another factor of production. The production of goods and services always involves people. The work people do to provide goods and services is called labor. Some of the work is physical. For example, construction workers use their muscle power to build a building. Labor also includes the people who use brainpower to design the building. Whether the work you do involves muscle power or brainpower does not matter. You are part of labor even as a part-time worker.

What is capital?

Capital is any resource used by humans to make other goods and services. There are two types of capital: **physical capital** and **human capital.** Physical capital is human-made objects used to make goods and services. They include buildings, machinery, tools, and equipment. Human capital is what a worker gains from education and experience. Going to school and learning new skills is an investment in human capital. Reading, working with a computer, and playing a musical instrument are all examples of human capital. People with more skills—greater human capital— usually earn more money than a person with few skills.

Often, physical capital and human capital are used together. Factory workers use their training as well as machines and equipment. Nurses and doctors make use of computers to check patients. They also use their special training and what they have learned from past experiences.

What are the benefits of capital?

Both physical and human capital are important. Physical capital, such as machines and tools, helps produce goods and services more easily. Workers become more productive because they can make more of the product for less money. Sometimes businesses give workers extra training. This adds to their human capital. It also makes them more productive.

Suppose a family of six people washes dishes by hand after every meal—breakfast, lunch, and dinner. In a 7-day week, that is a total of 21 meals. It takes two family members working together for 30 minutes to scrape, stack, wash, rinse, dry, and put away the dishes. So the family spends 21 hours a week cleaning dishes. They could have spent this time on other, more productive activities.

What happens when the family buys a dishwasher? They spend $400.00 on physical capital—the dishwasher. Now it takes one family member only 15 minutes after each meal to load the

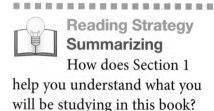

Reading Strategy
Summarizing
How does Section 1 help you understand what you will be studying in this book?

dishwasher. Then it takes another 15 minutes at the end of the day to put the dishes away. A job that used to take 21 hours now takes only 7 hours. This example shows the benefits of using capital:

1. *Extra time* The family saves 14 hours a week. This is time that can be used for doing other things.
2. *More knowledge* By learning how to use the dishwasher, family members can learn about using other appliances.
3. *More productivity* Family members can use their resources and labor for other skills or to spend more time together.

✔ **CHECKPOINT** *What are the factors of production?*

Why are resources scarce?

Economic resources are scarce because the resources used to produce them are scarce. This principle applies to a pair of blue jeans, an MP3 player, or a space shuttle.

We might also notice another factor about these resources. Each has many other uses. Individuals, businesses, and governments have to choose which use they most want.

Essential Questions Journal To continue to build a response to the Essential Question, go to your **Essential Questions Journal.**

SECTION 1 ASSESSMENT

Quick Write

Think of an item that you really would like to purchase. What things do you consider before making a purchase? Write a letter to a friend explaining your decision-making process.

 Guiding Question

1. Use your cause-and-effect chart to answer this question: How does scarcity force people to make economic choices?

Key Terms and Main Ideas

Directions: On a sheet of paper, write the answer to each question. Use complete sentences.

2. What is the difference between goods and services?
3. How does scarcity differ from a shortage?
4. What does an entrepreneur do?
5. What is a benefit of using both physical capital and human capital?

Critical Thinking

6. **Categorize** Identify the factor of production represented by each of the following: (a) clerks in a store, (b) a tractor, (c) a student in a cooking school. Explain.
7. **Draw Inferences** Computers can make companies more productive. Why would a company not buy new computers for all employees each year?

Objectives

- **Explain** why every decision involves trade-offs.

- **Summarize** the idea of opportunity cost.

- **Describe** how people make decisions by thinking at the margin.

Guiding Question

How does opportunity cost affect decision making?

Copy this concept web and fill it in as you read. Add more rectangles if necessary.

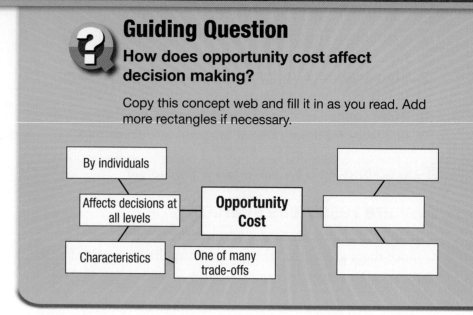

■ ■ ■ ■ ■ ■ ■ ■ ■ ■ ■ ■ ■ ■ ■ ■ ■ ■ ■ ■

trade-off
the alternatives that we give up when we choose one course of action over another

▶ **Economics and You** You are cleaning your bedroom. Boxes, clothes, and other items cover your bed, the floor, the entire room. Suddenly, your phone rings and a friend invites you to a party. You consider your options. You quickly decide that going to the party will be more fun than cleaning your room.

Later, tired but happy, you enter your bedroom. You realize that you now have to clear off your bed when all you want to do is sleep. Your decision to go to the party cost you the time you needed to clean up your room. Was the benefit of your choice worth the cost?

Principles in Action Every time we choose to do something, we give up the opportunity to do something else. Even a simple decision such as how late to sleep in the morning involves weighing costs and benefits. The Economics & You feature on page 11 shows how scarcity and choice can affect the ways you spend your time and what services are made available to you in your community.

What are trade-offs?

We have learned that a resource can only be used one way at a time. For example, if land is used to grow corn, it cannot be used as a golf course. Let's say that you have $20.00 in your pocket. If you use it to go to a movie, you cannot use the same money to take a friend out. In a **trade-off,** you give up one thing for another. The trade-off for going to the movie is not being able to take your friend out.

Why do businesses have to make trade-offs?

Every time a business decides how to use its land, labor, and capital, trade-offs are involved. A farmer who decides to grow corn cannot at the same time use the land to grow soybeans. If a furniture maker decides to use all the resources to make chairs, the same resources cannot be used to make tables or desks.

What trade-offs do governments make?

As we learned in Section 1, even governments have to make choices. Economists use the term **"guns or butter"** to describe the choice. *Guns* refers to military spending; *butter* refers to everyday goods that people buy. A country that spends a certain amount of money on "guns" cannot spend the same money on "butter."

☑ **CHECKPOINT** *What are trade-offs?*

What are opportunity costs?

Each possible use of the same resource is an opportunity. Every time we make a choice, we give up an opportunity, or chance to do something else.

Opportunity cost is what you give up to get something else. It is the second-best choice. Opportunity cost includes all costs, such as time and other activities.

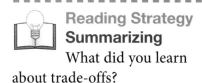

"guns or butter"
the idea that a country that produces guns has fewer resources to produce butter (consumer goods), and vice versa

opportunity cost
the most desirable alternative given up as the result of a decision

Reading Strategy
Summarizing
What did you learn about trade-offs?

Economics & YOU

Trade-offs

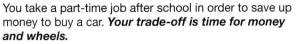

You take a part-time job after school in order to save up money to buy a car. *Your trade-off is time for money and wheels.*

CLOSED
Due to staff cuts

Public Library

Your town can afford to fix local roads or keep the library open on mornings and Saturdays—but not both. *The town council trades off full library service for road improvements.*

For example, after high school, you have many choices. One choice is to go on to college. Another choice is to work full-time. Going to college may mean that you will not have enough money to move out on your own. Finding a full-time job may mean more money in your pocket now but less in the future. In general, college graduates earn more money than people whose education ends with high school. There is a cost for giving up the other choice or opportunity. The opportunity cost is the cost of the next best choice, or the choice not taken.

How can using a decision-making grid help you?

It is often difficult to make choices. Using a decision-making grid like **Figure 1.2** can help you. In this example, we will look at Karen, a high school student. She is trying to decide whether to sleep late or get up early to study for a test. Karen likes to sleep. Getting up early is tough. However, she knows if she gets up early to study she will probably get a better grade.

Karen knows she has two choices. She could sleep late or she could get up early to study. Karen knows that there are trade-offs for her decision. She could decide to sleep longer. Then the trade-off will probably be a lower grade on the test. If she gets up early to study, the trade-off might be feeling tired all day. Choosing to get up early makes the opportunity cost the extra sleeping time. If she decides to sleep longer, the opportunity cost is the higher grade on the test.

Fig. 1.2 Decision Making at the Margin

GRAPH SKILLS

This graph shows that the opportunity cost of studying means an opportunity cost of one hour of sleep.

1. What is the benefit for one hour of extra study time?
2. At what point is Karen paying an added cost with little benefit?

Options	Benefit	Opportunity Cost
1st hour of extra study time	Grade of C on test	1 hour of sleep
2nd hour of extra study time	Grade of B on test	2 hours of sleep
3rd hour of extra study time	Grade of B+ on test	3 hours of sleep

What does it mean to think at the margin?

Think about folding a piece of paper to put in your pocket. Fold the paper in half and then in half again. It can just squeeze into your pocket and will lay fairly flat. Fold it in half two or three more times. It would fit more easily in your pocket but would also become more bulky. How many folds work best to make the paper fit in your pocket and lay flat once inside? When you decide how much more or less to do, you are thinking at the margin.

Deciding by thinking at the margin is just like making any other decision. You have to look at what you give up and what you will gain. This process is sometimes called **cost/benefit analysis.**

To make good decisions at the margin, you must weigh marginal costs against marginal benefits. Marginal refers to the extra cost or benefit of doing something. The **marginal cost** is the extra cost of producing one unit. The **marginal benefit** is the extra benefit of adding the same unit. If the marginal costs outweigh the marginal benefits, there is no profit in making more units. Therefore, the decision would be not to add any more units.

✅ **CHECKPOINT** *What is the difference between an opportunity cost and a trade-off?*

cost/benefit analysis
a process in which you compare what you will sacrifice and gain by a specific action

marginal cost
the extra cost of adding one unit

marginal benefit
the extra benefit of adding one unit

Reading Strategy
Summarizing
What are some important ideas you read about in this section?

 SECTION 2 ASSESSMENT

Essential Questions Journal
To continue to build a response to the Essential Question, go to your **Essential Questions Journal.**

Guiding Question

1. Use your completed concept web to answer this question: How does opportunity cost affect decision making?

Key Terms and Main Ideas

Directions: On a sheet of paper, write the answer to each question. Use complete sentences.

2. Why do all economic decisions involve trade-offs?

3. How does the phrase "guns or butter" show the idea of trade-offs?

4. Why do many economic decisions involve thinking at the margin?

5. Why is it important to compare marginal costs to marginal benefits?

Critical Thinking

6. **Analyze Information** Give an example of a decision that your school might have to make. Explain how the decision involves trade-offs.

7. **Identify Alternatives** A business owner has to decide whether to hire one or two additional workers. What marginal costs and benefits might the owner have to consider?

Objectives

- **Interpret** a production possibilities curve.
- **Explain** how production possibilities curves show efficiency, growth, and cost.
- **Explain** how a production curve shows a trade-off.

production possibilities curve
a graph that shows alternative ways to use an economy's productive resources

Guiding Question

How does a nation decide what and how much to produce?

Copy this concept web and fill it in as you read. Add more rectangles if necessary.

```
┌─────────────────┐                        ┌──────────────┐
│ Used to analyze │                        │              │
│   trade-offs    │                        └──────────────┘
└─────────────────┘      ┌────────────┐
                         │ Production │    ┌──────────────┐
┌─────────────────┐      │Possibilities│   │              │
│  Compares two   │──────│   Curve    │────│              │
│goods or services│      └────────────┘    └──────────────┘
└─────────────────┘
┌─────────────────┐      ┌────────────┐    ┌──────────────┐
│                 │      │            │    │              │
└─────────────────┘      └────────────┘    └──────────────┘
```

▶ **Economics and You** Your class decides to sponsor a community breakfast to raise money. Can you make more money by serving only eggs or only pancakes? Or should you offer both? To decide, you will have to look at the cost of things that go into the product, the number of workers you have, and the size of the kitchen. Also, does it take more time to scramble eggs or to flip pancakes? What you decide will affect how much money you make. Nations face similar decisions about what to produce. For nations, however, the effects of these decisions can be far more serious.

Principles in Action Economists use a tool known as a **production possibilities curve** to decide what and how much to produce. You will see how an imaginary country uses this tool to decide between producing two very different products: shoes and watermelons.

What is a production possibilities curve?

A production possibilities curve is another way of looking at trade-offs and opportunity costs. This is an economic model. It is a simple way to show the real world. A production possibilities curve shows the different ways an economy's resources can be used.

How is a production possibilities curve drawn?

To draw a production possibilities curve, we will look at a pretend country called Capeland. The government of Capeland must decide how best to use the country's scarce resources. Should they use the resources to make shoes or to grow watermelons?

Look at the graph in **Figure 1.3** below. The vertical axis shows how many millions of pairs of shoes could be made. The horizontal axis shows how many millions of watermelons could be grown. If Capeland uses all its resources to make shoes, it could make 15 million pairs. That is point *a* on the graph. But if Capeland instead uses all its resources to grow watermelons, it would grow 21 million tons of watermelon. This is represented by point *c* on the graph.

There is a third choice. The resources could be used to produce both shoes and watermelons. The table shows six different ways the people of Capeland could produce both products. Using the data from the table, we can put other points on the graph. Connecting the points creates a curve. This curved line is called a **production possibilities frontier** or curve. Any spot on the line represents a point at which Capeland is using all its resources to produce both the most watermelons and the most shoes.

How does the production possibilities curve show trade-offs?

Each point on the production possibilities curve shows a trade-off. Near the top of the curve, factories produce more shoes, but farmers grow fewer watermelons. Farther down the curve, farmers grow more watermelons, but fewer shoes are being produced.

production possibilities frontier
a line on a production possibilities curve that shows the maximum possible output an economy can produce

Fig. 1.3 Production Possibilities Curve

Watermelons (millions of tons)	Shoes (millions of pairs)
0	15
8	14
14	12
18	9
20	5
21	0

Action Graph
online

For an animated version of this graph, visit **PearsonSuccessNet.com**

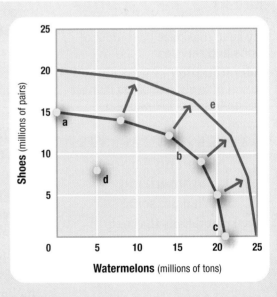

GRAPH SKILLS

The table shows six different combinations of watermelons and shoes that Capeland could produce using all of its resources. These figures have been used to create a production possibilities curve.

1. How much watermelon can Capeland produce if they are making 9 million pairs of shoes? What will the opportunity cost be if Capeland increases shoe production to 12 million?

2. Why would production at point *d* represent an underutilization of resources?

KEY

a. No watermelons; all possible shoes
b. A production possibilities frontier
c. No shoes; all possible watermelons
d. A point of underutilization
e. Future production possibilities frontier

Innovators

Steven Levitt

"I just wander through life looking for anything that interests me," says economist Steve Levitt. "And every once in a while I stumble onto something that turns into a research idea." This wide curiosity has led him to publish books and articles on topics from illegal drug use to sumo wrestling. Levitt uses economic principles to explore all human behavior.

Levitt is brilliant, but he also has his own way of doing things. He has shown a rare ability to observe human behavior and create mathematical models that predict future outcomes. He has done ground-breaking work on important "real world" issues. These include the effect of the prison system on criminal behavior and whether increasing the number of police lowers the crime rate.

Levitt has an ambition that may seem unusual for an economist. "I'd like to put together a set of tools that lets us catch terrorists," he says. For Levitt, catching terrorists is a matter of finding the right data.

Fast Facts

Steven Levitt (1967–)
Education: B.A. in Economics from Harvard; Ph.D. in Economics from M.I.T.

---

efficiency
the use of resources in such a way as to maximize the output of goods and services

underutilization
the use of fewer resources than an economy is capable of using

---

🔖 **Reading Strategy**
Summarizing
What are some important details that help you understand production possibilities curves?

These trade-offs are necessary, because resources are scarce. Remember, we always have to make choices because our wants and needs are greater than our resources. This is what economics is all about.

What else do production possibilities curves show?

Production possibilities curves tell us how efficient an economy is. **Efficiency** is the use of resources in a way that produces the most goods and services. It does this with the least waste of time, energy, and resources. Many governments invest in education so that their people can use and develop technologies that help increase efficiency. Sometimes, an economy is not efficient. If workers are laid off, the farms or factories where they worked will produce fewer goods. The drop-off in production is shown as a point inside the production possibilities curve. Any point inside the line shows **underutilization.** This means that fewer resources are being used than are available. Capital is being wasted in the form of workers that are not being used. For example, look at point *d* in the figure on page 15. Capeland is growing 5 million tons of watermelons and making 6 million pairs of shoes. This is much less than could be produced if the resources were used in a more efficient way.

Production possibilities curves show the cost involved in making a decision. Cost does not always mean money. To the economist, cost always means opportunity cost. Look at the figure again. We can see that the opportunity cost of choosing to grow 8 million tons of watermelons instead of zero is 1 million shoes.

 CHECKPOINT *What three kinds of information can be seen in production possibilities curves?*

What is the law of increasing costs?

Every decision has a cost, and there are trade-offs to every decision. Let's assume that farmland has been sold to build a factory. As the factory increases its production, it purchases more land from the farmer. To grow as much as before on less land, the farmer may have to buy more resources such as fertilizer, better seed, or more land. The **law of increasing costs** says that when production switches from one item to another, the opportunity costs increase. This is because more resources are needed to increase production of the second item.

 CHECKPOINT *Why do opportunity costs increase as production switches from one item to another?*

law of increasing costs
an economic principle stating that as production shifts from making one good or service to another, more resources are needed to increase production of the second good or service

 Reading Strategy
Summarizing
In your own words, tell what this paragraph is about.

SECTION 3 ASSESSMENT

Essential Questions Journal
To continue to build a response to the Essential Question, go to your **Essential Questions Journal.**

Word Bank
production possibilities curve
efficiency
production possibilities frontier

 Guiding Question

1. Use your completed concept web to answer this question: How does a nation decide what and how much to produce?

Key Terms and Main Ideas

Directions: On a sheet of paper, use the words from the Word Bank to complete each sentence correctly.

2. What shows alternative ways to use an economy's productive resources?

3. What is the line that shows the maximum possible output an economy can produce?

4. What is the term for the use of resources that makes the biggest output of goods and services?

Critical Thinking

5. **Summarize** Explain the law of increasing costs and provide an example.

Section 1—Scarcity and the Factors of Production

- Scarcity is the most basic economic problem because, in general, our wants are greater than what is available.

- A need is something we need to stay alive. A want is something that makes our lives better.

- Goods are manufactured things that people, businesses, and governments buy.

- Services refer to work done for other people for a fee.

- Entrepreneurs decide how to combine resources to create goods and services.

- Land, labor, and capital are the three main factors of production.

Section 2—Opportunity Cost

- In a trade-off, you give up one thing for another thing.

- An opportunity cost is the best alternative you give up when you decide to do something else.

- When you decide how much more or less to do, you are thinking at the margin.

Section 3—Production Possibilities Curves

- A production possibilities curve shows ways to use an economy's resources.

- Efficiency is the use of resources to produce the most goods and services with the least waste of time and energy.

Section 1
How does scarcity force people to make economic choices?

Section 2
How does opportunity cost affect decision making?

Section 3
How does a nation decide what and how much to produce?

Essential Question, Chapter 1
How can we make the best economic choices?

The Communist Manifesto

Karl Marx and Friedrich Engels were the leaders of a new social movement. They thought it would change history. In 1848, the two men published the Communist Manifesto, *a pamphlet that stated their beliefs. Marx and Engels called themselves Communists. They believed that the bourgeoisie (a class of business owners) were becoming much more powerful than the proletariat (a class of workers). They argued that the proletariat should overthrow the bourgeoisie. Their ideas would become a revolutionary force in the twentieth century.*

"The modern bourgeois society [middle class factory owners] that has sprouted from the ruins of the feudal society . . . has but established new classes, new conditions of oppression, new forms of struggle in place of the old ones. . . .

The discovery of America, the rounding of the Cape [of Good Hope in Africa], opened up fresh ground for the rising bourgeoisie. . . .

The feudal system of industry, in which industrial production was monopolized by closed guilds, now no longer (meets) the growing wants of the new markets. . . .

Meantime, the markets kept ever growing, the demand ever rising. . . . The place of manufacture was taken by the giant, MODERN INDUSTRY; the place of the industrial middle class by industrial millionaires, the leaders of the whole industrial armies, the modern bourgeoisie.

Modern industry has established the world market. . . . This market has given an immense development to commerce, to navigation, to communication by land. . . . [In] proportion as industry, commerce, navigation, railways extended . . . the bourgeoisie developed, increased its capital, and pushed into the background every class handed down from the Middle Ages.

The bourgeoisie . . . has resolved personal worth into exchange value, and . . . has set up that single, (excessive) freedom—Free Trade. . . .

The need of a constantly expanding market for its products chases the bourgeoisie over the entire surface of the globe. It must nestle everywhere, settle everywhere, establish connections everywhere.

The bourgeoisie has, through its exploitation of the world market, given a cosmopolitan character to production and consumption in every country."

Document-Based Questions

1. Why did Karl Marx and Friedrich Engels write the *Communist Manifesto?*
2. According to the authors, what is one reason that allowed the bourgeoisie to gain power?
3. List three areas that developed because of the growth in the world economy.
4. What freedom do the authors call "excessive"?
5. In your own words, explain why Marx thinks that communism is the best economic choice.

Directions: Choose the letter of the correct answer or write the answer using complete sentences.

Section 1–Scarcity and the Factors of Production

1. What are human-made resources that are used to produce other goods and services called?
   - **A.** factors of production
   - **B.** labor
   - **C.** capital
   - **D.** land

2. What word refers to work done for other people for a fee?
   - **A.** resources
   - **B.** shortages
   - **C.** goods
   - **D.** services

3. What are the things that people, businesses, and governments buy called?
   - **A.** resource
   - **B.** shortage
   - **C.** goods
   - **D.** services

4. What is economics?

5. Why do people have to make choices?

Section 2–Opportunity Cost

6. What is the extra cost of producing one unit called?
   - **A.** cost/benefit analysis
   - **B.** marginal cost
   - **C.** marginal benefit
   - **D.** opportunity cost

7. What is the extra benefit of adding one unit called?
   - **A.** cost/benefit analysis
   - **B.** marginal cost
   - **C.** marginal benefit
   - **D.** opportunity cost

8. What is the most desirable alternative given up as the result of a decision?
   - **A.** cost/benefit analysis
   - **B.** marginal cost
   - **C.** marginal benefit
   - **D.** opportunity cost

9. What does the term "guns or butter" refer to?

10. Why is there a trade-off for every decision?

11. What is the purpose of a decision-making grid?

Economics
on the go

Section 3—Production Possibilities Curves

12. What is the term for the use of fewer resources than an economy is capable of using?

    A. underutilization   **C.** production curves

    B. efficiency   **D.** production frontiers

13. Explain the law of increasing costs.

14. Why does underutilization result in wasted resources?

15. What does each point on a production possibilities curve show?

16. Cars that weigh more tend to be safer than lightweight cars. They also use more gasoline because they are heavier. Identify the trade-off and opportunity cost for choosing either one.

17. Your town can afford either to build a new library or pave 5 miles of a dangerous road. Explain what the trade-offs and opportunity cost would be for each decision.

 Exploring the Essential Question

Essential Question Project

18. Complete this activity to answer the Essential Question **How can we make the best economic choices?**

As you have learned, scarcity and opportunity cost lie at the heart of all economic decisions—including those you make. You have limited time and limited resources. Every time you make a choice, you give up something else. Using your worksheet, keep track of how you use your resources for the next three days.

Essential Questions Journal — To continue to build a response to the Essential Question, go to your **Essential Questions Journal.**

 Test-Taking Tip

Always try to restate directions in your own words. That way, you can make sure you know how to answer the questions.

Chapter **2** Economic Systems

Essential Question, Chapter 2

How does a society decide who gets what goods and services?

Economics on the go

To study anywhere, anytime, download these onlin resources at *PearsonSuccessNet.com* ➤

▶ All countries in the world face scarcity.

Each nation follows an economic system to deal with this problem. The systems the societies have depend on the importance they attach to efficiency, freedom, security, equity, and growth.

This chapter discusses the three questions that all societies must answer. You will learn about four different types of economic systems. Each economic system answers the three questions in a different way. The economic systems are traditional, free market, centrally planned, and mixed. You will read about the advantages and disadvantages of each.

Reading Strategy: Questioning

Asking questions as you read will help you find answers and remember more of the information. Questioning the text will also help you to be a more active reader. As you read, ask yourself:

Before Reading
• What is my reason for reading this chapter?
• What will I learn?

During Reading
• What decisions can I make about the facts and details?
• Do I understand what I am reading?

After Reading
• What connections can I make between this text and my own life?
• What still does not make sense to me?

In general, ask questions that begin with *Who, What, Where, When, How,* and *Why.*

Visual Glossary
online

Go to the Visual Glossary Online for an interactive review of **incentives.**

How the Economy Works
online

Go to How the Economy Works Online for an interactive lesson on **innovation and the economy.**

Action Graph
online

Go to Action Graph Online for animated versions of key charts and graphs.

Objectives

- **Identify** the three key economic questions that all societies must answer.

- **Analyze** what a society values by how a country answers the three economic questions.

- **Describe** a traditional economy.

Guiding Question

What goals and values affect how a society answers the key economic questions?

Copy this chart and fill it in as you read.

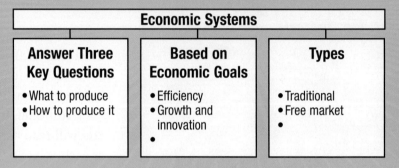

Economic Systems		
Answer Three Key Questions	**Based on Economic Goals**	**Types**
• What to produce • How to produce it •	• Efficiency • Growth and innovation •	• Traditional • Free market •

economic system
the structure that a society uses to produce and distribute both goods and services

▶ **Economics and You** When you go to a supermarket, you see rows of shelves stacked with many items. But imagine the government telling you that you could buy just one brand of cereal and one brand of soap. Or imagine that you had to depend only on what you and your neighbors could grow or make yourselves. In some societies, this is how needs and wants are met.

Principles in Action Each society has to answer three basic economic questions. As you will see, the way these questions are answered has a lot to do with people's freedom of choice.

What are the three basic questions all economic systems answer?

The choices we make as shoppers, workers, business owners, and government workers create the economy. Every society must answer the three basic economic questions:

- What should be produced?
- How should it be produced?
- Who should get the goods and services?

There are no right answers and no wrong answers. The way people answer these questions describes their **economic system.** An economic system is the structure that a society uses to produce and distribute goods and services. It is the way a society tries to provide for the wants and needs of its people.

What should be produced?

The first question is *what*. We need to decide what and how much should be produced. Even a rich country like the United States cannot produce everything it wants. People choose the kinds of goods and services to produce. They may decide to use resources to make cars. This means there are fewer resources to spend on other products like clothes and food. Maybe a country can make all of these things, but it still has to decide how much of each is best.

How should it be produced?

The second question is *how*. Now that we know what we will produce, we have to decide how to produce it. There are many ways to build a house. They can be built on the site or in a factory. The builders can use wood, bricks, or steel. Cars can be made using people or robots. How are the choices made? If times are good, business owners may want to increase capital resources. If many people are out of work, the owners may decide to spend money on human capital instead.

Who should get the goods and services?

The third question is *who*. We know what should be produced and how the goods will be produced. Now we must decide who should receive them. Should only those people with enough money to buy the goods and services get them? Should the government decide who receives them?

The answers to these questions depend on how the society distributes **income**. Income is the amount of money a person makes. **Factor payments** are the income people receive in return for supplying land, labor, or capital. Factor payments also include **profits** that business owners earn if the business does well. Profit is the amount of money a business keeps after all costs of production have been paid. The way a society distributes income tells a great deal about the society's values and goals.

 CHECKPOINT *What are the three basic economic questions?*

What do the three questions tell about a society?

All societies have economic goals. These goals include growth, efficiency, freedom, security, and equity. All societies may share these goals. However, they do not all agree on what is most important. The way a society answers the three economic questions tells us how important each goal is to that society.

■ ■ ■ ■ ■ ■ ■ ■ ■ ■ ■ ■ ■ ■ ■ ■

Reading Strategy
Questioning
    What details are important to understanding the three basic economic questions?

■ ■ ■ ■ ■ ■ ■ ■ ■ ■ ■ ■ ■ ■ ■ ■

income
the money a person makes

factor payment
the income people receive in return for supplying land, labor, or capital

profit
the amount of money a business keeps after all costs of production have been paid

Fig. 2.1 How the Economy Works

How can innovation lead to economic growth?

New resources, new inventions, new processes, new ways of doing business—all of these are innovations. Some innovations are small and limited in their effects. But every once in a while, an innovation comes along that revolutionizes the economy and society. One such innovation was the development of the microchip.

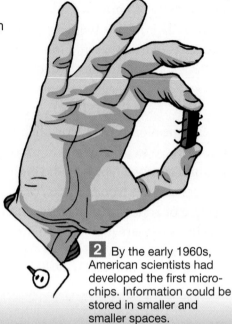

1 In the 1940s and 1950s, computers were huge. Most were located in military installations or university labs.

2 By the early 1960s, American scientists had developed the first micro-chips. Information could be stored in smaller and smaller spaces.

The Way Things Were

The Innovation

▪▪▪▪▪▪▪▪▪▪▪▪▪▪▪▪▪▪▪

standard of living
the way of living that is usual for a person, community, or country

innovation
bringing new methods, products, or ideas into use

What is economic growth?

A nation's economy must grow as its population grows. It must find jobs for the new people joining the workforce. A nation's economy must grow if the people are going to have more money. When income goes up, the nation improves its **standard of living.** The standard of living is the way of living that is usual for a person, place, community, or country.

Innovation plays a big role in economic growth. Innovation is the process of bringing new methods, products, or ideas into use. Think about the many changes that have happened just in your lifetime. Innovations like computers have changed our lives. They affect the way we work, shop, do business, find information, and talk with one another.

What is economic efficiency?

Because resources are always scarce, societies try to get the most out of the scarce resources they have. An economy is efficient, or wastes very little, when it correctly decides what to produce.

How the Economy Works
online

For an animated, interactive version of this feature, visit **PearsonSuccessNet.com**

3 By the 1980s, computers got smaller and cheaper to manufacture. The home computer had arrived…and ushered in a new period of economic growth.

New Markets: The home computer gave millions of buyers and sellers access to the Internet. Online marketing changed the world economy.

New Goods: Hundreds of products on the market—from MP3 players to GPS systems—make use of microchip technology.

New Services: The home computer gave rise to related businesses, such as computer stores and computer repair services.

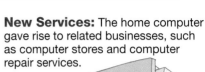

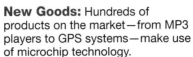

Check Your Understanding
1. Why was the microchip a turning point in the development of the Computer Age?
2. Describe another technological innovation that led to the creation of new goods or services.

Economic Growth

A manufacturer would be wasting resources making desktop computers if people mostly want laptops.

The goal of cutting down waste also involves the second and third economic questions. Producers always look for better ways to create goods and to offer them for sale. An economy that does not make the right goods in the right quantity for the right people at the right price is not efficient.

What is economic freedom?

How would you feel about laws that kept you from getting some kinds of jobs or buying certain items? Most people like to make their own choices. Still, there are many people in the world who do not have the economic freedom we have in the United States. Individual freedom is very important to Americans. We enjoy many freedoms, such as buying what we can pay for and working where we choose. We are also free to own property and free to start our own businesses.

safety net
a set of programs designed to
protect people who face economic
hard times

What is economic security?

Most people like to know they can depend on others. We want to know that we can get milk or bread every time we go to the grocery store. We like the feeling of knowing we will get paid every payday. Every economic system tries to make people feel safe or secure.

Part of feeling safe is knowing that we can get help if we need it. Many governments provide a **safety net.** This is a set of programs to protect people who face economic hard times such as injury or job loss. Most nations also give retired people some income to help them with financial support.

What is economic equity?

Equity, or fairness, is another economic goal. Not all societies define equity in the same way. Each society must decide how to divide its economic pie. In some countries, a small group of very rich families receives most of what is produced. The large number of poor people in these countries gets very little. Most developed countries have a large middle class. Almost everyone has a chance to get the goods and services produced. Some countries try to even out the amount of money workers earn. No one is very rich, but no one is very poor. In this way, every person shares in the nation's production. How the economic pie is divided shows how important equity is to the society.

What happens if goals conflict with one another?

Environmental protection, jobs for all workers, or protecting national industries may also be among a nation's economic goals.

Sometimes, economic goals conflict with one another. For example, providing a safety net for all citizens may slow economic growth. Protecting the environment may limit the economic freedom of some businesses. All nations must arrange their economic goals in order of importance. No matter how a nation ranks its goals, each choice comes with some kind of trade-off.

CHECKPOINT *What are two examples of economic goals?*

Traditional economies exist in small areas of the modern world. Like earlier generations, this Peruvian woman makes a living producing fine textiles. ▼

What is a traditional economic system?

Societies have developed four different economic systems. Each system answers the three economic questions in a different way. Each system also reflects the values of the societies in which these systems are found.

A **traditional economy** is the oldest and simplest economic system. In a traditional economy, people do things as they have in the past. In other words, the three basic economic questions are answered as they always have been. One of the advantages of a traditional economy is that everyone knows what is expected of them. What to produce is based on what was produced in the past. If you are born to a family of hunters, you hunt. If your family makes a living from farming, you farm. The way you produce goods is the same way the people who lived before you produced them. Custom and tradition help to decide who should get the goods and services produced.

Traditional economies exist on almost every continent. They are usually found in rural areas of the world, which are places away from cities. The economy is centered on a family or tribal group. The role that the men, women, and children play is often decided by tradition. In a traditional economy, change occurs very slowly. Often, the standard of living is low.

In the next three sections, you will learn about three other economic systems. They are the free market economy, the centrally planned economy, and the mixed economy.

 CHECKPOINT *What are the main economic activities in a traditional economy?*

traditional economy
the oldest and simplest economic system in which people do things as they have in the past

 Reading Strategy
Questioning
Ask yourself: "Did I understand what I just read?" If not, read the material about traditional economies again.

SECTION 1 ASSESSMENT

Essential Questions Journal — To continue to build a response to the Essential Question, go to your **Essential Questions Journal.**

 Guiding Question

1. Use your completed chart to answer the following question: What goals and values affect how a society answers the key economic questions?

Key Terms and Main Ideas

Directions: On a sheet of paper, write the answer to each question. Use complete sentences.

2. Why does a government provide a safety net for its people?

3. What must happen for a nation's standard of living to improve?

Critical Thinking

4. **Analyze Information** A clothing designer releases a new line of jeans. How are the three economic questions answered in the process of releasing this new product line?

5. **Draw Conclusions** (a) Why would it be inefficient for a manufacturer to produce audio cassettes instead of CDs today? (b) What resources would be wasted?

Objectives

■ **Explain** why markets exist.

■ **Analyze** a circular flow model of a free market economy.

■ **Identify** the advantages of a free market economy.

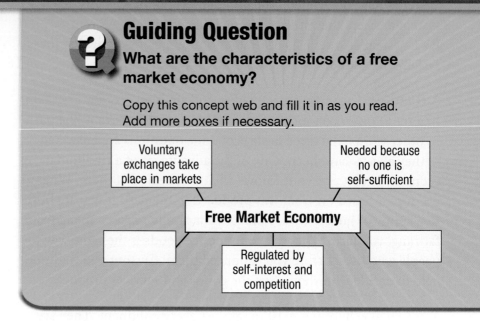

Guiding Question

What are the characteristics of a free market economy?

Copy this concept web and fill it in as you read. Add more boxes if necessary.

Voluntary exchanges take place in markets

Needed because no one is self-sufficient

Free Market Economy

Regulated by self-interest and competition

market
a place that allows buyers and sellers to exchange things

Reading Strategy
Questioning
What do you think you will learn by reading this section?

▶ **Economics and You** Do you value freedom? If you thought about the freedom of speech or right to a fair trial, you probably said yes. What about the freedom to own property, get a job, or spend your money the way you want? Americans also value economic freedom. It has shaped the system under which we live.

Principles in Action Economic freedom is the chief feature of a free market economy. In this section, you will see how the free market affects every household and community, including yours. You will also see how one entrepreneur used the free market to make a fortune selling something many people use—cosmetics.

Why do markets exist?

There are many different types of **markets**. A market is a place that allows buyers and sellers to exchange things. Does your town have a farmers' market? Is there a community bulletin board where you can post a sign advertising baby-sitting services? Have you heard of the New York Stock Exchange? All of these are examples of markets. Markets exist because no one is totally independent. None of us produces all we require to satisfy our needs and wants. You probably did not grow the cotton plants used to make the cloth for the shirt you are wearing. Instead, you bought your shirt at a store, which is a market. Markets allow us to exchange the things we have for the things we want.

What is specialization?

Specialization is when individuals and businesses do only what they do best. A baker specializes in making breads, cakes, and cookies. A nurse specializes in caring for the sick. An aircraft plant makes planes, not refrigerators. Specialization has several advantages:

1. Workers can be trained better.
2. Workers learn their skills better.
3. Production becomes more efficient.
4. Production increases.

What is a free market economy?

In a **free market economy,** decisions about the three economic questions are made by **voluntary exchange.** A voluntary exchange is a transfer that someone makes willingly. You make an exchange when you give another person something and you get something back. In a free market, buyers and sellers are free to make exchanges. Sellers get money for their goods and services. Buyers get products they want. Both buyers and sellers use their economic freedoms to satisfy their needs and wants.

specialization
when individuals and businesses do only what they do best

free market economy
an economic system in which decisions on the three economic questions are based on the principle of voluntary exchange

voluntary exchange
a transfer of goods, services, or ideas that someone makes willingly

Innovators

Mary Kay Ash

In 1963, Mary Kay Ash used her life savings of $5,000 to launch her "dream" company in Dallas, Texas. Her business plan for Mary Kay Cosmetics was simple but powerful. The firm trained women to sell quality cosmetics from their homes. Because sellers brought the product directly to busy homeowners, the firm was able to keep costs down. Ash rewarded top sellers with incentives like diamond-studded bumblebee pins and pink luxury cars.

The dream became hugely successful. Today, Mary Kay, Inc. earns $2.5 billion in wholesale and has 1.7 million sales reps in more than 30 countries. It has been on *Fortune*'s list of most admired companies.

At a time when males led the business world, Mary Kay Ash helped create wealth for hundreds of women. She handed out over $50 million in sales commissions each year. And she made each one of the women feel important.

Fast Facts

Mary Kay Ash (1918–2001)
Education: One year at the University of Houston
Claim to Fame: Founder of Mary Kay Cosmetics

household
a person or group of people who live together in the same place

firm
a business that uses resources in order to produce a product or service for sale

circular flow
a model that shows the process of exchanges between households and firms

factor market
an exchange in which firms purchase the factors of production from households

product market
an exchange in which households buy goods and services from firms

What is the circular flow model?

The participants in a free market economy are **households** and **firms.** A household is a person or group of people who live together in the same place. Households own the factors of production—land, labor, and capital. They are also buyers of goods and services.

A firm, or business, uses resources to produce a product or service for sale. Look at **Figure 2.2** below. The diagram is called a **circular flow** model. It shows how households and firms exchange money, resources, and products in the marketplace. The inner ring of the diagram shows the flow of resources and products. The outer ring shows the flow of money.

What are the factor and product markets?

The circular flow shows two markets, the **factor market** and the **product market.** Firms and households work together to give each other what they need.

Fig. 2.2 Circular Flow Model of a Market Economy

GRAPH SKILLS

A circular flow model shows the exchanges between households and firms.

1. What is the primary item that changes hands in the monetary flow?
2. Give one example from your own life of an exchange that takes place in the factor market.

Action Graph online

For an animated version of this graph, visit **PearsonSuccessNet.com**

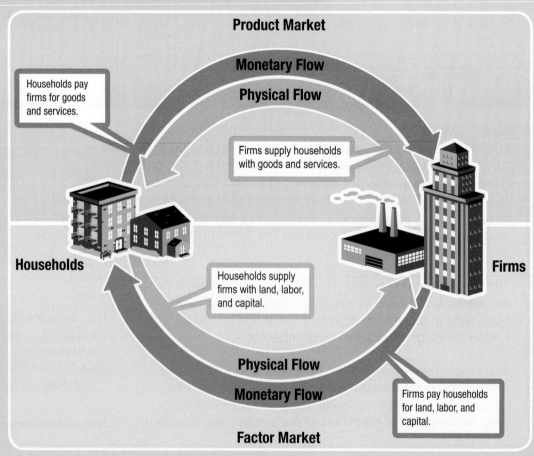

Product Market

Monetary Flow

Physical Flow

Households pay firms for goods and services.

Firms supply households with goods and services.

Households

Households supply firms with land, labor, and capital.

Firms

Physical Flow

Monetary Flow

Firms pay households for land, labor, and capital.

Factor Market

The bottom half of the figure on page 32 shows the factor market. In the factor market, firms buy or rent land. They pay their workers for labor. They also borrow money from households. Households supply firms with the land, labor, and capital they need.

The top half of the figure shows the product market. The product market involves buying and selling between households and firms. Firms sell products and provide services to households. Households buy the products and services made by firms.

✅ CHECKPOINT **What is the role of firms in the free market economy?**

How does competition adjust the marketplace?

In 1776, Adam Smith published one of the most important books on economics. It is called *The Wealth of Nations.* Smith observed that an economy is made up of many exchanges. In these exchanges, the buyer and seller consider only their **self-interest;** in other words, what is best for themselves. Self-interest is an individual's own personal gain.

Smith thought that the free market offered people **incentives.** An incentive is something that makes a person take a certain action. Consumers respond to the incentive of a lower price by buying more goods. Firms have the incentive to make products that people want to buy. This creates **competition.** Competition is like a contest between firms or individuals to sell a product or service. Smith said that this competition acts like an **"invisible hand"** that **regulates**, or controls, the marketplace.

✅ CHECKPOINT **Why is competition important in a free market?**

■■■■■■■■■■■■■■■■■■
Reading Strategy
Questioning
Think about the purpose of this text. Ask yourself: "Am I finding out what I expected about a free market economy?"
■■■■■■■■■■■■■■■■■■

self-interest
an individual's own personal gain

incentive
something that makes a person take a certain action

competition
the contest between firms or people to sell goods or services

invisible hand
Adam Smith's idea that competition should regulate the marketplace

regulate
to control or direct

◀ The phrase "carrot-and-stick" refers to the idea that a mule driver can make a donkey move forward by dangling a carrot in front or by hitting the donkey in the back with a stick. How is the carrot in this cartoon an incentive?

Fig. 2.3

" WELL OF COURSE YOU OUTPERFORMED ME. THE INCENTIVES WERE STACKED IN YOUR FAVOR. "

consumer sovereignty
the power of consumers to decide
what gets produced

What are the advantages of the free market?

You have learned that each society has economic goals and tries to meet them in different ways. Let's look at how the free market meets many of these goals.

1. ***Economic efficiency*** A free market economy can change quickly if conditions change. Producers make only the goods and services that consumers want when they want them.

2. ***Economic freedom*** Free market economies have a lot of economic freedom. Workers work where they want. Firms produce what they want. Individuals buy what they want.

3. ***Economic growth*** There is a lot of competition in free market economies. Entrepreneurs are willing to try new ideas if they think it will help them make more money.

4. ***Additional goals*** Free markets offer many goods and services. Consumers have a lot of power to decide what gets produced. This is called **consumer sovereignty.**

No country today has a pure, uncontrolled free market system. Some economic goals conflict with other goals. It is hard to balance the goals of economic equity and economic security. In Section 4, you will read about how the free market system has been changed to better meet all of the economic goals.

 CHECKPOINT *Why does the free market economy result in a wider variety of goods and services?*

SECTION **2** ASSESSMENT

Essential Questions Journal
To continue to build a response to the Essential Question, go to your **Essential Questions Journal.**

Quick Write

Mary Kay Ash (see the Innovators feature) said that for people to succeed in business, they need to have enthusiasm, discipline, willingness to work, determination, and appreciation of others. Write a short essay describing which of these qualities is your strength. How might you use it to achieve success in the free market?

Guiding Question

1. Use your completed concept web to answer this question: What are the characteristics of a free market economy?

Key Terms and Main Ideas

Directions: On a sheet of paper, write the answer to each question. Use complete sentences.

2. How does specialization make us more efficient?

3. What is the difference between a household and a firm?

4. Explain what Adam Smith meant by the "invisible hand" of the marketplace.

Critical Thinking

5. **Draw Conclusions** How can specialization benefit both buyers and sellers in a free market economy?

6. **Draw Inferences** Why do you think no country has a pure free market economy?

Objectives

- **Describe** how a centrally planned economy is organized.
- **Compare** socialism and communism.
- **Analyze** the use of central planning in the Soviet Union and China.
- **Identify** the disadvantages of a centrally planned economy.

Guiding Question

What are the characteristics of a centrally planned economy?

Copy this chart and fill it in as you read.

Characteristics of Centrally Planned Economies	
Features	**Disadvantages**
• Government owns all factors of production • No consumer sovereignty •	• Results in poor quality goods, shortages, and falling production • Efficiency suffers •

centrally planned economy
an economic system in which a group of central planners makes economic plans for the government

▶ **Economics and You** Suppose you lived in Cuba. Each month, the government would give you a booklet that allowed you to buy food at low prices. The problem is that this quantity of food usually lasts only about two weeks. To eat the rest of the month, you need to buy food at much higher prices. If you are like most Cubans, this is not easy. You earn very little money. Even if you had some money, you might not be able to buy the food. Shortages are common in Cuba.

Why is the situation in Cuba so different from that in the United States? One reason is that the two countries have different economic systems. Cuba does not have a market economy. It has a centrally planned one.

Principles in Action The chief feature of an economy like Cuba's is the amount of government control. In this section, you will see how the ideas of central planning were carried out in two powerful countries.

What is a centrally planned economy?

A **centrally planned economy** is very different from a free market economy. In a centrally planned economy, a group of central planners makes economic plans for the government. The planners make the decisions about how the resources are to be used. The government owns both land and capital. In a way, they also own labor. They decide where workers will work and how much they will earn.

command economy
another name for a centrally planned economy

socialism
a political and economic system in which the means of production are owned by the state

communism
a political and economic system in which the government owns all property and controls all resources

authoritarian
a type of government that requires everyone to obey and in which citizens have few rights

heavy industry
the large-scale production of basic products used in other industries

A centrally planned economy is sometimes called a **command economy.** The government commands, or directs, what goods and services will be produced. Usually the people living in these economies are not free. They are expected to follow the decisions made by the government. They do not have much power.

✔ **CHECKPOINT** *Who makes the key economic decisions in a centrally planned economy?*

What is socialism?

Countries with a centrally planned economy sometimes have a socialist government. **Socialism** is a political and economic system in which the means of production are owned by the state. Socialists believe that governments rather than individuals should own the centers of economic power. The government also controls services for the people.

✔ **CHECKPOINT** *In socialism, who has the power to control the economy?*

What is communism?

Communism is a political and economic system based on socialism. Under communism, the government owns all property and controls all resources. Communism comes mostly from the writings of Karl Marx. Marx said that capitalists such as factory owners gained all of their profits by the labor of workers. (Adam Smith believed capital was the most valuable factor of production.) Communist countries are **authoritarian.** Authoritarian governments require that everyone obey them. Their citizens have few rights.

What was life like in the former Soviet Union?

In 1917, there was a revolution in Russia. The Communist Party took control of the government. The communists gave Russia a new name. It became the Union of Soviet Socialist Republics (USSR), or the Soviet Union. In 1928, Soviet leader Joseph Stalin introduced plans to boost industry and agriculture. Soviet planners wanted to make the USSR a powerful industrial nation. The planners stressed **heavy industry.** This is the large-scale production of basic products, such as steel. This meant that the same resources could not be used to make the everyday products people needed. By shifting resources, the Soviet Union became an industrialized country in only a few years. Because the resources were used in heavy industry, goods such as clothing and shoes became scarce.

Communists in the USSR created large farms owned by the government. The central planners believed these large farms could produce more food with fewer workers. However, these large farms did not produce as much as the government had planned. The Soviet Union often did not have enough crops to feed its own people.

What is life like under communism in China?

China also had a communist revolution. The People's Republic of China was set up as a communist country in 1949. From 1949 to the late 1970s, government planners controlled every part of the economy. At first, they allowed some people to own their own farms. The government tried to build small factories to produce goods to be sold in nearby areas. But these goods were of poor quality and were expensive to make.

▲ Shortages were a common problem in the Soviet Union. Consumers would often wait in long lines at stores. When it was their turn, they might discover there was nothing to buy.

In the 1950s, the government forced many peasants onto large farms. Within a few years, farm production dropped a great deal. There were shortages of many food products. Leaders eventually loosened their control over workers on these farms. The government also sent many factory workers to work on farms. There was no longer a shortage, but China's economy still had many problems.

In the 1970s, Chinese leaders began moving away from central planning. They gave farmers more freedom to own more land. They offered bonuses to factory managers who made their products better. The country's new leaders invited foreign countries to invest in China. Chinese people were allowed to start small businesses and work for their own profit. As a result, China's economy began to grow.

Today, the Chinese government still owns firms in major industries. Government planners set prices of many basic goods. They also make the key economic decisions. Still, China allows far more economic freedom than in the past. China's economy has grown quickly because of such changes.

✔ **CHECKPOINT** *Who makes economic decisions in a communist government?*

▲ The Chinese government used posters like these. They encouraged workers to work hard and produce more.

Reading Strategy
Questioning
Ask yourself: "Did I understand what I just read?" If not, read the material again.

What are the disadvantages of centrally planned economies?

Centrally planned and free market economies share many of the same basic goals. However, centrally planned economies often struggle to meet these goals.

1. *Economic efficiency* In a centrally planned economy, the government owns all factors of production. The government fixes wages, so workers have few incentives to work hard. Government workers make economic decisions. They are slow to adjust to changing economic conditions.

2. *Economic freedom* Usually, command economies stress what is good for society over what is best for the individual. This means that there are fewer individual freedoms.

3. *Economic growth* Innovation is a key to economic growth. Command economies allow little innovation. Managers follow an approved government plan. Producers stress quantity rather than quality.

4. *Economic equity* A major goal of communism was economic equality. Goods and services were to be distributed fairly. However, people in government had more choices. Ordinary people suffered shortages and poorly made products.

5. *Additional goals* Central planning is successful in some ways. It can guarantee everyone a job. Also, communists in the USSR did increase production in heavy industries.

Many countries try to blend the best features of both centrally planned and free market economies.

 CHECKPOINT *Why do centrally planned economies tend to be inefficient?*

SECTION 3 ASSESSMENT

Essential Questions Journal To continue to build a response to the Essential Question, go to your **Essential Questions Journal.**

Guiding Question

1. Use your completed chart to answer this question: What are the characteristics of a centrally planned economy?

Key Terms and Main Ideas

Directions: On a sheet of paper, write the answer to each question. Use complete sentences.

2. What does a centrally planned economy oppose that a market economy encourages?

3. How do socialism and communism differ?

4. What are the characteristics of an authoritarian government?

5. Why is each of the following goals difficult to achieve in a centrally planned economy? (a) economic freedom (b) economic growth

Critical Thinking

6. **Recognize Ideologies** Which economic goal do you think was most important to Karl Marx: efficiency, growth, or equality? Explain.

7. **Draw Conclusions** (a) Who benefits most from a centrally planned economy and how? (b) Who suffers from such an economy and how?

Objectives

- **Explain** the rise of mixed economic systems.
- **Interpret** a circular flow model of a mixed economy.
- **Compare** the mixed economies of various nations with centrally planned and free market systems.
- **Describe** the role of free enterprise in the economy of the United States.

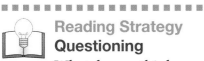

Reading Strategy
Questioning
    What do you think you will learn about by reading this section?

mixed economy
a market-based economic system in which the government has some involvement

laissez faire
the idea that government should not get involved in economic matters

Guiding Question
What are the characteristics of a mixed economy?

Copy this chart and fill it in as you read.

Mixed Economies	
Elements of Market System	**Elements of Centrally Planned System**
• Private property • Exchanges take place in market • •	• Government involved in factor market • Government involved in product market •

▶ **Economics and You** As an American, you expect a high degree of economic freedom. That still does not mean you can do whatever you want. It does not mean you can walk into a store and take a bag of chips. And it surely does not mean you get to decide whether or not to pay taxes. Why not?

Principles in Action Most economies today—including our own—blend a market system with some central planning. You will see why governments sometimes step in. In the Economics & You feature, you will see how government rules prevent you from freely buying certain items in the marketplace.

Why do we have mixed economies?

Pure forms of market economies or centrally planned economies do not exist. Only the traditional economic system really exists in its pure form. Most economies in the world are **mixed economies.** They are a blend of economic systems. Individuals and the government share in making economic decisions. The degree of government involvement varies from nation to nation.

What does "laissez faire" mean?

In the late seventeenth century, France had a king. The king's finance minister asked a merchant how the government could help business. The merchant answered *laissez nous faire,* which means, "Leave us alone." Ever since, **laissez faire** has become a motto for the free market economy. According to the policy of laissez faire, the government should not get involved in economic matters. Business decisions should be left to individuals.

What are the limits of laissez faire?

Even Adam Smith realized that some government involvement is necessary. We accept the idea that there are some things that are best left to the government. Among these are national defense, public education, and mass transit.

Why should economic freedom and economic control be balanced?

Remember that each society has economic goals. Some goals are easily met by the free market. Other goals need government involvement. Each nation must decide what it is willing to give up to meet its goals.

CHECKPOINT *What is one reason the government plays a role in the economy?*

What does the circular flow model for a mixed economy look like?

The circular flow model in Section 2 showed the process of exchanges between households and firms. To show how most mixed economies work, we must add government to our circular flow. **Figure 2.4** shows this.

Fig. 2.4 Circular Flow Model of a Mixed Economy

GRAPH SKILLS

This circular flow model shows how government typically interacts with households and firms in the marketplace.

1. According to this model, how does government affect the monetary flow in a mixed economy?

2. Give one real-life example of how government can interact with a firm in the product market.

Action Graph
online

For an animated version of this graph, visit **PearsonSuccessNet.com**

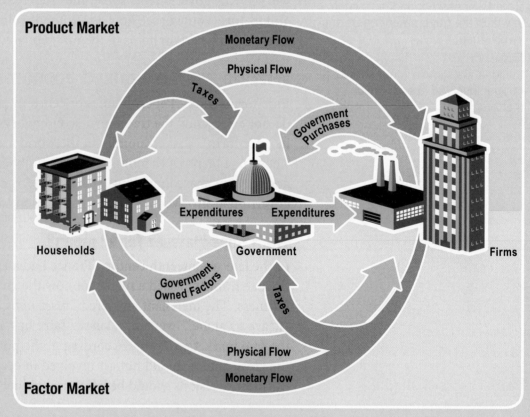

Product Market

Monetary Flow
Physical Flow
Taxes
Government Purchases
Expenditures   Expenditures
Households
Government
Firms
Government Owned Factors
Taxes
Physical Flow
Monetary Flow

Factor Market

What is the role of government in the factor market?

Governments buy land, labor, and capital from households in the factor market. For example, in 2006 the U.S. government paid 2.7 million employees $166.8 billion a year for their labor.

What is the role of government in the product market?

Governments buy goods and services from firms in the product market. Government offices need telephones and computers. Printing money requires many tons of paper and gallons of ink. The government buys most of these things from private firms.

How does money flow to and from the government?

The outer ring of the circular flow model in **Figure 2.4** shows the flow of money to and from the government. Governments collect taxes from both households and firms and transfer some of this money to firms and individuals.

 CHECKPOINT *How are governments involved in the product market?*

How can we compare mixed economies?

As you read earlier in this chapter, most modern economies are mixed. One way of comparing them is by how much the government is involved. In some economies, governments are very involved. In others, there is little government involvement. **Figure 2.5** shows a **continuum** of mixed economies in the world. A continuum is a continued series of things with no clear division between them.

In what mixed economies is the government very involved?

North Korea is a good example of a centrally planned economy. Like the former USSR, communist North Korea has an economy almost totally controlled by the government. Government-owned industries produce 95 percent of North Korea's goods. Most imports are banned, and foreign companies are not allowed.

In China, the government continues to play a large role in the economy. But China is now going through an **economic transition.** This is a period of change in which a nation moves from one economic system to another. In China's case, the transition involves privatizing government-owned firms. **Privatization** means selling government businesses or services to individuals. They are then allowed to compete in the marketplace. China has some central planning, but not as much as North Korea.

Fig. 2.5 Continuum of Mixed Economies

Centrally Planned

Free Market

Iran   Mexico   France   United Kingdom   Hong Kong

South Africa

North Korea   China   Germany   Canada   Singapore

Cuba   Russia   Poland   Japan   United States

GRAPH SKILLS

The degree of government intervention in the marketplace varies among nations.

1. Choose two nations on this continuum. Based on this diagram, write one sentence for each nation describing how its economic system differs from that of the United States.

2. Why is China a little bit farther to the right on this diagram than Cuba?

---

free enterprise system
an economic system in which investment decisions are made by individuals rather than being made by the government

Reading Strategy
Questioning
Think beyond the text. Consider your own thoughts and experiences as you read about different kinds of economies.

In what economies is there little government involvement?

Perhaps the economy closest to a free market economy is Hong Kong. In Hong Kong, the rule of laissez faire is followed. The government rarely interferes in the free market. There are few limits on foreign companies.

✅ **CHECKPOINT** *Why is China's economy more mixed than North Korea's?*

What is the role of government in the U.S. economy?

The U.S. economy is often described as a **free enterprise system.** Free enterprise means that investment decisions are made by individuals rather than by the government.

In the United States, the role of government is larger than in Hong Kong. It is much less than in North Korea. The U.S. government keeps order, provides important services, and promotes the general welfare. Overall, Americans enjoy a high level of economic freedom. In the next chapter, you will read more about free enterprise and the role the U.S. government plays in the economy.

✅ **CHECKPOINT** *Why is the United States said to have a free enterprise system?*

Buying and Selling in a Mixed Economy

You walk into a store, put down your money, and walk away with an MP3 player. *In our free market, you can buy most goods without government interference.*

Pharmacy

A druggist can sell only those medicines approved by the Food and Drug Administration. Regulations also determine what medicines can be bought only with a doctor's prescription. *In a mixed economy, the government restricts your ability to buy certain goods.*

SECTION 4 ASSESSMENT

Essential Questions Journal To continue to build a response to the Essential Question, go to your **Essential Questions Journal.**

Guiding Question

1. Use your completed chart to answer this question: What are the characteristics of a mixed economy?

Key Terms and Main Ideas

Directions: On a sheet of paper, write the answer to each question. Use complete sentences.

2. What is laissez faire?

3. Why is it difficult to balance economic freedom and economic control?

4. Why have some nations begun an economic transition to a free enterprise system?

Critical Thinking

5. **Make Comparisons** (a) How does laissez faire differ from a centrally planned government? (b) Do you think a pure laissez faire system could work? Why or why not?

6. **Make Comparisons** How does the American free enterprise system differ from North Korea's centrally planned system?

7. **Make Connections** In mixed economic systems, the government makes rules that apply to buying and selling products. Review the Economics & You feature. List some other goods and services that are affected by government rules.

Section 1–Answering the Three Economic Questions

- Every society asks three basic economic questions: What goods and services should be produced? How should these goods and services be produced? Who will consume these goods and services?

- Different societies answer these questions based on the importance they attach to their own economic goals.

Section 2–The Free Market

- Markets exist because no one produces all they require to satisfy their needs and wants.

- In a free market economy, self-interest is what leads people to act.

- Adam Smith believed that competition acted as an "invisible hand" to control the marketplace.

Section 3–Centrally Planned Economies

- In centrally planned economies, the central government provides answers for the three basic economic questions.

- Socialism and communism are two terms linked to centrally planned economies.

- Centrally planned economies have often had trouble meeting their economic goals.

Section 4–Mixed Economies

- Most modern economies are mixed economies.

- The idea that government should not get involved in economic matters is called *laissez faire,* or "leave alone."

- Mixed economies fall along a continuum. This ranges from North Korea at one end and Hong Kong at the other end.

- The U.S. economy has a free enterprise system.

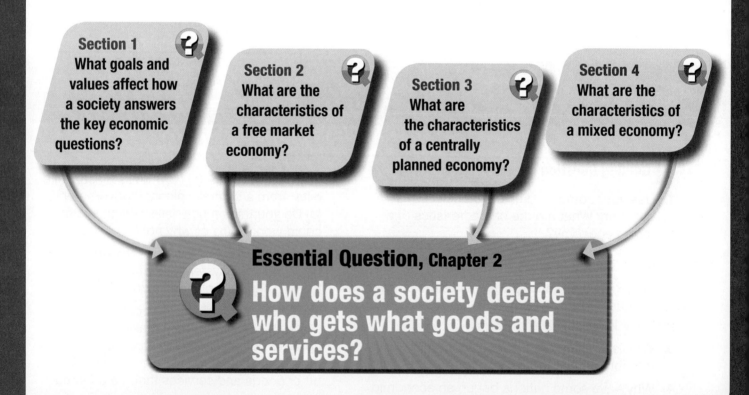

Section 1
What goals and values affect how a society answers the key economic questions?

Section 2
What are the characteristics of a free market economy?

Section 3
What are the characteristics of a centrally planned economy?

Section 4
What are the characteristics of a mixed economy?

Essential Question, Chapter 2

How does a society decide who gets what goods and services?

The Principles of Economics

Alfred Marshall was an important British economist from the late 1800s until he died in 1924. He studied economics for much of his life. He also taught political economics at the University of Cambridge in England. Two other famous economists, John Keynes and Arthur Pigou, were among Marshall's students.

In 1890, Marshall wrote a book called the Principles of Economics. *His book covered many parts of economics. Many of the economic terms that we use today come from Marshall's ideas. This passage is from a section of the book called "On Wants and Their Satisfaction."*

"Human wants and desires are countless in number and . . . various in kind: but they are generally limited and capable of being satisfied. The uncivilized man indeed has not many more [wants and desires] than the . . . animal; but every step in his progress upwards increases the variety of his needs together with the variety in his methods of satisfying them. He desires not [only] larger quantities of the things . . . but better qualities of those things; he desires a greater choice of things, and things that will satisfy new wants growing up in him.

. . . As man rises in civilization, as his mind becomes developed . . . his wants become rapidly more subtle and more various. . . .

As a man's riches increase, his food and drink become more various and costly; but his appetite is limited by nature, and when his expenditure on food is extravagant it is more often to gratify the desires of hospitality and display. . . .(T)herefore, although it is man's wants in the earliest stages of his development that give rise to his activities . . . each new step upwards is to be regarded as the development of new activities giving rise to new wants, rather than of new wants giving rise to new activities."

Document-Based Questions

1. Why is Alfred Marshall important to the study of economics?
2. What does the first sentence of the passage say about wants and desires?
3. According to Alfred Marshall, what happens to a person's wants as the person becomes more developed?
4. Why do wealthy people spend a great amount of money on expensive goods?
5. What role could scarcity play as a person's wants increase?

Directions: Answer the questions below using complete sentences.

Section 1–Answering the Three Economic Questions

1. What questions does every society have to answer about its economic system?

2. Why do you think traditional economies are most common in isolated places?

3. What is the purpose of a safety net?

4. Why does a country's economy have to grow as its population grows?

Section 2–The Free Market

5. What are two things Adam Smith discussed in his book *The Wealth of Nations?*

6. Why is it important for people and businesses to specialize in what they produce?

7. Why is economic efficiency important to a free market economy?

8. How does competition regulate the marketplace?

Section 3–Centrally Planned Economies

9. How much economic freedom is there in a centrally planned economy?

10. How are socialism and communism alike?

11. In 1928, why did Soviet planners decide to use their resources on heavy industry?

12. What happened when the Chinese government forced peasants onto large farms in the 1950s?

Section 4–Mixed Economies

13. What is one way to compare mixed economies?

14. What happens to a country during an economic transition?

15. Why can we say that Hong Kong is closest to having a free market economy?

16. Why is the U.S. economy said to be a free enterprise system?

17. Why are most of the major economies in the world mixed economies?

18. What are the two ways that households and firms interact in the factor market? In the product market?

 Exploring the Essential Question

Essential Question Activity

19. Complete the activity to answer the Essential Question **How does a society decide who gets what goods and services?**

Imagine that your class is advising leaders of a new nation, Ervola. The President of Ervola wants to know the best way to meet their economic goals. Political leaders want to use central planning. But business leaders want a laissez-faire approach. Which system will help Ervola meet the economic goals stated in Section 1 of this chapter? Use the format of a debate. First, team members should identify each economic goal and decide how their side plans to meet it.

(a) For the affirmative, a student team will argue for a strict command economy.

(b) For the negative, another student team will argue for a totally free market economy.

Essential Questions Journal To continue to build a response to the Essential Question, go to your **Essential Questions Journal**.

Test-Taking Tip

When studying for a test, work with a partner to write your own test questions. Then answer each other's questions. Check your answers.

Study anytime, anywhere. Download these files today.

Economic Dictionary online
Vocabulary Support in English and Spanish

Audio Review online
Audio Study Guide in English and Spanish

Action Graph online
Animated Charts and Graphs

Visual Glossary online
Animated feature

How the Economy Works online
Animated feature

Download to your computer or mobile device at PearsonSuccessNet.com

Chapter **3** American Free Enterprise

Essential Question, Chapter 3

What role should government play in a free market economy?

- **Section 1** Benefits of Free Enterprise

- **Section 2** Promoting Growth and Stability

- **Section 3** Providing Public Goods

- **Section 4** Providing a Safety Net

Economics on the go

To study anywhere, anytime, download these online resources at *PearsonSuccessNet.com* ➤

▶ **What is free enterprise?** What is the role of the consumer in the American economy? Does the Constitution say anything about taxes and consumer rights? How does the government work to promote economic strength and fight poverty?

In this chapter, you will find answers to all these questions and more. You will learn about the principles behind the free enterprise system.

Reading Strategy: Predicting

Previewing helps readers think about what they already know about a subject. It also prepares readers to look for new information. It helps readers think about what will come next. In other words, it gives readers a purpose for reading. Keep this in mind as you make predictions.

- Look at the chapter words, images, and graphs for clues about economics.

- Make your best guess about the content under each subhead before you read it.

- As you read, check your predictions. You may have to change your predictions as you learn more information.

Visual Glossary online

Go to the Visual Glossary Online for an interactive review of **free enterprise.**

How the Economy Works online

Go to How the Economy Works Online for an interactive lesson on **providing public goods.**

Action Graph online

Go to Action Graph Online for animated versions of key charts and graphs.

Objectives

- **Describe** the basic principles of the American free enterprise system.
- **Describe** the role of the consumer in the American economy.
- **Identify** how the Constitution protects free enterprise.
- **Explain** why the government may get involved in the marketplace.

■ ■ ■ ■ ■ ■ ■ ■ ■ ■ ■ ■ ■ ■ ■

Reading Strategy
Predicting
Preview the title of the section. Ask: "What do I think this section will be about?"

Guiding Question

What are the benefits of free enterprise?

Copy this chart and fill it in as you read.

Free Enterprise System	
Characteristics	Benefits
• Profit motive • Open opportunity • Equality under the law •	• Forces financial discipline • Encourages innovation •

▶ **Economics and You** Picture the many services and products you use every week. Somebody had to think of each one. Somebody figured out that people would rather rent DVDs from a Web site that offers thousands of choices than to go to a store that offers far fewer. Somebody invented a way to send photos as well as messages with cellphones. Now, suppose you had one of these great ideas. Could you put your plan into action? Every day, American entrepreneurs begin new businesses. These businesses earn profits, create jobs, and offer new goods and services.

Principles in Action The American free enterprise system allows people who have ideas and drive to start businesses and make them into a success. In this section, you will see how one immigrant built a successful business in the U.S. fashion industry. You will also learn about the important role that you, as a consumer, play in the free enterprise system.

What is the free enterprise system?

Today there are millions of businesses in America. Many were started by single entrepreneurs. They shared a dream. It was to earn a living and become successful or even rich.

The United States has long been thought of as a "land of opportunity." We are a country where anyone from any background can be a success. There are many reasons for the economic success of America. The most important may be the free enterprise system. In the free enterprise system, people enjoy many economic freedoms. People can own their own property.

They can set up businesses. They are free to buy and sell things. Consumers are the people who buy and use products. They can choose the best products at the lowest price.

Our free enterprise economy has several key characteristics. These include:
- the profit motive
- legal equality
- the right to private property
- voluntary exchange

■ ■ ■ ■ ■ ■ ■ ■ ■ ■ ■ ■ ■ ■ ■ ■ ■ ■ ■ ■

profit motive
the incentive that drives individuals and business owners to improve their material well-being

legal equality
the principle that everyone has the same legal rights

private property rights
the principle that people have the right to control their possessions and use them as they wish

What is the profit motive?

Profit is the money a business keeps after expenses are paid. Profits are very important to free enterprise. No business can last long if it does not make a profit. Entrepreneurs open businesses because they expect to make a profit. This hope of making a profit is called the **profit motive.** In the free enterprise system, business owners can run their businesses in the way they think best. They hope this will allow them to make the most profit. The system rewards the most efficient, productive, and innovative firms. They are the ones that make the biggest profit.

How does free enterprise ensure legal equality?

The free enterprise economy gives everyone the same rights. The idea that all people have the same rights under the law is called **legal equality.** The law treats everyone the same. Everyone has a chance to compete in the marketplace. In some countries, women and minorities do not have many rights.

What are private property rights?

In a free enterprise economy, people own and control property. This right is called **private property rights**. People and businesses are free to use their property in any way they choose, within the law. As an individual, you decide how to use your property. This includes property like the car or clothes you own. Businesses that use their resources wisely make a greater profit.

What is the principle of voluntary exchange?

An exchange is a transfer. You make an exchange when you give another person something and get something back. If you were not forced to make the exchange, it was a voluntary exchange. In free enterprise, buyers and sellers are free to make exchanges.

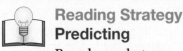

Reading Strategy
Predicting
     Based on what you have just read, what do you think the next three paragraphs will be about?

interest group
an organization that tries to persuade government officials to act in ways that help its members

patriotism
love of one's country

Both benefit from the exchange. Sellers get money for their goods and services. Buyers get products they want. Both buyers and sellers use their economic freedoms to satisfy their needs and wants. Voluntary exchange encourages competition. People and businesses often compete for the same resources. When you finish school, you will be competing with many others for jobs. Businesses compete to attract consumers. Competition is good. It encourages producers to make the best products for the least cost.

✔ **CHECKPOINT** *What are three key economic rights that Americans enjoy?*

What role do consumers play in the free enterprise system?

In the free enterprise system, consumers have the freedom to make their own economic choices. Consumers send a signal to businesses through voluntary exchange. They tell businesses what to produce and how much to make. Consumers also send a signal when they do not buy a good or service. They are telling the producer that they do not want the good or service or that it is priced too high.

Consumers can also make their wishes known by joining an **interest group.** This is a group that tries to persuade government officials to act in ways that help the group's members. One consumer interest group is the Consumers Union. It urges Congress to pass laws to protect consumers.

Businesses form interest groups as well. For example, the National Retail Federation represents an industry with more than 1.6 million U.S. retail companies. It tries to get laws passed that will help its many members.

✔ **CHECKPOINT** *How do consumers make their wishes known?*

What economic ideas exist in the U.S. Constitution?

The economic freedoms that Americans enjoy are an important source of **patriotism,** or love of one's country. The rights to own property or to become an entrepreneur are basic to liberty. They are as important as freedom of speech or the right to vote.

What does the Constitution state about private property rights?

The writers of the Constitution believed in the right to private property. One of the signers was John Adams of Massachusetts. He believed that "property must be secured or liberty cannot exist." He thought that there was no freedom if people were not allowed to own property. James Madison, often called the "father of the Constitution," believed that governments are set up in order to protect property.

The Constitution says that "no person shall be . . . deprived of life, liberty, or property, without due process of law; nor shall private property be taken for public use, without just compensation." It prevents the government from taking private property except when there is a public reason. For instance, suppose a state wants to add lanes to a highway. It may take land from people who own property along the highway. This right of a government to take private property for public use is called **eminent domain.** Even then, the government must pay the owner the fair value of the property that has been taken. This protection applies to businesses as well as to individuals.

What does the Constitution state about taxation?

The Constitution also spells out how government can tax individuals and businesses. It says that taxes collected from each state would be based on the number of people living in the state. No state is allowed to tax goods it buys from other states. The 16th Amendment gave the government the right to tax income. Both individuals and corporations pay income tax.

What does the Constitution state about contracts?

Finally, the Constitution guarantees people and businesses the right to make contracts. Contracts are legal agreements between people or businesses. This means that people or businesses cannot use the political process to change their contracts. The terms of someone's business agreement cannot be changed by a law.

✔ **CHECKPOINT** *What constitutional protections make it possible for Americans to conduct business?*

eminent domain
the right of a government to take private property for public use

Innovators

Oscar de la Renta

Born in the Dominican Republic, Oscar de la Renta showed a talent for art. His parents sent him to Spain to study painting. But he became fascinated with fashion and soon found work with a famous Spanish designer. His early career was spent designing for the rich.

In 1963, de la Renta moved to New York City. Like many entrepreneurs, Oscar de la Renta had a vision—and was willing to take risks to pursue it. For this enterprising immigrant, America truly proved to be a land of opportunity.

Oscar de la Renta has never lost his interest in the arts, giving generously of his time as a board member of New York's Metropolitan Opera and Carnegie Hall. Nor has he forgotten his Latin roots. He served as chairman of the Spanish Institute and helped build a school and day-care center for underprivileged Dominican children.

Fast Facts

Oscar de la Renta (1932–)
Education: Academy of San Fernando, Madrid, Spain
Claim to Fame: Successful fashion designer

---

public disclosure laws
laws that require companies to provide information about their products

public interest
the concerns of society as a whole

What is the role of government in the free enterprise system?

The government protects property rights, contracts, and other business activities. We also expect the government to protect us from economic problems that affect us all, such as pollution or unsafe foods.

Why does government have to provide information to consumers?

Another important role the government plays is keeping consumers informed. The government gives information to consumers in order to protect them from dangerous products. **Public disclosure laws** require companies to give consumers information about their products. You have probably seen information like this attached to some things you have looked at or bought. For example, every new car has a sticker that shows how much fuel the car will use. Refrigerators and air conditioners also come with information about how much energy they use. This information helps consumers make good decisions.

How does government protect the health, safety, and well-being of people?

The government also is interested in the well-being of all the people. This is called the **public interest.** The government passes laws controlling some business activities. For example, Congress and many states have passed laws protecting the environment. Gas stations, for example, have to follow strict rules on getting rid of waste oil. Makers of cars, medicine, and other products have to meet government standards.

The government protects consumers in many ways. Drugs must be safe and effective. Foods have to be produced in ways that will not make consumers sick. They come with information on what they are made of. Products like ladders and power equipment come with information to make sure they will be used safely.

Are there negative effects of government regulation?

During the 1960s and 1970s, several new governmental agencies were created to protect consumers and the environment. People wanted these protections. As a result, businesses had to spend more to make sure the new rules were followed. In the 1980s and 1990s, however, government cut back some government regulation. Today, the government tries to balance the concerns of businesses with the need to protect the public.

 CHECKPOINT *Why does the government place some limits on the freedom of businesses?*

SECTION 1 ASSESSMENT

Essential Questions Journal To continue to build a response to the Essential Question, go to your **Essential Questions Journal.**

Quick Write

Create a two-column list. On one side, write the basic personal and political rights guaranteed to Americans. On the other side, list basic economic rights under the free enterprise system. Then, write a paragraph explaining in your own words how the two sets of rights are linked.

 Guiding Question

1. Use your completed chart to answer this question: What are the benefits of free enterprise?

Key Terms and Main Ideas

Directions: On a sheet of paper, write the answer to each question. Use complete sentences.

2. How is the profit motive the driving force behind the American economy?
3. How does the principle of voluntary exchange promote market competition?
4. What is an interest group?
5. What is the right of eminent domain?

Critical Thinking

6. **Recognize Cause and Effect** How can inequality or discrimination hurt an economy's ability to maximize its human capital? Give two examples.
7. **Analyze** How do the decisions you make as a consumer affect the economy?

Objectives

- **Explain** why the government tracks and influences business cycles.

- **Describe** how the government promotes economic strength.

- **Analyze** the factors that increase productivity.

Guiding Question

How does the U.S. government encourage growth and stability?

Copy this chart and fill it in as you read. Add more boxes if necessary.

Promoting Economic Strength		
Employment	**Growth**	**Stability and Security**
• Goal: providing jobs for all able workers • Actions: steps to encourage job growth if needed	• Goal: • Actions: cut taxes or increase spending to promote growth •	• Goal: help investors and others feel secure • Actions:

------

macroeconomics
the study of economic behavior and decision making in a nation's whole economy

gross domestic product
the total value of all final goods and services produced in a country in a given year

microeconomics
the study of the economic behavior and decision making in small units, such as households and firms

▶ **Economics and You** Yesterday you bought a pack of gum . . . or a new guitar . . . or your first car. Your purchase was just one of millions of exchanges that took place across the country that day. This pattern of buying and selling is tracked by government economists. They use the information to see how well the American economy is doing.

Principles in Action Tracking economic data is one tool the government uses to promote economic growth and stability. As you will see, supporting education is another economic role taken by the government. You will also see how your involvement in elections can help shape the economy.

Why do governments track business cycles?

There are two branches of economics. In **macroeconomics,** economists look at the big picture. They study the overall economy using information such as unemployment, inflation, production, and price levels. One way of looking at an economy as a whole is to figure out the **gross domestic product** (GDP). The GDP is the total value of all final goods and services produced in a country in one year. It is an important measure of an economy. It allows us to make comparisons among different countries. It also allows us to see how the economy is doing compared to past years.

In **microeconomics,** economists look at the small picture. It is the bottom-up view of the economy. It focuses on individual households and firms.

The economy is always changing. Economists study trends in the GDP. They see that the GDP usually follows a pattern of ups and downs. This pattern is called the **business cycle.** You will learn a lot more about the business cycle in Chapter 12.

■ ■ ■ ■ ■ ■ ■ ■ ■ ■ ■ ■ ■ ■ ■ ■ ■ ■
business cycle
a period of macroeconomic expansion, or growth, followed by one of contraction, or decline

✔ **CHECKPOINT** *Why do governments track gross domestic product?*

How does the government try to promote economic strength?

The government has three goals as it tries to promote economic growth. These goals are high employment, growth, and stability.

What does the employment rate show?

The first goal is to ensure jobs for everyone who is able to work. The government tries to monitor the unemployment rate so that it is no higher than between 4 percent and 6 percent. If the unemployment rate rises higher than that, the government may take steps to create more jobs.

How is steady economic growth created?

The second goal is steady economic growth. The more the economy grows, the better it can produce the goods and services we need and want. Steady economic growth helps increase our standard of living. To help growth, the government may cut taxes or increase spending. Experts do not agree on which approach works best in promoting economic growth.

Why is economic stability important?

Consumers, producers, and investors feel better about the economy when economic conditions do not change much. Suppose people started worrying about the safety of their money in banks. What if there were a sudden jump in prices? If economic conditions change too fast, people will start worrying about the economy. Economic growth may slow or even stop.

✔ **CHECKPOINT** *What three goals does the government try to meet when promoting economic strength?*

Fig. 3.1 Gross Domestic Product, 1900–2006

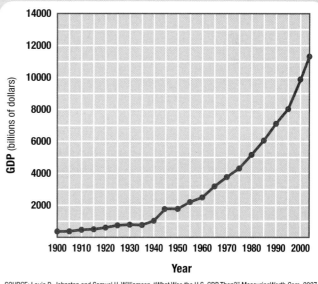

SOURCE: Louis D. Johnston and Samuel H. Williamson, "What Was the U.S. GDP Then?" MeasuringWorth.Com, 2007.

GRAPH SKILLS

A growing GDP is one sign of a healthy economy.

1. How much did the GDP grow between 1990 and 2006?
2. Which periods in this graph may represent downturns in the business cycle?

Action Graph
online

For an animated version of this graph, visit **PearsonSuccessNet.Com**

work ethic
a commitment to the value of work

obsolescence
a situation in which older products
and processes become out of date

Reading Strategy
Predicting
What technology do
you think you'll read about in
the next three paragraphs?

What affects productivity?

Americans enjoy one of the highest standards of living in the
world. This is the result of our high level of productivity. How
do we do it? One way is through the American **work ethic.** This
is our willingness to work hard, to learn, and to finish things we
start. Another way is by improving technology.

How does technology increase productivity?

Technology is the process used to make a good or service.
Improved technology is a key factor in increasing productivity.
Our GDP keeps increasing because we are always finding new
ways of doing things. The new technology gives American
businesses a big advantage over other countries.

American history is full of innovations that improved productivity.
Thomas Edison's perfection of the light bulb made it possible to
work even after dark. Henry Ford used the assembly line to make
cars that more people could afford. In recent times, computers
allow workers to do more work in less time.

Innovation often leads to **obsolescence.** This refers to older
products and processes becoming out of date. Workers, too, may
become obsolete. Telephone operators became unnecessary when
firms changed to dialing systems run by computers. Still, these
physical and human resources can be used in other ways. Old
factories can be changed into stores or apartments. Workers can
be trained to do other jobs.

How does the government promote productivity?

The government knows how important it is to keep our leadership
in technology. To make sure we do not lose our advantage, the
government promotes inventions and new ways of doing things.
The government sponsors many projects at universities. The
Morrill Acts of 1862 and 1890 created land-grant colleges. These
colleges received land and money to study "agriculture and the
mechanical arts." The Massachusetts Institute of Technology and
Texas A&M Universities were land-grant colleges. Land-grant
schools have been leaders in promoting new ideas.

The government produces new technologies itself. An example is the National Aeronautics and Space Administration (NASA). NASA is a U.S. government program that has sent spaceships and humans into space. Technology created by NASA has produced many spin-offs, or products with commercial uses. One NASA spin-off is a muscle stimulator for people with disabilities. Another is a scanner that allows firefighters to see "invisible flames" given off by alcohol or hydrogen fires.

▲ Americans patent thousands of inventions every year. These college entrepreneurs, Gavin McIntyre and Eben Bayer, created a new "green" insulation partly from mushrooms that they grew under their beds.

The government also encourages new ways of doing things by granting **patents** and **copyrights.** A patent gives the inventor of a new product the sole right to produce and sell it for 20 years. A copyright gives an author sole rights to publish and sell his or her work. Patents and copyrights encourage new ideas. They protect people's right to profit in the free market from things they create.

patent
a government license that gives an inventor the exclusive right to produce and sell a product

copyright
a government license that grants an author exclusive rights to publish and sell creative works

Economic growth cannot occur without individual effort. The work ethic is a commitment to the value and quality of hard work. The American work ethic has been a key ingredient in the nation's productivity and economic success.

✅ **CHECKPOINT** *How does improved technology help the economy?*

SECTION 2 ASSESSMENT

Essential Questions Journal
To continue to build a response to the Essential Question, go to your **Essential Questions Journal.**

 Guiding Question

1. Use your completed chart to answer this question: How does the U.S. government encourage growth and stability?

Key Terms and Main Ideas

Directions: On a sheet of paper, write the answer to each question. Use complete sentences.

2. Why is the government decision to increase or decrease spending a matter of macroeconomic policy?

3. How does gross domestic product provide a means to analyze economic growth?

4. Describe the business cycle.

5. How can innovation lead to obsolescence?

Critical Thinking

6. **Demonstrate Reasoned Judgment** Suppose you had a job you did not like. If the economy was in the downward part of the business cycle, would you be more or less likely to quit your job to look for a better one? Why or why not?

7. **Analyze Information** Identify three individual qualities and actions you think demonstrate a strong work ethic. Explain why you chose each one.

Objectives

- **Identify** examples of public goods.
- **Analyze** market failures.
- **Evaluate** how the government sets aside some resources by managing externalities.

■ ■ ■ ■ ■ ■ ■ ■ ■ ■ ■ ■ ■ ■ ■ ■ ■ ■

public good
a shared good or service for which it would be difficult to make consumers pay individually and to exclude those who did not pay

Guiding Question

Why does a society provide public goods?

Copy this chart and fill it in as you read.

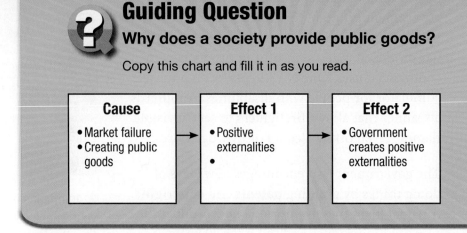

Cause	Effect 1	Effect 2
• Market failure • Creating public goods	• Positive externalities •	• Government creates positive externalities •

▶ **Economics and You** Roads, schools, dams, bridges, parks—suppose that federal, state, and local governments stopped providing all these services. What would your life be like without them? Now suppose that there was a paved road in your town, but you couldn't drive on it because your family had not chipped in to have the road built. How fair would a system like that be?

Principles in Action Even in a free market economy, the government must provide certain goods and services that the marketplace cannot.

What are characteristics of public goods?

Roads and bridges are examples of how government provides a **public good.** A public good is a shared good or service. One characteristic is that they are products and services available to everyone. Dams and national defense are other examples of public goods.

Would people be willing to pay for public services such as highways, police, fire protection, and the space program on their own? Probably not. The government forces us to pay our fair share in taxes. Otherwise, some people would benefit from them without paying for them.

Public goods have another characteristic. Many people can use them without cutting benefits to anyone else. Most of the time, increasing the number of consumers does not increase the cost of providing the public good. Suppose you are driving on a highway. Eight other drivers enter. The extra drivers do not reduce the road's benefits to you. They do not increase the government's cost of providing the road.

Public goods are paid for by the **public sector.** This is the part of the economy that deals with providing basic government services. The **private sector** is the part of the economy that is controlled or owned by individuals and businesses.

What are the costs and benefits of providing public goods?

Every time the government provides public goods, there are costs and benefits. When the government builds roads, it is an obvious benefit. Transportation is a vital part of the nation's **infrastructure.** This refers to the things necessary for a society to function.

There is also a cost to the public when the government builds roads. It is the economic freedom we give up as well as the physical cost of building a road.

What is the "free rider" problem?

A **free rider** is someone who benefits from what he or she does not directly pay for. You probably would not be willing to pay to build roads in another state. Yet, when the government builds a system of national roads, you share in the benefit. For example, the American system of roads makes it easier for trucking companies to bring goods to your state. And if you were traveling through another state on vacation, you would certainly drive on their roads. You receive the benefit even if you did not directly pay for it.

Everyone is better off if the government provides this service. The service is paid for by local taxes. Could the government rely on people to donate whatever they wanted to? Probably not. Some people would refuse to give any money.

 **CHECKPOINT** *What two characteristics do public goods have?*

Why are public goods examples of market failure?

Some economists call public goods an example of **market failure.** This describes a special situation in which the free market, operating on its own, does not efficiently distribute resources.

Recall how a successful free market operates: The choices about what goods get made, how they get made, and for whom the goods are made are chosen by individuals. The possibility of making a profit attracts producers.

public sector
the portion of the economy that involves the transactions of the government

private sector
the part of the economy that involves the transactions of individuals and businesses

infrastructure
the basic facilities that are necessary for a society to function and grow

free rider
someone who would not be willing to pay for a certain good or service but who would benefit from it anyway if it were provided as a public good

market failure
a situation in which the free market, operating on its own, does not distribute resources efficiently

Fig. 3.2 How the Economy Works

How are public goods created?

Some public goods are too costly for the free market to satisfy. In these cases, the government may intervene to provide public goods.

1 Farmers in Capp County have to drive an extra hundred miles to get their crops across the river. They want a new bridge built nearby.

Cost: $126 million

Benefit: Saves each farmer $5,000 a year

Public Need

Costs and Benefits

externality

an economic side effect of a good or service; it generates benefits or costs to someone other than the person deciding how much to produce or consume

Consider our road-building example. Are the features of the free market present? No. If a company did build a road, it could charge a high price for tolls because it would have no competition. Also, companies would probably not build roads in areas with few people. They would see no chance to earn profits. For that reason, this is an example of market failure.

 CHECKPOINT *Why are public goods examples of market failure?*

What are externalities?

Economic side effects are sometimes called **externalities**. They can be either helpful or harmful. They affect people other than the buyer and seller. Some of the helpful, or positive, externalities of building a bridge are shown in **Figure 3.3** on page 64.

Building a bridge is an example of the public sector. However, the private sector can also create positive externalities. For instance, if a computer company hires poor teenagers and trains them to be computer programmers then other companies benefit from hiring these workers without having to pay for their training.

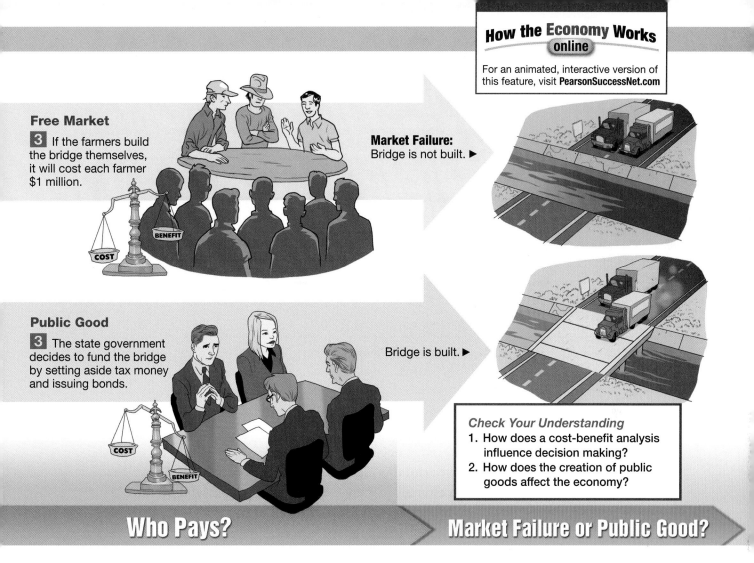

Free Market

3 If the farmers build the bridge themselves, it will cost each farmer $1 million.

BENEFIT

COST

Market Failure:
Bridge is not built. ▶

Public Good

3 The state government decides to fund the bridge by setting aside tax money and issuing bonds.

COST

BENEFIT

Bridge is built. ▶

Check Your Understanding
1. How does a cost-benefit analysis influence decision making?
2. How does the creation of public goods affect the economy?

Who Pays?

Market Failure or Public Good?

Of course, as **Figure 3.2** shows, producing goods and services can also have harmful economic side effects. These are called **negative externalities.** Negative externalities cause part of the cost of producing a good or service to be paid for by someone other than the producer.

✅ **CHECKPOINT** *How do negative externalities contribute to the cost of a product?*

How does the government respond to externalities?

The government tries to create positive externalities. Education, for example, benefits students. At the same time, society as a whole also benefits. This is because educated workers are generally well trained in their specific fields and can contribute more to the public good.

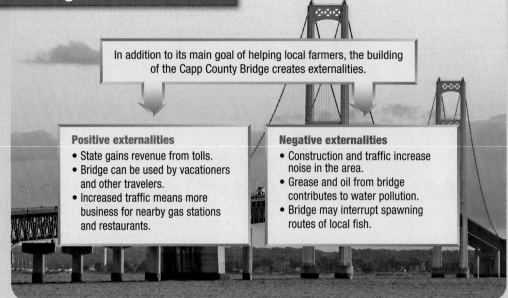

Fig. 3.3 Positive and Negative Externalities

CHART SKILLS

Building a bridge creates dozens of externalities, both positive and negative, depending on your point of view.

1. Why is use of the bridge by vacationers an externality?

2. Why would increased car traffic be considered a positive externality by some people and a negative externality by others?

In addition to its main goal of helping local farmers, the building of the Capp County Bridge creates externalities.

Positive externalities
- State gains revenue from tolls.
- Bridge can be used by vacationers and other travelers.
- Increased traffic means more business for nearby gas stations and restaurants.

Negative externalities
- Construction and traffic increase noise in the area.
- Grease and oil from bridge contributes to water pollution.
- Bridge may interrupt spawning routes of local fish.

The government tries to limit negative externalities, such as pollution. Acid rain is very harmful to all living things. Why is acid rain a negative externality? It is part of the cost of producing power and driving cars. Who pays for the cost of the trees, plants, and animals that are hurt? Not the people who produce the pollution. The cost is paid by all of us.

The federal government now requires new cars to have expensive antipollution devices. Actions like these force the producers of the pollution to pay for its costs.

 CHECKPOINT *What does the government do in response to externalities?*

SECTION 3 ASSESSMENT

Essential Questions Journal To continue to build a response to the Essential Question, go to your **Essential Questions Journal.**

 Guiding Question

1. Use your completed chart to answer the following question: Why does a society provide public goods?

Key Terms and Main Ideas

Directions: On a sheet of paper, write the answer to each question. Use complete sentences.

2. What are two characteristics of public goods?

3. What is an example of an action taken by the public sector? By the private sector?

4. Give an example of one positive and one negative externality.

Critical Thinking

5. **Analyze Information** Why is national defense an example of the free rider problem?

6. **Synthesize Information** Because of the interstate highway system, transportation costs are lower. How is this an example of positive externalities?

Objectives

- **Explain** the ways the United States might fight poverty.

- **Identify** how the government redistributes income.

- **Describe** how the government encourages private efforts to help the needy.

Guiding Question

How does government help the poor?

Copy this chart and fill it in as you read.

Government Help for the Poor			
Cash Transfers	In-Kind Benefits	Medical Benefits	Education
• Temporary aid for needy families • Social Security • Unemployment insurance • Workers' compensation	• Food giveaways • Food stamps • •	• Medicare • Medicaid •	• Aid to students with learning problems • Federal programs from preschool to college

Reading Strategy
Predicting

Preview the title of the section. Ask: "What do I think this section will be about?"

poverty threshold
an income level below that needed to support families

▶ **Economics and You** When you go to the store to buy something—whether it's a cellphone, a CD, or a pair of sneakers—you can usually find it. You are being helped by the free market system at work. Businesses are making enough profit to produce and sell the goods you want at a price you are willing to pay.

Principles in Action Prices are affected by the laws of supply and demand and by government action. Using the market for pizza as an example, you will see how free markets provide goods and services at the right price and in enough quantities. You will also see examples of how government actions affect the wages of some workers and the rent that some people pay.

What is poverty?

Poverty means being poor. During the last 30 years, the number of people living in poverty in the United States has risen. The government determines the **poverty threshold.** People below the poverty threshold have less income than what is needed to support families. The poverty threshold is adjusted on a regular basis. In 2006, the poverty threshold for a single parent under age 65, with one child, was $13,896. For a four-person family with two children, it was $20,444.

welfare
government aid to the poor

What is the government safety net?

As a society, we have some responsibility for our weakest members. We think it is important to take care of the very young, the very old, the sick, the poor, and the disabled. For these people, the government tries to provide a safety net. A safety net is a large net for catching anyone who falls. The government's safety net helps those people who fall into poverty. These programs are run by federal, state, and local governments. They try to raise people's standard of living by giving them the ability to purchase the goods and services they need and want.

What is the goal of government welfare programs?

Since the 1930s, the government has tried to fight poverty by providing **welfare.** The government collects taxes from individuals and redistributes some of the money to the poor. Welfare is government aid for those in need.

The nation's welfare system began under President Franklin Roosevelt during the Great Depression in the 1930s. Welfare spending greatly increased in the 1960s under President Lyndon Johnson's "War on Poverty."

Welfare spending really shot up in the 1970s and 1980s. Some people were worried that people on welfare were becoming unable or unwilling to get off welfare. They were dependent on it. Others claimed that income redistribution discourages productivity resulting in increased poverty. In 1996, Congress made major changes in the welfare system. New reforms limited the length of time people could receive welfare payments. The reforms gave states more freedom to experiment with other ways to fight poverty.

✅ **CHECKPOINT** *What is the goal of government welfare programs?*

Economics & YOU

Redistribution Programs

Public colleges and universities often have lower tuition than private schools. *You can pay less to attend a public college because states have redistributed tax money to support education.*

Social Security taxes are taken out of your paycheck. *The money you pay to Social Security is redistributed to senior citizens so they can maintain a decent standard of living.*

What are four programs that provide benefits to the poor?

State and federal governments provide **cash transfers.** These are direct payments of money to poor, disabled, or retired people. There are four main cash transfer programs.

cash transfers
direct payments of money by the government to poor, disabled, or retired people

1. *Temporary Assistance for Needy Families (TANF)* This program was part of the reforms Congress began in 1996. TANF stopped giving direct federal welfare payments to people. Instead, federal money goes to the states. They design and run their own welfare programs. States must follow federal rules. They must create work incentives and set a time limit for benefits. The goal of TANF is to move people from welfare into the workforce.

2. *Social Security* The Social Security program started in 1935. During the Great Depression, many older people lost their life savings and had no income. Social Security collects taxes from people who are now working. The money is then redistributed to current recipients. Most of the people who receive Social Security are retired people. People with disabilities who are unable to work, and, in some cases, the husband or wife and children of those with disabilities also receive benefits.

3. *Unemployment insurance* Another cash transfer is the unemployment insurance program. It is paid for by both the federal and state governments. Unemployment compensation checks give money to workers who have lost their jobs. Workers must show that they are trying to find work. As with TANF, states set the rules for this program. The program is supposed to supply help for only a short time. As a result, most states pay benefits to workers for only 26 weeks. When many people are out of work, however, the government may decide to pay the benefits for a longer time.

4. *Workers' compensation* This program provides a cash transfer of state funds to workers who are hurt on the job. Most employers have workers' compensation insurance. This covers employers against any future claims their employees might make.

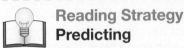
What are in-kind benefits?

The government also provides poor people with **in-kind benefits.** These are goods and services provided for free or at greatly lowered prices. The most common in-kind benefits include food giveaways, food stamps, subsidized housing, and legal aid.

The food stamp program helps low-income people buy food. Although it is a federal government program, it is run by state or local governments. People who qualify receive a plastic card with a magnetic memory strip. That strip contains a dollar amount. The information loaded on the card tells people how much food they can buy each month.

Legal aid is advice about the law that poor people can receive at no charge. They are given help with contracts and other business matters. A public defender is a free lawyer provided by the courts. Public defenders help poor people accused of a crime. They are paid with tax dollars. (The right of an accused person to have a lawyer is guaranteed by the Sixth Amendment.)

What medical benefits does the government provide?

The U.S. government also provides health insurance for older people, the disabled, and the poor. Medicare covers Americans over age 65 and people with disabilities. Medicaid covers some poor people who are unemployed or not covered by their employer's insurance plans. Medicare and Medicaid are run by the Social Security Administration. They are very expensive programs. We will look at them more closely in Chapter 14.

A program called the State Children's Health Insurance Program (SCHIP) provides health insurance for children who do not have insurance. SCHIP is paid for by both state and federal governments. States write the rules for the program. All state programs must follow federal guidelines. In 2008, this program covered more than 7.4 million children.

What aid does the government give to education?

Federal, state, and local governments all give aid to education. The federal government pays for programs from preschool to college. State and local programs aid students with learning problems. Education programs add to the nation's human capital and labor productivity by providing workers with training and skills.

CHECKPOINT *Identify four programs that provide cash benefits to the poor.*

How does the government encourage private action to help the needy?

Not only does the government help the poor directly, it also encourages private actions. Federal tax law encourages both individuals and corporations to give to charity. These donations can be used to lower the amount of taxes paid. This gives individuals and businesses an economic incentive to give money and property to relief organizations and other nonprofit groups such as churches, hospitals, colleges, libraries, or museums. In 2006, Americans gave $295 billion to charity.

The government may also provide **grants** to organizations that provide social services. A grant is money given by the government. It is given to a private individual or group in order to carry out a special project. Many people believe that private groups are more effective in helping people than the government is.

In 2001, President George W. Bush created the Office of Faith-Based and Community Initiatives. The purpose of this office was to help religious groups get money from the federal government. With money from the government, these groups are supposed to provide services to people in need. Some people felt that giving money to religious organizations violated the First Amendment.

✔ **CHECKPOINT** *How does the tax law provide an incentive to help the needy?*

grant
a financial award given by a government agency to a private individual or group in order to carry out a specific task

---

SECTION **4** ASSESSMENT

Essential Questions Journal To continue to build a response to the Essential Question, go to your **Essential Questions Journal.**

 Guiding Question

1. Use your completed chart to answer the following question: How does government help the poor?

Key Terms and Main Ideas

Directions: On a sheet of paper, write the answer to each question. Use complete sentences.

2. What is the poverty threshold? Why does it vary according to the number of people living in a household?

3. What are three examples of cash transfers?

4. How are unemployment insurance and workers' compensation alike?

5. What are in-kind benefits?

Critical Thinking

6. **Analyze Information** How does the TANF program seek to answer one of the common objections to the older welfare system?

7. **Draw Conclusions** Do you think tax incentives are necessary to encourage charitable giving? Explain your answer.

QUICK STUDY GUIDE

Section 1–Benefits of Free Enterprise

- The American free enterprise system is the result of several principles. These are the profit motive, the principle of open opportunity, legal equality, and economic rights. Economic rights include private property rights and the right of voluntary exchange.

- The U.S. Constitution protects property rights and the right to make contracts. It also gives the government the right to tax individuals and corporations.

Section 2–Promoting Growth and Stability

- Macroeconomics is the study of economic behavior and decision making in the whole economy of a nation. Microeconomics is the study of economic behavior and decision making in small units such as households and firms.

- The government tracks business cycles and promotes economic strength. Three main goals are high employment, growth, and stability. The government also encourages the development of new technology.

Section 3–Providing Public Goods

- Public goods are shared goods or services. It would be impractical to make consumers pay individually or to exclude those who did not pay for those services.

- Providing public goods produces positive and negative externalities. Positive externalities generate benefits to someone other than the person deciding how much to produce or to consume. Negative externalities are costs that are paid by someone other than the producer.

Section 4–Providing a Safety Net

- The government provides programs to help people who live in poverty. One of these programs is the welfare system. Redistribution programs provide direct payments through Temporary Assistance for Needy Families, Social Security, unemployment insurance, and workers' compensation.

- In-kind benefits are provided for free or reduced prices. These include Medicare and Medicaid as well as education programs. The government also encourages people to make charitable donations by providing tax deductions.

Section 1
What are the benefits of free enterprise?

Section 2
How does the U.S. government encourage growth and stability?

Section 3
Why does a society provide public goods?

Section 4
How does government help the poor?

Essential Question, Chapter 3
What role should government play in a free market economy?

Constitutional Amendments

When the United States won its independence from Great Britain, leaders had to set up a government for the new country. They decided to write the Constitution. This document gives certain rights to U.S. citizens. It also describes the powers and duties of the government. The writers of the Constitution knew that changes might have to be made from time to time. They included a part about amendments to the Constitution. In over 200 years since the Constitution was written, only 27 changes have been made. Three of these amendments are about a person's rights and responsibilities in a free market economy.

Amendment 4–Search and Arrest Warrants

The right of the people to be secure in their persons, houses, papers, and effects, against unreasonable searches and seizures, shall not be violated, and no warrants shall issue, but upon probable cause, supported by oath or affirmation, and particularly describing the place to be searched, and the persons or things to be seized.

Amendment 5–Rights in Criminal Cases

No person shall be held to answer for a capital, or otherwise infamous crime, unless on a presentment or indictment of a grand jury . . . nor shall any person be subject for the same offense to be twice put in jeopardy of life or limb; nor shall be compelled in any criminal case to be a witness against himself, nor be deprived of life, liberty, or property, without due process of the law; nor shall private property be taken for public use, without just compensation [payment].

Amendment 16–Income Taxes

The Congress shall have power to lay and collect taxes on incomes, from whatever source derived, without apportionment [sharing] among the several States, and without regard to any census or enumeration.

Document-Based Questions

1. Why is the Constitution important to United States citizens?
2. Based on Amendment 4, what does a police officer need to have in order to search another person's property?
3. How does Amendment 5 protect citizens?
4. According to Amendment 16, is money from a person's job the only source that can be taxed? Explain.
5. Of the three amendments described above, which one do you think is most important in a free market economy? Why?

Directions: Write your answers to the following questions using complete sentences.

Section 1—Benefits of Free Enterprise

1. What information is required by public disclosure laws?

2. Why is it important to have a law saying the government cannot overturn terms of existing contracts?

3. How does the government support free enterprise and protect the public interest?

4. How does the Constitution protect property rights?

Section 2—Promoting Growth and Stability

5. How do patents act as an incentive to develop new technology?

6. How does technological progress increase the GDP?

7. In your own words, describe the work ethic.

Section 3—Providing Public Goods

8. What is infrastructure? Give three examples.

9. How is national defense an example of the free rider problem?

10. Why are public goods examples of market failure?

11. What is the government doing to limit negative externalities such as pollution?

Section 4—Providing a Safety Net

12. How does the government work to raise the standard of living for people living in poverty?

13. Why is unemployment insurance considered a cash transfer?

14. Why are food stamps considered an in-kind payment?

15. What medical benefits does the government provide for older people, the disabled, and the poor?

16. How does the government help education programs?

Economics
on the go

Exploring the Essential Question

17. (a) What are the four basic principles of free enterprise? (b) How do these principles promote competition?

18. (a) What is the goal of government redistribution programs? (b) Should government redistribute income in a free market economy? Explain.

Essential Question Activity

19. Complete the following activity to answer the Essential Question **What role should government play in a free market economy?**

Divided into four groups, the class will look at one of the following topics: government regulation, encouraging economic growth, providing public goods, providing an economic safety net. Research your topic in print or in online news sources that illustrate government's role. The worksheet from your teacher or the electronic worksheet at **PearsonSuccessNet.com** lists reliable sources and keywords for your search.

After your group chooses a story, answer these questions: (a) How would you summarize the actions taken by businesses and the reasons for them? (b) How would you summarize the actions taken by government and the reasons for them? (c) How would you describe the externalities that resulted from each action?

Essential Questions Journal To continue to build a response to the Essential Question, go to your **Essential Questions Journal.**

 **Test-Taking Tip**

When your teacher announces a test, listen carefully. Write down the topics that will be included. Also write down the specific chapters or reading material you should review.

Unit 1 Challenge

Essential Question, Unit 1

How does economics affect everyone?

VIDEO
By Students For Students
For videos on Essential Questions,
go to *PearsonSuccessNet.com*

Some people think that economics does not affect them. In fact, it would be impossible to find anybody whose life is *not* touched by economics. Look at the opinions below, keeping in mind the Essential Question: How does economics affect everyone?

> Economics is, at root, the study of incentives: how people get what they want, or need, especially when other people want or need the same thing…. An incentive is simply a means of urging people to do more of a good thing and less of a bad thing. But most incentives don't come about organically. Someone—an economist or a politician or a parent—has to invent them. Your three-year-old eats all her vegetables for a week? She wins a trip to the toy store. A big steelmaker belches too much smoke into the air? The company is fined for each cubic foot of pollutants over the legal limit.
>
> —Steven D. Levitt and Stephen J. Dubner, *Freakonomics*

> Economics surely does not provide a romantic vision of life. But the widespread poverty, misery, and crises in many parts of the world, much of it unnecessary, are strong reminders that understanding economic and social laws can make an enormous contribution to the welfare of people.
>
> —Gary Becker, Nobel Prize acceptance speech, 1992

"The economy is slowing down. Last night the Tooth Fairy left me an IOU"

Essential Question
Writing Activity

Consider the different views of economics expressed in the sources on this page. Review what you've learned in this unit and your own life experiences about the effects of economics. *Then write a well-constructed essay expressing your view of how economics affects everyone.*

Writing Guidelines

- Address all aspects of the Essential Question Writing Activity.
- Support the theme with relevant facts, examples, and details.
- Use a logical and clear plan of organization.
- Introduce the theme by establishing a framework that is beyond a simple restatement of the question and conclude with a summation of the theme.

For help with Expository Writing, refer to the *Writing Skills Handbook* in the Reference section, page S-1.

Essential Questions Journal

To respond to the unit Essential Question, go to your **Essential Questions Journal**.

UNIT 2 How Markets Work

Essential Question, Unit 2

Who benefits from the free market economy?

Chapter 7
How does competition affect your choices?

Chapter 6
What is the right price?

Chapter 5
How do suppliers decide what goods and services to offer?

Chapter 4
How do we decide what to buy?

4 Demand

Essential Question, Chapter 4

How do we decide what to buy?

- **Section 1** Understanding Demand

- **Section 2** Shifts in the Demand Curve

- **Section 3** Elasticity of Demand

Economics
on the go

To study anywhere, anytime, download these online resources at *PearsonSuccessNet.com* ➤

▶ **Billions of consumers in the world demand goods and services every day.** Maybe you have waited in line at a store to buy a particular item that many people wanted. Your wants and needs have a lot to do with deciding what is produced. The things you and other consumers demand influence what goods and services are made.

In this chapter you will learn what the law of demand is. You will read about the substitution effect and the income effect and how they can change your spending patterns. You will find out how a change in the demand for one good can affect demand for a related good. You will also learn how the expectations of consumers, population growth, and advertising all affect the demand for goods and services.

Reading Strategy: Text Structure
Understanding how text is organized helps readers decide which information is most important. Before you begin reading this chapter, look at how it is organized.

- Look at the title, headings, boldfaced words, charts, graphs, and photographs.

- Look at the questions for clues about which information the chapter covers.

- Ask yourself: Does the text show a problem and solution, description, or sequence? Does it compare and contrast or show cause and effect?

- Summarize the text by thinking about its structure.

Visual Glossary
online

Go to the Visual Glossary Online for an interactive review of the **law of demand.**

How the Economy Works
online

Go to How the Economy Works Online for an interactive lesson on **elasticity of demand.**

Action Graph
online

Go to Action Graph Online for animated versions of key charts and graphs.

Objectives

- **Explain** demand.
- **Describe** how the substitution effect and the income effect influence decisions.
- **Identify** demand schedules.
- **Interpret** a demand curve using demand schedules.

Guiding Question

How does the law of demand affect the quantity demanded?

Copy this table and fill it in as you read.

	Demand	
	As the price of a good goes up . . .	As the price of a good goes down . . .
Law of demand	Quantity demanded goes down	
Substitution effect		People buy less of a substitute good
Income effect	Consumers feel poorer, so consumption of that good goes down	

demand
the desire to own something and the ability to pay for it

law of demand
consumers will buy more of a good when its price decreases and less when its price increases

Reading Strategy
Text Structure
Preview this section. Notice the headings, features, and boldfaced words.

▶ **Economics and You** If you have ever bought something, you can understand **demand.** Suppose you are shopping at the local mall. After visiting many stores, you find a watch you really like. But the watch costs a little more than you want to pay. Otherwise, it is perfect. You decide that you just have to have it. If you want the watch *and* you can pay for it, you have demand for that good.

Principles in Action Price changes always affect the quantity demanded. The Economics & You feature shows how a change in price serves as an incentive to buy something else instead.

What is demand?

Demand has two parts. First, consumers must be willing to buy. Then, they must have the ability to pay. Wanting something does not create demand. Suppose you go to an auto show and see a $50,000 sports car you like. You probably do not have $50,000 to pay for it. According to economists, you have not added to demand. In the same way, you might have $50,000. But if you are not willing to spend it on the sports car, demand is not affected.

What is the law of demand?

The **law of demand** is simple. It says that when the price of a good goes up, the quantity demanded goes down. If the price goes down, demand generally goes up. Producers are aware of this law. They know that if their prices rise too high, consumers will stop buying their goods and services.

Now ask yourself a question: Would you buy a slice of pizza for lunch if it cost $2.00? Many of us would. Some of us might even buy more than one slice. But would you buy the same slice of pizza if it cost $4.00? Fewer of us would buy it at that price. Even real pizza lovers might buy just one or two slices instead of three or four. How many of us would buy a slice for $10.00? Probably very few would do that. As the price of pizza increases, fewer of us are willing to buy it. That is the law of demand in action.

What is the substitution effect?

One factor influencing demand is the number of substitutes that exist and are demanded. For example, you could buy a nice car for much less than a $50,000 sports car. You could buy a different kind of food instead of pizza. When the price goes up, consumers usually decide to buy less of that good. They may also buy more of other goods. This is called the **substitution effect.** If the price of pizza goes up, people may start buying tacos instead.

What is the income effect?

Another factor is income, or how much money we make. What we choose to buy often changes when prices change. This is called the **income effect.** When the price of pizza increases, your limited budget just won't buy as much as it did in the past. It feels as if you have less money. When the price of pizza goes up, you spend more money on pizza but demand less of it. That is the income effect in action.

The substitution effect and the income effect both affect demand. Together, they explain how an increase in prices changes the quantity demanded.

CHECKPOINT *What happens to demand when prices increase?*

substitution effect
the reaction of consumers to an increase in a good's price by consuming less of that good and more of other goods

income effect
changes in consumption that result from changes in real income

Economics & YOU

The Substitution Effect

When the price of one good increases, people have an incentive to buy substitutes. *Your decision to purchase a less expensive lunch is the substitution effect in action.*

Roast Beef sandwich $4.50 $5.25

Chili $1.99

REDUCED

The substitution effect also applies when a drop in price creates a cheaper alternative. *Your purchase of the car with the reduced price is another example of the substitution effect.*

demand schedule
explains the law of demand in
table form

demand curve
a graph that shows the same
information as a demand schedule

market demand schedule
a table that lists the quantity of a
good all consumers in a market
will buy at each different price

What does a demand schedule look like?

A **demand schedule** explains the law of demand in a table. Look at **Figure 4.1**. It shows how price affects the demand for pizza. Let's look at a pretend student called Ashley. What if you took the numbers in Ashley's individual demand schedule and plotted them on a graph? The result would be a **demand curve**. **Figure 4.2** shows the same information as the demand schedules in **Figure 4.1**, but in graph form. Both the demand schedules and the demand curves show the same thing. Demand for pizza is greater when the price is lower.

What is a market demand schedule?

A **market demand schedule** shows the quantities demanded at each price by all consumers in the market. Pizza sellers can predict how many pizza slices they would sell at different prices. The schedule also shows the law of demand. The number of slices demanded falls as the price rises. The only difference between the individual and market demand schedules is that the market demand schedule shows the possible demands of all consumers rather than just one.

How do you read a demand curve?

Note that Ashley's demand curve in **Figure 4.2** shows only how the price of pizza affects the amount of pizza Ashley buys. It assumes that all other factors stay the same. In other words, Ashley's income, the price of other goods, and the quality of the pizza do not change.

The demand curves slope downward to the right. Follow the curve with your finger from the top left to the bottom right. You will notice that as prices fall, the quantity demanded jumps. This is just another way of stating the law of demand. Higher prices will always lead consumers to demand less. All demand schedules and curves show the law of demand.

Fig. 4.1
Demand Schedules

CHART SKILLS

Demand schedules show that demand for a good falls as the price rises.

1. How does individual demand for pizza change when the price falls from $3.00 to $2.00 a slice?

2. How does market demand for pizza change when the price rises from $3.00 to $4.00 a slice?

Market Demand Schedule	
Price of a slice of pizza	Quantity demanded per day
$1.00	300
$2.00	250
$3.00	200
$4.00	150
$5.00	100
$6.00	50

Individual Demand Schedule	
Price of a slice of pizza	Quantity demanded per day
$1.00	5
$2.00	4
$3.00	3
$4.00	2
$5.00	1
$6.00	0

Fig. 4.2 Demand Curves

GRAPH SKILLS

Ashley's demand curve shows the number of slices of pizza she is willing and able to buy at each price. The market demand curve illustrates demand for pizza in an entire market.

1. How many slices of pizza does Ashley demand when the price is $4.00 per slice?

2. How is the market demand curve similar to Ashley's demand curve?

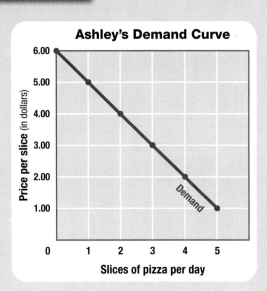

Ashley's Demand Curve

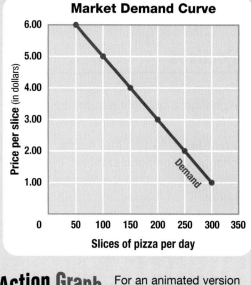

Market Demand Curve

Action Graph online For an animated version of this graph, visit **PearsonSuccessNet.com**

What are the limits of a demand curve?

In real life, market conditions often change. The market demand curve is only accurate for one specific set of market conditions. Even if the price for pizza stayed the same, demand might change. For example, a factory near a pizza restaurant might close. There would be fewer workers wanting pizza for lunch. In the next section, you will read how demand curves can shift because of changes in factors other than price.

 CHECKPOINT *What does a shift in the demand curve mean about a particular good?*

SECTION 1 ASSESSMENT

Essential Questions Journal To continue to build a response to the Essential Question, go to your **Essential Questions Journal.**

 Guiding Question

1. Use your completed table to answer this question: How does the law of demand affect the quantity demanded?

Key Terms and Main Ideas

Directions: On a sheet of paper, write the answer to each question. Use complete sentences.

2. What two qualities make up demand?

3. According to the law of demand, what will happen when the price of a good increases?

4. Under the substitution effect, what will happen when the price of a good drops?

5. What information about consumers does a market demand schedule show?

Critical Thinking

6. **Make Comparisons** Describe the difference between the substitution effect and the income effect.

7. **Draw Inferences** What can economists predict by creating a demand curve?

Objectives

- **Explain** the difference between a change in quantity demanded and a shift in the demand curve.
- **Identify** the factors that create changes in demand and that can cause a shift in the demand curve.
- **Describe** how change in the demand for one good can affect demand for another good.

■ ■ ■ ■ ■ ■ ■ ■ ■ ■ ■ ■ ■ ■ ■ ■ ■

ceteris paribus
a Latin phrase that means "all other things held constant"

Guiding Question

Why does the demand curve shift?

Copy this concept web and fill it in as you read.

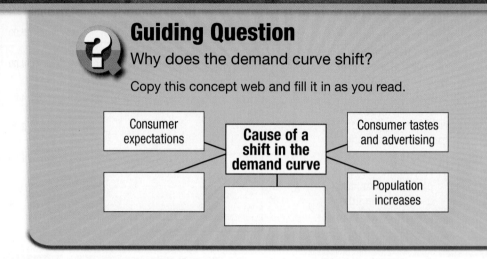

▶ **Economics and You** After reading about individual and market demand for pizza in Section 1, you may think about opening your own pizza shop. All you have to do is create a market demand schedule and pick the best price and quantity combination—right? However, as you may have guessed, several other factors can affect demand for a good at any price.

Principles in Action Changes in demand that are not connected to price can cause the entire demand curve to shift to either the left or the right. Section 2 describes factors besides price and quantity that may cause a shift in the demand curve. Shifts in the demand curve affect market equilibrium, as well as the prices of related goods.

What factors besides price affect demand?

When we counted the number of pizza slices that would sell as the price went up or down, we assumed that nothing besides the price of pizza would change. Economists call this ***ceteris paribus.*** It is a Latin phrase meaning "all other things held constant." The demand schedule took into account only changes in price. In this section, you will learn how economists consider the effect of other changes on the demand for goods like pizza.

If we consider other factors that affect demand, the whole demand curve shifts. A shift in the demand curve means that at every price, consumers buy a different amount than before. The shift of the entire curve is what economists call a change in demand.

✔ **CHECKPOINT** *What does a shift in the demand curve mean about a particular good?*

What can cause the demand curve to shift?

A demand curve is accurate when only the price changes. When other factors change, something else happens. We no longer move along the demand curve. Instead, the entire demand curve shifts. At every price, consumers buy a different quantity than before.

Let's suppose that the weather in Ashley's town suddenly becomes very warm. She wants to eat less pizza no matter what the price is. The graph on the left in **Figure 4.3** shows her original demand curve. Next to it is her new demand curve showing the changes because of the hot weather. This is a decrease in demand.

How do changes in income affect demand?

We have already learned that people's income affects what they buy. Most things we buy are **normal goods.** These are goods that we demand more of when our incomes go up, such as well-known name brands rather than store brands. Name brands are often thought to be better than store brands.

If Ashley's income increased, she would buy more normal goods at every price. A new demand schedule for Ashley would show a greater demand for pizza at every price. Plotting the new schedule on the graph would give us a curve to the right of Ashley's original curve. At each price, the demand would be higher. This shift to the right of the curve is called an increase in demand.

normal good
a product or good that consumers demand more of when their incomes increase

Reading Strategy
Text Structure
Notice that the section headings are written as questions. After you read each section, try to answer the question asked in the heading.

Fig. 4.3 Graphing Changes in Demand

GRAPH SKILLS
When factors other than price cause demand to fall, the demand curve shifts to the left. When demand increases, the demand curve shifts to the right.

1. If the price of a slice of pizza rose by $1.00, how would you represent the change on one of these graphs?

2. Advertisers show that eating pizza increases your popularity. How would you represent this on one of these graphs?

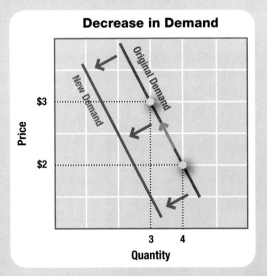

Decrease in Demand

Increase in Demand

Action Graph online

For an animated version of this graph, visit **PearsonSuccessNet.com**

inferior good
a product or good that consumers demand less of when their incomes increase

demographics
information such as age, race, gender, income level, and occupation of a population

There are also other goods called **inferior goods.** These are goods for which there is less demand when incomes go up. For example, if your income went up, you might buy less macaroni and cheese and more steak. You might buy a new car rather than a used one. The macaroni and the used car are inferior goods. The steak and a new car are examples of normal goods.

How do consumer expectations affect demand?

Let's say you have your eye on a new bicycle. You walk into a store to look at the bike. The salesperson tells you that the cost of the bike will go up next week. What will you do? Because you know the price is going up, you are more likely to buy the bike now. In other words, the consumer's expectation of a higher price has caused your demand to increase right away. What if the salesperson were to tell you that the price will go down next week? You probably would not buy the bike today. In other words, your demand would fall.

How do population increases change demand?

In many areas, population is growing. As the population increases, so does demand for goods and services. For example, a growing population will increase the demand for new homes. Demand for food and water will go up. A growing population will demand more schools, better roads, and improved transportation.

How is demographic information used?

Demographics is information such as the age, race, gender, income level, and occupation of a group of people. Businesses use this information to identify markets for their goods and services.

Consumers who expect a hurricane wait in line to buy plywood. Such natural disasters can create sudden demand for household goods. ▼

Growing ethnic groups, such as Asians and Latin Americans, can create shifts in demand for goods and services. In the United States, Hispanics made up about one half the population growth between 2003 and 2004. Hispanics, or Latinos, are currently the largest minority group in the United States. The U.S. Census Bureau estimates that by the year 2025, Hispanic Americans will make up 18.9 percent of the U.S. population. The purchasing power of Hispanics will grow. Firms will then devote more of their resources to creating goods and services for Hispanic consumers.

David Ogilvy

"It takes a big idea to attract the attention of consumers and get them to buy your product. Unless your advertising contains a big idea, it will pass like a ship in the night."

Those words reflect the life experience of their author, David Ogilvy. Ogilvy was a bright student who won a scholarship to Oxford University, in England. But he left Oxford in 1931, because he was, in his own words, a "dud." His brother Francis got him his first advertising job with a London ad agency. "I loved advertising," Ogilvy later wrote. "I studied and read and took it desperately seriously."

Ogilvy decided to seek his fortune in America. In 1938, he joined the staff of George Gallup's National Research Institute in Princeton, New Jersey. The experience convinced him that market research was the foundation of good advertising. In 1948, Ogilvy founded his own ad agency in New York. It eventually became known as Ogilvy & Mather. He wrote detailed ads that told a good story or introduced a memorable character. His ads helped generate demand and led to huge sales increases for his clients.

Ogilvy is remembered as a pioneer in the development of brand images. He said, "Every advertisement should be thought of as a contribution to the complex symbol which is the brand image."

Fast Facts

David Ogilvy (1911–1999)
Education: Oxford University (no degree)
Claim to Fame: Founded the advertising agency Ogilvy & Mather

How do changes in what people like affect demand?

Consumers sometimes change their minds about what they like and want. Fashions change. If consumers decide they prefer khakis to blue jeans, the demand for jeans changes. The demand curve for khakis also shifts.

In the past, many adults smoked cigarettes. When people learned that smoking was bad for their health, the demand for cigarettes went down. It was not only the price of the cigarettes that caused people to stop smoking. It was rather the change in what consumers liked and wanted.

Advertising may also affect what consumers like and demand. Companies spend a lot of money on advertising. They hope it will increase the demand for the goods and services they sell. When you see an ad on TV, you may want to buy the product. This shows how advertising creates demand.

 CHECKPOINT *If consumers expect the price of a good to rise, how will that affect the current demand for the good?*

complements
two goods that are bought and
used together

substitutes
goods that are used in place of
one another

Reading Strategy
Text Structure
How does the
checkpoint question help you
understand what you have read?

How do the prices of related goods affect demand?

The demand curve for one good can be affected by a change in the
demand of another good. There are two types of related goods that
affect demand: complements and substitutes.

Complements are two goods that are bought and used together.
If you are a skier, you need both skis and ski boots. If the price of
the boots goes up, it affects the sale of skis. Because skis cannot be
used without ski boots, the demand for skis will fall at all prices.

Substitutes are goods used in place of another. A snowboard is
a substitute for skis. A rise in the price of snowboards will cause
people to buy fewer snowboards. Therefore, they might buy skis
instead. Likewise, if the price of snowboards went down, the
demand for skis would drop.

 CHECKPOINT *If the demand for a good increases, what will
happen to the demand for its complement?*

SECTION **2** ASSESSMENT

Essential Questions Journal
To continue to build a
response to the Essential
Question, go to your
Essential Questions Journal.

Quick Write

Based on what you have read
in this section about shifts in
the demand curve, write a short
essay answering the following
questions: How did your
demand for a product or service
change based on something
other than price? What factors
were responsible for this
shift in demand? How might
these factors have affected
other people's demand for the
product or service?

Guiding Question

1. Use your completed concept web to answer this question:
   Why does the demand curve shift?

Key Terms and Main Ideas

**Directions: On a sheet of paper, write the answer to each
question. Use complete sentences.**

2. How is *ceteris paribus* related to demand curves?

3. What is a normal good?

4. Suppose weather forecasters predict a stormy winter. As
   a result, stores sell a lot of snow shovels and sleds. What
   factor caused demand for these items to rise?

5. Name at least three goods that could be bought as
   complements to hamburgers.

Critical Thinking

6. **Analyze Information** How are normal goods and inferior
   goods different?

7. **Recognize Cause and Effect** If demand for a good increases,
   what will happen to the demand for its substitute?

86 DEMAND

Objectives

- **Explain** how to figure out elasticity of demand.
- **Identify** factors that affect elasticity.
- **Explain** how firms use elasticity and revenue to make decisions.

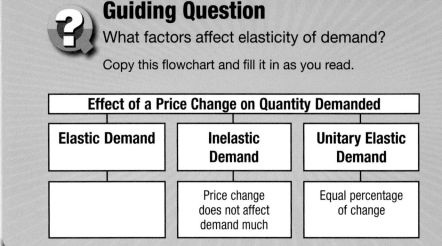

Guiding Question

What factors affect elasticity of demand?

Copy this flowchart and fill it in as you read.

Effect of a Price Change on Quantity Demanded		
Elastic Demand	**Inelastic Demand**	**Unitary Elastic Demand**
	Price change does not affect demand much	Equal percentage of change

Reading Strategy
Text Structure
Notice that red headings in each section ask general questions about a topic. The smaller blue headings ask more specific questions about the topic.

elasticity of demand
a measure of how consumers respond to price changes

▶ **Economics and You** Are there some things you would continue to buy, even if the price doubled or tripled? Are there other goods you would cut back on or stop buying if the price went up just a little? No matter how you answer these questions, economists have a way to describe your behavior.

Principles in Action How we react to a change in the price of a product affects overall demand for that good. Economists call this **elasticity of demand.** You will learn about several factors that can change demand for a product. You will also learn how these factors influence pricing and revenue.

What is elasticity?

Elasticity of demand measures how much buyers will cut back on demand for a good when the price rises. It also measures how much demand for a good increases when the price falls.

How does price affect elasticity?

Let's compare two products, candy bars and milk. Assume that the price of each goes up 20 percent. The cost of a 75-cent candy bar would increase to 90 cents. Milk that cost $3.00 a gallon would cost $3.60. How would these price increases affect demand? Economists would predict that the demand for the candy bars would fall much more than the demand for milk. Why? The demand for the candy is elastic, while the demand for the milk is not.

inelastic
describes demand that is not very sensitive to price changes

unitary elasticity
describes demand whose elasticity is exactly equal to 1

The law of demand tells us that a rise in prices causes demand to go down. It does not tell us how much the demand decreases. Economists use the term *elasticity* to measure the effect of the rise in price. Even a small change in the price causes a large change, or "stretch," in the amount demanded. When the price increase causes a large change in demand, the demand is said to be elastic. In other words, people are less likely to buy the product if the price goes up.

Some food items are good examples of elasticity. For example, the demand for lobster is elastic. Usually lobster is priced higher than beef or chicken. At the regular price, only a certain number of people will buy it. But if the store has a half-price sale, consumers will rush in to buy the lobster. Figure 4.4 shows how price changes affect the demand for lobster.

Why is the demand for some products inelastic?

The demand for some products is inelastic. **Inelastic** demand occurs when the price increase has little effect on demand. Milk is a good example. Most people consider milk to be a necessary part of their diets. Raising or lowering the price of milk is not likely to affect demand very much. Even if the price were cut in half, the amount demanded would not go up much. Likewise, if the price doubled, people would still buy milk. Sugar, salt, and bread are other examples of items with inelastic demand.

Sometimes the percentage change in quantity demanded is exactly equal to the percentage change in the price. This is known as **unitary elasticity.** Suppose the elasticity of demand for a magazine at $2.00 is unitary. When the price of the magazine rises by 50 percent to $3.00, the newsstand will sell exactly half as many copies as before.

 CHECKPOINT *Is demand for an expensive, unnecessary good with plenty of substitutes likely to be elastic, inelastic, or unitary elastic?*

What factors affect elasticity?

Several different factors can affect the elasticity of demand for a specific good.
1. *Is the product or service a luxury or a necessity?* Elasticity is greatest in goods and services we consider luxuries. Things we think of as necessities have little elasticity.
2. *Is a substitute available?* Juice, milk, and water are all substitutes for soft drinks. Demand is more elastic when many substitutes are available. Sometimes, consumers have few or no substitutes. For example, we have to buy medicine we need even if the price goes up. When few substitutes are available, demand is often inelastic.

Fig. 4.4 Elasticity of Demand for Lobster

Quantity Demanded (Tons of Lobster)

GRAPH SKILLS
As the price of lobster goes up, the demand for lobster drops. Elastic demand means the demand changes, or stretches, when the price changes.
1. At $2.00 per pound, about how many tons of lobster are demanded?
2. At $10.00 per pound, has demand for lobster increased or decreased?

3. *How much of the person's income does the purchase require?*
Some products do not cost much. You might not think twice
about buying something that only costs a few dollars, even
if the price has gone up a lot. The few dollars you spend are
only a small part of your total income. On the other hand,
you would spend a large part of your income to buy a home.
Does price affect your decision on which home to buy? Of
course it does! Price changes affect demand for expensive
products more than for things that do not cost much. A
10 percent increase in the price of a home affects you a lot.
A 10 percent increase in the price of a candy bar does not.

 CHECKPOINT *What factors affect elasticity of demand?*

Why does elasticity matter?

Elasticity matters because it affects **total revenue.** A company's
total revenue is the amount of money it receives for selling its
goods and services. This is determined by two factors: the price of
the goods and the quantity sold. Sellers may think they will always
earn more money if they charge more for their products. However,
we have learned that demand may be elastic. A price increase does
not make sense if it causes fewer people to want the product.

Let's go back to our pizza example. Pizza
has an elastic demand. If the price is
raised by 20 percent, the quantity sold
will drop by a larger percentage, say 50
percent. This drop will actually reduce
the firm's total revenue. **Figure 4.5** shows
this demand.

Companies that produce goods can use
their knowledge of elasticity of demand
to make pricing decisions that affect their
profits. If a company knows that demand
for its product is elastic at the current
price, it knows that an increase in price
would reduce total revenue. However, if a
company produces an inelastic product it
knows that consumers will have difficulty
finding a substitute for it. Remember
that if demand is inelastic, it will not
change much even if prices go up. If a
firm raises its price by 25 percent, the
quantity demanded will fall, but less than
25 percent. For instance, as you can see

 Reading Strategy
Text Structure
As you read the lesson,
use a graphic organizer to
illustrate the problem and its
possible solutions.

total revenue
the total amount of money a
company receives by selling
goods or services

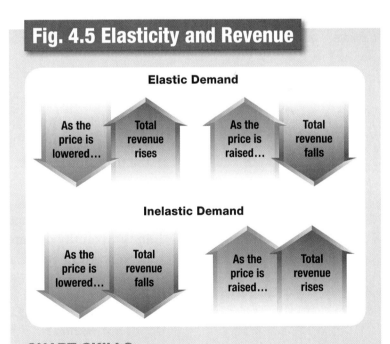

Fig. 4.5 Elasticity and Revenue

Elastic Demand

As the price is lowered… Total revenue rises

As the price is raised… Total revenue falls

Inelastic Demand

As the price is lowered… Total revenue falls

As the price is raised… Total revenue rises

CHART SKILLS
Elasticity of demand determines how a price change affects
total revenues.
1. Why will revenue fall if a firm raises the price of a good
whose demand is elastic?
2. What happens to total revenue when price decreases but
demand is inelastic?

Fig. 4.6 How the Economy Works

How does elasticity affect consumer demand?

On any given day, the average consumer faces a series of spending decisions. Elasticity of demand describes how strongly buyers will react to a change in the price of a good. How does elasticity of demand affect your decision to buy or not to buy?

2 You notice that the price of gasoline has increased by twenty cents a gallon. Your car runs on gasoline and there are no substitutes. Despite the increase, your demand for gasoline is **inelastic.**

1 The price of your morning latte has increased from $3 to $4. Instead of the latte, you buy a regular coffee for $2. Because a substitute is available, your demand for the latte is **elastic.**

Availability of Substitutes

in **Figure 4.6,** there is no substitute for gasoline. Even if the price of gasoline increases, if you want to drive your car, you must make this purchase. You may decide to buy less gasoline but nevertheless you must still buy it. In other words, the higher price makes up for the firm's lower sales. The total revenue goes up. **Figure 4.5** shows inelastic demand.

On the other hand, a decrease in the price will lead to an increase in the quantity demanded if demand is inelastic. However, demand will not rise as much, in percentage, as the price fell, and total revenue goes down.

✔ **CHECKPOINT** *When will an increase in price also increase a firm's total revenue?*

3 You need a new set of tires. The price for the same brand-name tire has increased by 20 percent. That price is too high, so you buy the cheaper tires. Your demand for the brand-name tire is **elastic.**

4 That new set of tires put a big dent in your budget. But you have a date, so takeout replaces dining out. Your demand for a restaurant dinner is **elastic.**

5 **Elasticity of Demand** Your demand for a good is **inelastic** if you buy the same amount or just a little less after a price increase. Your demand for a good that has increased in price is **elastic** if the good has many substitutes, takes a big bite out of your budget, or is a luxury.

Check Your Understanding
1. How does knowing the elasticity of demand for a good help entrepreneurs?
2. What changes might make demand for gasoline more elastic over time?

Share of Budget

Necessity Versus Luxury

SECTION 3 ASSESSMENT

Essential Questions Journal To continue to build a response to the Essential Question, go to your **Essential Questions Journal.**

 Guiding Question

1. Use your completed flowchart to answer the following question: What factors affect elasticity of demand?

Key Terms and Main Ideas

Directions: On a sheet of paper, write the answer to each question. Use complete sentences.

2. What is elasticity of demand?

3. If demand for a good is elastic, what will happen when the price increases?

4. If demand for a good is inelastic, how will a drop in price affect demand for the good?

5. Name three factors that determine a good's or service's elasticity.

Critical Thinking

6. **Analyze Information** How does the percentage of your budget you spend on a good affect its elasticity?

7. **Recognize Cause and Effect** Do higher prices always lead to increased revenues for a company? Explain.

Section 1—Understanding Demand

■ Demand describes the ability and desire to buy a good or service.

■ The law of demand says that when a good's price is lower, consumers buy more of it. When the price is higher, consumers buy less of it.

■ The substitution effect and the income effect are two different ways consumers can change their spending patterns.

■ A demand schedule lists the quantity of a good a person will purchase at various prices. A market demand schedule shows this same quantity for all consumers in the market.

■ A demand schedule shown as a graph is called a demand curve.

Section 2—Shifts in the Demand Curve

■ A demand schedule takes into account only changes in price *(ceteris paribus)*.

■ The whole demand curve shifts when other factors affect demand.

■ Consumers demand more normal goods when their incomes increase. They demand fewer inferior goods when their incomes increase.

■ Several things affect demand: consumer income expectations, population increases, demographics, and consumer tastes.

■ Complements are two or more goods bought and used together. Substitutes are goods used in place of others.

Section 3—Elasticity of Demand

■ Elasticity of demand measures how consumers respond to price changes.

■ Demand for a good that people will buy despite a price increase is inelastic. It does not change in response to price changes.

■ If people buy much less of a good after a small price increase, demand is elastic. It changes in response to a price change.

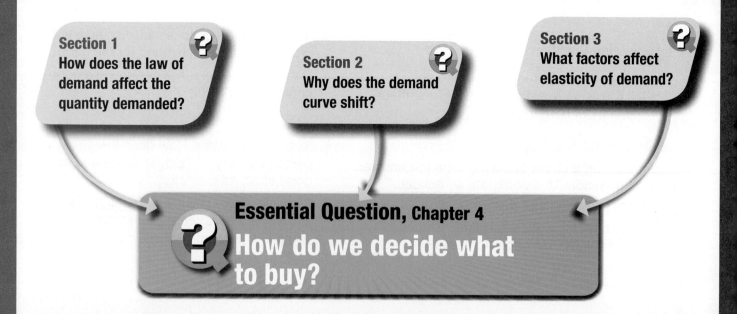

Section 1
How does the law of demand affect the quantity demanded?

Section 2
Why does the demand curve shift?

Section 3
What factors affect elasticity of demand?

Essential Question, Chapter 4
How do we decide what to buy?

Pumpkin growers in Texas say demand is up

By Betsy Blaney

In October 2008, heavy rains damaged some of the largest pumpkin crops in West Texas. This caused pumpkin supplies to be low at a time of the year when demand for pumpkins is traditionally high. Low supply coupled with high demand and the increased cost of production resulted in people paying higher prices for pumpkins than they had in previous years.

. . .Several heavy downpours across many parts of West Texas in the past few weeks came at inopportune times for pumpkin producers. . . .

. . .It's prime pumpkin time across the country with Halloween and Thanksgiving just around the corner.

Demand for pumpkins is at an all-time high, Texas agriculture officials said, and it's mostly because there are fewer pumpkins coming from Floyd County this year.

"Across the country, pumpkin prices are up in many places, though that could reflect increased production and transportation costs," said Gary Lucier of the U.S. Agriculture Department. . . .

Does the drop in acreage mean there might not be enough pumpkins to go around in Texas?

"I would suspect our supply will be short once we get to Halloween time," J.D. Ragland [a Texas AgriLife Extension Agent] said. "We've got pumpkins available now. Come get them while they last."

Prices are high because of a diminished supply. Pumpkins, which come in several varieties ranging in size from less than 2 pounds to as much as 300, this year are selling for an average of 13 cents a pound, Ragland said. The average price over the past 10 years is about 6 cents a pound. . . .

. . ."The drop in acreage this year is basic economics," Ragland said. "Everything done with the pumpkin needs to be done by hand," he said. "Hand labor is expensive."

Producers also had to water the crop earlier in the season, which added to their irrigation costs.

"Energy costs are just so high," Greg Carthel [a Texas pumpkin farmer] said, adding that running irrigation pumps prohibits many growers from planting more acres. . . .

Document-Based Questions

1. According to this article, what is the reason for the pumpkin shortage?
2. Why don't farmers plant more pumpkins?
3. What are some costs associated with the planting and distribution of pumpkins?
4. How is a drop in acreage "basic economics"?
5. Do you think pumpkin planters will profit from the increased price of pumpkins?

SOURCE: "Pumpkin Growers in Texas say demand is up" by Betsy Blaney, The Associated Press, October 20, 2008

Directions: Choose the letter of the correct answer or write the answer using complete sentences.

Section 1–Understanding Demand

1. What is demand?

2. According to the law of demand, what happens when the price of a good drops?

3. How would an increase in income affect the demand curve for a normal good?

4. What is the income effect?

5. What is the substitution effect?

6. What is a demand schedule called when it is represented as a graph?

   A. demand curve   **C.** law of demand
   B. curve schedule   **D.** consumer curve

Section 2–Shifts in the Demand Curve

7. What is the name for two goods that are bought and used together?

8. What is the name for a good used in place of another good?

9. What does a shift in the demand curve mean?

10. What things can cause a demand curve to shift?

11. What is an inferior good?

12. What kind of goods are most things we buy?

    A. abnormal   **B.** inferior   **C.** normal   **D.** excess

Section 3–Elasticity of Demand

13. What term do economists use to measure the effect of the rise in price?

14. Why would raising the price of a loaf of bread likely not have a great effect on demand?

15. What is the difference between a luxury and a necessity?

16. Is the demand for pizza elastic or inelastic? Why?

17. When elasticity of demand is exactly equal to 1, what is that demand called?

    A. equal elasticity   **C.** substitute elasticity

    B. unitary elasticity   **D.** total elasticity

 Exploring the Essential Question

18. Think about goods you buy regularly. Suppose the price of everything doubled. Which items would you continue to buy?

19. Suppose you are thinking about buying a new pair of shoes. The price of the shoes will not change. What other factors could affect your demand for the shoes?

Essential Question Activity

20. Complete this activity to answer the Essential Question **How do we decide what to buy?**
To determine how you spend your money, make a list of recent purchases. Include clothing, electronics, food, or entertainment. You will analyze your demand for these products. Use your list to gather the following information: (a) State why you bought a particular product. (b) Use your knowledge of Chapter 4 to list factors that may have contributed to your decision. (c) Note your elasticity of demand for each product. As a class, discuss the items on your lists. Why did you and your classmates buy these items? Why is there a demand for these items?

Essential Questions Journal To continue to build a response to the Essential Question, go to your **Essential Questions Journal.**

Test-Taking Tip

When studying for a chapter test, review the topics in the chapter. Then make up a practice test for yourself.

Chapter

5 Supply

Essential Question, Chapter 5
How do suppliers decide what goods and services to offer?

- **Section 1** Understanding Supply

- **Section 2** Costs of Production

- **Section 3** Changes in Supply

Economics
on the go

To study anywhere, anytime, download these online resources at *PearsonSuccessNet.com* ➤

▶ **Businesses such as warehouse stores are always making choices.** They have to decide what products or services to offer consumers. They have to figure out the costs of the resources involved in their businesses. How much of a product or service to offer is another choice. The success of a business depends on making the right choices.

This chapter will introduce you to the term *supply.* The idea of supply is key to business. You will learn how firms decide what to make, how much to make, and how to make a product or service. You will also read about the role of government in raising or lowering the cost of producing goods.

Reading Strategy: Visualizing
Visualizing is another strategy that helps readers understand what they are reading. It is like creating a movie in the mind. Use the following ways to visualize a text section:

• Think about experiences in your own life that may help you understand the images.

• Notice the order in which concepts are introduced.

Visual Glossary
online

Go to the Visual Glossary Online for an interactive review of **the law of supply.**

How the Economy Works
online

Go to How the Economy Works Online for an interactive lesson on **production costs.**

Action Graph
online

Go to Action Graph Online for animated versions of key charts and graphs.

Objectives

- **Explain** the law of supply.
- **Interpret** a supply schedule and a supply graph.
- **Examine** the relationship between elasticity of supply and time.

supply
the amount of goods available

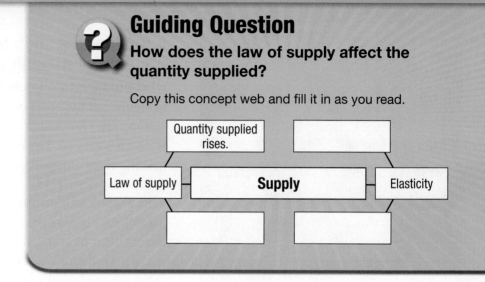

Guiding Question

How does the law of supply affect the quantity supplied?

Copy this concept web and fill it in as you read.

▶ **Economics and You** Suppose you were running a business. What would you do if you found that customers were suddenly willing to pay twice as much for your product? You might decide to work fewer hours. The higher prices would allow you to earn the same income. But if you were like most entrepreneurs, you would take advantage of the higher prices. You would produce more to increase your profit.

Principles in Action As prices rise, producers will offer more of a product. New suppliers will enter the market to earn a share of the profits. The markets for music and pizza show how higher prices increase the quantity supplied.

What is the law of supply?

Like the word *demand,* the word *supply* has a different meaning in economics than it does in everyday life. It has a specific meaning. **Supply** is the ability and willingness of sellers to make goods available for sale. *Ability* means the seller is able to produce and sell a product or service. *Willingness* means the seller wants to produce or sell it. Suppose you decide to make wooden toys to sell at Christmastime. You quickly find out that the job is harder than you thought. You lack the ability to produce the toys, so there is no supply. Then you learn that you have a competitor. He is selling the same toys for less than it costs you just to buy the materials you need. You may no longer be willing to make the toys. Again, this means there is no supply.

What is quantity supplied?

Economists use the term **quantity supplied** to describe how much of a good a producer is willing and able to sell at a set price. A producer may also be called a supplier, a company, or an owner. No matter what term is used, it refers to whoever supplies a product to the market.

You contribute to demand by being a consumer. You buy products and services. You also add to supply. You are a producer. You supply goods and services. If you bag groceries or make hamburgers in a paid job, you supply your labor. You are providing a service. If you are on a school team, you are also a producer. You supply a product that others may pay to see.

Imagine you are a farmer. You can grow corn or soybeans. Last year, the price of corn went up while the price of soybeans went down. What crop would you plant this spring? Most farmers would choose corn. Whether they knew it or not, they were using the law of supply.

The **law of supply** says as the price of a good rises, the quantity supplied will rise. As the price of a good goes down, so does the supply of the good. Farmers will not be willing to produce if they do not receive a fair price for their goods. This is also true of other producers. The law of supply, like the law of demand, is really common sense. Suppliers are willing to supply more of their goods at higher prices than they are at lower prices.

Why do firms increase production when prices rise?

Let's look at the market for music. In the late 1970s, disco music became popular. People began to pay more for disco recordings. Soon, more and more groups were making disco recordings. Groups that once recorded other types of music decided to record disco songs. New groups entered the market. Disco, however, was a fad for only a short time. By the early 1980s, disco music was gone. Stores were unable to sell their disco music.

This rise and fall in supply happens again and again in the music industry. In the early 1990s, grunge music became popular among students. Record labels soon hired many grunge groups. Music stores gave more space to grunge music. Fans of grunge paid more for the music as its popularity rose. However, in a few years, grunge was not as popular. Many groups broke up or moved on to new styles of music, such as rap, hip-hop, and independent rock, as these styles became popular.

quantity supplied
the amount a supplier is willing and able to supply at a set price

law of supply
the idea that producers offer more of a good as its price increases and less as its price falls

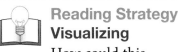

Reading Strategy
Visualizing
How could this paragraph be written differently to create a stronger picture in your mind?

supply schedule
a chart that shows the quantity of a good offered at each possible market price

variable
a factor that can change

In each of these examples, many musicians wanted to profit from what was popular. Their actions showed the law of supply. More of a good was produced as the price went up.

 CHECKPOINT *Why do firms increase production of a good when the price goes up?*

What is a supply schedule?

A **supply schedule** illustrates the law of supply using a chart. It is a chart that shows the quantity of a good offered at each possible market price. Suppose we are looking at a pizza business. **Figure 5.1** is an example of a supply schedule. The individual supply schedule compares two **variables,** or factors that can change. These factors are the price of a slice and the number of slices supplied per day by a pizza shop. The supply schedule shows the quantity of pizza slices the maker would supply at different prices. As the price goes from $1.00 to $6.00, the quantity supplied goes from 100 to 350. The pizza maker is much more eager to sell (supply) pizza slices at the higher price than at the lower price. At higher prices, the shop owner is willing to make more pizza. At lower prices, she will make less pizza. She will use her scarce resources to make other items that will give her more profit.

Fig. 5.1 Supply Schedule

Individual Supply Schedule

Price per Slice of Pizza	Slices Supplied per Day
$1.00	100
$2.00	150
$3.00	200
$4.00	250
$5.00	300
$6.00	350

Market Supply Schedule

Price per Slice of Pizza	Slices Supplied per Day
$1.00	1,000
$2.00	1,500
$3.00	2,000
$4.00	2,500
$5.00	3,000
$6.00	3,500

CHART SKILLS
The individual supply schedule lists how many slices of pizza one pizzeria will offer at different prices. The market supply schedule represents all suppliers in a market.

1. What does the individual supply schedule tell you about the pizzeria owner's decisions?
2. How does the market supply schedule compare to the individual supply schedule?

What is a market supply schedule?

Figure 5.1 shows an individual supply schedule for just one pizza shop. What if we wanted to see how price affected the quantity supplied by all firms in a market? We would create a **market supply schedule.** This kind of chart is helpful when we want to look at the total supply of pizza at a certain price in a large area, like a city. The market supply schedule for pizza in **Figure 5.1** shows the supply of pizza for an imaginary city. It looks like the supply schedule for a single pizza shop, but the quantities are much larger. Like the individual supply schedule, the market supply schedule shows the law of supply. Pizza shops supply more pizza at higher prices.

What is a supply curve?

A supply schedule can also be shown as a graph called a supply curve. The supply curve measures the quantity of the good supplied, not the quantity demanded. The demand curve shows that more people are willing to buy at lower prices than at higher prices. The supply curve shows that suppliers are more willing to sell at higher prices than at lower prices.

The key feature of the supply curve, as shown in **Figure 5.2**, is that it always rises from left to right. Follow one of the curves from left to right with your finger. It moves toward higher and higher production levels and higher and higher prices. This shows the law of supply, which says that a higher price leads to more production.

✔ **CHECKPOINT** *What are the two variables represented in a supply schedule or a supply curve?*

market supply schedule
a chart that lists how much of a good all suppliers will offer at various prices

Fig. 5.2 Supply Curves

GRAPH SKILLS
Supply curves always rise from left to right. As price increases, so does the quantity supplied, as predicted by the law of supply.

1. How many slices will one pizzeria produce at $3.00 a slice?

2. How does a producer create a market supply schedule or curve?

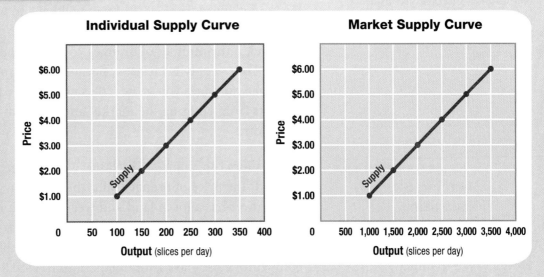

Action Graph online For an animated version of this graph, visit **PearsonSuccessNet.com**

elasticity of supply
a measure of the way quantity supplied reacts to a change in price

inelastic supply
when an increase in price has little effect on the supply demanded

What does elasticity of supply measure?

Just like demand, supply can be either elastic or inelastic. **Elasticity of supply** measures how changes in price affect the quantity supplied. The supply is elastic if a change in price has a big effect on the quantity supplied. If a change in price has little effect on the quantity supplied, the supply is inelastic.

Let's look at an example of elastic supply. On September 11, 2001, terrorists destroyed the World Trade Center in New York City. Many people wanted to show their love of the country by buying American flags. Consumers were willing to pay extra to get a flag. Demand for flags increased. How did this demand affect the supply of flags? Making flags is relatively easy and cheap. They can be made with resources that are common and readily available. Sewing flags is not difficult. They are usually made of cloth that is not expensive. Soon stores had many flags to sell. The price for flags went up, causing a large increase in supply.

Other goods may have an inelastic supply. **Inelastic supply** exists when a small increase in price has little effect on the supply demanded. Goods usually have an inelastic supply if a lot of time and money are required to produce them. In the short run, producers cannot easily change production, so supply is inelastic. In the long run, firms are more flexible, so supply is more elastic.

▲ Because the vines take three or four years to produce fruit, cranberries are another product for which supply is inelastic in the short term.

How does a business adjust to a change in price in the short run?

Let's say you grow oranges. In the short run, it would be hard for you to adjust to a change in price. Orange trees take several years before they grow fruit. If the price of oranges goes up, you can buy and plant more trees. But you will have to wait several years before this effort will pay off. In the short term, you might be able to increase the number of oranges you grow, but probably not by much. Your supply is inelastic, because you cannot easily change how many oranges you grow. The same factors also prevent new growers from entering the market and supplying oranges in the short term.

Reading Strategy
Visualizing
    What clues help you visualize how the elasticity of a product is determined?

In the short run, supply is inelastic whether the price goes up or down. If the price of oranges falls, there are few ways to cut supply. The grower has a lot of land and trees. The oranges will grow no matter what the price is. Even if the price drops a lot, the grower will probably pick and sell nearly as many oranges as before. His competitors also have a lot of land and trees. They won't drop out of the market unless they have to. In this case, supply is inelastic.

Some businesses have a more elastic supply. For example, a business that provides a service, such as a haircut, is highly elastic. Unlike oranges, the supply of haircuts is easily expanded or reduced.

If the price rises, barbershops and salons can hire workers fairly quickly or stay open later. New barbershops and salons will open. This means a small hike in price will cause a large increase in quantity supplied, even in the short term.

If the price of a haircut drops, some shop owners will lay off workers or close earlier. Others will leave the market. Quantity supplied will fall quickly. Because haircut suppliers can quickly adjust to change, the supply of haircuts is elastic.

How does a business adjust to a change in price in the long run?

Like demand, supply can become more elastic over time. In the short run, the orange grower could not easily produce more oranges when the price went up. In the long run, planting more trees can increase his supply. After several years, the orange grower will be able to sell more oranges at the higher market price.

What if the price drops and stays low for several years? The orange growers might decide to grow something else. In the long run, the supply of oranges will be more elastic. Like demand, supply becomes more elastic if the supplier has a long time to adjust to a price change.

 CHECKPOINT *How does a business that is highly elastic respond to a fall in prices?*

SECTION 1 ASSESSMENT

Essential Questions Journal To continue to build a response to the Essential Question, go to your **Essential Questions Journal.**

 Guiding Question

1. Use your completed concept web to answer this question: How does the law of supply affect the quantity supplied?

Key Terms and Main Ideas

Directions: On a sheet of paper, write the answer to each question. Use complete sentences.

2. What is the difference between supply and quantity supplied?

3. What does a supply schedule show?

4. What does a market supply curve show?

5. When the price of oil rises, what will happen to oil production in an oil-rich country?

Critical Thinking

6. **Draw Conclusions** Give examples of two variables, other than price, for each of the following markets: (a) a rock band's concert tour, (b) a bakery.

7. **Analyze Information** State whether you think the supply of the following services is elastic or inelastic, and explain why: (a) lawn-care service, (b) making movies.

Objectives

- **Explain** how firms decide how many workers to hire.
- **Analyze** the production costs of a firm.
- **Explain** how a firm decides how much to produce.
- **Identify** how a firm decides to stay in business or to shut down.

Guiding Question

How can a producer maximize profits?

Copy this table and fill it in as you read.

To Maximize Profit . . .	
Managing Labor	Setting Output
• Increase marginal returns. • Encourage specialization. •	• When prices rise, increase output to equalize price and marginal revenue. • •

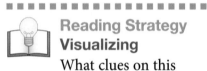

Reading Strategy
Visualizing
What clues on this page help you visualize the relationship between the number of workers and the number of beanbags per hour?

▶ **Economics and You** Looking at a beanbag factory is a good way of checking out labor and other production costs. The factory's physical capital is one sewing machine and one pair of scissors. It uses workers and materials, including cloth, thread, and beans. Each beanbag needs the same amount of materials. How does the company decide how many beanbags to produce?

Principles in Action Producers think about the cost of making one more unit of a good when deciding how to earn the most profits. Firms earn their highest profits when the cost of making one more unit of a good equals the market price of that good. In this section, you'll learn what happens when it costs more to make a product than it costs to buy it.

Fig. 5.3 Marginal Product of Labor

CHART SKILLS

The marginal product of labor is the increase in output added by the last unit of labor.

1. In this chart, why does the marginal product of labor increase with the first three workers?

2. Why does the marginal product of labor decrease with more than four workers?

Marginal Product of Labor

Labor (number of workers)	Output (beanbags per hour)	Marginal Product of Labor
0	0	—
1	4	4
2	10	6
3	17	7
4	23	6
5	28	5
6	31	3
7	32	1
8	31	−1

How do firms decide how many workers to hire?

The number of workers a firm hires will affect total production. For example, at the beanbag factory, one worker can produce four bags per hour. Two workers can make a total of ten bags per hour. Three workers can produce 17 bags an hour. The more workers, the more bags produced. The most will be produced with seven workers. The seven workers can make 32 bags per hour. What happens if the firm hires another worker? Production will drop to only 31 bags per hour. **Figure 5.3** shows the relationship between the number of workers in the factory and the hourly number of beanbags produced.

What is marginal product of labor?

The change in production produced by hiring one more worker is called the marginal product. The **marginal product of labor** is shown in **Figure 5.3**, column 3. The first worker to be hired produces four bags an hour. Her marginal product is four bags. The second worker raises production from four bags an hour to ten. Her marginal product of labor is six (ten bags – four bags produced by first worker = six). Looking at this column, we see that the marginal product of labor goes up for the first three workers. It rises from four to six to seven.

Why do marginal returns go up?

The marginal product of labor went up for the first three workers. This is because there are three steps in making a beanbag. Workers have to cut and sew cloth into the correct shape. They have to stuff it with beans. Then they sew the bag closed. A single worker doing all three steps can produce only four bags per hour. If a second worker is hired, each worker can specialize in one or two of the steps. This specialization saves time and makes the workers more efficient. Each becomes more skilled at her job. Specialization increases production per worker, so the second worker adds more to production than the first. The firm enjoys **increasing marginal returns.** **Figure 5.4** shows the effect on marginal returns.

marginal product of labor
the change in output from hiring one additional unit of labor

increasing marginal returns
a level of production in which the marginal product of labor increases as the number of workers increases

Reading Strategy
Visualizing
How do the figures on these pages help you better understand what you read?

Fig. 5.4 Marginal Returns

GRAPH SKILLS
Labor has increasing and then diminishing marginal returns.

1. What is the marginal product of labor when the factory employs five workers?
2. Why does the factory experience diminishing marginal returns with more than three workers?

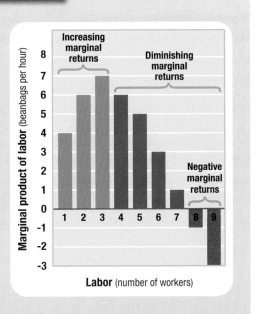

diminishing marginal returns
a level of production at which the marginal product of labor decreases as the number of workers increases

In our example, hiring three workers increases the benefits of specialization. Each worker can specialize in one step. The firm enjoys a rising marginal product of labor.

Why do marginal returns go down?

When workers four through seven are hired, the marginal product of labor still goes up. Each new worker adds to total production. However, as each worker joins the company, the increase in marginal product of labor gets smaller. The fourth worker increases production by six bags. The seventh worker only raises production by one bag. Why?

When there are only three workers, the firm benefits from specialization. Adding more workers lessens the benefits. Total production goes up, but at a lower rate. This is known as **diminishing marginal returns.** A firm with diminishing marginal returns of labor will produce less and less output from each new worker. In other words, adding more workers is not always a good thing. The increase in production eventually diminishes, or becomes smaller.

The firm has diminishing marginal returns because its workers have a limited amount of capital. The firm's capital is its single sewing machine and its one pair of scissors. With three workers, only one needs to use the sewing machine. Another worker uses the scissors. No one has to wait to get to use either the sewing machine or the scissors. If there are more than three workers, more than one will work at the sewing machine. So while one works, the other waits. She may use her time to cut the cloth or stuff bags. Still, every bag must be sewn at some point. She cannot do much to make production go faster.

The problem gets worse as more workers are hired. The capital stays the same. More time is wasted waiting for the single sewing machine or scissors. This means the extra workers will add less and less to total production.

What are negative marginal returns?

As **Figure 5.3** on page 104 shows, adding an eighth worker actually cuts production by one bag. Workers start getting in one another's way. Negative marginal returns means adding extra workers actually causes production to drop. The production process is no longer smooth.

▲ When workers specialize in specific tasks, output per worker increases. The firm enjoys increasing marginal returns.

✅ **CHECKPOINT** *How are diminishing marginal returns of labor related to the amount of capital?*

What are the costs of production?

Businesses need to know the costs of production when deciding how much to supply to the market. The costs of production have a big effect on how much profit a business will make. These costs fall into two groups: fixed and variable. **Figure 5.6** on page 108 shows the process that businesses follow.

What are fixed costs?

Every business has **fixed costs**. Fixed costs stay the same no matter how much is produced. Many fixed costs of doing business are obvious. Businesses usually pay rent. Bills for electric and gas power have to be paid. Firms have to pay for insurance. Money has to be set aside for taxes. Loans have to be paid back. All these are examples of costs that are fixed. Fixed costs also include machines and capital goods. Their costs are the same whether they are being used or not. These costs of doing business are sometimes called overhead.

What are variable costs?

Variable costs change with the amount of production. How much the business spends on raw materials can change from month to month. Workers' pay also goes up and down. If demand is strong, workers may work more hours. The business rewards them by paying them more. Labor and raw materials are the most common examples of variable costs.

fixed cost
cost that stays the same no matter how much is produced

variable cost
a cost that rises or falls depending on the quantity produced

Fig. 5.5 Production Costs

CHART SKILLS

Firms consider a variety of costs when deciding how much to produce.

1. Why is the marginal revenue always equal to $24?

2. What is the average cost when output is seven beanbags per hour?

Beanbags (per hour)	Fixed Cost	Variable Cost	Total Cost (fixed cost + variable cost)	Marginal Cost	Marginal Revenue (market price)	Total Revenue	Profit (total revenue – total cost)
0	$36	$0	$36	—	$24	$0	$–36
1	36	8	44	$8	24	24	–20
2	36	12	48	4	24	48	0
3	36	15	51	3	24	72	21
4	36	20	56	5	24	96	40
5	36	27	63	7	24	120	57
6	36	36	72	9	24	144	72
7	36	48	84	12	24	168	84
8	36	63	99	15	24	192	93
9	36	82	118	19	24	216	98
10	36	106	142	24	24	240	98
11	36	136	172	30	24	264	92
12	36	173	209	37	24	288	79

Fig. 5.6 How the Economy Works

What are production costs?

Production costs are the costs an entrepreneur must pay to run a business. Production costs are divided into two categories: fixed costs and variable costs.

1 Fixed Cost
Rent: Fixed costs are costs that do not change, no matter how much of a good is produced. The rent for the storefront is a fixed cost.

2 Fixed Cost
Manager: The new manager is essential to the operation of the store. The manager's salary is a fixed cost.

3 Variable Costs
Goods and electricity: Variable costs are costs that change as the level of production changes. The cost of all the merchandise the store sells is a variable cost. The cost of the electricity that the store uses during business hours is also a variable cost.

JACK'S SPORTING GOODS

COMING SOON

Fixed Cost

---

total cost
the sum of fixed costs and variable costs

How is total cost calculated?

We get the **total cost** of production by adding the fixed costs to the variable costs of production. It is called total cost because it is the total of all the costs of doing business. **Figure 5.5** on page 107 shows what it costs the firm to produce beanbags. The factory is fully equipped to produce beanbags. How does the cost of producing beanbags change the more beanbags the factory makes?

In our example, the fixed costs are the costs of the factory building and all the machinery inside. As shown in the second column in **Figure 5.5**, fixed costs are $36.00 per hour.

Variable costs include the cost of beans, fabric, and most of the workers. As shown in the third column, variable costs rise with the number of beanbags produced. The total cost is shown in the fourth column.

4 **Variable Cost**
Part-time workers: Some companies hire part-time workers, whose hours are reduced when business is slow. The salaries for part-time workers are a variable cost.

5 **Total Cost**
When fixed costs and variable costs are added together, the result is a firm's total cost—the amount of money needed to operate a business.

Check Your Understanding
1. Would an advertisement for the store that runs every week in a local newspaper be a fixed cost or a variable cost?
2. Is the separate storage space the owner rents for two months a fixed cost or a variable cost?

Variable Cost ▶ **Total Cost** ▶

What is marginal cost?

Marginal cost is the extra cost of producing one more unit. **Figure 5.5** shows that even if the firm is not producing a single beanbag, it still has fixed costs of $36.00 an hour. It costs the firm $8 more to make just one beanbag. Total cost is now $44.00 ($36 + $8 = $44). The marginal cost of the first beanbag is $8.00.

For the first three beanbags, marginal cost falls as the amount of production goes up. The marginal cost of the second beanbag is $4.00. The marginal cost of the third beanbag is $3.00. Each extra beanbag is cheaper to make because of increasing marginal returns. At four beanbags per hour, the marginal cost starts to rise. The marginal cost of five beanbags per hour is $7.00. The sixth costs $9.00. The seventh costs $12.00. The marginal costs rise because of diminishing returns. The firm no longer benefits from specialization. The returns keep becoming smaller as more and more workers share the limited resources.

marginal cost
the cost of producing one more unit of a good

✔ **CHECKPOINT** *Why does a factory owner who produces nothing still have production costs?*

marginal revenue
the additional income from selling one more unit of a good

average cost
the total cost divided by the quantity produced

How does a firm decide how much to produce?

Remember, a firm is in business to earn a profit. Profit is the money left over after all the costs of production have been paid. In other words, it is total revenue minus total cost. As you have read in Chapter 4, a firm's total revenue is the money the firm gets by selling its product. Total revenue is equal to the price of a good multiplied by the number of goods sold. Figure 5.5 shows total revenue when the price of a beanbag is $24.00.

Another way to find the best level of production is to find the point where marginal revenue is equal to marginal cost. **Marginal revenue** is the extra income from selling one more unit of a good. If the firm has no control over the market price, marginal revenue equals the market price. Let's say each beanbag sells at $24.00. This raises the firm's total revenue by $24.00, so marginal revenue is $24.00. According to the table in Figure 5.5, market price equals marginal cost with ten beanbags. This is the number of beanbags a firm could produce to earn the highest profit at $98 an hour. Profit is greatest when marginal revenue (price) is equal to marginal cost. As Figure 5.5 on page 107 shows, we can figure profit per hour by subtracting total cost from total revenue.

We can also calculate profit by comparing price and average cost. **Average cost** is total cost divided by the quantity produced. If the firm is producing ten beanbags per hour, the average cost is $14.20 ($142 [total cost] ÷ 10). Profit is the difference between market price and average cost ($24 − $14.20 = $9.80) multiplied by the quantity ($9.80 × 10 = $98).

▼ When a factory loses money, operating cost and revenue determine whether it remains open.

✔ **CHECKPOINT** *What is a firm's basic goal when it sets its level of output?*

When does a firm decide to shut down?

Sometimes businesses decide to shut down. How is this decision made? Let's say a firm is producing at the level of production that earns the highest profit. This is the level of production at which marginal revenue is equal to marginal cost. But if the market price is so low that the factory's total revenue is still less than its total cost, the firm is losing money. Should this firm continue to produce goods and lose money, or should its owners shut it down?

There are times when keeping a money-losing firm open is the best choice. The firm should remain open if the total revenue from the goods and services the factory produces is greater than the cost of keeping it open.

For example, let's say the price of beanbags drops to $7. The factory produces five beanbags per hour, the rate at which the profit is highest. At $7 a beanbag, the total revenue is $35 per hour. What is the factory's **operating cost,** or the cost of operating the factory? Operating cost includes the variable costs the owners must pay to keep the firm running. It does not include fixed costs, which the owners must pay even if the firm is closed.

According to **Figure 5.5** on page 107, if the firm produces five beanbags, the variable cost is $27 per hour. Keeping the firm open makes sense. The total revenue of $35 is more than the variable cost of $27. The owners would be left with $8 an hour ($35 − $27 = $8) which they could use to pay some of the fixed costs.

If the owners decide to shut down the firm, they still have to pay all its fixed costs. The total revenue would be zero because the firm produces nothing for sale. Therefore, the firm would lose $36 an hour, the amount of its fixed costs. The owners lose money whether they keep making beanbags or not. They would lose less money by keeping the firm open than by closing it. Of course, a business cannot operate at a loss forever. The firm can only stay in the market if the market price of beanbags is high enough to cover all the costs of production.

 CHECKPOINT *Under what circumstances should a firm keep a money-losing business open?*

SECTION 2 ASSESSMENT

Essential Questions Journal — To continue to build a response to the Essential Question, go to your **Essential Questions Journal.**

Guiding Question

1. Use your completed table to answer the following question: How can a producer maximize profits?

Key Terms and Main Ideas

Directions: On a sheet of paper, write the answer to each question. Use complete sentences.

2. What does marginal cost refer to?

3. What are examples of fixed costs and variable costs for a firm?

4. What is marginal revenue?

5. Is operating cost a fixed cost or a variable cost? Why?

Critical Thinking

6. **Synthesize Information** Suppose you are advising a company that is seeing diminishing marginal returns. Other than reducing staff, what steps would you recommend to improve its performance?

7. **Synthesize Information** Suppose your company has two office spaces, one twice as large as the other. Would you add the same number of employees to each facility? Why or why not?

Objectives

- **Explain** which factors can create changes in supply.
- **Identify** three ways the government can influence the supply of goods.
- **Explain** how firms choose a location to produce goods.

Guiding Question

Why does the supply curve shift?

Copy this table and fill it in as you read.

Supply	
Increases	Decreases
• Fall in the cost of an input	• Rise in the cost of an input
• New technology	•
•	•

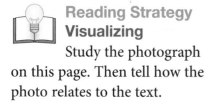

Reading Strategy
Visualizing
Study the photograph on this page. Then tell how the photo relates to the text.

▼ The higher input costs that dairy farmers pay for feed, labor, and fuel increase the price of milk and other dairy products.

▶ **Economics and You** You have learned how production costs can affect how much a firm produces and its profits. Inputs are the resources used in making a product. Their costs are a variable cost of production. The price of raw materials, machinery, and labor can change. These changing costs affect output, or how much is produced. They can either raise or lower the marginal cost of production. Changes in input costs will raise or lower the supply of a good at any price.

Principles in Action New technology can also change supply. Government actions can lead to a shift in the supply curve. Events around the world also can affect supply. The effect of input costs is the subject of the Economics & You feature.

How does the cost of resources affect supply?

In Chapter 1, we talked about the factors of production. We learned the three types of resources used in production. The three were natural resources, labor resources, and capital. Any change in the cost of these resources will affect supply. What happens if the price of the resources goes down? More can be produced because the goods are cheaper to make. Likewise, if the cost of the resources goes up, producers will make less. Why? Because the goods become more expensive to make.

New technology tends to lower the cost of production. Today's farmers, for example, are able to produce a great deal more than those in the past. New technologies such as pest control, better seed, and improved fertilizers and machines allow the farmer to grow more. The cost of production goes down. Because production costs are less, farmers are more willing and able to produce more. Technology lowers costs and increases supply at all price levels. The supply curve shifts to the right, as **Figure 5.7** shows.

✅ **CHECKPOINT** *How would a rise in the cost of inputs, such as raw materials, affect supply?*

How does government regulation affect supply?

Regulation is when government steps in to make rules. Some rules affect the safety of products. For example, there are many government rules for making cars. Starting in 1970, laws were passed to limit the amount of pollution cars produced. All cars now must use lead-free gasoline. Rules such as these raise the cost of making cars. Supply drops. The supply curve shifts to the left.

How do taxes affect supply?

The government has the power to affect the supplies of many goods. One way is through taxes. A tax is money that people and firms pay to help pay for the cost of government. Businesses think of taxes as an extra cost of producing goods and services. A raise in taxes has the same effect as an increase in the cost of resources. It makes production more expensive. As a result, producers make less. Supply drops.

Government can also reduce the supply of some goods by placing an excise tax on them. An **excise tax** is a tax on the creation or sale of a product. There are excise taxes on cigarettes and alcohol. Like any extra cost, an excise tax causes the supply of a good to drop. As **Figure 5.7** shows, the supply curve shifts to the left.

regulation
when a government makes rules that affect the production of a good or service

excise tax
a tax placed on the creation or sale of a product

Fig. 5.7 Shifts in the Supply Curve

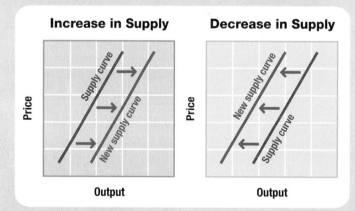

GRAPH SKILLS
Factors that reduce supply shift the supply curve to the left, while factors that increase supply move the supply curve to the right.
1. Which graph best represents the effects of higher costs?
2. Which graph best represents advances in technology?

For an animated version of this graph, visit PearsonSuccessNet.com

Reading Strategy
Visualizing

What words in these three paragraphs help you visualize what you are reading?

How do subsidies affect supply?

Governments sometimes pick out industries they believe are important to their countries. Many governments believe their countries should not depend on other countries for food. To encourage farmers to continue to produce, governments sometimes pay a **subsidy** to support a business or market.

In the United States, one type of subsidy is price supports to farmers. Price supports are government guarantees that farmers will receive a minimum price for their products. These subsidies have the opposite effect of taxes. They lower the cost of production and encourage businesses to continue production. This makes the supply go up and the supply curve shift to the right. If farmers did not receive government subsidies, many would give up farming. The supply would go down.

Developing countries provide subsidies to young industries to protect them from foreign competition. Countries like Indonesia and Malaysia have subsidized national car companies, even though imported cars were less expensive. In Western Europe, banks and national airlines were allowed to suffer huge losses with the promise that the government would cover their debts. In many countries, governments have stopped providing industrial subsidies in the interest of free trade and fair competition.

✔ **CHECKPOINT** *What happens to supply if sellers of a good expect the price of that good to rise in the future?*

Economics & YOU

Input Costs

Rising costs for wheat, fertilizer, and fuel make this box of cereal more expensive to produce. *As a result of higher input costs, you pay more for your morning bowl of cereal.*

You receive special offers and discount coupons by e-mail. *Technology helps companies reduce costs for advertising and postage.*

Where do firms produce?

The location of a business is important. For many firms, the cost of transportation is a key factor. They need to know the cost of shipping their products to markets. Sometimes, raw materials are expensive to move. It takes seven tons of tomatoes to produce one ton of sauce. It makes sense for the firm to locate close to the tomato fields. One ton of sauce costs a lot less to ship to consumers than seven tons of tomatoes to a factory far from the fields.

On the other hand, some firms locate close to consumers. Soft drinks are made by adding water to syrup. The cans of soda weigh a lot more than the syrup alone. It makes sense for the firm to locate close to its customers. The firm saves by having to transport soft drinks only a short distance. In general, if a product is bulky or spoils easily, a firm will locate near its customers.

There are other reasons why firms locate where they do. Some locate in places with lower energy costs or with many skilled workers. Many locate near cities because of the numerous services cities offer businesses.

 CHECKPOINT *When is a firm likely to locate near its consumers?*

SECTION 3 ASSESSMENT

Essential Questions Journal To continue to build a response to the Essential Question, go to your **Essential Questions Journal.**

Guiding Question

1. Use your completed table to answer this question: Why does the supply curve shift?

Key Terms and Main Ideas

Directions: On a sheet of paper, write the answer to each question. Use complete sentences.

2. What is a subsidy, and how do subsidies affect the supply curve?

3. What is an excise tax, and how do excise taxes affect the supply curve?

4. What effect do regulations have on the supply curve? Why?

5. Why would the government give a subsidy to support a farmer?

Critical Thinking

6. **Draw Conclusions** If regulation increases price and decreases supply, why does the government issue regulations?

7. **Analyze Information** (a) Why would an automaker want to have manufacturing plants in several different regions? (b) Why would a software company not necessarily want facilities in several different regions?

QUICK STUDY GUIDE

Section 1—Understanding Supply

- The law of supply states that when the price of a good rises, the quantity supplied of that good also rises. That is because existing firms produce more, and new firms join the market.

- A supply schedule shows the relationship between price and quantity supplied for a specific good. A supply curve is a graph showing this data. It rises from left to right.

- Elasticity of supply measures how suppliers respond to a price change. Time is the most important factor that determines whether the supply of a good is elastic or inelastic.

Section 2—Costs of Production

- The marginal product of labor is the change in output from hiring one more worker. It measures the output at the margin.

- Diminishing marginal returns is a decrease in output from each additional unit of labor.

- Adding another worker can decrease output when there are not enough resources. This is known as diminishing marginal returns.

- Producers have two main categories of costs. Fixed costs do not change. Variable costs rise or fall depending on the quantity produced.

- The basic goal of any firm is to maximize profits. Profit is total revenue minus total cost.

Section 3—Changes in Supply

- Any change in the cost of an input will affect supply. A rise in the cost of an input will cause a fall in supply because the good is more expensive to produce. A fall in the cost of an input will cause an increase in supply.

- Technology lowers costs and increases supply at all price levels.

- Governments have the power to affect supplies of many goods. They do this by placing taxes on goods.

- The location of a firm's suppliers or its consumers determines where the firm will locate. This is because of transportation costs.

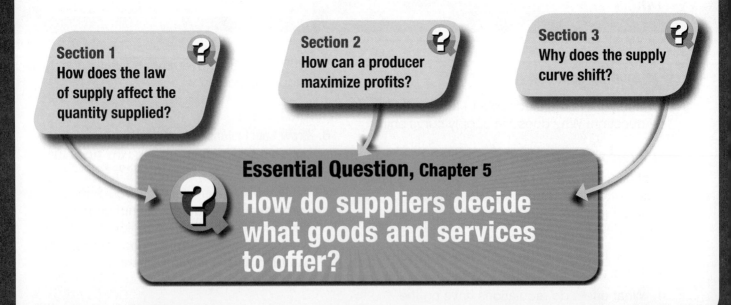

Section 1
How does the law of supply affect the quantity supplied?

Section 2
How can a producer maximize profits?

Section 3
Why does the supply curve shift?

Essential Question, Chapter 5
How do suppliers decide what goods and services to offer?

DOCUMENT-BASED ASSESSMENT

Klondike Gold Fields

Between 1897 and 1898, more than 100,000 people rushed to Dawson City and the Klondike to search for gold. Gold has a very limited supply, which is what, in part, makes it valuable. During the nineteenth century, in remote places like the Klondike, certain goods—such as specific types of food, tools, and clothing—were also in short supply.

SAN FRANCISCO, Cal., July 18—Joseph Ladue, the owner of the town site of Dawson City, Alaska, the nearest town to the Klondike section started last night for his home, in Plattsburg, N.Y. Besides owning the township of Dawson, where land is already selling for $5,000 a lot, Mr. Ladue brought with him enough gold dust to keep him in comfort for some time to come. Mr. Ladue said that there was no doubt of the richness of the gold diggings in the Klondike region. He thinks there is enough gold in the ground to keep all the miners who can work busy for the next twenty years. Mr. Ladue, however, issues a timely warning to the thousands who are preparing to rush to the gold fields this year. He says: "There are at present about 3,500 people in the country, and that number is about all that can be accommodated this winter. Provisions [supplies] are high [expensive], as it costs 10 to 15 cents a pound to land goods at Dawson City, and it is impossible to get more provisions in this year than will supply the present population. If miners rush up there this Summer, unless they take with them their own supplies, they will suffer great hardships. I advise every one going up to take supplies sufficient to last at least eighteen months... ."

Document-Based Questions

1. What town is nearest to the Klondike?
2. What does Mr. Ladue say about the supply of gold in the Klondike?
3. Why do you think supplies in the Klondike region are so expensive?
4. What do you think would happen to the supply of provisions if miners rushed to the Klondike?
5. How would increased demand for provisions impact the price of supplies?

SOURCE: "Klondike Gold Fields: Joseph Ladue of Plattsburg, N.Y. on the Wealth That is Being Discovered. Issues a Timely Warning," *The New York Times,* July 19, 1897.

Directions: Write the answer to the following questions. Use complete sentences.

Section 1–Understanding Supply

1. What is the law of supply?

2. What is a supply schedule?

3. What does elasticity of supply measure?

4. Give two examples of industries that would draw new firms into the market if profits of existing businesses rose.

5. Does the cable television industry have elasticity of supply? Why or why not?

Section 2–Costs of Production

6. What term describes the change in output at the margin?

7. What is a fixed cost? Give an example.

8. What is a variable cost? Give an example.

9. What is average cost?

10. What happens when marginal revenue equals marginal cost?

11. What questions must a factory owner ask when deciding to shut down a money-losing factory?

Section 3–Changes in Supply

12. How has technology lowered the cost of production?

13. What are subsidies?

14. How do future expectations of prices affect supply?

15. How does government control the supplies of many goods?

16. Why will a rise in the cost of raw materials cause a fall in supply at all price levels?

17. Why might a government rule limiting the amount of pollution a car can produce raise the cost of making cars?

Economics on the go

Exploring the Essential Question

18. What fixed and variable costs might a shoe repair shop have? How could you figure total revenue?

19. Why do producers have to consider the cost of resources when deciding what goods and services to offer?

Essential Question Activity

20. Complete the activity to answer the Essential Question **How do suppliers decide what goods and services to offer?**

For this activity, conduct a poll to determine which one good or service your community most needs. Interview three people in the community (family, friends, or other students) and have them identify the one good or service that best serves local needs. When everyone has completed the poll, the class will separate poll results into five different categories: entertainment, food establishments, medical services, recreational facilities, and other. Use the worksheet in your Essential Questions Journal or the electronic worksheet available at **PearsonSuccessNet.com** for instructions on how to conduct the poll.

| **Essential Questions Journal** | To continue to build a response to the Essential Question, go to your **Essential Questions Journal.** |

Test-Taking Tip

To study for a chapter test, use the headings within a chapter to write an outline. Review this outline to help you recall the information.

Chapter **6** Prices

? **Essential Question, Chapter 6**
What is the right price?

- **Section 1** Combining Supply and Demand

- **Section 2** Changes in Market Equilibrium

- **Section 3** The Role of Prices

Economics on the go

To study anywhere, anytime, download these onlin[e] resources at *PearsonSuccessNet.com* ➤

▶ **How are prices set?** How do you decide whether to buy something? Most consumers look at prices. Imagine how difficult shopping would be if there were no prices. You would not know whether you could afford to buy something or not. Prices are the way that buyers and sellers share information.

In this chapter, you will learn what equilibrium, or balance, means in the market. You will read about surpluses and shortages, and supply and demand. You will learn about the steps government sometimes takes to control prices. You will learn what rationing is and why it is used. You will find the answers to the questions "Why do prices change?" and "How does demand for an item affect its price?" And you will explore the reasons, or incentives, for people to work.

Reading Strategy: Inferencing
Sometimes the meaning of a text is not directly stated. You have to "read between the lines" to figure out what the text means. Use what you already know and what you just read to put the meaning together.

What I Know + What I Read = Inference

Visual Glossary
online

Go to the Visual Glossary Online for an interactive review of **equilibrium**.

How the Economy Works
online

Go to How the Economy Works Online for an interactive lesson on **shortage**.

Action Graph
online

Go to Action Graph Online for animated versions of key charts and graphs.

Objectives

- **Explain** how supply and demand create equilibrium in the marketplace.
- **Describe** what happens to prices when equilibrium is disturbed.
- **Identify** two ways that the government steps in to control prices.
- **Analyze** the impact of price ceilings and price floors on a free market.

■■■■■■■■■■■■■■■■■■■■

equilibrium price
the price that both buyers and sellers will accept

equilibrium
the point at which the demand for a product or service is equal to the supply of that product or service

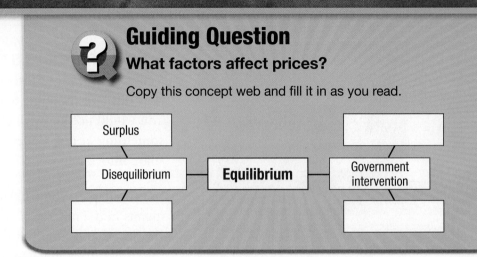

Guiding Question

What factors affect prices?

Copy this concept web and fill it in as you read.

▶ **Economics and You** When you go to the store to buy something—whether it's a cellphone, a CD, or a pair of sneakers— you can usually find it. You are being helped by the free market system at work. Businesses are making enough profit to produce and sell the goods you want at a price you are willing to pay.

Principles in Action Prices are affected by the laws of supply and demand and by government action. You will see how free markets provide goods and services at the right prices and in large enough quantities. You will see examples of how government actions affect prices and the wages of some workers.

How does a market reach equilibrium?

Supply and demand work together to set prices. Chapter 4 talked about demand. You learned that consumers buy less if the price goes up. Chapter 5 talked about supply. You read that producers want to sell more if the price goes up. It might look like buyers and sellers would never agree on a price. However, there is one price both will accept.

Supply and demand meet at the **equilibrium price**. This is the price that both buyers and sellers will accept. Look at **Figure 6.1.** This lists the supply of pizza slices available and the cost of each slice at one shop. There is only one point where the quantity supplied and quantity demanded are the same. At this point, the market is balanced. This point is called **equilibrium**. The equilibrium quantity is 200 slices of pizza per day. The equilibrium price is $3.00 per slice.

☑ **CHECKPOINT** *When is the market at equilibrium on a supply and demand schedule?*

What is disequilibrium?

Disequilibrium means that quantity supplied and quantity demanded are not balanced. This happens when there is more supply than demand. It also occurs when there is more demand than supply. Look again at **Figure 6.1** on this page. You can see that disequilibrium occurs at any price other than $3.00. It also occurs at any quantity other than 200. If the seller tried to sell pizza slices for $4.00, there would be fewer buyers. The sellers would have more pizzas than they could sell. If the pizza slices were sold for only $1.00, there would be more people wanting to buy pizza slices than there are slices available.

What is a shortage?

What would happen if the pizza sellers decided to lower the price to $2.00 per slice? At $2.00, the demand schedule shows that buyers would buy 250 slices. This number is more than the number producers are willing to sell at that price. They would be willing to sell only 150 slices. This causes a **shortage.** The shortage would be 100 slices. Shortages happen only when the price is less than the equilibrium price. Another name for shortage is excess demand. In other words, there is more demand for the cheaper pizza than the sellers are willing to sell at that price.

Why do prices rise when there are shortages?

If you were the pizza seller, what would you do? People seem to like your pizza. There are long lines of people wanting to buy. There is a shortage. This means that there are not as many pizzas available as there are buyers who want pizzas. Some buyers will offer to pay a higher price to get the scarce pizzas. These buyers are willing to pay more than other buyers. If you are the seller, you might want to work harder and make more pizzas. You know that you could earn more money for each slice of pizza you sell.

disequilibrium
any price or quantity not at equilibrium; when quantity supplied is not equal to quantity demanded in a market

shortage
a situation in which buyers want more of a good or service than sellers are willing to make available at a particular price

Fig. 6.1 Finding Equilibrium

GRAPH SKILLS

Market equilibrium is found at the price at which the quantity demanded is equal to the quantity supplied.

1. How many slices are sold at $2.00 per slice?
2. How many slices are sold at equilibrium?

Combined Supply and Demand Schedule

Price of a Slice of Pizza	Quantity Demanded	Quantity Supplied	Result
$1.00	300	100	Shortage from excess demand
$2.00	250	150	
$3.00	200	200	Equilibrium
$4.00	150	250	Surplus from excess supply
$5.00	100	300	
$6.00	50	350	

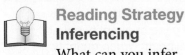
surplus
when quantity supplied is more than quantity demanded

price ceiling
a maximum price that can legally be charged for a good or service

price floor
the lowest price allowed for certain goods or services

rent control
a price ceiling placed on rent

What is a surplus?

What if the pizzeria owners thought they could sell pizza for $4.00 per slice? At that price, only 150 people are willing to buy. This would result in a **surplus** of 100 slices. Surpluses happen when what the seller is willing to supply is larger than what buyers are willing to buy at a price. Another name for surplus is excess supply.

A surplus means that the sellers are not able to sell as much as they hoped to sell. They have extra goods. The pizza makers may have to throw out unsold pizzas. This wastes valuable resources. Storing extra goods costs money. Many businesses try to avoid surpluses by lowering prices with clearance and end-of-season sales.

 CHECKPOINT *What market condition might cause a pizzeria owner to throw out slices of pizza at the end of the day?*

Why might government step in?

In a pure market economy, prices change according to supply and demand. There is competition in markets for resources and competition in markets for products. We learned in Chapter 2 that there are no pure market economies. Sometimes governments come between producers and consumers in order to protect them from big changes in market prices. Two ways they do this are to set **price ceilings** and **price floors**.

What is a price ceiling?

In some countries, the government sets the price of basic needs such as bread, milk, heating oil, and housing. The price ceiling is set below the equilibrium price. The government wants to make sure that all its citizens can afford basic needs. This seems like a good idea. But how do price ceilings affect the quantity supplied? We have learned what happens if prices are lower than the equilibrium price. Producers will not want to sell as much. They will use their scarce resources where they might make more money. Shortages may occur.

What is rent control?

Figure 6.2 shows housing-market data for a make-believe city. **Rent control** is a price ceiling placed on rent. Look at Graph A. The supply and demand curves for apartments meet at point *a*, where the rental price is $900.00 per month. At this equilibrium rent, consumers will demand 30,000 apartments and suppliers will offer 30,000 apartments for rent.

Suppose that the city government passes a law to limit the rent on apartments to $600.00 per month. This is below the equilibrium price. The effect on the market is shown in Graph B. At a price of $600.00, the number of apartments demanded is 45,000 (point *c*), and the number supplied is 15,000 (point *b*). At such a low price, many people will rent apartments instead of buying houses.

What is a price floor?

A price floor sets the lowest price allowed for certain goods and services. An example of a price floor is the **minimum wage.** This sets a minimum price that an employer must pay a worker for one hour of labor. The federal government sets a base level for the minimum wage. However, states can make their levels even higher.

How does the minimum wage affect business? Let's say the market equilibrium wage for low-skilled labor is $6.60 per hour. The minimum wage is set at $7.25 per hour. The result is a surplus of labor. Firms will employ fewer low-skilled workers than they would at the equilibrium wage rate. That is because the price floor on labor keeps the wage rate artificially high. If the minimum wage is below the equilibrium rate, it will have no effect. Employers would have to pay at least the equilibrium rate anyway to find workers in a free market.

minimum wage
the minimum price that an employer must pay a worker for an hour of labor

Fig. 6.2 The Effects of Rent Control

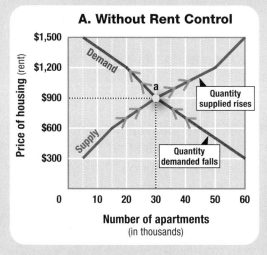

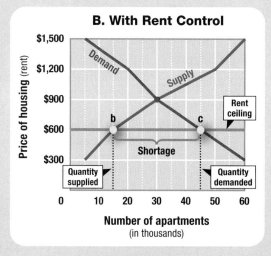

Action Graph
online

For an animated version of this graph, visit **PearsonSuccessNet.com**

GRAPH SKILLS

While rent control helps many tenants, it also creates disequilibrium in the housing market.

1. At what price is the market for apartments at equilibrium without rent control?

2. How does rent control lead to a shortage of desirable apartments?

KEY

a. The supply and demand curves for two-bedroom apartments meet at the equilibrium rent of $900 per month.

b. With rent control keeping rents at $600 per month, landlords are willing to supply 15,000 two-bedroom apartments.

c. With rent control keeping rents at $600 per month, potential tenants are seeking 45,000 two-bedroom apartments.

■ ■ ■ ■ ■ ■ ■ ■ ■ ■ ■ ■ ■ ■ ■

subsidy
a government grant often given to farmers to guarantee a certain price for their produce

financial aid
assistance in the form of grants and loans to help individuals in a time of need

■ ■ ■ ■ ■ ■ ■ ■ ■ ■ ■ ■ ■ ■ ■ ■

Reading Strategy
Inferencing
    After reading this section, what can you infer about the impact of price floors and price ceilings?

What are price supports?

Governments sometimes provide **subsidies,** or grants. One type of subsidy is price supports. The government promises that the price farmers receive for their produce will not fall below a certain amount. These price supports encourage farmers to grow more, because the government will step in to buy the surplus.

Congress voted to phase out most of these programs in 1996. Despite the effort to end price supports, many commodities remain relatively untouched by the new laws. For example, the Department of Agriculture has continued to buy tons of powdered milk. This way they keep the price from dropping below the set minimum. In response to low prices, the federal government also provides emergency **financial aid** to farmers. Without this help, some farmers would have to give up farming.

 CHECKPOINT *How does a minimum wage above the equilibrium rate affect the quantity of labor supplied?*

SECTION 1 ASSESSMENT

Essential Questions Journal
To continue to build a response to the Essential Question, go to your **Essential Questions Journal.**

Word Bank

disequilibrium

equilibrium

minimum wage

rent control

 Guiding Question

1. Use your completed concept web to answer this question: What factors affect prices?

Key Terms and Main Ideas

Directions: On a sheet of paper, write the word from the Word Bank that correctly answers each question.

2. When a market is balanced between supply and demand, what does it show?

3. When a market is not balanced between supply and demand, what does it show?

4. What is an example of a price ceiling?

5. What is an example of a price floor?

Critical Thinking

6. **Recognize Cause and Effect** (a) In a free market, what impact does excess demand have on consumers? (b) How does this differ from the effect on producers?

7. **Compare Points of View** Describe one argument for and one argument against rent control.

Objectives

- **Explain** why a free market naturally tends to move toward equilibrium.
- **Analyze** how a market reacts to an increase or decrease in supply.
- **Analyze** how a market reacts to an increase or decrease in demand.

Guiding Question

How do changes in supply and demand affect equilibrium?

Copy this concept web and fill it in as you read.

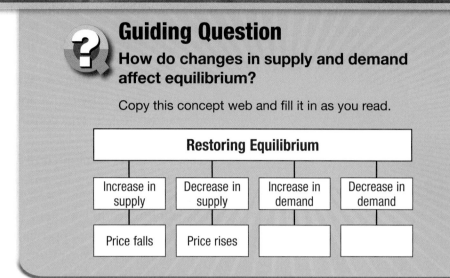

Restoring Equilibrium			
Increase in supply	Decrease in supply	Increase in demand	Decrease in demand
Price falls	Price rises		

▶ **Economics and You** Have you ever stood in a long line to buy concert tickets or the latest video game? Do you look at the signs at the gas pump to see if the price is up or down? Have you ever seen signs saying "Great Bargains… Everything Must Go!" in a store window? These are all part of the market system at work. And often, the one who gets the benefit—or pays the price—is you.

Principles in Action Changes in supply and demand upset the balance in the market and cause prices to change. Sometimes prices go up, sometimes prices go down. But either way, the principle of market equilibrium is at work. In this section, you will see how changes in supply and demand affect a variety of products, from digital cameras to toys.

The "sneaker blow-out" sign ▶ suggests that this store may be experiencing a surplus.

■■■■■■■■■■■■■■■■■■

Reading Strategy
Inferencing
What do you already know about equilibrium?

Why do markets move toward equilibrium?

Economists say that a market will move toward equilibrium. This means that the price and quantity will gradually move until they reach equilibrium levels. Why does this happen?

Remember that a shortage will cause firms to raise prices. Higher prices cause the quantity supplied to rise and the quantity demanded to fall. This continues until the two values are equal. However, a surplus will force firms to cut prices. Falling prices cause quantity demanded to rise and quantity supplied to fall. This continues until they are once again equal.

As you learned in Chapters 4 and 5, these changes are changes along a demand or supply curve. There are two factors that can push a market from equilibrium into disequilibrium. One is a shift in the entire demand curve. The second is a shift in the entire supply curve.

Look at **Figure 6.3** below. Notice how the supply curve shifted to the right from 2000. There is a different equilibrium price for each year shown on the graph.

✔ **CHECKPOINT** *What changes can push a market into disequilibrium?*

Fig. 6.3 Falling Prices and the Supply Curve

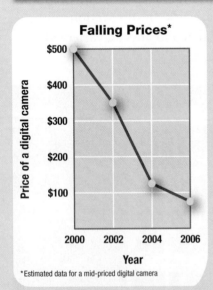

Falling Prices*

*Estimated data for a mid-priced digital camera

Action Graph online
For an animated version of this graph, visit
PearsonSuccessNet.com

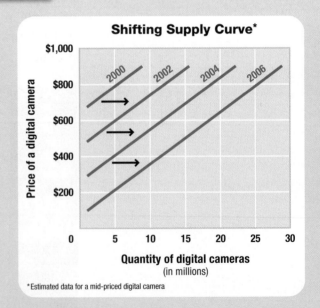

Shifting Supply Curve*

*Estimated data for a mid-priced digital camera

GRAPH SKILLS

These graphs use digital cameras as an example. As digital cameras became cheaper and easier to produce, the supply increased.

1. How much did the price of a camera drop between 2000 and 2006?

2. Based on these graphs, what is likely to happen to the supply curve for digital cameras in the future? What might change this trend?

What happens if there is an increase in supply?

In Chapter 5, you learned that there are factors that cause changes in supply. These factors include new technology, taxes and subsidies, and changes in the cost of resources and labor.

What happens when supply changes? Look at **Figure 6.4.** You can see that the entire supply curve shifts. There will be a new equilibrium price and quantity. Whenever the supply changes, the supply curve will shift. If the supply increases, the curve will shift to the right. If there is less supply, then the curve shifts to the left. To see what happens when the supply curve shifts to the right, we will look at a product that has gone through a huge market change in a short period of time. We will look at the market for digital cameras.

How did the increase in supply change the equilibrium price?

Figure 6.4 shows how the increase in supply caused disequilibrium. Supply and demand are now out of balance. The old equilibrium price is point *a*. We know that the supply increased. Camera makers are willing to offer four million digital cameras at the old equilibrium price. The market is in disequilibrium because fewer people are willing to pay that price. The increase in quantity supplied at the old equilibrium price is point *b*.

In this example, there has been no change in demand. The same number of people want to buy a digital camera as before. If the producers do not lower their price, there will soon be a surplus. Unsold cameras will begin to pile up in the warehouse. Producers do not want this. It costs money to store the surplus, and it wastes valuable resources.

As you read in Section 1, one of the ways suppliers will get rid of the surplus is to lower prices. As the price falls from $900.00 to $450.00, more people are willing to buy digital cameras. The quantity demanded rises. The combined movement of falling prices and increasing quantity demanded can be observed in **Figure 6.4.** It shows a change from point *a* to point *c*. Point *c* is the new equilibrium. The number of cameras offered equals the number of people willing to buy the camera at that price.

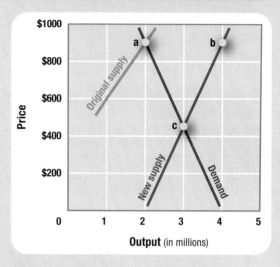

Fig. 6.4 A Change in Supply

GRAPH SKILLS

This graph shows how an increase in supply affects prices and demand.

1. What was the original equilibrium price?
2. What impact did the change in supply shown here have on the equilibrium price? Why?

For an animated version of this graph, visit **PearsonSuccessNet.com**

Fig. 6.5 How the Economy Works

How does a market react to a shortage?

When supply and demand are balanced, a market is at equilibrium. But a sudden change in supply or demand can result in a shortage. How does the market react?

1 Disequilibrium The market can be thrown out of balance.
Demand increases Wants or needs may increase demand. For example:
• More people need warm coats during a cold winter.
• Advertising creates a new fad.

Supply decreases An interruption in production can affect supply. For example:
• A natural disaster disrupts the flow of raw materials.
• Problems at the factory slow down production.

2 Whether the cause is an increase in demand or a decrease in supply, the result is the same: **shortage!**

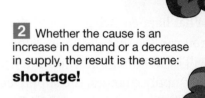

Shift in Supply or Demand

The supply curve has been moving to the right ever since the first digital cameras were sold. This shift will continue as long as technology changes and the cost of resources and labor goes down.

In real-life markets, equilibrium is always changing. New and better products are always being produced. Prices are always changing. You will notice this if you shop for a new camera. A digital camera costs less today than it did last year. The new camera may take better pictures and have new features. Sales are a way for camera makers and sellers to move out older cameras to make room for new ones.

✔ **CHECKPOINT** *What happens to the equilibrium price when the supply curve shifts to the right?*

BIG STORE
Z-CUBE ⚡ IS HERE

3 The immediate effects
of a shortage are obvious.
People line up at stores or
storm the Internet to buy the
hard-to-find item . . . and the
price goes up.

Z-CUBE
~~$149~~
$199

5 **A New Equilibrium** In time, supply
and demand will balance out again.
This may happen in two ways:

Quantity demanded decreases
- Fads end
- Higher prices drive buyers out of the
  market

Quantity supplied increases
- Problems in production are solved
- New suppliers fill in the gap

Whatever the cause, the hard-to-get
item is no longer so hard to get . . . and
the shortage ends.

4 If the shortage continues,
other suppliers will seek to enter
the market. Demand is up, prices
are up . . . and everybody wants a
piece of the profit.

Check Your Understanding
1. Why would a shortage of a product
   lead to a price increase?
2. What circumstances might lead to a
   shortage of bananas? Gasoline?
   Solar-powered cellphones?

The Market Reacts ➤

A New Equilibrium ➤

How did the decrease in supply change the equilibrium price?

A decrease in supply causes the supply curve to shift to the left.
Consider the market for cars. The cost of resources to make cars
sometimes goes up. Steel and rubber may cost more than in the
past. Workers may get raises. Higher taxes also affect the supply
of cars made. All of these raise the cost of producing a single car.
These changes cause the supply of cars to drop and the supply
curve to move to the left.

As the supply curve shifts to the left, suppliers raise their prices
and the quantity demanded falls. The new equilibrium point will
be a spot on the demand curve above and to the left of the old
equilibrium point. For you, the buyer, this means you will have to
pay more for the car. For the producers, this means they will sell
fewer cars.

✔ **CHECKPOINT** *What happens to price and quantity demanded when
the supply curve shifts to the left?*

fad
a product that becomes very popular for a very short period of time

search costs
the financial and opportunity costs consumers pay when looking for a good or service

How does an increase in demand shift the demand curve to the right?

Almost every year, there is a new **fad.** A fad is a product that becomes very popular for a very short time. Every year around November, a new doll, toy, or video game suddenly becomes popular. Everyone seems to want it. Sometimes, holiday shoppers wait in long lines for stores to open just to buy it.

As you read in Chapter 4, fads reflect buyers' tastes and the effects of advertising. Fads are real-life examples of a fast shift to the right in a market demand curve. Let's see how a sudden, unexpected jump in demand can affect the equilibrium.

As **Figure 6.6** shows, the fad causes a big increase in demand. The demand curve shifts to the right. This shift reflects a shortage at the original price of $24.00 (point *b*). Before the fad began, the quantity demanded and the quantity supplied were equal at 300,000 toys. This is shown as point *a* on the graph. But the fad created a greater demand. Now there is a shortage. On the graph, the shortage appears as a gap. Now there are 500,000 people wanting to buy at the $24.00 price level. This is shown as point *b* on the graph. The shortage is 200,000. If you went to the store to buy the product, you would see a lot of empty shelves. Shortages additionally result in **search costs.** These are costs that consumers pay to look for a good.

Fig. 6.6 A Change in Demand

GRAPH SKILLS

This graph shows how an increase in demand affects prices and supply.

1. What was the original equilibrium price?
2. What impact did the change in demand shown here have on the equilibrium price?

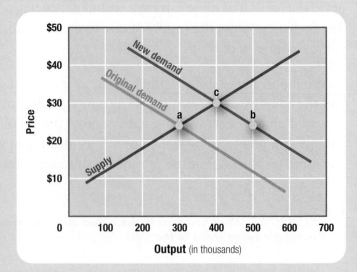

For an animated version of this graph, visit **PearsonSuccessNet.com**

What would you do if you were the firm producing the fad item? You would probably want to produce more to raise your profit. Point *c* on the graph shows the new equilibrium point. The new equilibrium price is higher, and the quantity supplied has increased. This means more of the product is available. The entire supply curve has shifted to the right.

✅ **CHECKPOINT** *How is equilibrium restored after a shortage?*

How did a decrease in demand change the equilibrium price?

Fads sometimes fade very fast. Demand can fall as fast as it rose. The shortage changes into a surplus. Now store shelves are full and there are few customers.

What would you do if you were the maker or seller of the fad item? You might lower the price on the number of fad toys you have in **inventory.** Inventory is the goods you have on hand. Price and quantity shift until a new equilibrium point is reached. The end of the fad is shown as point *a* on the figure on page 132. It brings us back to the original price of $24.00. That is the price that buyers were willing to pay and suppliers were willing to accept.

✅ **CHECKPOINT** *What happens to the demand curve when demand for a product decreases?*

inventory
the quantity of goods that a firm has on hand

Reading Strategy
Inferencing
How does what you already know about equilibrium help you understand what you have just read?

SECTION 2 ASSESSMENT

Essential Questions Journal To continue to build a response to the Essential Question, go to your **Essential Questions Journal.**

 Guiding Question

1. Use your completed concept web to answer this question: How do changes in supply and demand affect equilibrium?

Key Terms and Main Ideas

Directions: On a sheet of paper, write the answer to each question. Use complete sentences.

2. Is a shortage caused by excess supply or excess demand?

3. How do shortages create search costs?

4. What factors cause shifts in the supply curve?

Critical Thinking

5. **Make Inferences** As you travel from store to store looking for a good during a shortage, you pay search costs. What are two examples of search costs?

6. **Predict Consequences** A freeze destroys half of the coffee crop in South America. How would that affect the world's supply of coffee?

7. **Predict Consequences** What effect would the freeze in South America have on the worldwide demand for coffee?

Objectives

- **Identify** the many roles that prices play in a free market.

- **List** the advantages of a price-based system.

- **Explain** how a price-based system leads to a wider choice of goods and more efficient use of resources.

- **Describe** the relationship between prices and profit incentive.

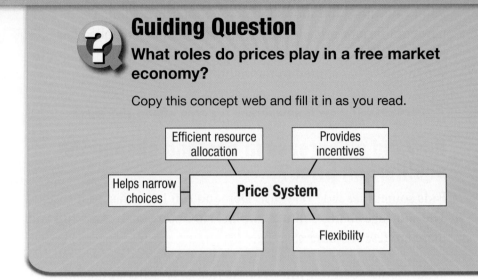

Guiding Question

What roles do prices play in a free market economy?

Copy this concept web and fill it in as you read.

- Efficient resource allocation
- Provides incentives
- Helps narrow choices
- **Price System**
- Flexibility

▶ **Economics and You** The price system is a balance of supply and demand. Consumers, producers, and sellers all play a role. How does the price system affect you as a consumer? Consider the following example.

You want to buy a pair of athletic shoes, so you go to a local mall to compare prices. A discount shoe store offers low-end sneakers for $20.00 At other stores, you find that you can spend as little as $50.00 for brand-name sneakers. You could also spend more than $200.00 for a pair of designer basketball shoes. Basing your decision on the available supply, the price, and your wants, you buy the $50.00 sneakers.

Later, through online research, you find a pair of sneakers similar to the pair you bought. But these are on sale for $5.00 less, including shipping. You buy the online sneakers with your credit card and return the sneakers you bought at the mall.

Principles in Action In a free market economy, prices offer a number of advantages to both consumers and producers. Simple purchases would be much harder without the price system to help us make good decisions. In this section, you will see how prices affect consumers and how producers respond. The Economics & You feature on page 138 shows how profits act as an incentive.

What is a price system?

Prices are important in a free market. They give information to both buyers and sellers. When you buy a purse for $200.00, you are sending the producer a message. The message is that you place a high value on the purse. If you go to a bookstore and find many discounted books, the seller is sending you a message. The message may be that the seller places a low value on these books. Or maybe business is bad. The seller hopes the low prices will bring more customers into the store. This communication between buyers and sellers is called the **price system.**

In a free market, prices are a tool to distribute goods and services. Prices help move land, labor, and capital into the hands of producers. Prices help move goods into the hands of buyers.

What are the advantages of the price system?

In Chapter 2, you learned about the three basic questions every economic system answers. Prices help determine the answers to what is produced, how it is produced, and who receives what is produced. An economy without prices would not operate very well. There are several reasons why prices are so important.

price system
the communication between buyers and sellers

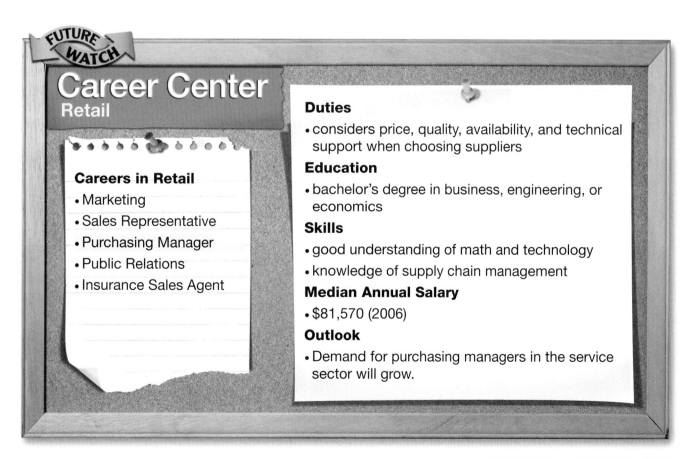

FUTURE WATCH

Career Center
Retail

Careers in Retail
- Marketing
- Sales Representative
- Purchasing Manager
- Public Relations
- Insurance Sales Agent

Duties
- considers price, quality, availability, and technical support when choosing suppliers

Education
- bachelor's degree in business, engineering, or economics

Skills
- good understanding of math and technology
- knowledge of supply chain management

Median Annual Salary
- $81,570 (2006)

Outlook
- Demand for purchasing managers in the service sector will grow.

What information does the price system provide?

Prices provide a common language for buyers and sellers. Prices tell businesses about the value customers put on certain products. They tell buyers the relative worth of goods. A jacket priced at $200.00 tells the consumer that it is valued more than a sweater priced at $100.00. To make good economic choices, buyers need to know the cost of the things they want. Producers base their decisions on prices too. They need to know the price of labor and other resources.

How do prices allow freedom of choice?

Producers and consumers have many choices available to them. Both can use substitutes for products that are too expensive. The market provides many goods and services in a wide range of prices.

What incentives do prices provide?

Have you ever been tempted to buy something because the price was too good to pass up? The low price was an incentive to you. The low price motivated you to buy. Prices are incentives for producers, too. Raising prices for goods that consumers like you want encourages businesses to increase production. Prices also provide incentives in markets for resources such as labor and capital. Increasing workers' pay encourages more people to apply for jobs or switch jobs. Lowering wages has the opposite effect.

How are prices like traffic lights?

You can think of prices as a traffic light. A high price is a green light. It tells producers that a product is in demand and they should produce more of that product.

But a low price is a red light. It tells suppliers that too much of a product is being produced. Low prices tell suppliers that they might want to produce a different product.

✔ **CHECKPOINT** *How does the price system provide incentives for both producers and consumers?*

■ ■ ■ ■ ■ ■ ■ ■ ■ ■ ■ ■ ■ ■ ■ ■ ■ ■

Reading Strategy
Inferencing
What can you infer about the way prices affect what you buy?

How do prices promote flexibility and efficiency?

Prices encourage resources to be used in the best way. Producers want to make things that consumers want to buy. Prices tell producers what consumers want most. If consumers are willing to pay high prices, they are telling producers that they are using their resources well. If consumers are only willing to pay low prices for goods, they are sending a different message. They are telling producers that resources are not being used efficiently. When there is a shift in supply or demand, the market can quickly adjust. It is flexible. It can change without breaking. Prices can be raised to solve the problem of shortage or lowered to prevent a surplus.

What causes supply shock?

During difficult times, sudden shortages may occur. For example, after a hurricane strikes, there may be a sudden shortage of almost all everyday needs. Such shortages are called **supply shocks.** A sudden shock creates a problem of excess demand. Suppliers can no longer meet the needs of consumers. The immediate problem is how to divide up the available supply of goods among consumers.

What is rationing?

One way of dealing with the problem of supply shock is **rationing.** Rationing is a system in which the government provides a fixed amount of limited supplies to each person. During World War II, supplies of many everyday things were limited. Much of the world's resources were used in the production of war material. To make sure that everyone received a fair share, the government issued ration coupons. These coupons could be exchanged for meat, butter, bread, and gasoline.

supply shock
a sudden shortage of a good
rationing
a system of allocating scarce goods and services using criteria other than price

Reading Strategy
Inferencing
What inference can you make about the difficulties of rationing?

During World War II, the federal government used rationing to control shortages. ▼

black market
an illegal market in which goods and services are sold above their legal price

invest
to use assets to earn income or profit

Economics & YOU

The Profit Incentive

SHREK 12

Movie producers are quick to create sequels of highly profitable films. *Your ticket purchase provides an incentive for the producer to make a sequel.*

High school athletes make an extra effort when they know a college scout is watching. *You profit by winning an athletic scholarship.*

A second way of dealing with sudden shortages is to raise prices. Prices act as a rationing device. They treat all consumers the same way. Scarce goods and services go to those who are willing and able to pay the price. They do not go to those who are unable or unwilling to pay the price.

What is the black market?

Rationing works better in theory than it does in practice. Rationing is often expensive because it requires many people to manage the system. A more serious problem is that it encourages **black markets.** A black market is an illegal market in which goods and services are sold above their legal price. Demand is high despite rationing. For example, during World War II, people wanted and needed more gasoline than was available. The high quantity demanded meant that some people bought gasoline on the black market. Some people needed less gasoline than their ration gave them. They sold their ration coupons to people who were able and willing to pay high prices for it. Black markets are often linked with rationing. They are not legal and governments try to stop them.

✔ **CHECKPOINT** *What impact does rationing have on the availability of goods?*

What is the profit incentive?

Capitalism, our economic system, provides people with an incentive to work. The incentive is often profit. Businesses want to provide a product that will make them money. Workers usually want jobs that pay them the most. We are often willing to work harder and longer if we are rewarded with more pay.

Remember, resources are scarce. The amount of land is limited. Landowners tend to use their scarce property in a way that will make them the most profit. Labor is also scarce. Workers tend to move to jobs in which they are paid the most for their labor. Investors use the scarce resource of capital wisely. They **invest** in businesses that will give them the highest return.

Why is Adam Smith important?

In 1776, Adam Smith wrote one of the most important books on economics. It is called *The Wealth of Nations.* Smith thought that people should be free to produce and sell products at a profit. They would work harder, produce more, and grow richer. Why do the baker and butcher provide us with food? Smith said the reason was to make a profit. Businesses make money when they provide people with the goods and services they want.

What are some market problems?

Three problems can occur in markets that can affect prices. The first is **imperfect competition.** Sometimes there are only a few firms selling a product. There might not be enough competition for sellers to lower prices. If there is only one seller or just a few sellers, the producer can usually charge a higher price. Real competition means prices are often lower.

A second problem is called externalities. You learned about these in Chapter 3. Negative externalities are side effects that can include unexpected costs. For example, say a new factory is built near where you live. People living near the new factory may suffer. There will be extra traffic and pollution from the factory. In this case, the producers do not pay the unexpected costs. The people living near the factory pay those costs.

A third problem is lack of information. Sometimes buyers and sellers do not have enough information to make the best choices.

✓ **CHECKPOINT** *Under what conditions may the free market system fail to give out resources efficiently?*

imperfect competition
a market structure in which only a few firms produce the same product

Reading Strategy
Inferencing
    After reading this paragraph, can you think of other ways that a factory could affect the environment?

SECTION 3 ASSESSMENT

Essential Questions Journal
To continue to build a response to the Essential Question, go to your **Essential Questions Journal.**

Quick Write

Look at the Economics & You feature in this section. It illustrates the profit incentive. List two or three examples of how the desire for profit motivates people. Then write a short essay answering the following questions:

Do you agree or disagree that incentives motivate people's actions?

How do incentives affect your daily life?

 Guiding Question

1. Use your completed concept web to answer this question: What roles do prices play in a free market economy?

Key Terms and Main Ideas

Directions: On a sheet of paper, write the answer to each question. Use complete sentences.

2. What is the communication between buyers and sellers called?

3. How does a supply shock affect equilibrium price?

4. How is rationing different from a price-based system?

5. Why do buyers and sellers conduct business on the black market?

Critical Thinking

6. **Summarize** (a) What is the quickest way to solve a shortage? (b) What is the quickest way to eliminate a surplus?

7. **Summarize** What are three problems that occur in markets that can affect prices?

Section 1–Combining Supply and Demand

■ Disequilibrium means that the market is not balanced. Equilibrium is when supply and demand are balanced.

■ A surplus is when the quantity supplied is more than the quantity demanded. A shortage is when the quantity demanded is more than the quantity supplied.

■ Government sometimes steps in and sets price ceilings and price floors to control prices. Examples of this are rent control and price supports to farmers.

Section 2–Changes in Market Equilibrium

■ A free market naturally moves to an equilibrium point. Changes in supply and demand cause prices to change. A shortage will cause prices to rise and quantity demanded to fall. A surplus causes prices to fall and quantity demanded to rise.

Section 3–The Role of Prices

■ The price system is a communication between buyers and sellers. A low price is an incentive to the consumer to buy a product. A high price encourages businesses to increase production.

■ Rationing is a system for dealing with sudden shortages. A sudden shortage will cause excess demand. When this happens, the government may ration supplies. It provides a fixed amount of supplies to each person.

■ Profit is an incentive for people to work. It is also the incentive for businesses to provide products that people want.

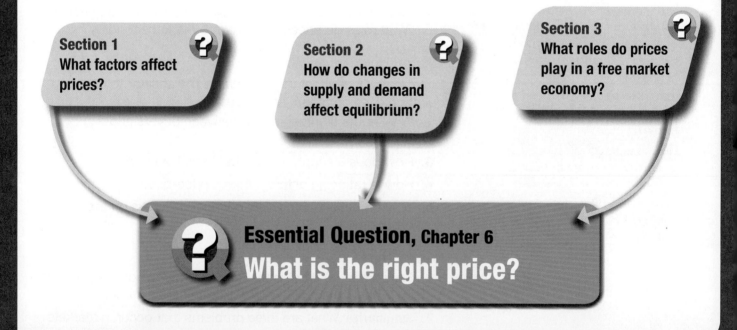

Section 1
What factors affect prices?

Section 2
How do changes in supply and demand affect equilibrium?

Section 3
What roles do prices play in a free market economy?

Essential Question, Chapter 6
What is the right price?

Wealth of Nations

Adam Smith is known as the father of modern economics. In 1776, he wrote a book called An Inquiry into the Nature and Causes of the Wealth of Nations. *Smith's book was written over two centuries ago, but many economists still think it is the best statement about capitalism. In this reading, Smith discusses the value of money and the price of labor.*

"Every man is rich or poor according to the degree in which he can afford to enjoy the necessaries, conveniences, and amusements of human life. But after the division of labour has once thoroughly taken place, it is but a very small part of these with which a man's own labour can supply him. The far greater part of them he must [gain] from the labour of other people, and he must be rich or poor according to the quantity of that labour which he can command, or which he can afford to purchase. The value of any commodity [good], therefore, to the person who possesses it, and who means not to use or consume it himself, but to exchange it for other commodities, is equal to the quantity of labour which it enables him to purchase or command. Labour, therefore, is the real measure of the exchangeable value of all commodities.

The real price of every thing, what every thing really costs to the man who wants to acquire it, is the toil and trouble of acquiring it. . . .

Labour was the first price, the original purchase-money that was paid for all things. It was not by gold or by silver, but by labour, that all the wealth of the world was originally purchased; and its value, to those who possess it, and who want to exchange it for some new productions, is precisely equal to the quantity of labour which it can enable them to purchase or command."

Document-Based Questions

1. According to the reading, what determines a person's wealth?
2. How is labor related to wealth?
3. How does the author define labor in this reading?
4. What does Adam Smith say about price?
5. Based on this reading, what can you infer about Smith's opinion of a free market?

SOURCE: *An Inquiry into the Nature and Causes of the Wealth of Nations,* 1776.

Directions: Choose the letter of the correct answer or write the answer using complete sentences.

Section 1–Combining Supply and Demand

1. What is the equilibrium price?

2. What is a surplus?

3. What situation creates a surplus?

4. What is the maximum price for particular goods and services called?

5. What is a government grant given to farmers to guarantee prices for their produce?

   A. surplus control   **C.** price floor
   B. subsidy   **D.** price ceiling

6. What is the minimum wage an example of?

   A. price floor   **C.** subsidy
   B. price ceiling   **D.** price support

Section 2–Changes in Market Equilibrium

7. How does a market react to an increase in supply?

8. How does a market react to a decrease in supply?

9. Why does a free market tend to move toward equilibrium?

10. Why does an increase in supply change the equilibrium price?

11. When the supply increases, what does the supply curve do?

    A. remains the same   **C.** shifts to the right
    B. shifts to the left   **D.** disappears

12. What will a surplus force firms to do to prices?

    A. increase   **B.** decrease   **C.** remove   **D.** avoid

Section 3–The Role of Prices

13. What is the price system?

14. Why must buyers know how much products cost?

15. What is rationing? Why is it done?

16. Despite rationing, demand for certain goods and services is high in what kind of market?

    A. bear   **B.** black   **C.** flea   **D.** farmers

17. How does profit act as an incentive?

Exploring the Essential Question

18. Governments sometimes step in to control prices. Who benefits most from a price ceiling? Who benefits most from a price floor?

19. What would happen if a seller raised the price of an item at a time when there was a market surplus?

Essential Question Activity

20. Complete this activity to answer the Essential Question **What is the right price?** Imagine that your class is planning to sell T-shirts to raise funds for disaster relief in a nearby community. Using the worksheet your teacher gives you or the electronic worksheet available at **PearsonSuccessNet.com**, gather the following information: (a) What is the cost of buying 1,000 plain white T-shirts in bulk? (b) What is the cost of having a special design printed on the shirts? (c) What is the average price that stores in your area charge for a printed T-shirt?

Using this information, decide what price you think people would be willing to pay for a T-shirt. You need to make enough money above your cost to make a donation. When you have made your decision, fill in your price on the worksheet. Write an explanation of how you arrived at the right price.

| **Essential Questions Journal** | To continue to build a response to the Essential Question, go to your **Essential Questions Journal.** |

Test-Taking Tip

When studying for a test, you will remember facts and definitions more easily if you write them down on index cards. Practice with a partner, using the index cards as flash cards.

Study anytime, anywhere. Download these files today.

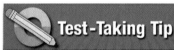

Economic Dictionary *online*
Vocabulary Support in English and Spanish

Audio Review *online*
Audio Study Guide in English and Spanish

Action Graph *online*
Animated Charts and Graphs

Visual Glossary *online*
Animated feature

How the Economy Works *online*
Animated feature

Download to your computer or mobile device at PearsonSuccessNet.com

Chapter 7 Market Structures

Essential Question, Chapter 7

How does competition affect your choices?

Economics on the go

To study anywhere, anytime, download these online resources at *PearsonSuccessNet.com* ➤

▶ **Competition is one of the most important parts of the free enterprise system.** For example, car companies compete with one another to sell cars. Competition between businesses is evident at car races, with logos and advertisements displayed on the cars. People also compete with one another because of scarcity. We compete with each other for the scarce resources and products available.

In this chapter, you will learn that the amount of competition a firm faces determines how it is set up. You will also learn about four market structures and how the government controls some competition.

▪▪▪▪▪▪▪▪▪▪▪▪▪▪▪▪▪▪▪▪▪▪▪▪▪▪▪▪▪▪▪▪▪▪▪▪

Reading Strategy: Metacognition
Metacognition means being aware of how you think and learn. Metacognition helps you figure out which strategy to use to better understand a text.

<u>Before Reading</u>
• Preview the section.
• Ask questions to identify your purpose for reading.
• Make predictions.

<u>During Reading</u>
• Identify the main idea.
• Visualize what is happening.
• Connect the text to your life.
• Ask questions about what you do not understand.

<u>After Reading</u>
• Summarize what you read.

Go to the Visual Glossary Online for an interactive review of **perfect competition.**

Go to How the Economy Works Online for an interactive lesson on **regulation.**

Go to Action Graph Online for animated versions of key charts and graphs.

Objectives

- **Describe** the four conditions that are in place in a perfectly competitive market.

- **List** two common factors that prevent firms from entering a market.

- **Describe** prices and output in a perfectly competitive market.

Guiding Question

What are the characteristics of perfect competition?

Copy this concept web and fill it in as you read.

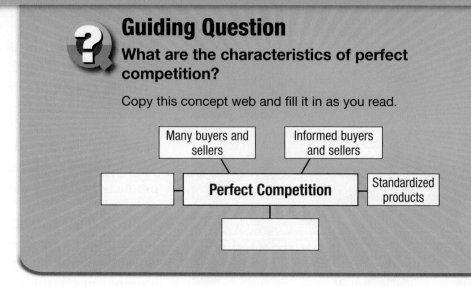

Reading Strategy
Metacognition

Before you read this section, think about what strategies you can use to improve your understanding of perfect competition.

----

perfect competition
a market structure in which a large number of firms all produce the same product, and no single seller controls supply or prices

▶ **Economics and You** You have decided to cook dinner. You shop for produce at the local farmers' market. You notice the variety of fruits and vegetables and that all the sellers charge the same price. On the way home, you wonder why buying a leather jacket, a car, or a high definition television is not as simple as buying fresh fruits and vegetables.

Principles in Action The farmers' market is a rare, real-world example of **perfect competition.** The goods are all the same and there are many buyers and sellers. However, you will learn about factors that prevent perfect competition in most markets.

What are the four characteristics of perfect competition?

Schools are places with a lot of competition. In a competition, you are trying to win or gain something that others want. Many students play sports. Your school teams compete against the teams of other schools. Students compete for places on the teams. Some compete to be in the school play or to become members of the school band. Not everyone can be on a team, in the play, or in the band. Often, more people are interested than there are positions available. In the study of economics, competition refers to the economic contest among buyers and sellers. They compete in the purchase and use of resources and products.

Perfect competitive markets are rare, if they exist at all. For perfect competition to exist, there must be the following four conditions:

1. Many buyers and sellers are in the market.
2. Sellers offer standardized products (products that are nearly the same).
3. Buyers and sellers must be well informed.
4. Sellers must easily be able to get into and out of the market.

Why must there be many buyers and sellers?

There must be many buyers and sellers for a product. Otherwise, the actions of any one buyer or seller would affect the entire market. When there are many buyers and sellers, each one has to accept the going market price set by supply and demand. Suppose a seller tries to raise the price even a little above the market price. That seller would not be able to sell much of the product. Consumers would buy from other businesses selling the product at the market price.

What is a standardized product?

The products of all the sellers have to be standardized, or nearly the same. If they are the same, buyers will not prefer the product of one business to that of any other. This means that buyers will be swayed by the price alone, not by special features of a product. In other words, there are no brands. For example, corn grown in one farmer's field is pretty much the same as corn grown in the neighbor's fields. A product that is pretty much the same regardless of who makes or sells it is called a **commodity.**

What do buyers and sellers need to know?

All buyers and sellers in a perfect competitive market are well informed. They know all there is to know about the product they are buying or selling. Buyers and sellers need to know who else is selling, at what price they are selling, and how much is being sold.

What does it mean to have free market entry and exit?

Factors that make it difficult for new firms to enter a market are called **barriers to entry.** In a free market, there can be no barriers for new firms to enter or leave the market. If profits can be made, new businesses will want to enter the market. If businesses are losing money, they will want to leave the market. There can be no government controls and no labor unions.

✔ **CHECKPOINT** *How does perfect competition ensure that prices are not determined by individual suppliers or consumers?*

commodity
a product, such as petroleum or milk, that is considered the same no matter who produces or sells it

barrier to entry
any factor that makes it difficult for a new firm to enter a market

Reading Strategy
Metacognition
Ask yourself questions as you read. This will help make sure you understand what you are reading.

▲ A landscaping company (left) has low start-up costs and minimal technical needs. It can easily enter a market. An auto repair shop (right) has high start-up costs and requires employees with a lot of technical skill. It will be more difficult for this type of business to enter the market.

imperfect competition
any market structure besides perfect competition

start-up costs
the expenses a new business must pay before it can begin to produce and sell goods

What prevents firms from entering a market?

Barriers to entry can lead to **imperfect competition.** Imperfect competition refers to any market structure besides perfect competition. Two factors that prevent firms from entering a market are start-up costs and technology.

What are start-up costs?

It takes money to open a business. To open a pizza shop, you would need to rent a store. You would also need to buy equipment like an oven and freezer. The costs that a new business must pay before it can open are called **start-up costs.** High start-up costs make it difficult to enter a market.

How does technology prevent firms from entering the market?

Some markets need a lot of technical skill. It takes years of training to become a carpenter or electrician. It would not be possible to compete if a person did not have the same skills as others in the market. Entrepreneurs need preparation and training in their specific field. Without it, they cannot be a success in the market.

✔ **CHECKPOINT** *Which barrier to entry can be overcome by education or vocational training?*

What happens to prices and output in a perfect competitive market?

Perfect competition keeps both prices and production costs low. Firms must use their resources in the most efficient way. They must keep production costs as low as they can. Prices in a perfect competitive market are also low. There are many suppliers selling almost the same product. Because of the competition, prices are set just above the sellers' cost of doing business. As you read in Chapter 6, this is market equilibrium. At equilibrium, a market is usually most efficient.

We saw in Chapter 5 that producers earn their highest profits under certain conditions. In a perfectly competitive market, no supplier can influence prices. Producers decide how much to produce (output) based on several factors. They decide how they can best use their land, labor, capital, and management skills.

✔ **CHECKPOINT** *How are output decisions made in a perfectly competitive market?*

Essential Questions Journal To continue to build a response to the Essential Question, go to your **Essential Questions Journal.**

SECTION 1 ASSESSMENT

 Guiding Question

1. Use your completed concept web to answer this question: What are the characteristics of perfect competition?

Key Terms and Main Ideas

Directions: On a sheet of paper, write the answer to each question. Use complete sentences.

2. What influences buyers in a perfectly competitive market?

3. When does imperfect competition occur?

4. What are two examples of barriers to entry in the magazine market?

5. How do start-up costs discourage entrepreneurs from entering a market?

Critical Thinking

6. **Draw Conclusions** Which of these markets come close to perfect competition: televisions, bottled water, pizza, or paper clips? Explain your choices.

7. **Predict Consequences** (a) What are commodities? (b) What would happen to a perfectly competitive market if it stopped dealing in commodities? Provide an explanation for your answer.

Objectives

- **Describe** what a monopoly is and give examples.
- **Describe** how monopolies, including government monopolies, are formed.
- **Explain** how a patent may affect a monopoly.
- **Explain** why monopolists sometimes practice price discrimination.

monopoly
a market in which a single seller has control

Reading Strategy
Metacognition
Notice the structure of this section. Look at the titles, headings, and boldfaced words.

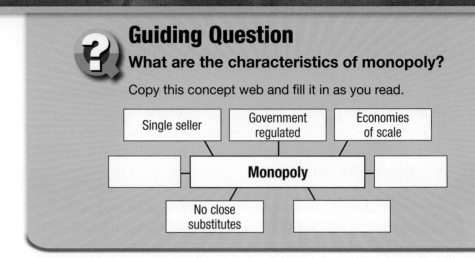

Guiding Question

What are the characteristics of monopoly?

Copy this concept web and fill it in as you read.

Single seller | Government regulated | Economies of scale

Monopoly

No close substitutes

▶ **Economics and You** The doctor tells you that you have a rare infection and that you must take a new medicine for 10 days. The drugstore charges you $97.35 for the medicine. That's almost $10.00 a pill! There are no substitutes, so you buy the medicine. Later, you learn that only one company has the right to produce that drug. The company says that it must charge a high price for the medicine to pay for the research and development costs of producing it.

Principles in Action Although there are different types of monopolies, all have a single seller that controls an entire market. This allows monopolies to control output, which results in consumers being charged higher prices.

What is a monopoly?

We are used to seeing a lot of competition in markets. Consumers benefit from competition. Competition gives consumers many choices. Sellers give consumers a choice of similar products. They know that if products are similar, consumers are likely to buy the products that offer the most quality for the lowest prices. Sometimes, however, there is no competition. This condition is called a **monopoly**.

A pure monopoly has three characteristics:
1. There is only one seller.
2. There are no close substitutes.
3. Getting into and out of the market is difficult.

The problem with monopolies is that they can take advantage of their market power and charge high prices. Given the law of demand, this means that the quantity of goods sold is lower than in a market with more than one seller. For this reason, the United States has outlawed some monopolistic practices, as you will read in Section 4.

In a perfect monopoly, there is only one seller of a good or service. Consumers must buy goods or services from that one producer.

What if there is no close substitute?

Suppose that there was only one carmaker in the world. If you wanted to buy a car, you would have to buy from that carmaker. Some people have to have a car. No substitute is available. They cannot take a bus or train. The carmaker has a monopoly. Anyone who needed a car would have to pay whatever price the one carmaker set.

Why is getting into and out of the market difficult?

There is only one way to keep a monopoly. New producers have to be kept out. Think about the example of the carmaker. A new producer might want to enter the market because of the high profits. Starting a new car company is not easy. Start-up costs are huge. Designing, building, and selling cars is not easy. The company with the monopoly has advantages over the new company.

Fig. 7.1 Monopoly

Number of firms:
One

Variety of goods:
None

Barriers to entry:
Complete

ENTRY

Control over prices:
Complete

Complete Control

CHART SKILLS

In a monopoly, one company controls the entire market.

1. Why is public water a monopoly?
2. Give two examples of other monopolies.

economies of scale
factors that cause a producer's average cost per unit to fall as more units are produced

What is the advantage of economies of scale?

Monopolies have what economists call **economies of scale.** These are the advantages that a firm has because of its size and control over the market. One advantage is that its size allows it to buy its materials in bulk. Another advantage is that the firm can take out loans at lower cost than other businesses. These factors lower the firm's cost of production.

A good example of economy of scale is hydroelectric plants. These plants generate electricity from a dam on a river. A large dam costs a lot of money to build. However, once the dam is built, the plant can produce more energy at a very low cost. All it has to do is let more water flow through the dam. The average cost of the first unit of electricity produced is very high because the cost of the dam is so high. As more power is produced, the fixed costs of the dam can be spread over more units of electricity. The average cost drops. In a market with economies of scale, bigger is better.

✅ **CHECKPOINT** *How can economies of scale affect a monopoly?*

Innovators

Andrew Carnegie

"The true road to . . . success in any line is to make yourself master in that line." Andrew Carnegie traveled that "true road."

Carnegie arrived in Pittsburgh in 1848, the son of poor Scottish immigrants. His first job as a telegraph operator for the Pennsylvania Railroad (PRR) began in 1853. He soon became the assistant to Thomas Scott, head of PRR's western division. He received $35 monthly.

Scott taught Carnegie to control costs and profit from related businesses. By 1865, Carnegie was earning $40,000 a year.

After the Civil War, Carnegie realized demand for steel would rise. He built a modern steel plant near Pittsburgh. Carnegie supplied steel for railroads, bridges, and naval ships. In 1901, when he sold the Carnegie Steel Company to J. P. Morgan for $480 million, it produced more steel than all of Great Britain.

Carnegie believed he should give away his great wealth. Before he died, he donated $350 million to establish 2,500 public libraries, support higher education, and promote world peace.

Fast Facts

Andrew Carnegie (1835–1919)
Education: 5 years of grade school
Claim to Fame: Founder, Carnegie Steel Company; philanthropist

What is a government monopoly?

The government creates some monopolies. Economists use the term **government monopoly** to refer to them. Why would the government want to give a company monopoly power? Let's look at patents, which is one way the government limits competition. A patent gives a company the right to sell a new good or service without competition. Patents protect inventions. They give inventors sole rights to the invention. In the United States, patents can be good for between 14 and 20 years. Inventors may sell or give away their rights. The patent is their property. A copyright is another government-approved monopoly. It gives writers and artists the sole right to sell or make copies of their works. Today, a copyright is good until 70 years after the author dies.

 CHECKPOINT *What government actions can lead to the creation of economic monopolies?*

How does a patent affect a monopoly?

Suppose you were a company trying to cure asthma. You hire many scientists to try to develop new drugs. Finally, after many years and great expense, the new drug is ready to go on the market. How would you feel if a competitor copied your new drug and sold it at a lower cost? The competitor did not have to pay any development costs. You would probably feel it is unfair that the competitor can benefit from your research without paying any of the costs. A patent allows your company to make up for the money it spent in developing the drug.

 CHECKPOINT *How do patents protect companies?*

Why do monopolies use price discrimination?

Monopolies do not charge all consumers the same price. Charging a different price to different consumers is known as **price discrimination.** It is based on the idea that each customer has a maximum price that he or she will pay for a good. Suppose a monopoly sets the good's price at the highest price anyone is willing to pay. In this case, the monopoly will sell only to the one customer willing to pay that much. If the monopoly sets a low price, there will be many customers. The monopoly will lose the profits it could have made from the customers who bought at the low price but were willing to pay more.

What is market power?

Although price discrimination is a feature of a monopoly, it can be practiced by any company with **market power.** Market power is the

government monopoly
a monopoly created by the government

price discrimination
a division of consumers into groups based on how much they will pay for a good

market power
the ability of a company to control prices and total market output

ability to control prices and total market output. Many companies have some market power without having a true monopoly. Market power and price discrimination may be found in any market structure except for perfect competition.

Are there limits to price discrimination?

For price discrimination to work, a market must meet three conditions. Firms that use price discrimination must have:

1. *Some market power* Price-discriminating firms must have some control over prices. For this reason, price discrimination is rare in highly competitive markets.
2. *Distinct customer groups* Price-discriminating firms must be able to divide customers into distinct groups based on how sensitive they are to price.
3. *Difficult resale* What if one set of customers could buy the product at the lower price and then resell it for a profit? The firms could not enforce price discrimination. The product must be hard to resell. Consumer goods like shoes, groceries, and clothes are easily resold. Price discrimination works best in marketing services that are used on the spot. A good example is a restaurant meal. Restaurants often practice price discrimination. They charge less for children or seniors.

Although most forms of price discrimination are legal, sometimes firms use price discrimination to drive other firms out of business. You will read more about this illegal form of price discrimination in Section 4.

Reading Strategy
Metacognition
Ask yourself, "What did I learn by reading this? What do I still want to know about price discrimination?"

 CHECKPOINT *What three conditions must a market meet for price discrimination to work?*

SECTION 2 ASSESSMENT

Essential Questions Journal To continue to build a response to the Essential Question, go to your **Essential Questions Journal.**

Guiding Question

1. Use your completed concept web to answer the following question: What are the characteristics of monopoly?

Key Terms and Main Ideas

Directions: On a sheet of paper, write the answer to each question. Use complete sentences.

2. Why must a monopoly supply a product that no one else supplies?

3. What is the problem with monopolies?

4. What is market power?

5. Why must firms be able to divide customers into distinct groups for price discrimination to work?

Critical Thinking

6. **Make Comparisons** How are nongovernment monopolies and government monopolies similar? How are they different?

7. **Summarize** In your own words, define the term *economies of scale*.

Objectives

- **Describe** characteristics and give examples of monopolistic competition.
- **Explain** how firms compete without lowering prices.
- **Understand** how oligopolies control markets.

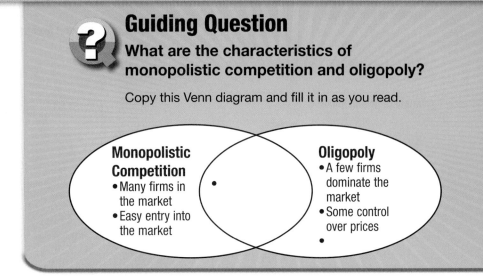

Guiding Question

What are the characteristics of monopolistic competition and oligopoly?

Copy this Venn diagram and fill it in as you read.

Monopolistic Competition
- Many firms in the market
- Easy entry into the market

Oligopoly
- A few firms dominate the market
- Some control over prices
-

▶ **Economics and You** At the supermarket, you roam the aisles. They are filled with many brands of soap, toothpaste, and paper towels. Although different companies make them, these everyday products are very much alike. To compete, producers look for ways other than price to make their products stand out.

Principles in Action Monopolistic competition is like perfect competition. Oligopoly is a market with only a few large producers. These are the market structures that we as consumers know well. The Economics & You feature in this section looks at some of the ways producers compete without involving price.

What is monopolistic competition?

Monopolistic competition is a common market structure. In it, many companies compete to sell products that are almost the same. Each firm has a monopoly over its own product.

Even though monopolistic competition and perfect competition are similar, there is a difference. The goods are enough alike that they can be substituted for one another. An example is the market for jeans. All jeans are made from the same type of cloth. However, buyers can choose from many different brands, colors, styles, and sizes. The markets for restaurants, cereals, shoes, and service industries are other examples.

✓ **CHECKPOINT** *How does monopolistic competition differ from perfect competition?*

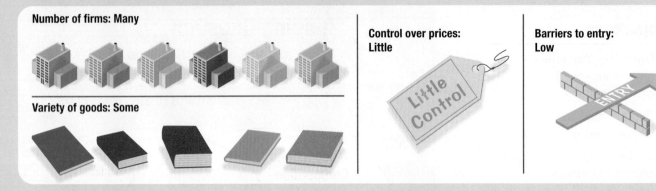

Fig. 7.2 Monopolistic Competition

Number of firms: Many

Variety of goods: Some

Control over prices: Little

Barriers to entry: Low

CHART SKILLS

Many firms provide a variety of goods in a monopolistically competitive market.

1. Why do firms in monopolistic competition have limited control over prices?

2. What features of a monopolistically competitive market are similar to a perfectly competitive market?

Reading Strategy
Metacognition

Note the details under this subhead. Summarize what you read to make sure you understand the conditions for monopolistic competition.

differentiation
making a product different from other, similar products

What conditions are necessary for monopolistic competition?

Monopolistic competition forms when these four conditions are met:

1. *Many firms* You will not find economies of scale in monopolistically competitive markets. They do not have high start-up costs. Firms can join the market quickly.

2. *Few barriers to entry* Firms in a monopolistically competitive market do not face the high barriers to entry discussed in Section 1. Patents no longer prevent competition. Maybe they have come to an end. It is also possible that each firm sells a product that is different enough that it is not protected by the patent.

3. *Little control over price* In a monopolistically competitive market structure, each firm's goods are a little different from everyone else's. Some people are willing to pay more for the difference. This gives firms some freedom to raise or lower their prices. However, unlike a monopoly, a monopolistically competitive firm has only limited control over price. If the price rises too high, consumers will buy a competitor's product. For example, some customers might be willing to buy a carton of brand-name orange juice even if it costs $.50 more per carton. What if the difference in price rose to $2.00 more per carton than the store brand? More people would buy the store brand of orange juice or some other drink.

4. *Differentiated products* Firms have some control over their selling price because they have **differentiation.** They can show the difference between their goods and other products.

Monopolistically competitive sellers often highlight the differences. They try to show how their product is better than their competitors. If they are successful, they profit.

☑ CHECKPOINT *Why is it easy for firms to enter and leave a monopolistically competitive market?*

How do firms compete in ways besides price?

Firms try not to compete on price alone. The other ways firms compete are called **nonprice competition.** There are four forms of nonprice competition:

1. *Physical features* These are the simplest ways to show how your products are different from the competition's. Products can be made in a new color, size, shape, or taste.
2. *Location* Some products can be differentiated by where they are sold. Gas stations, movie theaters, and grocery stores succeed or fail based on their locations.
3. *Service level* Some sellers offer more service than others. The business attracts more customers and earns higher profits.
4. *Advertising* Some firms use advertising to show how their product is different. For example, all gasoline is pretty much the same. However, firms use advertising to convince consumers that their brand of gas is cleaner or makes cars run better.

☑ CHECKPOINT *What keeps monopolistically competitive firms from making high profits?*

nonprice competition
a way to attract customers through style, service, or location, but not a lower price

Economics & YOU
Nonprice Competition

The designer athletic shoes are way more expensive than the sensible sneakers, but you buy them anyway. *The image and status associated with the designer shoe is a form of nonprice competition.*

Quick N Ez

The snacks would have cost less at the supermarket, but the Quick N EZ is so much closer to home. *The location of the convenience store is another example of nonprice competition.*

oligopoly
a market structure in which a few large firms dominate a market

collusion
an illegal agreement among firms to divide the market, set prices, or limit production

What is an oligopoly?

Another type of market is an **oligopoly.** An oligopoly has three main features:

1. *Few sellers in the market* In an oligopoly, a few large firms control the market for a product. Economists consider an industry an oligopoly if the four largest firms produce at least 70 to 80 percent of the output. A few examples of oligopoly are breakfast cereals, soft drinks, and major appliances.
2. *A nearly standardized product* The products sold by the oligopolies are almost the same. For example, cereals have almost the same ingredients. Imagine one company tries to come out with something new. It usually does not take long before the competition offers something just like it.
3. *Difficulty entering the market* The few large companies control the industry for several reasons. Start-up costs may be very high. Suppose you wanted to start a new airline. Airplanes are very expensive to buy and maintain. The biggest airlines own the best gates at the airport. Consumers know the large airlines. They are loyal to them and trust them. It is difficult for a new firm to enter the market.

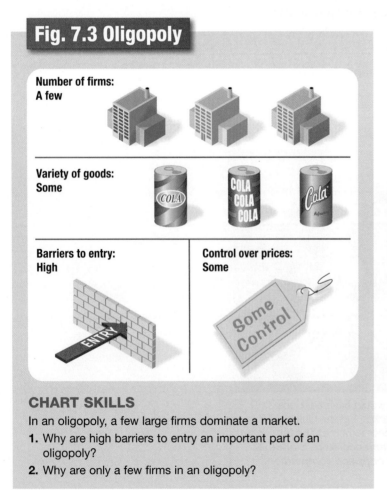

Fig. 7.3 Oligopoly

Number of firms:
A few

Variety of goods:
Some

COLA

COLA COLA COLA

Cola

Barriers to entry:
High

ENTRY

Control over prices:
Some

Some Control

CHART SKILLS

In an oligopoly, a few large firms dominate a market.

1. Why are high barriers to entry an important part of an oligopoly?
2. Why are only a few firms in an oligopoly?

How do oligopolies control the market?

You might be surprised to find that the major cereal brands sell for almost the same price. This is often true in oligopolies. The price each seller sets often depends on the price the other sellers set. Sometimes, one seller tries to lower the price to gain control of more of the market. This sets off a price war, causing a series of price cuts. Each seller tries to set a price lower than the competition to gain more of the market. This has sometimes happened in the airline industry. Consumers benefit from lower prices. The sellers, in this case the airlines, often lose money. They sell their services for less than their cost. Profits for the whole industry usually fall.

What is collusion?

Sometimes firms in an oligopoly break the law to keep profits high. One way is **collusion.** This is a secret agreement among competing firms to cooperate with one another. For example, the firms might divide the market by location. This way, each firm would be guaranteed a market with little competition.

Price fixing is an agreement to sell products for the same or similar prices. It is a type of collusion. The price is usually set higher than the price would be in a truly competitive market. A **cartel** is a formal organization among producers to agree to set prices and output. Although other countries permit them, cartels are illegal in the United States. Cartels can work only if every member keeps to its agreed production levels. If they do not, prices will fall, and firms will lose profits. However, each member has a strong incentive to cheat. They could produce more than they agreed to. If every cartel member cheats, too much product reaches the market, and prices fall. Cartels usually do not last very long.

■ ■ ■ ■ ■ ■ ■ ■ ■ ■ ■ ■ ■ ■ ■ ■ ■ ■ ■ ■

price fixing
an agreement among firms to sell at the same or very similar prices

cartel
a formal organization of producers that agree to coordinate prices and production

✔ **CHECKPOINT** *What role can market leaders play in an oligopoly?*

SECTION 3 ASSESSMENT

Essential Questions Journal
To continue to build a response to the Essential Question, go to your **Essential Questions Journal.**

Quick Write

Choose a product in a monopolistically competitive industry. Write an ad for your product for television, radio, newspapers, or the Internet. How can you persuade consumers to buy your product when many similar products are on the market? Write a paragraph answering these questions: Would you see an ad like this in a purely competitive market? Would you see this ad in a market with a monopoly? Explain your answers.

🤔 Guiding Question

1. Use your completed Venn diagram to answer the following question: What are the characteristics of monopolistic competition and oligopoly?

Key Terms and Main Ideas

Directions: On a sheet of paper, write the answer to each question. Use complete sentences.

2. What four conditions define monopolistic competition?
3. How does differentiation help monopolistically competitive firms sell their products?
4. How do economists determine if a market is an oligopoly?
5. How would price fixing and collusion help producers?

Critical Thinking

6. **Synthesize Information** (a) What are the advantages of a monopolistically competitive market for consumers? (b) What are some of the disadvantages?
7. **Draw Conclusions** (a) Name one way the government regulates oligopolies. (b) Why do you think the government has done this?

Objectives

- **Explain** how firms might try to increase their market power.
- **List** three market practices that the government regulates or bans to protect competition.
- **Define** deregulation and list its effects on several industries.

predatory pricing
selling a product below cost for a short period of time to drive competitors out of the market

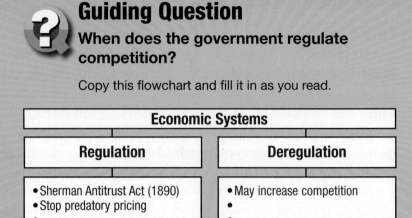

Guiding Question

When does the government regulate competition?

Copy this flowchart and fill it in as you read.

Economic Systems	
Regulation	**Deregulation**
• Sherman Antitrust Act (1890) • Stop predatory pricing •	• May increase competition • •

▶ **Economics and You** It is 1946, and cities are growing. In your job as a city planner, you propose building more streetcar lines for the city. A company called National City Lines buys your city's streetcar system. It shuts down the streetcars and replaces them with buses. Later, you learn that National City Lines was secretly getting help. The help came from companies that make buses, tires, and gasoline. All these companies now profit from the new bus system.

Principles in Action This series of events really took place after World War II in cities like Los Angeles and Baltimore. The federal government agreed that what National City Lines did was unfair. In this section, you will read about practices that limit competition. You will learn about the tools the government uses to stop these practices.

How might firms try to increase their market power?

Market power is the ability of a firm to control prices and total market output. If one firm or a few large ones control a market, it often has higher prices and lower output than markets with many sellers. The leading firms in a market can merge with one another or form a cartel to control prices and output. They might also practice **predatory pricing**. This means a firm sells a product below cost for a short period of time to drive competitors out of the market.

☑ **CHECKPOINT** *How does a market with only a few large firms act like a monopoly?*

How does government protect competition?

By the 1880s, many people demanded reforms of big business. Reformers are people who want to change a thing so it works better. More than half the U.S. Congressmen were reformers. Congress passed laws to try to control the problem of **trust** companies. A trust is an illegal grouping of companies that discourages competition. The Interstate Commerce Act was passed in 1887. It created the Interstate Commerce Commission (ICC) to regulate railroads. The ICC continued to regulate the railroads until it was done away with in 1995.

The Sherman Antitrust Act was passed in 1890. This law made it illegal for large companies to form monopolies. Unfortunately, the wording was not clear. Many trusts fought against the government in court and won. Ultimately, however, monopolies in both the tobacco and oil industries were broken up.

In 1982, the government broke American Telephone and Telegraph (AT&T) into seven smaller companies. Today, there are many competing firms in the telephone industry.

In addition to **antitrust laws,** the government can try to stop monopolies from forming. The government can block company **mergers.** A merger results when one business buys a competing business in the same industry. The government tries to predict what effect a merger will have on prices and services. It may decide not to approve the merger. It has taken some companies to court because it thinks the mergers will result in monopolies.

✔ **CHECKPOINT** *How does the government break up monopolies?*

trust
an illegal grouping of companies that discourages competition

antitrust laws
laws that encourage competition in the marketplace

merger
when two or more companies join to form a single firm

Fig. 7.4 Key Events in Federal Antitrust Policy

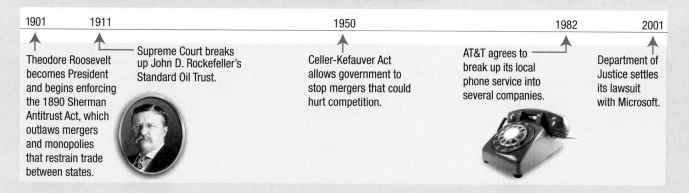

| 1901 | 1911 | 1950 | 1982 | 2001 |

Theodore Roosevelt becomes President and begins enforcing the 1890 Sherman Antitrust Act, which outlaws mergers and monopolies that restrain trade between states.

Supreme Court breaks up John D. Rockefeller's Standard Oil Trust.

Celler-Kefauver Act allows government to stop mergers that could hurt competition.

AT&T agrees to break up its local phone service into several companies.

Department of Justice settles its lawsuit with Microsoft.

Fig. 7.5 How the Economy Works

How is broadcasting regulated?

The Federal Communications Commission (FCC) is a government agency that regulates the broadcasting industry. The FCC issues licenses to radio and television stations. Creating a new television station requires FCC approval.

1 A broadcaster who wants to start a new television station begins with a search for an unused frequency. If a frequency can be found, the broadcaster files a petition with the FCC to add a new station. An attorney can help with the complex process.

2 The FCC grants or denies the broadcaster permission to apply for the station. Applications are filed online. The broadcaster must announce his application in a public notice. The FCC will conduct an electronic auction of licenses for broadcast stations.

Applying for a New Television Station

---

deregulation
the removal of some government controls over a market

What is deregulation?

In the late 1970s and 1980s, Congress passed laws to deregulate several industries. **Deregulation** means the government no longer controls the industry. Companies can set prices at whatever level they want. The government has deregulated, or removed control over, the airline, banking, railroad, and other industries.

Deregulation has had mixed success. It has increased competition in some industries. For example, many new firms are now in the airline, banking, and trucking industries. Lower prices in some industries have helped some consumers. However, deregulation has also raised costs in other industries. Deregulation of cable television has caused rates to go up. Many customers complain that service has become worse. There are now too many firms in the airline industry. Revenues have dropped and several firms have gone out of business. Thousands of people have lost their jobs. The health of the U.S. airline industry is not good.

Reading Strategy
Metacognition
Ask yourself, "What did I learn by reading this section? What do I still want to know about deregulation?"

☑ **CHECKPOINT** *What positive and negative outcomes have resulted from deregulating certain industries?*

G GENERAL AUDIENCE

PG PARENTAL GUIDANCE SUGGESTED

14 PARENTS STRONGLY CAUTIONED

MA MATURE AUDIENCE ONLY

How the Economy Works
online

For an animated, interactive version of this feature, visit **PearsonSuccessNet.com**

3 The FCC also sets broadcasting standards and monitors programs for indecent content. Stations that violate rules are subject to fines and penalties.

5 The FCC grants a construction permit to the highest bidder for the new station. The permit allows the station to broadcast before the FCC license has been issued.

4 Broadcasting without a license is illegal. The FCC shuts down illegal broadcasters and takes their equipment. Illegal operation of an unlicensed station may result in criminal prosecution.

CONFISCATED

Check Your Understanding
1. **Who can apply for a license to broadcast a television station?**
2. **What would happen if the FCC didn't limit the number of television broadcasters?**

Broadcasting Rules

FCC Approval

SECTION 4 ASSESSMENT

Essential Questions Journal

To continue to build a response to the Essential Question, go to your **Essential Questions Journal.**

 Guiding Question

1. Use your completed flowchart to answer this question: When does the government regulate competition?

Key Terms and Main Ideas

Directions: On a sheet of paper, write the answer to each question. Use complete sentences.

2. How does predatory pricing hurt competition?

3. What is the purpose of antitrust laws?

4. Why does the government sometimes try to prevent companies from merging?

5. How did deregulation change the airline travel industry?

Critical Thinking

6. **Predict Consequences** (a) Why might a firm not want to practice predatory pricing even if it was legal? (b) When might a firm try to practice predatory pricing?

7. **Make Inferences** (a) Why does the government step in to control markets? (b) Is this consistent with the idea of laissez faire and free markets? Explain your answer.

Section 1–Perfect Competition

- Perfect competition is a market structure in which a large number of firms all produce the same product. No single seller controls supply or prices.

- Perfect competition is found in markets that deal in commodities. Commodities are things such as wheat, sugar, and notebook paper.

Section 2–Monopoly

- A monopoly is a market in which a single seller dominates. Monopolies can take advantage of their market power and charge high prices.

- A government monopoly is created by the government. It can help protect artists, inventors, and other creative people.

Section 3–Monopolistic Competition and Oligopoly

- In monopolistic competition, many companies sell products that are similar but not identical.

- In an oligopoly, a few large firms dominate a market. Examples include the markets for air travel and soft drinks.

Section 4–Regulation and Deregulation

- The federal government has passed laws to promote competition and the breakup of corporate monopolies.

- Deregulation is the removal of some government controls over a market.

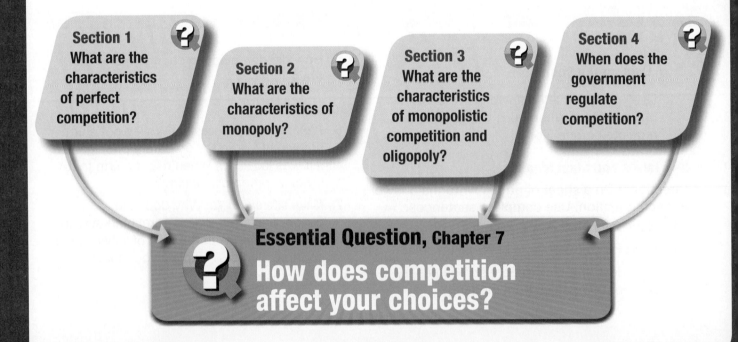

Section 1
What are the characteristics of perfect competition?

Section 2
What are the characteristics of monopoly?

Section 3
What are the characteristics of monopolistic competition and oligopoly?

Section 4
When does the government regulate competition?

Essential Question, Chapter 7
How does competition affect your choices?

The Sherman Antitrust Act

In 1890, the U.S. Congress passed the Sherman Antitrust Act. The act was created to restore competition and dissolve monopolies. It has been used in court cases for more than 100 years. In the late 1990s, the Sherman Act was used against a large U.S. computer software company. The Sherman Act reads, in part, as follows.

"Every contract . . . in the form of trust or otherwise, or conspiracy, in restraint of trade or commerce among the several States, or with foreign nations, is hereby declared to be illegal. Every person who shall make any such contract or engage in any such combination or conspiracy, shall be deemed guilty of a misdemeanor, and, on conviction thereof, shall be punished by fine not exceeding five thousand dollars, or by imprisonment not exceeding one year, or by both said punishments, at the discretion of the court.

Every person who shall monopolize, or attempt to monopolize . . . any part of the trade or commerce among the several States, or with foreign nations, shall be deemed [considered] guilty of a misdemeanor. . . .

Every contract, combination in form of trust or otherwise, or conspiracy, in restraint of trade or commerce . . . is hereby declared illegal.

The several circuit courts of the United States are hereby invested with jurisdiction to prevent and restrain violations of this act. . . .

Any property owned under any contract or by any combination . . . mentioned in section one of this act . . . shall be forfeited to the United States. . . .

Any person who shall be injured in his business or property by any other person or corporation by reason of anything forbidden or declared to be unlawful by this act, may sue . . . in any circuit court of the United States in the district in which the defendant resides or is found. . . ."

Document-Based Questions

1. Why was the Sherman Antitrust Act passed?
2. According to the Sherman Antitrust Act, how are people punished if found guilty of creating a monopoly?
3. What happens to property owned under a monopoly if the court finds the business guilty of creating a monopoly?
4. In your own words, explain the last paragraph of the document.
5. Do you think it is important to dissolve monopolies? Explain.

Directions: Choose the letter of the best answer or write the answer using complete sentences.

Section 1–Perfect Competition

1. Why must firms use land, labor, and other resources efficiently in a market with perfect competition?

2. What are two examples, other than technology and start-up costs, that could be barriers for a company to enter a market?

3. In a commodities market, why does competition among sellers result in the lowest prices possible?

4. On what factors do producers base their output decisions?

Section 2–Monopoly

5. Name the three characteristics of a monopoly.

6. What is a government monopoly?

7. What protection does a patent give an inventor?

8. How does the practice of price discrimination work?

Section 3–Monopolistic Competition and Oligopoly

9. What is the difference between perfect competition and monopolistic competition?

10. What happens during a price war?

11. Why does oligopoly present a challenge to government?

12. Why do cartels usually not last very long?

Section 4–Regulation and Deregulation

13. What is a trust?

14. What two big monopolies did the Sherman Antitrust Act break up?

15. How do some companies get around antitrust laws to gain control over their markets?

16. How can a corporate merger benefit consumers?

17. In the late 1970s and 1980s, the government decided to deregulate several industries. Name three of these.

? Exploring the Essential Question

18. With economies of scale, production costs continue to fall as output increases. What is the reason for this?

19. Suppose you opened a lemonade stand in your neighborhood. Soon your neighbor also opens up a lemonade stand. What could you do to compete with the other business?

Essential Question Activity

20. Complete this activity to answer the Essential Question **How does competition affect your choices?** As a class, decide on three features you would like to have on a high-tech product like a cellphone. Then, work in small groups to design that product, incorporating the features the class has selected. Using your worksheet, answer the following questions:

(a) What is the demand for your product? Who might want to buy the product? What price would you charge? How many could you sell at that price in a month or a year?

(b) What are the barriers to entry into this market?

(c) How will your product be different from similar products that are already on the market?

| **Essential Questions Journal** | To continue to build a response to the Essential Question, go to your **Essential Questions Journal.** |

Test-Taking Tip

Studying in small groups and asking questions of one another is one way to review for tests.

Unit 2 Challenge

Essential Question, Unit 2
Who benefits from the free market economy?

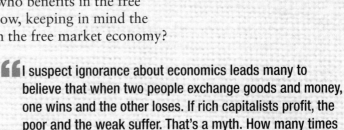

By Students For Students
For videos on Essential Questions,
go to *PearsonSuccessNet.com*

People have different opinions about who benefits in the free marketplace. Look at the opinions below, keeping in mind the Essential Question: Who benefits from the free market economy?

> "I'm all for a free economy, but competitors need to play by some rules. Congress has the power to regulate this trade through the commerce clause of the Constitution and needs to begin to do so."
>
> —Gatsby 999, msnbc.com

> "I suspect ignorance about economics leads many to believe that when two people exchange goods and money, one wins and the other loses. If rich capitalists profit, the poor and the weak suffer. That's a myth. How many times have you paid $1 for a cup of coffee and after the clerk said, "thank you," you responded, "thank you"? There's a wealth of economics wisdom in the weird double thank-you moment. Why does it happen? Because you want the coffee more than the buck, and the store wants the buck more than the coffee. Both of you win."
>
> —John Stossel, Real Clear Politics.com, "The Double Thank-You Moment," May 30, 2007

Essential Question
Writing Activity

Consider the different views expressed in the sources on this page and what you have learned about the operation of the free market. *Then write a well-constructed essay expressing your view of who benefits in a free market economy.*

Writing Guidelines

- Address all aspects of the Essential Question Writing Activity.
- Support the theme with relevant facts, examples, and details.
- Use a logical and clear plan of organization.
- Introduce the theme by establishing a framework that is beyond a simple restatement of the question and conclude with a summation of the theme.

For help in writing a Persuasive Essay, refer to the *Writing Skills Handbook* in the Reference section, page S-5.

Essential Questions Journal

To respond to the unit Essential Question, go to your **Essential Questions Journal**.

Essential Question, Unit 3

How can businesses and labor best achieve their goals?

Chapter 8
Why do some businesses succeed and others fail?

Chapter 9
How can workers best meet the challenges of a changing economy?

Chapter 8 Business Organizations

Essential Question, Chapter 8

Why do some businesses succeed and others fail?

- **Section 1** Sole Proprietorships

- **Section 2** Partnerships and Franchises

- **Section 3** Corporations, Mergers, and Multinationals

- **Section 4** Nonprofit Organizations

▶ **Workers and businesses are the heart of any economy.** Many kinds of businesses and jobs are out there. If you are not already part of the world of work, you will be soon. What job is best for you? This is not an easy thing to decide. Will your job be to provide a service or to make a product? What kind of business will you work for?

This chapter will discuss many kinds of businesses and how they are organized. More than 16 million businesses are in the United States today. Many of them are small businesses that one person owns. The biggest businesses are corporations. Businesses provide most of the goods and services produced for and sold to consumers.

Reading Strategy: Summarizing
As you read the text in this chapter, you will want to ask yourself questions to help you understand what you read. Ask questions such as:

- What is the chapter about?
- What new ideas am I being introduced to?
- Why is it important that I remember these ideas?

Visual Glossary
online
Go to the Visual Glossary Online for an interactive review of **corporation.**

How the Economy Works
online
Go to How the Economy Works Online for an interactive lesson on **how a small business grows.**

Action Graph
online
Go to Action Graph Online for animated versions of key charts and graphs.

Objectives

- **Explain** the characteristics of sole proprietorships.
- **Analyze** the advantages of a sole proprietorship.
- **Analyze** the disadvantages of a sole proprietorship.

Guiding Question

What are the risks and benefits of a sole proprietorship?

Copy this comparison chart and fill it in as you read.

Sole Proprietorships	
Benefits	Risks
• Ease of start-up • Relatively few regulations • Sole receiver of profit • •	• Unlimited personal liability • Limited access to resources • • •

business organization
the ownership structure of a company or firm

sole proprietorship
a business that one person (an entrepreneur) owns

▶ **Economics and You** You may be one of the lucky people who is able to turn something you really like to do into a business. Imagine launching a Web site that reviews video games or opening a baseball camp or a car detailing business. One of the biggest questions you will face is what is the best way for you to organize your business.

Principles in Action The easiest business to set up is the one in which you are the only owner. In this section, you will learn how being your own boss has both advantages and disadvantages. In the Economics & You feature, you will see how doing business with a sole proprietorship might affect you.

What is a sole proprietorship?

One type of **business organization** is a **sole proprietorship**. A sole proprietorship is a business owned by one person. That person keeps all the money that is earned but is also responsible for all its debts. There are far more single proprietorships than any other kind of business. In the United States, more than 70 percent of businesses are sole proprietorships. Most are very small. You probably could name dozens of sole proprietorships in your community. They include barbershops and hair salons, some restaurants, and the corner store. **Figure 8.1** shows characteristics of proprietorships.

Not everyone has what it takes to be an entrepreneur, or to start a business. Entrepreneurs often value achievement over money. Other characteristics of successful entrepreneurs include:

- a willingness to seek out responsibility and take risks
- belief in their ability to succeed and strong commitment to their goals
- optimism, high energy level, and focus on the future

Let's say you want to turn your idea into a new video game. First, you have to know whether your idea is practical. Your game idea may be great. However, if it costs more to make than you can charge for it, it will not make a profit. Your business will fail.

Starting a new business requires resources. Creating a new video game requires money. Before you start thinking about making the game, you have to find the money to pay for everything.

CHECKPOINT *What is the most common form of business organization found in the United States?*

Reading Strategy
Summarizing
What traits do you need in order to be a successful entrepreneur?

Fig. 8.1 Characteristics of Sole Proprietorships

GRAPH SKILLS
Most sole proprietorships take in relatively small amounts of money, or receipts.

1. What percentage of sole proprietorships is engaged in retail trade?
2. Why might more sole proprietors be engaged in services than in manufacturing?

For an animated version of this graph, visit
PearsonSuccessNet.com

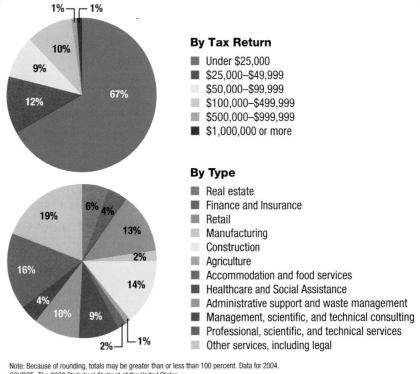

By Tax Return
- Under $25,000
- $25,000–$49,999
- $50,000–$99,999
- $100,000–$499,999
- $500,000–$999,999
- $1,000,000 or more

By Type
- Real estate
- Finance and Insurance
- Retail
- Manufacturing
- Construction
- Agriculture
- Accommodation and food services
- Healthcare and Social Assistance
- Administrative support and waste management
- Management, scientific, and technical consulting
- Professional, scientific, and technical services
- Other services, including legal

Note: Because of rounding, totals may be greater than or less than 100 percent. Data for 2004.
SOURCE: *The 2008 Statistical Abstract of the United States*

business license

written permission given by the local government that allows a business to open

What advantages do sole proprietorships have?

Owning your own business has several advantages. Sole proprietorships are easy to set up. They face few government rules. The owner does not have to share profits or control of the business with anyone else. They are also easy to end.

How are sole proprietorships formed?

The biggest advantage is that sole proprietorships are easy to form. Just about anyone can set up a business with a little paperwork. Sole proprietorships must meet the following requirements:

1. *Permission* Many local governments require sole proprietors to have a **business license** before opening a business. This is written permission given by the local government to open a business. Some professionals, such as doctors, need special licenses from the state.

2. *Site permit* Most sole proprietors do not open a business in their own homes. If they are using another building for the business, they must first get permission to use the site.

3. *Name* Sole proprietors must register a business name unless they are using their own name for the business.

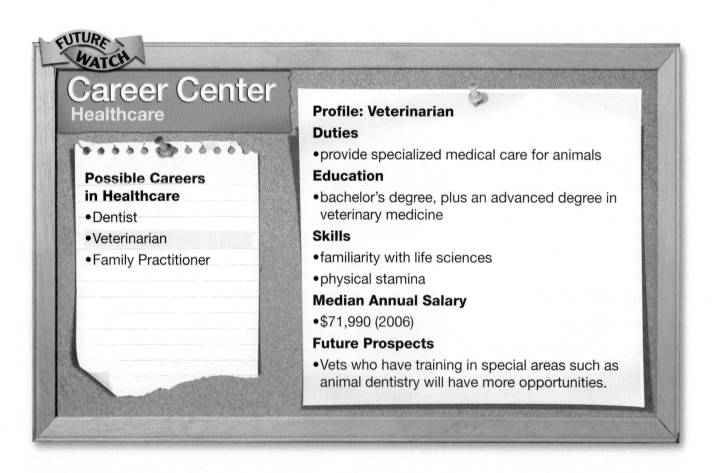

FUTURE WATCH

Career Center
Healthcare

Possible Careers in Healthcare
- Dentist
- Veterinarian
- Family Practitioner

Profile: Veterinarian

Duties
- provide specialized medical care for animals

Education
- bachelor's degree, plus an advanced degree in veterinary medicine

Skills
- familiarity with life sciences
- physical stamina

Median Annual Salary
- $71,990 (2006)

Future Prospects
- Vets who have training in special areas such as animal dentistry will have more opportunities.

Are there government rules for proprietorships?

All businesses have to follow government rules. However, sole proprietors have fewer rules than larger businesses. They may be subject to local **zoning laws.** Zoning laws are used to permit or prevent certain businesses from operating in certain areas. For example certain industries are not allowed to operate in residential areas.

Who receives the profits in a sole proprietorship?

In a sole proprietorship, the owner gets to keep all the profits after paying taxes. Most people start businesses of their own because they want to earn money.

Who controls a sole proprietorship?

Sole proprietors can run their businesses the way they want. They get to be their own boss. They decide what to sell and at what price. Single owners make all the management decisions. They get to make whatever changes they want. They decide what to charge for goods and services and when to open and close the business.

The sole proprietor can also decide when to shut the business down. If the owner decides to do something else, it is easy to put an end to the business. Of course, all owners must pay their debts before shutting down the business.

✔️ **CHECKPOINT** *Why are sole proprietorships easy to start and end?*

What are the disadvantages of sole proprietorships?

As with everything else, there are trade-offs with sole proprietorships. Along with the independence comes a high degree of responsibility.

What is unlimited personal liability?

The main disadvantage of owning your own business is **unlimited personal liability.** This means the owner is fully and personally responsible for paying all the money the business owes. If the business fails, the owner is still **liable,** or legally responsible. He or she may have to sell his or her home or car to pay off the debt.

zoning law
law that does not allow people to operate a business in certain areas

unlimited personal liability
when the owner of a business is responsible for paying all the money the business owes

liable
having legal responsibility

Economics & YOU

Sole Proprietorship

A clothing store owner takes pride in the quality of her customer service, wanting to make sure you get what you need. *You appreciate the personalized attention.*

SORRY WE'RE **CLOSED**
On Vacation
Back August 1

The store owner is on vacation. *You are inconvenienced.*

Reading Strategy
Summarizing

In your own words, describe the main features of a sole proprietorship.

limited capital
the limit on the amount of money to grow the business

fringe benefits
anything extra given to workers in addition to their wages, such as paid vacations, retirement plans, and medical insurance

Why is limited capital a problem in sole proprietorships?

Another disadvantage is **limited capital.** The single owner may not have extra funds to expand the business. Banks sometimes do not want to loan money to new businesses. The amount of money available to the business may be limited to what the owner has in savings. Human capital may be lacking, too. The sole proprietor, no matter how eager, may lack some of the skills necessary to be successful. Physical capital is also limited. Owners may not be able to buy the equipment and machines they need to make a profit.

Why do sole proprietorships have a limited life?

A third disadvantage is that sole proprietorships have a limited life. The business depends totally on the one owner. If the owner becomes sick or disabled, loses interest, or dies, the business ends. Sole proprietors have often had trouble finding and keeping good workers. Most cannot offer workers the **fringe benefits** that larger businesses can. Fringe benefits are benefits given to workers in addition to their wages.

✔ **CHECKPOINT** *What are the disadvantages of sole proprietorships?*

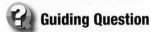

SECTION **1** ASSESSMENT

Essential Questions Journal To continue to build a response to the Essential Question, go to your **Essential Questions Journal.**

Guiding Question

1. Use your completed comparison chart to answer this question: What are the risks and benefits of a sole proprietorship?

Key Terms and Main Ideas

Directions: On a sheet of paper, write the answer to each question. Use complete sentences.

2. What is a sole proprietorship?
3. (a) What is liability? (b) What is the biggest disadvantage of a sole proprietorship?
4. What role do business licenses and zoning laws play in sole proprietorships?

5. Why do you think the desire for profit motivates people to start a sole proprietorship rather than starting a business with a partner?

Critical Thinking

6. **Draw Inferences** Why are sole proprietorships less able to offer benefits to workers?
7. **Analyze Information** (a) Name a sole proprietorship that would be subject to health codes. Why? (b) Name a business that would be subject to laws that regulate the disposal of dangerous chemicals. Explain.

Objectives

- **Compare** and contrast different types of partnerships.
- **Analyze** the advantages of partnerships.
- **Analyze** the disadvantages of partnerships.
- **Explain** how a business franchise operates.

Guiding Question

What are the risks and benefits of partnerships and franchises?

Copy this chart and fill it in as you read. Add more boxes if necessary.

Benefits and Risks	
Partnership	Franchise
• Easy, inexpensive to start up • Owners will have to share profits •	• Owner sacrifices some freedom • Financial help •

partnership
a business that two or more people own

general partnership
a partnership in which partners share equally in both responsibility and liability

▶ **Economics and You** Would you ever consider setting up your own business? Suppose you like the idea but aren't sure you want to be responsible for everything. You may be great at doing the job, but you may not want to do all the paperwork. Do you have to give up your dream?

Principles in Action Some business owners solve problems like this by taking on a partner. Others get help from larger businesses by entering a franchise arrangement.

What is a partnership?

A **partnership** is a business owned by two or more people. Usually, a written agreement is drawn up to create a partnership. This document is called a partnership agreement. In the United States, nearly 9 percent of all businesses are partnerships. There are three basic types of partnerships: general partnerships, limited partnerships, and limited liability partnerships. **Figure 8.2** shows characteristics of partnerships.

What is a general partnership?

In a **general partnership**, all partners share responsibility and liability equally. Many businesses in your community are probably owned by a general partnership. They may include many of the same types of businesses owned by a single person. Sometimes lawyers, accountants, and doctors form partnerships. Farms, construction companies, as well as family businesses, are often general partnerships.

limited partnership
a partnership in which only one partner is required to have both responsibility and liability

limited liability partnership
a partnership in which all partners are limited partners

articles of partnership
a partnership agreement; lists each partner's rights and responsibilities and how the partners will share profits or losses

What is a limited partnership?

In **limited partnerships**, there are both general partners and limited partners. General partners have unlimited liability, but limited partners do not. The general partners manage the business. The limited partners have no say in how the business is run. However, their liability is limited. Limited partners cannot lose more than they put into the business. A limited partnership must have at least one general partner. It can have any number of limited partners.

What is a limited liability partnership?

The **limited liability partnership** (LLP) is a newer type of partnership. It is designed for use by certain professionals such as accountants, lawyers, and architects. In this type of partnership, all partners are limited partners. An LLP works like a general partnership, except that all partners have limited liability. They are not responsible for the mistakes other partners make.

✓ **CHECKPOINT** *What is a partnership?*

What are the advantages of a partnership?

Partnerships are easy to establish and are subject to few government rules.

How difficult is it to set up a partnership?

A partnership is easy to start. Most partners work with a lawyer to draw up an agreement called **articles of partnership.** This spells out each partner's rights and responsibilities. It states how the partners will share profits or losses. Sometimes the partners do not write their own articles of partnership. In this case, they fall under the rules of the Uniform Partnership Act (UPA). This law sets up the rules for partnerships. It is used in most states.

Fig. 8.2 Characteristics of Partnerships

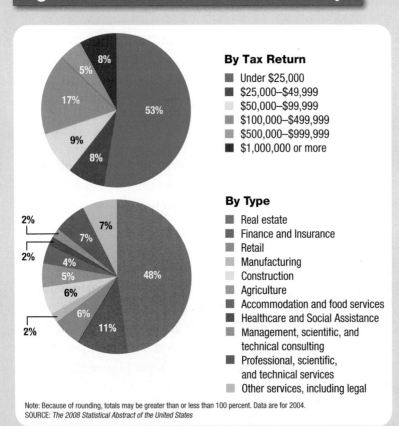

By Tax Return
- Under $25,000
- $25,000–$49,999
- $50,000–$99,999
- $100,000–$499,999
- $500,000–$999,999
- $1,000,000 or more

By Type
- Real estate
- Finance and Insurance
- Retail
- Manufacturing
- Construction
- Agriculture
- Accommodation and food services
- Healthcare and Social Assistance
- Management, scientific, and technical consulting
- Professional, scientific, and technical services
- Other services, including legal

Note: Because of rounding, totals may be greater than or less than 100 percent. Data are for 2004.
SOURCE: *The 2008 Statistical Abstract of the United States*

GRAPH SKILLS

Partnerships can range in size from a pair of house painters to an accounting firm with thousands of partners.

1. Using the data in these charts, describe partnerships in terms of industry and income.
2. Why do you think real estate businesses form the largest percentage of partnerships?

Action Graph online For an animated version of this graph, visit **PearsonSuccessNet.com**

Partnerships have few government rules they must follow. The government does not tell them how to manage their business. The partners can distribute the profits any way they want. But they must follow the partnership agreement or the UPA.

■ ■ ■ ■ ■ ■ ■ ■ ■ ■ ■ ■ ■ ■ ■ ■ ■ ■ ■ ■
asset
the money and valuables belonging to an individual or business

Why is a larger pool of assets helpful?

The partnership combines the funds and skills of the partners. By forming a business together, the partnership has more **assets** to invest than each would have alone. Assets are money and other valuables. Another advantage is that each partner could specialize in what he or she does best. For example, perhaps one partner is better at selling than the other. The second partner may be better at keeping the books. The partners can use their special skills to increase profits. Partnerships, like sole proprietorships, do not have to pay any special taxes.

☑ **CHECKPOINT** *What are the advantages of partnerships?*

What are the disadvantages of a partnership?

Partnerships have many of the same disadvantages as sole proprietorships. However, limited liability partnerships have fewer disadvantages than general partnerships.

What is unlimited liability?

The chief disadvantage of a partnership is unlimited liability. Like a sole proprietorship, the general partners are responsible for all the company's debt. If one of the partners runs off, the other partners are still liable for all of the company's debts. The partners may have to sell things they own to pay what the company owes. Limited partners stand to lose only as much as they put into the firm.

In a general partnership, the decisions made by any general partner affect all the partners. If a partner makes a mistake, all the general partners are liable. Of course, this is not a problem in limited liability partnerships.

Who has control of the business in a partnership?

In a general partnership, decision making is shared by all the general partners. Unlike businesses with only one owner, in a partnership no one partner has complete control.

Partners do not always see eye to eye. There is a chance that the partners will disagree on how best to run the business. The disagreement may cause the business to fail. Partners must learn to talk with one another to make sure the business survives.

Fig. 8.3 How the Economy Works

How can a **small business** grow?

All businesses begin with an idea to sell a product or service. Sole proprietors, working on their own, sometimes find that adding a partner will help them be more successful.

1 Calvin, an enterprising college student, has launched an online business, Hiyerminds.com. He creates and sells college survival kits to incoming freshmen. He keeps his costs down and makes a tidy profit. He is keeping up with a steady stream of orders and with his schoolwork.

2 Calvin finds that as his product becomes more popular, he can't manage the ordering and accounting part of the business. He decides to ask his friend Diego to join Hiyerminds.com as an equal partner. The partnership allows the business to expand.

Expansion

business franchise
a business that pays fees to a parent company in return for the right to sell a product or service

Reading Strategy
Summarizing
What are two advantages and two disadvantages of a partnership?

How long do partnerships last?

Partnerships may have a limited life. The partnership ends when one of the partners leaves or dies. A new partnership agreement must be drawn up if the business is to continue.

✅ **CHECKPOINT** *How does control of general partnerships differ from sole proprietorships?*

What is a business franchise?

A new form of business organization, a franchise, has become common in the last 25 years. A **business franchise** is an agreement between a person and a parent company. The parent company is called the franchiser. The person who buys the franchise is called the franchisee. Franchisees pay fees to the parent company. In return, they are given the right to sell a certain product or service. Under the franchise agreement, the franchiser develops the products and the systems to produce them. It also provides national advertising. Many businesses in your community may be franchises. They include hotels, fast-food restaurants, convenience stores, income tax service, and even jewelry shops.

3 After a few months, Calvin and Diego begin having many disagreements about how to operate the business. Customer service suffers.

How the Economy Works
online
For an animated, interactive version of this feature, visit **PearsonSuccessNet.com**

5 As a result, Calvin and Diego hire employees to assemble the kits. Calvin focuses on finding new customers and Diego manages the business.

4 Calvin and Diego realize that their differences are bad for business and threaten their income. They revise the articles of partnership to set new rules about individual responsibilities and their business goals.

Check Your Understanding
1. What basic change did Calvin make in his small business to enable it to grow?
2. How did his change create both advantages and disadvantages?

Conflict and Resolution

Further Expansion

What are the advantages of franchises?

Owning a franchise is a lot like owning your own business. It has some advantages over a sole proprietorship. The most important may be that the franchisee is usually buying into a successful business. The other advantage is that the franchiser helps make running the business easier. How?

1. *Management training and support* The parent company trains the franchise owners to manage their business better.
2. *Standardized quality* The parent companies require that certain rules be followed. For example, in a hamburger franchise, the meat is to be cooked in the same way.
3. *National advertising programs* Parent companies advertise all over the country. This helps make the product or service well known. The ads can also increase sales.
4. *Financial assistance* Some franchisers give loans to help people who want to start their own business but do not have enough money.
5. *Centralized buying power* Parent companies buy materials in large amounts. They pass on the savings to their franchisees.

Reading Strategy
Summarizing
This section has lists that identify advantages and disadvantages of franchises. How do these lists help you summarize the content?

What are the disadvantages of franchises?

The biggest disadvantage is that franchisees must give up some of their control. They have to follow the rules set up by the parent company. Other disadvantages include:

1. *High franchise fees and royalties* The cost of buying a franchise is often high. The franchisee often pays a share of the profits to the parent company called **royalties.**
2. *Strict rules* Franchise owners must follow all the rules set out in the franchise agreement. The agreement spells out such matters as store hours, workers' dress, and a way of doing things. If franchisees do not follow the rules, they may lose the franchise.
3. *Buying limits* Franchise owners must buy their supplies from the parent company or from other approved suppliers.
4. *Limited product line* The franchisee has no say on what products will be sold. Only approved products may be sold.

✔ **CHECKPOINT** *What are the advantages and disadvantages of owning a franchise?*

SECTION 2 ASSESSMENT

Essential Questions Journal

To continue to build a response to the Essential Question, go to your **Essential Questions Journal.**

Word Bank

articles of partnership

franchiser

franchisee

royalties

Quick Write

With a partner, draw up articles of partnership for a fictional business. Decide which type of partnership best suits your business and your personal preferences and skills.

Guiding Question

1. Use your completed chart to answer this question: What are the risks and benefits of partnerships and franchises?

Key Terms and Main Ideas

Directions: On a sheet of paper, write the term from the Word Bank that correctly completes each sentence.

2. Partners can work with an attorney to develop _____, or a partnership agreement.

3. Parent companies collect _____ from their franchises.

4. In a franchise, the local owner is called a(n) _____.

5. In a franchise, the parent company is called a(n) _____.

Critical Thinking

6. **Draw Inferences** Why might physicians and lawyers find limited liability partnerships attractive?

7. **Make Comparisons** How do general partnerships, limited partnerships, and limited liability partnerships differ from one another?

Objectives

- **Explain** the characteristics of corporations.
- **Analyze** the advantages of incorporation.
- **Analyze** the disadvantages of incorporation.
- **Compare** and contrast corporate combinations.
- **Describe** the role of multinational corporations.

Guiding Question

What are the risks and benefits of corporations?

Copy this Venn diagram and fill it in as you read. Add more ovals if necessary.

Publicly Held
- Benefits: limited liability for owners
- Risks:

All
- Benefits:
- Risks: can go out of business

Closely Held
- Benefits: owners have more control
- Risks:

---

corporation
a business that can be made up of many owners; the law allows it to act like a single person

charter
an official document issued by state governments that gives the right to create a corporation

share
a unit of stock in a company

stock
a certificate that signifies ownership in a corporation

▶ **Economics and You** Every day you use goods and services provided by a variety of businesses, both large and small. Did the bread you eat today come from a local bakery or a huge multinational food producer? Some goods can be provided by both. But what about the car or bus you took to school? Some products can be produced only by big businesses.

Principles in Action Some goods and services require huge amounts of capital. They require a special kind of business organization, or ownership structure. What form of business do these companies have? Most of these businesses are corporations.

What is a corporation?

A **corporation** is the form of business organization most difficult to understand. It can be made up of many owners, but the law allows it to act like a single person. This means that legally, a corporation has most of the same rights as a person. Corporations can own and sell property. They pay taxes. They enter into contracts. They can be sued in court. In the United States, about 20 percent of businesses are organized as corporations. They are important because they generate nearly 60 percent of the nation's income. **Figure 8.4** shows characteristics of corporations.

How are corporations formed?

To form a corporation, a person or group must apply for a **charter** from a state government. A charter is an official document that gives permission to create a corporation. After receiving the charter, the corporation is allowed to sell **shares** of **stock.** Stock is a sign of ownership in a corporation.

closely held corporation
a corporation that gives stock to only a few people, often members of the same family

publicly held corporation
a corporation that sells stock on the open market

When investors buy stock in a business, they are issued shares. Suppose the corporation decides to sell 10,000 shares. An investor who buys 1,000 shares owns one-tenth of the business. Everyone holding shares of the corporation is a stockholder and part owner of the corporation.

What are the two types of corporations?

Some corporations have only a few shareholders. Often, they are members of the same family. Their shares are seldom sold but are usually passed on to other family members. Such corporations are called **closely held corporations.** They are also known as privately held corporations.

The second type of corporation is the **publicly held corporation.** It has many shareholders. The stock can easily be bought or sold in markets called stock exchanges.

Who runs the corporations?

Almost all corporations are run in the same way. The shareholders elect a board of directors. The board of directors makes all the major decisions for the corporation. The day-to-day decisions are made by the corporate officers. The most important officers are

Fig. 8.4 Characteristics of Corporations

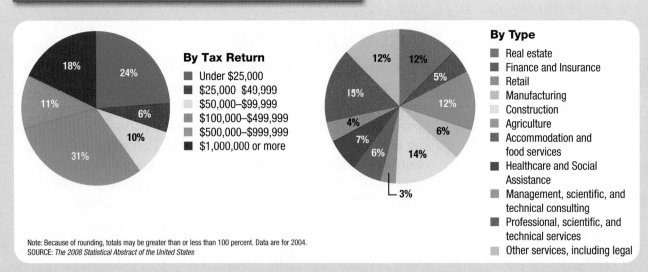

By Tax Return
- Under $25,000
- $25,000 $49,999
- $50,000–$99,999
- $100,000–$499,999
- $500,000–$999,999
- $1,000,000 or more

By Type
- Real estate
- Finance and Insurance
- Retail
- Manufacturing
- Construction
- Agriculture
- Accommodation and food services
- Healthcare and Social Assistance
- Management, scientific, and technical consulting
- Professional, scientific, and technical services
- Other services, including legal

Note: Because of rounding, totals may be greater than or less than 100 percent. Data are for 2004.
SOURCE: *The 2008 Statistical Abstract of the United States*

GRAPH SKILLS
Approximately 44 percent of corporations are engaged in construction, manufacturing, real estate, and retail business.

1. What incentives to incorporate do businesses have in these industries?
2. Firms that sell services make up a large part of corporations. What does this say about the U.S. economy?

Action Graph
online

For an animated version of this graph, visit
PearsonSuccessNet.com

the chief executive officer (CEO) and the chief financial officer (CFO). These officers run the corporation. They hire others to work in various departments of the corporation.

✔ **CHECKPOINT** *What is the role of corporate officers?*

What are the advantages of incorporation?

Forming a corporation, or incorporating, has advantages to both stockholders and the corporation itself.

What are the advantages to the stockholders?

Unlike sole proprietorships and partnerships, corporate liability is limited. With **limited liability**, investors can lose only as much money as they have invested. The investor who bought 1,000 shares in the new corporation can lose only what the shares cost. A shareholder's private property cannot be taken to pay the corporation's debts. This advantage is so important that corporations often add the abbreviation "Ltd."(for *limited*) to their company name.

A corporation allows easy transfer of ownership. Stockholders can easily enter or leave the corporation. They do this by simply buying or selling their shares in the corporation. Shareowners can sell their shares and get money in return. This is not true of other forms of business organizations.

What are the advantages for the corporation?

Corporations can raise capital by selling stock and **bonds.** A bond is a written agreement issued by a corporation. It states a promise to repay borrowed money with interest. Bonds are IOUs. You may be familiar with U.S. Savings Bonds. You pay the government $50.00 now. After several years, the government gives you back $100.00. Corporate bonds work the same way. Investors buy the bonds, and the corporation pays them back plus interest at a later date.

Corporations have unlimited life. Businesses owned by one person or a partnership end when their owners die. Corporations go on even if there is a change in ownership, management, or labor.

✔ **CHECKPOINT** *What are the four advantages of incorporating?*

■ ■ ■ ■ ■ ■ ■ ■ ■ ■ ■ ■ ■ ■ ■ ■ ■ ■ ■ ■

limited liability
when investors can lose only the money they have invested

bond
a type of loan that an investor buys from a company or from the government; the seller promises to pay back the investor's money plus a profit later

■ ■ ■ ■ ■ ■ ■ ■ ■ ■ ■ ■ ■ ■ ■ ■ ■ ■ ■ ■

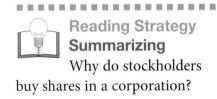

Reading Strategy
Summarizing
Why do stockholders buy shares in a corporation?

certificate of incorporation
a license to form a corporation issued by a state government

dividend
the investor's share of a company's profit

capital gain
the difference between the selling price and purchase price; it results in a financial gain for the seller

limited liability corporation
a type of business with limited liability for the owners; it does not pay corporate income tax

What are the disadvantages of incorporation?

Corporations are fairly expensive to set up. Usually, a lawyer is required to obtain a **certificate of incorporation,** or charter. Investors need to be found and stock sold. The costs are higher than organizing a sole proprietorship or partnership.

Why are corporations taxed twice?

Corporations are taxed twice. The corporation is taxed once on the money it earns. Often the stockholders receive a share of the profits in **dividends.** Dividends represent the investor's share of the profit. The investors have to pay taxes on their dividends.

Stockholders may sell shares. Sometimes they earn money and sometimes they lose. If they make money, they earn what is called a **capital gain.** The gain is also taxed.

Who controls a corporation?

The shareholders of a corporation do not control the business directly. Corporations are managed by the board of directors. Sometimes the board of directors does not always act in the best interests of the stockholders.

What laws must corporations follow?

Corporations must follow more state and federal laws than other forms of business organizations. Corporations must share information about how the business is run and how much money the firm made or lost.

How do limited liability corporations limit disadvantages?

Some businesses organize as **limited liability corporations** (LLCs). An LLC has some characteristics of a partnership and some characteristics of a corporation. LLCs have the advantage of limited liability just like all corporations. But they also have the tax advantages of a partnership. The owners do not pay corporate income taxes. Earnings pass to the owners, who must pay taxes on them. The owners of the LLC are called members. Many experts believe that the limited liability corporation will soon become the most common business form for small businesses.

✔ **CHECKPOINT** *What are the disadvantages of incorporating?*

Why do corporations sometimes combine?

Corporations sometimes merge, or combine. A merger occurs when one corporation buys a majority, or more than half of the stock of another corporation.

What are horizontal mergers?

Horizontal mergers join two or more firms providing the same goods or services. In 2004, Cingular, a wireless phone company, bought the wireless business of AT&T. This was a horizontal merger. The directors of the two corporations believed that combining the two firms would lower costs and make the business more efficient. As you read in Chapter 7, the government watches carefully to make sure the mergers will not create a monopoly.

What are vertical mergers?

Vertical mergers join two or more firms involved in different stages of producing the same good or service. A vertical merger allows a firm to operate better because the firm controls all phases of production. The government may stop a vertical merger if it believes the merger lessens competition. **Figure 8.5** illustrates horizontal and vertical mergers.

horizontal merger
when a business buys another business that provides the same goods and services

vertical merger
the combination of businesses involved in the different stages of producing the same good or service

Fig. 8.5 Horizontal Merger and Vertical Merger

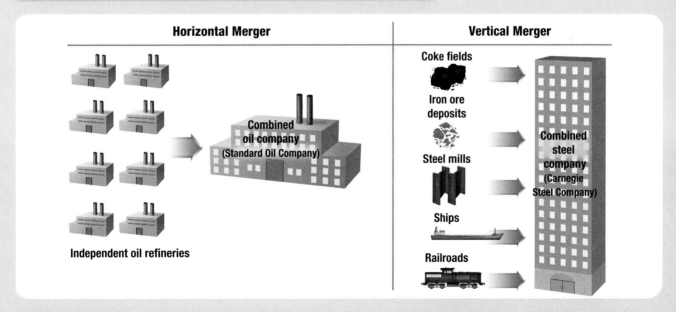

GRAPH SKILLS

Beginning in the 1880s, John D. Rockefeller's Standard Oil Company combined horizontally with 40 other oil refineries. The power gained by Standard Oil and similar monopolies prompted passage of the Sherman Antitrust Act in 1890. In 1899, Andrew Carnegie established the Carnegie Steel Company. He used the vertical merger to purchase companies that produced the raw materials needed to make steel, as well as companies that would move his products to market. Within a short time, Carnegie controlled the steel industry. Most vertical mergers, however, do not result in monopolies.

1. Explain the difference between horizontal mergers and vertical mergers.

2. What are some modern examples of horizontal mergers and vertical mergers?

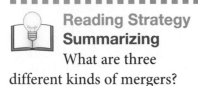

conglomerate
the business combination that brings together more than three businesses that make or provide unrelated goods or services

multinational corporation
a large corporation that operates in more than one country

Reading Strategy
Summarizing
What are three different kinds of mergers?

What is a conglomerate?

Sometimes firms buy other companies that make totally unrelated goods or services. A corporation made up of a number of different companies that operate in a variety of fields is called a **conglomerate.** The government usually allows this kind of merger because it does not cut down on competition.

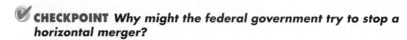 **CHECKPOINT** *Why might the federal government try to stop a horizontal merger?*

What are multinational corporations?

Corporations that operate in more than one country are called **multinational corporations** (MNCs). MNCs must obey laws and pay taxes in each country in which they operate. In the early 2000s, there were more than 64,000 multinational corporations.

What are the advantages of multinationals?

Multinationals allow us to buy products and services from around the world. We may work at corporations that do business in other countries. Often MNCs provide jobs for people in less developed countries. These jobs allow the people to enjoy a higher standard of living. Multinationals also spread new ways of doing things.

What are the disadvantages of multinationals?

Many people point out problems with multinational corporations. They think that big corporations have a bad influence in the countries where they operate. The MNCs do provide jobs, but critics say those jobs have low pay and bad working conditions.

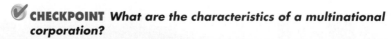 **CHECKPOINT** *What are the characteristics of a multinational corporation?*

SECTION 3 ASSESSMENT

| **Essential Questions Journal** | To continue to build a response to the Essential Question, go to your **Essential Questions Journal.** |

 Guiding Question

1. Use your completed Venn diagram to answer this question: What are the risks and benefits of corporations?

Key Terms and Main Ideas

Directions: On a sheet of paper, write the answer to each question. Use complete sentences.

2. What is stock?

3. How do bonds work?

4. Who makes most decisions in a corporation?

5. Why are corporations taxed twice?

Critical Thinking

6. **Analyze Information** How does a community benefit from an incorporated business?

7. **Draw Conclusions** (a) How do consumers benefit from multinationals? (b) How might a corporation benefit from becoming a multinational corporation?

Objectives

- **Identify** the different types of cooperative organizations.
- **Understand** the purpose of nonprofit organizations, including professional and business organizations.

cooperative
a business organization owned and operated by a group of individuals for their mutual benefit

Guiding Question

How are some businesses organized to help others?

Copy this chart and fill it in as you read. Add more bullets if necessary.

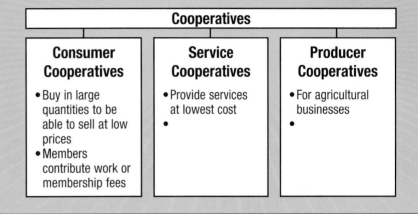

Cooperatives		
Consumer Cooperatives	**Service Cooperatives**	**Producer Cooperatives**
• Buy in large quantities to be able to sell at low prices • Members contribute work or membership fees	• Provide services at lowest cost •	• For agricultural businesses •

▶ **Economics and You** Museums, zoos, and hospitals are business organizations that benefit the public. Their main goal is to provide a service rather than to make a profit. If you meet certain criteria, you may join a credit union whose main purpose is to benefit its members. Although these various institutions may appear to be like other businesses, they are not quite the same.

Principles in Action Success in business is not measured only in dollars and cents. Some businesses are not organized to maximize profits. Instead their goals are to work for the good of all their members or to work for the good of society in general. In this section, you will learn about these business organizations.

What are cooperatives?

A **cooperative** is a business organization owned and operated by a group of individuals for their shared benefit. In other words, there are big advantages of working together.

All cooperatives have three basic characteristics:
- Membership is not forced and is open.
- The organization is owned and run by its members.
- Every member shares in the benefits.

Cooperatives, or co-ops, are a type of self-help. The members get together to provide goods and services at prices they can afford. Without the co-op, the goods and services might not be available to them. Co-ops are found in many industries including farming, energy, healthcare, insurance, and housing. About 120 million Americans belong to a co-op.

Since cooperatives are not corporations, they do not pay income tax. Members, of course, have to pay personal income tax on the money they earn from the co-op. The tax laws allow the co-op to invest up to 80 percent of its earnings. This money can be used to expand the work of the co-ops. The three main types of co-ops are consumer cooperatives, service cooperatives, and producer cooperatives.

▲ A farmers' co-op is an agricultural cooperative. Farmers combine resources to buy supplies at a discount, process their products, and then market and distribute those products.

■ ■ ■ ■ ■ ■ ■ ■ ■ ■ ■ ■ ■ ■ ■ ■ ■ ■

consumer cooperative
a retail outlet owned and operated by consumers that sells merchandise to members at reduced prices

service cooperative
a type of cooperative that provides a service rather than a good

Consumer Cooperatives

Stores that are owned and run by consumers are called **consumer cooperatives**. Another name for them is buying or purchasing co-ops. They sell goods to their members at a lower cost. Because they buy the goods they sell in large amounts, they can obtain the goods at a lower cost. They then pass the savings on to members by setting prices low. Some examples of consumer co-ops are discount price clubs and clubs that sell CDs or books. Some co-ops may require each member to work a certain number of hours. Others, like big discount price clubs, charge members a fee each year.

Service Cooperatives

A **service cooperative** is much like a consumer co-op. Its members join together to buy services instead of goods. The goal is not to earn money but to provide services at the lowest possible price. An example of a service co-op is a day-care center. Some companies cannot afford to set up day-care centers for their workers. By joining with other companies in a co-op, their workers can all benefit from a day-care center at affordable prices.

Producer Cooperatives

Producer cooperatives are most common among farmers. The farmers join together to try to get the highest possible price for their farm products. These groups market dairy products like milk and cheese. Other groups market grain, beef, and chicken. In a recent year, producer co-ops sold more than $70 billion worth of farm products.

 CHECKPOINT *How do members benefit from cooperatives?*

What are nonprofit organizations?

The majority of business organizations function to make a profit. **Nonprofit organizations** are more interested in **philanthropy** or providing a service than in making money. The American Red Cross is an example of a nonprofit. Its mission is to prevent and reduce suffering. It helps people after a disaster such as a flood or tornado. It collects and distributes blood to save lives. It supports men and women serving in the armed forces and their families. Other nonprofit organizations are most museums, places where people worship, YMCAs, and the Boy Scouts and Girl Scouts of America.

Nonprofit organizations receive most of their money through donations. Sometimes they sell products or charge a fee for their services. Their income is not taxed by the government.

producer cooperative
an agricultural marketing cooperative that helps members sell their products

nonprofit organization
an institution that functions much like a business but does not operate for the purpose of generating profit

philanthropy
an activity or organization whose purpose is to improve the social or economic welfare of humanity

 Reading Strategy
Summarizing
What are some important details that help you understand how co-ops work?

Innovators

Bill and Melinda Gates

Bill Gates had a vision. He founded the hugely successful Microsoft Corporation. He believed desktop computers could make big changes in business practices. Of course, he was right, and the world has rewarded him. In fact, according to *Forbes* magazine, he is the richest man in the world. Thankfully, he is using that fortune for good purposes. He is giving back through the Bill and Melinda Gates Foundation, the world's largest nonprofit corporation.

Philanthropy is only one part of the foundation's mission. Its goals include finding ways to use technology to improve people's quality of life. This unique "family business," which has been endowed with more than $28.8 billion, remains focused on three key areas. Those areas are a Global Health Program, a Global Development Program, and a U.S. Program geared primarily toward education.

Fast Facts
Melinda French Gates (1965–)
Education: B.A. and M.B.A. at Duke University

Fast Facts
William (Bill) H. Gates III (1955–)
Education: 2+ years at Harvard Univ.
Family Life: Married in 1994, three children
Claim to Fame: Founder of Microsoft Corporation, Cofounder of the Bill and Melinda Gates Foundation

professional organization
a nonprofit organization that works to improve the image, working conditions, and skill levels of people in particular occupations

business association
a group organized to promote the collective business interests of an area or group of similar businesses

Some nonprofit organizations provide services to a special group or to a special part of the country. These include professional business and trade associations, as well as labor unions.

What is the purpose of professional organizations?

Professional organizations bring together people who work in the same field. Many doctors belong to the American Medical Association. Lawyers may be members of the American Bar Association. The National Education Association brings teachers together. Their purpose is to improve the image and working conditions for members of the profession. Professional organizations keep members educated about the newest industry trends. They enforce a code of conduct for their members.

What is a business association?

A **business association** is a group that helps business in many ways. In most cities or states, the group is called the chamber of commerce. Your local chamber of commerce tries to bring new businesses to your area. It keeps business owners informed and helps them keep their businesses running smoothly.

The U.S. Chamber of Commerce is the world's largest business organization. It has more than three million business members. Like the local groups, it promotes U.S. business around the world and tries to keep members well informed.

Fig. 8.6

I NEVER PROMISED YOU HE COULD TALK... I SAID HE "CHATS."

RETURN POLICY

MARK PARISI   ATLANTIC FEATURE SYND. ©2002 MARK PARISI   offthemark.com

Another business organization is the Better Business Bureau (BBB). It is a nonprofit organization organized by local businesses. It protects the citizens and businesses in a community. The BBBs try to keep consumers from being cheated by unethical businesses, as in **Figure 8.6.** If you have a problem with a BBB member, you should report the problem to the organization. They will help you and the business owner solve the problem.

◄ An ethical and successful business will be clear about its return policies. It is in its best interest to keep a good relationship with its customers. Much of its success depends on repeat business.

What are trade associations?

Trade associations are nonprofit organizations that promote the interests of a single industry or trade. Trade associations offer lots of information to their members. They may give information about market trends. The American Marketing Association, for example, is one of the largest sales associations. It tries to promote the image of companies that sell American goods and services. All kinds of industries have trade associations that promote the common interests of members of their industry.

What is the role of labor unions?

A **labor union** is an organized group of workers. Their aim is to improve working conditions, hours, wages, and fringe benefits for members. You will read about the history and role of labor unions in the next chapter.

☑ **CHECKPOINT** *How are nonprofit organizations similar to and different from corporations?*

trade association
a nonprofit organization that promotes the interests of a particular industry

labor union
an organization of workers that tries to improve working conditions, wages, and benefits for its members

Reading Strategy
Summarizing
Look at the types of nonprofit organizations. How are all these ideas related?

SECTION 4 ASSESSMENT

Essential Questions Journal To continue to build a response to the Essential Question, go to your **Essential Questions Journal.**

Guiding Question

1. Use your completed chart to answer this question: How are some businesses organized to help others?

Key Terms and Main Ideas

Directions: On a sheet of paper, write the answer to each question. Use complete sentences.

2. What is an organization owned and operated by a group of individuals called?

3. What is a nonprofit organization?

4. What is a professional organization?

5. What kind of business organization is a chamber of commerce?

Critical Thinking

6. **Analyze Information** Do you think professional organizations and business associations benefit consumers? Explain your reasoning.

7. **Draw Inferences** Some professional organizations do not approve of advertising on the part of their members. State a case where you think advertising would be appropriate. State a case where you think it would be inappropriate.

Section 1–Sole Proprietorships

■ A sole proprietorship is a business owned by one entrepreneur. More than 70 percent of U.S. businesses are sole proprietorships.

■ Sole proprietorships are easier to set up than other businesses. There are few government rules, and the owner has control of the business.

■ The sole proprietor has unlimited personal liability. There may be limited capital, and the business can end when the owner dies or decides to close the business.

Section 2–Partnerships and Franchises

■ A partnership is a business owned by two or more people.

■ In partnerships, partners share responsibility and liability. In limited partnerships, only one partner needs to have responsibility and liability. In limited liability partnerships (LLPs), all partners are limited partners.

■ A business franchise is an agreement between a person and a parent company. The franchisee pays fees to the company for the right to sell certain products or services. The franchisee has to follow rules set up by the parent company.

Section 3–Corporations, Mergers, and Multinationals

■ A corporation is complicated. Shareholders elect a board of directors to make decisions.

■ Horizonal mergers join two or more firms that provide the same goods or services. Vertical mergers join firms involved in different stages of producing the same goods or services.

■ A multinational corporation operates in a number of different countries.

Section 4–Nonprofit Organizations

■ Cooperatives are owned and operated by a group of people for their mutual benefit.

■ Nonprofits do not operate to make a profit; instead, they provide services to help people.

■ Other types of organizations promote the interests of their members.

Section 1
What are thc risks and benefits of a sole proprietorship?

Section 2
What are the risks and benefits of partnerships and franchises?

Section 3
What are the risks and benefits of corporations?

Section 4
How are some businesses organized to help others?

Essential Question, Chapter 8
Why do some businesses succeed and others fail?

John D. Rockefeller, Sr.

John D. Rockefeller, Sr., was one of the wealthiest and most successful entrepreneurs in American history. But Rockefeller's family was not wealthy when he was a young boy. Rockefeller used his knowledge of business to create a leading company in the oil industry. The excerpts about Rockefeller's business life are from Titan: The Life of John D. Rockefeller, *by Ron Chernow.*

"On January 10, 1870, the partnership of Rockefeller, Andrews and Flagler was abolished [ended] and replaced by a joint-stock firm called the Standard Oil Company (Ohio). . . . With $1 million in capital—$11 million in contemporary [today's] money—the new company became an instant landmark in business history. . . . Already a mini-empire, Standard Oil controlled 10 percent of American petroleum refining. . . . From the outset, Rockefeller's plans had a wide streak of megalomania [a desire to do great things]. . . .

Now, on May 1, 1885, . . . Standard Oil moved into its . . . new fortress, a massive, granite, nine-story building. . . . Twenty-six Broadway soon became the world's most famous business address, shorthand for the oil trust itself, evoking its mystery, power, and efficiency. Standard Oil was now America's premier business, with a reach that ramified [spread] into a labyrinth of railroads, banks, and other businesses. . . .

Rockefeller was a unique hybrid in American business: both the instinctive, first-generation entrepreneur who founds a company and the analytic second-generation manager who extends and develops it. . . .

When Rockefeller receded from the business world in the mid-1890s, the average American was earning less than ten dollars per week. Rockefeller's average income—a stupefying [amazing] $10 million per annum [year] in those glory days before income taxes—defied public comprehension. Of more than $250 million in dividends distributed . . . between 1893 and 1901, over a quarter went straight into Rockefeller's coffers [account]. As Standard Oil shares took flight in the late 1890s, one periodical computed that Rockefeller's wealth had appreciated [increased] by $55 million in nine months."

When Rockefeller retired from business, he used his time to share his fortune with others. Rockefeller gave large amounts of money to churches, colleges, and universities, African American education, and medical research. When he died in 1937, Rockefeller was called by some, "the world's greatest . . . organizer in the science of giving."

Document-Based Questions

1. Who was John D. Rockefeller, Sr.?
2. How did Rockefeller's company, Standard Oil, become so powerful?
3. What was Twenty-six Broadway?

4. Do you think any companies today are as powerful as Standard Oil was in the late nineteenth century?
5. What details help you understand Rockefeller's success in business?

Directions: Write answers to each of the following questions. Use complete sentences.

Section 1—Sole Proprietorships

1. What is the greatest disadvantage of sole proprietorships?
2. Sole proprietors cannot usually offer benefits to workers. Why do some people choose to work for them rather than for large companies that offer benefits?
3. What is the purpose of a business license?
4. What is the purpose of zoning laws?

Section 2—Partnerships and Franchises

5. What does the Uniform Partnership Act require of owners?
6. How much is the government involved in partnerships?
7. What are business franchises?
8. Name an advantage and disadvantage a franchise owner faces.

Section 3—Corporations, Mergers, and Multinationals

9. What liability are stockholders subject to?
10. How can stockholders influence the actions of the corporation in which they have ownership?
11. How is a vertical merger formed?
12. Who benefits from the incorporation of a business?
13. What is the purpose of a charter?

Section 4—Nonprofit Organizations

14. What is a nonprofit organization? Give an example of one.
15. What are some ways a nonprofit can make use of the Internet to further its goals?

Economics
on the go

16. If cooperatives offer benefits to their members, why do you think everyone does not belong to them?

17. How do service co-ops and producer co-ops differ?

 Exploring the Essential Question

18. Why are some of the benefits of a sole proprietorship also its greatest disadvantages?

19. Identify the qualities of a successful entrepreneur. Choose the three you think are most important and explain why.

Essential Question Project

20. Complete either of the following activities to answer the Essential Question **Why do some businesses succeed and others fail?**

   - Conduct an interview with either a current or former sole proprietor, partner in a partnership, manager of a corporation, or a franchisee to uncover their personal view of the pros and cons of doing business. Focus on why they thought the business succeeded or failed.

   - Using information on the Internet or in a business magazine or newspaper, research why a specific entrepreneur or business succeeded or failed. Use your worksheet to guide how you collect information.

Essential Questions Journal	To continue to build a response to the Essential Question, go to your **Essential Questions Journal.**

 Test-Taking Tip

It is easier to learn new vocabulary words if you make them part of your speaking and writing in other discussions and subject areas.

Study anytime, anywhere. Download these files today.

Economic Dictionary online
Vocabulary Support in English and Spanish

Audio Review online
Audio Study Guide in English and Spanish

Action Graph online
Animated Charts and Graphs

Visual Glossary online
Animated feature

How the Economy Works online
Animated feature

Download to your computer or mobile device at PearsonSuccessNet.com

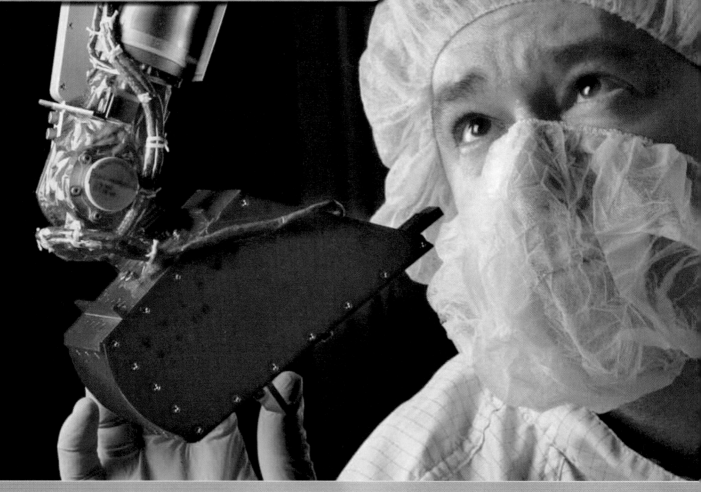

Essential Question, Chapter 9

How can workers best meet the challenges of a changing economy?

Economics
on the go

To study anywhere, anytime, download these online resources at *PearsonSuccessNet.com* ➤

▶ As part of the labor force, you will go to work. There are many different types of jobs. The labor force includes everyone who is at least 16 years old and working or looking for work. Some jobs pay well, while others do not. What is your dream job? What career goals do you have?

In this chapter, you will study some economic trends and how you might be affected. You will learn who makes up the labor force and why some people earn more than others. You will read about the protections and rights that workers have. Finally, you will learn about the history of labor unions, how they work, and the challenges they face.

■ ■

Reading Strategy: Questioning
As you read, ask yourself questions. For example, as you begin Section 1, ask yourself the following:

• Who is in the labor force?

• What jobs will probably grow in the future?

• How is my education related to the wages I will earn?

Asking questions will help you understand and remember more of the information.

Visual Glossary
online

Go to the Visual Glossary Online for an interactive review of **productivity of labor.**

How the Economy Works
online

Go to How the Economy Works Online for an interactive lesson on **collective bargaining.**

Action Graph
online

Go to Action Graph Online for animated versions of key charts and graphs.

Objectives

- **Describe** how trends in the labor force are tracked.
- **Analyze** occupational trends from the past and present.
- **Summarize** how the U.S. labor force is changing.
- **Explain** trends in the wages and benefits that are paid to U.S. workers.

labor force
all nonmilitary people who are employed or unemployed

Guiding Question
How do economic trends affect workers?

Copy this chart and fill it in as you read.

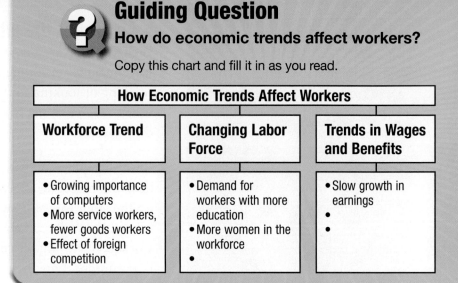

How Economic Trends Affect Workers

Workforce Trend	Changing Labor Force	Trends in Wages and Benefits
• Growing importance of computers • More service workers, fewer goods workers • Effect of foreign competition	• Demand for workers with more education • More women in the workforce •	• Slow growth in earnings • •

▶ **Economics and You** Have you considered how you want to earn a living when you get out of school? You may have been focused on a career goal for as long as you can remember. On the other hand, you may not have a clue. Is your goal to help others, earn a lot of money, or travel the world? Whatever career you decide on, you will have to be prepared for change.

Principles in Action Economic trends affect workers in many ways. Over the past 20 years, the U.S. economy has changed. It has moved from a manufacturing economy to a service economy. This change has resulted in a **labor force** that is better educated. The labor force includes all nonmilitary people who are employed or unemployed. Some industries, like technology and financial services, have grown a lot. The number of manufacturing jobs has declined.

How is the labor force tracked?

The Bureau of Labor Statistics (BLS) of the U.S. Department of Labor keeps track of the labor force. Economists consider people to be employed if they are 16 years or older and meet at least one of the following requirements:

- have worked at least 1 hour for pay in the past week
- have worked 15 or more hours without pay in a family business, such as a farm or a family-owned store
- have held jobs but are not working because of illnesses, vacations, labor disputes, or bad weather

People who have more than one job are counted only once.

The BLS counts the number of people working and those who are unemployed, or not working. People are counted as unemployed if the following are true:

1. They are temporarily without work.
2. They are not working but have looked for jobs within the last 4 weeks.

Some groups of people are not part of the labor force. One group is made up of people who once looked for work but have given up. Another group is made up of full-time students, parents staying home to raise children, and retirees. They are not considered unemployed and thus are not counted in the job figures. **Figure 9.1** summarizes the groups that make up the U.S. labor force. To be counted as unemployed, then, a person either must have work lined up for the future, or must be actively searching for a new job.

 CHECKPOINT *What important information can we learn from the Bureau of Labor Statistics?*

What are some occupational trends?

In the beginning, the United States was a nation of farmers. There were few jobs besides farming. The Industrial Revolution arrived in the Northeast in the 1800s. The coming of the machine age changed the economy. It created new jobs in mills making cloth, shoes, and other manufactured items.

By the 1900s, the U.S. economy had a lot of heavy manufacturing. New corporate empires were born. John D. Rockefeller entered the oil refining business in 1863. Andrew Carnegie began to work with steel in the 1870s. Henry Ford created his automobile company in 1903. Thousands of people worked for these huge firms. In the 1950s there was a boom in electronics, led by radio and television. Many new factory jobs were created. Thousands of people in the Northeast and Midwest worked for huge companies such as General Electric, Westinghouse, Carrier, and Goodyear.

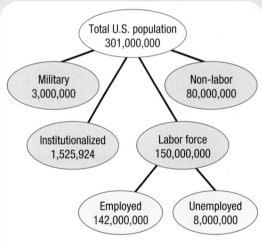

Fig. 9.1 Composition of the U.S. Labor Force

SOURCE: *The 2008 Statistical Abstract of the United States.*
Note: Total U.S. population includes 66.5 million children under 16 years old. That segment of the population is not reflected in this chart's labor and non-labor statistics.

GRAPH SKILLS

This flowchart shows how the Bureau of Labor Statistics defines who is in the labor force and who is employed or unemployed.

1. What parts form the total U.S. population?
2. How does being unemployed differ from not being part of the labor force?

The mass production of computers also created many new jobs. The so-called Information Age began in the 1970s. Many people worked making computers. There was also a big growth in jobs that used computers. Even some traditional jobs such as trucking, farming, and car sales required basic computer skills. By the early 2000s, more than half of American workers were using computers on the job. More than a quarter of all workers in the farming, forestry, and fishing industries, as well as manufacturing and construction, were using computers.

What are the three basic sectors of the labor force?

Economists group workers into three basic types, or **sectors.** The smallest sector in the United States today is the agricultural sector. Until about 100 years ago, it was the largest. In the past, many people earned a living by farming. Today, farm workers make up less than 3 percent of all workers. Yet today's farmers produce more goods than ever before. This increase in the efficiency of production has been made possible by new technology. Better seed, better farming techniques, better water management, and new machinery and equipment have all helped.

A second sector, manufacturing/construction, produces most of a country's goods. Around 1920, there was a change. It was the first time the number of jobs in this sector was greater than the number of jobs in agriculture. Many people left the farms for better-paying jobs in the cities.

The third sector of the labor force, the service sector, is the largest. It is still growing. People in the service sector include anyone doing a service for other people. This sector includes people who work in restaurants and shops. Other service industries are entertainment, education, and healthcare. Financial services like banking, insurance, and investment are also part of the service sector.

What are some effects of international competition?

While the service sector is growing, the manufacturing sector in the United States is shrinking. In 1990, almost 17.7 million Americans worked in manufacturing industries. Fifteen years later, the number had fallen to 14.2 million. Many workers have been laid off. Some plants have closed or moved. Some people lost their jobs because machines now do the jobs they used to do.

In the past, American workers in American factories made most goods sold in the United States. Today, capital and labor can be easily moved. American firms can build factories and hire workers in other countries. There, wages and other costs are lower. American stores can buy goods made in foreign countries to sell in the United States.

Many large firms have begun **outsourcing** work. Outsourcing is the hiring of overseas workers to do jobs that American workers used to do. This is a problem for Americans who used to work in the manufacturing sector. They have to find new work. Many go back to school or enter job-training programs to gain new skills.

How does the shift to service jobs show the effects of supply and demand?

Manufacturing jobs generally require few skills. Demand for skilled service workers is rising. As it does, their wages go up. These higher wages cause more people to train for these jobs to meet the demand. At the same time, the demand for manufacturing workers is going down. There is now a surplus of these workers. As the demand for them drops, so do their wages. They find that they must learn new skills if they want to earn more money.

In recent years, businesses have outsourced jobs of even highly skilled workers. By the early 2000s, companies were hiring many highly skilled workers overseas. Among these were computer engineers and software programmers. This trend has also affected other fields, such as auto design and medical services.

✔ **CHECKPOINT** *Why do companies engage in outsourcing?*

How is the labor force changing?

Not only have jobs changed—workers have also changed. In the 1950s, a typical American worker was a white male high-school graduate. He worked 40 hours a week. He probably hoped to stay at his job until retiring at age 65. Not anymore. Today, more women and minorities are in the workforce. Someone entering the workforce can expect to have four or five different jobs during his or her working life. Many retire at around age 62 or even earlier.

Reading Strategy
Questioning
Ask yourself, "How has international competition affected the U.S. economy?"

outsourcing
sending work to an outside source, often in another country, to cut costs

learning effect
the idea that education increases the efficiency of production and results in higher wages

How important is education?

To get jobs, people must have human capital. This is the education, training, and experience people have that make them useful on the job. More and more, a high-school diploma alone is not enough. To get and succeed at a job, people need more education. A good education, however, requires money, time, and effort. Those workers who have the education are rewarded for their hard work with higher pay.

Economists have two explanations for the connection between education and wages. One explanation is called the **learning effect.** It says that education increases the efficiency of production and thus results in higher wages. Look at the numbers in **Figure 9.2.** They show that college-educated workers have higher incomes than high-school dropouts. On average, the more education a person has, the higher his or her income. Some professional people such as doctors and lawyers have higher degrees. They earn more than people with bachelor's degrees.

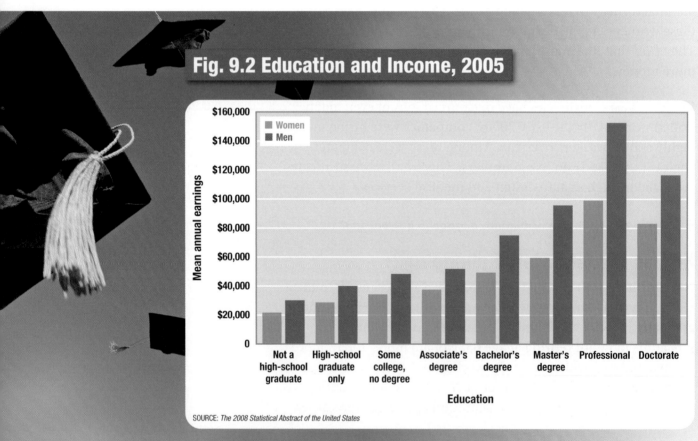

Fig. 9.2 Education and Income, 2005

SOURCE: *The 2008 Statistical Abstract of the United States*

Action Graph
online

For an animated version of this graph, visit **PearsonSuccessNet.com**

GRAPH SKILLS

This bar chart shows that higher levels of education correspond to higher income.

1. When do men and women see the greatest increase in income?

2. What can be concluded about the opportunity costs for men and women of moving up to that higher-paying level?

The second explanation is called the **screening effect.** It says that finishing college is a signal to employers. It shows that someone is intelligent and hardworking. Employers are looking for workers who have these qualities. According to this explanation, a college degree does not increase the efficiency of production. It just identifies people who may be good workers because of the skills they have.

screening effect
the idea that a college degree is a signal to employers that a person is intelligent and hardworking

contingent employment
a temporary or part-time job

How has the role of women in the labor force changed?

Women were not always looked at as an important part of the labor force. From early days in U.S. history, some women worked outside the home. Often, these women were unmarried farm workers. They were paid less than men and had few rights. In the 1860s, during the Civil War, women replaced men on farms and in factories. By 1930, more than 10 million women were in the labor force. Women most often worked as secretaries, typists, clerks, or servants in other people's homes.

During World War II, women again replaced men who left the farm and factory to go fight. After the war, the number of women workers dropped as the soldiers returned. The 1960s brought big changes. More and more women joined the labor force. In 1960, almost 38 percent of women belonged to the labor force. By 2005, that rate had jumped to nearly 60 percent.

What factors affect the number of women in the labor force?

Most of the growth in the U.S. labor force will come from women. There are several reasons why. One is that women are becoming better educated. Employers generally want workers with the best education. They are also willing to pay these workers more. More women want to work because they expect to earn more. Today, fewer jobs call for physical strength. Instead, jobs require brainpower and personal skills. This places men and women on equal footing.

Why is the number of temporary workers growing?

There is another important change in the labor force. Full-time workers are being replaced with part-time and temporary workers. These temporary and part-time jobs are known as **contingent employment.** In the past, many of these temporary workers were unskilled day workers. Now these workers include software engineers and attorneys. Companies hire them for a certain amount of time and for a set rate. When the workers complete the part of the project they were hired for, they are let go.

guest workers
foreign-born workers who are allowed to live and work in the United States for a set amount of time

Experts provide a number of reasons for the growing number of temporary employees.

1. ***Flexible work arrangements*** These allow firms to easily adjust their workforces to changing demand. When demand drops, they can lay off temporary workers or cut workers' hours. They do not have to pay unneeded workers. When business picks up, companies can rehire whatever workers they need.

2. ***Temporary workers in many industries are paid less*** Firms often pay their full-time workers better. Hiring more temporary workers cuts costs.

3. ***Letting temporary workers go is easier*** Laying off full-time workers is not easy and is costly. Many employers give full-time employees severance pay. This is the several weeks' worth of wages paid to laid-off workers when they are no longer needed. Employers do not have to make these payments to temporary workers.

4. ***Some workers might actually prefer temporary work*** Some workers may like temporary work better than full-time jobs. However, government studies show that most temporary workers would rather be working full time.

What effect do foreign-born workers have on the workforce?

In 2005, foreign-born workers amounted to about 22 million people, or almost 15 percent of all workers in the United States.

Many immigrant workers come to the United States to live permanently. Some foreign-born workers are **guest workers.** They are allowed to live and work in the United States for a set amount of time. The effect of these immigrants has caused much debate.

Some people think immigrant workers hold down the wages of Americans. The idea of supply and demand is at work here. As more immigrants enter the country, they increase the supply of workers. With greater supply than demand, employers can pay their workers less. Some say this causes wages of American-born workers to drop and increases competition for jobs.

Other people think immigrant workers fill an important role in the economy. Many immigrant workers do jobs that Americans are unwilling to do because the wages are low. As a result, important work gets done that would not be done otherwise. Also, companies that hire immigrants can charge less for their goods and services. This means that consumers pay lower prices for those same goods and services.

✓ **CHECKPOINT** *How are education and income connected?*

What are the trends in wages and benefits?

American workers are paid more than those in many other countries. In recent years, however, the growth in earnings has slowed. The government said that average weekly earnings in the United States in 1980 were $275. That is nearly $590 in today's dollars. This sounds like a lot, but the actual increase is much less. To be able to compare, economists have to figure in the effect of **inflation**—the rise of prices over time. If you adjust for inflation, average wages rose to just under $281 in 1980 dollars in July 2007. In other words, weekly wages went up only about $6 in 27 years.

Why have average wages not increased more?

One reason is average wages have not increased because of more competition from foreign companies. Increased competition in many industries, such as trucking and air travel, may have forced firms to cut employees' wages. The increased use of temporary work has also kept wages down.

inflation
increase in prices over time

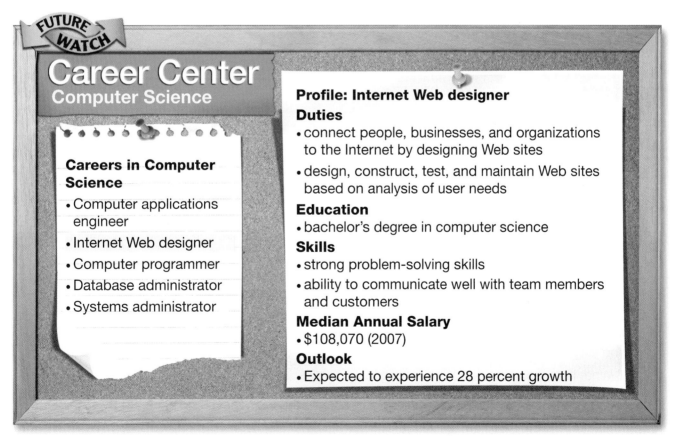

FUTURE WATCH

Career Center
Computer Science

Careers in Computer Science
- Computer applications engineer
- Internet Web designer
- Computer programmer
- Database administrator
- Systems administrator

Profile: Internet Web designer

Duties
- connect people, businesses, and organizations to the Internet by designing Web sites
- design, construct, test, and maintain Web sites based on analysis of user needs

Education
- bachelor's degree in computer science

Skills
- strong problem-solving skills
- ability to communicate well with team members and customers

Median Annual Salary
- $108,070 (2007)

Outlook
- Expected to experience 28 percent growth

benefits

anything besides wages provided to workers, such as paid vacations, retirement plans, and medical insurance

compensation

payment to an employee for his or her work with the company, including wages and benefits

What are benefits?

Fifty years ago, workers expected only their weekly wages from employers. Now, workers expect more **benefits**. Benefits are anything extra given to workers besides wages. The most common benefits are paid vacations, retirement plans, and medical insurance. For example, health insurance costs a lot of money. Many workers cannot pay for insurance by themselves. They expect their employers to help pay for the insurance.

By 2005, benefits added $7.87 an hour to the cost of workers. Benefits now make up nearly 30 percent of full-time workers' **compensation.** Compensation is payment given to an employee for his or her work with the company. Because compensation includes both wages and benefits, it adds up to a large cost for employers.

Employers are finding that the rising cost of benefits has cut into their profits. They are hiring more temporary workers and outsourcing more work to cut the cost of these benefits. If benefits costs continue to rise, companies may cut back or limit them. This, of course, will be very unpopular with workers.

 CHECKPOINT *What are three reasons American workers' wages have not risen more in recent years?*

SECTION 1 ASSESSMENT

Essential Questions Journal
To continue to build a response to the Essential Question, go to your **Essential Questions Journal.**

 Guiding Question

1. Use your completed chart to answer this question: How do economic trends affect workers?

Key Terms and Main Ideas

Directions: On a sheet of paper, write the answer to each question. Use complete sentences.

2. Who is included in the labor force?

3. (a) What is outsourcing? (b) What economic changes have brought it about?

4. The U.S. economy has changed from an economy based on agriculture to one based on manufacturing and then to an economy based on service industries. What has brought about these changes?

5. How has the Industrial Revolution affected American society?

Critical Thinking

6. **Draw Conclusions** Why do temporary workers earn less than other types of workers?

7. **Recognize Cause and Effect** What effect does the increase in benefits paid by employers have on workers' wages?

Objectives

- **Analyze** how supply and demand in the labor market affect wages.
- **Describe** why workers earn different wages.
- **Explain** why some people receive less than the equilibrium wage.
- **Identify** other factors affecting wage levels.

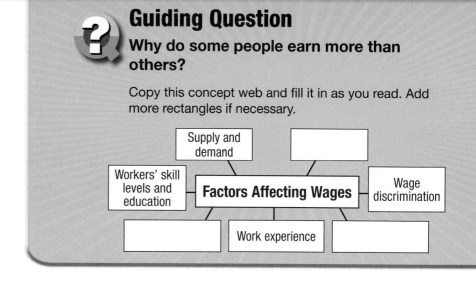

Guiding Question

Why do some people earn more than others?

Copy this concept web and fill it in as you read. Add more rectangles if necessary.

Supply and demand

Workers' skill levels and education

Factors Affecting Wages

Wage discrimination

Work experience

Reading Strategy

Questioning

You learned about supply and demand in Unit 2 of this text. Ask yourself, "How will that help me understand the labor market?"

derived demand

demand that depends on the demand for some other service or good

▶ **Economics and You** How important is it to you to earn a lot of money? If it is very important, then you had better think carefully about what you want to do for a living. Some jobs and professions are very well paid. A top-notch surgeon can charge $150,000 for one operation. A lawyer might make $600 for an hour-long consultation, while the clerk at the local store might make $8 an hour. What determines the size of your paycheck?

Principles in Action Some people earn more than others because workers' wages are largely a matter of supply and demand. Like eggs or airplanes or pet iguanas, labor is a commodity that is bought and sold. Wages are high for jobs where supply is low and demand is high. Doctors, for example, are in relatively short supply but in high demand. Relatively large numbers of people become sales clerks compared to the number of such jobs available. As a result, these workers earn less than doctors. In fact, workers' earnings—the price of labor—depend on conditions in the labor market.

How do supply and demand affect the labor market?

Private firms and the government demand labor. They hire workers to produce goods and services. In most labor markets, many firms compete with one another for workers.

Demand for labor is a **derived demand.** This means that the demand is derived from, or depends on, some other demand. For example, the demand for cooks in a market depends on the demand for restaurant meals.

productivity of labor
the amount of goods and services workers can produce in a given time period

How does the labor market affect wages?

Workers are usually paid based on the value of what they produce. For example, a cook who is productive, or gets a lot done, is more likely to be promoted to a higher paying job than one who works more slowly. **Productivity of labor** is the amount of goods and services workers can produce in a given time. Suppose a new restaurant opens. This increases the demand for cooks. The competition for cooks will push up the wages the cooks earn.

The supply of labor comes from people willing to work for wages. The graph to the left in **Figure 9.3** shows the law of supply. The higher the wage, the larger the quantity of labor supplied. In other words, the more a job pays, the greater the number of people who want that job.

Look at the demand curve for labor, shown at right in **Figure 9.3**. It shows how the law of demand affects the price of labor. The higher the price of labor, the lower the demand for workers. Restaurants are more likely to hire more cooks at $12 an hour than at $16 an hour. The lower cost means the restaurants can earn more profits.

What is the equilibrium wage?

When the market is in equilibrium, the quantity of a good supplied will equal the quantity demanded. There is also equilibrium in the labor market. It is called the equilibrium wage.

Fig. 9.3 Labor Supply and Demand

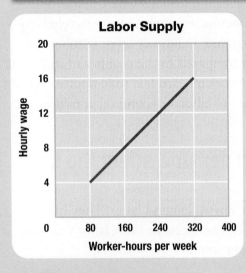

Action Graph
online

For an animated version of this graph, visit **PearsonSuccessNet.com**

GRAPH SKILLS

These graphs show (a) how the quantity of labor demanded varies depending on the price of labor, and (b) how the labor supply varies depending on the wage rate.

1. Why does the supply curve slope up to the right?
2. According to the demand curve, if each cook works a 40-hour workweek, how many cooks will be hired at $12 an hour and $20 an hour?

The **equilibrium wage** is the wage at which the quantity of labor demanded is equal to the quantity of labor supplied. On a graph, the equilibrium wage is the point at which the supply and demand curves cross. **Figure 9.4** shows this. Equilibrium occurs when employers can hire as many workers as are willing and able to work.

How does this affect how much you will earn working in a pet store or a grocery store next summer? It depends on supply and demand in your area. Maybe your local pet stores and grocery stores do not hire many extra workers during the summer. But there are a lot of teenagers who want to work. The result will be a relatively low wage. On the other hand, maybe stores want to hire a lot of teenagers. If only a few teens want to work, the wage will be higher.

✔ **CHECKPOINT** *What determines the equilibrium wage of labor in a particular market?*

Why do workers earn different wages?

The reason not all workers earn the same wage is simple. The supply and demand for different jobs are not the same. For example, many pro athletes earn millions of dollars. Why? The supply of star athletes is very small, but the demand is very great. On the other hand, people who work at amusement parks or in big discount stores earn little. The supply of these kinds of workers is greater than the demand.

Why are some skills valued more than others?

There are several other reasons why workers earn different wages. One is differences in ability. Very few people can write songs that others want to hear. Some people type faster than others. Others are good at selling. Some skills are valued more than others. The skills most valued get the best wages.

There are differences in effort and jobs. Some workers are willing to work long hours to earn extra money. Some jobs are very dangerous. The work of police officers and firefighters is dangerous. People in these jobs often earn more money than workers with less-dangerous jobs. Airline pilots are responsible for moving people safely from place to place over long distances. They receive higher pay than most workers.

Work experience makes a difference. Workers who have had the same job for a long time earn more money than new hires. Employers believe that experienced workers are better at their jobs than workers with less experience.

equilibrium wage
the point at which the quantity of labor demanded is equal to the quantity of labor supplied

Fig. 9.4 Equilibrium Wage

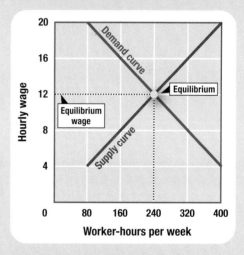

GRAPH SKILLS

This graph shows the wage at which the quantity demanded equals the quantity supplied.

1. Explain why a stable wage means stable restaurant prices.
2. Under what circumstances would the equilibrium wage be $8 an hour?

Action Graph
online

For an animated version of this graph, visit **PearsonSuccessNet.com**

unskilled labor
work that requires no special skills, education, or training

semiskilled labor
work that requires some training and education

skilled labor
work that requires special skills and training

professional labor
work that requires advanced skills and education

wage discrimination
treating a person differently and paying him or her less because of the social group to which he or she belongs

Education and training also affect differences in pay. Workers with more education or special training earn more than those with less education. College graduates earn a lot more money than high school graduates.

What are the four groups of skill level?

Jobs are often grouped into four skill levels:

1. *Unskilled labor* These jobs do not need special skills, education, or training. Workers in unskilled jobs have skills, but their jobs require little training. Someone who clears tables or welcomes people in a restaurant may be very skilled. However, that person's job is still grouped as unskilled. Unskilled workers include dishwashers, janitors, and farm workers. They are usually paid by the hour.

2. *Semiskilled labor* These jobs require some training and education. Semiskilled workers often work with machines and other types of equipment. They usually earn an hourly wage. They include lifeguards, cable TV workers, telephone operators, and many construction and factory workers.

3. *Skilled labor* These jobs need special skills and training. Skilled workers usually earn an hourly wage. They include auto mechanics, bank tellers, plumbers, and firefighters.

4. *Professional labor* These jobs require more skills and education than any other group. Professionals have college degrees and a lot of special training. Professionals are usually workers who receive a salary, or a fixed amount per year. Lawyers, doctors, teachers, dentists, bankers, and members of the clergy are professionals.

✔ **CHECKPOINT** *How do education, training, and experience affect wages?*

Why are some people paid less than the equilibrium wage?

Some people are paid less because of the social group to which they belong. For instance, sometimes women and members of minority groups receive lower wages than white male workers. This difference in pay is known as **wage discrimination.** Some employers tried to defend wage discrimination against women. They claimed that men needed the money to support families, while women were just working to earn extra money. Minority members were discriminated against because of prejudice. Prejudice is an opinion formed without knowledge or consideration of the facts. Both the U.S. government and many state governments have passed laws to end wage discrimination.

What laws have made wage discrimination illegal?

The U.S. Congress passed several antidiscrimination laws in the 1960s. One of these laws was the Equal Pay Act of 1963. This law required that men and women in the same workplace, doing the same job, receive the same pay. Title VII of the Civil Rights Act of 1964 was another important law. It made job discrimination on the basis of race, sex, color, religion, or nationality against the law. The Civil Rights Act also created the Equal Employment Opportunity Commission (EEOC). This group enforces the law. Workers who believe they have not been treated fairly can complain to the EEOC.

What does the term *glass ceiling* mean?

Despite these laws, women still earn less than men on average. The earnings gap has closed over the years but not completely. Some women still find they cannot rise to a position of leadership in a corporation. When women are prevented from advancing simply because they are female, it is called hitting a **glass ceiling.**

✔ CHECKPOINT *What groups have been hurt by wage discrimination?*

What other factors affect wages?

In addition to laws outlawing discrimination, several other factors can affect wages. These include minimum wage laws, workplace safety laws, employer actions, and labor unions.

In 1938, Congress passed the Fair Labor Standards Act. This law created a minimum wage. It set up a minimum wage of 25 cents an hour. Workers who worked more than 40 hours per week had to be paid **overtime.** Overtime was also paid if extra work was done on weekends or holidays. Many states and some cities also have minimum wage laws that set higher wages than the national law. Most of the time businesses must pay their workers the highest minimum wage. Because of these laws, employers may be forced to pay more than the equilibrium wage for unskilled labor.

Supporters of the minimum wage argue that it helps the poorest American workers earn enough to support themselves. Those who are against the minimum wage say it actually hurts poor people. It causes a drop in the number of unskilled workers demanded. In other words, workers will earn more, but companies will hire fewer of them.

glass ceiling
the limit believed to prevent women from rising to a position of leadership in corporations because they are women

overtime
extra money paid to employees for work beyond 40 hours per week or on weekends or holidays

What safety laws has Congress passed?

Congress has passed laws requiring certain safety standards in the workplace. These may also affect wages. If a law or policy makes the job safer, it is less dangerous. This may lower wages, because workers are willing to work for less when jobs are safer. Holding wages down cuts the employer's costs. Of course, it costs the employer money to make the workplace safer. These extra costs may be more than the savings from the lower wage.

How can employers' actions affect wage levels?

Employers may also take actions to try to affect wage levels. For example, a company might try to cut labor costs by having machines do the work of people. In other words, employers can replace human capital with physical capital.

Even organizations that cannot use technology to replace labor can reduce their costs in other ways. As you learned in Section 1, companies may outsource jobs to other countries where labor is cheaper. They may also choose to hire temporary workers.

How do unions affect wages?

A labor union is a group of workers who try to make sure workers are treated fairly. Labor unions work to improve working conditions, wages, and benefits for their members. Union members in the United States tend to earn higher wages than workers who do not belong to a union. In 2005, the average union wage was nearly $5 an hour higher than the average wage for nonunion wage earners. Union workers make $200 more in a 40-hour workweek than nonunion workers.

Economics & YOU

Safety and Minimum Wage Laws

Many jobs teenagers hold are closely regulated by the federal government. It restricts hours and sets safety standards for workers under 18. *It is against the law for teens to operate a forklift because of the dangers.*

RESTRICTED AREA
NO ONE UNDER 18 ALLOWED TO OPERATE MACHINERY

PRODUCE

Oranges
$1.69 lb

Some jobs, like stocking shelves, pay the minimum wage and are well suited for young workers.

Some economists believe that unions can lower the wages of nonunion members. In addition, some unions have used **featherbedding** when working on labor contracts. Featherbedding is when a union agrees to a labor contract that keeps unnecessary workers on a company's payroll. An example of this practice occurred in the railroad industry. Caboosemen were necessary in the early days of railroads. They rode at the back of the train to operate a rear brake that stopped the train. Eventually, new technology let the engineer at the front of the train operate the rear brakes. In spite of this new technology, unions kept caboosemen on the payroll using featherbedding.

Other economists argue that without the ability to organize, workers have little power compared to their employers. Unless the workers join together, employers can decide wage levels and working conditions. Because employers can usually find replacement workers, their employees have little real choice. The next section will trace the history of unions in the United States. It will discuss some of their advantages and disadvantages.

 CHECKPOINT *What three actions can employers take to reduce the cost of wages?*

 Reading Strategy
Questioning
Ask yourself, "What did I learn that helps me understand the labor force?"

featherbedding
the agreement of a labor union to a labor contract that keeps unnecessary workers on a company's payroll

SECTION 2 ASSESSMENT

Essential Questions Journal To continue to build a response to the Essential Question, go to your **Essential Questions Journal.**

Guiding Question

1. Use your completed concept web to answer this question: Why do some people earn more than others?

Key Terms and Main Ideas

Directions: On a sheet of paper, write the answer to each question. Use complete sentences.

2. Why is a demand for labor a derived demand?

3. If an advertising firm does not attract much business, how is its productivity affected?

4. How does skilled labor differ from professional labor? Give an example of each.

5. How does a labor union try to improve conditions for its worker members?

Critical Thinking

6. **Make Comparisons** Choose two occupations. One should pay high wages, and the other should pay low wages. Explain the reasons for the difference in wages in terms of supply and demand.

7. **Synthesize Information** How do employers benefit from workplace safety laws?

Objectives

- **Describe** why U.S. workers have formed labor unions.

- **Summarize** the history of the U.S. labor movement.

- **Analyze** reasons for the decline of the labor movement.

- **Explain** how labor and management negotiate contracts.

Guiding Question

How do labor unions support the interests of workers?

Copy this chart and fill it in as you read.

How Unions Promote Workers' Interests	
Features of Union Contract	**Tools for Persuading Companies**
• Better wages and benefits • Better working conditions • Job security for members •	• Collective bargaining • Strikes • Mediation •

▶ **Economics and You** What comes to mind when you think of Labor Day? Do you think of it as the holiday that marks the end of summer? The holiday began in 1882. Labor leader Peter J. McGuire suggested a day to celebrate the American worker. On September 5, 1882, some 10,000 workers marched in a parade in New York City. The parade was led by a labor group called the Knights of Labor. The Knights later urged making the day a holiday. Twelve years later, Congress made Labor Day a federal holiday to be spent any way workers wished.

Principles in Action Labor unions try to improve wages, benefits, and working conditions for workers. One of their most important goals is collective bargaining. In collective bargaining, representatives of labor and management sit down together to try to reach an agreement. Wages, benefits, and safety in the workplace are important to all workers, young and old.

Why do workers join labor unions?

Between the Civil War and 1900, the United States changed. It had been a nation of farmers. By 1900, it became the greatest industrial power in the world. The new business leaders had almost complete control over work hours and pay.

The workers wanted to do something to improve their working conditions. They organized themselves into labor unions. A labor union is a group of workers who join to promote their common good. Many workers thought that joining together gave them some control over their wages and working conditions. They knew it was hard for one worker to change how an employer acted. By banding together, workers had much more power.

Today, only about one out of eight workers in the United States belongs to a labor union. In the past, though, unions had a stronger influence on the nation's economy. The union movement took shape over the course of more than a century. It faced many obstacles along the way. **Figure 9.5** highlights some of the key events in the U.S. labor movement.

In this section, you will learn how labor unions rose to power in the United States. By knowing how they rose to power, you can better understand the role of labor unions today.

✔ **CHECKPOINT** *What is a labor union?*

What was work like in the 1800s?

Working conditions changed during the early and mid-1800s as a result of the Industrial Revolution. Labor unions developed largely as a result of these changes. Early factory jobs were very hard. Some people worked 12- to 16-hour days, 7 days a week. Pay was low, and working conditions were unsafe. Men, women, and young children worked in factories. Some of the machines were dangerous. Many people lost their sight, hearing, and even fingers, arms, and legs. Once they were hurt, workers often lost their jobs. They were not given any benefits.

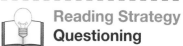
Reading Strategy
Questioning
Ask yourself, "What do I already know about working conditions in the 1800s that will help me understand the details in this paragraph?"

Fig. 9.5 Some Key Events in the U.S. Labor Movement

1869	1886	1900	1911	1919	1938	1947	1955
Knights of Labor founded	Haymarket Riot stirs antiunion feelings Samuel Gompers founds the American Federation of Labor (AFL)	International Ladies' Garment Workers Union (ILGWU) founded	Triangle Shirtwaist Company fire kills 146, spurring action on workplace safety	John L. Lewis becomes president of United Mine Workers	AFL splinter group becomes the independent Congress of Industrial Organizations (CIO) Fair Labor Standards Act creates minimum wage, bans child labor, requires overtime pay	Taft-Hartley Act allows states to pass right-to-work laws	AFL and CIO merge to create AFL-CIO

CHART SKILLS

The U.S. labor movement began in the 1800s. At that time, the rise of factories led to difficult and dangerous working conditions.

1. Why do you think violence marked the early years of the labor movement?
2. Describe the relationship shown above between labor laws and union membership in the 1900s.

Innovators

Walter Reuther

"There is no greater calling than to serve your fellow men. There is no greater contribution than to help the weak." Measured by his own words, Walter Reuther was a natural leader. Born to poor immigrant parents, Reuther had little formal education. But his upbringing fostered in him a sense of courage and conviction. This helped him fight for worker rights and become one of the greatest leaders in the American labor movement.

As a local union boss in the United Auto Workers, Reuther used sit-down strikes to help organize manufacturing plants. On May 26, 1937, Reuther and three colleagues clashed with Ford Motor Company security forces outside a plant in Detroit, Michigan. News reporters witnessed a bloodbath as Reuther and his friends were badly beaten. The incident caused public outrage against Ford and was a key factor in helping the UAW gain public sympathy and support for worker rights. It was a strategic victory.

Reuther went on to make the UAW a major labor force, eventually becoming its president in 1947. He was a pioneer. He was one of the first American labor organizers to successfully negotiate for benefits that American workers take for granted today: decent hourly wages, paid vacations, health insurance, and employer-paid pensions.

> ### Fast Facts
>
> **Walter Reuther (1907–1970)**
> **Education:** Received H.S. diploma from Detriot City College at age 22
> **Claim to Fame:** Early leader of the United Auto Workers

---

strike
the act of stopping work to argue for better pay, benefits, and working conditions

yellow-dog contract
contract that some employers forced their workers to sign that made the workers promise not to join a union

Why did unions become popular?

As early as the 1790s, some workers began organizing protests. Skilled workers such as shoemakers and carpenters began to form unions to protect their interests. The chief tool of these early unions was the **strike.** This is the act of stopping work to argue for better pay and working conditions. Employers reacted by firing and replacing workers who tried to organize.

The man who truly started the U.S. labor movement was Samuel Gompers. Gompers believed unions should focus on improving working conditions and getting workers higher pay. In 1886, Gompers founded the American Federation of Labor (AFL). The AFL focused on three goals: higher wages, shorter hours, and safer work environments.

What were employers' attitudes toward early unions?

Employers fired early union organizers because they saw them as threats to the company. Some employers forced workers to sign **yellow-dog contracts** before they would hire them. In the contracts, the workers promised not to join the union. If they joined the union later, they would be fired for not following the contract they had signed.

At first the government was against unions. Companies used **injunctions** to force striking employees back to work. An injunction is a court order preventing some activity. The government's use of injunctions against labor unions continued for many years. This made it harder for unions to organize workers. However, the government's attitude slowly began to change. Congress passed new laws protecting the rights of workers.

Why did union membership rise in the 1930s?

The 1930s and the Great Depression changed many things. Production fell. Many people were out of work. People lost their homes and businesses. To get the economy moving again, Congress passed new laws. These laws expanded workers' rights and contributed to a rise in union strength. Membership grew and was at its highest in the 1940s. At that time, 35 percent of the nation's nonfarm workforce belonged to a union.

☑ **CHECKPOINT** *Why did union membership rise in the 1930s?*

What led to the decline of the labor movement?

As they grew, some unions began to use their power unwisely. You read about featherbedding in Section 2. Some unions tried to keep unnecessary job positions in order to keep more members employed. As a result, some companies found that unions could get in the way of efficiency.

In an effort to limit union power, Congress passed the Taft-Hartley Act in 1947. This law let states pass **right-to-work laws.** These laws make it illegal to require a worker to join a union. Today, most right-to-work states are in the South.

Why is union membership dropping?

By 2002, union membership dropped to just 13.2 percent of the labor force. Right-to-work laws may be one of the several reasons for a decline in union membership in recent decades. There are a few other reasons why union membership is falling.

1. Unions are strongest among unskilled and semiskilled workers. These workers are still called **blue-collar workers.** The decline of blue-collar manufacturing jobs has caused many union jobs to disappear.
   Unions are weakest among **white-collar workers.** White-collar workers include professionals who usually earn a weekly salary. White-collar jobs are growing because of the market's shift toward service industries. Some white-collar workers who belong to unions work in the public sector.

injunction
a court order that prevents some activity

right-to-work law
a law against forcing a worker to join a union

blue-collar worker
someone who performs manual labor, often in a manufacturing job, and who earns an hourly wage

white-collar worker
someone who works in a professional or office job and who usually earns a weekly salary

Fig. 9.6 How the Economy Works

How can **collective bargaining** settle differences?

Conflicts commonly arise between workers and company management. If those conflicts are not resolved, then disgruntled workers can threaten to make it difficult for a company to operate. Collective bargaining allows a labor union and management to resolve their differences through a give-and-take process. This usually results in a new contract.

1 Each side defines an agenda before sitting down to negotiate. In the case of the local union, representatives meet to discuss strategy and concessions they wish to get from management. These contract disputes usually involve issues such as higher pay and better benefits. Management, on the other hand, will seek to win concessions from labor that will allow the company to increase efficiency and production, which could lead to higher profits.

2 Union leaders hold a series of negotiating sessions with management. Both sides list and explain their needs. To agree on a new contract, discussions revolve around strategies to satisfy those needs in ways that are beneficial for all.

Negotiations

Some people believe that workers such as teachers and postal workers should not be able to strike. Members of these unions disagree. They argue that unions are needed for these workers just as they are needed for other workers.

2. There have always been large numbers of union members in some industries, such as the steel industry. Industries such as car-making and textiles have been hurt by foreign competition in recent years. (The textile industry makes cloth products.) As a result, these industries have laid off workers. This reduction of workers has cut into union strength.

3. The changing labor market has added to the decline. A growing number of workers work part-time jobs. There are more female workers and teenage workers. All of these workers are less likely to join unions.

4. The shift in jobs to other parts of the country or to other countries is another reason for the loss of union jobs. Many large corporations outsource work to cheaper labor markets in other countries. Some industries have moved from the Northeast and Midwest to the South. The South is less friendly to unions.

3 Sometimes one side will decide it can't budge on one or more of its goals. For example, a union might believe that workers' pay is too low. Management decides it will compromise on job security and working conditions but will not yield on pay, because profits are down.

CONFLICT

4 If neither side concedes, negotiations break off. This can lead to one of several possible scenarios:

1. Both sides can agree to enter into mediation, where a neutral third party can help them settle their differences.
2. Workers can vote to go on strike.
3. Management can lock out workers.

Labor and management generally don't benefit from a prolonged work stoppage. Both sides often come back to the collective bargaining process to reach a new contract.

DEAL

NO DEAL

UNFAIR!

Contract

Check Your Understanding
1. Identify two actions that can lead to a work stoppage.
2. Why do you think both labor and management reach a point where they are willing to compromise?

Conflict Arises

Deal or No Deal

Labor leaders have another explanation for the drop in membership. They refer to job losses in manufacturing, construction, hotels and restaurants, and the airlines. Many workers in these jobs are union members. Since 2001, the United States has lost millions of manufacturing jobs. This has affected union membership.

Is there a lessened need for unions?

Some people argue that unions are no longer necessary. The government has passed laws making workplaces safer. The 40-hour workweek is standard. The government provides unemployment insurance and Social Security benefits. More employers offer benefits such as medical insurance and pension plans, even if their workers do not belong to a union.

✔ **CHECKPOINT** *Why is union membership declining?*

Ask, "How has my opinion about unions changed after reading this section?"

collective bargaining
representatives of labor and management sitting down together to try to reach an agreement

job security
a guarantee that workers will not lose their jobs

grievance
a worker complaint

For many striking workers, the rat is a symbol used to protest unfair work conditions and publicize that a business is using nonunion labor. Why might this symbol be seen as an example of the historical relationship between unions and management? ▼

How do unions help workers in the workplace?

Workers at a business vote on whether they will accept a union. When the majority of workers accepts a union, the union represents the workers at that company. When this happens, the company is required by law to work out a contract with the union.

What are major issues in collective bargaining?

Collective bargaining occurs when union and company management meet to work out an agreement. Labor almost always believes it should receive better pay and working conditions. Management often disagrees. Both sides benefit if an agreement can be reached. The agreement is called a contract. The contract spells out each side's rights and responsibilities.

What goals do unions aim for?

Generally unions come to the bargaining table with certain goals:

1. *Wages and Benefits* The union works out wage rates, overtime rates, planned raises, and benefits for all members. In seeking higher wages, the union knows that if wages go too high, the company may lay off workers to cut costs.

2. *Working Conditions* Labor is always trying to make its working conditions better. Workers want to work in a safe and clean workplace. They also want the job described clearly. Contracts usually set the number of hours in the normal workweek. In the contract, management agrees to pay workers overtime.

3. *Job Security* More and more, labor is calling for **job security.** Job security is a guarantee that workers will not lose their jobs. This guarantee lasts as long as the contract is in effect. It gives workers freedom from worry that they will lose their jobs. Sometimes, workers are willing to take lower pay in exchange for more job security. If a union member is fired for reasons that go against the contract, the union might file a complaint. These complaints are called **grievances.** Often a grievance committee listens to the complaint and tries to work out a solution.

When does a union decide a strike is necessary?

When a contract is about to end, sometimes parties cannot reach an agreement. When this happens, conflict grows. The union may ask its members to vote to approve a strike. The strongest weapon labor has is the strike. It is the refusal to work until the union's demands are met. Strikes, especially long ones, can cripple a company. Some firms use managers to keep production going. Management may also hire "strikebreakers," workers who do not belong to the union.

A long strike can also be bad for workers. They do not get paid while they are on strike. Many unions use money from union dues to make some payments to their members during a strike. These payments can help workers, but they are generally much less than the members would have earned while working.

Most of the time, the collective bargaining process goes smoothly. Actually, there are very few strikes. In 2004, there were only 22 major strikes in the United States. They involved about 100,000 workers, a small fraction of the nation's workforce.

What happens if a strike continues for a long time?

If a strike drags on, sometimes third parties are brought in to help. A **mediator,** a neutral third party, listens to the arguments. After hearing from both sides, the mediator suggests ways agreement can be reached. Neither side has to follow the mediator's suggestions. **Arbitration** is like mediation, except both sides agree ahead of time to go along with the arbitrator's decision.

CHECKPOINT *What issues are addressed in collective bargaining?*

mediator
a neutral third party who listens to arguments from both sides and suggests ways an agreement can be reached

arbitration
when both sides agree to have a neutral third party make a decision that is legally binding for both the company and the union

---

SECTION 3 ASSESSMENT

Essential Questions Journal To continue to build a response to the Essential Question, go to your **Essential Questions Journal.**

 Guiding Question

1. Use your completed chart to answer this question: How do labor unions support the interests of workers?

Key Terms and Main Ideas

Directions: On a sheet of paper, write the answer to each question. Use complete sentences.

2. What is the purpose of a strike?

3. How do right-to-work laws reduce the power of unions?

4. What is collective bargaining? Who usually decides which issues to discuss?

5. How do blue-collar workers and white-collar workers differ in the types of work they perform? Give an example of each.

Critical Thinking

6. **Make Comparisons** What is the difference between the need for labor unions now and in the 1800s?

7. **Analyze Information** Today, some white-collar professionals such as teachers and doctors belong to labor unions. Do you think this is a good idea? Why or why not?

Section 1–Labor Market Trends

- The labor force is all nonmilitary people who are employed or unemployed.

- The U.S. economy has shifted from a manufacturing economy to a service economy.

- As a result of international competition, outsourcing has increased.

- The idea that education increases productivity and results in higher wages is called the learning effect.

- The idea that the completion of college tells employers that a job applicant is intelligent and hardworking is called the screening effect.

- Temporary and part-time jobs are known as contingent employment.

- Guest workers are foreign-born workers who are allowed to live and work in the U.S. temporarily.

Section 2–Labor and Wages

- Derived demand is created by the demand for another good or service.

- Productivity is a measure relating a quantity or quality of output to the inputs required to produce it.

- Equilibrium wage is set when the supply of workers meets the demand for workers in the labor market.

- The unofficial barrier that sometimes prevents some women and minority members from advancing to the top of organizations run by white men is called a glass ceiling.

- Safety laws and minimum wage laws help protect workers.

Section 3–Organized Labor

- Labor unions were formed in response to changes in working conditions brought by the Industrial Revolution. Samuel Gompers started the labor movement in the United States. In 1886, he founded the American Federation of Labor.

- There are several reasons for the decline of the labor movement. These include the passage of right-to-work laws and a decline in blue-collar manufacturing jobs, where unions were strongest. Other institutions now provide many of the services that had been won by unions in the past.

Section 1
How do economic trends affect workers?

Section 2
Why do some people earn more than others?

Section 3
How do labor unions support the interests of workers?

Essential Question, Chapter 9

How can workers best meet the challenges of a changing economy?

Uniting America's Workforce—The Songs of Joe Hill

In the early 1900s, Joe Hill joined the Industrial Workers of the World (IWW), a group of labor activists. He supported their belief to give business profits to the workers and not to the wealthy business owners. Hill had worked in the dangerous jobs the IWW was fighting against. He used his experiences to write songs to boost the spirits of workers. He wrote lyrics to the music of popular tunes so that people would easily remember his songs. Hill's songs became anthems for struggling workers everywhere. The following song is an example of his lyrics.

Workers of the World, Awaken!

Workers of the world, awaken!
Break your chains, demand your rights.
All the wealth you make is taken
By exploiting parasites.
Shall you kneel in deep submission
From your cradles to your graves?
Is the height of your ambition
To be good and willing slaves?

Arise, ye prisoners of starvation!
Fight for your own emancipation;
Arise, ye slaves of ev'ry nation,
in One Union Grand.
Our little ones for bread are crying;
And millions are from hunger dying;
The end the means is justifying,
'Tis the final stand.

If the workers take a notion,
They can stop all speeding trains;
Every ship upon the ocean
They can tie with mighty chains;
Every wheel in the creation,
Every mine and every mill,
Fleets and armies of the nation,
Will at their command stand still.

Join the union, fellow workers,
Men and women, side by side;
We will crush the greedy shirkers
Like a sweeping, surging tide;
For united we are standing,
But divided we will fall;
Let this be our understanding—
"All for one and one for all."

Document-Based Questions

1. Who was Joe Hill?
2. What is the main idea of "Workers of the World, Awaken!"?
3. In verse two of the song, why does Hill say the workers are slaves? Do you agree or disagree with this assessment?

4. Why do you think workers liked Joe Hill's songs? Do you think employers liked his songs?
5. Do you think songs are still a good way to spread a message? Explain.

SOURCE: "Workers of the World, Awaken!," written by Joe Hill

Directions: Choose the letter of the correct answer or write the answer using complete sentences.

Section 1–Labor Market Trends

1. As the U.S. economy has changed, what has been the trend in jobs over the past 20 years?
   A. from manufacturing to farming
   B. from farming to manufacturing
   C. from manufacturing to service
   D. from service to manufacturing

2. What is the term for the idea that education increases a worker's productivity?

3. What are two advantages and two disadvantages of being a temporary worker?

4. What are two ways employers can cut the expense of offering benefits to their workers?

5. Who tracks the labor force?

Section 2–Labor and Wages

6. What is labor that requires no specialized training?
   A. professional   C. skilled
   B. semiskilled   D. unskilled

7. What is wage discrimination?

8. What is the glass ceiling?

9. What are possible reasons women often earn lower pay than men do?

10. What does compensation include?

Section 3–Organized Labor

11. What did Samuel Gompers do?

12. What settlement method requires a neutral person to meet with each side to find a solution both sides will accept?

Economics
on the go

13. Which settlement method asks a neutral third party to listen to both sides and then make a decision they must accept?

14. Why are unions weakest among white-collar workers?

15. Why would right-to-work laws be a reason for a decline in union membership?

16. What is the purpose of collective bargaining?

17. Why is job security important?

Exploring the Essential Question

18. Suppose you are a worker whose job has been outsourced. How will you find a new job?

19. There is a trend for employers to replace human capital with physical capital. How might this trend affect the workforce in the future?

Essential Question Activity

20. Complete the following activity to answer the Essential Question **How can workers best meet the challenges of a changing economy?** Imagine your uncle repairs shoes. New fashions and less demand for repair have reduced his business. Your uncle needs to find a new occupation. He does not have a college degree. Using the worksheet your teacher gives you, gather the following information. (a) Which of the occupations your uncle could now apply for has the most projected openings? (b) Which occupation pays the most? Could your uncle apply for this job now? If not, why not?

Essential Questions Journal
To continue to build a response to the Essential Question, go to your **Essential Questions Journal.**

Test-Taking Tip

Before you begin a test, look it over quickly. Try to set aside enough time to complete each section.

Unit 3 Challenge

Essential Question, Unit 3

How can businesses and labor best achieve their goals?

THE ESSENTIAL **VIDEO**
By Students For Students
For videos on Essential Questions,
go to *PearsonSuccessNet.com*

There are differing views on how business and labor can achieve their goals. Look at the opinions below, keeping in mind the Essential Question: How can businesses and labor best achieve their goals?

> **"**Slower labor force growth will encourage employers to [encourage] greater labor force participation among women, the elderly, and people with disabilities.... Rapid technological change and increased international competition spotlight the need for the workforce to be able to adapt to changing technologies and shifting product demand. Shifts in the nature of business organizations and the growing importance of knowledge-based work also favor strong non-routine [thinking] skills, such as abstract reasoning, problem-solving, communication, and collaboration.**"**
>
> —Lynn Karoly and Constantijn Panis, Rand Corporation

> **"**I think the low road is where somebody thinks of only their immediate self-interest in solving their particular problem no matter what it costs to somebody else. Which means you'll have an owner of a company that'll make money...by destroying the community.

> I think you can have a labor union that...has a problem of protecting wages, jobs of its own members even at the expense of a regional development strategy.**"**
>
> —Dan Swinney, Center for Labor and Community Research, Interview, 2005

"Gentlemen, nothing stands in the way of a final accord except that management wants profit maximization and the union wants moola."

Essential Question Writing Activity

Consider the different views of economics expressed in the sources on this page and what you have learned about the needs of business and labor. *Then write a well-constructed essay expressing your view of how business and labor can meet their goals.*

Writing Guidelines

- Address all aspects of the Essential Question Writing Activity.
- Support the theme with relevant facts, examples, and details.
- Use a logical and clear plan of organization.
- Introduce the theme by establishing a framework that is beyond a simple restatement of the question and conclude with a summation of the theme.

For help in writing a Persuasive Essay, refer to the *Writing Skills Handbook* in the Reference section, page S-5.

Essential Questions Journal

To respond to the unit Essential Question, go to your **Essential Questions Journal**.

4 Money, Banking, and Finance

Essential Question, Unit 4

How can you make the most of your money?

Chapter 11
How do your saving and investment choices affect your future?

Chapter 10
How well do financial institutions serve our needs?

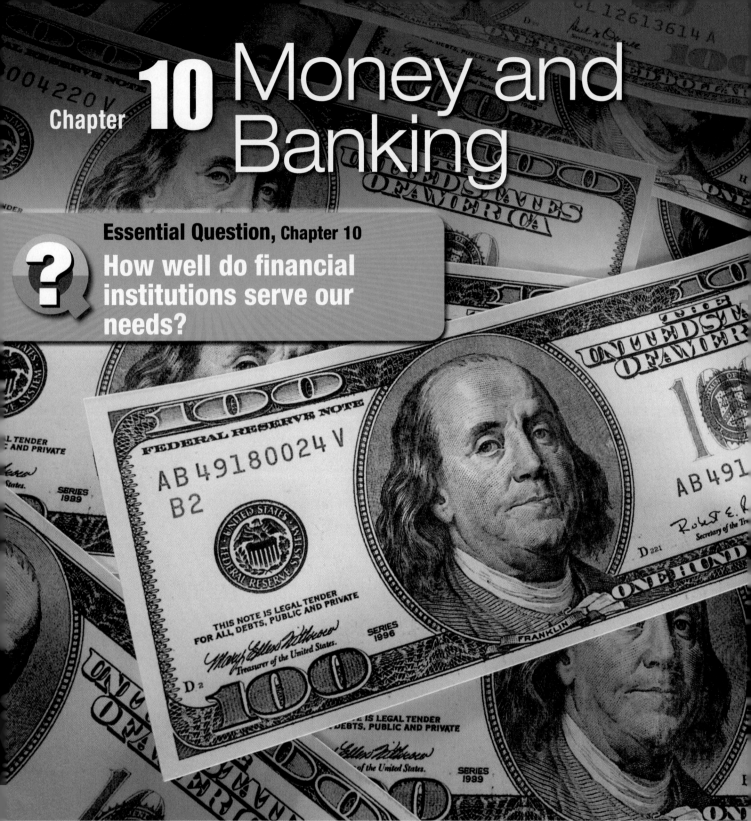

Chapter 10 Money and Banking

Essential Question, Chapter 10

How well do financial institutions serve our needs?

Economics
on the go

To study anywhere, anytime, download these onlin
resources at *PearsonSuccessNet.com* ➤

▶ **In the Middle Ages, people used mostly gold and silver coins for money.** These were heavy and hard to handle. They were easily stolen. Businesses found it easier to leave their coins with the local goldsmiths. The businesses received written receipts in exchange for the coins. Other businesses accepted the receipts for goods. They knew they could go to the goldsmiths, who would buy back the receipts and give them coins. In this way, a goldsmith gave services like those of a modern bank.

Banking involves a lot more than just putting money into a vault to keep it safe, however. In this chapter you will learn about the history of banking, different kinds of financial assets, and how banking works today.

Reading Strategy: Questioning
As you read, ask yourself questions. This will help you understand more of the information and be a more active reader. Ask yourself:

• Why are there so many different roles for money?

• When did banking get started in the United States?

• What can a bank do for me today?

Visual Glossary
online

Go to the Visual Glossary Online for an interactive review of **money**.

How the Economy Works
online

Go to How the Economy Works Online for an interactive lesson on **what happens when you put money in the bank**.

Action Graph
online

Go to Action Graph Online for animated versions of key charts and graphs.

Objectives

- **Describe** the three uses of money.
- **List** the six characteristics of money.
- **Analyze** the sources of money's value.

Uses

Money

Sources of value

Characteristics

portable

money
anything that serves as a medium of exchange, a unit of account, and a store of value

medium of exchange
anything that is used to determine value during the exchange of goods and services

Reading Strategy
Questioning
What are some important details that help you understand the different roles of money?

▶ **Economics and You** It has been a hot day, and you have been playing basketball. You are thirsty and stop at the local store. You grab a soda and fish around in your jean pockets for some money. You find a pen, keys, and a chewing gum wrapper, but, unfortunately, no money. Then you reach into your jacket pocket. Finally!—a crumpled dollar bill. You hand the money to the clerk and take a long, cold drink.

Principles in Action Money, like the dollar you used to buy the soda, serves us in many ways. It provides a way to compare values of goods and services. It serves as a store of value. Without it, we cannot get the things we need and want. That is not the whole story of money, as you will see. In fact, money has uses and characteristics that you might never have thought about.

What are the three uses of money?

No matter what form **money** takes, it tends to play three major roles. These roles are as a medium of exchange, a unit of account, and a store of value.

How does money act as a medium of exchange?

A **medium of exchange** is anything used to determine value during the exchange of goods and services. In a money-based economy, people exchange goods and services for money. For example, if you work, you exchange your labor for money. As a medium of exchange, money is something everyone will accept. Businesses and other people accept money in exchange for goods and services. You can use it to buy whatever you want. Money makes exchanges much easier.

Without money, people get goods and services through **barter.** This is the direct exchange of one set of goods or services for another. Barter is still used in many parts of the world. Many traditional economies in Asia, Africa, and Latin America use barter. It is also sometimes used in the United States. For example, a person might agree to mow a neighbor's lawn in exchange for vegetables from the neighbor's garden. In general, however, bartering is not practical in a modern economy.

Have you ever tried to barter with someone? Did each of you get what you wanted? Let's look at an example to show the difference between a barter economy and a money-based economy. Suppose money did not exist. You want to trade your portable DVD player for a mountain bike. Making an exchange would be tough. First, you need to find someone who wants to sell a mountain bike you want. That person would also have to want your DVD player. Second, this person needs to agree that your DVD player is worth the same as the bike. People in barter economies spend a lot of time and effort exchanging the goods they have for the goods they want.

How much easier would it be if you used money as a medium of exchange? All you would have to do is find someone willing to pay you $100.00 for your DVD player. Then you could use that money to buy a mountain bike from someone else. The person selling you the bike can use the $100.00 any way he or she wishes.

How does money serve as a unit of account?

Money also serves as a **unit of account.** That is, money is a way to compare the values of goods and services. For example, suppose you see a jacket on sale for $30.00. You know this is a good price. You have compared the cost of the jacket in this store with the cost in other stores. Every store in the United States shows prices in the same way, in dollars and cents. Other countries have their own forms of money that serve as units of account. Prices in Japan are listed in yen. Russia uses rubles. Mexico uses pesos.

How does money serve as a store of value?

Money also serves as a **store of value.** This means money keeps its value if you decide to hold on to—or store—it instead of spending it. Remember the DVD player you sold to buy a mountain bike? Maybe you did not have a chance to buy a bike right away. In the meantime, you can keep the money in your wallet or in a bank. The money is still valuable. It will be accepted as a medium of exchange weeks or months from now when you buy the bike.

barter
the direct exchange of one set of goods or services for another

unit of account
a way to compare the values of goods and services

store of value
something that keeps its value if it is stored rather than used

Suppose you are a baker. You have lots of cakes to sell. Your cakes will grow stale and spoil if they are not sold. They do not grow more valuable as they get older. You sell your cakes for cash. Unless you spend the money right away, it stores the value of the cakes you sold. You are storing the cake's buying power until you need it.

Money serves as a good store of value with one important exception. Sometimes economies have rapid inflation, or a general increase in prices. Suppose the United States has 10 percent inflation during one year. You sold your DVD player at the beginning of that year for $100. Inflation means that at the end of the year, the money you received has less value. Inflation has cut your buying power by 10 percent. Now your $100 will buy goods worth only $90. At the same time, inflation causes the price of a mountain bike to rise 10 percent. It now costs $110. The $100 you received at the beginning of the year no longer is enough to buy the bike. This shows that in a time of inflation, money does not function as well as a store of value.

✔ **CHECKPOINT** *Under what circumstance does money not serve as a good store of value?*

What are the six characteristics of money?

The coins and paper bills used as money are called **currency**. In the past, many other objects were used as currency. Cattle, salt, dried fish, furs, precious stones, gold, and silver were used as currency. None of these items would work well in our economy today. Each is missing at least one of the six characteristics of money today. Money must be durable, portable, divisible, uniform, limited in supply, and acceptable.

Why must money have durability?

Imagine how tough life would be if our money was made of a liquid that evaporated. We want money to be **durable,** to be able to last a long time. If money wore out fast or were easily destroyed, it would not serve well as a store of value. Money is printed on high-quality paper with high rag (cloth) content. Even then it wears out. When it does, new bills replace the old ones.

Without the portability, divisibility, and uniformity of our currency, sharing a restaurant bill would be very complicated. **What other characteristics are essential to a sound currency?** ▼

What does *portability* mean?

Imagine if money was as large and heavy as a bowling ball. It sure would make shopping a lot harder. People need to be able to take money with them to do business. Modern money is small and lightweight. It is **portable,** or easy to carry.

Why is divisibility important?

Divisible means "able to be divided." Not everything costs an even amount like one dollar or 25 cents. When you buy something, you do not often need to worry about having exact change. You know that when you pay with a larger bill, you will get change back. Making change is easy because of divisibility.

Why must money be uniform?

Maybe students at your school wear uniforms. Everyone's clothing is the same. Money is also **uniform.** One ten dollar bill is just as valuable as another. Imagine how confusing it would be if some dollar bills were worth more than others. All money is made very carefully to make sure that bills and coins of the same amount are uniform in size and weight.

Why must the supply of money be limited?

Suppose a society used a special kind of small stone as money. These rare stones have been found only on one beach. One day, however, someone finds a huge supply of stones just like them on a different beach. Now anyone can scoop them up by the handful. Because these stones are no longer in **limited supply,** but are easily available, they are no longer useful as currency.

In the United States, the Federal Reserve System controls the supply of money. The Federal Reserve is able to keep just the right amount of money available.

Why is acceptability important?

It is important that everyone in an economy accepts money in exchange for goods and services. **Acceptable** means "recognized as having value." When you go to the store, why does the clerk accept your money in exchange for a carton of milk? Your money is accepted because the store owner can spend it elsewhere to buy something he or she needs or wants.

☑ **CHECKPOINT** *What are the six characteristics of money?*

portable
easily carried
divisible
able to be divided
uniform
looking the same
limited supply
not easily available
acceptable
recognized as having value

Reading Strategy
Questioning
Ask yourself what might happen if money lacked one of these characteristics.

What are the sources of money's value?

Think about the bills and coins in your pocket. They are durable and portable. They are also easily divisible, uniform, and in limited supply. They are accepted throughout the country. As useful as they may be, however, bills and coins are just paper or a small amount of metal. What makes money valuable? The source of the money's value depends on whether it is commodity, representative, or fiat money.

What is commodity money?

Commodity money is an object that has value of its own and is also used as money. For example, some societies have used salt, cattle, and precious stones as commodity money. They are valuable because they are useful. If not used as money, salt can be used to keep food from spoiling and to make it taste better. Cattle can be killed for meat. Gems can be made into jewelry.

Several characteristics that make objects good sources of money are missing in commodity money. For example, it is often not portable, durable, or divisible. That's why commodity money works best in simple economies.

What is representative money?

Representative money uses objects that have value because the holder can exchange them for something else of value. For example, if your brother gives you an IOU, the piece of paper itself is worth nothing. The piece of paper simply shows what he has promised to you. The promise that he will do some of your jobs for a month may be worth quite a lot.

In the Massachusetts Bay Colony in the late 1600s, the colonists first used representative money. The colony's treasurer issued bills of credit to lenders to help pay for war. The bills of credit showed how much the colonists had loaned to the Massachusetts government. Holders of these bills could take their bills of credit to the treasurer. He would then pay them back in **specie**. Specie is money in the form of coins made of gold or silver.

Representative money has problems, too. During the American Revolution (1775–1783), the Second Continental Congress issued representative money called Continentals to pay for the war against England. The federal government was not able to buy the money back. The government had no power to collect taxes. People even began to say "not worth a Continental" to refer to things of no value.

▲ Commodity money

▲ Representative money

▲ Fiat money

Later, the U.S. government issued representative money in the form of silver and gold certificates backed by gold or silver. People who had bought the certificates could turn them in for gold or silver. This meant the U.S. government had to keep a big supply of gold and silver on hand in case there was a demand to change paper dollars to gold. The government used silver certificates until 1968. For the most part, the government stopped changing paper money into silver or gold in the 1930s.

What is fiat money?

On one side of a dollar bill is George Washington's picture. To the left of the picture are the words *This note is legal tender for all debts, public and private.* These words make it **fiat money.** Our money is valuable because our government says it is. Fiat money is still in limited supply, and therefore valuable, because the Federal Reserve controls its supply. If the money supply grows too large, the currency risks becoming less valuable because of inflation.

 CHECKPOINT *Why is commodity money not useful in our modern society?*

fiat money
objects that have value because the government has determined that they are an acceptable means to pay debts

Fig. 10.1

"Sorry. Cash only."

▲ To be useful as commodity money, the commodity must have some value. **Why are cattle more useful than frogs as commodity money?**

SECTION 1 ASSESSMENT

Essential Questions Journal To continue to build a response to the Essential Question, go to your **Essential Questions Journal.**

Guiding Question

1. Use your complete concept web to answer this question: How does money serve the needs of our society?

Key Terms and Main Ideas

Directions: On a sheet of paper, write the answer to each question. Use complete sentences.

2. What are the three uses of money? Which use do you think is the most important?

3. Which word describing money means it lasts a long time?

4. What kind of money is salt an example of?

5. What kind of money is a dollar bill?

Critical Thinking

6. **Analyze Information** (a) How does barter work? (b) How does this differ from the way money is used?

7. **Draw Inferences** Would gold be a good form of currency if scientists could create gold from sand? Explain.

Objectives

■ **Describe** the shifts between centralized and decentralized banking before the Civil War.

■ **Explain** how the government reformed the banking system in the later 1800s.

■ **Describe** how banking changed in the early 1900s.

■ **Explain** the causes of two recent banking crises.

bank
an institution for receiving, keeping, and lending money

national bank
a bank chartered by the national government

▲ Alexander Hamilton (top) and Thomas Jefferson held different views of how the new nation should satisfy its banking needs.

Guiding Question

How has the American banking system changed to meet new challenges?

Copy this flowchart and fill it in as you read.

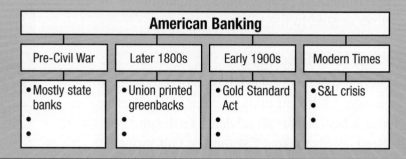

American Banking			
Pre-Civil War	Later 1800s	Early 1900s	Modern Times
• Mostly state banks • •	• Union printed greenbacks • •	• Gold Standard Act • •	• S&L crisis • •

▶ **Economics and You** Imagine that you need a large sum of cash to buy something. Do you get it from under your mattress or from a cookie jar? That is not likely today. In the past, many Americans kept their savings hidden in places like these. However, times have changed. Today, almost all Americans prefer to put their savings in a **bank,** an institution for receiving, keeping, and lending money.

Principles in Action Over time, the American banking system has changed to meet new challenges. In earlier days, people did not trust banks. In this section, you will see how the government made rules to end many dangerous banking practices. You will also see how American banking has developed over the years as the population has grown and changed.

What was U.S. banking like before the Civil War?

Many of the early leaders of the United States believed that a strong, centralized banking system was needed. The first Secretary of the Treasury, Alexander Hamilton, suggested that a **national bank** be created. The Bank of the United States was set up in 1791. It was the largest and most powerful bank in the United States. The bank collected fees and paid the bills for the federal government.

Why was the First Bank of the United States created?

There was a need for the First Bank of the United States. The government owed a lot of money from the Revolutionary War. The money system was confusing, because every state had a different form of currency. The bank was also successful in helping to bring order to banks chartered by the states.

Many people did not like the Bank of the United States. Some people believed it was too large and powerful. In 1811, Congress refused to renew its charter. As a result, the number of banks chartered by the states grew.

In 1811, there were about 100 state banks. A state, not the federal government, gave state banks the right to organize. State banks were all owned by individuals. These state banks printed their own paper money. This caused many problems. Notes issued by banks in one state might not be accepted by banks in other states. The money was supposed to be backed by silver and gold coins. However, many banks did not have enough gold and silver to back the money they printed. Many banks failed. Thousands of people were stuck with worthless paper money. Soon, people no longer trusted the banks and the money they issued.

Did the Second Bank of the United States solve all the problems?

In 1816, Congress set up the Second Bank of the United States to try to bring order back to the banking system. The bank had some success, but again, many people did not like it. President Andrew Jackson thought it favored rich and powerful people. To weaken it, he spoke out against the bank. He refused to renew its charter in 1832. He took all government money out of the Second Bank of the United States and put the money into smaller, state-chartered banks. Many of these banks were careless and made loans to people who never paid them back. This led to an economic slowdown called the Panic of 1837.

What banking problems developed during the Civil War?

When the Civil War (1861–1865) broke out, both the Union in the North and the Confederacy in the South printed paper money to pay their bills. Union money was black on one side and green on the other. This money quickly became known as **greenbacks.** Greenbacks were fiat money. They were backed only by the government's promise to repay the notes at some future date. People were worried, because they were not sure the greenbacks had any value.

Reading Strategy
Questioning
What would happen if every state had its own form of currency today?

greenback
a paper currency issued by the Union government during the Civil War

gold standard
a system in which paper money and coins are equal to the value of a certain amount of gold

The Confederacy did not have stable banks. It was soon unable to borrow money from Europe to pay for the war. It began to print more paper money. It printed so many Confederate dollars that they began to lose value. Today their only value is to collectors. By the end of the war in 1865, most banks in the South had closed.

☑ CHECKPOINT *Why did some leaders favor a strong central bank?*

How did Congress try to reform banking during the Civil War?

In 1863 and 1864, Congress passed the National Banking Acts to set up a system of national banks. The government checked each bank to make sure it was safe. The government set high standards for the banks. These banks were allowed to print official money.

☑ CHECKPOINT *What were national banks?*

Reading Strategy
Questioning
Do you think you would like a return of the Gold Standard Act? Explain.

How did banking change in the early 1900s?

Congress passed the **Gold Standard** Act in 1900. It set the value of the dollar at a certain amount of gold. People could go to the U.S. Treasury and exchange their dollars for gold. People knew they could cash in their paper money for gold. The act also prevented the government from printing more paper money than it could back in gold or silver.

Innovators

Amadeo P. Giannini
Amadeo Giannini was unlike other bankers of his time who cared only about the rich. Giannini built his bank by providing services to everyone.

He opened a small bank in 1904 in San Francisco. When an earthquake destroyed the city in 1906, Giannini's bank was also ruined. However, he put a plank across two barrels where his bank had stood and set up office. He offered loans to people whom the earthquake had affected.

By 1918, Giannini's bank had expanded across California. By the 1930s, he had merged with other banks. He soon controlled the Bank of America, the world's largest commercial bank.

Giannini himself had little interest in personal wealth. For many years, he underpaid himself, and he left only a small estate at his death. He feared that great wealth would cause him to lose touch with the ordinary people he served.

Fast Facts

Amadeo P. Giannini (1870–1949)
Education: no formal education beyond eighth grade
Claim to Fame: Founded the Bank of America, now the largest U.S.-owned bank

A gold standard also has disadvantages. Because gold is scarce, the amount of money in circulation is limited. This slowed growth in the economy. The United States went off the gold standard in 1933.

How did the Panic of 1907 help to create the Federal Reserve System?

The Panic of 1907 happened because many banks made bad loans and gave too much credit. People lost trust in banks. Many people panicked and demanded their money at the same time. This caused a **bank run.** The banks did not have enough cash to cover the demands of investors. Some banks were forced to close. The run on the banks caused panic and fear. Many businesses failed. Some who had deposited money in the banks lost their savings.

In 1908, Congress created a National Monetary Commission. Its job was to find ways to prevent panics from happening again. It made many suggestions to improve the banking system. The Commission's reports led to the creation of the Federal Reserve System.

How is the Federal Reserve System Organized?

The Federal Reserve Act was passed in 1913. It served as the nation's first true **central bank.** It created a banking system of 12 district banks throughout the country. All banks must meet the requirements set by the Federal Reserve System, or the Fed. The banks that belong to the Fed are called **member banks.**

The Fed has 12 regional districts. Each district has a Federal Reserve Bank with its own president. The district bank carries out the Fed's policies. The larger districts also have branch banks. As of 2008, there were 25 branch banks. Although each district Federal Reserve Bank is independent, they all work together as a team. They all have a common goal—to keep the economy stable and healthy.

The Federal Reserve Act also created **Federal Reserve notes.** This is the national currency we use today in the United States. Look at the top of a dollar bill. You will see the words *Federal Reserve Note.* You will learn more about the Fed and the important work it does in Chapter 16.

What banking reforms were passed after the Great Depression?

The Great Depression began in October 1929 and coincided with the U.S. stock market crash. Businesses were struggling and many people were out of work. Banks, stores, and factories closed.

bank run
a widespread panic in which many people try to get their paper money at the same time

central bank
a bank that can lend to other banks in time of need and regulates overall money supply

member bank
a bank that belongs to the Federal Reserve System

Federal Reserve note
the currency we use today in the United States

deregulate
to remove controls on

interest
the price paid for the use of borrowed money

principal
the amount of money borrowed

mortgage
a specific type of loan used to buy real estate

default
to fail to pay back a loan

Millions of Americans lost their jobs. They could not pay back money they had borrowed. There were runs on the banks. Many bank customers were afraid their banks would fail. They withdrew all of their money.

One of the first acts of the new President, Franklin D. Roosevelt, was to try to end the panic. On March 5, 1933, he declared a "bank holiday." He ordered all the banks closed. After they were all inspected, only safe banks were allowed to reopen. Later in 1933, Congress created the Federal Deposit Insurance Corporation (FDIC). The FDIC insures money deposited in banks. If a bank fails, the government will give each depositor up to $250,000 back.

✔ **CHECKPOINT** *How did the FDIC help to restore confidence in the banking industry?*

Economics & YOU

FDIC: How Your Deposit Is Protected

Most of us today take for granted that the money we put in banks is safe. Before 1933, however, Americans had less confidence that their money was safe. *When the stock market crashed in 1929, thousands of banks failed. The people who had money in those banks lost everything.*

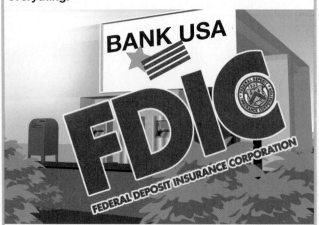

Today, your checking or savings at a bank is insured up to $250,000. *In the unlikely event that your bank fails, you will get your money back.*

What were the Savings and Loan and subprime mortgage crises?

In the late 1970s and 1980s, Congress passed laws affecting industries. One was to **deregulate,** or remove some controls on, several industries. This helped bring about a crisis in a class of banks known as savings and loans (S&Ls).

During the 1970s, S&Ls made long-term loans at low rates of **interest.** The amount borrowed is called the **principal.** By the 1980s, interest rates had risen. This meant that S&Ls had to pay large amounts of interest to their depositors. However, their returns on the money they had loaned out in the 1970s were low. The S&L industry started to make risky loans in the early 1980s. By the late 1980s, one third of all S&Ls were in trouble.

In late 2006, a new problem in the U.S. banking industry developed. This was the subprime mortgage crisis. The term *subprime* refers to loans made to borrowers with a bad credit history. **Mortgages** are loans used to buy property like a home. The interest rate is higher on a subprime loan. This is because there is a greater risk that the borrower may **default,** or not be able to pay back the loan. Many banks were willing to take the risk.

Beginning in the 1990s, the U.S. housing market boomed. Mortgage companies and banks began to offer subprime loans. By 2005, subprime loans made up more than one fourth of U.S. mortgages. Bankers tried to lessen their risk by "bundling" the mortgages to sell to investors. The value of these bundles depended on whether the individual homeowners could repay their loans.

In 2006, interest rates rose. Many people now found that they could not pay their mortgage. These people lost their homes through **foreclosures**. In a foreclosure, the bank takes over the property because the borrowers are unable to pay back their loans.

The sharp rise in foreclosures forced several large mortgage companies into bankruptcy. This hurt banks. Stock prices dropped. Financial institutions that had invested heavily in subprime mortgages laid off thousands of employees. In time, this led to the worst economic downturn since the Great Depression.

 CHECKPOINT *How did the rash of subprime mortgages endanger the U.S. economy?*

Reading Strategy
Questioning
Ask yourself: "Did I understand what I just read about banking crises?" If not, read the material again.

foreclosure
the seizure of property from borrowers who are unable to pay back their loans

---

SECTION 2 ASSESSMENT

Essential Questions Journal
To continue to build a response to the Essential Question, go to your **Essential Questions Journal.**

Quick Write

Write a short essay answering the following questions: What powers do you think the federal government should have to regulate banks? Why are these powers necessary?

 Guiding Question

1. Use your completed flowchart to answer the following question: How has the American banking system changed to meet new challenges?

Key Terms and Main Ideas

Directions: On a sheet of paper, write the answer to each question. Use complete sentences.

2. Identify the three functions of a bank.
3. Under the gold standard, how is the value of paper money and coins set?
4. As a central bank, what can the Federal Reserve System do for other banks?
5. Name one advantage of Federal Reserve notes.

Critical Thinking

6. **Synthesize Information** (a) When did the United States start issuing greenbacks? (b) What significant event happened at this time in history? (c) How are these two events related?
7. **Recognize Cause and Effect** How did laws passed during the Great Depression affect depositors' money?

Objectives

- **Explain** how the money supply in the United States is measured.
- **Describe** the functions of financial institutions.
- **Identify** different types of financial institutions.
- **Describe** the changes brought about by electronic banking.

money supply
all the money available in the United States economy

Guiding Question

What banking services do financial institutions provide?

Copy this concept web and fill it in as you read.

Storing Money	

Banking Services → Providing loans

Issuing credit cards

▶ **Economics and You** Suppose that it is Friday. You just got your paycheck for the week. You take it to the bank. You fill out a deposit slip and then stand in line and wait . . . and wait . . . and wait for the next available teller. Hold on a minute. That scene is so yesterday! You don't have time for standing in line. You deposit your check quickly at an ATM. Or better yet, you have your week's pay electronically deposited directly into your bank account.

Principles in Action Financial institutions provide these electronic services as well as many others suited to the computer age. They issue credit cards, make loans to businesses, and provide mortgages that allow people to buy homes. They also manage automated teller machines (ATMs). These machines allow a person to deposit or withdraw money at any time and in almost any place in the world. You will learn more about electronic transactions and other aspects of banking today in this section.

How is the money supply measured?

You know you can use currency—bills and coins—to buy things. Currency is money. So are traveler's checks, checking account deposits, and other substitutes for money. All of these make up the **money supply**: all the money available in the U.S. economy. To more easily keep track of these different kinds of money, economists use several ways of measuring the money supply. The main categories are called M1 and M2.

M1 measures only the money actually in use. This includes all currency and checking accounts. M1 is money people can easily get and use to pay for goods and services. An important feature of M1 is **liquidity.** This means the ability to be used as, or directly changed into, cash. Almost half of M1 is made up of currency. Another part of M1 is money held in checking accounts. These funds are sometimes called **demand deposits,** because checks can be paid "on demand," that is, at any time.

Other economists like a broader measure of the money supply. They use M2. **M2** includes all M1 money as well as other monies. These other monies include money market mutual funds, certificates of deposit, and savings accounts less than $250,000. **Money market mutual funds** pool savers' money to buy short-term government and corporate securities. M2 funds cannot be used as cash directly but can be made liquid fairly easily. M2 assets are also called near money.

✔ **CHECKPOINT** *Why are checking accounts also called demand deposit accounts?*

How do financial institutions operate?

Banks and other financial institutions are important in managing the money supply. They also perform many functions and offer a wide range of services to consumers.

How do banks store money?

Banks are a safe, convenient place for people to store money. The money is stored in fireproof vaults and insured. Private insurance protects against loss from robbery. FDIC insurance protects people from losing their money if the bank is unable to repay funds.

Savings accounts and checking accounts are the most common types of bank accounts. They are especially useful for people who need to make withdrawals from time to time. Savings accounts and some checking accounts pay interest at an annual rate.

Money market accounts and certificates of deposits (CDs) are special kinds of savings accounts. They pay a higher rate of interest than other accounts. Money market accounts allow you to write a limited number of checks. Interest rates are not fixed but can move up or down. CDs, on the other hand, offer a guaranteed rate of interest. Money put in a CD, however, cannot be removed until the end of a certain time period, such as one or two years. Customers who remove their money before that time pay a penalty.

M1
all the money actually in use
liquidity
the ability to be used as, or directly converted into, cash

demand deposit
money in a checking account that can be paid "on demand," or at any time
M2
includes M1 money plus all other monies, such as money market and savings accounts

money market mutual fund
a fund that pools money from small savers to purchase short-term securities

Fig. 10.2 How the Economy Works

How does the **fractional reserve system** work?

In fractional reserve banking, banks keep a fraction of their funds on hand and lend the remainder to customers.

1 It's been a good week at Acme Products, so owner Don Hennessey is able to deposit **$10,000** in his account at the Friendly Bank.

2 Marco Gonzalez wants to buy a car. Friendly Bank can lend him 80 percent of the money Don deposited, or **$8,000.** The bank holds 20 percent, or **$2,000,** in reserve.

Original Deposit   **Loans**

---

fractional reserve banking
a banking system that keeps only a fraction of funds on hand and lends out the remainder

How do bank loans work?

Banks also provide loans. As you have read, the first banks started doing business when goldsmiths issued paper receipts. These receipts showed that the goldsmiths were holding gold coins in safe storage for their customers. They would charge a small fee for this service. Goldsmiths realized that their customers seldom asked for all their gold on one day. Goldsmiths could then lend out some of the gold and still have enough to pay off customers who wanted their gold back. The goldsmiths kept just enough gold in reserve to cover demand. Today, a banking system that keeps only a fraction of funds on hand and lends out the rest is called **fractional reserve banking.** (See **Figure 10.2.**) Today's banks work much like the early banks. They lend money for many reasons. You might borrow money for home improvements or to attend college. The more money a bank lends out, the higher the profit that the bank might earn.

By making loans, banks help new businesses get started. Existing businesses borrow money to grow. Businesses invest in physical capital to increase production. This investment creates new jobs.

3 The car dealer who sold Marco the car puts the $8,000 in his bank account at the Even Friendlier Bank. The bank lends 80 percent, or **$6,400,** to Jack and Ginny Li, who are redecorating their living room. The bank holds the remaining **$1,600** in reserve.

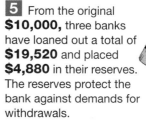

5 From the original **$10,000,** three banks have loaned out a total of **$19,520** and placed **$4,880** in their reserves. The reserves protect the bank against demands for withdrawals.

4 The owner of the furniture store deposits the $6,400 in the Friendliest of All Bank. The bank then lends 80 percent of $6,400, or **$5,120,** to C. S. Perkins to help him pay for college. The bank puts the remaining **$1,280** in reserve.

Check Your Understanding
1. By Step 3, how much of the original $10,000 is still being held in bank reserves?
2. What would happen if banks were required to keep all deposits in reserve?

Final Result

New workers may be hired. A business that gets a loan may help other businesses to grow. For example, suppose you and a friend want to start a window-washing business. Your business will need supplies like window cleaner and ladders. The companies that make your supplies will benefit.

Bankers must make sure the borrower is able to repay a loan. Suppose borrowers default. Then the bank may lose part or even all of the money it has loaned. Bankers therefore always face a trade-off between profits and safety. If they make too many bad loans that are not repaid, they may go out of business. This is what happened in 2008. There were so many bad loans that the government had to provide billions of dollars to help the banking system survive.

What is a mortgage?

A mortgage is a loan used to buy a building or land. Suppose the Lee family wants to buy a house for $250,000. The Lees are unlikely to have saved all the money they need to pay for the house. Like almost all homebuyers, they will need to borrow most of the money. The money they borrow is the mortgage.

The Lees can afford to make a down payment of 20 percent of the price of the house, or $50,000. After making sure the Lees are a good credit risk, their bank agrees to lend them the remaining $200,000 to buy the house. Mortgages usually last for 15, 25, or 30 years. Like all borrowers, the Lees must pay back the loan plus whatever interest the bank charges.

How do credit cards work?

Banks also issue **credit cards.** Banks that do so are loaning you the money to buy the things you want. Suppose you buy a sleeping bag and tent for $100.00 on May 3. Your credit card bill may not arrive until June. You do not actually pay for the gear until you pay that bill. In the meantime, however, the bank will have paid the store for your camping equipment. Your payment repays the bank for the "loan" of $100.00. What happens if you do not pay your credit card bill in full? You will end up paying a high rate of interest on that loan.

What is the difference between simple and compound interest?

As you have read, interest is the price paid for the use of borrowed money. The amount borrowed is called the principal. Simple interest is interest paid only on the principal. For example, if you deposit $100.00 in a savings account at 5 percent simple interest, you will earn $5.00 in a year.

Suppose you leave the $5.00 in interest in the bank, so that at the end of the year you have $105.00 in your account—$100.00 in principal and $5.00 in interest. Compound interest is interest paid on both principal and the interest added to it. That means that in the second year, interest will be paid on $105.00.

What is the biggest source of profit for banks?

The largest source of income for banks is the interest they receive from customers who have taken loans. Banks, of course, also pay interest on customers' savings and some checking accounts. They do not pay as much as they collect in interest. The difference in the amounts is how banks cover their costs and earn a profit.

✔ **CHECKPOINT** *Why are checking accounts more useful than CDs for people who must make frequent withdrawals?*

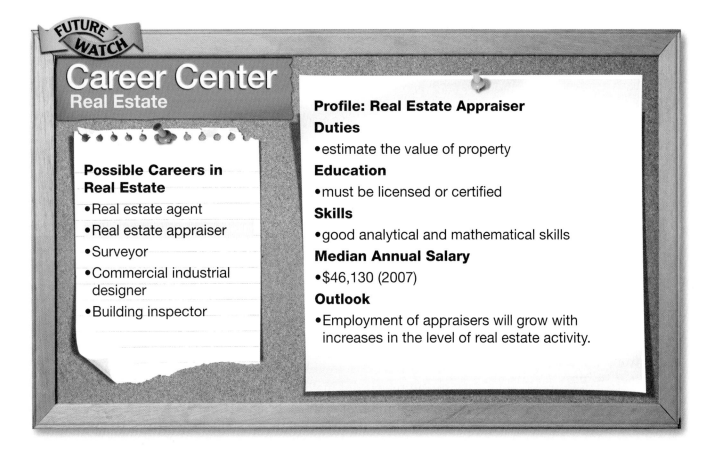

FUTURE WATCH

Career Center
Real Estate

Possible Careers in Real Estate

- Real estate agent
- Real estate appraiser
- Surveyor
- Commercial industrial designer
- Building inspector

Profile: Real Estate Appraiser

Duties
- estimate the value of property

Education
- must be licensed or certified

Skills
- good analytical and mathematical skills

Median Annual Salary
- $46,130 (2007)

Outlook
- Employment of appraisers will grow with increases in the level of real estate activity.

What are the five main types of financial institutions?

Many organizations manage money. These are called financial institutions. The five major financial institutions in the United States are commercial banks, savings and loan associations, savings banks, credit unions, and finance companies.

What services do commercial banks offer?

Commercial banks once served only businesses. Today, they offer many services. They accept deposits and make loans to individuals as well as to businesses. Commercial banks provide the most services and play the largest role in the economy of any type of bank. Today's banks use fractional reserve banking.

What are savings and loan companies?

Savings and loan companies (S&Ls) began in the 1800s. Members of S&Ls put money into a large general fund. Then they borrowed enough money to buy their own houses. Savings and loans are also called thrifts. This is because they originally let "thrifty" working-class people save up and borrow enough to buy their own homes. Now, S&Ls do many of the same things as commercial banks.

debit card
a card used to withdraw money
from a bank account

Reading Strategy
Questioning
How would your life be
different if there were no ATMs
or electronic banking?

Phone cards, gift cards, and mass
transit cards are useful stored-
value, or smart cards. ▼

What are savings banks?

Mutual savings banks (MSBs) also began in the early 1800s.
They accepted smaller deposits than commercial banks. Mutual
savings banks were owned by the depositors themselves, who
shared in any profits. Later, many MSBs began to sell stock to raise
additional funds.

What is the purpose of credit unions?

Credit unions operate like banks but are owned and controlled by
people who use their services. The owners often work for the same
company, labor union, or government agency. Some are open to
the entire community. Credit unions are often small. They offer
loans to their members at lower interest rates than do banks.

What do finance companies do?

Finance companies make loans to consumers. Consumers can
pay them back in regular, usually monthly, payments. These loans
spread the cost of major purchases like cars and large appliances
over a number of months. People who borrow from finance
companies sometimes fail to repay the loans. To cover this risk,
finance companies usually charge higher interest rates than banks.

✅ **CHECKPOINT** *Which type of financial institution plays the largest
role in the economy?*

What is electronic banking?

Banks began to use computers in the early 1970s to keep track of
accounts. Today, computers play a huge role in banking. The main
types of electronic banking are automated
teller machines (ATMs), debit cards, home
banking, automated clearinghouses, and
stored-value cards.

The first ATMs allowed customers to take
out cash from an account. Today, ATMs
take deposits, transfer money, make cash
advances to credit cards, and accept payments.
ATMs are one of the most common types of
electronic banking, available 24 hours a day.
They reduce the number of people who work
in a bank.

Debit cards work a lot like cash, but money
never changes hands. Banks give debit cards
to people who have checking accounts. Bank
customers can use a debit card at an ATM.

When you "swipe" your debit card, the card sends a message to your bank to debit, or subtract money from, your checking account. To prevent fraud, debit cards require customers to use a personal identification number (PIN).

More and more people are using the Internet to conduct business. Many financial institutions allow people to do many things from home. They can check account balances, transfer money, and pay their bills via the Internet.

Automated Clearing Houses (ACHs), located at Federal Reserve Banks and their branches, allow people to pay bills without writing checks. An ACH transfers money automatically from a customer's account to a **creditor's** account. People usually use ACHs to pay regular monthly bills, such as mortgage payments. They save time and the cost of a stamp and end any worries about forgetting to make a payment.

Smart cards, also called stored-value cards, are the newest form of electronic banking. Smart cards are much like debit cards. These cards have either a magnetic strip or a computer chip with account balance information. College students often use these to pay for cafeteria food, computer time, or photocopies. Other examples of smart cards are phone cards and gift cards.

creditor
a person or institution to whom money is owed

✔ **CHECKPOINT** *How does a debit card work?*

SECTION **3** ASSESSMENT

Essential Questions Journal To continue to build a response to the Essential Question, go to your **Essential Questions Journal.**

 Guiding Question

1. Use your completed concept web to answer this question: What banking services do financial institutions provide?

Key Terms and Main Ideas

Directions: On a sheet of paper, write the answer to each question. Use complete sentences.

2. What type of loan is used to buy real estate?

3. What is the price paid for borrowed money?

4. What do we call the ability of an asset to be used as cash?

5. What kind of account lets money be paid out at any time?

Critical Thinking

6. **Analyze Information** (a) What kinds of money are included in M1 and M2? (b) Why do economists use these categories?

7. **Make Comparisons** (a) In what ways are debit cards and stored-value cards similar? (b) How are they different?

Section 1—Money

- Money serves as a medium of exchange, a unit of account, and a store of value.

- Money has six characteristics. It is durable, portable, divisible, uniform, limited in supply, and acceptable.

- The source of money's value depends on whether it is commodity, representative, or fiat money.

Section 2—The History of American Banking

- Before the Civil War, each state bank issued its own paper money. Many banks did not have enough gold and silver to back this money.

- The First Bank of the United States was set up in 1791. Many thought it was too large and too powerful.

- The Second Bank of the United States was set up in 1816.

- The National Banking Acts of 1863 and 1864 set high standards for banks.

- The Federal Reserve System was the nation's first true central bank.

- The S&L and subprime mortgage crises have caused problems in recent years.

Section 3—Banking Today

- Two measures of the money supply are M1 and M2.

- The services that banks supply include storing, saving, and loaning money and issuing credit and debit cards.

- Commercial banks, S&Ls, savings banks, credit unions, and finance companies are the main financial institutions in the U.S.

- Electronic banking includes the use of ATMs, debit cards, home banking, automated clearinghouses, and stored-value cards.

Section 1
How does money serve the needs of our society?

Section 2
How has the American banking system changed to meet new challenges?

Section 3
What banking services do financial institutions provide?

Essential Question, Chapter 10
How well do financial institutions serve our needs?

Grameen Bank

This Nobel Lecture was given by the Nobel Peace Prize Laureate 2006, Muhammad Yunus (Oslo, December 10, 2006).

"All borrowers of Grameen Bank are celebrating this day as the greatest day of their lives. They are gathering around the nearest television set in their villages all over Bangladesh, along with other villagers, to watch the proceedings of this ceremony. This year's prize gives highest honour and dignity to the hundreds of millions of women all around the world who struggle every day to make a living and bring hope for a better life for their children. This is a historic moment for them.

The new millennium began with a great global dream. World leaders gathered . . . in 2000 and adopted . . . a historic goal to reduce poverty by half by 2015. Never in human history had such a bold goal been adopted by the entire world in one voice, one that specified time and size. But then came September 11 and the Iraq war, and suddenly the world became derailed from the pursuit of this dream, with the attention of world leaders shifting from the war on poverty to the war on terrorism. . . .

I became involved in the poverty issue . . . because poverty was all around me, and I could not turn away from it. In 1974, I found it difficult to teach elegant theories of economics in the university classroom, in the backdrop of a terrible famine in Bangladesh. . . . I wanted to do something immediate to help people around me,

even if it was just one human being, to get through another day with a little more ease. That brought me face to face with poor people's struggle to find the tiniest amounts of money to support their efforts to eke out a living. . . .

Grameen Bank was born as a tiny homegrown project run with the help of several of my students, all local girls and boys. Three of these students are still with me in Grameen Bank, after all these years, as its topmost executives. They are here today to receive this honour you give us.

I believe that we can create a poverty-free world because poverty is not created by poor people. It has been created and sustained by the economic and social system that we have designed for ourselves; the institutions and concepts that make up that system; the policies that we pursue. . . .

Let me conclude by expressing my deep gratitude to the Norwegian Nobel Committee for recognizing that poor people, and especially poor women, have both the potential and the right to live a decent life, and that microcredit helps to unleash that potential."

Document-Based Questions

1. What conditions made it difficult for Yunus to teach economics?
2. What is the effect of giving loans to women?
3. What does Yunus believe created poverty?
4. What happened to change the focus of world leaders from poverty to terrorism?
5. What group of people have benefited the most from Grameen Bank?

SOURCE: "Nobel Lecture, Oslo, December 10, 2006" by Muhammad Yunus from nobelprize.org

Directions: Write the answers to the following questions. Use complete sentences.

Section 1–Money

1. Why is money acceptable to people in the United States?

2. What objects have been used as commodity money?

3. What was the problem with the Continentals issued by the Continental Congress during the American Revolution?

4. What is representative money?

5. What is fiat money?

6. Would the use of commodity money be as practical now as it was in the past? Explain your answer.

Section 2–The History of American Banking

7. Why did some people not like the First Bank of the United States?

8. What did Andrew Jackson think of the Second Bank of the United States?

9. During the Civil War, what was the money the Union printed called? Why were there problems with it?

10. What was the purpose of the Federal Reserve Act of 1913?

11. Why did President Franklin D. Roosevelt declare a "bank holiday"?

12. Why did Alexander Hamilton want to create the Bank of the United States? Was the bank successful?

Section 3–Banking Today

13. What is a demand deposit?

14. How have computers changed the way banking works?

15. What are the main categories economists use for the money supply? How do they differ?

16. What does the term *fractional reserve banking* refer to?

17. What do you think is the most important thing that banks do?

Exploring the Essential Question

18. Explain how banks earn a profit.

19. What are the advantages of using a stored-value card?

Essential Question Project

20. Complete this activity to answer the Essential Question **How well do financial institutions serve our needs?** Imagine that after many years of service, you become the manager of the bank that serves your neighborhood. Your responsibility to the bank is to increase its profits. However, you also want to do good works in your community. Using your worksheet from **Pearson SuccessNet.com**, fill in the following information:

(a) In the first column, write the services you will offer your customers.

(b) In the second column, write how these services will benefit your neighborhood. For example, how might giving people mortgages be good for the neighborhood? Think about which services and benefits are most likely to attract customers to your bank. Based on your ideas, write an advertising slogan for your bank in the third column.

Essential Questions Journal To continue to build a response to the Essential Question, go to your **Essential Questions Journal.**

Test-Taking Tip

Always read test directions more than once. Underline words that tell how many examples or items you must provide.

Chapter **11** Financial Markets

Essential Question, Chapter 11

How do your saving and investment choices affect your future?

- **Section 1** Saving and Investing

- **Section 2** Bonds and Other Financial Assets

- **Section 3** The Stock Market

Economics on the go

To study anywhere, anytime, download these onlir resources at *PearsonSuccessNet.com* ➤

▶ **What do saving, investment, and the stock market mean to you?** To many people, saving means opening a savings account. You can open a savings account at any bank. An investment is the use of money to create more money. It is the use of money today to earn profit in the future. There are many different types of investments, such as trading in a crowded stock market. Investing is an important part of the free enterprise system. It allows people to make a profit and increase their wealth.

In this chapter, you will learn that you have many choices on how to use your money. You will see how you can make your money work for you. And you will read about the history of the stock market and how attitudes have changed over the years.

Reading Strategy: Predicting
As you read, make predictions about the text. It will be helpful to preview the text and consider what you already know about a topic. Ask yourself:

• What details will support the main idea?

• What topic might be covered next in this section?

• Was my prediction accurate? What new information could cause me to change my prediction?

Visual Glossary
online
Go to the Visual Glossary Online for an interactive review of **capital gains.**

How the Economy Works
online
Go to How the Economy Works Online for an interactive lesson on **the bond market.**

Action Graph
online
Go to Action Graph Online for animated versions of key charts and graphs.

Objectives

- **Describe** the role of investing in the free enterprise system.
- **Explain** how the financial system links savers and borrowers.
- **Explain** the role of financial institutions in moving funds from savers to borrowers.
- **Identify** the trade-offs among risk, liquidity, and return.

■■■■■■■■■■■■■■■■■■■■■■

investment
something bought for future financial benefit

? Guiding Question

What are the benefits and risks of saving and investing?

Copy this concept web and fill it in as you read. Add more rectangles if needed.

▶ Economics and You Right now, you are making a huge investment. You are investing your time and energy in your education. This investment may pay off later, when you start your career. In the same way, businesses and governments look to the future. When a firm builds a new plant, it is making an investment. It hopes to earn more money later. When the government builds a new dam, it is making an investment too. It is spending money to ensure that people will have electric power in the future.

Principles in Action There are both benefits and risks to savings and investment. The savings you put in the bank will grow with almost no risk. However, this section will point out that some investments can bring a much greater reward. On the other hand, they also carry more risk.

Why is investment an important part of free enterprise?

Investment is an important part of the free enterprise system. It is something bought for future financial benefit. It promotes economic growth and contributes to a nation's wealth. People deposit money in a savings account in a bank. The bank may then lend the funds to businesses. The businesses, in turn, may invest that money in ways that help them grow. Then, as the businesses grow, they create new products and provide new jobs.

✔ **CHECKPOINT** *What role does investment play in free enterprise?*

How does the financial system bring savers and borrowers together?

The **financial system** allows the transfer of money between savers and borrowers. They may be linked directly or through **financial intermediaries.** These institutions help channel funds from savers to borrowers. When people save, they are really lending money to others. To earn a profit, banks and other financial institutions lend the money that has been deposited in them. Depositors are given a passbook or other papers in return. These papers show that the saver has a claim against the borrower. These claims are called **financial assets** or securities.

Figure 11.1 shows how the financial system brings together savers and borrowers. On one side are savers. Households, individuals, and businesses lend their savings in return for financial assets. On the other side are investors. Governments and businesses borrow money to build roads, factories, and homes. Businesses borrow money to develop new products, create new markets, or provide new services.

✓ **CHECKPOINT** *How does a bank serve as a way for savers and borrowers to transfer money between them?*

financial system
the network of structures that allows for the transfer of money between savers and borrowers

financial intermediary
an institution that helps channel funds from savers to borrowers

financial asset
a claim on the property or income of a borrower

Fig. 11.1 Financial Intermediaries

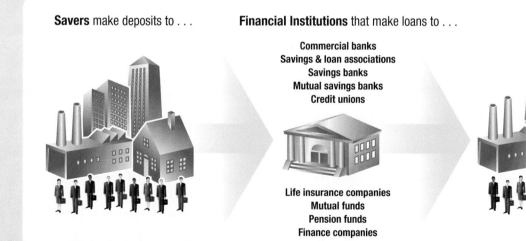

Savers make deposits to . . .

Financial Institutions that make loans to . . .

Commercial banks
Savings & loan associations
Savings banks
Mutual savings banks
Credit unions

Life insurance companies
Mutual funds
Pension funds
Finance companies

Investors

CHART SKILLS

Financial intermediaries include banks and other financial institutions. They accept funds from savers and make loans to investors. Investors include entrepreneurs, businesses, and other borrowers.

1. What advantages do financial intermediaries provide for savers?
2. What advantages do financial intermediaries provide for investors?

diversification
the strategy of spreading out investments to reduce risk

mutual fund
an organization that pools the savings of many individuals and invests it in stocks, bonds, and other financial assets

portfolio
a collection of financial assets

prospectus
an investment report

What are the advantages of working with financial intermediaries?

Savers and borrowers are usually linked through other institutions called financial intermediaries. Some financial intermediaries are banks, savings and loan associations, and credit unions. Life insurance companies, finance companies, and pension funds are also intermediaries. Intermediaries share risks, provide information, and provide liquidity.

Sharing risk Before you invest your money, you must decide how much of a risk taker you are. *Risk* refers to the chance of loss. Some investments have little risk. Savings accounts are almost risk free. Savers can take their money out whenever they choose. Other investments are more risky. Investors could lose some or all of the money from their investments. An example might be buying stock in a new company. If the investment turns out well, the investor earns a lot of money. If the investment turns out poorly, much of the money may be lost.

One way to cut down risk is by **diversification.** This strategy spreads investments to reduce risk. Spreading out investment money to different businesses rather than putting all the money into one business lowers the risk. Another way of lowering risk is by investing in a **mutual fund.** A mutual fund pools the savings of many individuals. It invests this money in a broad range of companies in the stock market. This way of investing is less risky than purchasing the stock of only one or two companies.

Providing information Financial intermediaries are also good sources of information. Your local bank collects information about borrowers. So do finance companies. Mutual fund managers know how the stocks in their **portfolios,** or collections of financial assets, are doing. The law requires all intermediaries to share this information with potential investors. The information is printed in an investment report called a **prospectus.**

The typical prospectus warns potential investors that "past performance does not necessarily predict future results." An investment that looks great today may not tomorrow. Financial intermediaries reduce the amount of time moneylenders and borrowers would spend looking for this information. Sometimes a prospectus can be long and have small type. The careful investor must study all of the information that has been provided.

Providing liquidity Financial intermediaries give investors more liquidity. Liquidity measures how quickly you can change your savings into cash. The easier it is to withdraw your funds, the more liquid the investment. Most investments are not very liquid.

 CHECKPOINT *How do financial intermediaries help lower risk?*

How are risk, liquidity, and return linked?

Risk, liquidity, and return are closely linked. How much investors receive for the use of their money is called the **return.** This is the extra money investors receive beyond their original investments. Before you invest, you should ask what the **rate of return** is. As we have learned, savings accounts often have a fixed rate of return. Many investments do not. Generally, the less risky and the more liquid an investment is, the lower the return. Investments that offer a high return often have high risk and low liquidity. Saving and investing, like many decisions, involve trade-offs.

 CHECKPOINT *Which investment has greater liquidity, a savings account or a certificate of deposit?*

 Reading Strategy
Predicting
Was your prediction accurate? If you need more information about saving and investing, see the Personal Finance Handbook at the back of this book.

return
the money an investor receives above and beyond the sum of money initially invested

rate of return
refers to the return stated as a percentage of the total amount invested

SECTION 1 ASSESSMENT

Essential Questions Journal To continue to build a response to the Essential Question, go to your **Essential Questions Journal.**

Quick Write

Read "Why is investment an important part of free enterprise?" and "How are risk, liquidity, and return linked?" in this section. Write a short essay answering the following questions: Why does our society need investment? How can businesses or other financial institutions attract the investors they need? Who benefits from these relationships?

 Guiding Question

1. Use your completed concept web to answer this question: What are the benefits and risks of saving and investing?

Key Terms and Main Ideas

Directions: On a sheet of paper, write the answer to each question. Use complete sentences.

2. What is investment?
3. What are the three parts of the financial system?
4. What is the main benefit of diversification?
5. What is the purpose of a prospectus?

Critical Thinking

6. **Summarize** What financial assets might be in a portfolio?
7. **Make Inferences** Rank the following investments from the least risky to the most risky: a certificate of deposit, stock in one company, and a mutual fund.

Objectives

- **Describe** the characteristics of bonds.
- **Identify** different types of bonds.
- **Describe** the characteristics of other types of financial assets.
- **List** four different types of financial asset markets.

savings bond
a bond issued by the government

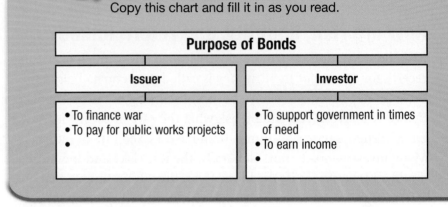

Guiding Question

Why are bonds bought and sold?

Copy this chart and fill it in as you read.

Purpose of Bonds	
Issuer	**Investor**
• To finance war • To pay for public works projects •	• To support government in times of need • To earn income •

▶ **Economics and You** It is 1942. The world is fighting World War II. The United States has thrown all its resources into defeating Germany and Japan. To keep the war going, the government needs money. To raise that money, the government begins selling **savings bonds.** Many Americans support the war by purchasing these "war bonds." Even though money is tight, you manage to do your part by bringing a few nickels and dimes to school to buy war stamps. Added to the money that other students bring, the school collects enough stamps to buy a bond.

Principles in Action

Why are bonds bought and sold? The war bonds helped pay for World War II. Governments or corporations sell other types of bonds to pay for projects. But unlike war bonds, most bonds are sold because the buyer expects to make a profit. The profit comes from the interest the bonds pay. In this section you will see how bonds are often a good investment. They pay a higher return than savings accounts but are almost as risk-free and safe.

What are bonds?

As you learned in Chapter 8, bonds are like IOUs. The federal government, cities and towns, and corporations sell them. When you buy a bond, you are lending money. In return for the loan, the seller promises to pay you back plus interest. You can keep and increase your savings if you hold the bond until it matures, or comes due. This may be several months or many years.

What are the three basic parts of bonds?

Bonds have three basic parts:

- *Coupon rate* The **coupon rate** is the interest rate a bond seller will pay to a buyer of the bond.
- *Maturity* **Maturity** is the time when the loan is to be repaid. Some bonds mature or must be paid off in a few years. Others do not have to be paid off for as long as 30 years.
- *Par value* **Par value** is the amount repaid to the investor when the bond matures.

Suppose you buy a $1,000 bond from the corporation Jeans, Etc. The investor who buys the bond is called the holder. The seller of a bond is the issuer. You are therefore the holder of the bond, and Jeans, Etc. is the issuer. These are the features of this bond:

- coupon rate: 5 percent, paid to the bondholder each year
- maturity: 10 years
- par value: $1,000

How much money will you earn from this bond and over what period of time? The coupon rate is 5 percent of $1,000 per year. This means you will receive 5 percent each year for 10 years. You would earn $50.00 (.05 × $1,000) each year, or $500.00 in interest over 10 years. In 10 years, the bond will have matured. Jeans, Etc. will then pay you back the money you loaned it when you bought the bond. You will receive the par value, or $1,000. Thus, for your $1,000 investment, you will have received $1,500 over a period of 10 years.

Not all bonds are held until they mature. Over their lifetimes they might be bought or sold, and their price may change. Because of these shifts in price, buyers and sellers are interested in a bond's yield. **Yield** is the rate of return on a bond if the bond is held to maturity.

What does it mean to buy bonds at a discount?

One way investors earn money is from interest on the bonds they buy. They can also earn money buying bonds at a discount. This is sometimes called a discount from par. Suppose Sharon buys a $1,000 bond at 5 percent interest. A year later, she wants to sell the bond. By that time, however, interest rates have gone up to 6 percent. No one will pay $1,000 for Sharon's bond at 5 percent interest when they could buy their own $1,000 bond at 6 percent interest. For Sharon to sell her bond at 5 percent, she will have to sell it at a discounted price. (See **Figure 11.2**.)

---

coupon rate
the interest rate a bond seller pays a bond buyer

maturity
the time a loan is to be repaid

par value
a bond's stated value, to be paid to the bondholder at maturity

yield
the annual rate of return on a bond if the bond is held until it matures

Fig. 11.2 Discounts From Par

1. Sharon buys a bond with a par value of $1,000 at 5 percent interest.

Bond purchase without discount from par

2. Interest rates go up to 6 percent.

3. Sharon needs to sell her bond. Nate wants to buy it, but is unwilling to buy a bond at 5 percent interest when the current rate is 6 percent.

4. Sharon offers to discount the bond, taking $40 off the price and selling it for $960.

5. Nate accepts the offer. He now owns a $1,000 bond paying 5 percent interest, which he purchased at a discount from par.

Bond purchase with discount from par

CHART SKILLS

Investors can earn money by buying bonds at a discount, called a discount from par.

1. How does interest affect bond prices?
2. Sharon buys the bond at $1,000 at 5 percent interest per year. She sells it five years later at $960. Would she necessarily have lost money on the purchase of her bond?

As you have seen in **Figure 11.2** on page 263, Nate buys Sharon's bond with a par value of $1,000 at a discount. Sharon sells it to Nate for only $960.00. When the bond matures, Nate will receive $1,000, the par value. He will also earn all the interest payments from the bond issuer plus the $40.00 discount.

Are all bonds rated the same?

How does an investor decide which bonds to buy? Bonds are rated by independent firms. The two biggest firms are Standard & Poor's and Moody's. They rate bonds. The highest rating goes to bond issuers who show they are able to repay the bonds with interest.

The highest investment rating is AAA in Standard & Poor's system and Aaa in Moody's. An investment-grade bond is considered safe enough for banks to invest in. The lowest rating generally means the bond is in default. This means the issuer has not kept up with interest payments or has failed to repay the money it borrowed.

A high bond rating usually means the issuer can sell the bonds even if the interest rate it pays is low. For example, a AAA ("triple A") bond may be issued at a 5 percent interest rate. A BBB bond, however, may be issued at a 7.5 percent interest rate. Buyers of both bonds are involved in trade-offs. The buyer of the AAA bond trades off a lower interest rate for lower risk. The buyer of the BBB bond trades greater risk for a higher interest rate.

What are the advantages and disadvantages to the issuer of bonds?

Bonds are good for the issuer for two main reasons:
1. Once the bond is sold, the coupon rate for that bond will not go up or down. For example, when Jeans, Etc. sold its bonds, it knew it would be making fixed payments for 10 years.
2. Unlike stockholders, bondholders do not own a part of the company. Stockholders share in a company's profits. Bondholders do not.

On the other hand, there are two main disadvantages to the issuer of bonds:
1. The company must make interest payments. It must pay the interest even in bad years when it does not earn much.
2. Suppose the firm is doing poorly. Then its bonds may be downgraded to a lower bond rating. The company may have to sell its bonds at a discount.

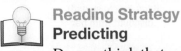

Reading Strategy
Predicting
Do you think that after you have read this section, you will be able to make good investment choices?

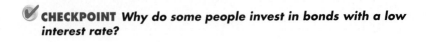

CHECKPOINT *Why do some people invest in bonds with a low interest rate?*

What are the main types of bonds?

There are many different types of bonds. The most common are savings bonds, Treasury bonds, municipal bonds, corporate bonds, and junk bonds.

What are savings bonds?

You may already know about savings bonds. Sometimes, they are given to young people as gifts. Savings bonds are bonds the U.S. government issues. They are usually issued in small amounts. The government uses the money it raises from the sale of savings bonds to help pay for projects such as government buildings, roads, and dams. Savings bonds have little risk to the bond holder and are a safe investment.

The federal government pays interest on savings bonds. However, unlike most other bond issuers, it does not send interest payments to bondholders regularly. Instead, the buyer purchases a savings bond for less than par value. For example, you can buy a $50.00 savings bond for only $25.00. When the bond matures, you receive the $25.00 you paid for the bond plus $25.00 in interest.

What are Treasury bonds?

The U.S. Treasury Department issues **Treasury bonds.** It also issues Treasury bills and notes (T-bills and T-notes). Some of these investments mature in a few months. Others take as long as 30 years to mature. Because they are backed by the U.S. government, there is little risk.

One possible problem with bonds is inflation. Inflation is a rise in the price of goods and services. Suppose a Treasury bond pays you 5 percent interest per year. If the inflation rate is 3 percent, you are really earning just 2 percent interest on the bond.

The **inflation-indexed bond** protects investors against inflation. It links the principal and interest to an inflation index. The index measures prices. If the index rises by 3 percent, this bond's par value will also rise by 3 percent. As a result, you will receive the return on the bond that you expected when you bought it.

What are municipal bonds?

Local governments issue **municipal bonds.** So do state governments. The bonds are sold to pay for such things as highways, state buildings, libraries, parks, and schools. Sometimes, these bonds are called *munis.* (See **Figure 11.3.**) Investors do not have to pay taxes on the money they earn. For this reason, munis may be a good investment.

Treasury bond
a government bond issued with a term of 10 to 30 years

inflation-indexed bond
a bond that protects investors against inflation by linking to an inflation index

municipal bond
a bond issued by state and local governments to pay for such things as highways, state buildings, parks, and schools

Fig. 11.3 How the Economy Works

What is the **function** of a **municipal bond?**

Companies or governments sell bonds to finance projects. Most bonds are bought because the buyer expects to earn interest on the investment. Here's the story of one bond, known as a municipal bond: It explains why it was issued and why it was bought.

1 The main state road connecting Mudville and Saltville is in terrible shape. People don't want to use it. The economies of both cities are suffering.

2 Mudville and Saltville and all the towns in between need a new road. But how can the citizens pay for it? The state steps in and proposes to repair the road and make it into a toll road. State residents vote to issue bonds.

The Problem

Financing the Solution

corporate bond
a bond sold to help raise money to make a business bigger

junk bond
a bond with high risk and, possibly, high yield

What are corporate bonds?

Corporations sell bonds to help raise money to make their businesses bigger. These **corporate bonds** are generally sold in amounts such as $1,000 or $5,000.

Corporate bonds have more risk than government bonds. Investors must be sure the corporation has enough money to pay back the bondholders. The ratings firms closely watch the corporations that issue bonds. They are also watched by the Securities and Exchange Commission (SEC). The SEC is a part of the government.

What are junk bonds?

Junk bonds are below investment-grade bonds. They offer high yields but have a high risk. Investors in junk bonds must know that some of the issuing firms may not be able to repay the bonds. Still, selling junk bonds made it possible for companies to start projects that otherwise would not have been possible.

✓ **CHECKPOINT** *What type of bond might have been used to fund the construction of your school?*

UNDER REPAIR

CASH

3 The bonds go on sale and sell well. The state's credit is good, and interest on the bond is tax exempt. There's enough money to begin construction on a new road.

5 Investors are happy because they receive a nice check every three months. The citizens of Mudville and Saltville are happy because the repaired road makes travel between the two cities easier.

4 With a new road, Mudville and Saltville prosper. Tolls from the road more than cover the interest that must be paid to bondholders.

Check Your Understanding
1. What is the cost and benefit of buying a municipal bond?
2. Why do you think bond issues like this one must be approved by voters?

Problem Solved

What are other types of financial assets?

Certificates of deposit (CDs) are a common form of investment. As you read in Chapter 10, CDs are available through banks. Small investors can deposit as little as $100.00 in a CD. Some CDs mature in just three months. Others mature in as long as six years. A short-term CD is very liquid. The trade-off is that it pays low interest. The long-term CD earns a higher interest. The trade-off is that investors cannot get to their savings for six years.

Money market mutual funds invest in short-term financial assets such as Treasury bills and CDs. Their main goal is protecting the investment. Money market mutual funds pay a higher interest rate than savings accounts. The trade-off for the higher interest is that money market mutual funds are a little more risky than savings accounts. They are not covered by FDIC insurance.

✔ **CHECKPOINT** *What is one advantage and one disadvantage of a money market mutual fund as compared with a savings account?*

capital market
a market in which money is lent for periods longer than a year

money market
a market in which money is lent for periods of one year or less

primary market
a market where newly issued financial assets can be redeemed only by the original holder

secondary market
a market where financial assets are allowed to be resold

Reading Strategy
Predicting

Was your prediction correct? If so, name two things you have learned about investing bonds. If not, what would you still like to learn about bonds?

How are financial asset markets classified?

Bonds, certificates of deposit, and money market mutual funds are traded on financial asset markets. There are two ways to group these markets. One is according to the length of time for which funds are lent. These include capital markets and money markets.

- Markets in which money is lent for longer than a year are **capital markets.** Financial assets traded here include long-term CDs and corporate and government bonds.
- Markets in which money is lent for one year or less are **money markets.** Financial assets traded here include short-term CDs and Treasury bills.

Markets may also be grouped by whether assets can be resold. This grouping includes primary and secondary markets.

- Newly issued financial assets that can be paid to the original buyer, such as savings bonds, are sold on **primary markets.** They cannot be sold by the original buyer to another buyer. Small CDs are also in the primary market.
- Financial assets that are allowed to be resold are sold on **secondary markets.** If there is a strong secondary market for an asset, the investor knows the asset can be resold for quick cash.

✔ **CHECKPOINT** *What are the two ways of classifying financial asset markets?*

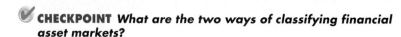

SECTION **2** ASSESSMENT

Essential Questions Journal
To continue to build a response to the Essential Question, go to your **Essential Questions Journal.**

❓ Guiding Question

1. Use your completed chart to answer this question: Why are bonds bought and sold?

Key Terms and Main Ideas

Directions: On a sheet of paper, write the answer to each question. Use complete sentences.

2. Identify the three components of bonds.

3. Why does the United States government issue savings bonds?

4. What is the advantage of an inflation-indexed bond?

5. Name two advantages and two disadvantages of bonds for their issuers.

Critical Thinking

6. **Draw Conclusions** When would selling bonds at a discount from par be a good investment?

7. **Draw Inferences** (a) How are bonds rated? (b) How do these ratings help investors?

Objectives

- **Identify** the benefits and risks of buying stocks.
- **Describe** how stocks are traded.
- **Explain** how stock performance is measured.
- **Describe** the Great Crash of 1929 and more recent stock market events.

■■■■■■■■■■■■■■■■■■■

stock exchange
a market where stocks can be bought and sold

Guiding Question

How does the stock market work?

Copy this chart and fill it in as you read.

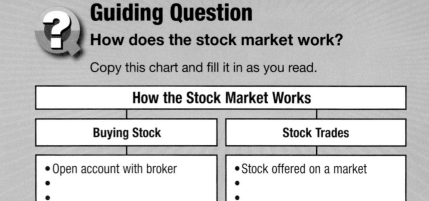

How the Stock Market Works	
Buying Stock	**Stock Trades**
• Open account with broker • •	• Stock offered on a market • •

▶ **Economics and You** You hear it on the news every day: "Stock prices fell today in heavy trading," or "The Dow surged today." Lots of long faces follow a drop in the stock market. A big rise makes most people happy. Many people are interested in the stock market. But is the stock market a place where you should invest your savings?

Principles in Action Much information and advice is available about investing in the stock market. The Internet lists stocks with the changes in price per share. Whether the stock market has gone up or down is big news. But just what is stock, how is it traded, and when is it a good investment?

What is the stock market?

As the twenty-first century began, more than half of all the households in America owned stock. Stocks are bought or sold on **stock exchanges.** These are markets for buying or selling stock. The New York Stock Exchange (NYSE) is the largest stock exchange in the world. It is located on Wall Street in New York City. Today, billions of shares of stock and bonds are exchanged every day.

The stock market is very important. It affects people's confidence about the future even if they do not own stock themselves. When the stock market is doing well, people feel good about the economy. When they feel good, they are willing to spend more money. Up to a certain point, the more they spend, the more the economy grows.

Companies need money to grow. Maybe they want to expand or develop new products. They could borrow money from a bank, but they would have to pay it back. Instead, they could sell bonds.

▲ To expand, companies need money. They may sell shares to investors. Some companies issue paper certificates.

■■■■■■■■■■■■■■■■■■■■

capital gain
the difference between a higher selling price and a lower purchase price that results in a financial gain for the seller

capital loss
the difference between a lower selling price and a higher purchase price that results in a financial loss for the seller

Another way a company can raise money without going into debt is by selling stock. Stock is usually sold in units known as shares. Not every company can issue stock. Only a business corporation can issue stock.

What are the benefits of buying stocks?

Most people who buy stocks are interested in a good return on their money. Investors can profit from stocks in two ways: from income or from growth. They can earn income by collecting dividends. As you have read in Chapter 8, many corporations pay out part of their profits as dividends to their stockholders. Dividends are usually paid quarterly (four times a year). Usually, companies that have been in business for a long time pay higher dividends. Newer firms tend to use profits to develop new products or to grow. They seldom pay dividends.

Investors can profit if the price of the stock goes higher than the price they paid. This is called a **capital gain.** Suppose you had $100.00. You bought 10 shares of a business. You paid $10.00 a share. The share price goes up to $15.00. You could sell the stock. Your profit would be $5.00 a share, or a capital gain of $50.00. Of course, stock prices go down too. Let's say the price of the stock drops to $5.00 and you decide to sell. Your **capital loss** is $5.00 a share, or a total of $50.00.

What is the difference between an income stock and a growth stock?

Some people buy stock that will give them extra income. Stock that gives investors income by paying dividends is called income stock. Other people are more interested in growth than income. They invest in companies that use their earnings to build the business. They benefit when the business (and its stock) grow in value over time. This type of stock is called growth stock.

How are common and preferred stock different?

Corporations issue both common and preferred stock. Both common and preferred shareholders own a portion of the company, but they have different rights. Owners of common stock can help elect the board of directors. They have a say on company policies. Owners of preferred stock are nonvoting owners of the company. There are two benefits to owning preferred stock. First, owners of preferred stock receive dividends before the owners

Innovators

Warren Buffett

"Why should I buy real estate when the stock market is so easy?" Warren Buffett believed he would be rich someday, and he was right. In 2008, shares in his investment company, Berkshire Hathaway, traded at more than $125,000 for a single share. To many people, he is the ultimate stock market expert, nicknamed "the Oracle of Omaha."

Buffett learned how to invest at Columbia University, where a professor taught him to pick his investments by doing his own research. "You're not right or wrong because 1,000 people agree with you or disagree with you," the professor said. "You're right because your facts and reasons are right."

Fast Facts

Warren Buffett (1930–)

Education: B.A./B.S. University of Nebraska; M.S. Columbia University

Claim to Fame: Very successful stock market investor and philanthropist, with personal assets worth more than $55 billion.

In 1965 Buffett purchased Berkshire Hathaway, a large manufacturer in the declining textile industry. Where others saw an aging dinosaur that was practically worthless, Buffett saw a business that could still produce large amounts of capital. Although the stock market valued Berkshire at $14.86 per share, Buffett knew the company was worth more. Using the excess capital from Berkshire, he went on to invest in a wide range of businesses. Like Berkshire Hathaway, the companies Buffett has bought are exceptional values. Today Buffett focuses on a new venture—giving his money away. In 2006, he donated 80 percent of his fortune to charities.

of common stock. Second, if the company goes out of business, preferred stockholders may receive some of their investments back before common stockholders do.

Why do stock prices change?

Some newspapers list stocks and bonds and their prices. For stocks, the opening price, high, low, and closing price are listed. Sometimes, the high and low price for the last 52 weeks (one running year) is also included. The value of every stock is always changing. When the price of a stock rises, that stock is up. When the price drops, that stock is down.

Generally, the value of stock goes up if the company makes a profit. If investors think it will do better in the future, its value may also go up. Another factor affecting stock prices is how confident people feel about the U.S. economy and the world economy. Stock prices cannot be predicted. A good rule to remember is that companies with growing profits are most likely to be the best investments.

✔ **CHECKPOINT** *What are two ways an investor can make a profit from buying stocks?*

Reading Strategy
Predicting
Remember that a prediction is not just a guess. As you read about Warren Buffett, think about the predictions he made that earned him money.

stockbroker
a person who links buyers and sellers of stock

brokerage firm
a business that specializes in trading stocks

futures
contracts to buy or sell commodities or financial assets at a particular date in the future at a price specified today

stock option
contract that gives investors the right to buy or sell stock and other financial assets at a particular price until a specified future date

call option
a contract for buying stock at a particular price until a specified future date

How are stocks bought and sold?

To buy and sell stock, investors must open an account with a **stockbroker.** A stockbroker has a license to buy and sell stocks. You must be at least 18 years old to open an account. Parents can open accounts for younger investors. Of course, you must fill out forms and deposit money in the account.

Stockbrokers work for **brokerage firms.** These businesses buy and sell stock. Stockbrokers receive a fee for every stock bought or sold.

What is a stock exchange?

A stock exchange is a market for buying and selling stock. The New York Stock Exchange is the largest and most powerful exchange in the country. The NYSE handles trading of stocks and bonds for the top companies in the United States and in the world.

The National Association of Securities Dealers Automated Quotations (NASDAQ) system was created in 1971. Now it handles more trades on average than any other American market. It links buyers and sellers via a network of computers.

In addition, a large number of people trade stocks on the Internet. They use online brokerage firms or special trading software.

How can investors use futures and options?

Futures are contracts to buy or sell commodities or financial assets at a date in the future at a price set today. For example, a buyer and seller might agree today on a price of $4.50 per bushel for soybeans. Actually, the beans will not reach the market until six or nine months from now. The buyer pays part of the money today. The seller agrees to deliver the goods in the future. Many of the markets in which futures are bought and sold are linked with grain and livestock exchanges. These markets include the New York Mercantile Exchange and the Chicago Board of Trade.

An investor could profit from buying futures if the price goes up. For example, if the price of soybeans goes up to $5.50 per bushel, the investor is paying a dollar less than new buyers. The investor could also sell his futures contract to another buyer for profit.

An *option* is a choice. **Stock options** give the holder the right to buy or sell stock at a set price or a set period of time. The option to buy shares of stock until a set time in the future is known as a **call option.** For example, you may pay $10.00 per share today for a call option. The call option gives you the right to buy a certain stock at a price of, say, $100.00 per share. Let's say that at the end of six months, the price has gone up to $115.00 per share. Your option still allows you to buy the stock for $100.00. You thus earn $5.00 per share ($15.00 minus the $10.00 you paid for the call option). If, on the other hand, the price has dropped to $80.00, you can disregard the option and buy the stock for $80.00. Of course, you lose the $10.00 you paid for the option.

The option to sell shares of stock at a time in the future is called a **put option.** Suppose you, as the seller, pay $5.00 per share for the right to sell at $50.00 per share a stock you do not yet own. If the price per share falls to $40.00, you can buy the share at that price. But you can require the buyer who signed the contract to pay the agreed-on $50.00. You would then earn $5.00 per share on the sale ($10.00 minus the $5.00 you paid for the put option). If the price rises to $60.00, however, you can disregard the option and sell the stock for $60.00.

✅ **CHECKPOINT** *What two kinds of contracts allow investors to buy and sell commodities or financial assets at some later date?*

How is stock performance measured?

One of the most popular measures of stock market performance is the Dow Jones Industrial Average (DJIA). People often call it "the Dow." It is the average selling price of 30 of the top stocks in the NYSE. The DJIA goes up and down all the time. By checking the changes in the Dow, investors get a fair picture of how the stock market is doing.

The S&P 500 (Standard & Poor's 500) gives a bigger picture of stock performance than the Dow. It tracks the price changes of 500 different stocks to measure how well the overall stock market is doing. Most of the S&P 500 are stocks listed on the NYSE, but some of its stocks are traded on the NASDAQ.

Bears are cautious animals. They usually do not move too fast. Bulls are bold animals. They sometimes charge right ahead. Investors who believe the stock market will go down are called bears. Bearish investors buy stock cautiously. Investors who believe the stock market will go up are called bulls. Bullish investors charge ahead and put more of their money in the market. In a **bear market,** the prices of most stocks are falling. In a **bull market,** the prices of most stocks are going up.

✅ **CHECKPOINT** *What do investors tend to do during a bull market?*

---

put option
a contract for selling stock at a particular price until a specified future date

bear market
a market in which the prices of most stocks are falling

bull market
a market in which the prices of most stocks are rising

Risk vs. Return: Stocks and Bonds

Your grandmother, who does not like risk, gave you a savings bond when you were in grade school. *The rate of return is fixed, so you know exactly what the bond will be worth when you cash it in.*

You decide to take some money from your pay and buy a few shares of stock. *You can't predict how your stock will perform, so the possible risk and return are both greater than if you bought bonds.*

What was the Great Crash of 1929?

The 1920s saw a long-term bull market. This period ended with the crash of the stock market in 1929. This collapse is called the Great Crash of 1929.

When President Herbert Hoover took office in 1929, the United States economy seemed to be in excellent shape. The stock market was soaring. However, there were some signs of trouble. A small number of companies and families held much of the nation's wealth. Many farmers and workers were poor. Many ordinary people went into debt buying consumer goods on credit. In addition, industries were producing more goods than consumers could buy. Some industries developed large amounts of surplus goods. Prices began to decline.

How did speculation impact the stock market?

The practice of **speculation** grew. Speculation is making high-risk investments using borrowed money with the goal of profiting from changes in price. This was the first time that ordinary people could try their hand in the stock market. Stockbrokers started using a practice called "buying on margin" to attract these investors. The investors bought stock for a fraction of its price and borrowed the rest from a brokerage firm.

In September 1929, the Dow had reached an all-time high. Then, the Dow dropped. When stock prices continued to fall, the public started to panic. Stocks continued to lose their value, and investors all over the country raced to take out their money. On October 29, 1929, 16.4 million shares were sold. At the time, that was a record. The average number of shares sold every day had been 4 to 8 million. The Great Crash had begun. The Great Crash was one cause of the Great Depression. Millions of Americans lost their jobs, homes, and farms.

▲ Panicked investors sold large numbers of stock shares (bottom), causing the Great Crash. Many investors lost everything (top).

How did attitudes toward stocks change after the Great Depression?

After the Great Depression, many people avoided stocks. They thought stocks were risky investments. Gradually, however, Americans became more comfortable with stock ownership. The stock market grew steadily, and investors prospered.

Stocks crashed again on October 18, 1987. However, this time the market bounced back, and the effect on the economy was much less severe. Starting in 1990, stock prices began to soar because of a growing economy and a technology boom. But again prices began dropping when investors became worried. The investors wondered if new companies could earn enough money to justify their high stock prices. Those prices began dropping.

In 2001, an economic downturn and the terrorist attacks of September 11 further battered the stock market. This was followed by the fall of a company called Enron. This enormous company had lied about profits for years to cover up huge losses. In response, Congress passed the Sarbanes-Oxley Act to make sure financial reports are accurate.

In 2006, the stock market once again recovered. In 2008 and 2009, however, the collapse of several large institutions and tightening credit markets coincided with the stock market falling. As always, nobody can predict how the stock market will behave in the future.

 CHECKPOINT *What was the Great Crash of 1929?*

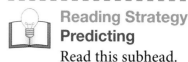
Reading Strategy
Predicting
Read this subhead. Then predict how attitudes about stocks changed after the Great Depression.

SECTION **3** ASSESSMENT

Essential Questions Journal

To continue to build a response to the Essential Question, go to your **Essential Questions Journal.**

Guiding Question

1. Use your completed chart to answer this question: How does the stock market work?

Key Terms and Main Ideas

Directions: On a sheet of paper, write the answer to each question. Use complete sentences.

2. Describe the job of a stockbroker.

3. Identify two major U.S. stock exchanges.

4. What is a capital gain? A capital loss?

5. How did speculation contribute to the Great Crash of 1929?

Critical Thinking

6. **Predict Consequences** Would you buy stock during a bear market? Why or why not?

7. **Make Inferences** (a) Name the main causes of the Great Crash of 1929. (b) What lessons can investors learn from the crash?

Section 1–Saving and Investing

- Investing is an important part of the free enterprise system. It promotes economic growth and contributes to a nation's wealth.

- Financial intermediaries link savers and borrowers. These institutions share the risks with investors, provide information, and provide liquidity.

Section 2–Bonds and Other Financial Assets

- Bonds have three basic parts: the coupon rate, maturity, and the par value. Bonds are relatively safe investments, but they may also lose some of their value and be harder to sell.

- Several types of bonds include savings bonds; Treasury bonds, bills, and notes; municipal bonds; corporate bonds; and junk bonds.

- Other financial assets include certificates of deposit and money market mutual funds.

- Financial asset markets are classified in different ways: as capital markets and as money markets, and as primary and secondary markets.

Section 3–The Stock Market

- Benefits of buying stock include earning money from dividends and reselling the stock for more than the investor paid for it.

- Risks of buying stock include earning lower profits because the firm selling the stock may earn lower profits than expected or even lose money. Investors could also lose money by selling their stock at a lower price than they paid for it.

- Stocks are traded on a stock exchange. People may work with stockbrokers, who work for brokerage firms. The New York Stock Exchange and the NASDAQ are the most powerful stock markets in the United States.

- The Great Crash of 1929 saw the collapse of the stock market, which was one cause of the Great Depression. After the Great Depression, people avoided stocks, but attitudes then began to change. The stock market today continues to have its ups and downs.

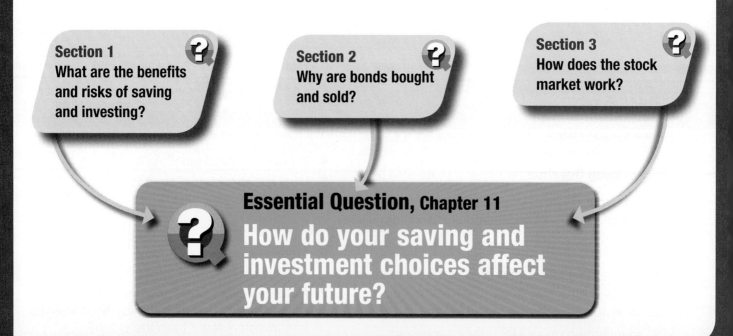

Section 1
What are the benefits and risks of saving and investing?

Section 2
Why are bonds bought and sold?

Section 3
How does the stock market work?

Essential Question, Chapter 11
How do your saving and investment choices affect your future?

Franklin D. Roosevelt's 1933 Inaugural Speech

When U.S. President Franklin D. Roosevelt gave his inaugural speech on March 4, 1933, the world was in the middle of the Great Depression. People were out of money. Jobs were scarce. Banks were in crisis. The outlook was grim, but Roosevelt urged Americans to think positively. He gave a plan for recovery in his speech.

"We face our common difficulties. They concern . . . only material things. Values have shrunken to fantastic levels; taxes have risen; our ability to pay has fallen; government of all kinds is faced by serious curtailment [decrease] of income; the means of exchange are frozen in the currents of trade; . . . farmers find no markets for their produce; the savings of many years in thousands of families are gone.

More important, a host of unemployed citizens face the grim problem of existence, and an equally great number toil with little return. Only a foolish optimist can deny the dark realities of the moment. . . .

Our greatest primary task is to put people to work. . . . It can be [done] in part by . . . accomplishing greatly needed projects to stimulate and reorganize the use of our natural resources. . . .

We must act and act quickly. . . .

. . . There must be a strict supervision of all banking and credit and investments; there must be an end to speculation with other people's money, and there must be provision for an adequate but sound currency. . . .

I am prepared under my constitutional duty to recommend the measures that a stricken nation in the midst of a stricken world may require. . . .

But in the event that the Congress shall fail, . . . and in the event that the national emergency is still critical, . . . I shall ask the Congress for . . . broad executive power to wage a war against the emergency. . . ."

Document-Based Questions

1. Describe the U.S. economic situation in 1933.
2. What five common difficulties did Americans face, according to Roosevelt's speech?
3. What did Roosevelt say was the government's greatest task?
4. How did Roosevelt want to change the banking system?
5. Do you think the words of this speech were important to the American people? Explain.

SOURCE: Inaugural Address of the President, Washington, D.C., March 4, 1933 http://www.archives.gov/digital_classroom/lessons/fdr_inaugural_address/images/address_logif from the National Archives.

Directions: Write the answer to the questions using complete sentences.

Section 1—Saving and Investing

1. What is the main advantage of mutual funds?
2. What are the advantages of bonds for investors?
3. What is a portfolio?
4. Why would a borrower or saver use financial intermediaries rather than work directly with financial institutions?
5. How does diversification lower the risk for investors?

Section 2—Bonds and Other Financial Assets

6. Which is more liquid, a business or a bond? Explain.
7. What is the difference between the primary market and the secondary market?
8. How does the U.S. government use funds from the sale of savings bonds?
9. Why are CDs attractive to small investors?
10. Are U.S. Treasury bonds a risky investment? Explain.
11. What risk do investors face if they keep their bonds until maturity? If they sell them before maturity?

Section 3—The Stock Market

12. Why do corporations sell stock?
13. How are income stock and growth stock different?
14. How are common stock and preferred stock different?
15. What determines the size of dividends that corporations pay investors?

Economics on the go

16. Why do people buy stock, even though it is considered risky?

17. Describe the attitude of people toward the stock market after October 29, 1929. Has this attitude changed in recent years?

Exploring the Essential Question

18. How are the advantages and risks of investing in bonds similar to and different from those of investing in stocks?

19. Do you think a stock market crash like the Great Crash of 1929 could happen again? Explain.

Essential Question Activity

20. Complete this activity to answer the Essential Question **How do your saving and investment choices affect your future?**

Imagine you have turned 21. A relative you have never met has died, leaving you $5,000. The will states you must provide an investment plan to meet your expected financial needs when you are 30 years old. Answer these questions to help you:

(a) What career do you expect to be in? How much money will you be earning? (b) What financial responsibilities will you have? (c) How much money will you need from your investments? Will you depend on that income, or can you risk losing some of it?

Diversify your investments between relatively safe and relatively high return investments, depending on your predicted needs.

> **Essential Questions Journal** To continue to build a response to the Essential Question, go to your **Essential Questions Journal.**

 Test-Taking Tip

Look for details in the directions that ask for the correct form of the answer. For example, some directions may ask for a paragraph. Others may require only a sentence or phrase.

Unit 4 Challenge

Essential Question, Unit 4

How can you make the most of your money?

There are many differing opinions about how individuals can make the most of their money. Look at the opinions below, keeping in mind the Essential Question: How can you make the most of your money?

VIDEO By Students For Students
For videos on Essential Questions, go to *PearsonSuccessNet.com*

"Legend has it that Albert Einstein once called compound interest the most powerful force in the universe. Compound interest is the engine that can turn even meager savings into a nice nest egg over time. Inattention to debt puts you on the wrong side of that equation. You spend dollars that could be put to work making you wealthy. You want to be on the right side—the side that uses debt to make money but avoids debt when it hurts.... Stop watching your money go up in smoke."

—Mary Dalrymple, "Habits for Wealth: Dump Your Debt Habit"

"I don't know what the stock market will do tomorrow. (And, let me be equally clear, neither does anyone else.) Bad things may happen tomorrow. Certainly, bad things will happen on some days.... You get a great return [from stocks] by noticing that the day-to-day price of the market doesn't have much to do with the real long-term value of the best companies within that market. You get an even better return than the market averages by never mixing up three very important facts: Extreme stock market pessimism is great for buyers, extreme exuberance is great for sellers...and stocks are long-term investments."

—John Casper, "Lessons Learned"

Essential Question Writing Activity

Consider the different views of economics expressed in the sources on this page and what you have learned about banking and financial institutions. **Then write a well-constructed essay expressing your view of how you can make the most of your money.**

Essential Questions Journal

To respond to the unit Essential Question, go to your **Essential Questions Journal**.

Writing Guidelines

- Address all aspects of the Essential Question Writing Activity.
- Support the theme with relevant facts, examples, and details.
- Use a logical and clear plan of organization.
- Introduce the theme by establishing a framework that is beyond a simple restatement of the question and conclude with a summation of the theme.

For help with writing a Persuasive Essay, refer to the *Writing Skills Handbook* in the Reference section, page S-5.

5 Measuring Economic Performance

Essential Question, Unit 5

Why does it matter how the economy is doing?

Chapter 13
How much can we reduce unemployment, inflation, and poverty?

Chapter 12
How do we know if the economy is healthy?

Chapter 12 Gross Domestic Product and Growth

Essential Question, Chapter 12

How do we know if the economy is healthy?

Economics on the go

To study anywhere, anytime, download these online resources at *PearsonSuccessNet.com* ➤

▶ **You pick up a newspaper.** You read that the economy is "slowing down." What exactly does that mean? How is the health of the economy measured? Economists try to predict the future. They help the government make decisions about keeping the economy healthy. In a way, economists are like doctors. They take measurements to check the health of the economy. If they find a problem, they suggest ways to fix it.

In this chapter, you will learn many ways to measure an economy. You will also learn about the phases of the business cycle, how saving and investing relate to economic growth, and how technology affects progress.

Reading Strategy: Visualizing
Visualizing is like creating a movie in your mind. It will help you understand the content you read.

For example, you could visualize the business cycle as a roller coaster. The cycle goes up (expansion), reaches the top (peak), falls (contraction), and bottoms out (trough). The cycle then repeats itself, like a roller coaster running around a track.

Also, look at the figures, photographs, and descriptive words. These will help you visualize what is happening.

Visual Glossary online

Go to the Visual Glossary Online for an interactive review of **Gross Domestic Product.**

How the Economy Works online

Go to How the Economy Works Online for an interactive lesson on what causes a **recession.**

Action Graph online

Go to Action Graph Online for animated versions of key charts and graphs.

Objectives

- **Explain** how gross domestic product (GDP) is measured.
- **Distinguish** between nominal and real GDP.
- **List** the main limitations of GDP.
- **Identify** factors that influence GDP.
- **Describe** other output and income measures.

Guiding Question

What does GDP show about the nation's economy?

Copy this chart and fill it in as you read. Make four statements about GDP and list four drawbacks to this economic measure.

About GDP	Drawbacks to GDP
• Describes the total output of an economy • Can be based on expenditures or income •	• Both methods of calculation are imperfect • Nominal GDP misleading • Doesn't measure "well-being"

Gross Domestic Product (GDP)

national income accounting
a system economists use to collect and organize macroeconomic statistics on production, income, investment, and savings

▶ **Economics and You** How much attention do you pay to the economic news? If you are like most people your age— or even most Americans in general—your answer is probably, "Not much." After all, you would have to be a genius to keep track of GDP, GNP, NNP, NI, DPI, and the rest of the economic alphabet soup. And you might think who cares anyway?

But whether or not you care, GDP, NI, and the rest do affect you. What's more, you affect them. Every time you buy a shirt, rent a movie, or get a paycheck, you toss your bit into the alphabet soup.

Principles in Action Economists have developed many tools to monitor the nation's economic performance. They even have a way to measure how much money families like yours have to spend. You will learn what these measures tell us—and don't tell us—about the economy.

What is the gross domestic product?

In order to track the U.S. economy, economists use a bookkeeping system called **national income accounting.** With this system, they collect and organize economic facts. They study overall production, income, investment, and savings. The information is collected by the U.S. Department of Commerce. It is available in the form of the National Income and Product Accounts (NIPA). The information in NIPA is used to make an economic plan of action. You will read how the government does this in Chapters 15 and 16.

Gross domestic product (GDP) is the most important measure of the economy. GDP is the dollar value of all final goods and services produced in a country in a given year. To help you understand GDP, let us look at each part of this definition:

- **Dollar value** refers to the total of the selling prices of all goods and services produced in a calendar year. The selling prices of everything produced are added up to calculate GDP. This includes goods and services produced by individuals, businesses, and the government.

- **Final goods and services** are goods and services sold to the final user. This can be confusing. Let's use a car as an example. The carmaker has to buy steel, plastic, glass, and other things that go into its cars. These are not figured into GDP because they are **intermediate goods.** Intermediate goods are goods that have not reached the final user. They are goods used to make final goods. The final user in our example is the person who buys the car. By using only the value of final goods and services, economists avoid counting the values of goods more than once.

- **Produced in a country** is especially important to remember. Because we are trying to find the country's gross *domestic* product, we can look only at the goods and services produced within that country. For example, the GDP of the U.S. economy includes cars made in Ohio by a Japanese car company. It does not include cars made in Brazil by an American company.

- **In a given year** takes into account when a good is produced. Suppose your neighbor sells a used car. When the car was originally made, it was counted in the GDP of that year. Thus, it cannot be counted again this year when it is resold. After all, the car was produced only once. However, suppose your neighbor put new brakes on the car this year before selling it. The value of the brakes would be included in this year's GDP.

How is GDP calculated?

Government economists estimate how much will be spent in one year on four groups of final goods and services:

1. consumer goods and services
2. business goods and services
3. government goods and services
4. net exports

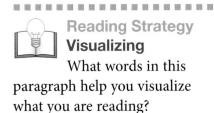

Reading Strategy
Visualizing
What words in this paragraph help you visualize what you are reading?

gross domestic product
the dollar value of all final goods and services produced within a country's borders in a given year

intermediate goods
goods used in the production of final goods

durable goods
goods that last for a relatively long time

nondurable goods
goods that last a short period of time, such as food, light bulbs, and sneakers

expenditure approach
a way of calculating GDP in which economists estimate the annual amount spent on four categories of final goods and services

income approach
a way of figuring GDP that adds up all the incomes in the economy

Fig. 12.1 Expenditure Approach

❶ Suppose an economy's entire output is cars and trucks.

❷ This year the economy produces:

10 cars at $15,000 each = $150,000
+ 10 trucks at $20,000 each = $200,000
_____
Total = $350,000

❸ The economy's GDP for this year is $350,000.

CHART SKILLS

The expenditure approach is a practical way of calculating GDP.

1. What would the GDP be if the entire output was 15 cars at $15,000 each and 11 trucks at $20,000 each?
2. Using the expenditure approach, explain how a new housing complex would add to the GDP.

Two of these categories need explanation. First, keep in mind that consumer goods include two kinds of goods. The first kind is **durable goods.** These are goods that last a long time, such as refrigerators and cars. The second kind is **nondurable goods.** These goods last a short period of time, such as food and sneakers.

Exports are goods produced in the country but purchased in other countries. Net exports are all these goods minus imports. Imports, of course, are goods produced in another country. Since they were made in another country, they belong to the gross domestic product of that country.

What is the expenditure approach?

One way to calculate GDP is called the **expenditure approach,** or output-expenditure approach. In this system, the values of those four groups of final goods and services are added up. **Figure 12.1** shows how GDP is figured using the expenditure approach.

What is the income approach?

The second way to calculate GDP uses the **income approach.** It calculates GDP by adding up all the incomes in the economy. The idea behind this approach is that the selling price of goods and services that a firm sells represents income for the firm's owners and workers. As **Figure 12.2** on the next page shows, each purchase creates income for producers and consumers.

Suppose that your neighbor bought a newly built house for $200,000. That $200,000 is income shared by all the people who helped build the house. This includes the builder, the bricklayer, the roofer, and the window installer. Each of these people may get only a small share of the house's selling price. However, if we added up all those shares, they would total $200,000. This is how much income the sale created. This is also true for all goods and services. Thus, we may calculate GDP by adding up all income earned in the economy, as shown in **Figure 12.2.**

In theory, both the income approach and the expenditure approach should give us the same total. In fact, there are usually differences because of mistakes in collecting information. Economists who work in the federal government try to work out those differences. They first calculate GDP using both approaches. Then they compare the two totals and make adjustments. This gives them a more accurate result.

✅ **CHECKPOINT** *Why are imports not included in GDP?*

What is the difference between nominal GDP and real GDP?

Look at **Figures 12.1** and **12.2**. They show **nominal GDP**. This is the GDP measured in today's prices. Because it is based on today's prices, nominal GDP is also called current GDP. To calculate nominal GDP, we just add up the current prices of everything that has been produced this year. **Figure 12.1** shows how the definition of nominal GDP applies to the small economy that produces only cars and trucks.

There is a problem with the information about nominal GDP in **Figure 12.3** on page 288. The GDP of Year 2 is higher than that of Year 1. This is true even though the same number of cars and trucks were produced in the two years. The difference is the rise in prices. The price increases make the GDP look higher in the second year. This is misleading. To correct this, economists use **real GDP**. This is GDP adjusted for changes in price.

Look at the third section of **Figure 12.3**. Notice that GDP in Year 2 is based on the prices from Year 1. By using real GDP, economists know whether an economy is actually producing more goods and services, even if the prices of those items have changed.

✔ **CHECKPOINT** *What problem is solved by using real GDP?*

What are some limitations of GDP?

Using GDP as the measurement of how well a country is doing creates some problems. GDP leaves out some economic activity. For example, it does not count illegal goods and services. Income from illegal gambling goes unreported. So do "under the table" wages that some companies pay workers to avoid paying business and income taxes. Because there is no record of this activity, it does not count in the GDP.

GDP also does not count legal business for which there is no record. Let's say a plumber agrees to fix your leaky toilet if you agree to wash and wax his car. No money is involved. It is not included in GDP.

Fig. 12.2 Income Approach

❶ Suppose an economy's entire output is cars and trucks.

❷ All employed citizens, therefore, would work in the car and truck industry or for its suppliers.

❸ The combined selling price of all the cars and trucks reflects the money paid to all the people who helped build the vehicles.

❹ The economy's GDP for this year, then, is the sum of the income of all its working citizens, or $350,000.

Engineers Designers Planners Assembly-line workers Managers Suppliers (metal, glass, and so on)

Combined income = $350,000

CHART SKILLS

The income approach is generally a more accurate way of calculating GDP than the expenditure approach.

1. What would the economy's GDP be if the auto company in the example also had to pay $15,000 in fees to an advertising agency?
2. Using the income approach, explain how a new housing complex would add to the GDP.

■ ■ ■ ■ ■ ■ ■ ■ ■ ■ ■ ■ ■ ■ ■ ■ ■ ■ ■

nominal GDP
GDP measured in current prices
real GDP
GDP adjusted for price changes

Fig. 12.3 Nominal and Real GDP

CHART SKILLS

Calculating nominal and real GDP may provide different results. Increases in real GDP reflect actual increases in output without the misleading effects of price increases.

1. How much did real GDP increase in the second year if output stayed the same but prices increased by $1,000 for each car and $1,500 for each truck?

2. Using Year 1 as the base year, calculate the real GDP for Year 3 in which 15 cars and 14 trucks were sold.

Year 1: Nominal GDP	Year 2: Nominal GDP	Year 2: Real GDP
❶ Suppose an economy's entire output is cars and trucks.	**❶** In the second year, the economy's output does not increase, but the prices of the cars and trucks do:	**❶** To correct for an increase in prices, economists establish a set of constant prices by choosing one year as a base year. When they calculate real GDP for other years, they use the prices from the base year. So we calculate the real GDP for Year 2 using the prices from Year 1:
❷ This year the economy produces:	10 cars at $16,000 each = $160,000	
10 cars at $15,000 each = $150,000	+ 10 trucks at $21,000 each = $210,000	10 cars at $15,000 each = $150,000
+ 10 trucks at $20,000 each = $200,000	_____	+ 10 trucks at $20,000 each = $200,000
_____	Total = $370,000	_____
Total = $350,000	**❷** This new GDP figure of $370,000 is misleading. GDP rises because of an increase in prices. Economists prefer a measure of GDP that is not affected by changes in prices. So they calculate real GDP.	Total = $350,000
❸ Because we have used the current year's prices to express the current year's output, the result is a nominal GDP of $350,000.		**❷** Real GDP for Year 2, therefore, is $350,000.

Think of the many services that people produce and use themselves but never sell. These include things like taking care of children, cleaning the house, doing laundry, and fixing the family car. None of these activities is included in GDP.

Another problem with GDP is that it does not measure well-being. *Well-being* refers to health and happiness. Does a country with a GDP twice the size of another mean its people are twice as healthy and happy?

Reading Strategy
Visualizing

As you read this example, notice the words that help you visualize well-being.

Let's look at an example. A typical American family might have a bigger home, more cars, and more appliances than a family living in Mexico. This might be because both parents work and spend their money buying many goods. They may eat many of their meals in restaurants. Maybe in the Mexican home, only the father works. The mother has more time to spend with the children. She prepares meals at home. Is the American family healthier and happier? Not always.

All these limitations suggest that even though GDP is a valuable tool, it is still not a perfect measure of the economy. Nevertheless, it is valuable because it allows us to compare how the economy is doing over a period of time. For this reason, economists and people in government closely watch the nation's GDP.

✔ **CHECKPOINT** *What are two economic activities GDP does not take into account?*

What factors make GDP go up or down?

The two factors that make the economy as a whole go up or down are aggregate supply and aggregate demand. **Aggregate supply** is the total amount of goods and services in the economy available at all possible price levels. Think of aggregate supply as a supply curve for the whole economy. **Aggregate demand** is the amount of goods and services in the economy that will be bought at all possible price levels. It includes all spending by individuals, firms, and the government.

How do price levels impact aggregate supply and aggregate demand?

In a nation's economy, as the prices of most goods and services change, the **price level** changes. The price level is the average of all prices in the economy. Firms react to changing price levels by changing how much they produce. For example, let's say the price level goes up. This means the prices of most goods and services are rising. This gives firms an incentive to increase production. After all, at higher prices, selling more goods and services usually creates bigger profits. But what if the price level drops? Companies' profits will shrink. This causes firms to cut back output.

You can see this effect in the aggregate supply (AS) curve in **Figure 12.4**. As the price level rises, real GDP rises. As the price level falls, real GDP falls.

As prices in the economy move up and down, they affect how much individuals and businesses buy. Compare the two graphs in **Figure 12.4**. Notice that the curve showing aggregate demand moves in the opposite direction of the curve for aggregate supply.

Let's take a closer view at what this means. Suppose that on average, prices (the price levels) go down. This gives consumers more purchasing power. This is because the real value of money rises as price levels drop. The dollars we hold are worth more at lower price levels than they are at higher price levels. Therefore, falling prices increase wealth and demand.

On the other hand, as the price level rises, purchasing power goes down. Fewer goods and services will be demanded. All consumers have less money to spend. The downward slope of the aggregate demand curve shows that consumers cut their expenditures. Cuts in business spending on capital investment, government spending, and foreigners' demand for export goods also cause the curve to slope downward.

aggregate supply
the total amount of goods and services in the economy available at all possible price levels

aggregate demand
the amount of goods and services that will be purchased at all possible price levels

price level
the average of all prices

What is the aggregate supply/aggregate demand equilibrium?

When we put together the aggregate supply (AS) and aggregate demand (AD) curves, we can find the AS/AD equilibrium in the economy as a whole. Look at the third graph in **Figure 12.4**. The point where the AS and AD_1 curves cross shows an equilibrium price level of P_1 and an equilibrium real GDP of Q_1.

Now think how GDP might change. Any shift in either the AS or AD curve will cause real GDP to change. For example, the graph shows aggregate demand falling from line AD_1 to line AD_2. As a result, the equilibrium GDP (Q_2) falls, and so does the equilibrium price level (P_2).

Any shift in aggregate supply or aggregate demand will affect real GDP and the price level. In the next section, we will discuss some factors that may cause such shifts.

✅ **CHECKPOINT** *What four types of demand are included in aggregate demand?*

Fig. 12.4 Aggregate Supply and Demand

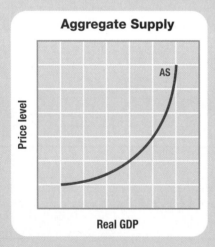

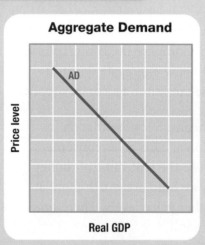

GRAPH SKILLS

Aggregate supply and demand represent supply and demand on a nationwide scale. The right-hand chart shows what happens to GDP and the price level when aggregate demand shifts from AD_1 to AD_2.

1. What do the positive (upward to the right) and negative (downward to the right) slopes of these curves mean?

2. If a country goes to war, causing an increase in government demand for all kinds of goods, how might real GDP and the price level be affected?

For an animated version of this graph, visit **PearsonSuccessNet.com**

Fig. 12.5 Measurements of the Macroeconomy

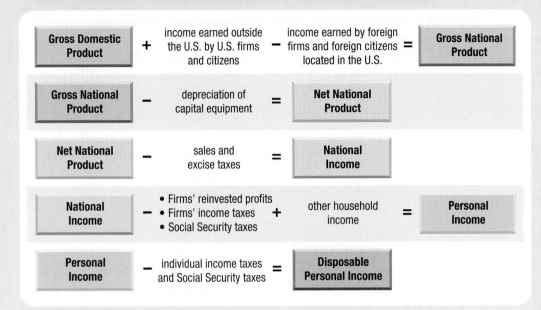

Gross Domestic Product	+ income earned outside the U.S. by U.S. firms and citizens	− income earned by foreign firms and foreign citizens located in the U.S.	= Gross National Product
Gross National Product	− depreciation of capital equipment	= Net National Product	
Net National Product	− sales and excise taxes	= National Income	
National Income	− • Firms' reinvested profits • Firms' income taxes • Social Security taxes	+ other household income	= Personal Income
Personal Income	− individual income taxes and Social Security taxes	= Disposable Personal Income	

What are other output and income measures?

As you have read, our system of National Income and Product Accounts provides many ways of measuring the nation's economy. GDP is the most important measure of income and output, but economists also look at other measures. Many of these other measures come from GDP. **Figure 12.5** shows how GDP is used to determine five other economic measures.

The first is **gross national product** (GNP). Just as with GDP, there are two ways to figure GNP. One is to add up the yearly income earned by U.S.-owned firms and U.S. citizens. The second is to add up the market value of all goods and services produced by Americans in one year. Study **Figure 12.5** to see how GNP is related to GDP.

GNP does not account for **depreciation.** Depreciation is the loss of the value of capital equipment that results from normal wear and tear. For example, think about what happens to the value of a new car. After a year, the new car is worth less than it was when it was new. Its value has depreciated. This is also true of physical capital like machines in a factory. The cost of replacing physical capital lowers the value of our net product. GNP minus the cost of depreciation of capital equipment is called net national product (NNP). NNP measures the net output for one year, or the output made after the adjustment for depreciation.

gross national product
the annual income earned by U.S.-owned firms and people

depreciation
the loss of the value of capital equipment that results from normal wear and tear

NNP does not exclude taxes, another cost of doing business. After subtracting sales and excise taxes and making some other minor adjustments to NNP, we get another important statistic, called national income (NI).

The last economic measure is called personal income (PI). PI is calculated by taking national income and subtracting what firms reinvest in the business and the income taxes and Social Security taxes they pay. They also subtract other household income. What remains is all the income received by households. After adding other income, such as Social Security benefits, we obtain PI.

Finally, we want to know how much money people actually have to spend after they pay *their* taxes. This figure is called disposable personal income (DPI). To find DPI, we take personal income and subtract individual income taxes. The DPI tells us how much money people have available to spend or save.

See how far we have come? We began with GDP, the value of all final goods and services produced in a year. This is a very large figure. We end up knowing how much cash Americans have to spend or invest. All this information is valuable to economic planners, legislators, investors, and businesses.

✓ CHECKPOINT *What does disposable personal income show?*

Essential Questions Journal

To continue to build a response to the Essential Question, go to your **Essential Questions Journal.**

SECTION 1 ASSESSMENT

Guiding Question

1. Use your completed chart to answer this question: What does GDP show about the nation's economy?

Key Terms and Main Ideas

Directions: On a sheet of paper, write the answer to each question. Use complete sentences.

2. How do U.S. economists use the system of national income accounting?

3. (a) What is the difference between intermediate goods and final goods? (b) Why are intermediate goods not included in GDP?

4. What is the difference between nominal and real GDP?

5. How does gross domestic product (GDP) differ from gross national product (GNP)?

Critical Thinking

6. **Summarize** (a) List four factors that make up GDP. (b) Describe how these factors are used to determine GDP for a specific year.

7. **Draw Conclusions** (a) What incentive do rising prices give firms? (b) What might prevent firms from earning increased profits during a time of rising prices?

Objectives

- **Identify** the four phases of a business cycle.

- **Describe** four key factors that keep the business cycle going.

- **Explain** how economists predict changes in the business cycle.

- **Analyze** the effect of business cycles in U.S. history.

Guiding Question

What factors affect the phases of a business cycle?

Copy this table and fill it in as you read to explain what economic factors influence the phases of a business cycle.

Business Investment	Interest Rates and Credit	Consumer Expectations	External Shocks
• Increased investment boosts aggregate demand, gross GDP • Decreased investment cuts AD, causing GDP decline	• Low rates make businesses more willing to borrow •	• High confidence increases spending •	• Disruptions of oil supply, wars, and drought cause GDP to decline •

expansion
a period of economic growth as measured by a rise in real GDP

economic growth
steady, long-term rise in real GDP

▶ **Economics and You** Sometimes, you don't have to read the newspaper to tell how the economy is doing. You can see the signs all around you. They may be "help wanted" signs in front of local stores. When the economy is doing well, businesses hire more people. Or they may be "closed" or "going out of business" signs in the windows of those same businesses. You might even get an idea by counting the number of "for sale" or "foreclosure" signs where you live. The ups and downs of the economy affect us all.

Principles in Action The national economy has cycles of good times, then bad times, and then good times again. Economists try to predict what the economy will do in the future. They want to make the good times last longer and keep the bad times brief. In this section, you will learn what factors affect these ups and downs. You will also see how the actions of ordinary consumers and borrowers can affect the phases of the economy.

What are the four phases of the business cycle?

The business cycle is usually divided into four phases, or stages. **Figure 12.6** on the next page shows the four stages.

The first stage, **expansion,** is a period of **economic growth.** Economists define economic growth as a steady, long-term growth in real GDP. Businesses begin to increase production. New workers are hired. Consumer spending increases. As spending goes up, production again increases and new jobs are created.

Fig. 12.6 Tracking a Business Cycle

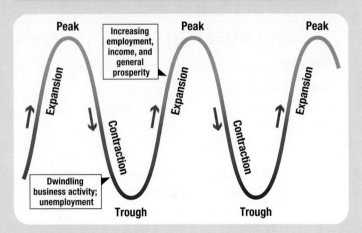

CHART SKILLS

A business cycle reaches a peak, then falls into a contraction. When the contraction phase reaches the low point, new expansion begins.

1. What is the low point of the cycle called? What is the period of increasing business activity called?
2. In which part of a business cycle do you think the United States is right now? Provide evidence to support your conclusion.

 For an animated version of this graph, visit **PearsonSuccessNet.com**

peak
the height of an economic expansion; the point at which real GDP stops rising

contraction
a period of economic decline marked by a fall in real GDP

trough
the lowest point of an economic contraction, the point at which real GDP stops falling

recession
long economic contraction

depression
a recession that is especially long and severe

stagflation
a decline in real GDP combined with a rise in the price level

The highest point in the cycle is the **peak.** The economy is booming. Most people looking for work can usually find it. People and businesses have money to spend. Business is producing as much as it can. Investment is high and new workers are being hired. Demand is high, so prices are increasing. This is the highest point of an economic expansion.

When GDP stops growing, the cycle begins the **contraction** phase. Real GDP begins to fall. Consumers begin to spend less. Businesses may lay off workers. Investment in new buildings and equipment slows. Production is cut.

The lowest point in the business cycle is the **trough.** Production of goods and services is at its lowest point. Consumer demand is very low. Unemployment is at its highest level. Times are tough. Many businesses fail, and jobs are hard to find. This is the point at which real GDP stops falling. During a contraction, GDP is always falling. However, other conditions may vary. Economists have created terms to describe different kinds of contractions. These include:

- *Recession* If real GDP falls for at least six straight months, the economy is said to be in a **recession.** A recession is a long economic contraction. Recessions generally last from 6 to 18 months. During recessions, the number of people out of work may reach between 6 percent and 10 percent.
- *Depression* A very long and severe recession is called a **depression.** The United States has had several depressions in its history. The largest depression in the twentieth century was the Great Depression. It lasted more than 10 years. In 1933, the worst year, nearly one out of every four workers was out of work. Many businesses failed. About 4,000 banks closed, and many people lost their life savings.
- *Stagflation* **Stagflation** combines parts of two words: *stag*nant and in*flation*. *Stagnant* means not growing. *Inflation* means a sharp increase in prices. Stagflation refers to an economy that is not growing but which has rising prices. Real GDP (output) drops, and prices rise (inflation).

✔ **CHECKPOINT** *What are the four phases of a business cycle?*

What keeps a business cycle going?

The shifts that occur during a business cycle have many causes. Some are more easily predicted than others. Often, two or more factors will combine to push the economy into the next phase of a business cycle. Typically, a sharp rise or drop in one of four main economic factors will set off a change in the business cycle. These four main economic factors are business investment, interest rates and credit, consumer expectations, and external shocks.

How does business investment keep a business cycle going?

When the economy is expanding, firms expect sales and profits to keep rising. Therefore, they may invest heavily. They may build new plants and equipment. Or they may expand old plants to increase production. All of this spending creates more output and jobs. This helps increase GDP and keeps the expansion going.

At some point, however, firms may decide they have expanded enough. Maybe demand for their products is dropping. They cut back on investment spending. The result is that aggregate demand falls. GDP and price levels decline. The drop in business spending affects other parts of the economy. Industries that produce capital goods slow their own production and begin to lay off workers. Other industries might follow. This causes the number of people out of work to increase. Jobless workers cannot buy new cars, eat at restaurants, or perhaps even pay their rent. Unless the economy begins to expand again, there will be a recession.

How do credit and interest rates keep a business cycle going?

In the U.S. economy, consumers often use credit to buy "big ticket" items like new cars and houses. This is a big benefit. Credit also has a cost. The cost of credit is that financial institutions charge their customers interest. Interest is money paid for borrowing money. Consumers are less likely to buy new cars or houses if the interest rates are high.

Interest rates are important to businesses, too. When interest rates are low, companies are more willing to borrow money. They might buy new equipment or expand their factories. By making new investments, they often add jobs to the economy. When interest rates go up, business borrowing goes down. When investment dries up, the economy stops growing. One result of rising interest rates, then, is less output. This may lead to a contraction phase.

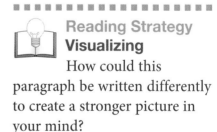

Reading Strategy
Visualizing
How could this paragraph be written differently to create a stronger picture in your mind?

Fig. 12.7 How the Economy Works

What causes a recession?

Recessions are an inevitable part of the business cycle. A number of conditions and events may trigger a recession–or deepen a recession that has already begun.

2 Despite the best efforts of government and business, recessions occur. Here are four possible reasons:

1 The economy has enjoyed an extended period of growth. Businesses are expanding, spending is up, and unemployment and inflation are largely under control.

External shock War breaks out in a nation where U.S. banks and businesses have invested heavily. This nation is also an important supplier of goods to the United States.

Business investment The war cuts into the assets of many U.S. firms. They lay off workers and cut back on plans to expand.

Peak

Contraction

Let's look at an example of the effect of interest rates on the business cycle. In the early 1980s, high interest rates helped bring on a long economic slowdown. Some credit card interest rates reached 21 percent. As a result, many Americans could not buy expensive items they usually bought on credit. When consumers cut down their spending, the economy entered a recession. The unemployment rate was more than 9 percent—the highest since the Great Depression. You can see why economists watch interest rates closely. The rise and fall of these rates has a great effect on consumer and business spending and on real GDP.

Interest rates and credit
As the war and threat of recession continue, banks are slower to extend credit. Interest rates creep up.

Consumer expectations
Predictions about a long recession discourage people from spending.

3 As these factors feed into one another, unemployment rises and business activity dwindles. In time, though, the cycle will move into a new phase of expansion.

Check Your Understanding
1. How can interest rates help bring on a recession?
2. Look at the four headings following step number 2. For each one, identify a condition that might lead to an economic expansion.

Trough

How do consumer expectations keep a business cycle going?

Consumer spending is influenced partly by consumers' expectations. When people are afraid the economy is slowing down, they may start spending less. They may start saving for a rainy day. They begin to worry that they may lose their jobs and that their income will be less. This cut in spending can actually help bring on a contraction.

High consumer confidence has the opposite effect on the economy. People expect good jobs. They believe their incomes will rise. Thus, they will buy more goods and services. This pushes up GDP.

How do external shocks keep a business cycle going?

External shocks are the things that upset the economy from the outside. Of all the factors that affect the business cycle, external shocks are probably the hardest to predict. External shocks can affect an economy's aggregate supply in big ways.

Let's look at an example of an economic shock. Suppose that the nation's supply of imported oil was suddenly cut off. The price of any remaining oil would skyrocket. This would affect many parts of the economy. Oil is used to produce many goods. Trucks, trains, and airplanes all use gasoline, which is made from oil. Bad shocks like an oil shortage will force firms to reduce production and raise prices. In other words, GDP declines and the price level rises.

Of course, not all external shocks are bad. The discovery of a large deposit of oil is a good shock. It contributes to a nation's wealth. A good growing season creates bigger harvests. These drive food prices down. Good shocks tend to shift the aggregate supply curve to the right. They lower the price level and increase real GDP.

External shocks usually come without much warning. The other key factors that can push an economy from one phase of the business cycle to another are more predictable. Economists are able to track business investment, interest rates, and consumer expectations to better predict changes in the business cycle.

CHECKPOINT *How are external shocks different from the other factors that affect the business cycle?*

How can business cycles be predicted?

Predicting changes in a business cycle is tough. For example, in the summer of 1929, an officer of General Motors made a prediction. He said the United States was about to begin the biggest industrial expansion in its history. Three weeks later, the stock market crashed. (See **Figure 12.9** on page 301.) Soon the country was in the worst depression in American history.

Fig. 12.8

CREDIT CARD SERVICE DESK

ACTUALLY, SIR, THE "GOLD" PART OF YOUR GOLD CARD REFERS TO THE INTEREST RATE, NOT THE CREDIT LIMIT.

E-mail:BobThaves@aol.com
©2000 Thaves/Dist. by NEA, Inc.
www.comics.com

7-31
THAVES

Economists today know a lot more about how our economy works. However, making economic predictions is still tricky. It is not easy to guess how real GDP will change. Many factors affect output in a modern economy. It is important for government and business decision makers to make correct guesses. When they are right, they can react quickly to changes in a business cycle. If businesses expect a contraction, they may put off building new factories. If government economists expect a contraction, they may take steps to try to prevent a recession.

leading indicators
a set of key economic variables that economists use to predict future trends in a business cycle

Economists use many tools to make these predictions. The most important tool is **leading indicators.** This is information about the economy that is used to make predictions about the business cycle.

The stock market is one leading indicator. Usually, the stock market goes down before a recession begins. For example, there was a crash of the NASDAQ exchange in 2000. The recession of 2001 followed. Another example occurred in 2008 when the Dow Jones sharply declined. This was, in part, because of changing oil prices, a decline in the value of people's houses, and a tightening credit market. Some experts pointed to this as a sign that a recession was about to begin.

Interest rates are another indicator. As you have seen, interest rates have a strong effect on consumer and business spending.

The Conference Board, a private business research organization, keeps an index of 10 leading economic indicators. These include stock prices, interest rates, and manufacturers' new orders of capital goods. Economists closely watch this index, which is updated monthly. However, like the other important tools used to predict changes in the business cycle, it is not always right.

✔ **CHECKPOINT** *Why is it difficult to predict future business cycles?*

What are some business cycles in U.S. history?

Before the 1930s, many economists believed that when an economy declined, it would quickly recover on its own. This explains why President Hoover felt little need to change his economic policies when the U.S. stock market crashed in 1929. The crisis, however, did not just go away.

Figure 12.9 shows that the Great Depression did not rapidly cure itself. Rather, it was the most severe economic downturn in the history of industrial capitalism. Between 1929 and 1933, GDP fell by about one fourth. Unemployment rose sharply. In fact, one out of every four workers was jobless, and those who could find work often earned very low wages.

Looking at the economy over time, you will see that economic activity in the United States really does follow a cycle. It goes up and down. The GDP grows in some periods and gets smaller in others. No economic downturns since the 1930s, however, have been nearly as bad as the Great Depression.

When have recessions occurred?

We have had recessions, though. In the 1970s, an international cartel, the Organization of Petroleum Exporting Countries (OPEC), stopped oil from being shipped to the United States. The price of oil went up 400 percent! As oil prices shot up, the economy quickly contracted into a period of stagflation. There was another recession in the early 1980s. High interest rates and other factors caused real GDP to fall. More than 9 percent of the labor force was out of work in the early 1980s.

Following a brief recession in 1991, the U.S. economy grew steadily. Much of this growth was fueled by the rise of Internet companies, called "dot.coms" after part of their Internet addresses. As the dot.com boom of the 1990s ended, however, U.S. growth slowed. In March 2001, the country slipped into a recession. Economists hoped this decline would not last long. But then the terrorist attacks of September 11, 2001, resulted in a sharp drop in consumer spending. The hotel, airline, and tourism industries were especially affected. Many companies blamed their performance problems on the terrorist attacks of September 11.

What is the business cycle today?

The economy did recover, though. By late 2003, it was booming. GDP grew at a rate of 7.5 percent over three months. After that, growth slowed. High gasoline prices in 2006 caused the economy to slow even further. In 2007, many people began to worry about difficulties in the home mortgage market. By 2008, the value of homes decreased and people ended up owing more money on their mortgages than the homes were actually worth. This began to affect the banking industry. The mortgage crisis pushed the stock and bond markets lower. People, banks, and businesses had a difficult time getting credit and taking out loans. Overall spending began to decline. Experts predicted that the business cycle was entering a phase of prolonged contraction.

✔ **CHECKPOINT** *What was a lasting effect of the Great Depression?*

Fig. 12.9 U.S. Real GDP, 1925–1945

U.S. Real GDP, 1925–1945

GDP (in billions of 2000 dollars) vs. Year

- Stock market crashes
- U.S. enters World War II

SOURCE: Louis D. Johnston and Samuel H. Williamson, "The Annual Real and Nominal GDP for the United States, 1790–Present." Economic History Services, October 2005, URL: http://www.eh.net/hmit/gdp/

▲ Declining GDP and high unemployment were two major signs of the Great Depression. It was the longest recession in U.S. history.

Reading Strategy
Visualizing
Study the photograph on this page. Then tell what you think the information on this page will be about.

Essential Questions Journal — To continue to build a response to the Essential Question, go to your **Essential Questions Journal.**

SECTION 2 ASSESSMENT

 Guiding Question

1. Use your completed table to answer this question: What factors affect the phases of a business cycle?

Key Terms and Main Ideas

Directions: On a sheet of paper, write the answer to each question. Use complete sentences.

2. (a) What is a business cycle? (b) In its trough phase, what has happened to the economy?

3. How can interest rates push a business cycle into a contraction?

4. What is the difference between a recession, a depression, and stagflation?

5. Why is the stock market considered to be a leading indicator of economic change?

Critical Thinking

6. **Analyze Information** As a consumer, would you prefer to be in a peak or a trough? Why? As a producer, at which point would you prefer to be?

7. **Draw Conclusions** (a) Why did Hoover believe the economy would quickly recover? (b) What role did World War II play in ending the Great Depression?

Objectives

- **Analyze** how economic growth is measured.
- **Explain** what capital deepening is and how it adds to economic growth.
- **Analyze** how saving and investment are related to economic growth.
- **Summarize** the effect of government on economic growth.
- **Identify** the causes and effects of new technology.

■■■■■■■■■■■■■■■■■■■■■■■

real GDP per capita
real GDP divided by the total population of a country

Guiding Question

How does the economy grow?

Copy this table and fill it in as you read to explain how an economy grows.

Changes in Real GDP	
Causes of Growth	**Causes of Decline**
• Capital deepening (more business investment) • High saving rate •	• Less business investment • Lower saving rate • •

▶ **Economics and You** A hundred years ago, most American families would have had an icebox to keep their food cold. A wood-burning stove would heat the house. They probably would have used a horse for transportation. Today, many of us think of a refrigerator-freezer, a microwave oven, and a car as things we must have. Clearly, most Americans are much better off today than they were 100 years ago. Why is this so?

Principles in Action

The answer is economic growth. This has allowed us to have more and better goods and services than our parents had. In this section, we will describe how economic growth allows an entire society to improve its quality of life.

How is economic growth measured?

Economic growth is an increase in real GDP from one year to the next. Remember that the figures for real GDP can be misleading. They may not look at the effect of rising prices or increases in population. Many economists believe that **real GDP per capita** is a more useful figure. It takes into account population growth. It is figured by dividing real GDP by the number of people in the country. (*Per capita* means "for each person.") It gives us a better idea of how well off the average person is.

For example, let's look at two countries. India is a large country with more than a billion people. Ireland is a small country with fewer than 4 million people. India's GDP is much larger than that of Ireland. Yet the real GDP per capita of Ireland is much higher than India's. We can probably say that the average person in Ireland is better off than the average person in India.

The basic measure of a nation's economic growth rate is the percentage change in real GDP over a period of time. For example, real GDP for the United States in 1996 was $8.3 trillion. In 2006, it was $11.3 trillion. The economic growth rate for this 10-year period was about 36 percent.

Every country wants its economy to grow. Economic growth means there is an increase in goods and services. Economic growth results in an improved standard of living. The standard of living includes what people have to eat, as well as their housing and clothing. The things people own—such as cars, television sets, computers, telephones, and the like—are also included.

Every society tries to improve the standard of living for its people. People with a high standard of living have more money to spend. They have more goods and services to choose from. They do not have to work all the time just to feed and clothe themselves and their families. They have more time to spend with their family and to enjoy themselves.

✅ **CHECKPOINT** *How is high GDP per capita linked to quality of life?*

What is capital deepening?

Physical capital is the equipment used to produce goods and services. With more physical capital, each worker can be more productive. He or she can produce more output per hour of work. Economists use the term *labor productivity* to describe the amount of output produced per worker.

Even if the size of the labor force does not change, more physical capital will lead to more output. The more output, the more economic growth. This process of increasing the amount of capital per worker is called **capital deepening.** It is one of the most important ways modern economies grow. Refer to **Figure 12.10** to see how capital deepening can help create economic growth.

Human capital is the skills and knowledge a worker learns on the job through education and experience. It also leads to more output. Firms and workers themselves can deepen human capital through training programs and on-the-job experience. Better trained and more experienced workers can produce more output per hour. Capital deepening also tends to increase workers' earnings.

✅ **CHECKPOINT** *What is human capital, and how does it add to capital deepening?*

■ ■ ■ ■ ■ ■ ■ ■ ■ ■ ■ ■ ■ ■ ■ ■ ■ ■ ■ ■
capital deepening
the process of increasing the amount of capital per worker

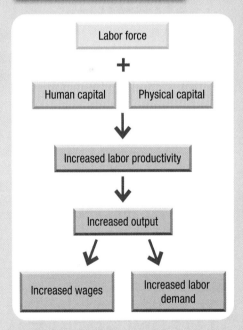

Fig. 12.10 Capital Deepening

CHART SKILLS

There are many benefits of capital deepening, as shown here.
1. What is capital deepening?
2. Suppose that you own a small clothing shop. Why should buying a new line of clothing and providing special training for sales staff result in capital deepening?

saving
income that is not spent

saving rate
the percentage of after-tax income
that is not spent

Reading Strategy
Visualizing
How does Figure 12.11
help you understand how saving
leads to capital deepening?

How is saving linked to capital deepening?

Saving is income that is not spent. The **saving rate** is the percentage of after-tax income that is not spent. If a family earns $50,000 and spends $47,500, its saving rate is 5 percent.

Figure 12.11 shows how saving adds to GDP by creating capital. Shawna had an after-tax income of $30,000 last year, but she spent only $25,000. That left her with $5,000 available for saving. She used some of her savings to buy shares in a mutual fund. She put the rest of the money into a savings account.

Through her mutual-fund firm, her bank, and other intermediaries, Shawna's $5,000 was made available to businesses. The firms could borrow the money. They used the money to invest in new plants and equipment. So, when Shawna chose to save some of her income, the money she saved could be used for business investment. The higher the saving rate, the more money available to businesses to borrow for investment.

Higher saving, then, leads to higher investment. This leads to higher amounts of capital per worker. In other words, higher saving leads to capital deepening. Now we can understand why most nations encourage saving. In the long run, more saving will lead to higher output and income for the population. This raises GDP and the standard of living.

The United States has a low saving rate. To get the investment funds they need, businesses and the government borrow from other countries that have higher saving rates.

✓ **CHECKPOINT** *How is saving linked to capital deepening?*

Fig. 12.11 How Saving Leads to Capital Deepening

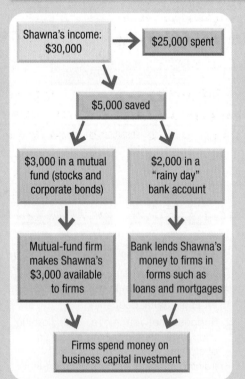

CHART SKILLS
Saving leads to capital deepening by providing funds for financial institutions to invest.

1. How much money has Shawna made available for investment in this example?
2. If people saved a high proportion of their incomes, how might the economy be affected?

How does government affect capital deepening?

Government can affect capital deepening in several ways. If government raises tax rates, households will have less money. People will not be able to save as much. This reduces the money available to businesses for investment.

But what if government invests the extra tax revenues in public goods, such as roads and communications satellites? Spending on infrastructure, that is, highways, bridges, sewers, and so on, increases investment. To see why, let's look at what the average household saves.

Suppose that, on average, households save 10 percent of their income. In this case, household saving (and investment) drops by 10 cents for every extra dollar in tax revenue the government collects. However, the government has an extra dollar in taxes to invest in infrastructure. The result is an increase in total investment of 90 cents. This kind of spending, then, is capital deepening, because the government is taxing its citizens to provide investment goods.

✔ **CHECKPOINT** *Do higher tax rates increase or reduce investment?*

What role does technology play in economic growth?

Another key source of economic growth is new technology. We normally use the term *technology* to mean new inventions or new ways of doing something. It allows us to increase production without using more resources.

New technology may result from new scientific knowledge. It can be a new invention that allows workers to produce goods more efficiently. It could even be a new method for organizing production. All these advances raise a nation's productivity. Increased productivity means producing more output with the same amounts of land, labor, and capital. The technology allows a society to enjoy higher real GDP per capita, which leads to a higher standard of living.

Economics & YOU

Economic Growth

When the economy is on the upswing, financial institutions are more likely to lend money. *A strong economy means you have greater access to loans that help pay for education.*

Many economists see teen spending as a huge source of future economic growth. *When you spend money responsibly, you help the economy expand.*

Innovators

Jerry Yang

"On the outside, Yahoo is a fun and irreverent place, but on the inside we are extremely competitive." It has become a familiar story. Two engineering students meet in college and turn their personal hobby into a technology-based start-up company. The company grows beyond all expectations and alters the lives of its founders, employees, users, and shareholders. And in this case the company, Yahoo! Inc., changes the face of business on a global scale.

Jerry Yang was born in Taiwan in 1968. He moved to the U.S. with his mother and brother at the age of 10. He cofounded Yahoo! with another Stanford University student, David Filo, while studying for a doctoral degree at Stanford in 1994. By 2008, Microsoft, the giant software company, had offered more than $45 billion to take it over.

Yang and Filo created Yahoo! to organize their own Internet searches. When they showed their new program to friends, Yang and Filo realized its huge business potential. Today Yahoo! is an Internet giant with more than 500 million users worldwide and a well-respected brand name. It is a starting point for many consumers as they search the Web. Yahoo! offers personalized home pages, e-mail, music, news, and more. In a global economy that requires many office workers to access, organize, and manage information on a daily basis, Yahoo! has proved its great value to society.

Reading Strategy
Visualizing

What clues on this page help you visualize the effects of technology on economic growth?

technological progress
an increase in efficiency gained by producing more output without using more input

Increased productivity that does not use more resources but results from new technology is called **technological progress.** Technological progress is an important source of economic growth. Economists agree there are two major causes:

1. *Scientific research* Scientists are always hunting for new or improved ways of producing things. They are also interested in improving physical capital. This research results in better goods and services.

2. *Innovation* When new products and ideas are successfully brought to market, output goes up. This boosts GDP and business profits. Yet innovation is not cheap. Most companies are willing to carry out research only if they know they will profit from the products they develop. This is the reason government issues patents. A patent is an exclusive right to produce and sell a product for a certain period of time.

Government aids innovation in other ways. The National Science Foundation, the National Institutes of Health, and other organizations conduct research that is sponsored by the government.

Additional causes of technological progress include the following:

3. *Scale of the market* Larger markets provide more incentives for innovation. In larger markets, the chance to earn a profit is greater. For this reason, there are usually more advances in technology in larger economies.

4. *Education and experience* Firms increase their human capital by providing education and on-the-job experience for workers. Human capital makes workers more productive. This increases economic growth. A more educated, experienced workforce can handle new technology better.

5. *Natural resource use* Increased use of natural resources can create a need for new technology. For example, new technology can turn raw materials thought to be of no value into usable resources. New technology can allow us to obtain and use resources more efficiently. It allows us to develop new resources and discover new resource reserves.

 CHECKPOINT *How is technological progress related to economic growth?*

SECTION 3 ASSESSMENT

Essential Questions Journal To continue to build a response to the Essential Question, go to your **Essential Questions Journal.**

Quick Write

In the mid-1800s, railroad companies borrowed money from foreign investors to create a transcontinental rail line. The completed railroad earned enough money to pay off the loans and return a profit. What other communication and transportation systems from the past might have had similar effects? Write a paragraph analyzing these effects.

Guiding Question

1. Use your completed table to answer this question: How does the economy grow?

Key Terms and Main Ideas

Directions: On a sheet of paper, write the answer to each question. Use complete sentences.

2. (a) What is real GDP per capita? (b) Why do economists measure it?

3. What is capital deepening?

4. What role does saving play in economic growth?

5. What happens when the U.S. has a low saving rate?

Critical Thinking

6. **Analyze Information** (a) What is real GDP per capita unable to measure? (b) How does that limit economists' knowledge of individuals' standard of living?

7. **Draw Conclusions** (a) What is the connection between saving and capital deepening? (b) Is it possible for capital deepening to occur without saving?

Section 1–Gross Domestic Product

- The most important measure of the economy is gross domestic product (GDP). It is the dollar value of all final goods and services produced in a country in a given year.

- Nominal GDP is measured in current prices. Real GDP is expressed in unchanging prices.

- The price level is the average of all prices in the economy. Aggregate supply is the total amount of goods and services in the economy available at all possible price levels. Aggregate demand is the amount of goods and services in the economy that will be purchased at all possible price levels.

Section 2–Business Cycles

- Business cycles are major changes in real GDP, above or below normal levels. The typical cycle has four phases: expansion, peak, contraction, and trough.

- A recession is a long economic decline. A depression is an especially long and severe recession. Stagflation is a decline in real GDP combined with a rise in the price level.

- Leading indicators are a set of key economic variables economists use to predict future trends in a business cycle. Economic activity in the United States follows patterns of growth alternating with periods of decline.

- The United States has experienced several recessions, but none has been as severe as the Great Depression of the 1930s.

Section 3–Economic Growth

- Economists measure economic growth using real GDP divided by the total population of a country. This does not, however, measure people's quality of life.

- One of the most important sources of growth in modern economies is capital deepening. This is the process of increasing the amount of capital per worker.

- Higher saving leads to higher investment. This leads to capital deepening, which raises the standard of living.

- If population grows while the supply of capital remains constant, the result will be lower living standards. Technological progress is an important source of economic growth. It results in increased efficiency and innovation.

Section 1
What does GDP show about the nation's economy?

Section 2
What factors affect the phases of a business cycle?

Section 3
How does the economy grow?

Essential Question, Chapter 12
How do we know if the economy is healthy?

"A New $5 Bill Enters Circulation Today"

The U.S. Treasury issues redesigned paper currency to help prevent counterfeiting. The $10 bill was introduced on March 2, 2006; the $20 bill on October 9, 2003; and the $50 bill in late 2004. All have new security features. The following is an excerpt from a press release announcing the new $5 bill.

"WASHINGTON, D.C. (March 13, 2008)—The first new $5 bill was issued by the Federal Reserve today during a commemorative transaction at President Lincoln's Cottage at the Soldiers' Home in Washington, D.C., a historic site used by the former president as a White House summer retreat. Officials from the Federal Reserve Board, U.S. Treasury, Bureau of Engraving and Printing and U.S. Secret Service ushered the new $5 bill into circulation. . . .

President Lincoln's Cottage at the Soldiers' Home in Washington, D.C., which has recently been restored and is now open to the public, was chosen as the location to spend the first new $5 bill because of its historic significance to President Lincoln, the subject of the bill's portrait. President Lincoln established the United States Secret Service the same evening he was assassinated [April 14, 1865] and made safeguarding the nation's currency from counterfeiters the agency's primary mission. . . .

As with the redesigned $10, $20 and $50 bills that preceded it, the new $5 bill features an American symbol of freedom printed in the background. The Great Seal of the United States, featuring an eagle and shield, is printed in purple on the front of the bill. Additional design elements include:

• The large, easy-to-read number "5" in the lower right corner on the back of the bill, which helps those with visual impairments distinguish the denomination, has been enlarged in the new $5 bill design and is printed in . . . purple ink. . . .

• Small yellow "05's" are printed to the left of the portrait on the front of the bill and to the right of the Lincoln Memorial vignette on the back.

The new $5 bill's most noticeable design difference is the addition of light purple in the center of the bill, which blends into gray near the edges. Because color can be duplicated, consumers and cash-handlers should use the key security features—on the new $5 bill, the watermarks and security thread—not color, to check the authenticity of paper money."

Document-Based Questions

1. Why was President Lincoln's Cottage chosen as the place to spend the first new $5 bill?

2. What is the American symbol of freedom printed in the background of the new bill?

3. Why is the number 5 enlarged on this new bill?

4. What is the most noticeable design difference in the new bill?

5. What are the security features on the new bill?

SOURCE: 2008 The Department of the Treasury Bureau of Engraving and Printing

Directions: Choose the letter of the best answer or write the answer using complete sentences.

Section 1–Gross Domestic Product

1. What does GDP measure?

2. How do the expenditure approach and income approach calculate GDP? Why do economists use both approaches?

3. Why is real GDP a better measure than nominal GDP?

4. In what four areas does aggregate demand decline when the price level increases?

5. What does GNP measure?

6. What is DPI, and how is it calculated?

Section 2–Business Cycles

7. Why do economists try to predict the business cycle?

8. When real GDP stops rising, what phase has the business cycle reached?

    A. expansion   **B.** peak   **C.** contraction   **D.** trough

9. What are three types of contractions?

10. How does a drop in business spending affect other parts of the economy?

11. How do high interest rates affect the business cycle?

12. How do fears about the future affect GDP?

13. Do external shocks positively or negatively affect the economy? Explain.

14. What are three leading economic indicators?

15. How did World War II affect the business cycle?

Section 3—Economic Growth

16. How is real GDP per capita different from real GDP?

17. How does capital deepening lead to economic growth?

18. How are you helping businesses expand when you put money into a savings account?

19. When can an increase in tax rates help the economy grow?

20. How does scientific research affect economic growth?

 Exploring the Essential Question

21. GDP does not take into account nonmarket activities. How can a nonmarket activity get shifted to the market?

22. Give examples of one illegal and one legal activity not counted in GDP.

Essential Question Activity

23. Complete the activity to answer the Essential Question **How do we know if the economy is healthy?** You are going to take the current pulse of the U.S. economy. Track your data over a three-year period. Using your worksheet, work in groups to gather the following information: (a) What trend does the real GDP of the United States reveal? (b) Was there a contraction phase? If so, how long did it last? (c) At what point during these three years did the rate of inflation peak?

Essential Questions Journal To continue to build a response to the Essential Question, go to your **Essential Questions Journal.**

Test-Taking Tip

Read test directions carefully. Do not assume you know what you are supposed to do.

Chapter 13 Economic Challenges

Office / Administrative

Skilled Trades

ARCHITECTURE AND ENGINEERING

AND FINANCIAL

CLEANING / JANITORIAL / HOUSEKEEPING

OFFICE / ADMINISTRATIVE
INCLUDES JOB LISTINGS FOR CUSTOMER SERVICE REPS

CONSTRUCTION / SKILLED TRADES

PROFESSIONAL AND Legal

Management

Personal Care / C Health

nction / Assembly

Sales and Marketing

PROFESSIONAL / LEGAL

MANAGEMENT POSITIONS

DUCTION / SSEMBLY

SALES AND MARKETING

Job Opportun

- **Section 1** Unemployment

- **Section 2** Inflation

- **Section 3** Poverty

Economics
on the go

To study anywhere, anytime, download these onlin resources at *PearsonSuccessNet.com* ➤

▶ **The economy of the United States is the largest in the world.** People in many other countries admire our high standard of living. Yet even the United States economy has some problems. Pick up a daily newspaper. Some stories are about companies closing and people losing their jobs. Other stories discuss rising food and gas prices. The number of poor people living in the United States seems to be growing.

This chapter discusses the economic challenges of unemployment, inflation, and poverty. Even if these problems do not directly affect you, they have a great effect on the community in which you live.

Reading Strategy: Inferencing
You can make inferences by thinking "beyond the text." When the meaning is not directly stated, you need to infer, or make a good guess about, what something means. Add what you already know to what you read. Then you are making an inference.

Go to the Visual Glossary Online for an interactive review of **inflation.**

How the Economy Works
online

Go to How the Economy Works Online for an interactive lesson on **structural unemployment.**

Go to Action Graph Online for animated versions of key charts and graphs.

Objectives

- **Define** frictional, seasonal, structural, and cyclical unemployment.
- **Describe** how full employment is measured.
- **Explain** why full employment does not mean that every worker is employed.

frictional unemployment
unemployment that happens when people must search a long time to find a job

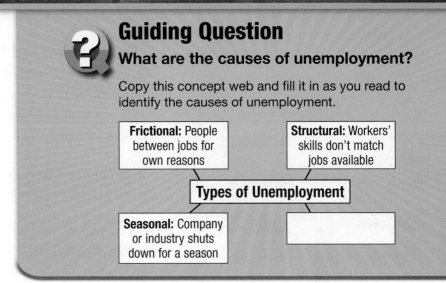

Guiding Question

What are the causes of unemployment?

Copy this concept web and fill it in as you read to identify the causes of unemployment.

Frictional: People between jobs for own reasons

Structural: Workers' skills don't match jobs available

Types of Unemployment

Seasonal: Company or industry shuts down for a season

▶ **Economics and You** Many people face unemployment at some point in their lives. Even if you have a job, unemployment affects you. It is a national economic issue. Economists measure the health of the economy by counting the number of people who are out of work. Government decision makers pay close attention to these numbers. If the numbers are too high, the government acts to get people back to work.

Principles in Action Many factors cause unemployment.
There are different kinds of unemployment. You will read about a woman who believes in helping people find and succeed in their jobs.

What does it mean to be unemployed?

Most students assume that they will find a job once they are finished with their schooling. Jobs provide wages. With wages, people can buy some of the goods and services they need and want. However, not everyone who wants a job will find one. The people who want jobs but cannot find them are the unemployed. Unemployment always exists, even in a growing economy. Economists identify four different types of unemployment. They are frictional, seasonal, structural, and cyclical unemployment.

What is frictional unemployment?

Frictional unemployment occurs when people take time to find a job. For example, after you finish your schooling, you may need some time to find a job. In the following examples, all three people are considered frictionally unemployed.

- Hannah was not satisfied working as a nurse in a large hospital. Last month, she left her job to look for a position at a small health clinic.
- Since Jose graduated from law school three months ago, he has interviewed with different law firms to find the one that best suits his needs and interests.
- Liz left her sales job two years ago to care for an aging parent. Now she is trying to return to the workforce.

None of these three people has found work right away. While they look for work, they are frictionally unemployed.

What is seasonal unemployment?

Some jobs are needed for only certain seasons. In general, **seasonal unemployment** happens when industries slow or shut down for a season. It can also be a result of harvest schedules, demand for holiday workers, or vacations.

Gregory is a bricklayer for a small construction company. Every winter, Gregory's boss lays off all seven of his workers. In the spring, he hires them back again for the new construction season. Gregory and his co-workers are examples of people who experience seasonal unemployment.

The lives of seasonally unemployed workers can be tough. Many workers travel throughout the country. They pick fruits and vegetables as different crops come into season. They are known as migrant workers. They know their work will end when winter arrives. If the weather is bad, these workers can have periods of unemployment even during the harvest season.

What is structural unemployment?

The structure of the American economy has changed over time. Two hundred years ago, most people were farmers. As the country developed an industrial economy, farmworkers moved to cities to work in factories. Today, more people work in service industries than in manufacturing.

All these shifts lead to big changes in the labor market. When the structure of the economy changes, workers need new skills to succeed. Workers who do not have the necessary skills lose their jobs. **Structural unemployment** occurs when workers do not have the skills needed for the jobs that are available. **Figure 13.1** on the next page shows an example of three workers affected by structural unemployment.

seasonal unemployment
unemployment that happens when industries shut down for a season

structural unemployment
unemployment that happens when workers' skills do not match those needed for the jobs available

Fig. 13.1 How the Economy Works

How do workers deal with structural unemployment?

The United States has shifted from a manufacturing economy to a service economy. Many workers do not have the skills needed for jobs in the new technology-based industries. Structural unemployment occurs when workers' skills don't match the jobs that are available.

1

Reginald's position as an accounting manager was eliminated after the company upgraded to a new computer software program.

Jennifer's job was outsourced when the furniture manufacturer she worked for moved to another country.

Matthew's job as a landscaper was eliminated when the Parks Department's budget was cut.

2 **Reginald** contacts former associates and gets a couple of interviews.

Jennifer realizes she needs to get training in another field.

Matthew searches online for a new job but discovers that his high school education leaves him unqualified for many positions.

Structural Unemployment

globalization
the shift from local to global markets as countries seek foreign trade and investment

There are five major causes of structural unemployment.

- *The development of new technology* New inventions and ideas often push out older ways of doing things. For example, downloading music has hurt the sales of CDs. Firms making CDs have laid off workers. Those workers must find other kinds of jobs.
- *The discovery of new resources* New resources replace old resources. This affects the industries that provide them. When oil was discovered in Pennsylvania in 1859, it hurt the whale-oil industry. Many whaling ship crews lost their jobs.
- *Changes in consumer demand* Consumers often stop buying one product in favor of another. Many people now favor sneakers over regular shoes. As a result, there are far fewer jobs in traditional shoemaking.
- *Globalization* The world economies are more interconnected. This is called **globalization.** As a result of globalization, companies often move parts or all of their businesses to other countries where costs are lower.

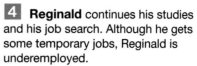

For an animated, interactive version of this feature, visit **PearsonSuccessNet.com**

4 **Reginald** continues his studies and his job search. Although he gets some temporary jobs, Reginald is underemployed.

Jennifer finds a good position as a technician at a pharmaceutical company.

Matthew will earn more money as a plumber than he did as a landscaper.

3 **Reginald's** recent experience inspires him to earn a degree in business technology management.

Jennifer gets into a federal job-training program for people who have lost their jobs due to globalization. She is studying to become a biomedical technician.

Matthew, who likes to work with his hands, takes a friend's advice and enrolls in a technical school. He is training to become a plumber.

Check Your Understanding
1. Identify three causes of structural unemployment.
2. How can the education system help reduce structural unemployment?

Retraining   **Employment**

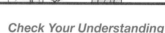

This practice is called outsourcing. Celia, for example, spent many years working on an automobile assembly line in Michigan. When her company moved much of its auto assembly work to Mexico, where labor is less expensive, Celia lost her job. More recently, outsourcing has affected call center operators and computer programmers.

- *Lack of education* People who drop out of school may be unemployed, employed part-time, or stuck in low-wage jobs. For example, Martin barely managed to graduate from high school. When a local store hired him as a clerk, he had trouble using the computerized checkout register. The store manager fired Martin after just two months because he did not have the skills needed for the job.

The government knows that computer technology, globalization, and other structural changes threaten the futures of many workers. As a result, it develops job-training programs to help workers gain new skills, especially computer skills.

Reading Strategy
Inferencing
What can you infer about the way schooling affects the kind of job a person can get?

Retraining takes time, however. Learning the new skills may not be enough to ensure that the trainees will gain high-wage jobs. Some companies offer their own training programs. In this way, they can teach trainees the special skills the company needs.

What is cyclical unemployment?

Unemployment goes up during recessions and depressions. It falls when the economy improves. This is known as **cyclical unemployment.** During recessions, the demand for goods and services drops. Production slows down. This causes the demand for labor to drop. Companies begin to lay off employees. Many of these laid-off workers will be hired back when the recession ends.

The best example of cyclical unemployment in the twentieth century was the Great Depression. During the Great Depression, one out of every four workers was unemployed. Many remained out of work for years. To help these unemployed workers, Congress passed the Social Security Act of 1935. It gave cash payments to people who could not support themselves. It also set up a program of unemployment insurance. Today, unemployment insurance still gives weekly payments to workers who have lost their jobs.

Innovators

Janice Bryant Howroyd

"I realized that I enjoyed helping people get temporary and permanent jobs." Careers are all about making a commitment. In 1978, Janice Bryant Howroyd rented a small office in Beverly Hills, California. She launched ACT•1 Personnel Services, an employment services agency. From the beginning, her focus was on providing employers with qualified employees and developing long-term business relationships.

Today the company is approaching $1 billion in annual revenue. Initially, Howroyd focused on the entertainment field. Soon her business expanded to include the technical, clerical, engineering, and accounting industries.

New technology has become a key to Howroyd's success. Her management-solutions company, Agile•1, created a new timekeeping system. Howroyd also owns two continuing-education schools. She wants to supply clients with employees who have basic academic skills, as well as higher-order thinking skills such as problem solving and decision making. It's no surprise that ACT•1's motto is "pride in performance."

Fast Facts

Janice Bryant Howroyd (1952–)
Education: North Carolina A&T State University, University of Maryland, North Carolina State University
Claim to Fame: Founder, CEO, of ACT•1 Personnel Services

How can factors outside the economy affect unemployment?

Sometimes events outside the economy can cause unemployment. The September 11, 2001, terrorist attacks may have cost the country 1.5 to 2 million jobs. Many of the lost jobs were in the travel and tourism industries. About 20 percent of the lost jobs were in the airline industry. In Manhattan, the area around the World Trade Center site was especially hard-hit. New York City lost some 150,000 jobs.

Events in nature can also affect employment. In August 2005, Hurricane Katrina hit the Gulf Coast region. This powerful storm caused a lot of damage. Thousands of people lost their jobs. Many families moved to other areas. Months later, unemployment among people affected by Hurricane Katrina was still high.

 CHECKPOINT *Why do policy makers not take steps to lower frictional and seasonal unemployment?*

How is employment measured?

The amount of unemployment in the nation is an important clue to the health of the economy. For this reason, the government keeps careful track of how many people are unemployed and why. To measure employment, the United States Bureau of the **Census** conducts a monthly household survey for the Bureau of Labor Statistics (BLS). This survey is called the Current Population Survey. Interviewers poll 60,000 families about employment during that month. This sample is designed to represent the entire population of the United States. The BLS, a branch of the U.S. Department of Labor, analyzes the data from the survey. It identifies how many people are employed and how many are unemployed. Using these numbers, the BLS computes the **unemployment rate**, or the percentage of the nation's labor force that is unemployed.

How is the unemployment rate figured?

The civilian labor force is made up of people age 16 and older who are not institutionalized or in the military and who have a job or are actively looking for a job. To determine the unemployment rate, the BLS adds up the number of employed and unemployed people. That figure equals the total labor force. Then it divides the number of unemployed people by the total labor force and multiplies by 100. As **Figure 13.2** shows, the result is the percentage of people who are unemployed.

■ ■ ■ ■ ■ ■ ■ ■ ■ ■ ■ ■ ■ ■ ■ ■ ■ ■ ■

census
an official count of the population

unemployment rate
the percentage of the nation's labor force that is unemployed

Fig. 13.2 Calculating the Unemployment Rate

To calculate the unemployment rate, use the following formula:

Number of people unemployed

divided by
number of people in the total civilian labor force **multiplied by** 100

For example,
if the number of people unemployed = 7 million and the number of people in the civilian labor force = 151.4 million

then,
$$7 \div 151.4 = .046$$
$$.046 \times 100 = 4.6$$

Therefore,
the unemployment rate is 4.6%

SOURCE: Bureau of Labor Statistics

CHART SKILLS

To calculate the unemployment rate, follow the steps in this figure.

1. In May 2008, the civilian labor force was 154.5 million. Of this number, 8.5 million were unemployed. What was the unemployment rate?

2. Does the unemployment rate accurately reflect the number of people who are unemployed? Explain.

■ ■ ■ ■ ■ ■ ■ ■ ■ ■ ■ ■ ■ ■ ■ ■ ■ ■ ■

full employment
a situation when no cyclical
unemployment exists

underemployed
working at a job which needs far
fewer skills than a worker has

For example, in May 2008, the figures showed that 154.5 million people were working, and 8.5 million were unemployed. The total labor force, therefore, was 163 million. If we divide 8.5 million by 163 million and then multiply the result by 100, we get 5.2 percent. This is the unemployment rate for that month.

What is "seasonally adjusted" unemployment?

The monthly unemployment rate is usually "seasonally adjusted." This means the rate has taken into account the level of seasonal unemployment. This step allows economists to better compare unemployment rates from month to month. This comparison helps them see how economic conditions are changing.

The unemployment rate is only an average for the nation. It may be higher or lower in different parts of the country. Some areas, such as the coal-mining regions of the southeastern United States, have a higher-than-average unemployment rate.

 CHECKPOINT *How is the unemployment rate calculated?*

What does full employment mean?

Look at **Figure 13.3.** Notice that the unemployment rate does not fall below 4 percent in any year. As you read earlier, there is always some unemployment. Most economists agree that an unemployment rate of around 4 to 6 percent is "normal" or "natural." A "normal" economy would still experience frictional, seasonal, and structural unemployment. In other words, **full employment** is the level of employment reached when no cyclical unemployment exists.

What is underemployment?

Full employment means nearly everyone who wants a job has a job. But not all those people are happy with their jobs. They may work at low-skill, low-wage jobs. But they may be highly skilled or educated in a field with few jobs. They are **underemployed.** They work at jobs that require far fewer skills than they have. Or they work part time, but they want full-time work.

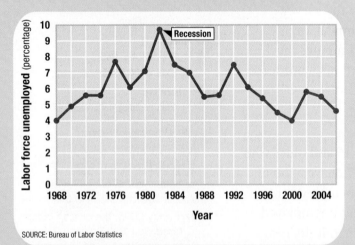

Fig. 13.3 Unemployment Rates, 1968–2006

SOURCE: Bureau of Labor Statistics

GRAPH SKILLS

The unemployment rate reached a 40-year peak in 1982.

1. In which years was the unemployment rate between 4 and 6 percent, a normal rate for a healthy economy?
2. Why does a high unemployment rate indicate a recession?

For example, Jim studied geology in college. Geology is the study of the physical features of the Earth. When he left school, Jim could not find a job as a geologist. Jim found a part-time job that did not pay well. He could not use the geology skills he had learned. He was underemployed.

Celia, the auto worker described earlier, was also underemployed. After her company sent her auto-assembly job to Mexico, she could not find a job like it where she lived. She was forced to take a low-skill, low-wage job.

Underemployment also describes people who want a full-time job but have not been able to find one. Many part-time workers and seasonal workers fit this group.

Why are some workers discouraged?

Some people, especially during a long recession, give up hope of finding work. These **discouraged workers** have stopped looking for work. They may depend on other family members or savings to support them. Although they are without jobs, discouraged workers are not counted in the BLS's unemployment rate. This is because they have not actively looked for work in the previous four weeks.

✔ **CHECKPOINT** *What kinds of unemployment are expected even in a normal economy?*

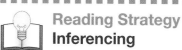

Reading Strategy
Inferencing
What can you infer about the difficulty of finding a job when the unemployment rate is up?

discouraged workers
unemployed people who are not actively looking for work because they have been seeking employment for a long time

SECTION 1 ASSESSMENT

Essential Questions Journal To continue to build a response to the Essential Question, go to your **Essential Questions Journal.**

Guiding Question

1. Use your completed concept web to answer the following question: What are the causes of unemployment?

Key Terms and Main Ideas

Directions: On a sheet of paper, write the answer to each question. Use complete sentences.

2. What factors affect seasonal unemployment?

3. What is cyclical unemployment?

4. What is globalization?

5. Why is there always some unemployment even with full employment?

Critical Thinking

6. **Make Comparisons** What are frictional unemployment and structural unemployment? Give an example of each.

7. **Test Conclusions** Two years ago, Edwin was in a car accident and needed six months to recover. After his recovery, he spent a year trying to find work in his former occupation, medical technology. He was not able to find a position, even though the economy was booming. Which of the four kinds of unemployment best describes Edwin's situation? Explain.

Objectives

- **Explain** the effects of rising prices.
- **Understand** how price indexes are used to compare changes in prices over time.
- **Identify** the causes and effects of inflation.
- **Describe** recent trends in the inflation rate.

Guiding Question

What are the causes and effects of inflation?

Copy this table and fill it in as you read to explain the causes and effects of inflation.

Inflation	
Causes	**Effects**
• Growth of the money supply • Changes in aggregate demand, as during wartime • Changes in aggregate supply	• Decreases purchasing power • •

▶ **Economics and You** At first, you hardly notice the changes. You pay more for lunch at your favorite place to eat. Clothing is more expensive. A ticket for the movies costs two dollars more. You realize that the price of everything seems to be higher. Your money doesn't buy as much as it did just a few months ago.

Principles in Action Economists believe prices rise for many reasons. Maybe the supply of money has increased. Perhaps demand has changed. It could be that production costs have gone up. This section's Economics & You shows how higher prices can affect your life.

How does inflation affect consumers?

Josephine and Jack Barrow have owned the same house for the past 50 years. Last week they had a real estate agent estimate how much their home is worth. The Barrows were shocked. Their house, which they had bought for $12,000, was worth nearly $150,000—a rise in value of more than 1,100 percent.

How could the value of a house, or anything else, go up so much? The main reason is inflation. Inflation is a general increase in prices. Over the years, prices generally go up.

The Barrows were happy they could get so much money for their house. Then they realized inflation had raised the prices of other houses, too. As a result, they could not buy a house like it in their area for $12,000 or even $120,000. Inflation had also raised wages and the prices of most other goods and services.

Inflation affects purchasing power. **Purchasing power** is the ability to buy goods and services. As prices go up, the purchasing power of money goes down. That is why $12,000 buys much less now than it did 50 years ago.

✔ **CHECKPOINT** *Why does purchasing power decrease over time?*

What is a price index?

Housing costs are just one factor economists look at when they study inflation. The economy has thousands of goods and services, with millions of individual prices. How do economists compare the changes in all these prices to measure inflation? The answer is that they do not compare individual prices. Instead, they compare price levels at different points in time. The price level is a measure of the general level of prices of goods and services in the economy as a whole.

Economists use a **price index** to help them calculate the price level. A price index is a measurement. It shows the average price of a group of goods. The average price changes from one month to another. By comparing the average prices, economists can see how much prices have changed over time.

How does the consumer price index help measure inflation?

The best-known index is the **consumer price index** (CPI). The CPI measures how much the prices of necessary items are changing. The information is collected each month by the BLS. It uses a **market basket** that a typical urban consumer might buy. This market basket includes food, housing, clothing, transportation, medical care, personal care, and entertainment. (See **Figure 13.4.**) By looking at the CPI, consumers, businesses, and the government can compare the average price of a group of goods this month with what the same goods cost months or even years ago. About every ten years, the items in the market basket are updated to account for changes in what consumers are buying.

purchasing power
the ability to buy goods and services

price index
a measurement that shows the average price of a group of goods

consumer price index
a measurement that shows how much the prices of necessary items are changing

market basket
items a typical urban consumer might buy, used for tracking the average price of a group of goods from month to month

Fig. 13.4 CPI Market Basket Items

Category	Examples
Food and drinks	Cereals, coffee, chicken, milk, restaurant meals
Housing	Rent, homeowners' costs, fuel oil
Apparel and upkeep	Men's shirts, women's dresses, jewelry
Transportation	Airfares, new and used cars, gasoline, auto insurance
Medical care	Prescription medicines, eye care, physicians' services
Entertainment	Newspapers, toys, musical instruments
Education and communication	Tuition, postage, telephone services, computers
Other goods and services	Haircuts, cosmetics, bank fees

SOURCE: Bureau of Labor Statistics

CHART SKILLS
The CPI market basket helps economists calculate the average inflation rate for the country.

1. Why might a family see an inflation rate that is higher or lower than the national average?
2. Which categories of market basket items are currently experiencing sharp price increases?

Fig. 13.5 Inflation Rate, 1970–2006

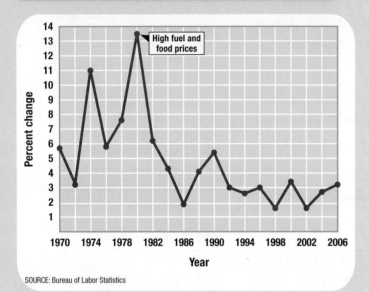

SOURCE: Bureau of Labor Statistics

GRAPH SKILLS

An inflation rate of 1 to 3 percent usually causes no problems. Sharp increases in 1974 and 1980 resulted from rising oil and food prices.

1. In what years was the inflation rate so high that economic planning was difficult?
2. Why does inflation hit lower- and fixed-income families hardest?

■■■■■■■■■■■■■■■■■■■■

inflation rate
the monthly or yearly percentage rate of change in prices

core inflation rate
inflation after the effects of food and energy prices are removed

hyperinflation
inflation that is out of control

quantity theory
the theory that inflation is caused by having too much money is in the economy

How is the inflation rate calculated?

Economists also calculate the **inflation rate.** This is the monthly or yearly percentage rate of change in prices. Economists use a formula to figure the inflation rate. It takes into account how much prices have gone up based on the CPI.

What are different types of inflation?

Inflation rates in the United States have changed greatly over time. When the inflation rate stays between 1 and 3 percent, it does not usually cause problems for the economy. When the inflation rate is more than 5 percent, however, problems develop.

As you can see in **Figure 13.5,** the inflation rate sometimes spikes, as in 1974 and 1980. These spikes happened partly because prices for food and oil jumped. People who study long-term trends in the inflation rate ignore these spikes in food and fuel prices because they usually do not last long. Economists use the **core inflation rate.** This is the rate of inflation after removing the effects of food and energy prices.

By far the worst kind of inflation is **hyperinflation,** or inflation that is out of control. During periods of hyperinflation, inflation rates can go as high as 100 or even 500 percent per month. Money loses much of its value. This level of inflation is rare. When it happens, the entire economy may collapse.

 CHECKPOINT *How do economists calculate the inflation rate?*

What are the three causes of inflation?

Nobody can explain every increase in price levels. However, economists have several explanations about what causes inflation.

The **quantity theory** of money states that inflation is caused by having too much money in the economy. Therefore, the money supply should be carefully controlled. Some economists believe the key to stable prices is to increase the supply of money at the same rate the economy grows. The money supply must be kept in line with the nation's productivity as measured by real GDP.

A second explanation for inflation looks at aggregate demand. Aggregate demand is the amount of goods and services in the economy that will be bought at all possible price levels. Inflation can occur when the demand for goods and services is greater than the supply. During wartime, for example, the government needs a lot of military supplies. This puts pressure on producers. The heavy demand for new equipment, supplies, and services makes those items more valuable. This pushes prices up. Wages also rise as the demand for labor increases along with the demand for goods.

A third cause of inflation is changes in aggregate supply. Inflation occurs when producers raise prices to meet higher costs. Higher prices for raw materials can cause costs to increase. Workers' wages are the largest single cost of production for most businesses. When wages go up, businesses often have to raise prices.

Let's look at an example of how higher wages are linked to inflation. Jen works at Am-Gro Fertilizer. She belongs to the union. Her union pushed for a raise because the cost of living had gone up. Through collective bargaining, it won a large wage increase from the company. The increased cost of labor led Am-Gro to raise its prices to keep its profits at the same level.

Remember that inflation results in a loss of purchasing power. When the prices for goods and services go up, workers need higher wages to keep up with rising prices. If businesses give workers more money, the businesses may be forced to raise their prices to earn a profit. The higher prices lead to more inflation and then to another round of higher wages. The process continues, with wages and prices constantly going up. Because the pattern repeats itself in the same way over and over, the process is called a **wage-price spiral.** The effect of a wage-price spiral on Am-Gro Fertilizer is shown in **Figure 13.6** on page 326.

✔ **CHECKPOINT** *What are the three causes of inflation?*

What are some effects of inflation?

The most noticeable effect of inflation is the loss of purchasing power. In a period of inflation, a dollar will not buy the same amount of goods it did in the past. Suppose a worker earns $500 a week. She spends it on things she wants and needs. If the prices of these things go up, her wages will no longer buy as much. When there is no inflation, her $500 will buy the same amount of goods it did last year. If the inflation rate is 10 percent, however, $500 will buy only $450 worth of goods.

wage-price spiral
a pattern of higher prices leading to more inflation and then to a round of higher wages, repeated over and over

Economics & YOU
Inflation

Instead of a cross-country vacation to see the Grand Canyon, your family takes some day trips. *Due to higher prices caused by inflation, your family cannot afford to travel across the country.*

You ask your boss if you can work extra hours at your part-time job. *You need the money because inflation has reduced the purchasing power of your paycheck.*

fixed income
income that does not go up even when prices go up

People living on fixed incomes are especially hard-hit by inflation. A **fixed income** is income that does not go up even when prices go up. For example, retired people usually are on fixed incomes. Much of their income comes from savings or a pension fund. The amount they receive each month is fixed, or the same each month. Inflation eats away at the purchasing power of that check. In addition, many retired people receive Social Security benefits. Unlike pensions, Social Security benefits are adjusted to keep up with inflation.

Inflation also affects interest rates. People earn a set amount of interest on money in their savings accounts. Their true return depends on the rate of inflation. For example, Sonia had her savings in an account that paid 7 percent interest. At the same time, the yearly inflation rate was 5 percent. As a result, the purchasing power of Sonia's savings that year went up by only 2 percent. She needed 5 percent interest to keep up with inflation.

When a bank's interest rate matches the inflation rate, savers break even. The amount they gain from interest is taken away by inflation. However, if the inflation rate is higher than the bank's interest rate, savers lose money.

✔ **CHECKPOINT** *What happens when income does not keep pace with inflation?*

Fig. 13.6 The Wage-Price Spiral

CHART SKILLS

Inflation can lead to a wage-price spiral of increasing prices.

1. Why do rising food prices encourage a wage-price spiral?
2. How might globalization and outsourcing affect the wage-price spiral?

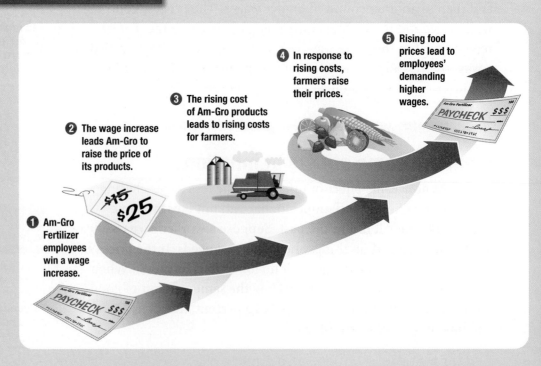

❶ Am-Gro Fertilizer employees win a wage increase.

❷ The wage increase leads Am-Gro to raise the price of its products.

❸ The rising cost of Am-Gro products leads to rising costs for farmers.

❹ In response to rising costs, farmers raise their prices.

❺ Rising food prices lead to employees' demanding higher wages.

What has been the trend in inflation in recent years?

The United States has had fairly low inflation since the 1960s. In the late 1990s, unemployment was low. Often, low unemployment leads to higher inflation. Because workers are scarce, companies have to offer higher wages. Rising wages can push the inflation rate up. However, in this period, inflation was less than 3 percent.

In the early 2000s, the economy entered a period of recession and slow growth. Inflation fell to less than 2 percent. Prices at times seemed to be falling. Some experts even predicted a period of **deflation.** Deflation is the opposite of inflation. It is a general drop in the price level. However, the economy recovered.

Despite the economic growth, inflation remained low. Rising energy prices in 2007 pushed the CPI a little higher than in 2006. Through most of 2007, however, the annual inflation rate was still under 4 percent.

By mid-2008, people were worried about inflation. Prices rose, and the CPI went up by 1.1 percent in June. It was the largest one-month gain in more than 25 years. Higher fuel and production costs pushed the inflation rate above 4 percent. As a result, people bought fewer expensive goods like cars, appliances, or homes.

✔ **CHECKPOINT** *What has been the trend in inflation in recent years?*

Reading Strategy
Inferencing
What do you already know about inflation?

deflation
a general drop in the price level

SECTION 2 ASSESSMENT

Essential Questions Journal To continue to build a response to the Essential Question, go to your **Essential Questions Journal.**

❓ Guiding Question

1. Use your completed table to answer the following question: What are the causes and effects of inflation?

Key Terms and Main Ideas

Directions: On a sheet of paper, write the answer to each question. Use complete sentences.

2. How does inflation influence a consumer's purchasing power?

3. What is the consumer price index (CPI)? Why is it important?

4. What is hyperinflation?

5. What causes a wage-price spiral, and what can it lead to?

Critical Thinking

6. **Draw Inferences** (a) What categories of goods and services are included in the CPI market basket? (b) What is the purpose of including these categories?

7. **Make Comparisons** (a) How is the core inflation rate different from the inflation rate? (b) What is the purpose of calculating these two separate rates?

Objectives

- **Define** who is poor, according to government standards.
- **Describe** the causes of poverty.
- **Analyze** how income is distributed in the United States.
- **Summarize** what the government is doing to fight poverty.

Guiding Question

What factors affect the poverty rate?

Copy this table and fill it in as you read to explain the causes of poverty.

Causes of Poverty	
Lack of education	Less education equals lower wages
Location	
Discrimination	Unfair treatment because of several factors
Growth of low-skill service jobs	

▶ **Economics and You** The United States has millions of people living in poverty. It also has one of the highest per-person GDPs in the world. How can that be? Looking at poverty rates among different groups of Americans reveals some reasons.

Principles in Action In general, you are at greater risk of living in poverty if you come from a single-parent home, live in the inner city, or do not have at least a high school education. Other factors, including the way income is spread, affect the poverty rate.

How do we know who the poor are?

Living in a state of poverty means being poor, or lacking enough resources such as food, shelter, and clothing. During the last 30 years, the number of people living in poverty in the United States has risen.

The U.S. Census Bureau collects a lot of information about the American people. Its economists then look at the information and organize it. One thing they look at is how many families and households live in poverty. The census bureau defines a *family* as a group of two or more related people who live in the same home. A *household* is all people who live in the same home, regardless of whether they are related. According to the census bureau, 37.3 million people living in rural areas are poor. More than 16 percent of people living in cities are poor. Some experts believe these numbers are really much larger.

What is the poverty threshold?

The government has a way of defining which people are poor. It says a family is poor whose total income is not enough to satisfy the family's minimum needs. The U.S. Census Bureau calculates what this minimum level is. This is known as the poverty threshold. The **poverty threshold** is the income level below which income is not high enough to support a family or household.

The poverty threshold, or poverty line, is not the same for all families. For example, in 2006, the poverty threshold for a single parent under age 65 with one child was $13,896. For a family of four with two children, it was $20,444. If a family's total income is below the poverty threshold, everyone in the family is counted as poor.

How is the poverty rate figured?

Poverty rates for different groups are shown in **Figure 13.7**. The **poverty rate** is the percentage of people who live in households with incomes lower than the official poverty threshold.

We can use poverty rates to discover whom the government considers to be poor. Poverty rates can also be used to learn the factors that seem to cause poverty. As you have read in Chapter 3, poverty rates differ sharply by group:

- *Race and ethnicity* The poverty rate among African Americans and Hispanics is more than double the rate for white Americans.

poverty threshold
an income level below that which is needed to support a family or household

poverty rate
the percentage of people who live in households with income lower than the official poverty threshold

Fig. 13.7 Poverty Rates by Group, 2006

GRAPH SKILLS

African Americans, Hispanics, Native Americans, and households headed by women are likelier than other groups to earn incomes below the poverty level.

1. Which group has the highest poverty rate?
2. Why do you think differences in poverty rates exist among groups?

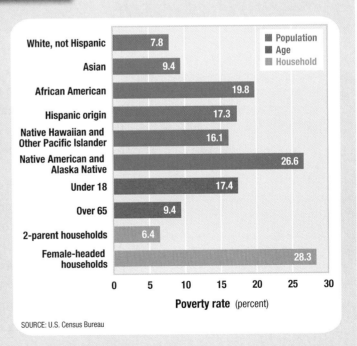

SOURCE: U.S. Census Bureau

▲ Limited job opportunities and lower levels of education are some of the factors that contribute to rural poverty.

- **Type of family** Families with a single mother have a poverty rate almost five times greater than that of two-parent families.
- **Age** The percentage of children living in poverty is much higher than that for any other age group. Young adults make up the next largest group.
- **Residence** People who live in the inner city have double the poverty rate of those who live outside the inner city. There is also much poverty in rural areas.

✅ **CHECKPOINT** *Which group has the highest percentage living in poverty?*

What are the main causes of poverty?

As you have read in Section 1, millions of Americans are unemployed for many reasons. While they are out of jobs, their families may fall below the poverty threshold. Many other poor adults are not even considered a part of the labor force. Some suffer from poor health. They may be unable to work. Some may be discouraged workers who are no longer looking for work.

Many poor adults do have jobs, however. In fact, more than half of poor households have someone who works at least part time. One in five has a full-time, year-round worker. These working poor usually earn low wages or cannot work as many hours as they would like. For example, Ray makes $9.00 an hour as a full-time clerk in a clothing store. While he is at work, his wife stays home with their two young children. Ray works 40 hours per week, and his salary is higher than the minimum wage. Yet he earns only $18,720 a year. This is below the poverty threshold for a family of four.

There are several reasons that people are poor. One is a lack of education. The average income of high school dropouts in 2006 was $25,912. This was just above the poverty threshold for a family of four in that year. High school graduates earned about two thirds more than the dropouts. College graduates earned more than three times as much. In general, the more education people have, the higher their income.

A second cause of poverty may be location. In most American cities, African Americans and Hispanics live mostly in the inner cities. This is far from the higher wage jobs in suburban areas. Many people who live in inner cities do not own cars. Often, public transportation is not available or convenient. As a result, people who live in the inner city often earn less than people living outside the inner city. Getting to available jobs is also hard for many people living in rural areas.

Another cause of poverty may be discrimination. Discrimination is unfair treatment because of a person's race, sex, religion, age, or physical condition. White workers generally earn more than minority workers. Men often earn more than women. There may be several reasons why. There may be differences in hours worked, education, and work experience. Another factor, however, may be discrimination. Economists agree that today there is less discrimination than there was in the past.

The loss of manufacturing jobs is another cause of poverty. Less-educated people could once earn good wages working in factories. Globalization and the rise of the service economy are two reasons there is less U.S. manufacturing today. More workers with less education now work in low-skill service jobs. Wages are often not as high as they were for factory jobs.

Changes in family structure are another cause of poverty. In the past, most families had both a mother and father. Today, there are a growing number of single-parent families. These families are more likely to live in poverty than two-parent families. That is especially true when the single parent is a mother. The growing number of divorces has also changed family structure. The divorce rate has been climbing since the 1960s. So has the number of children born to unmarried parents.

✅ **CHECKPOINT** *What are three causes of poverty?*

How is income distributed?

To fully understand poverty in the United States, you need to understand **income distribution.** This is how the nation's total income is spread among its population.

The distribution of income in the United States is shown in **Figure 13.8** on page 332. These figures do not factor in the effects of taxes or noncash government aid. This aid can take many forms, including housing subsidies, healthcare, or food stamps. **Food stamps** are government-issued coupons that people exchange for food.

Look at the table on the left side of **Figure 13.8.** To get the numbers in the table, economists take four steps.
1. First, they rank the nation's households according to income.
2. Second, they divide the list into fifths, or quintiles, with equal numbers of households in each fifth. The lowest fifth, which appears at the top of the list, includes the poorest 20 percent of households. The highest fifth, which appears at the bottom of the list, includes the richest 20 percent of households.

Reading Strategy
Inferencing
Does what you already know about poverty help you understand what you just read? Why or why not?

income distribution
the way the nation's total income is spread out among its population
food stamps
government-issued coupons that people exchange for food

Lorenz Curve
a graph that shows the distribution of income in the economy

3. Third, they find out each group's average income. They do this by adding up the incomes of all the households in the group and then dividing by the number of households.

4. Finally, they find out each group's share, or percentage, of total income. This number is calculated by dividing the group's total income by the total income of all the groups. The second column in the table in **Figure 13.8** shows each group's share. The third column is the total of that fifth plus those fifths below it. For example, the two lowest fifths of households earned 12 percent of total income.

Compare the share of the poorest fifth with that of the richest fifth. You will see that the richest fifth receives nearly 15 times the income of the poorest fifth.

What is the Lorenz Curve?

Now look at the graph on the right side of **Figure 13.8**. It shows the numbers for shares of total income. When they are plotted on a graph, they form a curve. This graph, called the **Lorenz Curve,** shows the distribution of income in the economy.

Let's see what this Lorenz Curve tells us. The straight line running diagonally across the graph shows complete equality. If there were complete equality, each quintile would receive one fifth of total income. That means the lowest 20 percent of households would receive 20 percent of total income, as shown by point A1. The lowest 40 percent (the first two quintiles) would receive 40 percent of total income. It is shown by point A2.

Fig. 13.8 Income Distribution, 2006

Action Graph online — For an animated version of this graph, visit PearsonSuccessNet.com

GRAPH SKILLS
The table (right) shows family income ranked by category. When shown on a Lorenz Curve (far right), this information shows how U.S. income is distributed.

1. What percent of total income did the lowest three fifths of households earn in 2006?

2. How would taxes and government programs affect the Lorenz Curve?

Percent of Total Income, 2006

Quintile	Percent of income for quintile	Cumulative: Percent of income for this and lower quintiles
Lowest fifth	3.4%	3.4%
Second fifth	8.6%	12.0%
Third fifth	14.5%	26.5%
Fourth fifth	22.9%	49.4%
Highest fifth	50.5%	100.0%

Note: Because of rounding, totals may be greater than or less than 100 percent.
SOURCE: U.S. Census Bureau

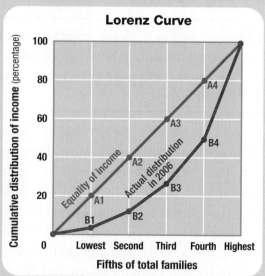

Lorenz Curve

For 2006, the Lorenz Curve, or the red line on the graph, shows that the distribution of income was not equal. For example, look at point B1. It shows that the lowest 20 percent, or one fifth, of households received just 3.4 percent of the nation's total income. Point B2 shows that the lowest 40 percent, or two fifths, of households received only 12 percent of the income. The area on the graph between the blue and red lines shows how far income distribution is from being equal. The closer the two lines are, the more equal the distribution of income is. The more the Lorenz Curve bends away from the blue line, the less equal the distribution of income is.

What is the income gap?

Some people earn more money than others. As you can see from **Figure 13.8**, the richest fifth of American households earned more income (50.5 percent) than the bottom four fifths combined. This is not too surprising. People have different skills and talents. Some are well-educated, and some have little education. In a market economy, people with skills and talents that are in high demand earn a lot of money. People who have few skills for which there is little demand earn much less.

The difference between what the richest and the poorest Americans earn is called the income gap. Over the last 25 years, the income gap in the United States has been growing larger. Since 1977, the share earned by the top 1 percent has more than doubled. At the same time, the share of income earned by the three lowest fifths has gone down by 12 percent.

Why are there such differences in income among Americans? Here are some reasons.

- *Differences in skills and education* Some people are more highly skilled than others, so they earn higher wages. Labor skills are linked to education and training.
- *Inheritances* Some people inherit, or receive from their parents or other relatives, large sums of money. They earn income by investing it. Others inherit businesses that produce income from profits.
- *Field of work* The demand for labor determines wages. People who produce goods with a low market value usually earn lower wages.

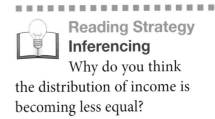

Reading Strategy
Inferencing
Why do you think the distribution of income is becoming less equal?

✔ **CHECKPOINT** *What can economists learn from income distribution?*

enterprise zone
area where companies can locate
and not have to pay certain state,
local, and federal taxes

How has government tried to reduce poverty?

The government spends billions of dollars on programs designed to reduce poverty. This money is spent mainly on cash assistance, education, medical benefits, and non-cash benefits such as food stamps and subsidized housing.

Critics of antipoverty programs say that much of the money is wasted. Many argue that the programs themselves harm the very people they are intended to help. One new policy gave tax refunds to low-income families with children. Job training programs, another new policy, help low-income people learn skills that are needed to earn an adequate income.

What are some new approaches that can be used to reduce poverty?

In recent years, the government has tried new ideas to reduce poverty. One of these is the creation of **enterprise zones.** These first became popular in the 1980s. Companies can locate in these areas and not have to pay certain state, local, and federal taxes. There are also fewer rules on business operations. These zones help businesses by lowering costs. They help people living in the areas by making it easier for them to find work near their homes. Many of these zones are located in cities. By providing jobs to people, these zones can help rebuild rundown areas in inner cities.

Many people are poor because they do not have needed skills. Federal and state governments have designed job-training programs to help workers who lack skills. The federal government has set a minimum wage since 1938. The minimum wage is the lowest wage a worker can be legally paid.

The government also has programs to help poor people find housing they can afford. Sometimes, the government helps renters by paying part of their rent directly to landlords. In another program, poor people receive coupons that cover part of the rent they pay. The third approach is government-owned housing. The rent that is paid is much lower than for private housing.

How has the welfare system changed?

Poor people often cannot afford basic needs, such as food and medical care. The United States has long had a welfare system. It provides for those basic needs, especially for children and the elderly. That system was changed in 1996 when President Bill Clinton signed the Personal Responsibility and Work Opportunity Reconciliation Act.

Some people thought the old welfare system encouraged poor people to remain unemployed to keep receiving aid. The new law set up a program called Temporary Assistance for Needy Families (TANF). TANF ended cash assistance for poor families. Instead, the federal government today provides **block grants,** or lump sums of money, to the states. The states have to design and operate programs to move most poor adults from depending on welfare to working. TANF also set a 5-year limit on how long a person would get benefits.

TANF is meant to move people from welfare to **workfare.** Workfare is a program requiring work in exchange for help from the government. It was hoped this change would reduce poverty. Supporters argued that once a person had a first job, he or she would be better able to find another, higher paying job. Poor Americans would learn new labor skills and be able to qualify for other jobs.

 CHECKPOINT *What was the goal of TANF?*

block grant
lump sum of money provided to states for poor families

workfare
a program requiring work in exchange for government help

SECTION 3 ASSESSMENT

Essential Questions Journal
To continue to build a response to the Essential Question, go to your Essential Questions Journal.

Guiding Question

1. Use your completed table to answer the following question: What factors affect the poverty rate?

Key Terms and Main Ideas

Directions: On a sheet of paper, write the answer to each question. Use complete sentences.

2. How is the poverty threshold related to the poverty rate?

3. Explain how a family can include working adults but still have an income below the poverty threshold.

4. How does lack of education contribute to poverty?

5. Describe at least three ways in which the government tries to fight poverty.

Critical Thinking

6. **Draw Conclusions** (a) What kinds of families are likely to live in poverty? (b) Why do you think these families have a greater risk of being poor?

7. **Synthesize Information** (a) How did the Personal Responsibility and Work Opportunity Reconciliation Act of 1996 change the assistance the government provides to poor families? (b) What are some benefits and some drawbacks of these new programs? Explain.

Section 1–Unemployment

- Frictional unemployment happens when people must search a long time to find a job.

- Structural unemployment happens when workers' skills do not match the skills needed for the jobs available.

- Seasonal unemployment happens when industries shut down for a season.

- Cyclical unemployment goes up during recessions and depressions and falls when the economy improves.

- Full employment in a market economy is a rate of unemployment of 4 to 6 percent.

Section 2–Inflation

- Inflation is a general increase in prices. It causes a decrease in purchasing power.

- The price index is a measurement that shows the average price of a group of goods. The consumer price index (CPI) measures the average price of a group of consumer goods.

- Items that a typical urban consumer might buy are called a market basket. This measurement is used for tracking the average price of a group of goods from month to month.

- The inflation rate is the monthly or yearly percentage rate of change in prices. The core inflation rate is the rate after removing the effects of food and energy prices. Hyperinflation is out-of-control inflation.

Section 3–Poverty

- The poverty threshold is an income level not high enough to support a family or household. The poverty rate measures the percentage of people who live in households with income lower than the poverty threshold.

- Income distribution measures the way the nation's total income is spread among its total population.

- Enterprise zones are areas where companies can locate and not have to pay certain state, local, and federal taxes.

- Workfare is a program requiring work in exchange for help from the government.

Section 1
What are the causes of unemployment?

Section 2
What are the causes and effects of inflation?

Section 3
What factors affect the poverty rate?

Essential Question, Chapter 13

How much can we reduce unemployment, inflation, and poverty?

DOCUMENT-BASED ASSESSMENT

U.S. says $4 gas not going away

By H. Joseph Hebert

The economy affects everyone. When the price of an inelastic good increases, all consumers suffer. The following article shows how rising energy costs is an economic challenge.

WASHINGTON—The nationwide average for gasoline prices should peak at $4.15 a gallon this summer [of 2008], the government says, finally an encouraging word for motorists who might be thinking the cost of filling up will just keep climbing. . . .

A drop in gasoline inventories, concerns about hurricanes that could disrupt Gulf of Mexico supplies and high oil prices have contributed to a belief that the upward spiral of gasoline costs will continue at least for a few months, according to [Guy] Caruso [head of the federal Energy Information Administration]. . . .

Motorists are paying $4.05 a gallon on average nationwide and considerably more in some parts of the country, according to a survey of gas stations by AAA [the American Automobile Association] and the Oil Price Information Service. That's an increase of nearly $1 a gallon since January. . . .

"The consensus view," said Rep. Edward Markey D-Mass. [Chairman of the House Select Committee on Energy Independence and Global Warming] . . ., "is that oil above $100 a barrel is going to be with us for some time."

. . . Predicting future oil and gasoline prices is highly uncertain with the volatile [unstable] global oil markets, Caruso acknowledged.

His agency bases its gasoline projections on assumptions of future oil prices, expectations of demand and economic trends. It has revised its figures several times since fall because it did not anticipate the huge surge in global oil costs. . . .

. . . A panel of energy experts told the House [of Representatives] hearing that consumers shouldn't expect quick fixes.

They said one answer is more conservation and a shift to alternative fuels, transitions that would take time. Caruso told lawmakers that new auto fuel economy requirements and the increased use of ethanol and other alternative fuels are expected to produce "a substantial reduction" in oil use and oil imports over two decades. . . .

Document-Based Questions

1. What was the nationwide average price for gasoline in the summer of 2008?
2. Why does the author believe gasoline prices could spiral upward?
3. How does a drop in oil supply (or inventories) impact the price of gasoline?
4. Why is predicting future oil prices risky?
5. In your own words, explain why energy costs are an economic challenge.

SOURCE: H. Josef Hebert, "U.S. says $4 gas not going away," The Associated Press, June 12, 2008

Directions: Write the answer using complete sentences.

Section 1–Unemployment

1. What is globalization?

2. What is full employment?

3. How is full employment related to the unemployment rate?

4. What did the government do to help unemployed workers during the Great Depression?

5. What might happen if the economy reached full employment?

6. How does the census help the Bureau of Labor Statistics determine the unemployment rate?

Section 2–Inflation

7. What are three possible effects of inflation?

8. What might cause inflation in food prices?

9. How would you react to higher food prices?

10. What is the worst kind of inflation? Why?

11. What is deflation?

12. According to the quantity theory, what causes inflation?

Section 3–Poverty

13. What are the most recognized causes of poverty?

14. What kinds of assistance might a poor family be able to get from the government?

15. What has happened to the income gap over the last 25 years?

16. What are three reasons for differences in income among Americans? Do you think these differences are a problem? Why or why not?

17. What does a Lorenz Curve for 2006 show about the distribution of income in the United States?

Exploring the Essential Question

18. Why is the poverty rate among African Americans and Hispanics more than double the poverty rate for white Americans?

19. What is the best way to help the working poor?

Essential Question Activity

20. Complete this activity to answer the Essential Question **How much can we reduce unemployment, inflation, and poverty?**

Your teacher will divide your class into three groups. Each group is advising the President of the United States on ways the federal government can help reduce unemployment, inflation, and poverty. Using the worksheet your teacher gives you or the electronic worksheet available at **PearsonSuccessNet.com**, answer the following questions:

(a) Globalization is accelerating, and America's manufacturing base is disappearing. How can we reduce unemployment? (b) What strategy or strategies would you recommend to reduce inflation? (c) What strategy or strategies would you recommend to reduce poverty? What are the benefits and drawbacks of your plan?

Essential Questions Journal To continue to build a response to the Essential Question, go to your **Essential Questions Journal.**

 **Test-Taking Tip**

When choosing answers from a Word Bank, complete the items you know first. Then study the remaining answers to complete the items you are not sure about.

Unit 5 Challenge

Essential Question, Unit 5

Why does it matter how the economy is doing?

THE ESSENTIAL

VIDEO
By Students For Students
For videos on Essential Questions, go to *PearsonSuccessNet.com*

Does economic news about GDP or inflation really matter to ordinary people? Plenty of people think that it does. Look at the opinions below, keeping in mind the Essential Question: Why does it matter how the economy is doing?

"Economists readily concede that GDP is not a one-number-fits-all view of what's going on. Some suggest changes to make it more useful and more accurate…. 'What we need to end up with is two separate accounts [of the economy]—a market price account and a quality of life account,' says Rob Atkinson, an economist in Washington…. 'It is an opportunity to think more accurately about our economic well-being.'"

—Mark Trumbull, "Does GDP Really Capture Economic Health?" Christian Science Monitor, March 12, 2008

"The U.S. economy is taking hits from all directions, or that's how it seems to many Americans…. Home foreclosures are multiplying. People with houses can't sell them. Home prices and sales dropped dramatically in January, and there's no sign of improvement soon. Banks no longer provide easy credit. Stock-market investments are on a roller-coaster ride. Pay checks don't buy as much today as yesterday…. Americans want to know what will turn the economy around. They want help and answers—from Congress and the president."

—*Miami Herald*, February 29, 2008

"I DON'T UNDERSTAND HOW HIGH INTEREST RATES AND THE NATIONAL DEFICIT AFFECT MY ALLOWANCE."

Essential Question
Writing Activity

Consider the different views of economics expressed in the sources on this page and what you have learned about measuring economic performance. *Then write a well-constructed essay expressing your view of why it is important to keep track of the economy.*

Writing Guidelines

- Address all aspects of the Essential Question Writing Activity.
- Support the theme with relevant facts, examples, and details.
- Use a logical and clear plan of organization.
- Introduce the theme by establishing a framework that is beyond a simple restatement of the question and conclude with a summation of the theme.

For help in writing a Persuasive Essay, refer to the *Writing Skills Handbook* in the Reference section, page S-5.

Essential Questions Journal

To respond to the unit Essential Question, go to your **Essential Questions Journal**.

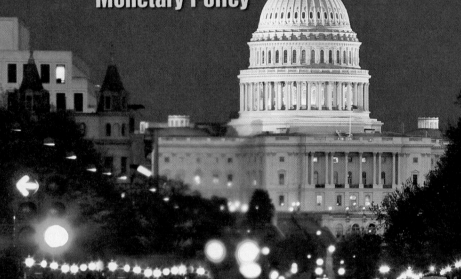

6 Government and the Economy

Essential Question, Unit 6

What is the proper role of government in the economy?

Chapter 14
How can taxation meet the needs of government and the people?

Chapter 15
How effective is fiscal policy as an economic tool?

Chapter 16
How effective is monetary policy as an economic tool?

Chapter 14 Taxes and Government Spending

Essential Question, Chapter 14

How can taxation meet the needs of government and the people?

Economics on the go

To study anywhere, anytime, download these online resources at *PearsonSuccessNet.com* ➤

A huge project like a dam can cost the U.S. government millions of dollars. The government needs taxes to build a project like this. Depending on what actions it takes, the government can strengthen or weaken the health of the economy. Many government decisions affect the economy. How much money will the government raise in taxes? How much will it spend? On what will it spend the money? The answers to all these questions are important to economic health.

In this chapter, you will read about the many different kinds of taxes. You will learn about the role of the American government in the economy. You will also read about federal, state, and local budgets.

■■■

Reading Strategy: Metacognition
Metacognition means "being aware of the way you learn." You can use metacognition to become a better reader by doing these things as you read:

• Visualize what is happening in the text. If something doesn't make sense, go back and read it again.

• Note the main idea of each paragraph and the details that support it.

• Make predictions. Ask yourself, "What do I already know about this topic?"

• At the end of each section, summarize what you have just read.

Go to the Visual Glossary Online for an interactive review of **progressive taxes.**

How the Economy Works
online

Go to How the Economy Works Online for an interactive lesson on the **federal income tax.**

Go to Action Graph Online for animated versions of key charts and graphs.

Objectives

- **Identify** what gives the government the right to tax.
- **Explain** the different kinds of tax structures and tax bases.
- **List** the characteristics of a good tax.
- **Identify** who bears the burden of a tax.

Guiding Question

What are the features of a tax system?

Copy this concept web and fill it in as you read.

- - - - - - - - - - - - - - - - - - -

Reading Strategy
Metacognition

Before you read this section, think about what strategies you can use to better understand taxes.

- - - - - - - - - - - - - - - - - - -

tax
a required payment to a local, state, or national government

▶ **Economics and You** You are looking forward to getting your first paycheck. You figure that at $7.00 an hour, you should be getting $140.00 for the 20 hours you worked. When you open the envelope, however, you find that the check is for much less than $140.00. Where did the money go? The answer is . . . taxes! The federal government and most state governments collect taxes on money you earn. Is this fair?

Principles in Action Fairness is one of the main features of a tax system. But what is fair to one person may not be fair to another. For example, at first glance, it may seem fair that all Americans should be taxed at the same rate. However, in this section, you will learn why most Americans believe that the person who earns more money should pay a higher percentage of income in taxes. This idea lies at the base of our income tax system.

What gives the government the right to tax?

Taxes are as old as civilization. Taxpayers' dislike of taxes goes back as far. Anger against taxes was one of the reasons American colonists declared their independence from Britain. Though they disliked taxes, they also understood that governments need taxes. When the U.S. Constitution was written, the federal government was given the right to tax. The money raised by taxes is used to pay for the many things government does.

What is the purpose of taxes?

A **tax** is a payment of money by people or businesses to a local, state, or national government. Everyone—citizen or not—has to pay them. Taxation is the main way all three levels of government pay their bills.

The income a government receives from taxes and other nontax sources is called **revenue.** What if there were no taxes? The government would not be able to pay for the many services we expect. For example, we expect the government to provide an army, highways, schools, and police. We also expect it to help take care of people in need. These goods and services cost money. All members of our society share these costs by paying taxes.

What are the limits on the government's right to tax?

The Constitution also limits the federal government's power to tax. Two of those limits are in Article One. First, the purpose of a tax must be "for the common defense and general welfare." It must be used for the good of all the people. It cannot benefit just a few people. Second, federal taxes must be the same in every state. The federal gas tax, for example, cannot be 4 cents a gallon in Maryland and 10 cents a gallon in South Dakota.

Other parts of the Constitution also limit the kinds of taxes Congress can gather. Congress cannot tax churches, because that would go against the freedom of religion guaranteed by the First Amendment. Another part of the Constitution says Congress cannot tax goods or products being sent out of the country. The government can collect taxes only on imports—goods brought into the United States. Congress can stop certain goods, such as technology or weapons, from being exported.

 **CHECKPOINT** *Why does the government collect taxes?*

What are tax structures and tax bases?

Economists identify three different tax structures. These are proportional tax, progressive tax, and regressive tax. Then economists also describe a tax according to the object taxed. This is called the tax base.

What is a proportional tax?

A **proportional tax** is sometimes called a flat tax. It is stated as a percentage. Suppose the United States had a flat tax. The tax rate would be the same no matter what a person's income was. Leslie Wilson, a corporate executive, earns $350,000 a year. Tony Owens, a nurse, earns $50,000 a year. What if the United States had a proportional tax of 6 percent? Leslie would pay 6 percent of $350,000, or $21,000, in taxes. Tony would pay 6 percent of $50,000, or $3,000.

revenue
the income received by a government from taxes and other nontax sources

proportional tax
a tax for which the percentage of income paid in taxes remains the same at all income levels

progressive tax
a tax for which the percentage of income paid in taxes increases as income increases

regressive tax
a tax for which the percentage of income paid in taxes decreases as income increases

tax base
the income, property, good, or service that is subject to a tax

individual income tax
a tax based on a person's earnings

corporate income tax
a tax based on the amount of profit a company makes

property tax
a tax based on real estate and other property

sales tax
a tax based on goods or services that are sold

What is a progressive tax?

The federal income tax is a good example of a **progressive tax**. The more money a person earns, the greater the percentage paid in taxes. People with higher incomes pay a higher percentage than people with smaller incomes. Leslie earns more than Tony, so she pays a higher percentage of her income in taxes than Tony does.

What is a regressive tax?

Most taxes, other than income taxes, are regressive. With a **regressive tax**, the higher the income, the smaller the percentage of income paid as taxes. Let's say Leslie and Tony decide to buy new computers. The price of each of the computers is $1,000 with an 8 percent sales tax. The sales tax for both is $80. The $80 Tony pays is a higher percentage of his income than the $80 Leslie pays.

What is the tax base?

A **tax base** is the income, property, good, or service being taxed. Different taxes have different bases. The **individual income tax** is based on what a person earns. The **corporate income tax** uses a company's profits as its base. The **property tax** is based on real estate and other property. The tax base for the **sales tax** is goods or services that are sold. When the government decides to create a new tax, it first decides what the base will be for the tax. Will it be income, profits, property, sales, or some other category?

 CHECKPOINT *Is the federal income tax proportional, progressive, or regressive?*

What are the characteristics of a good tax?

Economists generally agree on what makes a good tax. It should have four characteristics: simplicity, efficiency, certainty, and equity, or fairness.

- *Simplicity* Tax laws should be simple and easy to understand. It should be easy for taxpayers and businesses to keep records. They should be able to pay taxes on a regular schedule.
- *Efficiency* It should also be easy for government to collect taxes without spending too much time or money. At the same time, paying taxes should be easy. It should not take up too much time or cost too much money in fees.
- *Certainty* Taxpayers need to know when a tax is due, how much money is due, and how the tax should be paid.
- *Equity* The tax system should be fair. No one should bear too much or too little of the tax burden.

Although everyone agrees that a tax system should be fair to taxpayers, people often disagree on what "fair" really means. Over time, economists have proposed two different ideas about how to measure the fairness of a tax: the benefits-received principle and the ability-to-pay principle. According to the benefits-received principle, a person should pay taxes based on the level of benefits he or she expects to receive from the government. The ability-to-pay principle is the idea behind a progressive income tax: people who earn more income pay more taxes.

✓ **CHECKPOINT** *What are the four characteristics of a good tax?*

Who bears the tax burden?

Government tax policies affect individuals, businesses, and even whole regions. The policies may help some regions more than others. It is important to think about who actually bears the burden of the tax. Taxes affect more than just the people who send in the checks to pay them.

Suppose the government taxes gasoline $.50 per gallon and collects the tax from service stations. You may think that only the service stations pay the tax, because they mail the checks to the government. Graphs A and B in **Figure 14.1,** however, show that the answer is not so simple. Graph A shows the effect of a gasoline tax when demand is inelastic. Graph B reflects elastic demand.

Both graphs show two supply curves: an original supply line and a line showing the effect of the $.50 tax. A tax on a good like gasoline increases the cost of supplying the good. The supply of the good then goes down at every price level. This shifts the supply curve to the left.

Fig. 14.1 Elasticities of Demand and Tax Effects

GRAPH SKILLS

If demand for a good is relatively inelastic (Graph A), a new tax will increase the price by a relatively large amount, and consumers will pay a large share of the tax.

1. Under what conditions, elastic or inelastic demand, would the price of the good increase from $1.00 to $1.10?

2. Who bears the burden of a tax if demand is relatively elastic?

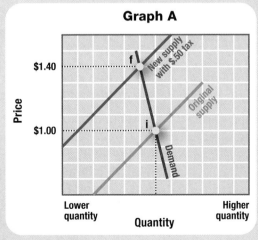

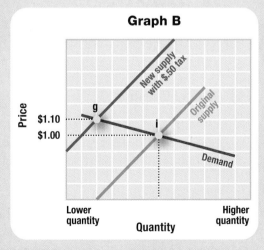

 For an animated version of this graph, visit **PearsonSuccessNet.com**

incidence of a tax
the final burden of a tax

Reading Strategy
Metacognition
Ask yourself if what you just read about taxes makes sense. If not, go back and read the text again.

Before the tax, the market was in equilibrium. Consumers bought gas at $1.00 per gallon. This is shown as point *i* on both graphs. Let's say demand for gas is relatively inelastic. Consumers will buy about the same amount no matter the price. The effect of the tax is to raise the price of each gallon by $.40, a pretty big jump. Consumers pay the largest share of the tax. The service stations pay only a small part. This is shown in Graph A.

What if demand is relatively elastic? (Consumers will buy much less if the price goes up.) The demand curve will be relatively flat, as in Graph B. Consumers will pay only a small part of the tax. In this case, the service stations pay the largest part of the tax.

This example shows the **incidence of a tax**—that is, the final burden of a tax. Government officials thinking about a new tax have to consider who will actually bear the burden. As in the previous example, producers can pass on a part of the tax to consumers. Generally, the more inelastic the demand, the easier it is for the seller to shift the tax to consumers. The more elastic the demand, the harder it is. In this case, the seller bears most of the tax burden.

 CHECKPOINT *Who bears the greater burden of a tax when demand is inelastic?*

SECTION 1 ASSESSMENT

Essential Questions Journal To continue to build a response to the Essential Question, go to your **Essential Questions Journal.**

 Guiding Question

1. Use your completed concept web to answer the following question: What are the features of a tax system?

Key Terms and Main Ideas

Directions: On a sheet of paper, write the answer to each question. Use complete sentences.

2. Where does the U.S. government get the power to impose taxes today?

3. What is a government's revenue?

4. Name two limits the Constitution places on the government's power to tax.

5. What is the tax base for the sales tax?

Critical Thinking

6. **Analyze Information** Suppose Michelle earns $40,000 and Rosa earns $100,000 a year. Under a proportional tax, who would pay a greater percentage of her income in taxes?

7. **Make Comparisons** How do progressive taxes work? How are progressive taxes different from regressive taxes?

SECTION 2 Federal Taxes

Objectives

- **Describe** the process of paying individual income taxes.
- **Identify** the basic characteristics of corporate income taxes.
- **Explain** the purpose of Social Security, Medicare, and unemployment taxes.
- **Identify** other types of taxes.

Guiding Question
What taxes does the federal government collect?

Copy this table and fill it in as you read.

Federal Taxes	
Individual Income	Taxes paid throughout year. Employers withhold taxes from pay. Individuals file taxes. Tax is progressive.
Corporate Income	
Social Insurance	Retirement funds; also benefits for surviving family members
Excise	Tax on certain U.S. goods
Estate	
Gift	Tax on money and property of a person who has died, if over $1.5 million

Reading Strategy
Metacognition
As you read, notice the structure of this chapter. Look at the titles, headings, and boldfaced words.

▶ **Economics and You** The United States has a government "of the people, by the people, and for the people." For our government to work well, it needs the backing of the American people. If you work and pay income taxes, you are helping support the work of the government.

Principles in Action The income tax is just one of the many taxes collected by the federal government. As you will read in this section, federal revenue also comes from a number of other taxes. These include corporate income taxes, social insurance taxes, excise taxes, estate and gift taxes, and taxes on imports.

How important is income tax?

The government's main source of revenue is from the tax on individuals' taxable income. As **Figure 14.2** on the next page shows, about 39 percent of the federal government's revenues come from the payment of individual income taxes.

The amount of federal income tax a person owes is figured every year. In theory, the federal government could wait until the end of the year to collect income taxes. In reality, that would be a problem for both taxpayers and the government. The government has to pay regularly for rent, supplies, services, and workers' salaries, as do other businesses. If all the nation's taxpayers paid their taxes at one time, it would be harder to pay these expenses.

Fig. 14.2 Federal Revenue

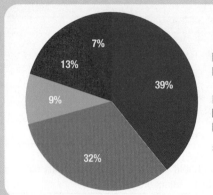

- Personal income taxes
- Social Security, Medicare and unemployment, and other retirement taxes
- Borrowing to cover deficit
- Corporate Income taxes
- Excise, customs, gift, and miscellaneous taxes

39%
7%
13%
9%
32%

SOURCE: The Internal Revenue Service, U.S. Department of Treasury

GRAPH SKILLS

The main sources of government revenue are the taxes shown on this graph.

1. What are the largest sources of federal revenue shown on the graph?
2. How many federal revenues do not come from individual and corporate income taxes?

withholding
taking tax payments out of an employee's pay before he or she receives it

tax return
a form used to file income taxes

taxable income
the earnings on which taxes must be paid; total income minus exemptions and deductions

tax deduction
a variable amount taxpayers may subtract from their gross income

personal exemption
a set amount taxpayers may subtract from their gross income for themselves, their spouse, and any dependents

What is "pay-as-you-earn" taxation?

Many people might have trouble paying their taxes all at once. For this reason, federal income tax is collected in a "pay-as-you-earn" system. This means individuals usually pay most of their income tax throughout the year. A small amount is taken out of every paycheck. This is called **withholding.** Employers are responsible for collecting this money. After withholding the money, the employer sends it to the federal government.

How do you file a tax return?

At the end of the year, workers receive a report from every company they worked for. It tells how much money has been withheld. Workers use the information to complete a **tax return.** A tax return is a form used to file income taxes. On it, you declare your income and figure out how much of that income is taxable.

People and corporations pay taxes based on **taxable income.** It is the income after deductions and exemptions have been taken out. **Tax deductions** are costs that you can subtract, or deduct, from your total, or gross, income. Deductions include such items as interest on a mortgage, donations to charity, major medical expenses, and state and local tax payments. An exemption is an exact dollar amount that is not taxed. Taxpayers can claim a **personal exemption** for themselves and each dependent. A child is considered dependent if he or she is under the age of 19, shares a house with his or her parents, and does not provide more than half of his or her own financial support. In some cases, full-time students under the age of 24 are also considered dependent children.

All federal income tax returns must be sent to the Internal Revenue Service (IRS). Individuals must file a tax return by mid-April each year. If too much of their income was withheld, the government will send them a tax refund. If too little was taken out, they will have to pay the government what they owe.

What are tax brackets?

The federal income tax is a progressive tax. In other words, the more taxable income you earn, the greater percentage of your income you pay in taxes. The tax rate is different if a person is single or married. The 2008 tax rate schedules are shown in **Figure 14.3**. Both schedules have six rates stated as a percentage. The rate is stated in the column headed "the tax is." Each applies to a different range of income, or tax bracket. For example, married couples who filed a return together (a joint return) and had a taxable income of $16,050 or less paid 10 percent income tax. The highest rate is 35 percent. It was paid by high-income single people or married couples with a taxable income of more than $357,700. Each year, the IRS publishes new tax rate schedules. These show any changes in the federal tax law.

✓ **CHECKPOINT** *What is the difference between a personal exemption and a tax deduction?*

Fig. 14.3 Federal Income Tax Rates, 2008

Schedule	If your taxable income is over –	but not over –	the tax is	of the amount over –
Schedule X – use if your filing status is single	$0	$8,025	10%	$0
	$8,025	$32,550	$802.50 plus 15%	$8,025
	$32,550	$78,850	$4,481.25 plus 25%	$32,550
	$78,850	$164,550	$16,056.25 plus 28%	$78,850
	$164,550	$357,700	$40,052.25 plus 33%	$164,550
	$357,700	no limit	$103,791.00 plus 35%	$357,700
Schedule Y – use if your filing status is married filing jointly	$0	$16,050	10%	$0
	$16,050	$65,100	$1,605.00 plus 15%	$16,050
	$65,100	$131,450	$8,962.50 plus 25%	$65,100
	$131,450	$200,300	$25,550.00 plus 28%	$131,450
	$200,300	$357,700	$44,828.00 plus 33%	$200,300
	$357,700	no limit	$96,770.00 plus 35%	$357,700

SOURCE: Internal Revenue Service, the U.S. Department of Treasury

TABLE SKILLS

According to these sample individual income tax tables, a single individual with $5,000 of taxable income would pay $5,000 x .10, or $500 in taxes.

1. If you are single, at what rate would you pay taxes on income over $32,550 and less than $78,850?

2. What would be the tax for a married couple filing jointly with $75,000 in taxable income?

▲ A taxpayer races to get an April 15 postmark on her tax return. **What items are included in a person's tax return?**

Why is it difficult to determine a corporation's taxable income?

Like individuals, corporations must pay federal income tax on their taxable income. Corporate taxes made up over 10 percent of federal revenues in recent years.

It is difficult to determine a corporation's taxable income. Businesses can take many deductions. That is, they can subtract many expenses from their income. For example, companies deduct the cost of employees' health insurance. Many other costs of doing business can also be subtracted.

Like individual income tax rates, corporate income tax rates are progressive. In 2007, rates began at 15 percent on the first $50,000 of taxable income. On the highest corporate income, above $18,333,333, the tax rate was 35 percent.

✔ **CHECKPOINT** *Why is it difficult to determine a corporation's taxable income?*

What other taxes are taken out of workers' paychecks?

Anyone who works knows that his or her take-home pay is much less than the gross income. As you have learned, a certain amount is taken out for federal income taxes. Some money is also withheld for FICA. FICA stands for Federal Insurance Contribution Act. Most of the FICA taxes you pay go to the Social Security program. Social Security is money the government pays mostly to retired and disabled workers. More than 50 million Americans receive Social Security payments each month.

FICA taxes also fund Medicare. The Medicare program is a national health insurance program. It helps pay for healthcare for people age 65 and older. It also covers people who are not able to work.

The federal government and the states also collect an unemployment tax. Employers pay it. The tax pays for administering state unemployment insurance programs. Suppose workers are laid off from their jobs through no fault of their own. They can file an unemployment compensation claim. They collect benefits for a fixed number of weeks. To collect unemployment benefits, unemployed persons usually must show that they are actively looking for another job. State and federal unemployment taxes pay for the unemployment program.

✔ **CHECKPOINT** *What are the FICA taxes?*

What are other types of taxes?

What are the taxes on gasoline and cable television service called? If you inherit money from your great aunt, will you have to pay a tax? Why are some imported products so expensive? To answer these questions you need to look at excise taxes, estate taxes, gift taxes, and protective tariffs.

What are excise taxes?

An **excise tax** is a tax on certain goods made in this country. The goods taxed are often luxuries, but not always. There are excise taxes on perfume, alcohol, and tobacco. Sometimes an excise tax helps pay for services for the people who buy an item. For example, the excise tax on gasoline helps pay for roads. Businesses sometimes pay excise taxes, too. For example, airlines pay excise taxes on the tickets they sell. Businesses that process natural resources such as lumber and natural gas pay them. Gas and electric companies also pay excise taxes.

What is an estate tax?

When a person dies, he or she can leave property and money to family and friends. An **estate tax** is a tax on the total value of property and money that was left. The persons receiving property or money from the person who dies may have to pay the estate tax.

What is a gift tax?

A **gift tax** is a tax on the money or property one living person gives another. The goal of the gift tax is to keep people from avoiding estate taxes by giving away their money before they die. The tax law sets limits on gifts. The law says a person can give someone up to $12,000 a year tax-free.

How are taxes used?

The main purpose of taxes is to pay for the cost of government. Taxes also have several other uses. They can protect certain businesses. Such a tax is called a protective **tariff.** Tariffs are taxes on imported goods (foreign goods brought into the country). Tariffs raise the price of foreign goods. Consumers are more likely to buy American products if those goods are cheaper than imported ones. You will read more about tariffs in Chapter 17.

Taxes can be used to get people to do or to stop doing certain things. Taxation used to discourage or encourage certain types of behavior is called a **tax incentive.**

excise tax
a tax on certain goods made in this country

estate tax
a tax on the total value of the money and property of a person who has died

gift tax
a tax on the money or property one living person gives another

tariff
a tax on imported goods

tax incentive
a tax used to discourage or encourage types of behavior

tax credit
an amount that taxpayers may subtract from the total amount of their income tax

Reading Strategy
Metacognition
Ask yourself, "What did I learn by reading this section? What do I still want to know about the different kinds of taxes?"

Taxes used to stop people from doing something are often called sin taxes. For example, we know smoking may cause cancer. Alcohol abuse can also cause health problems. The government tries to discourage people from smoking or drinking alcohol. To do this, it taxes cigarettes and liquor. This raises their prices. The high costs sometimes stop people from drinking and smoking.

Taxes can also be used to encourage certain activities. Congress has tried to get businesses and individuals to lower their energy costs. The government offers **tax credits** to businesses and individuals who buy equipment that uses less energy. This lowers the amount of tax they owe. It gives businesses an incentive to build factories and install machines that save energy. Some homeowners also earn tax credits. They receive tax credits for home improvements such as replacing their old windows.

✅ **CHECKPOINT** *Why is there a tax on gasoline?*

SECTION 2 ASSESSMENT

Essential Questions Journal To continue to build a response to the Essential Question, go to your **Essential Questions Journal.**

Quick Write
Based on what you have read in this section about tax incentives, write a short essay about the following: What behavior do you think the government should encourage or discourage in its tax policy? Suggest tax incentives that could help you achieve your goal.

 Guiding Question

1. Use your completed table to answer this question: What taxes does the federal government collect?

Key Terms and Main Ideas

Directions: On a sheet of paper, write the answer to each question. Use complete sentences.

2. What form do taxpayers use to file income taxes?
3. Would a person earning $15,000 a year and a person earning $300,000 a year be in the same federal income tax bracket? Why or why not?
4. When would you have to pay a gift tax?
5. What is a tax incentive?

Critical Thinking

6. **Predict Consequences** (a) Explain how "pay-as-you-earn" taxation works. (b) Why is this system important? (c) What might happen if the government did not use this system to collect income taxes?
7. **Make Comparisons** How are the systems similar for collecting Social Security and Medicare taxes?

Objectives

- **Distinguish** between mandatory and discretionary spending.
- **Describe** the major entitlement programs.
- **Identify** types of discretionary spending.
- **Explain** the effect of federal aid on state and local governments.

■ ■ ■ ■ ■ ■ ■ ■ ■ ■ ■ ■ ■ ■ ■ ■

mandatory spending
spending that Congress is required by law to do

discretionary spending
spending about which Congress is free to make choices

■ ■ ■ ■ ■ ■ ■ ■ ■ ■ ■ ■ ■ ■ ■ ■

Reading Strategy
Metacognition
Note the main ideas and important details of these three paragraphs. Summarize what you have read to make sure you understand it.

Guiding Question

How does the federal government spend its income?

Copy this chart and fill it in as you read.

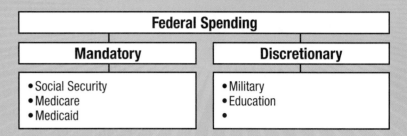

Federal Spending	
Mandatory	**Discretionary**
• Social Security • Medicare • Medicaid	• Military • Education •

▶ **Economics and You** Suppose you received a million dollars to spend each year. So much money! So many choices! Where would you begin? The federal government, with a budget of around $2.8 trillion, faces a similar "problem" every year.

Principles in Action By taking part in elections, the American public gives government officials clear guidelines on how the federal government should spend its income. As you will read, government spending meets numerous needs. However, the American people have decided that much of the money should be spent for our health and welfare.

What are mandatory spending and discretionary spending?

The U.S. government spends nearly $3 trillion a year. Where does the money go? The federal budget is a book with thousands of pages. It gives details about how the government spends its money. The government breaks down its spending into two large groups.

The first group is **mandatory spending**. This refers to money that lawmakers are required to spend. For example, the law requires that the government pay for Social Security programs. Congress is also required to pay interest on the money the government owes.

The second group is **discretionary spending**. This is spending about which the government has some choices. For example, Congress can choose to spend more or less on the military. It can increase or cut spending on education.

Fig. 14.4
Federal Spending, 2006

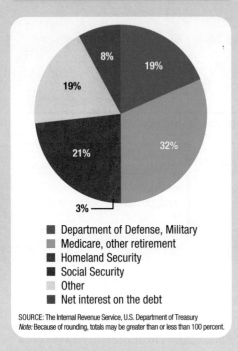

- Department of Defense, Military
- Medicare, other retirement
- Homeland Security
- Social Security
- Other
- Net interest on the debt

SOURCE: The Internal Revenue Service, U.S. Department of Treasury
Note: Because of rounding, totals may be greater than or less than 100 percent.

GRAPH SKILLS

The federal government spends the funds it collects from taxes and other sources on a variety of programs.

1. Which are the three largest categories of expenditure in the federal budget?

2. On which areas does the federal government spend more: military and homeland security or the needs of the elderly and retired?

■■■■■■■■■■■■■■■■■■■■

entitlement
social welfare program that people have a right to if they are eligible

means-tested
the practice of giving lower, or no, entitlements to people who have higher incomes

In recent years, the percentage of mandatory federal spending has grown. That leaves less money for discretionary spending. The graph in **Figure 14.4** shows some of the different categories of federal spending.

✓ **CHECKPOINT** *What is the difference between mandatory and discretionary spending?*

What are entitlement programs?

Except for interest on the national debt, most of the mandatory items in the federal budget are for **entitlement** programs. Entitlements are social welfare programs that people are entitled to. People have the right to benefits if they are eligible. Of course, the more people who qualify, the higher the mandatory spending. This makes managing costs a big problem.

Some, but not all, entitlements are **means-tested.** This means that people with higher incomes may receive lower benefits or no benefits at all. Medicaid, for example, is means-tested. It helps only low-income families or people unable to pay for their health needs themselves. Social Security is not means-tested. A retired person who has worked and paid Social Security taxes is entitled to certain benefits. It does not matter whether the person had a high-paying job or a low-paying one. People who have served in the military and retired federal workers are entitled to receive pensions from the government.

Entitlements are a part of government spending that Congress cannot change. Once Congress has set the requirements, it cannot control how many people become eligible for benefits. Congress can only try to keep costs down by changing the law.

How does Social Security work?

More than $500 billion a year is spent on Social Security. About 50 million Americans receive monthly Social Security checks. Most of the payments go to retired people. Many of those retirees depend on their Social Security checks to support themselves. (See **Figure 14.5** on page 358.)

The Social Security system faces a big problem soon. This is because American workers pay into the system through taxes. Those taxes pay benefits for people who are no longer working. That is, the money you pay into Social Security today supports people who have already retired. It does not go into a fund for your own retirement.

For the system to work well, there must be enough paying workers to support all the retired workers getting benefits. Until recently, the system has worked well. There were always more workers paying in than people getting benefits. The problem is the large number of people born after World War II. The people born between 1946 and 1964 are known as baby boomers. As they start to retire, there will be fewer workers to support them. But unless something is done, you might receive only limited benefits from Social Security when you are ready to retire.

How do Medicare and Medicaid work?

Medicare costs the government hundreds of billions of dollars each year. Medicare serves about 42 million people. Most of them are 65 years and older. The program pays for hospital care and for much of the cost of doctors and medical services. It also pays for medical services for people who suffer from certain disabilities and diseases. (See **Figure 14.5** on the next page.)

Like Social Security, Medicare is mostly paid for by taxes withheld from people's paychecks. Most people on Medicare also make a monthly payment to help pay for the program.

Innovators

Frances Perkins
"The large majority of our citizens need protection against the loss of income due to unemployment, old age, death of the breadwinners and disabling accident and illness, not only on humanitarian grounds, but in the interest of our national welfare."

With these words, delivered on national radio in 1935, Labor Secretary Frances Perkins unveiled an extraordinary plan for "social insurance"—the plan that became our Social Security program. Perkins helped write the Social Security Act and later developed other key entitlement programs.

Perkins fought for the rights of workers throughout her long career. In 1929, as Industrial Commissioner of New York State, she reduced the number of hours a woman was allowed to work in a factory to 48. Later, as the first female Cabinet member, she helped win workers the right to form unions and to earn a guaranteed minimum wage. Her greatest achievement was the Social Security Act.

Fast Facts
Frances Perkins (1880–1965)
Education: Columbia University, M.A. in economics and social history
Claim to Fame: Secretary of Labor, 1933–1945; wrote the legislation for Social Security

Fig. 14.5 How the Economy Works

Where do your **federal taxes** go?

Not everybody is happy about all the taxes taken from their paychecks. However, taxes give the government the money it needs to operate.

1 **Federal spending** is financed by deductions from your paycheck. Among the largest of the expenses are defense spending, the Social Security program, and the Medicare program.

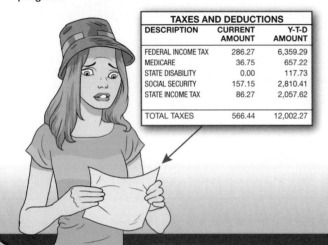

TAXES AND DEDUCTIONS		
DESCRIPTION	CURRENT AMOUNT	Y-T-D AMOUNT
FEDERAL INCOME TAX	286.27	6,359.29
MEDICARE	36.75	657.22
STATE DISABILITY	0.00	117.73
SOCIAL SECURITY	157.15	2,810.41
STATE INCOME TAX	86.27	2,057.62
TOTAL TAXES	566.44	12,002.27

2 **Defense spending** makes up about one fifth of the federal budget. It is a discretionary item and can be changed each year by government planners. However, because it pays for the salaries of everyone in the armed forces, as well as for weapons, planes, and ships, it has generally gone up each year.

The Deductions

Defense

Medicare costs have been going up. This is partly because of expensive technology but also because people are living longer. The basic problem facing Medicare is the same as that facing Social Security. In 1995, four people were paying Medicare taxes for every person on Medicare. By 2050, there will only be two people paying taxes for every person getting benefits.

State and federal governments spend more than $200 billion every year on Medicaid. Medicaid benefits mostly low-income families. It pays most of the medical services for America's poorest people. The federal government shares the costs of Medicaid with state governments. The federal share of the costs ranges from 50 percent to 76 percent. In 2004, about 57.6 million people were eligible for Medicaid—about 20 percent of Americans. The number of people covered by Medicaid was 55 million.

3 **Social Security** is the largest category of federal spending. It is one of the government's most important and successful programs, providing more than $500 billion in benefits to Americans each year.

4 **Medicare** provides benefits to people who are 65 years or older or who suffer from certain disabilities. Total Medicare spending reached $431.5 billion in 2007.

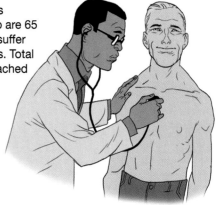

These deductions from paychecks can be unwelcome, but the programs they pay for are essential to the well-being of the United States.

Check Your Understanding
1. Why does the federal government take money from the paychecks of American workers?
2. List two areas where the money aids the safety and security of Americans. List two areas where the deductions improve the quality of life of Americans.

Social Security

Medicare

The government also spends more than $350 billion on other mandatory programs. These programs include:
- food stamps
- unemployment compensation
- child nutrition
- child tax credits
- student loans
- retirement/disability programs for government workers, the Coast Guard, and the military

✔ **CHECKPOINT** *Which entitlement program costs the federal government the most money?*

Reading Strategy
Metacognition
Remember to look at the charts and graphs. Also note the descriptive words. This will help you visualize what you are reading.

What are big types of discretionary spending?

One of the biggest categories of discretionary spending is national defense. As you can see from the graph in **Figure 14.4** on page 356, defense spending consumes about 19 percent of the federal budget.

The Department of Defense (DOD) spends most of the defense budget. It pays the salaries of all the men and women in the U.S. Army, Navy, Air Force, and Marines. It also pays all the nonmilitary people working in the DOD. Defense spending, of course, buys all the equipment and supplies the military needs. Building and keeping up our military bases and equipment are also part of the defense budget.

There are many other types of government discretionary spending. Here are some of the many programs that could be called "everything else":

- education and training
- scientific research
- student loans
- national parks and monuments
- law enforcement
- environmental cleanup
- housing and transportation
- aid after floods, earthquakes, fires, or bad weather
- aid to other countries
- payments to help farmers

This part of the federal budget also pays the salaries of the millions of people who work for the federal government. They include the President, members of Congress, Cabinet secretaries, and federal judges. They also include park rangers, FBI agents, file clerks, meat inspectors, and many others.

 CHECKPOINT *About how much of the federal government's budget goes toward defense?*

How does federal aid affect state and local governments?

Some federal tax dollars also find their way to state and local governments. In total, about $404 billion a year is divided among the states. This is an average of about $1,400 for each U.S. citizen.

As you have read, state and federal governments share the costs of Medicaid and unemployment compensation. They also share in paying for other social programs.

Federal money also goes to the states for education, lower income housing, and building highways. It also helps pay for mass transit, healthcare, employment training, and many other programs.

Federal grants-in-aid help pay for public projects. States must use these federal funds only for the specific purpose. Beginning in the early 1980s, many grant-in-aid programs were changed to block grants. As you have read in Chapter 13, block grants are lump sums of money to be used for the public good. They have fewer rules and restrictions than grants-in-aid.

When Hurricane Katrina slammed into Louisiana, Mississippi, and Alabama in 2005, those states turned to the federal government for help. Congress gave the states $116 billion to help recover from the damage caused by the hurricane.

IF YOUR SENATOR HAD CLOUT, THIS WOULD BE A $50,000,000 CONSTRUCTION PROJECT, INSTEAD OF A $5,000,000 ONE!

▲ In recent years, responsibility for more social programs has been passed from the federal government to the states. **What point is the cartoonist making about financing for these programs?**

 CHECKPOINT *Why did states ask the federal government for help after Hurricane Katrina struck?*

 SECTION **3** ASSESSMENT

Essential Questions Journal

To continue to build a response to the Essential Question, go to your **Essential Questions Journal.**

❓ Guiding Question

1. Use your completed chart to answer this question: How does the federal government spend its income?

Key Terms and Main Ideas

Directions: On a sheet of paper, write the answer to each question. Use complete sentences.

2. What are means-tested entitlements?

3. Name three examples of federal discretionary spending.

4. Whose retirement benefits are funded by the money today's workers are now paying into Social Security?

5. What services does Medicaid provide, and who benefits from these services?

Critical Thinking

6. **Draw Conclusions** (a) What problems do entitlement programs cause? (b) Why might it be difficult for lawmakers to change entitlement programs?

7. **Draw Inferences** Why might some members of Congress have pushed for additional government programs related to healthcare?

Objectives

- **Explain** how states use a budget to plan their spending.
- **Identify** where states spend their taxes.
- **List** the major sources of state tax revenue.
- **Describe** local government spending and sources of revenue.

Guiding Question

How do local governments manage their money?

Copy this table and fill it in as you read.

Revenue Collection		Revenue Spending	
State	Local	State	Local
• Sales tax • Income tax • Corporate income tax •	• Property tax • Sales tax • Excise tax •	• Education • Transportation • Public safety •	• Public schools • Police and fire protection • •

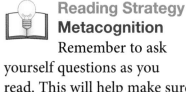

Reading Strategy
Metacognition
Remember to ask yourself questions as you read. This will help make sure you understand what you are reading about budgets.

budget
a plan that estimates future spending and saving

operating budget
a budget for day-to-day spending

▶ **Economics and You** Imagine that you and your family are thinking about colleges. Which one offers the courses you want? How much does it cost? You have found that state colleges cost much less than private schools. The reason is that your state government pays part of the cost of running the state colleges. In fact, this is one of the largest areas of state government spending.

Principles in Action When citizens vote in local elections, they help decide how they want their local taxes spent. In this section, you will see what voters think is most important. For example, in Economics & You, you will see that although few taxpayers like school tax increases, these taxes pay for programs that are important to good education.

Why is a budget important?

Like families and individuals, governments must plan for their spending ahead of time. That planning involves making a **budget.** A budget is an estimate of how much money the government will take in and how much it will spend. While the federal government has just one budget for planned revenue and expenses, states have two budgets: operating budgets and capital budgets.

What is an operating budget?

A state puts together an **operating budget** to plan for all of its day-to-day spending. Those expenses include salaries of state employees. It also includes supplies such as computers and paper. Taking care of state parks is also part of the operating budget.

What is a capital budget?

A state also creates a **capital budget** to plan for major long-term projects. If the state builds a new bridge, the money comes from this budget. Long-term borrowing or the sale of bonds meets most of these expenses.

What is a balanced budget?

In most states, the governor prepares the state budget. The legislature then discusses and approves the budget. Unlike the federal government, 49 states require balanced budgets. In these budgets, revenues must equal spending. These laws, however, apply only to the operating budget, not to the capital budget. That makes it easier to balance a state budget than to balance the federal budget.

✔ **CHECKPOINT** *Would a state's operating budget or capital budget pay for a new courthouse?*

Where are state taxes spent?

All states spend money on education, highways, police protection, and state parks, but there are differences among the 50 states. **Figure 14.6,** on the next page, shows other important ways states spend their money.

How do state taxes support education?

Every state has at least one public state university. Taxes support these universities. Some states, such as California, have many state colleges and universities. In many states, tax dollars also support two-year community colleges and other schools.

State governments also help local governments, which run public elementary, middle, and high schools. The total amount of money spent for each student is different from state to state. The national average is $8,701 for each student every year.

How do state taxes pay for public safety?

All states have a state police force. The state police enforce traffic laws and help in emergencies. State police also have a crime lab. This helps the local police catch lawbreakers. State governments build and run prisons. These prisons house people found guilty of breaking state laws.

■ ■ ■ ■ ■ ■ ■ ■ ■ ■ ■ ■ ■ ■ ■ ■ ■ ■

capital budget
a budget for spending on major long-term projects

Fig. 14.6 State Revenue and Spending, 2004–2005

CHART SKILLS

Individual income taxes, sales and other taxes, insurance premiums, and local and federal funds are major sources of state revenue.

1. What are the three largest categories of state government spending?

2. What percentage of state government spending goes toward education and public welfare?

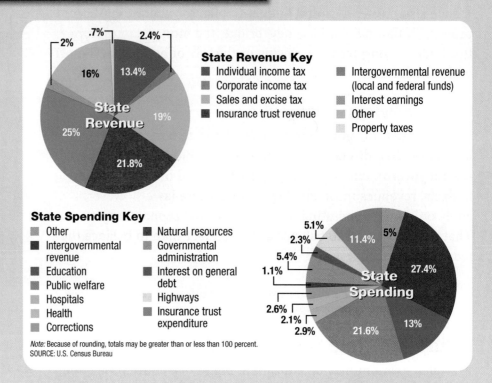

State Revenue Key
- Individual income tax
- Corporate income tax
- Sales and excise tax
- Insurance trust revenue
- Intergovernmental revenue (local and federal funds)
- Interest earnings
- Other
- Property taxes

State Revenue: .7%, 2.4%, 2%, 13.4%, 16%, 19%, 25%, 21.8%

State Spending Key
- Other
- Intergovernmental revenue
- Education
- Public welfare
- Hospitals
- Health
- Corrections
- Natural resources
- Governmental administration
- Interest on general debt
- Highways
- Insurance trust expenditure

State Spending: 5.1%, 2.3%, 5.4%, 1.1%, 2.6%, 2.1%, 2.9%, 11.4%, 5%, 27.4%, 13%, 21.6%

Note: Because of rounding, totals may be greater than or less than 100 percent.
SOURCE: U.S. Census Bureau

How do state taxes pay for highways and transportation?

Building and keeping up highway systems is another major state expense. State crews keep roads and bridges in good repair. Some money for roads comes from the federal government. In turn, states give some money to federal and interstate highway systems.

States pay at least some costs of other kinds of transportation. For example, they pay part of the cost of waterways and airports. Money for such projects may also come from federal and local government budgets.

How do state taxes support public welfare?

States look after the health and welfare of their residents. State funds support some public hospitals and clinics. State workers inspect water supplies and test for pollution.

States help pay for many of the federal programs that help individuals, such as unemployment benefits. States determine their own benefits. They can meet local needs better than the federal government can. For example, during a local business slowdown, they may decide to give benefits for a longer time.

Which state taxes benefit arts and recreation?

If you've hiked in a state forest or stopped for a picnic in a state park, you've enjoyed another benefit of state tax dollars. States set aside historical sites and recreation land for people to visit. They also run museums and help support music and arts programs.

How do state taxes keep governments running?

Administration costs are related to running state government. State tax revenues pay the salaries of all state workers. This includes everyone in state government and all state judges. It also includes secretaries, park rangers, professors in state universities, and many other state workers.

✔ **CHECKPOINT** *Where does a state get the money to fund public schools, prisons, and highway construction?*

Where do states get their revenues?

For every dollar a state spends, it must take in at least a dollar in revenue. Otherwise, its budget would not be balanced. The 50 states now take in more than $500 billion a year from taxes. Sales and individual income taxes provide the largest part of state revenues. **Figure 14.6** shows the sources of state revenue.

There are limits on the states' power to tax. States cannot tax imports or exports. They also cannot tax goods sent between states. Nonprofit organizations, religious groups, and charities are usually **tax exempt.** This means they do not have to pay taxes.

How important is the sales tax?

As **Figure 14.6** shows, sales taxes are a main source of revenue for state governments. As you read in Section 1, a sales tax is a tax on goods and services. The tax—a percentage of the purchase price—is added on at the cash register and paid by the purchaser.

All but a few of the 50 states collect sales taxes. Their sales tax rates range from 2.9 to 7.25 percent. Some local governments have their own additional sales tax. In every state, a sales tax is not collected on some products. For example, many states do not charge sales tax on basic needs such as food and clothing.

Some states place excise taxes on some products and activities. Some are sin taxes. They are taxes on products like alcoholic drinks and cigarettes. Other taxes apply to hotel and motel rooms, cars, rental cars, and insurance policies. Many states also tax gasoline. This state gasoline tax is in addition to the federal tax.

■ ■ ■ ■ ■ ■ ■ ■ ■ ■ ■ ■ ■ ■ ■ ■ ■ ■ ■
tax exempt
not required to pay taxes

■ ■ ■ ■ ■ ■ ■ ■ ■ ■ ■ ■ ■ ■ ■ ■ ■ ■ ■

Reading Strategy
Metacognition
Ask yourself, "Where do states get their revenues?" Try to predict what you will learn. At the end of the section, ask yourself, "Was my prediction correct?"

Do all states have an individual income tax?

All but seven states have individual state income taxes. For the states that do, individual income taxes are an important source of state revenue. People pay this state income tax in addition to the federal income tax. Two states tax only dividend and interest income. **Figure 14.6,** on page 364, shows that individual income taxes make up about 13 percent of a state's revenue.

Some states tax incomes at a flat percentage rate (that is, as a proportional tax). Some charge a percentage of a person's federal income tax. These states have a progressive tax structure like the federal income tax.

How do states collect corporate income taxes?

Most states collect income taxes from corporations that do business in the state. Some states tax business profits at a flat percentage rate. A few charge progressive rates. They tax businesses with higher profits at higher tax rates.

As you can see from **Figure 14.6,** corporate income taxes make up only about 2 percent of state tax revenues. Nevertheless, corporate income taxes can influence a state's economy. Low corporate taxes attract entrepreneurs and new businesses to a state. So do well-educated workers and good public services. Politicians keep this fact in mind when deciding what taxes to create.

Economics & YOU

School Taxes

School taxes make up the largest part of the local taxes Americans pay. Across the country, increases in school taxes have far outpaced the national rate of inflation. *No one enjoys paying taxes, but schools will have to cut services if they are not funded.*

School taxes pay for a wide range of in-school and after-school activities. *You have more choices when funding is sufficient.*

What are other state taxes?

Businesses pay many other state taxes and fees besides the corporate income tax. Do you want to be a hairdresser, a carpenter, or a building contractor? If so, you will have to have a license. A license is a kind of tax people pay to carry on different kinds of business within a state.

Some states charge a transfer tax when documents such as stock certificates are transferred and recorded. Other states tax the value of the stock shares that corporations issue.

As you read in Section 2, the federal government taxes the property of a person who has died. Some states also charge an inheritance tax. This is a tax paid by a person who receives money from someone who died.

Some states also tax property. That includes real estate, or real property—land and any buildings on land a person owns. It also includes personal property. This property can be moved. Examples include jewelry, furniture, and boats. Some states even tax property such as bank accounts, stocks, and bonds. Today, however, most property taxes, especially on real estate, are gathered by local governments.

✔ **CHECKPOINT** *Which two categories of tax provide the largest contribution to state revenues?*

How do local governments get and spend revenue?

Your local government is the level of government closest to you. It plays a big part in everyday life. Local governments hire police and firefighters. They build roads, libraries, hospitals, and jails. They pay teachers.

You probably think of local government as a town or city. There are many other types too. These include townships, counties, and special districts, such as school districts. Today, there are more than 87,000 local government units in the United States. Together they collect about $390 billion in yearly tax revenues.

What are the jobs of local government?

Local governments have many important jobs. **Figure 14.7** shows the major expenses of local government. In many areas, they run the public school systems. They are responsible for fire protection and law enforcement (local police, county sheriff's departments, or park police). They run public libraries, airports, and hospitals. Many local governments manage parks, public beaches, swimming pools, and zoos. They make sure the public's health is taken care of by inspecting restaurants. They check the water supply to make sure it is safe. They keep up the sewer system. Some operate a system of buses and trains. They run elections including registering voters, preparing ballots, and counting the votes. Local governments also keep records of births and deaths.

What are the major sources of revenue for local government?

Property taxes bring in a large portion of local revenue. They are paid by property owners in local communities to help fund important services. An official called a **tax assessor** determines

Fig. 14.7 Local Revenue and Spending, 2007

CHART SKILLS

Property taxes and state and federal funds (intergovernmental revenue) are the major sources of local revenue.

1. What are the three largest categories of local government spending?

2. What percentage of local government spending goes toward fire protection and parks and recreation?

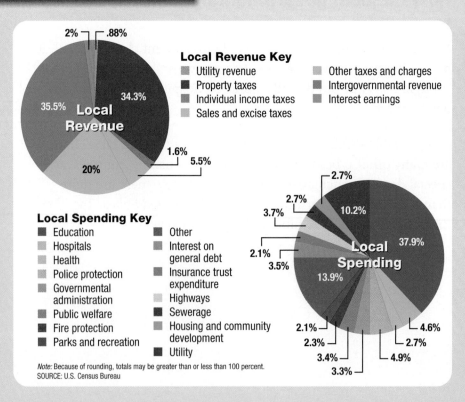

Local Revenue Key
- Utility revenue
- Property taxes
- Individual income taxes
- Sales and excise taxes
- Other taxes and charges
- Intergovernmental revenue
- Interest earnings

Local Revenue: 2%, .88%, 34.3%, 35.5%, 20%, 1.6%, 5.5%

Local Spending Key
- Education
- Hospitals
- Health
- Police protection
- Governmental administration
- Public welfare
- Fire protection
- Parks and recreation
- Other
- Interest on general debt
- Insurance trust expenditure
- Highways
- Sewerage
- Housing and community development
- Utility

Local Spending: 2.7%, 2.7%, 3.7%, 10.2%, 37.9%, 2.1%, 3.5%, 13.9%, 2.1%, 2.3%, 3.4%, 3.3%, 4.9%, 2.7%, 4.6%

Note: Because of rounding, totals may be greater than or less than 100 percent.
SOURCE: U.S. Census Bureau

the value of the property for tax purposes. The property tax rate is usually stated in terms of so much per $1,000 of assessed value. Most of the money raised by property taxes pays for education.

What are other local taxes?

Local taxes are much like the taxes states have. Besides taxing property, local governments often have sales, excise, and income taxes. These taxes affect not only people who live in a community but also visitors. In fact, many of these taxes are designed to raise revenue from visitors.

Suppose you go on a school trip to New York City. The room rate for your hotel is $200 a night. When you see the bill in the morning, however, it's $230.25. Three different taxes have been added. They raise the cost of the room by $30.25. Many other cities have taxes aimed at tourists and business travelers. Besides hotel taxes, they collect taxes on rental cars, airport taxes, and taxes on movie or theater tickets.

☑ **CHECKPOINT** *What type of tax is a main source of funding for public schools?*

SECTION 4 ASSESSMENT

Essential Questions Journal To continue to build a response to the Essential Question, go to your **Essential Questions Journal.**

 Guiding Question

1. Use your completed table to answer this question: How do local governments manage their money?

Key Terms and Main Ideas

Directions: On a sheet of paper, write the answer to each question. Use complete sentences.

2. What is a balanced budget?

3. List at least four programs and services on which states spend their money.

4. What kinds of organizations are tax exempt? What does this mean?

5. Identify at least three kinds of state taxes and fees that businesses pay.

Critical Thinking

6. **Predict Consequences** (a) Suppose a state operating budget included more spending than revenue. What action might lawmakers take to balance the budget? (b) Suppose the operating budget included more revenue than spending. How might lawmakers react?

7. **Draw Inferences** Explain the differences between real property and personal property.

Section 1–What Are Taxes?

- A tax is a required payment to a local, state, or national government. The U.S. Constitution gives the federal government the power to collect taxes.

- A proportional tax is the same percentage for all income levels. A progressive tax is a percentage of income that increases as income increases. A regressive tax is a percentage of income that decreases as income increases.

- According to economists, a good tax should be simple, efficient, clear, and fair.

Section 2–Federal Taxes

- The federal government receives about 39 percent of its income from the payment of individual income taxes.

- Corporate taxes have made up just over 10 percent of federal income in recent years.

- The federal government withholds money from a person's wages to pay for Social Security, Medicare, and unemployment taxes.

Section 3–Federal Spending

- Mandatory spending refers to money that Congress is required to spend. This makes up about two thirds of federal spending.

- Discretionary spending refers to money about which Congress is free to make some choices.

- Entitlement programs include Social Security, Medicare, and Medicaid.

- Defense spending consumes about 19 percent of the federal budget.

Section 4–State and Local Taxes and Spending

- States have an operating budget for day-to-day spending needs. The capital budget covers spending on major investments such as bridges.

- State taxes are spent on education, public safety, highways and transportation, public welfare, arts and recreation, and administration.

- Local spending includes schools, police and firefighters, libraries, airports, hospitals, beaches, zoos, and social services.

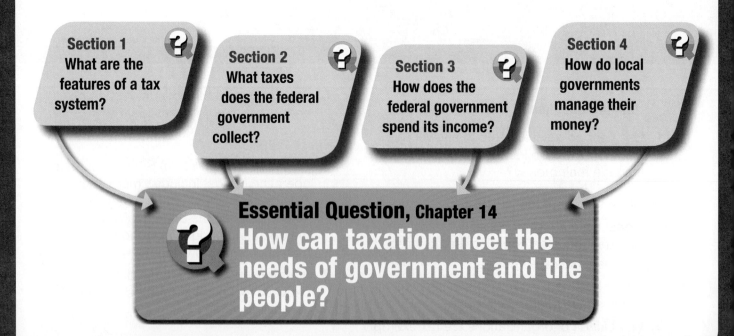

Section 1 What are the features of a tax system?

Section 2 What taxes does the federal government collect?

Section 3 How does the federal government spend its income?

Section 4 How do local governments manage their money?

Essential Question, Chapter 14
How can taxation meet the needs of government and the people?

October 29, 1929—Black Tuesday

In late October 1929, the American stock market was losing money. Finally, on October 29, the market crashed. Historians call this day Black Tuesday. The stock market crash affected people all over the world. It started the Great Depression, which lasted through the 1930s. The New York Times reported the crash in its October 30 edition, as follows:

"Stock prices virtually collapsed yesterday, swept downward with gigantic losses in the most disastrous trading day in the stock market's history. Billions of dollars in open market values were wiped out as prices crumbled under the pressure of liquidation [selling] of securities which had to be sold at any price. . . .

From every point of view, in the extent of losses sustained, in total turnover, in the number of speculators wiped out, the day was the most disastrous in Wall Street's history. . . .

It was estimated that 880 issues [stocks], on the New York Stock Exchange, lost between $8,000,000,000 and $9,000,000,000 yesterday. . . .

There were two cheerful notes, however. . . . One was the brisk rally of stocks at the close. . . . The other was that the liquidation has been so violent, as well as widespread, that many bankers, brokers and industrial leaders expressed the belief last night that it now has run its course. . . .

The market on the rampage is no respecter of persons. It washed fortune after fortune away yesterday and financially crippled thousands of individuals in all parts of the world. It was not until after the market had closed that the financial district began to realize that a good-sized rally had taken place and that there was a stopping place on the downgrade for good stocks.

The market has now passed through three days of collapse, and so violent has it been that most authorities believe that the end is not far away."

Document-Based Questions

1. What was Black Tuesday?
2. What historical time period began because of the stock market crash?
3. How much money was estimated to have been lost on the New York Stock Exchange?
4. Name one positive outcome of Black Tuesday.
5. How were people all over the world affected by the stock market crash?

Directions: Write your answers to the following questions. Use complete sentences.

Section 1—What Are Taxes?

1. Explain how a regressive tax works.

2. What is the tax burden?

3. What are two things that make a good tax?

4. What does it mean if a tax system is efficient? Why is it important that taxation be efficient?

Section 2—Federal Taxes

5. How can a person determine his or her taxable income?

6. If you get a part-time job, what taxes will you probably pay on your earnings? How will the government collect these taxes?

7. How do tax incentives encourage helpful behavior?

8. Contributions to charities are tax deductible. Explain the reason for this tax policy.

Section 3—Federal Spending

9. List at least three programs in which state governments and the federal government share funding.

10. What do you think are the three most important forms of discretionary spending?

11. Why are both Medicare and Medicaid considered entitlement programs? How much money is spent on these programs?

12. How are mandatory spending and discretionary spending different? How can a mandatory spending program be changed into a discretionary spending program?

Section 4—State and Local Taxes and Spending

13. What has to happen for a state to balance a budget?

14. What kinds of organizations are usually tax exempt?

15. How are property taxes used?

16. What is the job of a tax assessor?

17. What are the main sources of state revenue? How do they differ from the main sources of local revenue?

 ## Exploring the Essential Question

18. How might the characteristics of a good tax conflict with each other?

19. Do you think taxes are fair or unfair? Explain.

Essential Question Activity

20. Complete this activity to answer the Essential Question **How can taxation meet the needs of government and the people?** Suppose you are on the local town council. The community will have $59 million in revenue in the coming year. The estimated spending needs are done for all budget categories—education, fire and police, maintenance, and so on. Using the worksheet your teacher gives you or the electronic worksheet available at **PearsonSuccessNet.com**, answer the following questions: (a) What is the difference between your spending needs and your revenue? (b) Can you best meet this shortage by raising taxes, cutting services, or combining the two? What are the advantages and disadvantages of each alternative? (c) Create a budget and tax proposal.

Essential Questions Journal To continue to build a response to the Essential Question, go to your **Essential Questions Journal.**

 ## Test-Taking Tip

If a word on a test is new to you, take the word apart. Compare the parts to other words you know.

Chapter **15** Fiscal Policy

Essential Question, Chapter 15
How effective is fiscal policy as an economic tool?

- **Section 1** Understanding Fiscal Policy

- **Section 2** Fiscal Policy Options

- **Section 3** Budget Deficits and the National Debt

Economics on the go

To study anywhere, anytime, download these online resources at *PearsonSuccessNet.com* ➤

▶ **Economists agree that steady economic growth is good.** They want jobs for every person who wants to work. They also believe that high productivity and stable prices are good goals. Many government decisions affect the economy. In this chapter, you will learn about how the U.S. government budget uses spending and taxes to try to create a strong and stable economy.

Reading Strategy: Summarizing
When summarizing, a good reader asks questions about what he or she is reading. When reading this chapter, ask yourself the following questions:

- Why am I reading about fiscal policy?

- Whom does fiscal policy affect?

- What is the most important idea related to fiscal policy?

Visual Glossary
online

Go to the Visual Glossary Online for an interactive review of **fiscal policy.**

How the Economy Works
online

Go to How the Economy Works Online for an interactive lesson on **the national debt.**

Action Graph
online

Go to Action Graph Online for animated versions of key charts and graphs.

Objectives

- **Describe** how the government makes fiscal policy decisions.
- **Analyze** how expansionary and contractionary fiscal policies affect the economy.
- **Identify** the limits of fiscal policy.

Guiding Question

What are the goals and limits of fiscal policy?

Copy this table and fill it in as you read.

Fiscal Policy	
Goals	**Limits**
• Increase economic growth	• Difficult to change spending levels
• Create jobs	•
•	•

fiscal policy
the government's use of spending and taxes to make the economy grow faster or slower

▶ **Economics and You** The prom is next month. You have worked hard so you can afford to go. You've saved money from your part-time job and have not spent any of your allowance for weeks. When you add up your savings, you have all the money you need. And then Aunt Marilyn gives you a gift that more than covers the cost of the prom. Now, you don't have to spend any of your money. You must be wealthier than the U.S. government!

Well that's not likely. The federal government takes in and spends huge amounts of money. In fact, it spends about $2.8 *trillion* a year. That's an average of $7.7 billion every day. This is a tremendous flow of cash into and out of the economy. It has a huge effect on aggregate demand and supply in the economy.

Principles in Action The government uses that spending in ways that will help the economy. It does this through its fiscal policy. In this section, you will learn about the goals and limits of fiscal policy. You will learn why many economists believe higher taxes at times can be good for the economy. You will also learn why other economists believe it is almost impossible to use fiscal policy effectively.

What is fiscal policy?

Fiscal policy is the government's use of spending and taxes to influence the economy. It can be used to make the economy grow faster or slower. Fiscal policy can be used to help everyone who wants to work to get a job. It is important in keeping the economy steady. The government's fiscal policy decisions determine how much to spend and how much to tax.

These decisions are among the most important the government makes. The government makes these decisions each year during the creation of the federal budget. **Figure 15.1** shows an artist's idea of President George W. Bush's fiscal policy.

What is the federal budget?

A budget is a plan for spending and saving money. Just as you may have a personal budget, the government must also have a budget. This is called the **federal budget.** The federal budget estimates how much money the federal government will take in and spend in a year. A good budget has several key qualities. It has to be flexible, ongoing, and clearly stated. The government's budget is its spending plan for 12 months. It starts on October 1 and ends September 30 of the next year. This period is called the **fiscal year.**

Why is the budget important?

The federal budget tells us the national priorities. High priorities receive attention before anything else. In other words, they tell us what is most important. For example, finishing school has a higher priority than getting married for most high school students. Likewise, if the government decides to spend more on education, it means the government thinks good schools are important. Cutting spending on a program does not mean the program is not important. It means it has a lower priority, at least at the time.

Work begins on the budget more than one year before the money is spent. Both the President and Congress look at the budget carefully. Deciding which programs to fund and which to cut is hard. Some groups become upset because the budget leaves out things that are important to them. Rarely is everyone happy with the final budget. It is always a compromise. This means that to settle differences and reach agreement, all groups have to give up something they may want.

What is the budget process?

The President proposes the budget to Congress, but Congress must approve it. The proposed budget reflects the President's priorities. For example, the President may have to decide whether to support a new weapons system or a program to help senior citizens, or both.

federal budget
a written document that estimates how much money the federal government will take in and spend in a year

fiscal year
any 12-month period used for budgeting purposes

President George W. Bush took office during an economic slump. He believed tax cuts would lead to economic growth. He thought people would have more money to spend. **Does the cartoonist believe Bush's plan will work?** ▼

Fig. 15.1

Reading Strategy
Summarizing
Summarize the details that help you understand the federal budget.

■ ■ ■ ■ ■ ■ ■ ■ ■ ■ ■ ■ ■ ■ ■ ■

appropriation bill
a bill that allows a specific amount of spending by the government

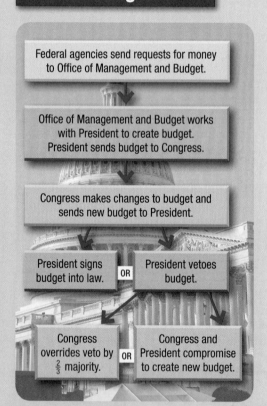

Fig. 15.2 Creating the Federal Budget

> Federal agencies send requests for money to Office of Management and Budget.
>
> Office of Management and Budget works with President to create budget. President sends budget to Congress.
>
> Congress makes changes to budget and sends new budget to President.
>
> President signs budget into law. **OR** President vetoes budget.
>
> Congress overrides veto by $\frac{2}{3}$ majority. **OR** Congress and President compromise to create new budget.

CHART SKILLS

Congress and the White House work together to put together a federal budget.

1. Who takes the first step in the budget process?
2. What happens to the proposed budget if the President vetoes it?

Of course, the President does not have time to make every minor budget decision. Most details are left to the budget director and the White House staff. Congress makes its own version of the budget. It can expand or cut programs. **Figure 15.2** shows the process.

What does the Office of Management and Budget do?

The budget director heads the Office of Management and Budget (OMB). It prepares the President's budget. It begins work more than a year and a half before the beginning of the fiscal year. The OMB reports to the President on the economy. The budget director may suggest fiscal policies to follow.

What is the President's role in the budget?

The President suggests general spending targets for each government department. After the President sets the targets, the departments plan their budgets. OMB officials meet with each department to work out details. The President reviews each department's plans and makes the final changes.

What is the role of Congress in the budget?

Congress and the President do not always agree on priorities. They often disagree over the budget. Both the Senate and the House of Representatives have budget committees. They look at the President's budget and make changes. Subcommittees look at specific parts of the budget. The Congressional Budget Office (CBO) helps Congress evaluate the budget. Congress approves the final budget by passing a set of **appropriation bills.** These bills give each government agency the money it needs for the year.

What happens after Congress approves the budget?

Like all bills, all appropriation or spending bills are sent to the President. If the President signs them, they become law. The President may reject, or veto, appropriation bills he does not approve. In 1996, Congress gave the President the power to veto certain budget items. Before then, the President had to accept or reject the budget as a whole. A bill can still become law even if the President vetoes it. This happens only if two thirds of Congress votes to override the President's veto.

CHECKPOINT *What two offices help the President and the Congress make budget decisions?*

How does the government use fiscal policy to encourage economic growth?

The circular flow model shows how a change in one part of the economy can cause changes in another. Suppose the government increases its spending on highways. The effect is to create more jobs. More working people means more total spending in the economy. This is called **expansionary policy.**

Another expansionary policy is using tax cuts. Suppose the government decides to lower taxes. This gives consumers and businesses more money to spend. By increasing spending, the economy expands.

CHECKPOINT *What is expansionary fiscal policy?*

How does the government use fiscal policy to slow down the economy?

The President and Congress might use fiscal policy to slow down spending if they believe prices are rising too fast. The government might spend less. It could raise taxes. Both actions reduce the amount of money in the economy available to buy goods and services. This kind of policy is called **contractionary policy.**

CHECKPOINT *What is contractionary fiscal policy?*

expansionary policy
a government financial policy used to encourage economic growth, often through increased spending or tax cuts

contractionary policy
a government financial policy used to get the economy to slow down, often through decreased spending or higher taxes

 Reading Strategy
Summarizing
In your own words, summarize the effects of expansionary policy and contractionary policy.

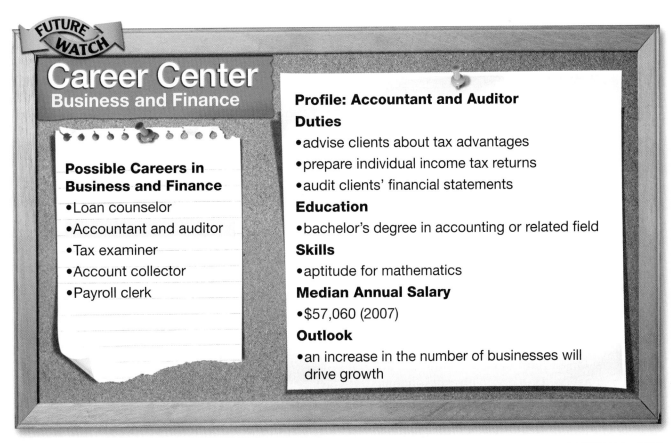

FUTURE WATCH

Career Center
Business and Finance

Possible Careers in Business and Finance
• Loan counselor
• Accountant and auditor
• Tax examiner
• Account collector
• Payroll clerk

Profile: Accountant and Auditor
Duties
• advise clients about tax advantages
• prepare individual income tax returns
• audit clients' financial statements
Education
• bachelor's degree in accounting or related field
Skills
• aptitude for mathematics
Median Annual Salary
• $57,060 (2007)
Outlook
• an increase in the number of businesses will drive growth

Why is changing spending levels difficult?

Increasing or decreasing the amount of federal spending is not easy. Many entitlements are in the federal budget. This spending is set by law. More than half the federal budget is set aside for programs such as Medicaid, Social Security, and veterans' benefits. The government cannot change spending for entitlements under current law. Also, it must continue to pay the interest on the national debt. As a result, any important spending cuts must come from the smaller, discretionary spending part of the federal budget.

Although changes in fiscal policy affect the economy, changes take time. First, government officials have to decide when and how to change fiscal policy. Then, they have to put changes in the federal budget. Finally, time is needed for the policy to affect the economy.

By the time the change takes effect, the economy might be moving in the opposite direction. For example, in the middle of a recession, the government could propose huge public spending on highways. But the economy could recover before construction begins. In a case like this, a change in fiscal policy might create a new problem. Suppose the government continued to spend lots of money on highways in the middle of a recovery. The result might be high inflation and a labor shortage.

CHECKPOINT *Why is it so difficult for government to change spending levels?*

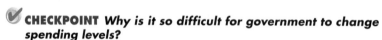

SECTION 1 ASSESSMENT

Essential Questions Journal — To continue to build a response to the Essential Question, go to your **Essential Questions Journal.**

 Guiding Question

1. Use your completed table to answer this question: What are the goals and limits of fiscal policy?

Key Terms and Main Ideas

Directions: On a sheet of paper, write the answer to each question. Use complete sentences.

2. Explain fiscal policy and how it relates to the federal budget.

3. What is a budget?

4. What is an appropriation bill?

5. What is expansionary policy?

Critical Thinking

6. **Summarize** What are the basic steps in the federal budget process?

7. **Synthesize Information** How do entitlement programs affect the federal budget?

Objectives

- **Compare and contrast** classical economics and Keynesian economics.
- **Explain** the basic ideas of supply-side economics.
- **Describe** the role fiscal policy has played in American history.

Guiding Question

What economic ideas have shaped fiscal policy?

Copy this flowchart and fill it in as you read.

Fiscal Policy Options

Classical Economics
- Free markets regulate themselves.
- Fiscal policy is limited.
-

Keynesian (Demand-side) Economics
- Government can affect demand.
-
-

Supply-side Economics
- Government should have a small role in economy.
-
-

classical economics
the idea that free markets will regulate themselves

▶ **Economics and You** Most likely you've heard classical music on the radio. Perhaps you've even played it in an orchestra. Music lovers have enjoyed this serious, formal style of music for hundreds of years. Today, more people listen to rock and hip-hop. But these kinds of music have not been around as long as classical music. These styles have not stood the test of time.

Principles in Action The same might be said for the newest ideas of economics. As you will read in this section, classical economics has been around a long time. But other economic ideas have developed to challenge classical economics. These new schools of thought have also offered the government additional fiscal policy choices.

What is classical economics?

Throughout this book, you have read about how a free market economy works. In a free market, people act in their own self-interests. This causes prices to rise or fall so the market always returns to equilibrium. This idea that free markets regulate themselves is at the center of **classical economics.** Adam Smith, David Ricardo, and Thomas Malthus all added basic ideas to classical economics. For more than 100 years, classical economics influenced government ideas about economics. Some parts of classical economic thought are still followed today.

Reading Strategy
Summarizing
Summarize what classical economists believe about the economy.

The Great Depression, which began in 1929, made some people question the classical ideas. Prices fell over several years. Demand should have increased enough to encourage production as consumers took advantage of low prices. Instead, demand fell. People lost their jobs. Bank failures wiped out their savings. According to classical economics, the market should have reached equilibrium, with everyone working. It didn't. Millions of workers lost their jobs and faced many difficulties. Farmers lost their farms. In the middle of this depression, corn sold for about 80 or 90 cents per bushel. Apples and beef were equally expensive.

The Great Depression pointed out a problem with classical economics. It did not make clear how long the market would take to return to equilibrium. Classical economists knew it could take some time. They looked to the "long run" for equilibrium to be reached. One British economist who was not willing to wait for the economy to recover on its own was John Maynard Keynes (pronounced "kaynes").

✔ **CHECKPOINT** *What event ended the dominance of classical economics over government economists?*

What ideas did Keynes have about economics?

Keynes developed a new theory of economics to explain the Great Depression. He presented his ideas in 1936 in a book called *The General Theory of Employment, Interest, and Money.* Many economists believe this is the most important book about economics written in the twentieth century. Keynes believed in active government involvement in the marketplace. He thought it was the best way to make the economy grow and stabilize. Economists who agree with Keynes believe it is the government's job to smooth out the bumps in business cycles. They believe the economy could be stabilized through the use of government spending and monetary policy. To help the economy grow, government could increase spending and cut taxes. To stop inflation, government spending could be cut and taxes increased. Keynes did not believe in the classical economic view of waiting for the long run. He wanted to give government a tool it could use in the short run.

Classical economists had always looked at the equilibrium of supply and demand for individual products. In contrast, Keynes focused on the economy as a whole.

Keynes looked at how much the entire economy could produce. **Productive capacity** is the most production possible over a period of time without increasing inflation. It is often called full-employment output.

Keynes explained why the depression was continuing. He said it was because neither consumers nor businesses had an incentive to spend enough to cause an increase in production. Why would a company spend money to increase production when demand for its products was falling? How could consumers increase demand when they had barely enough money to live? The only way to end the depression, Keynes thought, was to find a way to boost demand.

What is demand-side economics?

Economists who agreed with the idea that demand drives the economy believe in **demand-side economics.** Demand-side economists believe the government's actions can increase demand. They believe the government has a key role in the economy. They support the government's efforts to create jobs. For example, suppose the government decides to spend billions of dollars on new roads. Many new construction jobs would be created. The new workers would spend the money they earned. This would increase total demand and encourage businesses to increase production, thus creating more jobs. The result is that the economy starts to grow.

productive capacity
the most production possible over time without increasing inflation

demand-side economics
a school of thought based on the idea that demand for goods drives the economy

Economics & YOU

The Effect of Taxes

Paycheck $539.15

Sometimes, when the economy is overheated, the government increases taxes on individuals. *Tax increases can be painful because they leave you with less money to spend on goods and services or to save for the future.*

These tax increases do more than help stabilize the economy and move it on to the next phase of the business cycle. *They also provide the government with more resources to pay for a wide variety of public services.*

Reading Strategy
Summarizing
What will help you understand Keynesian economics?

Keynesian economics
a school of thought that uses demand-side theory as the basis for encouraging economic action

multiplier effect
the idea that every one dollar change in fiscal policy creates a change greater than one dollar in the national income

During the Great Depression, the Civilian Conservation Corps (CCC) employed more than 2 million young men in jobs such as planting forests and digging irrigation ditches. **How did the CCC meet the goals of Keynesian economics?** ▼

How could recessions and depressions be avoided?

Keynesian economics uses demand-side theory as the basis for encouraging action to help the economy. Keynes argued that fiscal policy can fight the problems of both recession and inflation. He said the federal government should track the total spending by consumers, businesses, and government in the economy. The government should watch for the possibility of a recession. If it looked as if the country was moving toward a recession, the government should increase its own spending. This extra spending should continue until spending by individuals returns to a higher level. Or the government can cut taxes. This would result in increases in spending and investment by consumers and businesses. Recall that raising government spending and cutting taxes are expansionary fiscal policies.

President Franklin D. Roosevelt carried out expansionary fiscal policies after his election in 1932. His New Deal put people to work. They built dams, planted forests, and built schools across the country. The government paid for all of these projects.

Many people argue that programs like the New Deal did not create new jobs. Such public works projects only shift employment from the private to the public sector. The two major political parties in the United States disagree over Keynes's ideas. Republicans generally have favored using tax cuts to get the economy to grow. Democrats, generally, have favored more expansive government programs.

What is the multiplier effect?

Although difficult to control, fiscal policy is a powerful tool. The key to its power is the **multiplier effect.** This is the idea that every one dollar change in fiscal policy creates a greater than one dollar change in the national income. This is true whether there is an increase in spending or a decrease in taxes. In other words, the effects of changes in fiscal policy are multiplied.

Suppose the federal government finds that business investment is dropping. It fears a recession. To prevent a recession, the government decides to spend an extra $10 billion.

The extra $10 billion of government spending will increase demand and income. When the government buys an extra $10 billion of goods and services, an extra $10 billion of goods and services have been produced. However, the GDP will increase by more than $10 billion.

Here's why: Businesses that sold the $10 billion in goods and services to the government have earned an extra $10 billion. These businesses will spend their additional earnings on wages, raw materials, and investment. Their workers, other suppliers, and stockholders all receive money. These people will spend part of it, perhaps 80 percent, or $8 billion. The businesses that benefit from this second round of spending will then pass it back to households. Households will again spend 80 percent of it, or $6.4 billion. The next round will add an additional $5.12 billion to the economy, and so on. When all these rounds of spending are added up, they total an increase of about $50 billion in GDP.

Suppose that a tourist spends $100 on a hotel room. The hotel owner uses some of the $100, say $70, to pay workers and suppliers. The workers and suppliers spend their money on such things as groceries. Of that $70, let's say $30 stays in the local economy. Because of the multiplier effect, the $100 has grown to $200 ($100 + $70 + $30 = $200). In other words, the multiplier effect is the ripple effect caused by the respending of money.

✔ **CHECKPOINT** *How did Keynes think the government should influence the economy?*

What is supply-side economics?

Not all economists agree with demand-side economics. Some believe in **supply-side economics.** It is based on the idea that the supply of goods drives the economy. Supply-side economists believe in laissez faire. They believe government controls make it hard for businesses to operate well. They say reducing controls will give businesses incentives to increase production. Prices will drop because the supply of goods and services increases. Businesses will hire more workers as their production goes up. Supply-side economists favor tax cuts, which encourage people and businesses to spend and invest more. This increased demand will cause the economy to grow.

Supply-side economists often use the Laffer curve to show the harmful effects of taxes. It is named after the economist Arthur Laffer. The Laffer curve shows the relationship between the tax rate and the total tax revenue the government collects. Revenue depends on both the tax rate and the health of the economy. The Laffer curve shows that high tax rates may not bring in much revenue if they cause the economy to slow down. The Laffer curve is shown in **Figure 15.3** on page 386.

✔ **CHECKPOINT** *How does supply-side economics link taxation to employment levels?*

Fig. 15.3 Laffer Curve

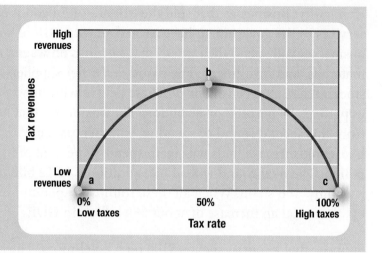

How has fiscal policy been used in U.S. history?

Recall that Keynes presented his ideas during the Great Depression. President Herbert Hoover, however, believed in classical economics. He thought the economy was basically sound and would return to equilibrium on its own. The man who followed him, President Franklin D. Roosevelt, was much more willing to increase government spending to get the country out of the depression. The Democratic Party won big victories in the 1932 and 1934 elections. This helped Roosevelt start several programs to pump money into the economy.

Keynes's theory was fully tested during World War II. As the United States geared up for war, a huge jump in government spending occurred. The government spent large sums of money to feed soldiers and equip them. Soldiers needed everything from warplanes to rifles to medical supplies. This money was given to the private sector in exchange for goods. The additional demand for goods and services moved the country out of the Great Depression. This was just as Keynesian economics had predicted. After the war, Congress created the Council of Economic Advisers (CEA). The CEA was a group of three respected economists who could advise the President on economic policy.

Between 1945 and 1960, the U.S. economy was healthy and growing. Still, there were a few minor recessions. The last recession continued into the term of President John F. Kennedy, with unemployment at 6.7 percent.

Walter Heller, Kennedy's chief financial policy adviser, wanted to lower the number of people out of work. He convinced Kennedy that tax cuts would create demand and cause the economy to grow.

As **Figure 15.4** on page 388 shows, tax rates were high in the early 1960s. The highest individual income tax rate was about 90 percent. Today, it is lower than 40 percent. Kennedy agreed with Heller to cut taxes. The tax cuts were popular.

Some of Kennedy's tax cuts were passed in 1964, after he was killed. At the same time, the Vietnam War raised government spending. Over the next two years, the economy grew rapidly. GDP increased by more than 4 percent a year. There is no way to prove that the tax cut caused this increase. But the result is what Keynesian economics had predicted.

Keynesian economics was used many other times in the 1960s and 1970s to try to adjust the national economy. One Keynesian economist, John Kenneth Galbraith, had an important influence on economic thinking. Galbraith was a strong supporter of public spending. He served as economic adviser to Presidents Roosevelt, Kennedy, and Lyndon Johnson. Under Johnson he helped develop a social welfare program called the Great Society.

Innovators

John Kenneth Galbraith

"The conventional [usual] view serves to protect us from the painful job of thinking."

John Kenneth Galbraith was the world's most famous economist for the last half of the twentieth century. He was also a keen observer of politics and social life and author of a number of best-selling books.

During World War II, President Roosevelt selected Galbraith to lead the Office of Price Administration. This gave him total control over the prices charged by U.S. companies.

After the war, Galbraith wrote a number of widely read books about the government's role in society. He favored an active government, using funds provided by a progressive income tax and high sales taxes. He warned against "the affluent [rich] society" that produced an excess of goods for the rich. He believed this type of society neglected the public sector—education, roads and bridges, parks, and concert halls.

Galbraith advised President John F. Kennedy. Later, he inspired President Lyndon B. Johnson's Head Start program. This was an early childhood education program for poor children.

Galbraith's long service to America did not go unnoticed. He received the Presidential Medal of Freedom twice. This is the nation's highest civilian (nonmilitary) honor.

Fast Facts

John Kenneth Galbraith (1908–2006)
Education: Ph.D., University of California at Berkeley
Claim to Fame: Wrote about the dangers of an affluent society, won the Presidential Medal of Freedom twice

Fig. 15.4 Top Marginal Tax Rate, 1925–2007

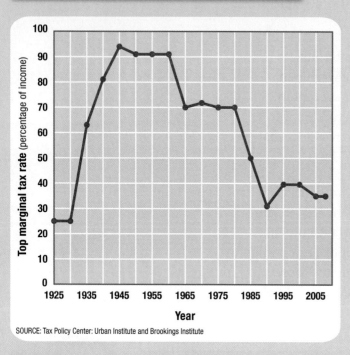

SOURCE: Tax Policy Center: Urban Institute and Brookings Institute

GRAPH SKILLS

Tax rates varied widely throughout the last century.
1. When were top marginal income tax rates at their highest?
2. What has the trend been in tax rates since 1985?

In the late 1970s, Keynesian fiscal policy was still in place. There was a major increase in the number of people out of work. Inflation was rising. When Ronald Reagan became President in 1981, he favored supply-side economics. Among his economic advisers was Milton Friedman, a former professor of economics. An anti-Keynesian, Friedman pushed for more laissez-faire policies.

In 1981, Reagan proposed a tax cut that reduced taxes by 25 percent over three years. In a short time, the economy recovered. Reagan agreed with Friedman that government should not spend its way out of a recession. For many reasons, however, government spending continued to rise each year while Reagan was in office.

 CHECKPOINT *How have Keynesian and anti-Keynesian ideas influenced Presidents?*

SECTION 2 ASSESSMENT

Essential Questions Journal To continue to build a response to the Essential Question, go to your **Essential Questions Journal.**

 Guiding Question

1. Use your completed flowchart to answer this question: What economic ideas have shaped fiscal policy?

Key Terms and Main Ideas

Directions: On a sheet of paper, write the answer to each question. Use complete sentences.
2. What is classical economics?
3. In what way is full employment related to productive capacity?
4. What is the multiplier effect?
5. How can low taxes encourage investment?

Critical Thinking

6. **Make Comparisons** Compare and contrast Keynesian and supply-side economics.
7. **Synthesize Information** How did the policies of Keynes work when applied during the Great Depression?

Objectives

- **Explain** the importance of balancing the budget.
- **Analyze** how budget deficits add to the national debt.
- **Summarize** the problems the national debt causes.
- **Identify** how political leaders have tried to control the deficit.

Guiding Question

What are the effects of budget deficits and national debt?

Copy this cause-and-effect chart and fill it in as you read.

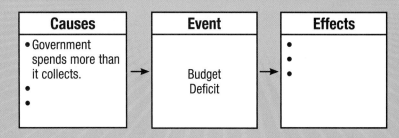

Causes	Event	Effects
• Government spends more than it collects. • •	Budget Deficit	• • •

deficit
when the amount spent is more than the amount taken in

budget surplus
when the amount of money spent is less than the amount collected

budget deficit
when the amount spent is more than the amount collected

▶ **Economics and You** Have you ever watched someone use a credit card? If so, you might have some idea how easy it is to spend money you don't have. If you fail to pay the full credit-card bill each month, the amount you owe—plus interest—keeps going up. Soon you could face a mountain of debt.

The federal government often spends more than it has. You have been reading about how the government uses spending as a fiscal policy tool to improve the economy.

Principles in Action The government's spending more than it has can lead to a growing national debt. You will learn about the national debt in this section. The How the Economy Works feature shows how that debt was created. The costs of this debt must be measured against the benefits of higher government spending.

How is the budget balanced?

The basic tool of fiscal policy is the federal budget. It has two parts: revenue (taxes) and expenditures (spending programs). If taxes equal government spending, the budget is balanced. However, it is unusual for a government to have an exactly balanced budget. Most of the time, budgets are either in **deficit** or surplus. A **budget surplus** occurs when the government spends less than it collects in taxes. More often, the government spends more than it collects. This is called a **budget deficit.** The deficit can grow or shrink because of forces beyond the government's control. Surpluses and deficits can be very large figures. The record occurred in fiscal year 2008: $455 billion. (See **Figure 15.5** on page 390.)

Fig. 15.5 Budget Surpluses and Deficits, 1950–2008

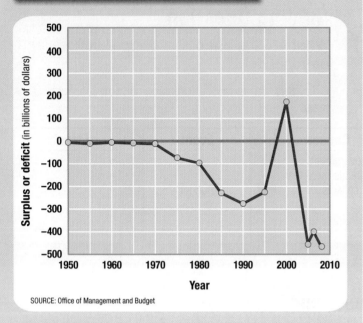

SOURCE: Office of Management and Budget

GRAPH SKILLS

Budget deficits swelled in the early 2000s due to recession, tax cuts, and defense spending.

1. In which of the years shown on the graph did the budget have a surplus?
2. What was the dominant trend in deficits in the late 1990s?

■ ■ ■ ■ ■ ■ ■ ■ ■ ■ ■ ■ ■ ■ ■ ■ ■ ■ ■ ■

hyperinflation
very high inflation

How does the government respond to budget deficits?

When the government does not take in enough revenue to cover its expenses for the year, it can do two things: (1) create money and (2) borrow money.

The government can create new money to pay salaries for its workers and benefits for citizens. It can simply print more money. The Federal Reserve can also create money electronically by depositing money in people's bank accounts. The effect is the same. This can work for relatively small deficits but can cause problems when there are large deficits.

When the government creates more money, it increases the amount of money in use. This increases the demand for goods and services. Output may increase. But there is a point at which the economy is producing all it can. Output cannot increase any more. The increase in money will mean there are more dollars but the same amount of goods and services. Prices will rise. A greater amount of money will be needed to buy the same amount of goods and services. The result is inflation.

Covering large deficits by printing more money can cause very high inflation, called **hyperinflation.** This happened in Germany and Russia after World War I. Brazil and Argentina in the 1980s and the Ukraine in the 1990s also experienced hyperinflation. If the United States had hyperinflation, a shirt that cost $30 in June might cost $400 in December.

Why might the government borrow money?

The federal government can also borrow money to pay for the extra spending. The government borrows money by selling bonds. A bond is a promise to repay money in the future, with interest. Consumers and businesses buy bonds from the government.

U.S. Savings Bonds (EE Bonds) allow millions of Americans to lend small amounts of money to the federal government. In return, they earn interest on the bonds for up to 30 years. Recall from Chapter 11 that other common forms of government borrowing are Treasury bills, notes, and bonds. **Treasury bills** are short-term bonds that have maturity dates of 26 weeks or less. **Treasury notes** have terms of 2 to 10 years. Treasury bonds mature 30 years after issue.

Federal borrowing lets the government pay for large projects. Wise borrowing allows the government to create more public goods and services. Federal borrowing also has disadvantages.

☑ **CHECKPOINT** *What is the most common way for the federal government to cover a large deficit?*

What is the national debt?

Like people, when the government borrows more than it has, it goes into debt. The **national debt** is the total amount of money the federal government owes all bondholders (lenders). Every year that there is a budget deficit and the federal government borrows money to cover it, the national debt will grow.

The United States first went into debt in 1790. The government decided to take over Revolutionary War debts. By the end of 1790, the debt was just over $75 million. World War II caused a huge increase in the national debt. It rose from $40 billion to $279 billion. Wars such as the Korean War and the Vietnam War made the debt even greater. The first five years of the Iraq War cost roughly $600 billion. The national debt in 2008 was more than $10.6 trillion.

Many people are confused about the difference between the deficit and the debt. The deficit occurs when the government spends more money than it has in one fiscal year. The debt, on the other hand, is the total amount of money the government owes. Each deficit adds to the total debt. Each surplus subtracts from the total debt.

☑ **CHECKPOINT** *What is the difference between a deficit and a debt?*

■■■■■■■■■■■■■■■■■■

Treasury bills
government bonds with a maturity date of 26 weeks or less

Treasury notes
government bonds with a term of 2 to 10 years

national debt
the total amount of money the federal government owes to all bondholders

■■■■■■■■■■■■■■■■■■

Reading Strategy
Summarizing
What are some ways the government deals with budget deficits?

Fig. 15.6 How the Economy Works

What causes the national debt to spiral?

The national debt is the amount of money the U.S. government owes the people and institutions who hold its bonds, bills, and notes. In the past 30 years, the national debt has grown enormously. Here is why.

1 Each year, the federal government has to pay for hundreds of essential services, from military protection to healthcare. Tax revenues pay for most of these expenses. But in most years, there is a gap between revenue and expenditures.

INTEREST

U.S. BONDS

2 To make up the gap, the government borrows money. It issues Treasury bonds, bills, and notes. The interest paid on this money becomes part of the federal budget.

Expenses

Borrowing

---

crowding-out effect
the loss of funds for private investment caused by government borrowing

What are some problems of a national debt?

The first problem with a national debt is that it cuts down the amount of money available for businesses to invest. To sell its bonds, the government must offer a high interest rate to attract buyers. Individuals and businesses are attracted by the high interest rates and the safety of investing in the government. They use some of their savings or profits to buy government bonds.

We have seen that the government often has to borrow money to pay its bills. However, every dollar the government borrows is one dollar less that businesses can borrow. Less money is available for companies to use to expand their factories, conduct research, and develop new products. As a result, interest rates rise. This loss of funds for private investment caused by government borrowing is called the **crowding-out effect.** Government borrowing "crowds out" other people and businesses that need to borrow. A national debt can hurt investment and slow economic growth over the long run.

3 Economic downturns
or external shocks such as natural
disasters may add unplanned costs
to the federal budget. This leads to
even more borrowing.

4 As the government
borrows more, the slice of the
federal budget taken up by
interest payments grows. The
more interest, the greater the
gap between revenue and
expenses. The greater the
gap, the more the government
borrows.

5 Large deficits over a period of
years have caused the national debt
to spiral to enormous proportions.
However, economists differ on
whether this large debt is a
serious problem to the
U.S. economy.

Check Your Understanding
1. How does borrowing lead to greater
   interest payments and greater debt?
2. How important do you think it is to
   immediately reduce the national debt?

More Expenses   More Borrowing

The second problem with a high national debt is that the
government must pay interest to bondholders. The more the
government borrows, the more interest it has to pay. Paying the
interest on the debt is sometimes called servicing the debt. Over
time, the interest payments have become large. In 2004, the federal
government spent more than half a trillion dollars servicing
the debt. An opportunity cost is also involved. Dollars spent
servicing the debt cannot be spent on something else, like defense,
healthcare, or infrastructure.

A third problem involves foreign ownership of the national debt.
Most of the national debt is money that the government owes
itself. The government uses bonds as a savings account for holding
Social Security, Medicare, and other funds. Foreign governments,
including Japan, China, and the United Kingdom, own about a
quarter of the debt. Some people are afraid that a country like
China could use its large bondholdings to hurt the U.S. economy.

For example, there is a danger some countries might stop buying the bonds or start selling them off. Others disagree. They argue that selling off U.S. assets would harm their own economies. They also argue that foreign states own too little of the debt to cause any problems.

Some people believe the national debt is not a big problem. It is important to remember that government spending has helped the economy out of depression and recession many times. Deficit spending may help create jobs and encourage economic growth. However, a budget deficit can be an effective tool if it is used for a short time only. Most people agree that large budget deficits year after year have more costs than benefits.

✔ **CHECKPOINT** *What are some of the problems of having a huge national debt?*

What has been done to reduce deficits?

There are several reasons why controlling the deficit is not easy. As we have seen, much of the budget consists of entitlement spending. Another large part of the budget is money that has to be set aside to pay interest to bondholders. Finally, special interest groups are against cutting special programs out of the budget. A special interest group is an organization that attempts to influence lawmakers in the group's favor. For example, union members may band together to try to get Congress to help workers.

■ ■ ■ ■ ■ ■ ■ ■ ■ ■ ■ ■ ■ ■ ■ ■ ■ ■

Reading Strategy
Summarizing
In your own words, explain how the government has tried to reduce deficits.

The National Debt Clock was first displayed in 1989 in New York City. It continually ticks off the growing national debt plus each family's share. Other cities and the Internet have similar "clocks." **Why do you think someone decided to build the National Debt Clock?** ▶

Worries about the budget deficits of the mid-1980s caused Congress to pass the Gramm-Rudman-Hollings Act. It created automatic across-the-board cuts in federal spending if the deficit was greater than a certain amount. However, the act did not apply to some parts of the budget. For example, interest payments and many entitlement programs were not included. The Supreme Court said some parts of the law were unconstitutional.

In 1990, a new budget system replaced Gramm-Rudman-Hollings. The 1990 Budget Enforcement Act created a "pay-as-you-go" system (also known as PAYGO). It required Congress to find a way to raise more money before it could spend on new programs that would add to the deficit.

Some people have suggested amending the U.S. Constitution to require a balanced budget. In 1995, Congress almost approved a balanced budget amendment. Supporters argued that requiring the budget to be balanced would force the government to be more careful about its spending. Opponents said a constitutional amendment would make it harder to deal with rapid changes in the economy such as those faced by the nation in 2008.

 CHECKPOINT *Why do some people oppose a constitutional amendment requiring a balanced budget?*

SECTION 3 ASSESSMENT

Essential Questions Journal — To continue to build a response to the Essential Question, go to your **Essential Questions Journal.**

Guiding Question

1. Use your completed cause-and-effect chart to answer this question: What are the effects of budget deficits and national debt?

Key Terms and Main Ideas

Directions: On a sheet of paper, write the answer to each question. Use complete sentences.

2. How does a Treasury note differ from a Treasury bill?

3. What is hyperinflation?

4. How might a budget deficit be related to the national debt?

5. What is PAYGO?

Critical Thinking

6. **Analyze Information** Explain the crowding-out effect that results from national debt.

7. **Analyze Information** What are two possible problems with having a national debt?

Section 1–Understanding Fiscal Policy

■ Fiscal policy decisions are among the most important decisions facing the government.

■ The federal budget is a plan to pay for the federal government's expenditures.

■ The fiscal year of the federal government runs from October 1 to September 30.

■ The government uses expansionary fiscal policy to encourage growth.

■ The government uses contractionary fiscal policy to reduce growth.

Section 2–Fiscal Policy Options

■ Classical economics has to do with the idea that free markets regulate themselves.

■ John Maynard Keynes believed the government should act to make the economy grow. His theory uses demand-side economics.

■ Demand-side economics has to do with the idea that demand for goods drives the economy.

■ Supply-side economics is based on the idea that the supply of goods drives the economy.

■ Supply-side and demand-side economics have been used successfully in U.S. history.

Section 3–Budget Deficits and the National Debt

■ A budget surplus occurs when the government spends less than it collects in taxes.

■ A budget deficit occurs when the government spends more than it collects in taxes.

■ The national debt is the total amount of money the federal government owes bondholders.

■ A budget deficit is the amount of money the government borrows for one budget. Each deficit adds to the debt.

■ The government has tried different ways to reduce budget deficits.

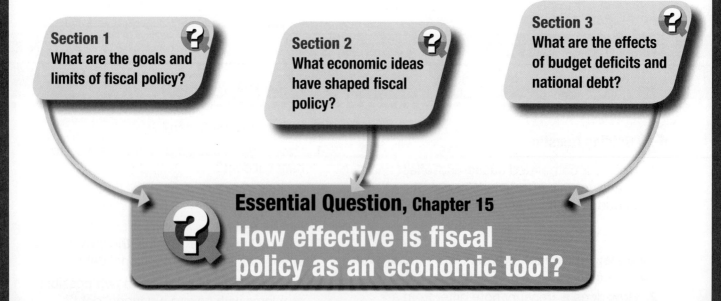

Section 1
What are the goals and limits of fiscal policy?

Section 2
What economic ideas have shaped fiscal policy?

Section 3
What are the effects of budget deficits and national debt?

Essential Question, Chapter 15
How effective is fiscal policy as an economic tool?

President Bush Discusses Economy, Growth Package

In January 2008 President George W. Bush spoke to the United States. By this time, the U.S. economy was slipping into a recession. President Bush wanted to let the people know what his government was doing to solve the recession. He hoped to reassure people about the future.

"Over the past several months I've held a series of meetings with my economic team on the outlook for the U.S. economy. And before I left for the Middle East, I directed them to conduct a thorough assessment of our economic condition, consult with members of Congress, and provide me with their recommendations about any actions we might need to take.

The economic team reports that our economy has a solid foundation, but that there are areas of real concern. Our economy is still creating jobs, though at a reduced pace. Consumer spending is still growing, but the housing market is declining. Business investment and exports are still rising, but the cost of imported oil has increased. . . .

In recent months, we've taken steps to shore up the housing market, including measures to help struggling homeowners avoid foreclosure and to keep their homes. . . . I have concluded that additional action is needed. To keep our economy growing and creating jobs, Congress and the administration need to work to enact an economic growth package as soon as possible.

This growth package must be big enough to make a difference in an economy as large and dynamic as ours—which means it should be

about 1 percent of GDP. This growth package must be built on broad-based tax relief that will directly affect economic growth—and not the kind of spending projects that would have little immediate impact on our economy. This growth package must be temporary and take effect right away— so we can get help to our economy when it needs it most. And this growth package must not include any tax increases. . . .

In a vibrant economy, markets rise and decline. We cannot change that fundamental dynamic. As a matter of fact, eliminating risk altogether would also eliminate the innovation and productivity that drives the creation of jobs and wealth in America. Yet there are also times when swift and temporary actions can help ensure that inevitable market adjustments do not undermine the health of the broader economy. This is such a moment. . . .

I'm optimistic about our economic future, because Americans have shown time and again that they are the most industrious, creative, and enterprising people in the world. That is what has made our economy strong. That is what will make it stronger in the challenging times ahead."

Document-Based Questions

1. What did President Bush's economic team tell him about the economy?
2. What two problems affect the economy?
3. What is the size of the growth package President Bush proposes?
4. What does President Bush say about an economy in which people take no risks?
5. What does President Bush say about the economic future of America?

SOURCE: "President Bush Discusses Economy, Growth Package," found at *http://www.whitehouse.gov/news/releases/2008/01/20080118-1.html*

Directions: Write your answers to the following questions. Use complete sentences.

Section 1—Understanding Fiscal Policy

1. What is a fiscal year?
2. What are some limits of fiscal policy?
3. Who helps the President prepare the budget?
4. Why would the government want to slow economic growth?
5. Why must spending cuts come in the discretionary budget?

Section 2—Fiscal Policy Options

6. How do classical economics and Keynesian economics differ?
7. What is demand-side economics?
8. What was President Franklin Roosevelt's New Deal?
9. Generally, what action have Republicans favored to get the economy growing?
10. Generally, what action have Democrats favored to get the economy growing?
11. Who was Milton Friedman?

Section 3—Budget Deficits and the National Debt

12. What are the benefits and the drawbacks of enacting a balanced budget amendment?
13. What is a budget deficit?
14. What kind of government bond is a short-term bond?
15. What kind of government bond has a term of 2 to 10 years?
16. In your own words, explain the crowding-out effect.
17. Why might people like to use a "pay-as-you-go" plan?

Economics on the go

Exploring the Essential Question

18. List three ways governmental fiscal policy affects your daily life.

19. How effective has the federal budget been as a tool of fiscal policy?

Essential Question Activity

20. Complete this activity to answer the Essential Question **How effective is fiscal policy as an economic tool?**

Work in small groups. Each group will research the administrations of Presidents from John F. Kennedy to the current President. Using the worksheet in your Essential Questions Journal or the electronic worksheet available at **PearsonSuccessNet.com,** gather the following information:

(a) Identify the President by political party and the number of years in office.

(b) Identify the main economic goals and challenges under that administration.

(c) Evaluate how successful that administration was at meeting its goals.

| **Essential Questions Journal** | To continue to build a response to the Essential Question, go to your **Essential Questions Journal.** |

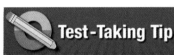 **Test-Taking Tip**

Drawing a picture, chart, or diagram is one way to help you understand a difficult test question.

Chapter **16** The Federal Reserve and Monetary Policy

Essential Question, Chapter 16

How effective is monetary policy as an economic tool?

- **Section 1** The Federal Reserve System

- **Section 2** Federal Reserve Functions

- **Section 3** Monetary Policy Tools

- **Section 4** Monetary Policy and Macroeconomic Stabilization

Economics on the go

To study anywhere, anytime, download these onlir resources at *PearsonSuccessNet.com* ➤

▶ **The U.S. government created the Federal Reserve System to manage the nation's money.** By managing the money well, the Federal Reserve helps to keep the economy stable. Nicknamed the "Fed," the Federal Reserve is the nation's central bank.

This chapter will discuss why the Federal Reserve was created, how it works, and what it does. You will learn what makes the Fed an important part of the government. You will also learn about the tools the Fed uses to control the money supply.

Reading Strategy: Questioning

Be an active reader. Ask yourself questions as you read. Asking questions will make you stop and think about what you have just read. You will remember more of what you have read, too. As you read, ask yourself:

- Why am I reading this text?
- How can I connect this text to my own life?
- What decisions can I make about the facts and details in this text?

Visual Glossary
online

Go to the Visual Glossary Online for an interactive review of **monetary policy.**

How the Economy Works
online

Go to How the Economy Works Online for an interactive lesson on the **business cycle.**

Action Graph
online

Go to Action Graph Online for animated versions of key charts and graphs.

Objectives

- **Describe** banking history in the United States.
- **Explain** why the Federal Reserve Act of 1913 led to reform.
- **Describe** the structure of the Federal Reserve System.

How is the Federal Reserve System organized?

Copy this concept web and fill it in as you read.

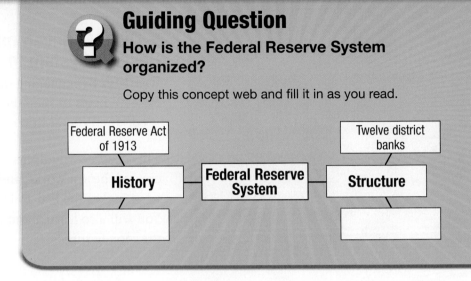

What details are important to remember about the Federal Reserve System?

▶ **Economics and You** It is Saturday night, and you have gone out to a movie with friends. Now everyone wants to get a pizza. You find that you have only a dollar and some change left. What can you do? If you have an ATM card, you can get cash out of your bank account. Here's a crazy thought—what if your bank runs out of money? What can it do?

Principles in Action As you will see in this section, when American banks need emergency cash, they turn to the Federal Reserve System for a loan. The Federal Reserve System performs many important services for banks, for the federal government, and for the national economy.

What is the history of the Federal Reserve System?

In 1907, the United States experienced an economic panic. In banking terms, a panic is a widespread fear of financial loss. Serious banking problems caused the Panic of 1907. Many banks made bad loans and gave too much credit. Many people no longer trusted banks. A lot of people wanted to take their money out at the same time. The banks did not have enough cash to give all of them their money back. Some banks were forced to close. The nation's banking system was in trouble.

After the Panic of 1907, Congress created the National Monetary Commission. Its job was to find ways to stop economic panics from happening again. People wanted to know their banks were safe. They wanted the government to manage bank activities.

The Commission's suggestions led to the creation of the Federal Reserve System. Bankers, business owners, and leaders agreed that the system needed reform. However, they could not agree on the type of reform. Some people wanted a central bank that bankers controlled. The Progressive reformers wanted government control over banking. President Woodrow Wilson sided with the Progressives. On December 23, 1913, the Federal Reserve Act was passed.

Why is there more than one Federal Reserve bank?

Many countries have one central bank. At the time the Fed was created, many people were worried about the national government having too much power. They believed one central bank was a bad idea. For this reason, the Federal Reserve Act created a decentralized system. This means power was spread out. Twelve district banks make up the Federal Reserve System.

Why was there a need for more reform?

The creation of the Fed restored people's trust in the banking system again. It was created to prevent financial hard times like the Great Depression. However, the Fed was forced to learn through trial and error. It was not able to prevent the Great Depression. The twelve regional banks acted on their own. The actions each bank took often canceled out those of another bank.

For example, in 1929 and 1930, the Governors of the Federal Reserve Banks of New York and Chicago wanted the Fed to lower interest rates. Many business loans had lost value as a result of the stock market crash. Lower interest rates would make more money available to banks. However, the Federal Reserve Board of Governors were against lowering interest rates. Concerned about the growth of the stock market, the board favored the opposite approach. They also restrained the New York board from taking strong action. Many economists believe that the failure of the Fed to act contributed to the deepening of the financial crisis.

In 1935, Congress changed the way the Fed was set up so the system could work better. These reforms created the Federal Reserve System as we know it today. The new Fed enjoyed more centralized power so that the twelve district banks were able to work more closely with one another.

✔ **CHECKPOINT** *Why did the Fed fail to prevent the financial crises that led to the Great Depression?*

How is the Federal Reserve System set up?

The Federal Reserve Act created a banking system of twelve district banks located throughout the country. The act required all national banks to become members. State banks could choose to become members. However, all banks had to meet the requirements set by the Federal Reserve System.

Each of the approximately 2,600 Fed member banks pays a small amount of money to join the system. In return, it receives stock. This stock earns the bank dividends from the Fed at a rate of up to an annual fixed rate of 6 percent. Since 1980, all banks receive services from the Fed, even if they are not Fed members. These services include loans to banks that need short-term cash.

Figure 16.1 shows how the Fed is organized. A Board of Governors controls the system. The board makes the key decisions for the nation's banking system. The Board of Governors is made up of seven members. The President appoints them, but they must be approved by the Senate. The President also chooses two of the seven members to serve as chair and vice chair. They are each appointed for a four-year term but can be reappointed.

The governors serve for fourteen years. Normally, only one new member is chosen every even-numbered year. This allows the board to make necessary, but maybe unpopular, decisions. Also, this prevents any one President from appointing a full Board of Governors. The board meets in Washington, D.C.

Fig. 16.1 Structure of the Federal Reserve System

CHART SKILLS

About 40 percent of all U.S. banks belong to the Federal Reserve System.

1. From what two levels of the Fed structure does the Federal Open Market Committee draw its membership?
2. How does the structure of the Fed reflect a compromise between centralized power and regional powers?

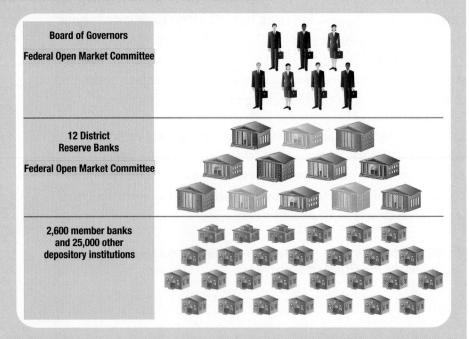

Board of Governors
Federal Open Market Committee

12 District
Reserve Banks
Federal Open Market Committee

2,600 member banks
and 25,000 other
depository institutions

Each of the twelve regional districts has a Federal Reserve Bank. Each district bank has its own president. The district bank carries out the Fed's policies. The larger districts also have branch banks. Although each district Federal Reserve Bank is independent, they all work together as a team to keep the economy healthy.

Why is the Fed called a "bankers' bank"?

The Fed is a bank for banks. It serves all banks that are members of the system. It does not serve businesses or private citizens directly. Even though it was created by federal law, the government does not own it. The Fed is part of the government, so, in a sense, the American people own it. Banks in each of the twelve regions use the Fed in much the same way people use their own banks.

What is monetary policy?

The decisions the Fed makes about money and banking make up **monetary policy.** It refers to the actions the Fed takes. These actions influence the level of real GDP and the rate of inflation in the economy.

What is the Federal Open Market Committee?

The Federal Open Market Committee (FOMC) makes key decisions about interest rates. It decides what the money supply should be. At least eight times a year, the committee meets to review the health of the economy. The committee decides whether to speed up or slow down the economy. The committee's decisions are based on research by the staff of the Federal Reserve Board.

 CHECKPOINT *What is the role of each of the twelve Federal Reserve banks?*

 Reading Strategy
Questioning
As yourself: "Did I understand what I just read about the Federal Reserve System?" If not, read the material again.

monetary policy
the decisions the Fed makes about money and banking

SECTION 1 ASSESSMENT

Essential Questions Journal To continue to build a response to the Essential Question, go to your **Essential Questions Journal.**

 **Guiding Question**

1. Use your completed concept web to answer this question: How is the Federal Reserve System organized?

Key Terms and Main Ideas

Directions: On a sheet of paper, write the answer to each question. Use complete sentences.

2. What is the Fed?

3. How many district reserve banks are there?

4. Which type of bank is required to belong to the Federal Reserve System? Which can join the Federal Reserve System voluntarily?

5. What is monetary policy?

Critical Thinking

6. **Summarize** Describe the panic of 1907.

7. **Make Inferences** Why do you think the Federal Reserve is part of the government?

Objectives

- **Describe** how the Federal Reserve serves the federal government.
- **Explain** how the Federal Reserve serves banks.
- **Describe** how the Federal Reserve regulates the banking system.
- **Explain** the Federal Reserve's role in regulating the nation's money supply.

■■■■■■■■■■■■■■■■■■■■

Reading Strategy
Questioning
   What do you already know about the Bureau of Engraving and Printing?

Guiding Question

What does the Federal Reserve do?

Copy this flowchart and fill it in as you read.

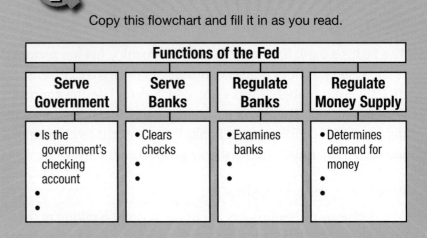

Functions of the Fed

Serve Government	Serve Banks	Regulate Banks	Regulate Money Supply
• Is the government's checking account • •	• Clears checks • •	• Examines banks • •	• Determines demand for money • •

▶ **Economics and You** Your summer job is going great. You like the work, and it pays well. The only problem is the paychecks are handed out just once a month. You really need that first paycheck. Finally, the end of the month arrives. You rush to your bank to cash your paycheck. But the bank teller has an unpleasant surprise for you. The bank will not give you the money until the check clears. It will take at least two days, the teller says, for the check to clear.

Principles in Action The teller doesn't explain the delay. He or she probably does not know that the Fed handles most of the check clearing in the United States. In addition to your check, the Fed will process another 18 billion checks this year. Another function of the Fed, as you will read in Economics & You, is to issue money. In this section, you will learn about the many things the Fed does.

How does the Fed serve government?

The Federal Reserve System's biggest customer is the U.S. government. The Fed handles the Treasury Department's "checking account." The Treasury deposits government funds in the Fed, including all tax deposits. It also handles all outgoing government payments. These include Social Security checks, pension checks, and other benefits.

The Treasury also sells and buys back U.S. government securities. These include savings bonds and Treasury notes and bonds. These bonds are part of the government's debt. The U.S. Treasury sells bonds to get the money it needs to pay for services such as defense, food stamps for poor people, highways, and medical care for the aged and poor.

The Fed also issues the nation's currency. The Bureau of Engraving and Printing produces paper money, and the U.S. Mint produces coins. The district banks distribute the money to their member banks. Take a look at the money you have in your wallet or purse. Notice that each bill is labeled "Federal Reserve Note." Each bill has an emblem and a code showing which of the district banks issued it.

The Fed controls and regulates the banking system of the United States. All twelve district banks have teams of bank examiners. Their job is to make sure the banks follow the rules. They check bank records and look carefully at the loans and investments the banks have made. The examiners can pressure banks that are not following the rules to change the way they do business.

 CHECKPOINT *What does the Federal Reserve do in its role as the government's banker?*

How does the Fed serve its member banks?

The Fed provides important services to its member banks. As the banker's bank, it offers the same services consumers get from their banks. It supplies cash and it lends money.

The Fed manages the flow of money among the district banks and member banks. Each day, the Fed handles millions of payments. Some of these are paper checks. Many others are electronic money transfers. In these electronic transfers, money changes hands through computers. The Fed keeps track of all these payments through a service called **check clearing.** The Fed collects a service fee for each check it processes.

Just as you may sometimes have to borrow money, banks sometimes borrow money. Suppose that a large number of a bank's customers suddenly wanted their money. Banks may find themselves short on cash on paydays, at vacation time, and during the holiday season. These are times when people spend a lot of money. At times like these, banks might be forced to borrow money. It may also happen when many people are out of work.

check clearing
the process by which banks record whose account gives up money and whose account receives money

▲ The Federal Reserve is the banker for the U.S. government. Among its many functions, it processes Social Security checks and income tax refunds. **What are some of its other responsibilities?**

reserves
funds that banks keep in accounts with the Fed, called federal funds

federal funds rate
the interest rate banks charge one another for loans

reserve requirements
the amount of funds banks must hold in reserve

discount rate
the rate the Fed charges banks for loans to banks

net worth
total assets minus total liabilities

Usually, banks lend one another money, using money from their reserve balances. **Reserves** are funds banks keep in accounts with the Fed. They are called federal funds. The interest rate banks charge one another for these loans is the **federal funds rate.**

Banks can also borrow from the Federal Reserve. They do so often, especially in bad times such as recessions. The Federal Reserve sometimes makes emergency loans to commercial banks so they can maintain required reserves. **Reserve requirements** are the amount of funds banks must hold in reserve. This money must be in the bank's vaults or at the closest Federal Reserve Bank. The Fed charges a **discount rate** for these loans. You will read more about the role of the discount rate in the economy of the United States in Section 3.

CHECKPOINT *What is check clearing?*

How does the Federal Reserve regulate financial institutions?

The U.S. banking system operates as a fractional reserve banking system. Banks hold in reserve only a fraction of their funds. They hold back just enough to meet customers' daily needs. Banks lend out most of the rest of the money. They earn money by charging interest. Each financial institution that holds deposits for customers must report daily to the Fed about its reserves and activities. The Fed uses these reserves to control how much money is in use at any one time.

The Fed also checks banks from time to time to make sure they are obeying all the rules. Bank examiners can force banks to sell bad investments. Loans that will not be repaid must be declared as losses. Sometimes, examiners find that a bank is a problem bank. They may check it more often. Examiners may take the same action for banks that have low **net worth.** Net worth equals total assets minus total liabilities.

CHECKPOINT *What do banks do with most of their customers' deposits?*

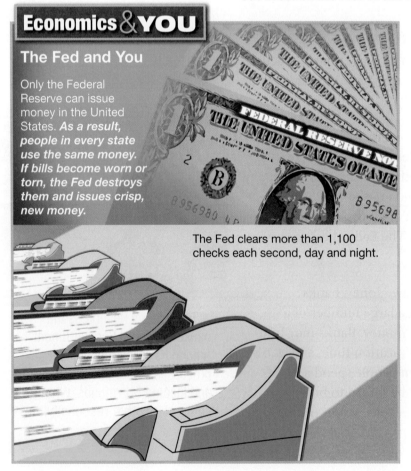

Economics & YOU

The Fed and You

Only the Federal Reserve can issue money in the United States. *As a result, people in every state use the same money. If bills become worn or torn, the Fed destroys them and issues crisp, new money.*

The Fed clears more than 1,100 checks each second, day and night.

How does the Fed regulate the money supply?

The best-known role of the Fed is controlling the U.S. money supply. The Fed tries to balance the flow of money and credit with the needs of the economy.

You will recall that economists and the Fed watch several indicators of the money supply. M1 measures only the money actually in use. M2 includes the funds counted in M1 plus money market accounts and savings accounts. The Fed's job is to look carefully at M1 and M2 and to figure out the likely demand for money.

The laws of supply and demand affect money, just as they affect everything else in the economy. Too much money in the economy leads to a general rise in prices, or inflation. Inflation means it will take more money to buy the same goods and services. Too little money in the economy leads to a general fall in prices, or deflation. The Fed tries to balance the money supply so inflation and deflation are controlled.

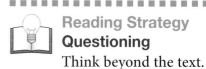

Reading Strategy
Questioning
Think beyond the text. Consider your own thoughts and experiences as you read.

In an ideal world, the Fed would change the money supply just to match the demand for money. If the Fed could do this, the country would experience very low rates of inflation and deflation. Ideally, the economy would remain at full employment.

The Fed uses its tools to stabilize the economy as well as it can. In the next section, you will read about the tools that the Fed can use to help the economy function at full employment without contributing to inflation.

✔ **CHECKPOINT** *What do M1 and M2 measure?*

SECTION 2 ASSESSMENT

Essential Questions Journal — To continue to build a response to the Essential Question, go to your **Essential Questions Journal.**

 **Guiding Question**

1. Use your completed flowchart to answer this question: What does the Federal Reserve do?

Key Terms and Main Ideas

Directions: On a sheet of paper, write the answer to each question. Use complete sentences.

2. How does check clearing work?

3. What is the difference between the federal funds rate and the discount rate?

4. How is net worth calculated?

5. How do the laws of supply and demand affect money?

Critical Thinking

6. **Analyze** What relationship does the Fed have with the Treasury Department?

7. **Evaluate** (a) How does the Federal Reserve control the amount of money in use? (b) Should state governments control the amount of money in use instead of the Federal Reserve?

Objectives

- **Describe** the process of money creation.
- **Explain** how the Federal Reserve carries out its monetary policy.
- **Explain** why the Fed favors one monetary policy tool over the others.

Guiding Question

How does the Federal Reserve control the amount of money in use?

Copy this chart and fill it in as you read.

Controlling the Money Supply		
Tools	**To increase it**	**To decrease it**
Reserve requirements		Raise requirements
Discount rate	Lower the rate	
Open market operations		

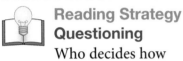

Reading Strategy
Questioning
Who decides how much money is in use?

money creation
the process of manufacturing currency and putting it into use

▶ **Economics and You** Suppose you have a checkbook that allows you to write as many checks as you wish for any amount you want. You do not need to worry about whether you have money in your account. The checks will always be cashed, no matter how much you spend. Of course, no person has an account like that. However, the Federal Reserve, through its monetary policy tools, comes close.

Principles in Action The Federal Reserve has the power to create money. It also has the power to cut the supply of money in use. The Fed controls the amount of money in use to keep the American economy steady. How does the Federal Reserve do this? You will learn how in this section.

What is money creation?

The U.S. Department of the Treasury manufactures money, in the form of currency. The Federal Reserve puts this money into use. How does this money get into the economy? The process is called **money creation.** It is carried out by the Fed and by banks all around the country. In Chapter 15, we discussed the multiplier effect of government spending. The multiplier effect in fiscal policy states that every one dollar change in fiscal policy creates a change greater than one dollar in the economy. The process of money creation works in much the same way.

How do banks create money?

Money creation does not mean the printing of new bills. Banks create money not by printing it but by doing their business.

For example, suppose that you take out a loan of $1,000.00. You decide to deposit the money in a new checking account. Once you have deposited the money, you have a balance of $1,000.00. Because checking accounts like yours are included in M1, the money supply has now increased by $1,000.00 This is where the process of money creation begins.

You already know banks earn money by charging interest on loans. Your bank will lend part of the $1,000.00 you deposited. The most a bank can lend is based on the **required reserve ratio** (RRR). This is the percentage of deposits banks are required to keep in reserve. The Fed sets the RRR to make sure banks will have enough money in case depositors want to take their money out.

Suppose in our example that the RRR is 10 percent. This means that of your $1,000.00, the bank is required to keep 10 percent, or $100.00, in reserve. It can lend out the remaining $900.00.

Let's say the bank lends that $900.00 to Elaine. She deposits it in her checking account. Elaine now has $900 she didn't have before. Elaine's $900.00 is now included in M1. You still have your $1,000.00 in your account. Your $1,000.00 deposit in the bank and the loan to Elaine have caused the money supply to increase. It now totals $1,900.00 ($1,000 + $900 = $1,900).

Now suppose Elaine uses the $900.00 to buy Josh's old car. Josh deposits the $900.00 from Elaine into his checking account. His bank keeps 10 percent of the deposit, or $90.00, as required reserves. It will lend the other $810.00 to its customers. The $810.00 is added to the money supply. This means the money supply has now increased by $2,710.00. This all was possible because of your first $1,000.00 deposit ($1,000 + $900 + $810 = $2,710). (See **Figure 16.2** on the next page.)

What is the money multiplier process?

This money creation process will continue until the amount the bank can loan out becomes very small. Economists use the **money multiplier formula** to figure out the total amount of new money that can be created and added to the money supply.

required reserve ratio
the percentage of deposits banks are required to keep in reserve

money multiplier formula
the formula economists use to figure out the total amount of new money that can be created and added to the money supply

When you deposit money in the bank, you are not only increasing your net worth, you are also increasing the money supply of the United States. **Explain how your deposit begins the process of money creation.** ▼

Fig. 16.2 Money Creation

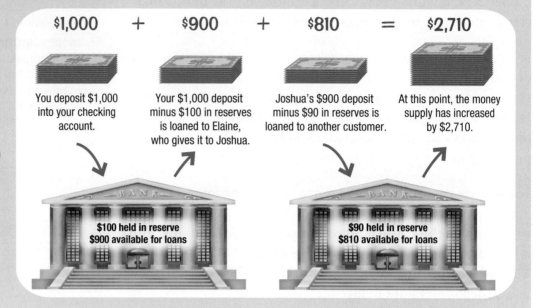

$1,000   + $900   + $810   = $2,710

You deposit $1,000 into your checking account.

Your $1,000 deposit minus $100 in reserves is loaned to Elaine, who gives it to Joshua.

Joshua's $900 deposit minus $90 in reserves is loaned to another customer.

At this point, the money supply has increased by $2,710.

$100 held in reserve
$900 available for loans

$90 held in reserve
$810 available for loans

CHART SKILLS

In this example of money creation, the money supply increases to $2,710 after four rounds.

1. In this example, what is the RRR?

2. Suppose Joshua deposited only $500 of Elaine's payment into his account. How much would the money supply increase then?

■ ■ ■ ■ ■ ■ ■ ■ ■ ■ ■ ■ ■ ■ ■ ■ ■ ■

excess reserves
reserves that are more than the required amounts

As of 2008, banks in the United States had no reserve requirement on the first $9.3 million of deposits. They were required to hold 3 percent in reserves on deposits between $9.3 million and $43.9 million. The reserve requirement for deposits of more than $43.9 million was set at 10 percent.

In the real world, people do not put all their cash into the banking system. The money multiplier process does not apply to this other money. Also, banks sometimes hold **excess reserves.** These are reserves of more than the required amounts. These excess reserves are a way for banks to make sure they will always be able to meet their customers' demands and the Fed's reserve requirements.

✓ **CHECKPOINT** *How do banks create money just through the business of making loans?*

How does adjusting reserve requirements affect the economy?

The Fed carries out its monetary policy in three ways. The first is by adjusting reserve requirements. Raising or lowering the reserve requirements allows the Fed to control the flow of money and credit. This is not the monetary policy tool the Fed likes to use the most. In fact, it is not used often.

The Fed might increase reserve requirements if it decides prices are rising too quickly. If it raises reserve requirements, the cost of borrowing money goes up. Banks have less money to lend. Fewer consumers and businesses can afford to borrow money. Money becomes scarce.

On the other hand, if the Fed wants to increase economic growth, it can lower the reserve requirements. The Fed might decide to do this because it believes the economy is slowing down and more people are out of work. When the Fed lowers reserve requirements, banks have more money to lend.

✔ **CHECKPOINT** *What happens when reserve requirements are raised or lowered?*

How does the discount rate affect the money supply?

A second way the Fed can affect the money supply is by changing the discount rate. It is the price banks must pay to borrow money from the Federal Reserve. Borrowing from the Fed is often referred to as "going to the discount window." The phrase comes from an earlier time when bankers came to the Federal Reserve Bank and borrowed money from a clerk. The clerk stood behind protective glass. Now, all borrowing is done through electronic transfers.

By raising or lowering the discount rate, the Fed influences the banks' ability to lend. If the discount rate is high, banks think twice before making loans. When the discount rate rises, the **prime rate** rises too. The prime rate is the interest rate banks charge their best customers. Smaller and less-important borrowers find loans even harder to get. The higher the cost of credit, the fewer people there are willing to pay for it. The Fed tends to raise the discount rate if it wants to slow down the economy.

Lowering the discount rate is a sign that the Fed thinks the economy is slowing down. Lowering the rate encourages banks to borrow more. This gives them more money to make loans to customers. It has the same effect as lowering the reserve requirements.

Today, the discount rate is used mainly to make sure enough money is available in the economy. For example, during a recession, there may not be enough money available in the banking system to supply loans businesses and individuals need. In that case, the banks can borrow at the discount rate from the Fed.

■ ■ ■ ■ ■ ■ ■ ■ ■ ■ ■ ■ ■ ■ ■ ■ ■ ■ ■ ■

prime rate
the interest rate banks charge their best customers

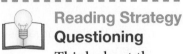
open market operations
the buying and selling of
government securities to alter the
supply of money

Today, the Fed mostly uses small changes to the federal funds rate as a way to carry out its monetary policy. The federal funds rate is the interest rate banks charge one another for loans.

In late 2008, the Fed lowered its federal funds rate to nearly zero. By doing so, it signaled that it was fighting a recession by making large amounts of money available to businesses and consumers.

The Fed keeps the discount rate above the federal funds rate. Banks usually borrow from one another at the federal funds rate. Only if they need extra reserves will they turn to the Federal Reserve and borrow at the higher discount rate.

✓ **CHECKPOINT** *What is the main tool the Federal Reserve uses to adjust the money supply?*

Why are open market operations the Fed's most important monetary policy tool?

Open market operations are the monetary policy tools most often used by the Federal Reserve. The term **open market operations** refers to the Fed's buying and selling of U.S. government securities. These securities are Treasury bills, notes, and bonds. Through its open market operations, the Fed adjusts the amount of money in use.

How does the Fed try to speed up the economy?

If the Federal Open Market Committee decides the economy needs to speed up, it will put more money into use. It does this by buying government securities from investment companies. When it buys government bonds and other securities, it pays for them by depositing money into banks and other financial institutions. Then the banks have more money to lend. In this way, funds enter the banking system. This starts the money creation process.

As more money and credit become available, companies are more likely to increase production and start new construction. The effect is to create economic growth. The hope is that people will spend more money. Trade will increase and so will the number of jobs. (See **Figure 16.3.**)

Fig. 16.3 Open Market Operations

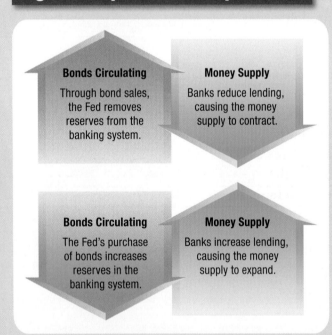

Bonds Circulating
Through bond sales, the Fed removes reserves from the banking system.

Money Supply
Banks reduce lending, causing the money supply to contract.

Bonds Circulating
The Fed's purchase of bonds increases reserves in the banking system.

Money Supply
Banks increase lending, causing the money supply to expand.

CHART SKILLS
Open market operations are the most often used monetary policy tools.
1. When the Fed sells government securities to bond dealers, does that increase or decrease the amount of money in circulation?
2. How do open market operations differ from reserve requirements?

Why might the Fed want to slow economic growth?

Sometimes the economy grows too fast. There is too much money in use, causing inflation. The Fed tries to cool off the economy by cutting back on the money supply. It does this by selling government securities to investment companies, receiving from them checks drawn on their accounts. After the Fed processes these checks, the money is taken out of circulation.

When the Fed sells bonds, consumers pay for the bonds by having money taken out of their banks. Banks still have to maintain their required reserve ratio. This means the banks have less money and credit to offer their customers. Borrowing becomes more expensive. The money multiplier process is working in the opposite direction. More money is taken out of the money supply than the original cost of the government securities that were bought.

Reducing the money supply may lessen inflation. It may also cause a drop in trade, slow economic growth, and put more people out of work.

 CHECKPOINT *Why are open market operations the Fed's preferred monetary policy tools?*

SECTION 3 ASSESSMENT

Essential Questions Journal To continue to build a response to the Essential Question, go to your **Essential Questions Journal.**

 Guiding Question

1. Use your completed chart to answer this question: How does the Federal Reserve control the amount of money in use?

Key Terms and Main Ideas

Directions: On a sheet of paper, write the answer to each question. Use complete sentences.

2. How does money creation work?

3. What is the required reserve ratio (RRR)?

4. Describe the money multiplier formula.

5. Why do some banks hold excess reserves?

Critical Thinking

6. **Explain** (a) How do banks create money? (b) How does the required reserve ratio affect the amount of money banks can lend?

7. **Make Inferences** When the Fed cuts interest rates, what effect does it expect to have on businesses and consumers?

Objectives

- **Explain** how monetary policy works.
- **Describe** the problem of timing in carrying out monetary policy.
- **Explain** why the Fed's monetary policy can involve predicting business cycles.
- **Contrast** two general approaches to monetary policy.

Guiding Question

How does monetary policy affect economic stability?

Copy this concept web and fill it in as you read.

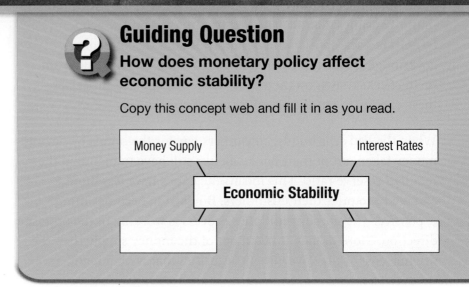

monetarism
the belief that the money supply is the most important factor in the entire economy

▶ **Economics and You** Have you ever asked a parent for money—maybe a raise in your allowance or cash to buy concert tickets? If so, you know that timing is everything. For example, if your parent has just paid a big bill for home or car repairs, you know that is the wrong time to ask for spending money.

Principles in Action As you will see in this section, timing is also important to the Fed. Good timing is needed for the Fed to be able to bring economic stability. Bad timing can destroy it. In How the Economy Works, you will see how the Fed deals with the many factors that can make its monetary policy succeed or fail.

How does monetary policy work?

Some economists are big believers in monetary policy. They believe in **monetarism.** This is the belief that the money supply is the most important factor in the entire economy. Monetary policy influences macroeconomics (the working of the economy as a whole).

Monetary policy changes the supply of money. The supply of money, in turn, affects interest rates. Interest rates affect the level of investment and spending in the economy.

▲ The interest rate is always the cost of money. If the money supply is higher, the interest rate will be lower. **What happens to the interest rate when the money supply is low?**

What is the relationship between the money supply and interest rates?

It is easy to see the cost of money if you are borrowing it. The cost of borrowing money—the price borrowers pay—is the interest rate. Even if you spend your own money, the interest rate still affects you because you are giving up interest by not saving or investing. Thus, the interest rate is always the cost of money.

The market for money is just like any other market. It is ruled by supply and demand. If the supply of money is higher, the price—the interest rate—is lower. If the supply of money is lower, the price is higher. In other words, when the money supply is high, interest rates are low. When the money supply is low, interest rates are high.

Innovators

Milton Friedman

As economic adviser to Presidents Nixon and Reagan, Milton Friedman argued that less government is better government. The policies he recommended have lowered income tax rates, helped control inflation, and decreased unemployment. His ideas are taught in most economics textbooks today. That was not always the case. For the first half of the twentieth century, the ideas of John Maynard Keynes dominated economic thought. Keynes believed government spending was the key to economic health, and government should emphasize fiscal policy in managing the economy.

In sharp contrast, Friedman argued that market forces must operate freely. In the view of Friedman and other monetarists, the government, through the Federal Reserve Board, must control the supply of money available to banks. Friedman argued that the most important power of the Fed is to grow or shrink the money supply by buying or selling government securities. The differences between supply siders such as Friedman and demand siders such as Keynes are some of the most important economic issues of our times.

Fast Facts

Milton Friedman (1912–2006)
Education: Ph.D., Columbia University, economics
Claim to Fame: Nobel Prize, Economic Science; Presidential Medal of Freedom

Reading Strategy
Questioning
Why is monetary policy an important factor in the economy?

What is the relationship between interest rates and spending?

In Chapter 12, you learned that interest rates are an important factor in spending in the economy. When interest rates are low, businesses usually increase investment spending. This is because it costs less to borrow at lower interest rates.

If the economy as a whole is slowing down, the Federal Reserve may want to stimulate, or expand, it. The Fed will follow an **easy money policy.** That is, it will increase the money supply. Having more money available to lend will lower interest rates. More firms are likely to increase investment spending. If the money supply becomes too large, the result may be overborrowing and overinvestment.

If the economy grows too fast, it may cause high inflation. In such a case, the Fed may introduce a **tight money policy.** That is, it will cut the money supply. The cut in the money supply pushes interest rates up. Higher interest rates make it more likely that firms will cut their investment spending. This brings real GDP down too.

✔ **CHECKPOINT** *How are monetary policy, money supply, and interest rates connected?*

Why is timing important?

Monetary policy, like fiscal policy, must be carefully timed. Bad timing can cause bad economic times to get worse instead of better. To see why, look at **Figure 16.4.**

The green curve in **Figure 16.4A** shows the business cycle. The Fed tries to keep the economy stabilized. In other words, it wants the economy to be well balanced and to hold steady over time. The

Fig. 16.4 Business Cycles and Stabilization Policy

GRAPH SKILLS

The timing of monetary policy measures can intensify the business cycle.

1. Which troughs are lower, business cycles with proper timing or ones with improper timing?

2. What are the effects of proper timing and improper timing?

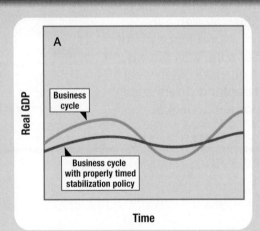

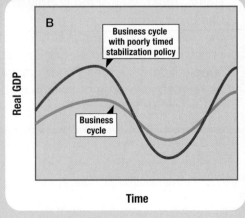

Fed's goal is to even out the highs and lows of the cycle. The Fed tries to lessen inflation in the peaks and to cut down the effects of recessions in the troughs. The red curve in **Figure 16.4A** shows the effects of good timing.

But what if the stabilization policy is badly timed? It can actually make the business cycle worse, not better. For example, suppose the Fed is slow to see that the economy is going into a recession, as shown by the green line in **Figure 16.4B**.

It takes time to do what is necessary to get the economy moving again. By the time the steps are taken to expand the money supply, the economy may already be coming out of the recession on its own. If the money supply grows at the same time the economy is expanding, the result could be high inflation. This would be bad timing. It would also be bad timing if the Fed waited too long before expanding the money supply. In this case, the economy may have slowed down so much that businesses do not want to borrow no matter what the interest rate is. As you can see, there are a couple of problems in the timing of macroeconomic policy. These are called policy lags, or delays.

What are inside lags?

The **inside lag** is the time it takes to carry out monetary policy. Such lags happen for two reasons. First, it takes time to see there is a problem. Economists use computer models to predict economic trends. Still, they cannot know for sure that the economy is headed into a new phase of the business cycle until it is already there. Experts may disagree. It can take up to a year before they agree that the country may be in serious economic trouble. Even if economists agree there is a problem, it takes time to bring about change. This also causes inside lags.

It is easier to change monetary policy than fiscal policy. Fiscal policy includes changes in government spending and taxation. Both Congress and the President need to take action. Congress must discuss and agree on new plans. The plans must then get the President's approval. This could take a lot of time.

In comparison, it is much easier to change monetary policy. The Federal Open Market Committee meets at least eight times each year to discuss monetary policy. Once it has decided that changes are needed, the FOMC can act almost right away. It can change the supply of money through discount rate changes or through open market operations.

■ ■

 Reading Strategy
Questioning
Ask yourself, "How does this information affect my life?"

■ ■

inside lag
the time needed for monetary policy to go into effect

Fig. 16.5 How the Economy Works

How does the **Fed** make **monetary policy?**

Monetary policy may be explained simply as the steps the Federal Reserve Board takes to control the business cycle and make sure that the economy remains prosperous and stable.

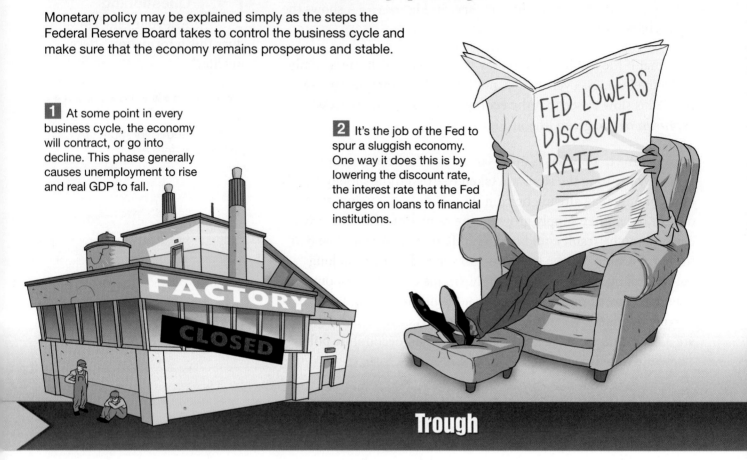

1 At some point in every business cycle, the economy will contract, or go into decline. This phase generally causes unemployment to rise and real GDP to fall.

2 It's the job of the Fed to spur a sluggish economy. One way it does this is by lowering the discount rate, the interest rate that the Fed charges on loans to financial institutions.

FED LOWERS DISCOUNT RATE

Trough

---

outside lag
the time it takes for monetary policy to have an effect

What are outside lags?

Changes in policy take time to become effective. This time period is known as the **outside lag.** It is also different for monetary and fiscal policy. For fiscal policy, the outside lag lasts as long as is needed for new government spending or tax policies to take effect. This time period can be relatively short. For example, to get the economy moving, Congress sometimes approves tax rebates. This returns some of the money taxpayers have sent to the government. The idea is that most people will spend their rebates and the economy will get a boost. One computer model showed that an increase in government spending would increase GDP after just six months.

Outside lags can be much longer for monetary policy. Firms take months or even years to make large investment plans. For example, deciding to invest in a new factory is a big decision. Thus, the effect of a change in interest rates may not affect investment spending completely for several years. Several studies suggest that it takes more than two years before the change of monetary policy is felt completely.

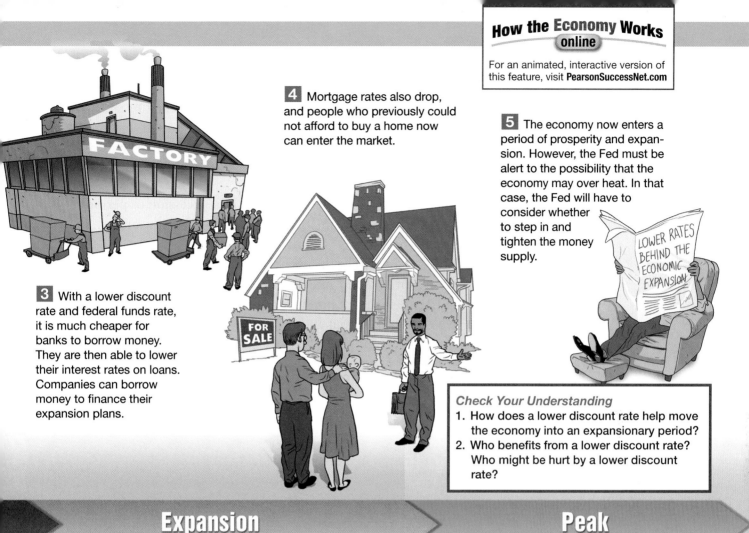

4 Mortgage rates also drop, and people who previously could not afford to buy a home now can enter the market.

5 The economy now enters a period of prosperity and expansion. However, the Fed must be alert to the possibility that the economy may over heat. In that case, the Fed will have to consider whether to step in and tighten the money supply.

3 With a lower discount rate and federal funds rate, it is much cheaper for banks to borrow money. They are then able to lower their interest rates on loans. Companies can borrow money to finance their expansion plans.

Check Your Understanding
1. How does a lower discount rate help move the economy into an expansionary period?
2. Who benefits from a lower discount rate? Who might be hurt by a lower discount rate?

LOWER RATES BEHIND THE ECONOMIC EXPANSION

Expansion   **Peak**

Given the longer inside lag for fiscal policy and the longer outside lag for monetary policy, it is hard to know which policy has the shorter total lag. It is often difficult for the President and Congress to agree on fiscal policy. Because of this, we rely more on the Fed to use monetary policy to stabilize the economy.

CHECKPOINT *What problem can result from expanding the money supply after the economy has already emerged from recession?*

Why is predicting business cycles important?

The Federal Reserve does not only react to current trends. It must also anticipate changes. An expansionary policy, if enacted at the wrong times, may push an economy into inflation, and reduces its positive impact. This is the chief danger of using an easy money policy to get the economy out of a recession.

An inflationary economy can be fixed by a tight money policy. Timing is again crucial. If the policy takes effect as the economy is already cooling off on its own, the tight money could turn a mild contraction into a full-blown recession.

The decision to use monetary policy must be based partly on what we expect from the business cycle. Some recessions do not last long. Periods of inflation may also be temporary. Because the timing of monetary policy is so important, in some cases it may be wiser to allow the business cycle to correct itself rather than risk making a change that is badly timed.

The key question is this: How long will the recession or period of inflation last? Economists do not agree on the answer to this question. The estimates for the United States economy range from two to six years. Since the economy may take quite a long time to recover on its own from an inflationary peak or a recessionary trough, there is time for policymakers to guide the economy back to stable levels of output and prices.

CHECKPOINT *How would the Fed most likely respond if it predicted that a recession would soon turn into an expansion?*

Fig. 16.6

▲ Ben Bernanke, chair of the Fed, uses one of his tools to make the economy stable. **What action does the cartoonist suggest Bernanke has taken?**

What are the two approaches to monetary policy?

In practice, the lags discussed here make monetary and fiscal policy difficult to apply. One approach favors a policy of taking swift action. This is called interventionist policy. The second approach is laissez faire. Laissez-faire economists believe the economy will self-adjust without taking any new actions. Economists who believe that recessions last for years usually favor intervention. They will recommend fiscal and monetary policies to move recovery along.

The rate of adjustment may also vary over time, making policy decisions even more difficult. This debate over which approach to take with monetary policy will probably never be settled to the satisfaction of all economists.

 CHECKPOINT *How do the two different approaches to monetary policy differ from each other?*

Essential Questions Journal
To continue to build a response to the Essential Question, go to your **Essential Questions Journal.**

SECTION 4 ASSESSMENT

Quick Write

With a partner, prepare a debate on monetary policy. One of you should write an argument for an interventionist approach, encouraging action. The other should write an argument for a laissez-faire approach, discouraging action. Use information from your textbook.

 Guiding Question

1. Use your completed concept web to answer this question: How does monetary policy affect economic stability?

Key Terms and Main Ideas

Directions: On a sheet of paper, write the answer to each question. Use complete sentences.

2. What do monetarists believe about the money supply?
3. Why would the Federal Reserve want to enact an easy money policy?
4. Why would it enact a tight money policy?
5. What are inside lags, and why do they occur?

Critical Thinking

6. **Explain** What are outside lags, and why do they occur?
7. **Draw Conclusions** (a) Why do business cycles make monetary policy difficult to time? (b) What could happen if monetary policy is enacted at the wrong time?

Section 1–The Federal Reserve System

- Congress created the Federal Reserve System, or Fed, after the Panic of 1907 caused problems for many banks.

- The Fed helped restore confidence in the banking system, but it failed to prevent the Great Depression.

- The United States is divided into twelve Federal Reserve districts. One Federal Reserve Bank is located in each district.

Section 2–Federal Reserve Functions

- The Fed serves as the banker for the U.S. government. It maintains a checking account and serves as a financial agent for the U.S. Treasury Department.

- The Fed provides services such as check-clearing, safe-guarding bank reserves, and lending reserves to banks.

- The Fed makes sure banks keep money in reserve and controls how much money is kept in circulation.

- The Fed tries to keep the money supply stable.

Section 3–Monetary Policy Tools

- The U.S. Department of the Treasury manufactures money in the form of currency. The process of money creation involves reserve requirements, the discount rate, and open market operations.

- The most used of the Fed's policy tools is open market operations. This refers to the Fed's buying and selling of U.S. securities.

Section 4–Monetary Policy and Macroeconomic Stabilization

- Monetary policy controls the supply of money. The supply of money affects interest rates.

- When monetary policy is timed well, it smooths out the business cycle. When it is not timed well, it can make the business cycle worse.

- The Fed must decide when to take action based on its expectations of the business cycle. Sometimes the economy corrects itself without any help from the Fed.

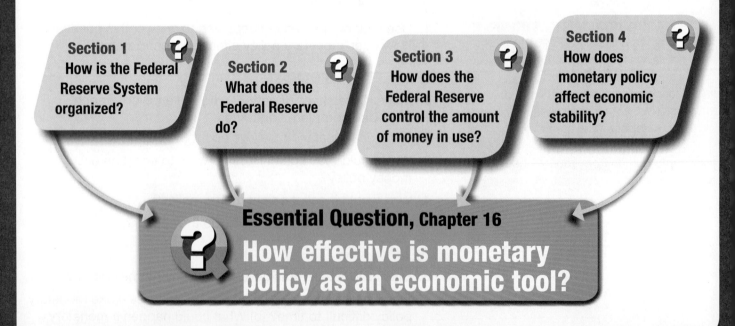

Section 1
How is the Federal Reserve System organized?

Section 2
What does the Federal Reserve do?

Section 3
How does the Federal Reserve control the amount of money in use?

Section 4
How does monetary policy affect economic stability?

Essential Question, Chapter 16
How effective is monetary policy as an economic tool?

DOCUMENT-BASED ASSESSMENT

Financial Markets, the Economic Outlook, and Monetary Policy

In 2008, the chair of the Fed, Ben Bernanke, spoke about the poor U.S. economy. In his speech, he discussed some of the reasons for the conditions. He also discussed some actions the Fed had taken to improve the situation.

"Since late last summer, the financial markets in the United States and in a number of other industrialized countries have been under considerable strain. . . .

. . . Perhaps an even greater challenge was posed by a sharp and protracted correction in the U.S. housing market, which followed a multiyear boom in housing construction and house prices. Indicating the depth of the decline in housing, according to the most recent available data, housing starts and new home sales have both fallen by about 50 percent from their respective peaks. . . .

Banks have become more restrictive in their lending to firms and households. More-expensive and less-available credit seems likely to impose a measure of financial restraint on economic growth. . . .

. . . The demand for housing seems to have weakened further, in part reflecting the ongoing problems in mortgage markets. In addition, a number of factors, including higher oil prices,

lower equity prices, and softening home values, seem likely to weigh on consumer spending as we move into 2008.

. . .The same increase in oil prices that may be a negative influence on growth is also lifting overall consumer prices and probably putting some upward pressure on core inflation measures as well. Last year, food prices also increased exceptionally rapidly by recent standards, further boosting overall consumer price inflation. . . . As you know, the [Federal Open Market] Committee cut its target for the federal funds rate . . . at the October and December meetings. In total, therefore, we have brought the funds rate down by a percentage point from its level just before financial strains emerged. The Federal Reserve took these actions to help offset the restraint imposed by the tightening of credit conditions and the weakening of the housing market. . . . "

Document-Based Questions

1. How much does Bernanke say house sales fell in 2008?
2. What will happen if credit is more expensive and less available?
3. Which factors might cause consumers to spend less?
4. How did the Fed try to improve the situation?
5. People pay close attention to the Fed chair's words. What effect do you think this speech might have had on the economy? Explain.

Source: "Financial Markets, the Economic Outlook, and Monetary Policy," Chairman Ben S. Bernanke, January 10, 2008, found at *http://www.federalreserve.gov/newsevents/speech/bernanke20080110a.htm.*

Directions: Write the answer to the following questions using complete sentences.

Section 1–The Federal Reserve System

1. Why was the Federal Reserve System created?

2. Why do the terms of the members of the Board of Governors of the Federal Reserve System start and end at different times?

3. What does the term *monetary policy* refer to?

4. Why was the Fed unable to prevent the Great Depression?

Section 2–Federal Reserve Functions

5. What are two services the Federal Reserve offers banks?

6. What are two regulations that the Federal Reserve places on banks?

7. Why does the Treasury Department auction off government bills, bonds, and notes?

8. What happens if the Fed finds that a bank has made too many risky investments?

Section 3–Monetary Policy Tools

9. What effect would a reduction in the required reserve ratio (RRR) have on banks?

10. Explain the money multiplier.

11. Why are open market operations the most commonly used actions taken by the Fed?

12. Describe one of the three tools the Fed uses to adjust the amount of money in the economy.

Section 4–Monetary Policy and Macroeconomic Stabilization

13. What is monetarism?

14. Why is it difficult to predict business cycles?

15. How is a tight money policy different from an easy money policy?

16. Why does monetary policy have long outside lags?

17. Do you think a laissez-faire approach or a hands-on approach works better? Explain.

 Exploring the Essential Question

18. What helps determine whether monetary policy should be used?

19. Why do the district Federal Reserve Banks work more as a team now than they did in the 1930s?

Essential Question Activity

20. Complete this activity to answer the Essential Question **How effective is monetary policy as an economic tool?**

Work in groups to gather information about the use of monetary policy to stimulate, downsize, or otherwise stabilize economies. Using the worksheet your teacher gives you or the electronic worksheet available at **PearsonSuccessNet.com,** gather the following information: (a) What steps did the United States take to prevent a recurrence of the Panic of 1907? (b) How did the Federal Reserve Board attempt to deal with the Great Depression? How successful was it? (c) How effective was the Federal Reserve Board in controlling the double-digit inflation of the late 1970s?

Essential Questions Journal
To continue to build a response to the Essential Question, go to your **Essential Questions Journal.**

Test-Taking Tip

When answering a set of questions about a drawing or diagram, you may find that the answer to one question may be useful in answering the others.

Study anytime, anywhere. Download these files today.

Economic Dictionary online
Vocabulary Support in English and Spanish

Audio Review online
Audio Study Guide in English and Spanish

Action Graph online
Animated Charts and Graphs

Visual Glossary online
Animated feature

How the Economy Works online
Animated feature

Download to your computer or mobile device at **PearsonSuccessNet.com**

Unit 6 Challenge

Essential Question, Unit 6

What is the proper role of government in the economy?

VIDEO
By Students For Students
For videos on Essential Questions,
go to *PearsonSuccessNet.com*

People have different opinions about what the government's role in the economy should be. Look at the opinions below, keeping in mind the Essential Question: What is the proper role of government in the economy?

" Government spending should be significantly reduced. It has grown far too quickly in recent years, and most of the new spending is for purposes other than homeland security and national defense. Combined with rising entitlement costs associated with the looming retirement of the baby-boom generation, America is heading in the wrong direction. To avoid becoming an uncompetitive European-style welfare state like France or Germany, the United States must adopt a responsible fiscal policy based on smaller government. "

—Daniel J. Mitchell, "The Impact of Government Spending on Economic Growth"

" Global competition, rising health costs, longer life spans with weaker pensions, less secure employment, and unprecedented inequalities of opportunity and wealth are calling for a much broader, more inclusive approach to helping all of us meet these challenges, one that taps government as well as market solutions…. We can wield the tools of government to build a more just society, one that preserves individualist values while ensuring that the prosperity we generate is equitably shared. "

—Jared Bernstein, *All Together Now: Common Sense for a Fair Economy*

Essential Question
Writing Activity

Consider the different views of economics expressed in the sources on this page and what you have learned about government and the economy. *Then write a well-constructed essay expressing your view of the economic role of the government.*

Essential Questions Journal

To respond to the unit Essential Question, go to your **Essential Questions Journal**.

Writing Guidelines

- Address all aspects of the Essential Question Writing Activity.
- Support the theme with relevant facts, examples, and details.
- Use a logical and clear plan of organization.
- Introduce the theme by establishing a framework that is beyond a simple restatement of the question and conclude with a summation of the theme.

For help in writing a Persuasive Essay, refer to the *Writing Skills Handbook* in the Reference section, page S-5.

Essential Question, Unit 7

How might scarcity divide our world or bring it together?

Chapter 18
Do the benefits of economic development outweigh the costs?

Chapter 17
Should free trade be encouraged?

Chapter 17 International Trade

Essential Question, Chapter 17

Should free trade be encouraged?

- **Section 1** Absolute and Comparative Advantage

- **Section 2** Trade Barriers and Agreements

- **Section 3** Measuring Trade

Economics on the go

To study anywhere, anytime, download these online resources at *PearsonSuccessNet.com* ➤

▶ **In 2007, goods worth nearly $4 trillion were shipped into and out of the United States.** People in other countries bought American goods worth about $1.6 trillion. Americans spent more than $2.3 trillion to buy goods produced in other countries. The chief trading partners of the United States are Canada, Mexico, China, Japan, the United Kingdom, and other countries in Europe.

This chapter discusses the importance of international trade. You will learn about trade barriers and agreements. You will also read about the balance of trade and how trade is measured.

Reading Strategy: Predicting

When reading, the best way to predict is to preview the text before you begin. Previewing helps you think about what might happen next. It also forces you to seek new information. In this way, previewing motivates you to continue learning.

Visual Glossary
online

Go to the Visual Glossary Online for an interactive review of **free trade.**

How the Economy Works
online

Go to How the Economy Works Online for an interactive lesson on the **benefits of trade.**

Action Graph
online

Go to Action Graph Online for animated versions of key charts and graphs.

Objectives

- **Evaluate** how the unequal distribution of resources affects trade.

- **Apply** the concepts of specialization and comparative advantage to explain why countries trade.

- **Summarize** the position of the United States in world trade.

- **Describe** the effects of trade on employment.

Reading Strategy
Predicting

Consider the section guiding question: Why do nations trade? Start by scanning the subheads and images in this section. Look for clues that will help you answer this question. As you read, don't forget to make your best guess about what you will learn next.

Guiding Question

Why do nations trade?

Copy this cause-and-effect chart and fill it in as you read.

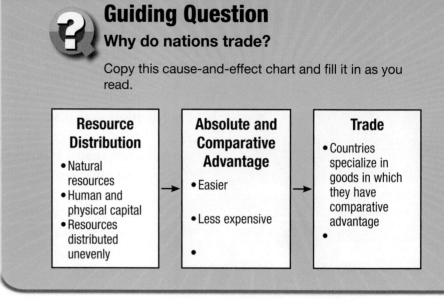

Resource Distribution
- Natural resources
- Human and physical capital
- Resources distributed unevenly

Absolute and Comparative Advantage
- Easier

- Less expensive

-

Trade
- Countries specialize in goods in which they have comparative advantage
-

▶ **Economics and You** Have you used a computer or bought a pair of jeans lately? There is a good chance the computer and the jeans were made outside the United States. Why do Americans buy so many goods from overseas? Wouldn't it make more sense for us to produce everything we need ourselves?

Principles in Action The answer to these questions lies in an economic idea you already know about: factors of production. In this chapter, you will look at how resources are unevenly distributed. This will help you better understand why nations trade. You will also learn how one Japanese entrepreneur built a business empire by selling electronics worldwide.

How are resources distributed?

Trade occurs because people want or need things they cannot get in their own country. Each country has different resources. Factors of production are the resources used to make goods and services. They include land (natural resources), labor, and capital (both human and physical).

Countries do not have the same natural resources. Some countries have a lot of oil. Others have none at all. Some have a climate that allows them to grow many different foods. Others have a harsh climate that allows them to grow only a few crops. It makes sense that the country with lots of oil would sell its oil. A country with a good climate for crops might exchange food to get the oil it needs. By trading, both countries benefit.

Human capital is different from labor. Labor refers to the size of a nation's workforce. Human capital is the knowledge and skills workers get through education and experience. One measure of human capital is literacy. This is the percentage of people who can read or write. A country with high literacy is likely to have an educated, skilled workforce.

Physical capital includes factories, machinery, and computers. It also includes roads and bridges. Countries with a well-developed transportation system and good physical capital are better able to produce and transport goods. **Figure 17.1** shows that the amount of resources differs greatly from one country to another. For example, the United Kingdom has less than one fifth the land area of Peru but nearly twice as many airports. So, at least in this area, the United Kingdom has more physical capital than Peru does.

✔ **CHECKPOINT** *What are the factors of production?*

How are trade and specialization linked?

Let's say there was no trade among countries. People could use only goods and services they produced. Some countries like the United States have a lot of resources. Even so, the resources might not be able to provide Americans with all the products they want.

Fig. 17.1 Resource Distribution, 2008

	India	Peru	United Kingdom	United States
Total area (sq km)	3,287,590	1,285,220	244,820	9,826,630
Farmable land	48.83%	2.88%	23.23%	18.01%
Natural resources	Coal, iron ore, manganese, mica, bauxite, titanium ore, chromite, natural gas, diamonds, petroleum, limestone, farmable land	Copper, silver, gold, petroleum, timber, fish, iron ore, coal, phosphate, potash, hydropower, natural gas	Coal, petroleum, natural gas, iron ore, lead, zinc, gold, tin, limestone, salt, clay, chalk, gypsum, potash, silica sand, slate, farmable land	Coal, copper, lead, molybdenum, phosphates, uranium, bauxite, gold, iron, mercury, nickel, potash, silver, tungsten, zinc, petroleum, natural gas, timber
Population	1.1 billion	29,180,900	60,943,912	303,824,640
Labor force	516.4 million	9.839 million	30.89 million	153.1 million
Literacy rate	61%	87.7%	99%	99%
Telephones (main lines and cellphones)	334.84 million	18.09 million	105.67 million	418.2 million
Airports	346	237	449	14,947

SOURCE: *CIA World Factbook, https://www.cia.gov/library/publications/the-world-factbook/index.html*

CHART SKILLS
Like all countries, the countries shown on this chart possess different natural, human, and physical resources.

1. Which resource on this list is most closely related to human capital?
2. Which nation has the most farmable land? Which has the largest percentage of farmable land?

Fig. 17.2 How the Economy Works

How do specialization and trade benefit nations?

Every nation in the world engages in trade—even nations that have the ability to be self-sufficient. One reason is that specialization increases the number of products available to all.

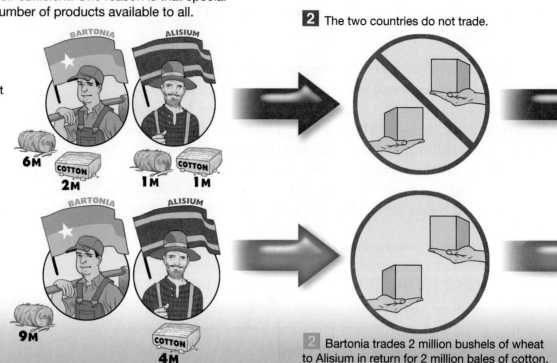

1 Left on its own, Bartonia can produce 6 million bushels of wheat and 2 million bales of cotton in a year. Alisium can produce 1 million bushels of wheat and 1 million bales of cotton.

BARTONIA
6M
COTTON
2M

ALISIUM
1M
COTTON
1M

1 Bartonia switches all of its cotton production to wheat. Alisium switches all of its resources to producing cotton.

BARTONIA
9M

ALISIUM
COTTON
4M

2 The two countries do not trade.

2 Bartonia trades 2 million bushels of wheat to Alisium in return for 2 million bales of cotton.

Production

Trade

export
goods or services that are sold to other countries

import
a good or service brought in from another country for sale

For example, maybe you enjoy bananas with your breakfast. Growing bananas in the United States would be difficult and costly. It makes more sense for the United States to grow the crops that grow best here. The United States can buy products, like bananas, that grow best elsewhere. Trade allows countries to specialize in producing certain goods and services. These can be traded for another country's specialties.

Every economy specializes in one or more areas. All economies import and export the goods and services they do not have or cannot produce. An **export** is a good or service sold to another country. An **import** is a good or service bought from another country. For example, some Arab countries have a lot of oil but few factories. Japan has little oil but many factories. Japan exports its goods and services to the Arab countries in return for their oil. It is better for countries to specialize in some products and to trade others. To see why, look at absolute and comparative advantage, discussed on the next two pages.

✓ **CHECKPOINT** *How does specialization create a need for trade?*

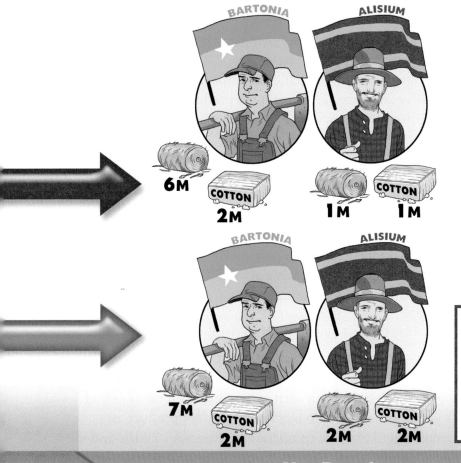

BARTONIA   ALISIUM

6M COTTON   COTTON
    2M   1M   1M

3 The two countries end up only with what each of them can produce.

BARTONIA   ALISIUM

7M COTTON   COTTON
    2M   2M   2M

3 Both countries end up with more than they would have if they had not specialized and traded.

Check Your Understanding
1. Which nation has a comparative advantage in producing wheat? Cotton?
2. What effect might trade between Bartonia and Alisium have on **(a)** production efficiency, **(b)** consumer choice, and **(c)** standard of living?

How the Economy Works
online

For an animated, interactive version of this feature, visit PearsonSuccessNet.com

Net Result

What is absolute advantage?

Suppose you are a 7-foot-tall basketball player. You certainly have an advantage over a 6-foot player. No matter how good the smaller player is, the taller player always has an advantage. It requires less effort for the tall player to make a basket. Such an advantage is called an absolute advantage.

In the same way, one country can have an absolute advantage over another country. A country has **absolute advantage** if it can produce something more easily and cheaply than a trading partner using the same resources. For example, the United States and Canada have an absolute advantage over Mexico in producing corn and wheat. Both the United States and Canada have a lot of rich, flat farmland. It is easy to use large farm machinery on that kind of land. No matter what Mexico does, it cannot overcome the absolute advantage that Canada and the United States have in growing corn and wheat.

absolute advantage
the ability to produce a product or service more easily and cheaply than trading partners that use similar resources

✔ **CHECKPOINT** *What is an absolute advantage?*

comparative advantage
the ability to produce a product or service at a lower cost and more efficiently than another country

law of comparative advantage
the idea that a nation is better off when it produces goods and services for which it has a comparative advantage

interdependence
the shared need of countries for resources, goods, services, labor, and knowledge that are supplied by other countries

What is comparative advantage?

Similarly, some countries have a comparative advantage over others. A country has a **comparative advantage** if it can produce a product or service more cheaply and efficiently than another country. Comparative advantage is the ability to produce an item at a lower opportunity cost. This is what is given up when a good is produced.

The United States and China both can make shoes and airplanes, but their resources are limited. If each decides to make shoes, they cannot make as many airplanes. Making shoes requires labor. Making airplanes requires technology that the United States has. It costs the United States more to make shoes. The United States can make airplanes faster and cheaper. The United States has a comparative advantage in making airplanes. It is better off making airplanes with the same resources.

What is the law of comparative advantage?

The **law of comparative advantage** says a country is better off when it provides goods and services for which it has a comparative advantage. Each nation can then use the money it earns selling those goods and services to buy those it cannot produce as efficiently. Based on their comparative advantages, China and the United States will trade with each other. The United States gets shoes, and China gets airplanes.

How is the world becoming more interdependent?

International trade has led to greater economic interdependence among nations. **Interdependence** is the shared need of countries for resources, goods, services, labor, and knowledge supplied by other countries. Countries increasingly depend on one another.

Changes in one country's economy affect other economies. A long dry period in Brazil would hurt its coffee growers. But coffee growers in Costa Rica may benefit. They might sell more coffee.

Interdependence also appears when one country's economy grows. Suppose Mexico's economy grows. This results in more jobs and higher wages for Mexican workers. With more money to spend, these workers are likely to demand more goods. Some of these goods may not be made in Mexico. When Mexicans buy those goods, they help the economies of Mexico's trade partners.

✓ **CHECKPOINT** *What determines which goods and services a country should specialize in producing?*

How does the United States rank in world trade?

The United States enjoys a comparative advantage in producing many goods and services. It is the world's second largest exporter, close behind Germany. One reason is the wide range of American exports, from soybeans to telecommunications equipment. Another reason is that the United States is a world leader in technology such as software, chemicals, and medical testing supplies.

The United States is also the world's leading exporter of services. These include education, computer and data processing, financial services, and medical care. Exports of services have grown rapidly over the last decade. The United States exports more to its neighbors, Canada and Mexico, than to any other nation.

The United States is also the world's top importer. In 2007, it imported more than $2.3 trillion in goods and services. That amount is more than the combined total of imports by Germany and China, the next two largest importers. You might be surprised to see how much the United States imports from China.

✔ **CHECKPOINT** *How does the United States rank in world exports and imports?*

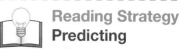

Reading Strategy
Predicting
    After reading this section, do you have a better idea of why your nation trades? How close were you to your original prediction?

Innovators

Akio Morita

"I knew we needed a weapon to break through to the U.S. market," remembered Akio Morita. The Japanese entrepreneur had cofounded a telecommunications company in 1946. But the firm found few buyers in Japan, a country still recovering from war. After visiting America, Morita dreamed of creating an original product for the booming U.S. economy. "It had to be something different," he realized.

The solution came quickly. Company engineers developed a radio that could fit into a person's pocket. Morita recognized that the radio could help establish a global brand name. He changed the corporate name to something easy to say and remember: Sony.

The Sony Corporation went on to create other innovative products, like the Walkman. Morita also formed multinational partnerships that led Sony into new areas such as entertainment and finance. By the time he died in 1999, he had built a global business empire.

Fast Facts

Akio Morita (1921–1999)
Education: Osaka Imperial University, 1944
Claim to Fame: Founder of Sony Corporation

How does trade affect employment?

Trade allows nations to specialize in producing a limited number of goods. It also gives consumers more goods from which to choose. However, specialization also strongly affects a nation's workers. The effect may be negative (loss of jobs), positive (creation of new jobs), or both.

In the last 20 years, international trade has affected the U.S. labor force. During the 1970s, for example, Japan developed new robot technologies. It had a highly skilled and productive workforce. This gave Japan a comparative advantage in making cars. As a result, Japanese cars became less expensive than many American cars. More consumers bought Japanese cars. American car companies lost business. They had to cut their workforces. Many American auto workers lost their jobs.

Businesses and governments often help laid-off workers. They try to retrain or relocate them. However, these two options are not easy, especially for older workers or workers with families. In some cases, retraining or relocation is not possible. Some workers may be forced to take lower-paying jobs or face long periods without jobs.

Job loss is not the only possible result of trade. If American exports grow, so will demand for workers to make those products. Workers who lost jobs can try to find work in those growing industries.

 CHECKPOINT *What could a worker do who loses a job because of international trade?*

SECTION 1 ASSESSMENT

 To continue to build a response to the Essential Question, go to your **Essential Questions Journal.**

 Guiding Question

1. Use your completed cause-and-effect chart to answer the following question: Why do nations trade?

Key Terms and Main Ideas

Directions: On a sheet of paper, write the answer to each question. Use complete sentences.

2. What effect does the distribution of resources have on trade?

3. How do absolute advantage and comparative advantage differ?

4. According to the law of comparative advantage, what goods should a nation choose to produce?

5. How does opportunity cost determine comparative advantage?

Critical Thinking

6. **Recognize Cause and Effect** What effect might the invention of an inexpensive sugar substitute have on the trade of other countries? Why?

7. **Analyze Information** Why do you think worker retraining and relocation may not be the best option for laid-off workers?

SECTION 2 Trade Barriers and Agreements

Objectives

- **Define** different types of trade barriers.
- **Analyze** the effects of trade barriers on economic activities.
- **Summarize** arguments in favor of protectionism.
- **Evaluate** the benefits and costs of participation in international trade agreements.
- **Explain** the role of multinationals in the global market.

Reading Strategy
Predicting

Think about the question asked at the beginning of this section: "Would you take part in a march to protest trade?" To answer this question, preview this section. Reflect on how much trade affects your life.

trade barrier
something that keeps a foreign product or service out of a country

Guiding Question

What are the arguments for and against trade barriers and agreements?

Copy this chart and fill it in as you read.

Arguments	
For trade barriers and against trade agreements	**Against trade barriers and for trade agreements**
• **Jobs:** Need barriers to protect jobs from going to other countries • **Industries:** Need time to become efficient producers • **Security:** • **Multinationals:**	• **Competition:** • **Prices:** Provide wider variety of less expensive goods • **Efficiency:** • **Risk:**

▶ **Economics and You** Would you take part in a march to protest trade? That's what more than 100,000 citizens of Costa Rica did in September 2007. They were protesting a trade agreement their government was about to sign with the United States. To the marchers, their government's plan of action was not just an economic idea. It was also an important force in their lives. The same is true for you—whether you know it or not.

Principles in Action Today, many people favor increased foreign trade, while others fear its effects. In this section, you will understand why some countries put up limits, or barriers, on trade. You will also see how trade policies can affect how much things cost.

What are trade barriers?

In Section 1, what happened when China used its comparative advantage to make shoes? American shoemakers had to lay off workers, and many shoemakers went out of business.

Businesses want to be protected from foreign competition. Workers want to keep their jobs even if other countries can make the same products more efficiently. Voters and businesses often pressure government leaders to create **trade barriers**. A trade barrier restricts, or limits, trade. It is a way of keeping a foreign product or service out of a country. Four common trade barriers are tariffs, quotas, sanctions, and embargoes.

customs duty
a tax on goods bought overseas and brought back to the U.S.

import quota
limit on the amount of a good that can enter a country

sanction
action a nation or group of nations takes to punish or put pressure on another nation that places limits on trade

embargo
the act of cutting off all trade with another country

How do tariffs limit trade?

A tariff is a tax on imported goods. Tariffs were the main source of money for the federal government until the early 1900s. As you can see from **Figure 17.3**, however, tariffs are much lower today.

If you have traveled overseas, you may have had to pay a tax on foreign goods you brought back to the United States. These taxes are called **customs duties.** They are another form of tariff.

How do quotas and voluntary export restraints limit trade?

Countries sometimes use import quotas to reduce the number of imports. **Import quotas** limit the number of certain goods that can enter the country. Suppose the United States had an import quota on computers made in China. A small quota allows a small number of Chinese computers into the country. This would allow American makers of computers to sell more, even though they might be more expensive.

Sometimes, foreign countries offer to limit the sale of their goods in another country. This is called a voluntary export restraint (VER). They do this to keep good relations and stay friendly. The exporting nations know that if they did not limit trade, bad feelings might arise. Using a VER also lowers the risk that the importing country will create trade barriers against the goods.

What are sanctions and embargoes?

Sanctions are limits on trade by one or several countries against some other country. Their purpose is to pressure a nation to change politically. Sometimes a country cuts off all trade with another country. This type of sanction is called an **embargo.** It is intended to cause economic strain on a country. Embargoes are usually more political than economic. For example, the United States has had an embargo against Cuba since the 1960s. It is meant to pressure Cuba's leaders to end their dictatorship.

✅ **CHECKPOINT** *How are voluntary export restraints and quotas different?*

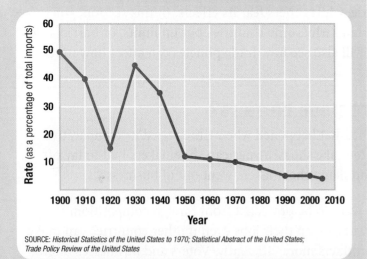

Fig. 17.3 Average Tariff Rates, 1900–2005

SOURCE: *Historical Statistics of the United States to 1970; Statistical Abstract of the United States; Trade Policy Review of the United States*

GRAPH SKILLS

One purpose of a high tariff is to shield American producers from foreign competition.

1. Describe the overall trend in tariff rates since 1930.
2. Why was it safer for American manufacturers to charge higher prices in 1900 than in 2000?

Why are trade wars harmful?

Trade barriers may backfire and cause conflict between countries. A country that puts tariffs on goods made in other countries often finds that tariffs are placed on goods it makes. The result is sometimes a **trade war**. This is a conflict between countries. Both are trying to improve their own import-export position. Trade wars often cause economic problems for both sides.

Probably the most damaging trade war in American history began during the Great Depression. In 1930, Congress passed the Smoot-Hawley Act. It raised average tariff rates on all imports to 50 percent. Congress hoped the tariff would protect American workers and businesses from foreign competition and help the economy recover.

The opposite effect took place, however. Other countries raised tariffs on American-made goods. The trade war decreased international trade and made the worldwide depression worse. Most economists blame the Smoot-Hawley Act for increasing the number of Americans who were out of work.

✔ **CHECKPOINT** *Why are trade wars harmful?*

What arguments favor restricting trade?

Limiting trade gives consumers fewer choices. Without trade, there would be no imports. All goods and services would have to be made within the country. The quality of life would go down. What arguments, then, support trade restrictions?

One argument is **protectionism.** Protectionism is the use of trade barriers to protect home industries from foreign competition. Those favoring protectionism use three main arguments to support their view.

The first argument is that restrictions help save jobs. This is because restrictions shelter workers in industries that foreign competition may hurt. For example, some argue that the United States needs restrictions because of cheap labor in other countries. Workers in some countries are paid much less than workers in the United States. This gives these countries a big advantage because they can sell their goods for much less. American producers argue that without trade restrictions, they will be forced out of business.

trade war
a conflict in which a country places tariffs on foreign goods and, in return, finds that tariffs are placed on its own goods

protectionism
the use of trade barriers in order to protect domestic industries from foreign competition

Reading Strategy
Predicting
After you have read the head on the left, stop and think. Why would a country or industry want to limit trade? Then read to see if you were correct.

infant industry
an industry that is in the early stages of development

free trade
the lowering or removal of protective tariffs and other trade barriers between nations

Another argument is that restrictions protect **infant industries.** These are new industries, which usually take time to develop fully. Developing countries sometimes limit trade on goods made elsewhere. They know their new industries cannot compete with industries in more developed countries. Early in American history, this argument was used to support protective tariffs for the young United States.

The third argument is that certain industries may require protection because their products are considered essential to defending the country. For example, oil is an important resource. In wartime, it is necessary to have a large supply. The United States uses about 20 million barrels of oil a day. Limiting imports might encourage U.S. companies to find substitutes for oil or to hunt for new sources within the United States. Oil produced in America could be saved for defense.

 CHECKPOINT *Why would one country want to restrict trade with another country?*

What arguments favor free trade?

Many people understand why their country restricts trade. The same people may oppose trade barriers raised by other countries. Every country wants to protect its industries and jobs. But people still want a variety of goods and services. The answer, according to some economists, is free trade. (See **Figure 17.4.**) **Free trade** is trade without barriers or regulation. Protective tariffs and other trade barriers between two or more nations are either lowered or removed.

Those who favor free trade say countries with the lowest trade barriers have the highest standard of living. Their people enjoy a higher quality of goods and a greater variety. They pay lower prices for goods.

No country allows completely free trade. The United States and Canada are two countries with few trade restrictions. Consumers in both countries benefit from the goods that flow in from many other countries.

What are the roots of free trade?

United States President Franklin D. Roosevelt believed that high tariffs were one of the causes of the Great Depression. He urged Congress to do something in order to increase trade. Congress passed the Reciprocal Trade Agreements Act of 1934. It gave the President the power to lower American tariffs by as much as 50 percent.

Fig. 17.4

"Take us to your leader...we've come to negotiate a free trade agreement with earth."

▲ Free trade agreements require a great deal of discussion between the parties involved.

The President can reduce a tariff if the trading partners reduce their tariffs on American goods by the same percentage. This is called a reciprocal trade agreement because both sides agree to the same terms of trade.

That law also allowed Congress to give most-favored-nation (MFN) status to a trading partner. All countries that are MFNs get the same lowered tariff that the United States gives another MFN. For example, suppose the United States agrees to lower the tariff on imported cheese from one MFN. The law requires it to lower the tariff for cheese for all other MFNs.

How was the World Trade Organization formed?

At the end of World War II, twenty-three countries signed the General Agreement on Tariffs and Trade (GATT). They thought the way to stop future wars was to promote international trade. Through a series of trade meetings since 1947, tariffs have been cut and other trade barriers reduced among these countries.

In 1994, after talking for nearly eight years, the then 123 nations of GATT reached a new agreement. They agreed to cut tariffs on capital goods and products like prescription drugs and computer chips. Import quotas on textiles and clothing would end over a period of time. Fewer restrictions would be placed on farm products. Trade barriers on such services as accounting would be loosened. All countries that signed the agreement said they would protect patents, copyrights, and trademarks. Those countries created the World Trade Organization (WTO) in 1995. It enforced the agreement and eventually replaced GATT.

Today, the World Trade Organization also acts as a referee. It enforces the rules agreed on by the member countries. The WTO settled the beef war and the steel tariff disputes between the United States and the European Union (EU).

What is the European Union?

The European Union is an organization that links European countries both economically and politically. It is an example of a **regional trade organization.** These organizations work toward lowering or getting rid of trade barriers among their members. The EU grew out of a customs union created after World War II in some western European countries. Now this organization is the largest trading union in the world. By 2008, the EU included twenty-seven countries—almost all Europe. This includes Poland, Hungary, Romania, and other nations the Soviet Union once controlled.

regional trade organization
an organization that works toward lowering or removing trade barriers among its members, which are located in the same region

free-trade zone
a region where a group of countries agrees to reduce or end trade barriers

What is NAFTA?

Other nations have created a **free-trade zone**. A free-trade zone is a region where a group of countries agrees to reduce or end trade barriers. An example is the North American Free Trade Agreement (NAFTA). It created a free-trade zone linking the United States, Canada, and Mexico. This agreement took effect in 1994. The three countries removed many trade barriers and pledged to phase out the rest. Now products from the three members of NAFTA cross international borders as easily as they cross state borders. The agreement has made it easier for each country to sell its goods and services. Exports and imports have increased for all three NAFTA members. Investments also have increased, especially in Mexico. Mexico and Canada have become the two biggest trading partners of the United States.

Some people argue that NAFTA has resulted in a loss of American jobs and damage to the environment. In 2004, the Congressional Research Service reviewed the effects of NAFTA. It found that NAFTA had little effect on the number of jobs in the United States and only a small effect on wages.

What other regional trade organizations exist?

In 2003, the U.S. government reached a free-trade agreement with five nations of Central America. At the time, the deal was called the Central American Free Trade Agreement (CAFTA). The next year, when the Dominican Republic joined the pact, the name was changed to DR-CAFTA. Costa Rica became a member of DR-CAFTA in late 2007.

About 100 regional trading organizations operate in the world today. They include the following, as shown in **Figure 17.5:**

- *APEC* The Asia-Pacific Economic Cooperation includes twenty-one countries that border the Pacific Ocean, including the United States. They have signed a nonbinding agreement to reduce trade barriers.
- *MERCOSUR* The Southern Common Market is similar to the EU in its goals. Its members are Brazil, Paraguay, Uruguay, Argentina, and Venezuela.
- *CARICOM* The Caribbean Community and Common Market includes countries from South America and the Caribbean.
- *ASEAN* The ten-member Association of Southeast Asian Nations wants to establish a free-trade zone similar to the EU.

✔ **CHECKPOINT** *Which countries are involved in NAFTA?*

Why are some countries concerned about multinational corporations?

A multinational is a large corporation that sells goods and services throughout the world. For example, an automobile company might design its cars in the United States. It might import parts from Asia. The cars themselves might be put together in an assembly plant in Canada. Even if you buy the car from an American company, it is not a purely American product.

Many goods besides cars are produced globally. Some brands of athletic shoes are designed in the United States but are made in East Asia. Some personal computers are designed in the United States with parts from the United States, but the computers are assembled overseas.

Fig. 17.5 Major Trade Organization Members

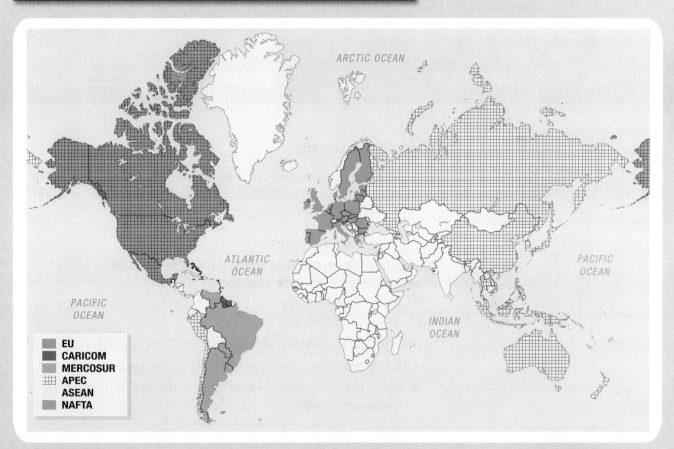

Legend:
- EU
- CARICOM
- MERCOSUR
- APEC
- ASEAN
- NAFTA

MAP SKILLS

Many countries are members of regional trade organizations.

1. To which two trade organizations does the United States belong?

2. What do the nations belonging to APEC have in common? Why do you think they would be interested in signing a trade agreement?

Action Graph online

For an animated version of this map, visit **PearsonSuccessNet.com**

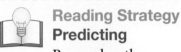

Reading Strategy
Predicting
Remember the prediction you made at the beginning of this section. Looking back, did you fully understand how trade influences parts of your life? What can you change or add to your previous understanding of trade?

Building factories in a foreign country benefits both the host nation and the multinational. By locating in another country, the corporation avoids some shipping fees and tariffs. It may also benefit from cheaper labor. The host nation gains jobs, of course, and tax revenue.

On the other hand, host nations worry about the effects of multinationals on their countries. In a small country with a less developed economy, multinationals can gain too much political power. Host nations also worry that multinationals could drive out local industries. They fear that multinationals will take advantage of the workers. To protect their industries, some host nations have created rules for multinationals. They require that the multinationals limit the percentage of their products that can be sold locally.

 CHECKPOINT *Why are some nations concerned about having multinational corporations in their countries?*

SECTION 2 ASSESSMENT

Essential Questions Journal
To continue to build a response to the Essential Question, go to your **Essential Questions Journal.**

Quick Write

Suppose you were a member of Congress considering a bill that would place higher tariffs on imported video game systems. Write a brief speech you would deliver for or against the bill. Base your argument on economic principles.

 Guiding Question

1. Use your completed chart to answer the following question: What are the arguments for and against trade barriers and agreements?

Key Terms and Main Ideas

Directions: On a sheet of paper, write the answer to each question. Use complete sentences.

2. Describe two ways trade barriers or free trade can affect you as a consumer.
3. What is the difference between an import quota and a tariff?
4. What are three arguments in favor of protectionism?
5. What happens when two countries decide to sign a free-trade agreement?

Critical Thinking

6. **Analyze Information** What are the advantages of international trade agreements? What might be some disadvantages?
7. **Synthesize Information** Give three examples from this section to show how trading partnerships and relationships change over time.

Objectives

- **Explain** how exchange rates change.
- **Describe** the effect of various exchange rate systems.
- **Define** balance of trade and balance of payments.
- **Analyze** the causes and effects of the U.S. trade deficit.

Guiding Question

How do exchange rates affect international trade?

Copy this chart and fill it in as you read.

Effect of Exchange Rates on Trade	
Effect of Appreciating Currency	**Effect of Depreciating Currency**
• Value of currency rises, making goods produced in a country more expensive. • Exports go down. •	• Value of currency falls, making goods produced in a country cheaper to other nations. •

▶ Economics and You It's happened to everyone. You buy something in a store. The clerk hands you your change. When you get outside, you notice something funny about one of the quarters. You've been given a Canadian quarter.

Maybe you feel cheated. But should you? Is this Canadian quarter worth less than a U.S. quarter—or more? How would you find out? These questions may seem unimportant when you're dealing with just a single quarter. But if you were dealing with hundreds or thousands of dollars, the questions might be very important.

Principles in Action The difference in value between an American dollar and a Canadian dollar changes daily. You will see how these changes have a huge effect on imports and exports. In the Economics & You feature, you will also see how changes in the value of the dollar can directly affect what you spend.

Why are foreign exchange rates necessary?

There are hundreds of countries in the world. Each one has its own government. Most have their own form of money, a national currency. Just as dollars are used everywhere in the United States, other countries use national currencies within their borders. International trade is more complex than buying and selling within one country. To trade, countries need to determine how much their currency is worth compared to other currencies.

■■■■■■■■■■■■■■■■

exchange rate
the value of a nation's currency in relation to a foreign currency

appreciation
a "strengthening" or increase in the value of a currency

The value of a nation's currency in relation to a foreign currency is called the **exchange rate.** The exchange rate lets you convert prices from one currency to prices in another currency.

Exchange rates are listed in major newspapers and on the Internet. **Figure 17.6** shows a sample table of exchange rates. If you read down the first column, you will see what one U.S. dollar can be exchanged for: a little more than one Australian dollar (1.12), less than one euro (.70), and so forth. An exchange rate table shows what one U.S. dollar is worth on one particular day. Remember, the rates change daily or even hourly.

What is the difference between a strong currency and a weak currency?

You have probably heard newscasters talk about a strong or weak dollar. What do these terms mean? Which one is good news for the economy, and which one is bad news?

An increase in the value of a currency is called **appreciation.** When a currency appreciates, it becomes "stronger." Consider the exchange rate between the dollar and the Japanese yen. Suppose it increases from 100 yen per dollar to 120 yen per dollar. This means each dollar can buy more yen. Because the dollar increased in value, we say the dollar has appreciated against the yen.

Fig. 17.6 Sample Foreign Exchange Rates

	U.S. $	Aust. $	U.K. £ (pound)	Canadian $	Japanese ¥ (yen)	€uro	Mexican Peso	Chinese Yuan
U.S. $	1	.88	2.04	1.00	.008	1.42	.09	.13
Australian $	1.12	1	2.30	1.13	.009	1.60	.10	.15
U.K. £ (pound)	.49	.43	1	.49	.004	.69	.04	.07
Canadian $	.99	.88	2.03	1	.008	1.42	.09	.13
Japanese ¥ (yen)	114.97	101.81	234.41	115.44	1	163.47	10.52	15.34
€uro	.70	.62	1.43	.71	.006	1	.06	.09
Mexican Peso	10.93	9.68	22.29	10.98	.095	15.54	1	1.46
Chinese Yuan	7.449	6.63	15.28	7.52	.065	10.65	.69	1

SOURCE: *X-rates.com* accessed on Friday, September 28, 2007
Note: These data are highly time sensitive and can change hourly.

CHART SKILLS

This chart shows exchange rates on a single day. Read down the first column of the chart to find out what one U.S. dollar was worth in various foreign currencies. Read across the top row to find out how much a selected foreign currency was worth in U.S. dollars.

1. On this day, how much was one U.S. dollar worth in Chinese yuan? Canadian dollars?
2. How much was a euro worth in pesos?

People in Japan will have to spend more yen to buy a dollar's worth of goods from the United States. Americans who travel to Japan can buy more goods and services for the same amount of dollars than they could before the dollar appreciated.

When a nation's currency appreciates, its products become more expensive in other countries. For example, a strong dollar makes American goods and services more expensive for the Japanese. Japan will therefore probably import fewer products from the United States. As a result, total U.S. exports to Japan will probably go down. In contrast, a strong dollar makes foreign products less expensive for U.S. consumers. American consumers are likely to buy more imported goods.

A decrease in the value of a currency is called **depreciation.** You might also hear depreciation referred to as "weakening." Suppose the exchange rate fell to 80 yen per dollar. You would get fewer yen for each dollar. In other words, the dollar has depreciated against the yen.

When a nation's currency depreciates, its products become cheaper to other nations. A depreciated, or weak, dollar means American-made goods are now less expensive to foreign consumers. A weak dollar usually results in increased exports. At the same time, other nations' products become more expensive. If the dollar depreciates, consumers in the United States will probably buy fewer imported goods.

What is the foreign exchange market?

When a company in the United States sells computers in Japan, that company is paid in yen. It must, however, pay dollars to its workers and suppliers in the United States. The company must change its yen into dollars. This exchange takes place on the foreign exchange market. International trade would not be possible without this market.

The **foreign exchange market** is the market for buying and selling national currencies. It is made up of about 2,000 banks and other financial institutions. They make it easier to buy and sell foreign currencies. These banks are located in big cities worldwide. They are closely linked to one another by telephones and computers.

✔ **CHECKPOINT** *What are the likely effects of the U.S. dollar becoming stronger?*

depreciation
a "weakening" or decrease in the value of a currency

foreign exchange market
the market for buying and selling national currencies

fixed exchange-rate system
a system in which governments try to keep the values of their currencies constant

flexible exchange-rate system
a system in which changes in the exchange rate are determined by supply and demand

What is the fixed exchange-rate system?

One system used in exchanging foreign currencies is called the **fixed exchange-rate system.** In this system, the currency of one nation is constant against that of another.

In a typical fixed exchange-rate system, one country has a strong and dependable currency. Other countries fix, or peg, their exchange rates to this currency. Let's say the economy of one country grows much faster than another. Then, the countries would probably agree to change the exchange rate.

This system was introduced at the Bretton Woods Conference in 1944. The conference brought together 44 countries that had fought together in World War II. They agreed to peg their currency to the U.S. dollar. To make the new system work, the conference set up the International Monetary Fund (IMF). Today, the IMF promotes international monetary cooperation, currency stabilization, and trade.

What happened to the fixed exchange-rate system?

The fixed exchange-rate system was used from 1944 to 1971. It worked well as long as international trade patterns stayed the same. By the late 1960s, worldwide trade was growing and changing rapidly. At the same time, the war in Vietnam was causing inflation in the United States.

What is the flexible exchange-rate system?

In 1971, the Netherlands and West Germany abandoned the fixed exchange-rate system. Other countries followed these two. By 1973, even the United States had adopted a system based on flexible exchange rates. Under a **flexible exchange-rate system,** the exchange rate is not fixed. Instead, it is determined by supply and demand.

Today, the countries of the world use a mixture of fixed and flexible exchange rates. Most major currencies—including the U.S. dollar and the Japanese yen—use the flexible exchange-rate system. This system accounts for the day-to-day changes in currency values you read about earlier in this section.

✓ **CHECKPOINT** *How are exchange rates set in a fixed exchange-rate system?*

Economics & YOU

The Value of the Dollar

A weak dollar makes it more expensive to visit another country whose currency is stronger. *Your family may decide to postpone its vacation until the dollar is stronger.*

A weak dollar means goods produced in foreign countries and sold in the United States become more expensive. *Even if you do not travel, the exchange rate affects your purchasing power.*

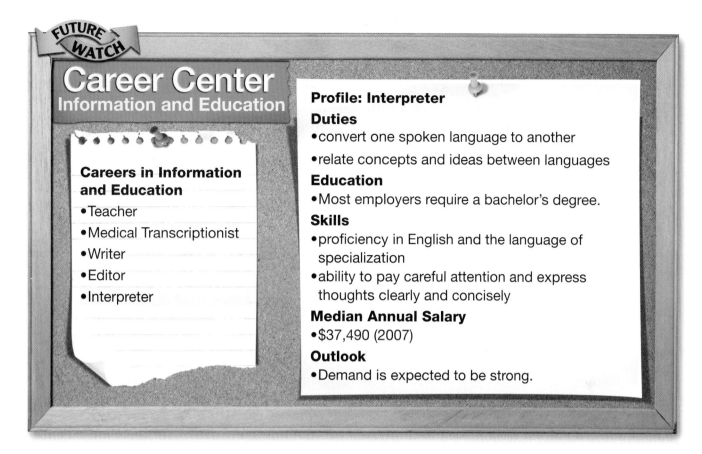

Career Center
Information and Education

Careers in Information and Education
- Teacher
- Medical Transcriptionist
- Writer
- Editor
- Interpreter

Profile: Interpreter

Duties
- convert one spoken language to another
- relate concepts and ideas between languages

Education
- Most employers require a bachelor's degree.

Skills
- proficiency in English and the language of specialization
- ability to pay careful attention and express thoughts clearly and concisely

Median Annual Salary
- $37,490 (2007)

Outlook
- Demand is expected to be strong.

What are the balance of trade and balance of payments?

The difference between the value of a country's imports and exports is its **balance of trade.** A country that sells more than it buys from other countries has a positive balance of trade. This is known as a **trade surplus.** A country that buys more than it sells has a negative balance of trade, or a **trade deficit.**

Nations seek to have balanced trade. That is, they hope the value of imports roughly equals the value of exports. By balancing trade, a nation protects the value of its currency. Some countries have a trade deficit over an extended period of time. One result is that the value of its currency falls.

One way of correcting a trade deficit is to limit imports. Another way is to increase the number or value of exports. Trading partners may react by raising tariffs.

Economists look at the balance of payments to get a more complete picture of international trade. **Balance of payments** is the value of all money exchanged between a country's economy and the rest of the world. Imports and exports are the largest part of a nation's overall balance of payments.

balance of trade
the difference between the value of a country's exports and imports

trade surplus
a favorable balance of trade that occurs when a country exports more than it imports

trade deficit
an unfavorable balance of trade that occurs when a country imports more than it exports

balance of payments
the value of all money exchanged between a country's economy and the rest of the world

Reading Strategy
Predicting
Was your predicted answer to the guiding question accurate? What details would make your prediction more specific?

✔ **CHECKPOINT** *What causes a trade surplus?*

What causes the U.S. trade deficit?

Exports from the United States in 2007 were valued at more than $1.6 trillion. This is a huge sum. At the same time, it imported goods worth more than $2.3 trillion. As a result, the United States has a large trade deficit. (See **Figure 17.7.**)

Until the mid-1970s, the United States had a positive balance of trade. The U.S. trade deficit began in the late 1970s. The Organization of Petroleum Exporting Countries (OPEC) raised the price of oil. The United States imports most of the oil it uses. Thus, it had to spend a lot more money on this important resource.

The United States suffered record trade deficits in 1986 and 1987. In the early 1990s, the trade deficit began to fall. By the late 1990s, however, the deficit had skyrocketed to record levels. One reason was a new increase in oil prices. Another reason was that in the booming economy, Americans bought a lot of imported goods.

The trade deficit totaled more than $711 billion in 2007. The largest trade deficits were with China, Japan, Germany, Canada, Mexico, and oil-exporting nations such as Venezuela. Imports of oil made up more than a third of the deficit.

What are the effects of the U.S. trade deficit?

When Americans import more than they export, more dollars end up in the hands of foreigners. Those foreigners can then use these extra dollars to buy American land, stocks, bonds, and other assets. Because of America's trade deficits, people from other countries now own a large part of the U.S. economy. Many Americans are afraid this threatens America's independence and safety.

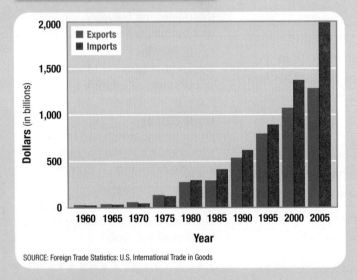

Fig. 17.7 U.S. Balance of Trade, 1960–2005

- ■ Exports
- ■ Imports

SOURCE: Foreign Trade Statistics: U.S. International Trade in Goods

GRAPH SKILLS

Although the United States has a large trade deficit today, that was not always true.

1. What was the difference between imports and exports in 1960? In 1980? In 2005?
2. During what year shown here did the United States begin to show a trade deficit?

For an animated version of this graph, visit **PearsonSuccessNet.com**

Some economists worry that foreign countries might not always support the trade deficit. They worry that the levels of U.S. imports keep rising and America's foreign debt is growing. This might cause overseas investors to think twice before buying American assets. If this happened, the flow of money into the United States would slow down. In 2000, a government group studied the deficit. It said having a large trade deficit was bad. It also said the United States could not continue to have such large deficits in the future.

Can a balance of trade be restored?

One thing the government could do to lower the trade deficit is to cut the exchange rate. As you saw, when the dollar is weak, American products become cheaper to buy for foreigners. Imports from other countries become more expensive. As a result, exports rise and imports fall. Another thing the government could do to reduce the trade deficit is cut back spending.

Individuals could help cut the deficit by choosing to buy fewer foreign goods, even though American goods would cost more. American companies could try to sell more products overseas. None of these choices is easy, but they would result in fewer dollars ending up in foreign hands.

 CHECKPOINT *What has been the trend in the U.S. balance of trade in recent decades?*

SECTION 3 ASSESSMENT

Essential Questions Journal — To continue to build a response to the Essential Question, go to your **Essential Questions Journal.**

Guiding Question

1. Use your completed chart to answer this question: How do exchange rates affect international trade?

Key Terms and Main Ideas

Directions: On a sheet of paper, write the answer to each question. Use complete sentences.

2. What is an exchange rate?

3. What effect do appreciation and depreciation have on the price of goods?

4. What happens to currencies in the foreign exchange market?

5. How do a fixed exchange-rate system and a flexible exchange-rate system differ?

Critical Thinking

6. **Recognize Cause and Effect** Explain how each of the following Americans might react to a rise in the value of the U.S. dollar and why: (a) a farmer who exports crops, (b) a consumer shopping for a new car, (c) the owner of a store selling imported food.

7. **Recognize Cause and Effect** Explain how each of the following has contributed to the growth of the U.S. trade deficit: (a) consumer demand, (b) dependence on foreign oil, (c) exchange rates.

Section 1–Absolute and Comparative Advantage

■ A country's natural resources, climate, and geographic location help determine which goods and services it produces. Resources are distributed unequally.

■ Trade allows countries to specialize in producing a limited number of goods. At the same time, trade allows a country to consume a greater variety of goods.

■ Absolute advantage lets one country produce something more cheaply than another country using the same resources. Comparative advantage lets one country produce something more cheaply or efficiently.

■ International trade has led to greater interdependence. It has also positively and negatively affected the U.S. economy.

Section 2–Trade Barriers and Agreements

■ Trade barriers prevent foreign products or services from freely entering a country's territory. Barriers include tariffs, quotas, sanctions, and embargoes.

■ Trade wars often cause economic trouble for the countries involved.

■ Some people favor restricting trade. Others favor free trade. Free-trade organizations include the EU, NAFTA, and about 100 others.

■ Multinational corporations can lower the price of goods. However, less developed countries worry that multinationals might gain too much political power.

Section 3–Measuring Trade

■ The value of a country's currency in relation to a foreign currency is called the exchange rate. Fixed and flexible exchange-rate systems are two ways countries exchange currency.

■ Exchange rates can affect a country's balance of trade. This is the relationship between the value of its exports and the value of its imports.

■ Until the 1970s, the United States had a positive balance of trade. By 2007, the trade deficit was more than $711 billion. Some people worry that the situation will be negative for the United States.

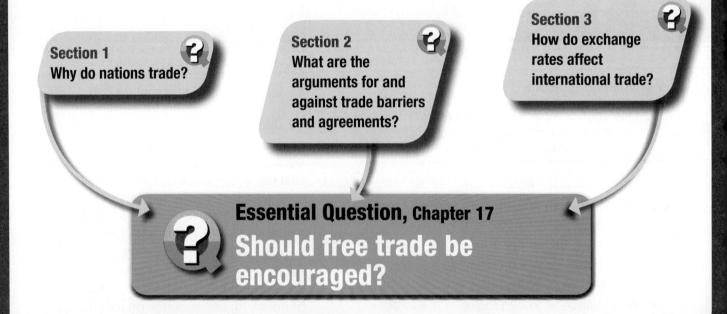

Section 1
Why do nations trade?

Section 2
What are the arguments for and against trade barriers and agreements?

Section 3
How do exchange rates affect international trade?

Essential Question, Chapter 17
Should free trade be encouraged?

Fair Trade Myths

As awareness of fair trade grows, so do many wrong ideas about it. The following are some popular myths about fair trade and the realities behind them.

"**Myth:** Fair trade is about paying developed world wages in the developing world.
Reality: Fair wages are determined by a number of factors, including the amount of time, skill, and effort involved in production, minimum and living wages in the local context, the purchasing power in a community or area, and other costs of living in the local context.

Myth: Fair trade siphons off American jobs to other countries.
Reality: Fair trade seeks to change the lives of the poorest of the poor who frequently lack alternative sources of income. As North American fair trade organizations grow, they employ more and more individuals in their communities. Most fair trade craft products stem from cultures and traditions which are not represented in North American production. Most fair trade commodities, such as coffee and cocoa, do not have North American-based alternatives.

Myth: Fair trade is a form of charity.
Reality: Fair trade promotes positive and long-term change through trade-based relationships which seek to empower producers to meet their own needs. Its success depends on independent, successfully-run organizations and businesses—not on handouts. While many fair trade organizations support charitable projects on top of their work in trade, the exchange of goods remains the key element of their work.

Myth: Fair trade results in more expensive goods for the consumer.
Reality: Most fair trade products are competitively priced in relation to their conventional counterparts. Fair trade organizations work directly with producers, cutting out exploitative middlemen, so they can keep products affordable for consumers and return a greater percentage of the price to the producers.

Myth: Fair trade refers only to coffee.
Reality: Fair trade encompasses a wide variety of agricultural and handcrafted goods, including baskets, clothing, cotton, footballs, furniture, jewelry, rice, toys, and wine. While coffee was the first agricultural product to be certified fair trade in 1988, fair trade handicrafts have been on sale since 1946."

Document-Based Questions

1. What is fair trade?
2. How is a fair wage determined?
3. Who benefits from fair trade practices?
4. How does fair trade bring about change?
5. How do fair trade organizations keep their products affordable?

Directions: Write the answer using complete sentences.

Section 1–Absolute and Comparative Advantage

1. What is one way to measure a country's human capital?

2. What are imports and exports?

3. What is the ability to produce something more easily and cheaply than a trading partner can?

4. What is the law of comparative advantage?

5. What is it called when a change in one country's economy affects other countries' economies?

6. Why do you think the United States leads the world in imports and exports?

7. Do you think specialization is good or bad for countries?

Section 2–Trade Barriers and Agreements

8. What are embargoes and sanctions?

9. What is it called when two countries put tariffs on each other's goods?

10. Give one argument in favor of restricting trade.

11. What was the GATT?

12. NAFTA has increased trade and investments in Mexico, Canada, and the United States. Why do you think some people still disapprove of NAFTA?

13. What do you think might happen if a multinational gained too much power in a less developed country's economy?

Section 3–Measuring Trade

14. What happens to a country's imports when its currency weakens? What happens when the currency strengthens?

15. Where was the fixed exchange-rate system introduced?

16. What happens to a country's currency when it imports more than it exports?

17. What happened to the balance of trade when OPEC raised the price of oil in the 1970s?

18. How could buying American products help change the balance of trade?

 Exploring the Essential Question

19. How do you think someone who sells Japanese cars would react to rising values of the dollar? How about someone who sells American cars?

Essential Question Activity

20. Complete the activity to answer the Essential Question **Should free trade be encouraged?** For this activity, the class will be divided into six groups. One group will represent the members of a Senate committee that is discussing a free-trade agreement with China. The other groups will represent one of the following: (1) economists at the WTO, (2) a U.S. consumer interest group, (3) a U.S. automaker, (4) a labor union, and (5) an organization of environmentalists. The senators prepare their questions. The other groups develop positions for or against the agreement. Using the worksheet in your Essential Questions Journal or the electronic worksheet found at **PearsonSuccessNet.com**, gather the following: (a) How do the speakers think the agreement will affect the people or businesses they represent? (b) How will the agreement affect the people of each senator's state? (c) How will the agreement affect the country as a whole?

Essential Questions Journal To continue to build a response to the Essential Question, go to your **Essential Questions Journal.**

Test-Taking Tip

When you read a multiple-choice question, look for words such as *most likely, generally, major,* and *best.* Decide which answer choice best fits the meaning of these words.

Study anytime, anywhere. Download these files today.

Economic Dictionary online
Vocabulary Support in English and Spanish

Audio Review online
Audio Study Guide in English and Spanish

Action Graph online
Animated Charts and Graphs

Visual Glossary online
Animated feature

How the Economy Works online
Animated feature

Download to your computer or mobile device at PearsonSuccessNet.com

Chapter 18 Development and Globalization

- **Section 1** Levels of Development

- **Section 2** Issues in Development

- **Section 3** Economies in Transition

- **Section 4** Challenges of Globalization

Economics on the go

To study anywhere, anytime, download these onlir resources at **PearsonSuccessNet.com** ➤

▶ **Every day you make economic decisions that affect your life.** Governments also make economic decisions. Their choices affect hundreds of thousands of people. Most countries see economic growth as a positive goal to work toward. But the transition to becoming an economically developed country is slow and difficult. One country still struggling with economic development is Colombia. To become more developed, the Colombian government decided to open its markets to international trade. It has also lowered tariffs, participated in regional trade agreements, and encouraged private investment. It has eased import restrictions and welcomed foreign investment. As a result, Colombia is one of the most industrialized countries in Latin America. Not everyone has benefited from these activities, however. About 65 percent of the population still lives below the poverty line. Colombia is not a special case. Many countries in Latin America, Africa, and Asia struggle to change from less developed countries to developed nations. The difficult choices they make today will echo in the future.

Reading Strategy: Text Structure
The way a text is organized can help readers determine which information is essential to understand. Before you begin reading, page through this chapter to see how it is organized. Pay special attention to the title, headings, boldface words, charts, and graphs. When reading, jot down notes, using the text's structure to guide you. When you are finished, summarize what you have read.

Visual Glossary
online

Go to the Visual Glossary Online for an interactive review of **globalization**.

How the Economy Works
online

Go to How the Economy Works Online for an interactive lesson on **the stages of economic development**.

Action Graph
online

Go to Action Graph Online for animated versions of key charts and graphs.

Objectives

- **Understand** what is meant by developed nations and less developed countries.
- **Identify** the tools used to measure levels of development.
- **Describe** the characteristics of developed nations and less developed countries.

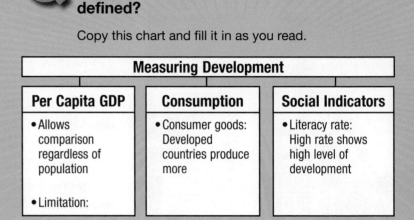

Guiding Question

How is a nation's level of development defined?

Copy this chart and fill it in as you read.

Measuring Development		
Per Capita GDP	**Consumption**	**Social Indicators**
• Allows comparison regardless of population • Limitation:	• Consumer goods: Developed countries produce more	• Literacy rate: High rate shows high level of development

development
the process by which a nation improves the economic, political, and social well-being of its people

developed nation
a nation with a high average level of well-being

less developed countries
nations with a low average level of well-being

▶ **Economics and You** Have you ever given money to help poor people in other countries? Each year, Americans of all ages give money and time to do so. The need is real. About 3 billion people—about half the world's population—are poor.

Principles in Action There are big differences between rich nations—such as the United States and Canada—and poorer nations like Ethiopia or East Timor. In this section, you will learn about some of these differences and why they exist.

What is meant by development?

The countries of the world have different levels of development. **Development** is the process by which a country improves the economic, political, and social well-being of its people. It is important to remember that *development* refers to a nation's well-being. It is not a way to judge the worth of a nation or its people. A developed country is not better than one that is less developed. Being developed, however, allows a nation to better feed, clothe, and shelter its people.

The United States, Canada, Japan, Australia, New Zealand, and most of Western Europe are called **developed nations.** They are nations with a high average level of well-being.

Poorer countries in the world are called **less developed countries** (LDCs). On average, their level of well-being is much lower. LDCs include the world's poorest countries, such as Bangladesh, Nepal, Haiti, and nations of central and southern Africa.

One group of LDCs has made great progress toward developing their economies. These are called **newly industrialized countries** (NICs). They include Mexico, Brazil, several countries in Eastern Europe, Saudi Arabia, and some former republics of the Soviet Union. Some NICs have seen their economies grow because they are rich in resources, especially oil. Saudi Arabia, for example, has earned a great deal of money from selling oil and oil products. Other NICs have turned to manufacturing.

In terms of growth, the NICs have pulled ahead of the poorer LDCs. Still, their people do not yet have the high standard of living of developed nations.

newly industrialized countries
less developed countries that have made great progress toward developing their economies

per capita GDP
a nation's gross domestic product divided by its population

CHECKPOINT *How do NICs differ from developed nations and LDCs?*

How is development measured?

Economists can measure a nation's level of development in many different ways. They can look at the production of goods and services. Other signs of development are how much energy is used and what people do to earn a living. There are also important social indicators.

What is per capita GDP?

You read about gross domestic product in Chapter 12. GDP is the total value of all final goods and services produced within an economy in a year. GDP alone, however, is not the best way to compare the living standards of nations. Instead, economists use **per capita GDP.** This is a nation's GDP divided by its population. As **Figure 18.1** shows, per capita GDP can be different from one nation to another.

Why is per capita GDP a better measure of development? Japan and India illustrate why GDP alone cannot be used to compare countries. The GDPs of Japan and India are about the same—about $4.28 trillion for Japan and about $2.98 trillion for India. Yet Japan enjoys a high standard of living, while India's standard of living is relatively low.

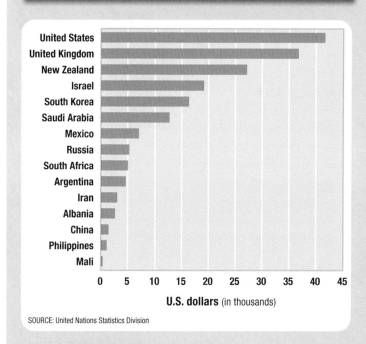

Fig. 18.1 Per Capita GDP of Selected Nations, 2005

U.S. dollars (in thousands)

SOURCE: United Nations Statistics Division

GRAPH SKILLS

Per capita GDP is calculated by dividing a nation's gross domestic product by its population.

1. In 2005, how much larger was the per capita GDP of the United States than that of Albania?
2. Iran has a much larger population than New Zealand. What does this graph suggest about the economies of the two nations?

The reason for this difference is population size. Japan has 127.7 million people. Thus, its per capita GDP is around $33,577 ($4.28 trillion divided by 127.7 million). India has about 1.1 billion people. Its per capita GDP is only around $2,659. These figures show that the average person in Japan has more income than the average person in India.

Still, per capita GDP is not a perfect measure of a nation's economic health. Per capita GDP does not take into account how income is distributed. Every nation has some people who are richer than others. In many LDCs, the gap between rich and poor is especially wide.

The World Bank, an international organization, uses a measure called per capita gross national income (GNI). Using this measure, the World Bank groups nations as high income, middle income, and low income. The map in **Figure 18.2** shows how these nations are spread out.

Fig. 18.2 Levels of Development

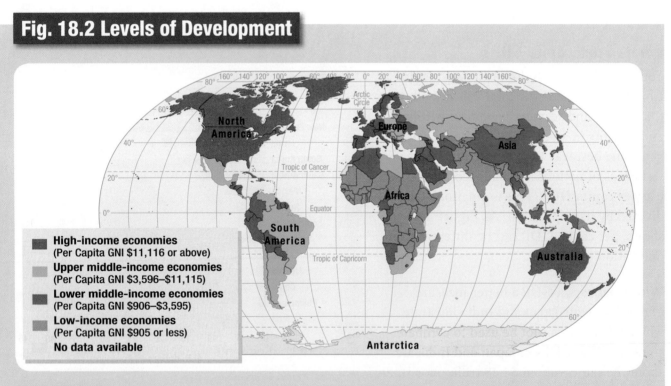

High-income economies
(Per Capita GNI $11,116 or above)

Upper middle-income economies
(Per Capita GNI $3,596–$11,115)

Lower middle-income economies
(Per Capita GNI $906–$3,595)

Low-income economies
(Per Capita GNI $905 or less)

No data available

MAP SKILLS

Although income is only one measure of development, it gives a good indication of a nation's standard of living.

1. What is the average income level of the United States? Australia?

2. Based on this map, make one generalization about the relationship between geographic location and level of development.

For an animated version of this graph, visit **PearsonSuccessNet.com**

How does energy use measure development?

Energy use is another way to measure development. The amount of energy a nation uses depends on how much industry it has. **Industrialization** is the organization of an economy to make, or manufacture, things. Industry usually needs large amounts of energy. The more industry, the more energy used. A country that uses a low level of energy tends to be one with little industry. Most of the people are farmers working with simple tools and few machines.

How does labor force measure development?

Another sign of low development is a high number of people working in agriculture. Why is that? It means most people are raising food just for themselves. Few are available to work in industry. As a result, there is little chance for workers to specialize. But specialization makes an economy work better. If a nation cannot produce specialized goods to sell, it has little cash income.

How do consumer goods measure development?

Developed countries can produce more consumer goods than less developed countries. Having consumer goods shows that people have enough money to meet their basic needs and still have enough left over to buy other goods. Thus, one way to study development is to measure how many people in a country own certain products. Some of the products measured are computers, cars, refrigerators, TVs, washing machines, or telephones.

What are social indicators?

Economists also look at three social indicators to measure a nation's level of development. These indicators give us information about the people who live in that country. The first is the **literacy rate.** This is the percentage of people over age 15 who can read and write. In general, the more people who can read and write, the higher a country's level of development. Countries that have a well-educated population are usually more productive than countries in which many people cannot read or write.

Another social measure of development is **life expectancy,** the average expected life span of an individual. People in LDCs often do not live as long as people in developed countries. Their lives are shortened by lack of food, lack of medical care, poor housing, and disease.

■ ■ ■ ■ ■ ■ ■ ■ ■ ■ ■ ■ ■ ■ ■ ■

industrialization
the organization of an economy to manufacture things

literacy rate
the percentage of people over age 15 who can read and write

life expectancy
the average expected life span of an individual

■ ■ ■ ■ ■ ■ ■ ■ ■ ■ ■ ■ ■ ■ ■ ■

Reading Strategy
Text Structure
Several social indicators help to measure a nation's level of development. Which words help you understand these indicators?

Fig. 18.3 How the Economy Works

What are the stages of economic development?

All over the world, economic development commonly follows a pattern. The change may be rapid or it may take generations. The number of people who benefit also varies from place to place.

1 Society has a traditional economy, with no formal economic organization or monetary system. Economic decisions are based on tradition.

2 People adopt new living patterns and economic activities, often as the result of outside intervention. Industries are introduced. Cultural traditions begin to crumble as people begin to find work in new industries.

Primitive Equilibrium

Transition

---

infant mortality rate
the number of deaths in the first year of life per 1,000 live births

Reading Strategy
Text Structure
   The section subheadings are written as questions. Use the text within those subheads to determine the characteristics of developed and less developed nations.

A third social indicator is a country's **infant mortality rate.** This is the number of deaths in the first year of life per 1,000 live births. For example, in the United States, out of every 1,000 babies born in a year, 6.4 of them die before they reach their first birthdays. This means the United States has an infant mortality rate of 6.4. Often, LDCs have high infant mortality rates.

 CHECKPOINT *How is energy use related to development?*

What are characteristics of developed nations?

Developed nations have high per capita GDPs. The majority of the people are neither very rich nor very poor. In general, people enjoy more economic and political freedom than do those in less developed countries. **Figure 18.3** shows the different stages of economic development.

3 New industries grow and profits are reinvested. As the economy expands, the society enters the international market. The traditional economic system continues to decline.

4 Economy is focused on consumer goods and public services. Basic human needs are met easily, but some people get left behind.

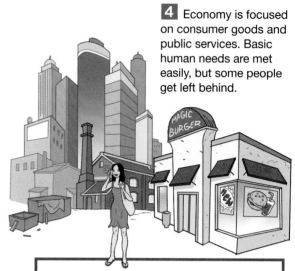

> **Check Your Understanding**
> 1. What impact does development have on cultural traditions?
> 2. Why do you think economists use the word *equilibrium*, or balance, to describe the traditional economy?

Takeoff and Semidevelopment

Highly Developed

How does quality of life measure development?

Developed countries have a high quality of life. Consumer spending is high. For example, in the United States, the average home has more TVs than people living in them. More than 60 percent of homes have computers.

The people of developed nations are generally healthy. There is low infant mortality and high life expectancy. Literacy rates are high. Most children stay in school until they are 18, and many go on to college.

How does high productivity measure development?

Developed countries have high productivity. Few people work on farms, but farmers produce a lot. Agriculture has largely become a high-tech big business. Since only a few people are needed in agriculture, more people can work in industry and services. The farmers are productive because they use technology and many machines that perform specialized functions.

subsistence agriculture
level of farming in which a person raises only enough food to feed his or her family

How do cities and infrastructure show development?

Most people in developed countries live in cities and towns and have done so for many years. New York, London, Tokyo, and other major cities are centers of banking and trade. A much smaller percentage of people live in rural areas.

Developed countries have good infrastructure. This includes everything needed for an economy to work well. Power plants are a part of infrastructure. Power is necessary to produce goods. Transportation and communication systems are also part of the infrastructure. They make it easier to transfer products, services, people, and ideas. Schools and banks are part of the infrastructure too. Schools increase literacy. Banks make the safe transfer of financial assets easier.

 CHECKPOINT *Why is there high productivity in the agricultural industry in developed nations?*

What are characteristics of less developed countries?

LDCs are different from one another. The people who live in less developed countries speak different languages. They practice different religions. Their histories, cultures, and traditions are different. But they also have much in common.

Why is low productivity a characteristic of LDCs?

LDCs have low per capita GDPs and limited economic development. Most people work in **subsistence agriculture**. This means they grow crops mainly to feed themselves and their families. Subsistence agriculture requires a lot of labor. This leaves fewer workers available to work in industry or services.

Unemployment rates are high in less developed countries, often around 20 percent. Much of the labor force is underemployed. People who are underemployed have work but not enough to support themselves or their families. They work less than eight hours a day.

How does quality of life show development?

Most of the people in LDCs cannot afford to buy many consumer goods. They do not earn enough money to buy these goods. Consumer goods that are produced are often shipped out of the country and sold in more developed nations.

A less developed country has few schools for its children. Resources for schools are limited. Many children have to work on the family farm. This limits the time they can spend in school, so literacy rates in LDCs are low. In Nepal, for example, only about 49 percent of the people more than 15 years old can read and write. Compare this figure with the United States, where the literacy rate is nearly 100 percent.

In the world's poorest countries, housing is often of poor quality. The people often do not have enough food to eat. There are few doctors and little medical care. This leads to high infant mortality rates and short life expectancy.

Most LDCs have other characteristics in common. In the next section, you will read about some of the difficult challenges less developed countries face.

CHECKPOINT *Why do most people in LDCs have few goods?*

SECTION 1 ASSESSMENT

> **Essential Questions Journal**
> To continue to build a response to the Essential Question, go to your **Essential Questions Journal.**

 Guiding Question

1. Use your completed chart to answer this question: How is a nation's level of development defined?

Key Terms and Main Ideas

Directions: On a sheet of paper, write the answer to each question. Use complete sentences.

2. What is a developed nation?

3. What are the differences between less developed countries, newly industrialized countries, and developed nations?

4. Why is per capita GDP a good tool to measure relative development?

5. Why is life expectancy a good tool to measure development?

Critical Thinking

6. **Draw Conclusions** How is literacy related to human capital?

7. **Synthesize Information** Explain why each of the following would be an important tool to enhance a country's rate of development: (a) a new airport, (b) high-speed Internet.

SECTION 2 Issues in Development

Objectives

- **Identify** the causes and effects of rapid population growth.
- **Analyze** how political factors and debt make development difficult.
- **Summarize** the role investment and foreign aid play in development.
- **Describe** the work of some international economic institutions.

Guiding Question

What factors harm or help development?

Copy this chart and fill it in as you read.

Factors Affecting Development	
Factors	**Effect**
Population growth	High rate makes development more difficult.
Physical capital	
Human capital	• Education and training •
Political factors	
Economic factors	Large loans can lead to spiraling debt.

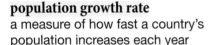

population growth rate
a measure of how fast a country's population increases each year

▶ **Economics and You** Even in a developed nation like ours, some people cannot read well or don't eat a healthy diet. Imagine what your life would be like if you never even had a chance to go to school. Imagine if not having enough food made it more likely you would not live to adulthood. Many people your age face these conditions worldwide.

Principles in Action

Illiteracy and not having enough food are just two factors that make development difficult. In this section, you will see what LDCs and the world community are doing to improve conditions and encourage economic growth.

How is population growth measured?

One problem facing LDCs is high population growth rates. The **population growth rate** measures how fast a country's population grows in a given year. It takes into account several things: the number of babies born, the number of people who die, and the number of people who move into or out of a country. It is stated as a percentage.

Compare the growth rates shown in **Figure 18.4.** The average population growth of less developed countries is around 1.8 percent. This may sound low to you, but at this rate, the population of LDCs will increase by nearly two thirds from 2007 to 2050. That is more than 20 times the population growth of developed nations.

What causes rapid population growth?

Rapid population growth has several causes. Life expectancy in many LDCs is rising. People are living longer. However, birth rates have not dropped much. When there are more births than deaths, the population grows.

The population of many LDCs is young. Many women are of childbearing age. (See **Figure 18.4**.) As these women have children, the population continues to grow. Many developed countries have an older population. Fewer women have children, so population growth is much smaller.

Why is rapid population growth a problem for LDCs?

LDCs know they have to deal with their high birthrates. It is difficult to raise the standard of living unless population growth can be controlled. Having more people means more jobs are needed. Healthcare, education, and infrastructure all have to be increased.

Reading Strategy
Text Structure
As you read, remember to look for visual clues that help you understand the order of the text. Headings, boldfaced words, and charts and graphs can help you make sense of what you are reading.

Fig. 18.4 Population of Selected Nations

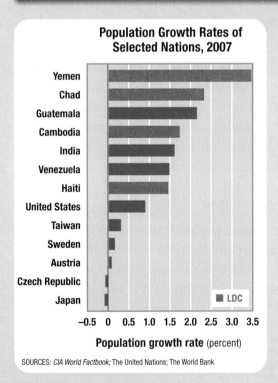

Population Growth Rates of Selected Nations, 2007

SOURCES: *CIA World Factbook;* The United Nations; The World Bank

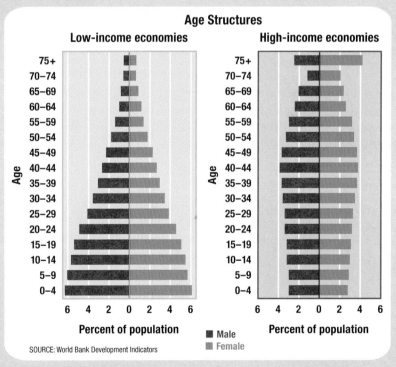

Age Structures

SOURCE: World Bank Development Indicators

GRAPH SKILLS

The graph on the left shows rates of population growth for selected nations. The graphs in the middle and on the right show how age distribution is related to national income.

1. In which nations is the population growing at a rate about double that of the United States?

2. Based on these graphs, what shape would you expect Guatemala's age structure to have?

Action Graph
online

For an animated version of this graph, visit **PearsonSuccessNet.com**

To improve the lives of its people, a nation has to create a higher per capita GDP. Economic output must grow faster than the population grows. This is not easy. It is difficult for an LDC to develop its economy. A main reason is that LDCs lack some of the factors of production.

✔ **CHECKPOINT** *Why is rapid population growth a problem for LDCs?*

How are factors of production and development linked?

In parts of Africa, Asia, and Latin America, physical geography makes development difficult. Natural resources are not evenly spread throughout the world. Some nations do not have many mineral resources or rich farmland. Temperatures may be too hot or cold for farming. There is often not enough rain. Nature is often unkind. There are many floods, hurricanes, and earthquakes.

Sometimes, LDCs have resources. The problem is that LDCs may not be able to use their resources efficiently. Technology can help LDCs develop their resources. Technology, however, costs a lot, and most LDCs do not have the capital to buy it.

How does physical capital affect development?

LDCs have low productivity. One of the main reasons is the lack of physical capital. Without capital, industry cannot grow. Farmers produce just enough to feed themselves. Subsistence farmers earn so little money that they have no savings. As a result, they do not have the cash to buy machines and tools that would make their farms more productive. They have little money to pay for goods and services that would raise their standard of living.

How do education and training affect development?

To produce more than enough to live on, a nation needs an educated workforce. Education and training allow people to develop new skills. They can learn to use new technologies. Many LDCs have low literacy rates. **Figure 18.5** compares figures for education and literacy of the United States and several other countries.

There are two main reasons why literacy rates in LDCs are low. First, few children get even as much as four years of schooling. Many children are forced to leave school early because they are needed at home to work on family farms. Second, in many LDCs, women are thought of as less important than men. Few women can read and write. Many women in these countries begin raising children at an early age. Those who do work earn low wages.

Fig. 18.5 Education and Literacy

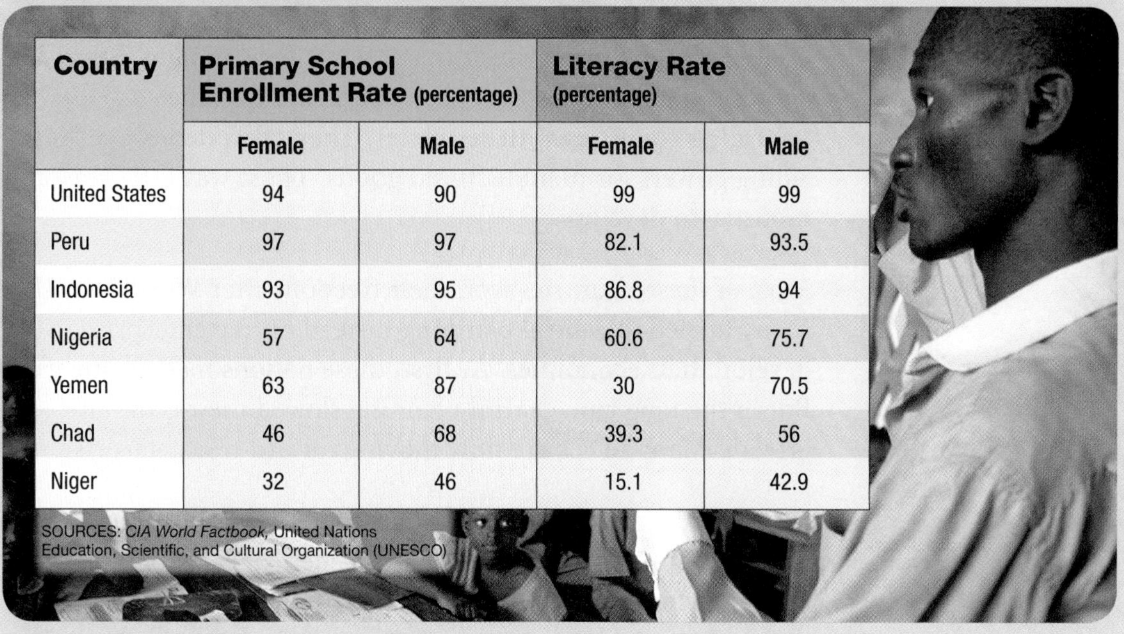

Country	Primary School Enrollment Rate (percentage)		Literacy Rate (percentage)	
	Female	Male	Female	Male
United States	94	90	99	99
Peru	97	97	82.1	93.5
Indonesia	93	95	86.8	94
Nigeria	57	64	60.6	75.7
Yemen	63	87	30	70.5
Chad	46	68	39.3	56
Niger	32	46	15.1	42.9

SOURCES: *CIA World Factbook,* United Nations Education, Scientific, and Cultural Organization (UNESCO)

CHART SKILLS

Education and literacy rates vary from country to country. These rates can also vary between men and women in the same country.

1. What percentage of male children attend school in Nigeria? In which nation can the smallest percentage of the population read and write?

2. Based on these charts, which two nations show the greatest inequality in education between men and women? What effect might this have?

How do nutrition and health affect development?

Many people in less developed countries are affected by **malnutrition.** This is consistently not having enough food to eat. People who are always hungry have little energy and are often sick. This makes them less productive than they could be. Many children, too, are malnourished. This damages their physical and mental development. It hurts their chances of being productive workers once they become adults.

malnutrition
consistently not having enough food to eat

Other factors affect the health of people in many LDCs. Garbage and sewage may not be collected. This spreads disease. Many countries have high rates of infection by HIV, the virus that causes AIDS. About 70 percent of the people infected with HIV/AIDS live in Africa. Many people have died. The deaths of many farmers have cut farm production. The number of orphans and old people that need care has grown. Caring for these people and their families puts a strain on the resources of many LDCs. Taking care of them costs money that could be spent on schools or the infrastructure.

✔ **CHECKPOINT** *How does education contribute to development?*

What political factors have slowed development?

Political factors may also slow a nation's development. Many LDCs are former colonies of European countries. Colonies supplied the ruling countries with resources. They often depended on the ruling powers for manufactured goods. There was little reason for industry to develop.

Most of these countries won their freedom after World War II. Many turned to central planning instead of free enterprise to develop their economies. At first, these nations made some gains. But in the long run, central planning slowed their economic growth. Many LDCs are now moving toward free enterprise.

Many governments are corrupt. Corruption has held back development in many LDCs. Some leaders have taken huge sums of money for their private use. They live in luxury while large numbers of their people remain poor.

Many LDCs have civil unrest. This is when people fight the government because they are unhappy with conditions in their country. Millions of people have died after years of fighting. Millions more have been forced to flee their homes. The unrest causes a loss of workers. Resources and infrastructure are destroyed.

Finally, in almost all LDCs, there is a huge gap between the richest and poorest citizens. In some countries, economic policies favor people who live in the cities, even though most people live in rural areas. In some LDCs, leaders favor one ethnic group—typically their own. In some cases, governments have actually tried to kill members of other ethnic or religious groups.

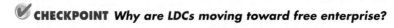 **CHECKPOINT** *Why are LDCs moving toward free enterprise?*

How can development be financed?

Building an infrastructure, providing education and healthcare, and creating industry all require large sums of money. There are several ways an LDC can get these funds. These include internal financing, foreign investment, borrowing, and foreign aid.

What is internal financing?

Internal financing is capital that comes from the savings of a country's own citizens. As you read in Chapter 11, when savers deposit money in banks, banks lend the money to firms. Firms invest in both physical and human capital so that they can expand. This creates new jobs. Job growth improves workers' standard of living. They buy more goods and services. This encourages businesses to expand more. As a result, the whole economy grows.

Most LDCs have a low savings rate. Many people do not earn enough money to save. The few people who are rich often keep their money in foreign countries. As a result, most poor countries turn to foreign sources to pay for development.

What is foreign investment?

Investment capital that comes from other countries is called **foreign investment.** There are two types of foreign investment: direct investment and portfolio investment.

Foreign direct investment happens when investors start a business in another country. For example, multinational corporations often build factories in LDCs. Multinationals do this because labor is cheap. They also do it to take advantage of the natural resources the LDC has.

As you have seen, there are good and bad things about multinationals. Some economists say the people of the LDC who work for the foreign corporation are better off than they would be doing other work. Their wages give them cash they can use to buy goods. This can help the country's economy grow. Other people believe multinationals take advantage of workers. They pay workers in LDCs less than they pay workers in their own countries. Opponents also say multinationals hurt a nation's economic growth because they take profits out of the country.

Sometimes, foreign investors buy shares in another country's financial markets. This is known as **foreign portfolio investment.** For example, an American investor might buy shares in a mutual fund. The mutual fund then buys stock in a foreign company. That company can use the funds to build another plant or to pay for research and development. This helps the economy of the LDC to develop, but it also creates some problems. Because the investors live in another country, some or all of the company's profits may be taken out of the LDC.

internal financing
capital that comes from the savings of a country's citizens

foreign investment
capital that comes from other, more developed, countries

foreign direct investment
when investors start a business in another country

foreign portfolio investment
buying shares in another country's financial markets

Each year, the government-owned Bank of Namibia holds a meeting to discuss issues related to the nation's economic development. ▼

Fig. 18.6 U.S. Foreign Aid, 2006

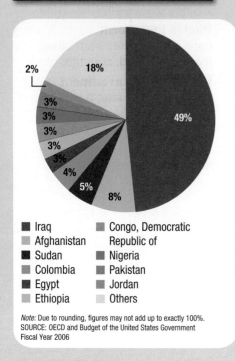

2%
18%
3%
3%
3%
3%
3%
4%
5%
8%
49%

- Iraq
- Afghanistan
- Sudan
- Colombia
- Egypt
- Ethiopia
- Congo, Democratic Republic of
- Nigeria
- Pakistan
- Jordan
- Others

Note: Due to rounding, figures may not add up to exactly 100%.
SOURCE: OECD and Budget of the United States Government Fiscal Year 2006

GRAPH SKILLS

This pie graph shows the ten countries that received the most foreign aid from the United States in 2006.

1. Identify the amount of foreign aid each of these countries received: Iraq, Colombia, Congo.
2. Why might providing aid to Afghanistan benefit the United States?

How does borrowing affect LDCs?

In the 1970s and 1980s, many LDCs received loans from foreign governments and private banks to finance development. Some of that money was poorly spent because of corruption or lack of experience.

Changes in the world economy also caused problems for the LDCs. Rising oil prices affected them. They had to borrow more money to buy the fuel they needed. Also, many of the loans were issued in—and had to be repaid in—U.S. dollars. When the value of the dollar increased in the 1980s, many LDCs found it impossible to repay their loans. Once again, many were forced to borrow even more. As a result, the foreign debt grew. In some countries it was greater than the annual gross domestic product.

What is foreign aid?

Sometimes, rather than making loans to developing nations, foreign governments give money and other forms of aid. For instance, many developed nations give money to build schools, roads, systems to provide clean and safe water, and other infrastructure. These foreign aid grants do not need to be repaid. **Figure 18.6** shows the countries that receive the most U.S. foreign aid.

Foreign aid is sometimes given just to help poor people in other countries. Sometimes, developed nations have military, political, economic, and cultural reasons to give aid to LDCs. After World War II, for example, the United States gave aid to countries in Africa, Asia, and Latin America. The United States was trying to block the influence of the Soviet Union in those areas. In the early 2000s, the United States gave aid to Iraq and Afghanistan. American leaders hoped to fight international terrorism by promoting democracy there.

✔ **CHECKPOINT** *Why is internal financing difficult for LDCs?*

How do international organizations help LDCs?

Several international economic organizations are trying to improve the quality of life in LDCs. The most important are the World Bank, the United Nations Development Program (UNDP), and the International Monetary Fund (IMF). Some nongovernmental groups give economic help and advice too.

The World Bank is the largest provider of development help to LDCs. It raises money on world financial markets. The wealthier member nations also give money to the World Bank. The World Bank uses these funds to offer loans and other resources to more than 100 LDCs. Since its founding in 1940, it has loaned billions of dollars to developing countries.

The **United Nations Development Program** was created in 1965. It controls most of the UN development projects around the world. These projects affect farming, mining, fishing, forestry, and manufacturing. Their goal is to reduce poverty through development. This program gives 90 percent of its resources to 166 low-income nations, where 90 percent of the world's poorest people live.

The International Monetary Fund (IMF) is an international organization of 185 member countries. As you learned in Chapter 17, the IMF was founded in 1946 to stabilize international exchange rates. Today, the IMF has expanded its role in the world economy. It promotes development by offering advice and technical help to LDCs. It also assists when LDCs need help in paying their international debt.

If a country has trouble repaying a debt, the IMF may arrange a rescheduling plan. **Debt rescheduling** is an agreement between the lending nation and the borrowing country. The lending nation gives the borrowing nation more time to repay the debt. Sometimes, it may forgive, or dismiss, part of the loan. In return, the LDC agrees to accept a **stabilization program,** changing its economic ways to meet IMF goals.

Why do some people disagree with some World Bank and IMF policies?

Both the World Bank and the IMF have had some successes. Some people, however, believe the policies of these agencies actually hurt the people they are meant to help. The World Bank and the IMF push the LDCs to adopt free market economies. They may ask the LDCs to lower trade barriers and get rid of subsidies. Countries are told to raise interest rates or to lower the value of their currencies to better control the money supply. To cut budget deficits, LDCs are forced to cut spending on education, healthcare, and welfare. The result may be economic progress, but it comes at a great cost to the poor people of the LDCs.

■ ■ ■ ■ ■ ■ ■ ■ ■ ■ ■ ■ ■ ■ ■ ■ ■ ■ ■

United Nations Development Program
an international program to control UN development projects

debt rescheduling
an agreement between lending nations and borrowing countries that lengthens the time of debt repayment

stabilization program
an agreement between a borrowing country and the IMF in which the LDC agrees to change its economic ways to meet IMF goals

Reading Strategy
Text Structure
How did the structure
of this section help you
understand it?

How do nongovernmental organizations help LDCs?

Some private aid groups also work to help the LDCs build
their economies. **Nongovernmental organizations** (NGOs) are
independent groups that raise money for development programs.
Examples are the Red Cross, CARE, and the World Wildlife Fund.

Some NGOs give food or medical help after floods, earthquakes,
or wars. Others try to promote development. For example, Heifer
International gives animals to families in less developed countries.
Families use these animals to produce and sell products such as
wool, milk, or honey.

✔ **CHECKPOINT** *Why do some people agree with stabilization*
programs? Why do some disagree with them?

	To continue to build a
Essential Questions Journal	response to the Essential Question, go to your **Essential Questions Journal.**

SECTION **2** ASSESSMENT

Quick Write

Suppose that you are an
economist with the World
Bank, International Monetary
Fund, or United Nations
Development Program. Write
a memo to the president of
your group explaining what
steps the organization should
take to combat corruption in
less developed countries. Also,
explain why these steps need to
be taken.

 Guiding Question

1. Use your completed chart to answer this question: What
   factors harm or help development?

Key Terms and Main Ideas

**Directions: On a sheet of paper, write the answer to each
question. Use complete sentences.**

2. Why do less developed countries have a high population
   growth rate?

3. Why are literacy rates relatively low in LDCs?

4. Why do many LDCs need to rely on foreign investment rather
   than internal financing?

5. What is the difference between foreign direct investment and
   foreign portfolio investment?

Critical Thinking

6. **Solve Problems** Suppose that you are the head of a less
   developed country. Which obstacle to development do you
   think you should tackle first? Why?

7. **Draw Conclusions** Do you think it would be more beneficial
   for a country to take a loan to fund new development or to
   invite in foreign investors? Explain.

Objectives

- **Identify** the characteristics of economic transition.

- **Describe** the political and economic changes that have taken place in Russia since the fall of communism.

- **Analyze** the reasons for rapid economic growth in China and India.

- **Summarize** the economic challenges facing Africa and Latin America.

privatization
the sale or transfer of government-owned businesses to individuals

Guiding Question

How has economic change affected different countries?

Copy this chart and fill it in as you read.

Russia	China	Brazil	Mexico
• Yeltsin: rapid switch to market	• Free market centers • Crime and pollution have increased. • •	• Natural resources: iron, timber, land and climate	• • • •

▶ **Economics and You** Change is always challenging. Suppose suddenly you and every American had to pay to attend high school. This would cause all sorts of problems for many families. But if somebody gave you a million dollars, you might face different sorts of problems. You might be tempted to spend the money on the wrong things. Friends and family might ask you for many things.

The same is true of nations. Economic change—even change for the better—always brings new challenges.

Principles in Action

Today, many countries are having economic transition, or change. Some are enjoying rapid growth, while others are changing their entire economic systems. In this section, you will look at the changing economies of Russia, China, India, and countries of Africa and Latin America. In addition, the Economics & You feature shows some ways economic change around the world may affect you.

What are three challenges in moving to a free market economy?

For many nations, the biggest economic change is moving from central planning to a market-based economy. In a centrally planned, or command, economy, the government owns and controls the factors of production. In a market-based economy, individuals own and control the factors of production. One of the first steps in moving to a market economy is to sell or transfer government-owned businesses to individuals. This process is called **privatization.**

A government can privatize businesses in several ways. It could simply sell the business to one owner. It could also sell shares to investors. It could give citizens a voucher (a ticket) that can be used to buy shares in whatever businesses they wish.

Privatization does not always go smoothly. The only businesses that will survive in a free market are those that can earn a profit. No one will want to buy businesses that do not earn a profit. This may cause people to lose their jobs. Other jobs will be created as the economy grows. However, the change will be difficult at first for workers used to jobs guaranteed by the government.

Fig. 18.7

Cheer up. Things will change when we get a FREE market economy.

BREAD LINE →

UNEMPLOYMENT LINE →

▲ Russia and other communist countries have had problems changing to free market economies. According to the cartoon, what problems did Russia face before and after the change?

The system of laws also has to change as the economy moves to a market economy. Centrally planned economies have no need to protect private property rights. This is because there is no private property. A free market economy needs such protections. As a result, the government must create new laws that ensure a person's right to own and transfer property. Changing the legal system in this basic way takes time.

In a planned economy, workers are used to being taken care of by the government. Many have guaranteed jobs at which they do not have to worry about making quality goods. They only need to meet government quotas. In the free market, there are no such guarantees. As a result, workers in a changing economy need to learn to work differently.

Not surprisingly, people comfortable with central planning often worry about how change will affect them. They might be against changing to the free market out of fear and not knowing how it will turn out.

✅ **CHECKPOINT** *Why is a country's transition to privatization not always smooth?*

How did Russia's economy change?

Russia has faced all of the challenges described above. It was once part of the Soviet Union, the world's most powerful communist nation. But in 1991, Soviet communism—and the Soviet Union itself—collapsed. Russia began the difficult transition to a free market economy.

Under communism, government planners managed the Soviet economy. The nation became an industrial giant and a military superpower. The planners pushed heavy industry. One result was that the Soviet people suffered shortages of consumer goods. The few goods they did get were often of low quality.

In the late 1980s, Mikhail Gorbachev became the Soviet leader. He faced big problems. The Soviet economy was falling apart. People spent hours a day standing in line to buy food and clothing. Gorbachev began a series of big political and economic changes. He tried to introduce some features of a market economy. The transition to a free market economy created problems, however (see **Figure 18.7**). People lost government jobs, benefits, and pensions they thought were guaranteed to them. Many older people had to live on the little they had saved. Some Russians started their own businesses and did well. Still, most people were unhappy with conditions in their country.

At the same time, some officials and army officers feared that the central government was becoming weak. If the Soviet Union broke up, they would lose their power. In 1991, they tried to bring back old-style communism. The attempt backfired. A new leader, Boris Yeltsin, led thousands of Russians against the army and the police. On December 1, 1991, Ukraine, one of the 15 Soviet republics, declared its independence. Within days, other Soviet republics declared their independence, too. The Soviet Union broke up into many different countries.

The largest of the new nations was the Russian Republic. Yeltsin was elected president. He promised to move Russia toward a market economy. Life improved, but many people still suffered. When Yeltsin lifted price controls in 1992, prices tripled. People on fixed incomes, such as retirees, could not afford to buy basics like food and clothing.

In the new Russia, most wealth went to cities such as Moscow. The uneven way income was spread led to calls for more change. It also led to corruption and a rise in organized crime.

The world was eager to help Russia change. Billions of dollars in financial aid flooded into the country from the World Bank, the IMF, and independent investors. However, this aid was not used efficiently. There was poor management and a lot of corruption. By 1998, the Russian economy was a mess. Debt was high. Few investors were willing to invest. Russia was in an economic crisis.

Eventually, Russia's economy recovered. The government still kept tight controls. Huge sums of money poured in as the world price for oil jumped. By 2007, according to the IMF, Russia had the world's seventh largest national economy. Much of the nation's foreign debt had been repaid. Economic growth led to growing consumer demand. New laws were passed to protect investments. This has encouraged foreign investors to start new businesses in Russia.

Reading Strategy
Text Structure
Look for the words in this section that help you understand the change in Russia's economy. As you read, jot down notes in your chart.

Reading Strategy
Text Structure
Summarize what you have learned about changes in Russia.

special economic zone
designated regions that operate under different economic laws from the rest of the country in order to attract foreign investment and promote exports

There are still some problems. Russia's economy relies on the export of natural resources. If the prices of these goods drop, export income will fall. In recent years, Russian leaders have brought back government control over many parts of the economy. The transition to a market economy is far from complete.

CHECKPOINT *How did communism end in the Soviet Union?*

How has China's economy changed?

In 1949, after a long civil war, communists took power in China. The government tried to control every part of Chinese life. Government planners made all key decisions about the economy. They told the Chinese people what to grow, where to live, where to work, and even what books to read. The leaders wanted to make China an industrial power without any help from other countries.

In 1979, Chinese leader Deng Xiaoping introduced a new plan for economic change. He let people once again own businesses and property. He invited foreign countries to invest in China. Deng began using the tools of the free market to increase productivity.

He gave farmers and factory managers more freedom to make decisions about what to produce and how much to charge for it. He also rewarded farmers, managers, and workers who increased output. With such incentives, production increased.

Most of China's growth has taken place in the coastal areas of southwest China. In the 1970s, Deng created four free market centers called **special economic zones.** Industries in these areas pay lower taxes. This encouraged foreign companies to invest. Chinese businesses could operate freely as well, with managers making most of their own investment and production decisions. This idea proved successful. China now has hundreds of these zones.

Economics & YOU

Economic Growth in Asia

Since the 1970s, Chinese manufacturing and foreign trade have skyrocketed. *Many of the clothes you buy today were imported from China.*

MADE IN CHINA

India

Many American companies have outsourced customer service jobs to countries where labor costs are cheaper. *When you call for computer tech help, you may be speaking to an operator in India.*

USA

Today, China's economy is one of the fastest growing in the world. Chinese cities are full of people who can choose from a wide variety of consumer goods. The economic changes have led to huge economic growth. China once lagged far behind most nations of Europe and North America. Now, China has the world's second most productive economy, after the United States. As you can see from **Figure 18.8,** China is a major exporter of goods and a key trading partner of the United States.

Still, development has brought some problems. Cities have grown quickly. Huge fields that once grew rice are now industrial areas with factories, apartments, schools, and traffic jams. Crime and pollution have increased. The poor complain that the government is no longer providing jobs and healthcare for everyone. In addition, growth has not reached all parts of the country. There are still many poor people and many people without work in rural areas (where two thirds of China's people live).

Economic development has not meant political freedom. Chinese citizens still do not have many political rights. The only elections are at the local level. The government tightly controls the press. People who fight for more individual freedoms are often put in prison.

 CHECKPOINT *What free market reforms did Deng Xiaoping introduce in China?*

How has India's economy changed?

India, too, has experienced rapid economic growth. A former British colony, India struggled economically after winning independence. In the 1990s, India's government began to invite foreign investment and promote other free market practices.

These new practices encouraged Indian companies to expand. One area of growth was in high-technology industries. Many software companies opened new plants in India. India is now one of the world's biggest exporters of computer software. Workers in India offer technical support to computer users around the world. Manufacturing is growing as well.

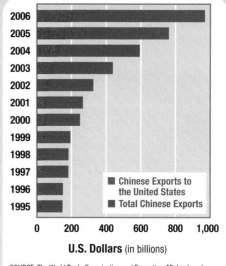

Fig. 18.8 Chinese Exports, 1995–2006

- Chinese Exports to the United States
- Total Chinese Exports

U.S. Dollars (in billions)

SOURCE: The World Trade Organization and Ferrantino, Michael, and Zhi Wang. "Accounting Discrepancies in Bilateral Trade: The Case of China, Hong Kong, and the U.S." *The Office of Economics (Working Paper),* The U.S. International Trade Commission, April 2007.

GRAPH SKILLS
Since China began to adopt free market policies, the export of Chinese products to the world market has skyrocketed.

1. How much did the value of Chinese exports to the world grow between 1995 and 2006?
2. What percentage of China's exports went to the United States in 2000? In 2006?

The economic growth is resulting in a large and growing middle class. India's middle class provides a growing market for consumer goods. Although India had no shopping malls before 1999, it now has more than one hundred. As the middle class seeks more (and more expensive) goods, local and foreign producers compete to meet that demand.

Still, as with China, India's growth is not complete. Farmers make up about 60 percent of the labor force. There is a growing gap between the rich and the poor. This is true of almost all nations with developing economies. Well-educated people living in the cities benefit the most from growth. One fourth of India's people live on less than $1 a day. Most of them are uneducated subsistence farmers.

✔ **CHECKPOINT** *What is one result of economic growth in India?*

What economic challenges does Africa face?

Like Asia, Africa is home to many poor countries. Many countries south of the Sahara are among the poorest countries in the world. Their economies are based largely on subsistence farming. They have low literacy rates. Many people do not get enough food to eat. Poor health and especially high rates of HIV infection slow down development. Many countries have huge international debts. Civil unrest is a big problem in some countries. In East Africa, there is ethnic conflict in many nations. Some nations have been fighting a civil war for many years.

Only two African nations have large economies—Nigeria and South Africa. Nigeria has more people than any country in Africa. It has large oil deposits and has benefited from high oil prices. The problem is that the economy depends too much on oil revenue. Oil makes up 20 percent of the GDP and 95 percent of foreign exchange earnings. It pays for 65 percent of Nigeria's yearly budget. This overdependence on oil has slowed growth in other areas.

Nigeria also suffers from political corruption and ethnic conflict. In 2007, new leaders took power in Nigeria. They promised to improve the economy and standard of living.

Like Nigeria, South Africa has an economy of two levels. One level is modern with a well-developed infrastructure. The other level is poorly developed. In the 1990s, South Africa shifted from longtime rule by the white minority to black majority rule. In the transition, economic growth slowed. Unemployment remains

Innovators

Wangari Muta Maathai

"I always felt that our work was not simply about planting trees," said Wangari Maathai. Maathai was the first African woman to win the Nobel Peace Prize. "It was about inspiring people to take charge of their environment, the system that governed them, their lives, and their future."

Maathai founded the Green Belt Movement (GBM). She wanted to promote economic development while preserving Kenya's forests for future generations. Maathai believes that Kenya, without its forest, could eventually become a desert wasteland. The GBM also created jobs by hiring thousands of poor women to plant trees in rural Kenya.

Early on, the Kenyan government was against the Green Belt Movement. It wanted to sell the forests to foreign developers. Police were sent to peaceful GBM demonstrations. Maathai herself was severely beaten.

After years of conflict, the Green Belt Movement triumphed. GBM has now planted more than 30 million trees and provided jobs for 80,000 people. Maathai was elected to Kenya's parliament in 2002. She continues to search for ways to improve living standards for both current and future generations.

Fast Facts

Wangari Muta Maathai (1940–)
Education: Ph.D., Veterinary Medicine, University of Nairobi
Claim to Fame: Founder of Green Belt Movement

---

high, and there are still many poor people. Still, South Africa has one of the 25 most productive economies in the world. It is rich in natural resources and has a strong manufacturing base.

 CHECKPOINT *What are reasons for continued poverty in Africa?*

What economic challenges does Latin America face?

In Latin America, the two biggest success stories are Brazil and Mexico. Both countries are rich in natural resources. Both are trying not to depend too much on their resources. They are taking steps to develop other industries. Venezuela, another large country, has gone a different way.

Brazil exports iron ore and timber. Its land and climate are good for growing coffee and soybeans. In recent years, Brazil has become a major manufacturing power. It produces everything from cars and trucks to shoes. Though it lacks oil reserves, it is a big producer of ethanol. More than 40 percent of the fuel that powers Brazilian cars comes from ethanol made from sugarcane. Brazil has also built cars that can run on gasoline or ethanol.

 Reading Strategy
Text Structure
What words and phrases in the above feature help you understand how Maathai's work has progressed over the years?

Mexico is rich in resources. Its most important natural resource is oil. It also has natural gas and silver. It produces rich crops of cotton and coffee. Like Brazil, Mexico has increased its manufacturing. Today, nearly one of every six workers is employed in manufacturing. Tourism is another important industry. People come to Mexico for its sunshine, beautiful beaches, and scenery. They also visit the remains of Mexico's ancient cultures.

Mexico and Brazil have tried to diversify, or give variety to, their economies. This has freed 80 percent or more of their labor forces from farm work. New jobs in manufacturing and service industries have helped these two economies grow.

Like Mexico, Venezuela has large deposits of oil. Its leadership has turned a different direction, though. President Hugo Chavez has shifted the economy away from the market system to socialism. Chavez has promised to use money from the sale of oil and gas to end poverty and improve healthcare and education. These advances have yet to be seen, however.

 CHECKPOINT *Which countries in Latin America have built the strongest economies?*

Essential Questions Journal To continue to build a response to the Essential Question, go to your **Essential Questions Journal.**

SECTION **3** ASSESSMENT

 Guiding Question

1. Use your completed chart to answer this question: How has economic change affected different countries?

Key Terms and Main Ideas

Directions: On a sheet of paper, write the answer to each question. Use complete sentences.

2. What is privatization?

3. Why do governments switching to a market economy need new laws?

4. How did Russia's economy change after the collapse of communism?

5. What was the purpose of China's special economic zones?

Critical Thinking

6. **Synthesize Information** How can a nation ease the transition from a command economy to a free market economy?

7. **Predict** China has been criticized for stopping dissent and for other violations of human rights. Do you think that will affect its trade relationships with other nations? Why or why not?

Objectives

- **Define** globalization and identify factors that promote its spread.
- **Explain** four problems linked to globalization.
- **Describe** three challenges globalization creates.
- **Identify** the characteristics needed for American workers and companies to succeed in the future.

Reading Strategy
Text Structure
Make use of a concept web to fill in the effects of globalization.

globalization
the growing connection of producers, consumers, and financial systems around the world

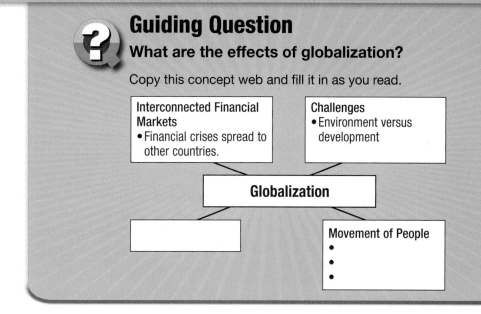

Guiding Question

What are the effects of globalization?

Copy this concept web and fill it in as you read.

Interconnected Financial Markets
- Financial crises spread to other countries.

Challenges
- Environment versus development

Globalization

Movement of People
- •
- •
- •

▶ **Economics and You** By now, you have seen many examples of how the world's economies are connected. You pick up the telephone to get tech support for your computer, and the call is answered in India. You eat a banana that was grown in Costa Rica. You fill your car with gas that is made from oil from Saudi Arabia. The value of the dollar goes down, and the cost of a vacation goes up. The list goes on and on.

Principles in Action The economies of the world's nations are interconnected in many ways. Whether we like it or not, they are going to remain interconnected. The global economy creates new issues we must take into account. In this section, you will look at many of these issues.

What causes globalization?

Have you heard people say the world is getting smaller every day? They mean the world is becoming more interconnected. Countries are linked economically more than ever. Producers, consumers, and financial systems around the world are connected. This is known as **globalization.** Globalization is not new. In the Middle Ages, the Asian spice trade connected Europe, Asia, and Africa. The voyages of Columbus led to the colonization of the Americas. The Age of Imperialism that began in the late 1800s strengthened the links between the economies of Europe and the United States and those of Africa and Asia. Still, globalization today is taking place at a much faster pace than in the past.

How do rapid transportation and communication aid globalization?

What do the taming of camels, the invention of the compass, and the creation of the Internet have in common? All are examples of innovation. They allowed greater movement of products, people, and ideas.

In the past, camels and ships made it possible to trade across vast deserts and oceans. Today, jet airplanes allow producers to sell goods in faraway markets. This would have been impossible in the past. For example, many of the fresh flowers for sale in the United States come from the Netherlands or Colombia.

It has never been so easy to communicate with people in faraway places. This has sped the pace of globalization. Thanks to satellite communications, customers and suppliers on opposite sides of the world can talk quickly and clearly. Computers give people information about products in other countries. Investors in one country can get up-to-date information and use it to buy stocks on financial markets anywhere.

How has the expansion of the free market affected globalization?

As you read in Section 3, many nations have moved away from central planning to free market economies. As a result, there are many more free market economies in the world. The fall of communism in the Soviet Union and Eastern Europe allowed nations that had once been locked out of world trade to enter the global marketplace. The opening of new markets has created new global economic ties.

The new free market economies are more open to foreign investment. In 1975, the value of foreign investment worldwide totaled about $23 billion. In the past few years, there has been a sharp increase. According to the United Nations, the total value of global foreign investment in 2006 was $1,306 billion. This is 38 percent higher than in 2005.

How do trading blocs promote globalization?

Many nations have signed regional trade agreements. The creation of trading groups, or blocs, has changed how nations compete in the global market.

The United States is the world's most productive single economy. Its output is far greater than that of any single nation in Europe. However, the combined output of the 27 nations that make up the

Fig. 18.9

"GLOBALISATION RISKY? HOW D'YOU MEAN?"

▲ Increasing interdependence carries risks as well as opportunities. **What point is this cartoon making about globalization?**

European Union (EU) is competitive with that of the United States. People, goods, and services can flow freely among members of the EU. This makes it work almost like one single economy.

The North American Free Trade Agreement (NAFTA) is a trade agreement signed by Mexico, Canada, and the United States. It created one large free-trade area in North America. The three countries removed many trade barriers and agreed to phase out the rest. By making it easier to trade with one another, the three countries hope to discourage companies from making deals with other trading blocs.

Trading blocs do not remain fixed. The EU has grown to include more and more nations. It is also working to develop trade ties with other regions. In the same way, members of NAFTA are reaching out to more of Latin America.

▲ Globalization began long ago. Here a caravan travels the 14th-century Silk Road. It linked the economies of China and Southwest Asia. Do you think the pace of globalization has gotten faster? Explain.

✔ **CHECKPOINT** *In what way have modern communications contributed to globalization?*

What are some issues in globalization?

"Arguing against globalization," said former UN Secretary-General Kofi Annan, "is like arguing against the laws of gravity." Though globalization is a fact of modern economic life, it has also created some challenges.

What happens when financial markets are connected?

In 2007, many American financial firms lost money. Some went out of business. This was the result of making too many risky home mortgage loans. Some investors worried this would cause a recession, so they sold their stocks. Heavy losses on the New York Stock Exchange worried investors elsewhere in the world. They, in turn, sold stocks on European and Asian exchanges.

The ripple effect caused by this American financial crisis has happened before. In the past, economic problems in Mexico, Japan, Russia, and Argentina have had the same effect on world financial markets.

▲ Banks are among the most influential multinational corporations. The Sanwa Bank of Japan and the Puerto Rico-based Banco Popular have branches in dozens of countries.

Financial problems in one country affect people in another because world financial markets are closely connected. Investors around the world watch the values of stocks in many different markets. They move quickly to buy the stock of promising companies in whatever country they find them. They sell their stocks just as quickly at any sign of trouble.

Another reason problems in one country affect people in another is the booming trade in currencies. Most of the world now follows a flexible exchange-rate system. The values of different national currencies go up or down every day. Investors holding money in the currency of a country may sell it if its value drops. If many investors sell a lot of a country's currency at the same time, that country's economy will suffer.

These effects hurt investors who risk their money in the hope of earning profits. They also affect ordinary people. Banks buy assets in other countries. If the value of those assets falls, the banks have less money to loan people in their own countries.

How do multinational corporations affect globalization?

There are both good and bad sides of multinational corporations. Some economists argue that these companies have helped the countries where they set up operations. For example, multinationals have been credited with much of the development of Eastern Europe after the fall of communism. Multinationals can introduce technology to developing countries. They offer jobs, train the labor force, and give related services and industries a chance to develop.

Others argue that multinationals do little to aid LDCs. They point out that most of the profits do not go to the LDC. They go to the foreign owners of the corporation. Others say multinationals create far fewer jobs than they claim. Many of the industries require few workers. They use a lot of machines. Only a few jobs are created. Working conditions are often much worse than in developed countries. This is because many LDCs do not have the tough labor laws most developed countries have.

Another area of disagreement is wages. Generally, wages in LDCs are low compared to wages in industrialized nations. Supporters of multinationals argue that the lower wages are fair because the cost of living in LDCs is also lower. Also, many of the people who work for multinationals might not have jobs at all otherwise. Those who oppose multinationals argue that the companies take unfair advantage of workers by paying them such low wages.

Does globalization cause job loss?

We have looked at how globalization affects LDCs. However, globalization affects people in developed nations too. They worry about losing jobs to workers in other countries.

In the global economy, companies may move parts of their operations to other countries. This practice is known as **offshoring.** Offshoring may involve just one part of a firm's operations. For example, an American bank might hire a call center in India or Kenya to handle its telemarketing. Total offshoring is when a manufacturer closes a plant in the United States to build one in another country. In either case, some jobs are lost.

☑ **CHECKPOINT** *What problems can result from interconnected financial markets?*

■ ■ ■ ■ ■ ■ ■ ■ ■ ■ ■ ■ ■ ■ ■ ■ ■ ■

offshoring
the movement of all or part of a company's operations to some other country

How are migration and globalization linked?

People have always moved from place to place in hopes of finding a better life. Globalization has increased migration. This is the movement of people from one place to settle in another place.

Much of this migration takes place within the country itself. In many countries, there are more jobs in cities than in rural areas. As a result, large numbers of people in villages are moving to cities. In 1950, less than 20 percent of the people in Africa and Asia lived in cities. By 2005, nearly 40 percent did. Today, 13 of the world's 20 largest cities are located in LDCs. Each of them has more than 10 million people.

This movement of millions of people to cities has caused several problems. Cities are growing so fast they cannot provide enough housing, schools, and sanitation for all the people. There is poverty, crime, and disease.

Each year, millions of workers leave LDCs hoping to find jobs in developed nations. This migration affects the economy of both the LDC and the developed nation.

Most immigrants come legally. They work hard and add to the country's GDP. However, they sometimes experience discrimination from natives. Native-born workers may be angry with them because natives view the newcomers as competition for jobs. Other people come illegally. This worries some natives who believe the newcomers are a danger to the country's safety. Illegal immigration also strains public resources. The immigrants create a need for more schools, medical care, housing, and other services.

remittance
cash payment sent by workers who have migrated to a new country to family members in their home country

"brain drain"
migration of the best-educated people of less developed countries to developed nations

Migration also affects the LDC. Once they find work, many immigrants send regular cash payments to their families back home. These **remittances** help poor families in the LDCs survive.

At the same time, many well-trained and educated people also leave LDCs for better-paying jobs in developed nations. The LDC loses valuable human capital because of this **"brain drain."** This may hurt future economic development.

 CHECKPOINT *How does migration affect LDCs?*

What new challenges does globalization create?

Globalization is creating new opportunities and new challenges for the world's economies. Many challenges are sources of tension between the developed world and the developing world.

What conflict do the developed and developing world have?

One challenge globalization creates is conflict between the developed and developing worlds. Leaders in LDCs—and even newly industrialized countries—argue that international trade and financial policies favor the wealthier nations.

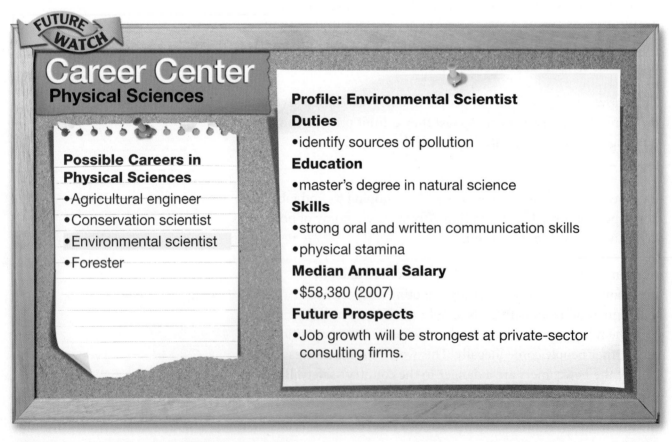

FUTURE WATCH

Career Center
Physical Sciences

Possible Careers in Physical Sciences
- Agricultural engineer
- Conservation scientist
- Environmental scientist
- Forester

Profile: Environmental Scientist
Duties
- identify sources of pollution

Education
- master's degree in natural science

Skills
- strong oral and written communication skills
- physical stamina

Median Annual Salary
- $58,380 (2007)

Future Prospects
- Job growth will be strongest at private-sector consulting firms.

They charge that the trade rules set by the World Trade Organization favor developed nations at their expense. They also claim that the International Monetary Fund asks them to make unfair changes. They say these changes make life for their poor people more difficult.

About two dozen countries have joined to give developing economies a chance to express their views. They formed an organization called the Group of 20 (G-20). The G-20 includes financial officials from growing nations such as China, India, Brazil, and Mexico. It also includes representatives from the United States and the EU. The G-20 provides a way for developed and developing countries to talk about important issues such as economic growth and the fight against terrorism.

What conflict does environmental protection create?

A second challenge globalization creates has to do with the environment. Developing and developed countries also disagree about it. Environmentalists, mostly based in developed nations, worry that rapid development can cause environmental damage. They try to promote **sustainable development.** This is the goal of meeting current development needs without using up the resources needed by future generations. On the other hand, many people in LDCs argue that they must use their resources now for their economies to grow.

Developed and developing countries disagree about **deforestation,** or large-scale destruction of forests. Many developing nations are clearing forests rapidly. They sell the timber. They use the money they earn to pay for other projects that create jobs for their people. Cleared land can be used for farming and other purposes. However, scientists in developed countries warn that deforestation destroys rare animals and plants. They also believe it adds to global warming.

How is competition for resources a challenge?

A third challenge is the competition for scarce resources. In some areas of the world, it is becoming more difficult to find enough water. Some experts warn that we are running out of oil and gas. They say we must find new supplies of these fuels or different sources of energy. If we do not, the experts believe the world's economies will stop working.

sustainable development
the goal of meeting current development needs without using up future resources

deforestation
large-scale destruction of forests

Fig. 18.10

© Mike Baldwin / Cornered

"Can Billy come out and compete in the global economy?"

▲ Staying competitive in a global marketplace is one of the main economic challenges facing Americans now and in the future. Why might this little boy be afraid to 'come out and play'? What might happen if he doesn't?

Even if these resources do not run out, the shortage of water and fuel can cause problems. The price of these vital resources will rise. People in poorer countries will not be able to pay the higher prices. If this happens, it will be even harder for the LDCs to emerge from poverty.

✅ **CHECKPOINT** *How can environmental protection conflict with economic development?*

What challenges does globalization pose to the United States?

Globalization poses challenges even for our own economy. For the United States to compete in global markets, American workers must be ready to meet changes in the workplace.

Information now drives the economy of the United States and the world. Workers need to learn how to use all sorts of information. Getting as much education as possible is a good first step. The need for education does not end when people find jobs. Workers must constantly keep up-to-date with new technology. In this way they remain productive in their jobs. Some workers will lose their jobs. They will have to learn completely new skills.

Another feature of the American workplace is the changing face of American workers. A growing percentage of American workers are foreign-born. There are more Asian Americans and Latinos than in the past. This trend will probably continue. To be productive, American workers must be ready to work closely with people of different backgrounds.

How has globalization increased the pressure to compete?

Globalization has increased economic competition. Consumers in developing nations demand more products and services. As you read, the growth of India's middle class has led to a boom in shopping malls. In Africa, the number of people who own cellular phones rose from 2 million in 1998 to nearly 80 million by 2004. This has created more competition as firms from many different countries enter the marketplace.

Competition affects business relationships too. A business might have a long relationship with a nearby supplier. However, if a different supplier can give lower prices or better service, the business will deal with that supplier. That new supplier could be located in the next town or on the other side of the world.

For all these reasons, American companies need to stay competitive. Business managers are always trying to cut costs and increase profits. They must ensure high productivity to avoid wasting money and work. They need to be constantly on the lookout for better ways to meet customer needs. Only by staying competitive can American companies succeed.

How has globalization increased the pressure to innovate?

Growing competition encourages innovation. The companies that develop new products or new ways of doing things can quickly gain a large share of the world market. For example, in 1996, two young American entrepreneurs began work on the Internet search engine company that became Google. Ten years later, the company had worldwide sales of $10.6 billion.

Still, introducing innovation and enjoying its success is not the end of the story. Any new product or service can quickly be replaced by a newer one. Other entrepreneurs are just as hungry to succeed. Writer Thomas Friedman says the new economic world is like a race that competitors must run over and over again. Winning one race does not guarantee winning a later one.

✅ **CHECKPOINT** *How can U.S. workers help firms stay competitive?*

Essential Questions Journal
To continue to build a response to the Essential Question, go to your **Essential Questions Journal.**

SECTION 4 ASSESSMENT

 Guiding Question

1. Use your completed concept web to answer the following question: What are the effects of globalization?

Key Terms and Main Ideas

Directions: On a sheet of paper, write the answer to each question. Use complete sentences.

2. How has the spread of market economies helped promote globalization?

3. Why are some Americans concerned about offshoring?

4. How does increased migration lead to "brain drain"?

5. Why is deforestation controversial?

Critical Thinking

6. **Recognize Cause and Effect** (a) What role has communications technology played in globalization? (b) How might communications be related to changing consumer demands around the world?

7. **Draw Conclusions** Should immigration be encouraged or discouraged? Explain.

QUICK STUDY GUIDE

Section 1–Levels of Development

- Nations with a high average level of well-being are called developed nations. Countries with a lower level are less developed countries (LDCs).

- Economists use per capita GDP to compare the living standards of nations.

- Generally, LDCs have low energy use and a large part of the population works in agriculture

- Literacy rate, life expectancy, and infant mortality show a nation's level of development.

Section 2–Issues in Development

- A country must expand its job opportunities, healthcare, education, and transportation as its population grows.

- Physical geography, natural resources, and climate can be problems for some LDCs.

- Many LDCs are poor and need foreign sources to fund development.

- Some LDCs use internal financing.

Section 3–Economies in Transition

- Under communism, Russia's government planners controlled the Soviet economy. In 1991 the Soviet republics became independent.

- In the 1970s, China's communist leader created special economic zones.

- India's economy has grown since the 1990s, in part because of high-technology industries.

- Some countries in northern Africa have become productive, but many nations still suffer from poverty and political conflicts.

- Brazil's and Mexico's economies have branched out into new industries.

Section 4–Challenges of Globalization

- Globalization has both advantages and disadvantages for countries.

- Multinationals may positively or negatively affect LDCs.

- Migrants often leave their home LDC to look for better jobs.

- Conflict between developed and less developed countries includes sustainable development, deforestation, and competition for resources.

- Globalization increases pressure to compete and to innovate.

Section 1
How is a nation's level of development defined?

Section 2
What factors harm or help development?

Section 3
How has economic change affected different countries?

Section 4
What are the effects of globalization?

Essential Question, Chapter 18

Do the benefits of economic development outweigh the costs?

Rachel Carson's *Silent Spring*

Rachel Carson was one of the first environmentalists. In the 1930s, she began studying ocean life and wrote many articles about marine biology. After World War II, Carson turned her focus to the use of pesticides. These were becoming common as the industry continued to develop. Carson wrote her most famous book, Silent Spring, *in 1962 to warn people about the deadly effects of these pesticides. The book was controversial, but it made many people think about the environment for the first time. Carson died of breast cancer in 1964, but her fight to protect the Earth continues today. Read the excerpt from* Silent Spring *below.*

"For the first time in the history of the world, every human being is now subjected to contact with dangerous chemicals from the moment of conception until death. . . . [The chemicals] have been recovered from most of the major river systems and even from streams of groundwater flowing unseen through the earth. Residues of these chemicals linger in soil to which they may have been applied a dozen years before. They have entered and lodged in the bodies of fish, birds, reptiles, and domestic and wild animals so universally that scientists carrying on animal experiments find it almost impossible to locate subjects free from such contamination. They have been found in fish in remote mountain lakes, in earthworms burrowing in soil, in the eggs of birds—and in man himself. . . .

All this has come about because of the sudden rise and prodigious [huge] growth of an industry for the production of man-made or synthetic chemicals with insecticidal properties. . . .

If a huge skull and crossbones were suspended above the insecticide department the customer might at least enter it with the respect normally accorded death-dealing materials. But instead the display is homey and cheerful. . . ."

Document-Based Questions

1. Who was Rachel Carson?
2. Why did Carson write the book *Silent Spring*?
3. According to Carson, where were the dangerous chemicals found?
4. What event caused the increase in contamination of people and animals?
5. Do you think people have become more concerned today with the environment since Carson's book was written? Explain.

SOURCE: *Silent Spring* by Rachel Carson, Houghton Mifflin Company, 1962.

Directions: Write the answers to the following questions. Use complete sentences.

Section 1–Levels of Development

1. What three conditions help determine the quality of life in a less developed country?

2. How is subsistence agriculture related to development?

3. How is literacy related to economic development?

4. Why do people want to know about development?

Section 2–Issues in Development

5. How do LDCs benefit from debt rescheduling?

6. Explain one political factor that slows development.

7. What is the result of malnutrition in less developed countries?

8. Do you think receiving help from the IMF or from an NGO is better for LDCs? Explain.

Section 3–Economies in Transition

9. What successes and failures has Russia had in establishing a free market economy?

10. What successes and failures has China had in establishing a free market economy?

11. What economic challenges face many African nations?

12. Does a free market system make governments better? Explain.

Section 4–Challenges of Globalization

13. Describe three characteristics of globalization.

14. What is sustainable development?

15. What is a regional trade agreement?

16. Do you think better technology always helps LDCs? Explain.

17. Why is a "brain drain" bad for LDCs?

Economics on the go

Exploring the Essential Question

18. Pick two countries discussed in this chapter. How were their economic transitions and challenges similar or different?

19. Suppose you were the leader of a developing nation. Would you favor clearing more forestland to provide immediate jobs and income or preserving the forest for future generations? Explain.

Essential Question Activity

20. Complete the activity to answer the Essential Question **Do the benefits of economic development outweigh the costs?**

The class will be divided into ten groups. Each will act as officials at the IMF. Each group will investigate economic conditions in a different LDC. Use the library or Internet to find social, economic, and political information about your country. Using the worksheet in your Essential Questions Journal or the one found at **PearsonSuccessNet.com,** gather the following information about your country: (a) current social and economic conditions, (b) resources or economic advantages, (c) economic problems, (d) political system. Each group will decide on a development plan for its country and present its recommendations to the rest of the class.

| **Essential Questions Journal** | To continue to build a response to the Essential Question, go to your **Essential Questions Journal.** |

 ## Test-Taking Tip

Take time to organize your thoughts before answering a question that requires a written answer.

Unit 7 Challenge

Essential Question, Unit 7

How might scarcity divide our world or bring it together?

VIDEO
By Students For Students
For videos on Essential Questions,
go to *PearsonSuccessNet.com*

In the global economy of the future, will scarcity lead to further interdependence—or will it lead to conflict? Look at the opinions below, keeping in mind the Essential Question: How might scarcity divide our world or bring it together?

> "Preliminary research indicates that scarcities of critical environmental resources—especially of cropland, freshwater, and forests—contribute to violence in many parts of the world. These environmental scarcities usually do not cause wars among countries, but they can generate severe social stresses within countries, helping to stimulate... ethnic clashes, and urban unrest. Such civil violence particularly affects developing societies because they are, in general, highly dependent on environmental resources and less able to buffer themselves from the social crises that environmental scarcities cause."
>
> —Thomas F. Homer-Dixon, *Environment, Scarcity, and Violence*

> "The potential exists to provide an adequate and sustainable supply of quality water for all, today and in the future. But there is no room for complacency. It is our common responsibility to take the challenge of today's global water crisis and address it in all of its aspects and dimensions."
>
> —Jacques Diouf, UN Food and Agriculture Organization Director-General, March 2007

arcadio/CAGLECARTOONS.COM/2008-IV.

Essential Question Writing Activity

Consider the different views of economics expressed in the sources on this page and what you have learned about the global economy. *Then write a well-constructed essay expressing your view of the impact of scarcity on the world economy.*

Essential Questions Journal

To respond to the unit Essential Question, go to your **Essential Questions Journal**.

Writing Guidelines

- Address all aspects of the Essential Question Writing Activity.
- Support the theme with relevant facts, examples, and details.
- Use a logical and clear plan of organization.
- Introduce the theme by establishing a framework that is beyond a simple restatement of the question and conclude with a summation of the theme.

For help in writing a Persuasive Essay, refer to the *Writing Skills Handbook* in the Reference section, page S-5.

498 UNIT REVIEW

FUTURE WATCH Personal Finance Handbook

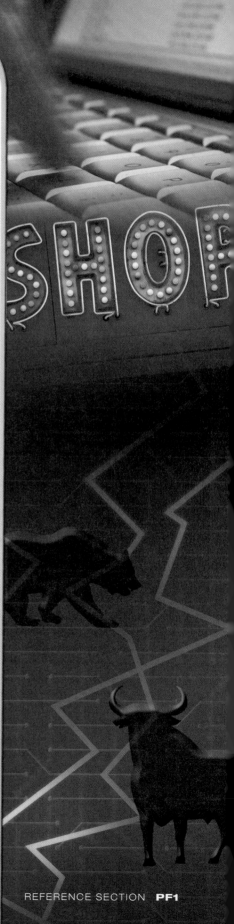

Your Fiscal Fitness: An Introduction

No pain, no gain. It applies as much to fiscal fitness as it does to physical fitness.

Think Long-Term

If you start investing $40 a week at a 5 percent rate of return, in 20 years you will have accumulated $17,800. Imagine you get a higher return, say 7 percent. By the time you retire in 45 years, you would have $163,688.

"Whoa! Slow down! 20 years? Retirement? I'm still living at home! I don't even own my first car yet! Who do you think you are—my parents?"

If that's your reaction, you're not alone. A great many high school students do not think much about their financial future. They also don't like to get stern lectures from Mom or Dad—whether it's about financial planning or about those 5,000 extra text messages that appeared on last month's cellphone bill.

But let's face it: free room and board doesn't last forever. Often, it comes to an end soon after you get handed a diploma. At some point in the not-too-distant future, the bills in the mail will be yours.

Responsible financial citizens are not born that way. Even adults must learn to comparison shop, avoid impulse buying, and put money aside they would rather spend on fun. Chances are, they made mistakes along the way. They wish you could avoid the same errors.

Take a Checkup

Start by looking at your own money habits. Are you a big spender? Moderate saver? Do you save anything at all? The answer is easy to figure out. If you have an unexpected windfall, a bigger-than-expected birthday check, or an opportunity to earn overtime money, what do you do with the money? Save it all? Save half? See what you can buy now?

Mess up your credit rating now, and you could pay the price until you're in your 30s. You might find yourself living at home after college and beyond. (Which sounds cooler—writing a check for your own apartment, or paying rent for the same bedroom you had in the sixth grade?)

Skip the Fats, Go for the Protein!

Personal finance, like athletics, requires discipline. Developing solid fiscal muscle involves training or budgeting, short- and long-term goal setting, and patience.

GO FIGURE

$269,040

The estimated cost of raising a child born in 2007 through age 17

SOURCE: United States Department of Agriculture. "Expenditures on Children by Families, 2007"

ON TRACK TO FINANCIAL CITIZENSHIP

Discipline is one of the qualities that defines a winner. If you want to come out on top, learn the rules of good financial citizenship and put them into action.

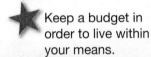 Keep a budget in order to live within your means.

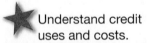 Understand credit uses and costs.

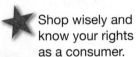 Shop wisely and know your rights as a consumer.

Preparing for a long race often involves delayed gratification. An athlete will sacrifice fast food because it's bad for the health, but healthy eating will pay off in the long run. The same is true of investing in your future. It may mean putting off purchases today for financial security later.

That's easy to say but hard to do. You and your dollars are the target of marketers and advertisers, especially of high-tech products. About 75 percent of U.S. teenagers own a cellphone, 60 percent have an MP3 player, and 43 percent have a car.

The Long Race

The impulse to get what we want now is far stronger than the desire to save for something months or years down the road. You may have to "trick" yourself into saving by promising yourself a reward when you have met certain goals.

Obstacles

What could slow your progress? One speed bump is credit card abuse. Many people struggle to pay their credit card balance in full every month. They let matters slide—failing to balance their checkbooks, check their credit card statements, or keep an eye on bank fees and interest rates. You want to develop the fiscal awareness that will keep you out of trouble.

★ Develop short- and long-term financial goals.

Savvy Savers Today's teens spend more than previous generations of teens. This 2007 survey, however, shows that many teens do understand the importance of saving and have begun to develop good saving habits.

What percentage of your income, from a job or your allowance, do you save?

Response	Percentage
I save at least 75% of my income every month.	15.6
I save 25–75% of my income every month.	51.4
I save less than 25% of my income every month.	21.9
I do not save any of my income.	11.2

Note: 1,512 teens between the ages of 13 and 18 were surveyed.
SOURCE: *Junior Achievement Personal Finance 2007: Executive Summary*

Grow Your Money

Despite the difficulty of thinking long-term, 65 percent of teens admit they want to learn how to grow their money. This is good news. Even better, 84 percent of teens average $1,044 in savings. Fueling those savings is their attitude that the future is now. Savings could translate into a car and college in the short run and a secure life and retirement in the years to come. With the right attitude, you're ready for basic training.

In no time at all, the following words will be part of your conversation. *Budgeting*—learning to spend your income so there's something left over to invest. *Compounding*—how saving a little now can translate into big money later in life. *Investing*—why the stock market can be both friend and foe. (Over the last 50 years or more, the stock market has averaged a higher return than bank accounts or bonds.)

Are You Ready?

1. How can your own spending habits help or hinder you?
2. What are some key steps to staying on a good financial track?

 To learn more about this topic, visit **PearsonSuccessNet.com**

Wise Choices for Your Money

Learning how to live within your means will help you make the most of what you have and to plan for a more secure future.

Budgeting 101

A **budget** is a plan for spending and saving. The word may conjure images of driving a junk car or eating canned spaghetti every night. The reality can be the opposite. In fact, most millionaires use a budget to manage their money. And most of them started early.

Spending Awareness

Surveys show that almost half of Americans between the ages of 13 and 18 know how to budget their money. That's the good news. The bad news is more than half don't. Which group do you fall into? Take this quick quiz:

1. How much money did you spend on beverages—from coffee or water to energy drinks—last week?
2. How much money will you spend on gas next week?
3. How long will it take you to save for the most expensive thing you'd like to buy?

If you could answer these questions without much trouble, you've already taken the first steps to good money management. If you didn't have a clue, maybe it's time to think about making a budget.

Good Habits Start Early

Did you ever ask for money to spend on concert tickets—or a piece of jewelry, or a ski trip— only to hear "You don't need it, and we can't afford it"? Odds are you didn't think of it as an economics lesson. But according to surveys, students who learned about money management at home scored higher than those who learned about it only in school.

A Balancing Act

Budgeting is a balancing act between income and expenses. It also means weighing your needs against your wants.

Income and Expenses

To begin creating a budget, follow these steps.

1. List your earnings per month from all sources. Add these up to calculate your expected monthly income.

2. For one month, record everything you spend, from chewing gum to car payments. Collect receipts or write everything in a notebook. Don't leave anything out (including savings!).
3. At the end of the month, organize your spending into categories such as food, entertainment, and car payments. Total the amount in each category.
4. List your income and expenses. If your expenses are less than your income, you're doing fine. If not, take a hard look at where your money is going.

Needs and Wants

Right now, many of your basic needs are probably part of the household budget. Still, some of your personal funds may go toward needs such as car insurance, lunches, or college savings. The rest goes toward buying things you want. So, if you are looking to cut expenses, focus first on the wants.

Consider Michelle, a high school senior. She works 20 hours a week at a department store, where she earns $10.00 an hour. Her **net income**—that is, her take-home pay after taxes—is $150. Her monthly necessities include $40 for her cellphone bill, $60 on average for gas, and $65 a month on car insurance. Michelle has already set aside $300 for her prom and hopes to have $500 by the time prom rolls around. To stay within her budget, she gives up her daily soda habit, saving almost $30 a month. She and her friends also decide to rent

What's in Your Budget? This budget shows the typical spending for a single earner, living alone. Budgets change according to lifestyle and income. What doesn't change is the need to save and pay for essentials, such as housing and food.

- 24% Housing
- 14% Food
- 6% Health
- 6% Clothing
- 17% Transportation
- 5% Entertainment/Recreation
- 11% Insurance
- 4% Charity
- 13% Savings and Investment

SOURCE: www.personalfinancebudgeting.com; National Foundation for Consumer Credit

movies rather than go out. This trade-off will allow them to rent a limousine to go to their prom.

Michelle has planned for a long-term goal and budgeted correctly. She has drawn a fine line between needs and wants.

If you find it difficult to stay within your budget, enlist a friend or family member to review your expenditures each week to keep on track. Try not to rationalize impulse buys. Consider them your sworn budget enemies!

Long-Term Rewards

Err on the side of responsibility. Live within your means and save a set percentage of your income. Some budget counselors suggest allotting 80 percent for needs, 10 percent for wants, and 10 percent for savings. Do that and you might find yourself with a tidy savings within a few years.

Spend without a plan and you might end up deep in debt. U.S. consumer debt topped an estimated $2.2 trillion dollars in 2005, or $7,400 per American. Learning to budget now may spare you from being part of this grim statistic later.

Budget Boosters

1. Keep a spending journal for one week: Include every latte, vending-machine snack, and music download.

2. Identify needs: bills, car payment, and so on.

3. Downsize or eliminate impulse buys such as coffee and soda.

4. Make saving a priority and a habit.

5. Add to your savings weekly, even if just a small amount.

6. Identify a long-term want and start saving for it. (You'll be surprised how fast those fast-food outings diminish when you set your mind on something.)

7. Prioritize and pay down any debt-including that $5 you owe your sister.

8. Use cash—not a credit card—for daily spending.

9. During vacations or the summer, pick up some extra hours at work.

10. Spend less than you make.

Are You Ready?

1. What are the steps for creating a budget?
2. Why are people with a budget more likely to be financially secure than those who don't have a budget?

 WebQuest online

To learn more about this topic, visit **PearsonSuccessNet.com**

Checking Up on Checking Accounts

Park your cash where it counts, and make your bank work for you.

The Right Bank

Banks are everywhere. Often they face each other at busy intersections in a community or are tucked in the corner of a supermarket. Every bank wants your business. How do you choose among them?

The Basic Requirement

You want to use a bank that is insured by the **Federal Deposit Insurance Corporation** (FDIC). The FDIC protects your money and the interest it has earned (up to the insurance limit) if your bank fails. For an account held by an individual, the limit is $250,000. Although banks are generally considered to be financially sound, the financial crisis has caused some banks to fail.

Endless Variety

It may be impossible for you to believe, but not so long ago even the biggest cities offered only a few different TV channels. That was it for choices. The services banks offer have grown in a similar way to the expansion of TV entertainment options. Although banks may look similar, their services are not one-size-fits all. The bank that is closest to home may not have the services that best meet your needs. First, you have to figure out what you want and then figure out where to get it.

GO FIGURE

500 million

The number of checks forged annually in the United States, with losses totaling more than $10 billion

SOURCE: Ernst & Young

How to Write a Check

All bank checks have the same basic layout and require the same information. To avoid problems with checks:
1. Write clearly.
2. Do not cross out or write over a mistake.
3. Tear a check with errors into small pieces, and write *Void* next to the check number in your check register.
4. Never write a check for more than your account balance.

Use words to write the payment amount.

Write the name of the payee.

Write the current date.

Use numerals to enter the payment amount.

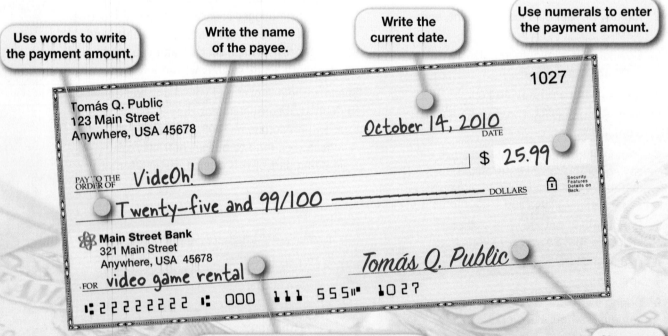

Write additional information about the payment or payee, such as a reason or an account number.

Sign your check.

The Right Services

One universal need is convenient and safe access to your money. Checking accounts, debit cards, and direct deposit have made both readily available.

Checking Accounts

To open a checking account, you will need identification, such as a birth certificate or a driver's license and a Social Security number. You will also need money to deposit.

Which checking account meets your needs?

Basic checking: Best bet for customers who use a checking account to pay some bills and use a debit card for some daily expenses.
Drawback: Monthly maintenance fees may apply unless you retain a minimum balance or enroll in direct deposit. Some banks may limit the number of checks you can write each month and charge you a per-item fee if you go over the limit.

Free checking: The operative word here is *free,* meaning a no-strings-attached account with no monthly service charges or per-item fees, regardless of the balance or activity.
Drawback: The "free" part may be an introductory offer that expires in six months or a year.

Checking with overdraft protection: If you write checks for more than the balance of your deposits, the bank will lend you the money to pay the check, up to a preset limit.
Drawback: This service comes with hefty fees.

Debit Cards

Most banks offer debit cards with a checking account. It has a credit card logo and the look and feel of a credit card, but there is a major difference. The money you spend is deducted from your checking account balance. Debit cards are also used to withdraw money from ATMs, giving you access to your money 24/7. If you use an ATM from a bank other than your own, you will likely be charged a fee. You could pay $2 or more to use your own money. Convenience comes with a price.

Direct Deposit

Banks and employers encourage people to use direct deposit. A win-win for you and the

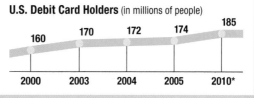

Debit Card Nation It's hard to beat convenience, and the rise in debit card usage confirms it. More than likely, you are one of 185 million Americans who use a debit card to access their checking accounts.

U.S. Debit Card Holders (in millions of people)

2000	2003	2004	2005	2010*
160	170	172	174	185

*Projected   SOURCE: *The 2008 Statistical Abstract of the United States*

environment, this paperless transaction lets your employer deposit your paycheck directly into your bank account. An employer may ask for your Social Security number, a voided check containing your bank's routing number, and your account number. Direct deposit saves you a trip to the bank and protects you from lost or stolen funds.

Keeping Track

When you open a checking account, you will receive a checkbook that includes sequentially numbered checks and a check register, or a booklet in which you'll record your account transactions. Every time you write a check, make a deposit, or use an ATM, you should take a few seconds to write it down. It is also important to save your ATM receipts. They are the only proof of how much you withdrew if the bank makes a mistake.

Each month the bank will send you a statement in the mail or online of the activity on your account. It lists deposits, withdrawals, ATM transactions, interest paid, and fees charged. Check your statement as soon as it arrives, comparing the transactions on the bank statement to your own records to make sure they agree. Most banks allow you to look at your activity 24/7 online.

For more banking tips, check out fdic.gov

Are You Ready?

1. How can you choose a checking account?
2. What are some fees banks place on checking accounts?

WebQuest online

To learn more about this topic, visit **PearsonSuccessNet.com**

Banking Online

You shop online. You chat online. You game online. Why not bank online?

Modern Banking

Once upon a time, people had to go to the bank to deposit money, transfer money from one account to another, or withdraw money from an account. They had to write a check or use cash to pay bills. This has become ancient history. As one of today's online banking customers, you can access your accounts, pay your bills, and transfer funds from one account to another 24 hours a day. Internet banks also offer the environmentally friendly option to stop paper records, allowing you to access your statements, canceled checks, and notices online only. You can even arrange automatic bill payment. Although you may receive a bill in the mail or in your e-mail, the amount you owe is automatically deducted from your bank account on a predetermined date. You save time, postage, and the possibility of missing a payment and so getting late fees.

Internet bank fees can be as much as 80 percent less than those of traditional banks. They may also offer checking, savings, or money market and CD accounts that yield higher interest rates than traditional banks.

A major benefit is the ability to find these good deals by comparison shopping online. By getting in the habit of looking for the lowest interest rates on loans and the highest interest rates on savings, wise consumers will see their money increase. Add a little compound interest, and the pace of progress will pick up.

Be Responsible

Although you may choose to bank online, every month you will get a statement from your financial institution. It is your responsibility to check this against your online transactions and report any discrepancies to your bank. Laws regulating **electronic funds transfer** (EFT),

GO FIGURE

67.9
million

The number of U.S. households that paid bills or banked online in 2008, up from 27.3 million in 2002.

SOURCE: "2008 Consumer Banking and Bill Payment" survey by Fiserv

Online Banking Tips

Online transactions offer layers of encrypted protection to safeguard your transaction and privacy.

* Make sure your computer is protected with the latest versions of antivirus and antispyware software.
* When banking online, ALWAYS double-check the Web site.
* When creating a password, avoid the obvious, including first names, birthdays, anniversaries, or Social Security numbers.
* Change passwords on a routine basis.
* Make sure all other browser windows are closed during your transaction.
* Exit a banking site after completing your online transactions and empty your computer's cache.
* Use Paypal. If your bank doesn't offer online bill pay, this online escrow service distributes your money fee-free to registered clients.
* Visit the U.S. government's site onguardonline.gov for further tips to protect yourself against online fraud.

a system for transferring money from one bank to another, protect you in case of fraud. To be protected by the law, you must report errors in transactions within 60 days of receipt of your bank statement. No matter how careful banks are not to make errors, no one is perfect.

If you use **automatic bill pay,** it is your responsibility to have enough funds in the account to cover the transaction. Some procedures of online banking are still affected by the business hours of the bank. If you transfer funds to cover your bills, the money may not show up in your account unless you have made the transfer the previous day before a specific time. A deposit made at 1 A.M. may not show up on your account until the next business day. Plan your transactions accordingly, particularly if you wait until the last moment to pay your bills.

Gone Phishing

Phishing is a scam that uses fake Web sites to gain personal and financial data to commit fraud. You can take several steps to protect yourself.

▶ Online banking transactions should be done through the bank's Web site only.

▶ Never respond to e-mails from your "alleged" bank that request account numbers, passwords, or other sensitive information.

▶ If you suspect fraud, phone your bank to determine if it's a legitimate communication from the bank. If not, alert them to the scam.

If you think you can't be fooled, think again. Phishing techniques can be elaborate. Many even set up Web pages intended to look like your financial institution's Web site to earn your trust.

Traditional Banking

Why would anyone still use a brick-and-mortar bank? There are a number of reasons.

While Internet-only banks receive high marks for convenience, they can be inconvenient.

▶ To fund an account, you have to mail in a check, arrange for direct deposit, or make

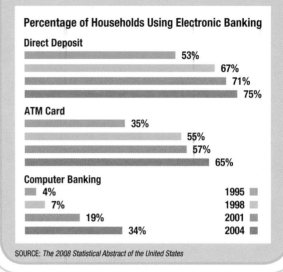

Online Revolution In 1995, Wells Fargo became the first financial institution to offer online statements. By 2012, about 82 million Americans will bank online. This chart shows trends in some methods of e-banking.

Percentage of Households Using Electronic Banking

Direct Deposit: 53% (1995), 67% (1998), 71% (2001), 75% (2004)
ATM Card: 35% (1995), 55% (1998), 57% (2001), 65% (2004)
Computer Banking: 4% (1995), 7% (1998), 19% (2001), 34% (2004)

SOURCE: *The 2008 Statistical Abstract of the United States*

a transfer from another bank. This is not a problem, of course, with banks that also operate a physical branch.

▶ Not being able to speak with someone face to face is another inconvenience. Some customers prefer to deal with people who know them personally. Phoning or communicating by e–mail is not to everyone's liking.

▶ Another drawback is the difficulty of finding fee-free ATMs, although online banks often have ATM networks for their customers to use at minimal cost.

▶ Lack of paper checks is a fourth issue. Internet-only banks offer a bill-pay service. But payments have to be scheduled ahead of time and take several days to process. As a result, you have to keep close tabs on your account to ensure you have money to cover the payments.

Are You Ready?

1. What are the advantages of online banking?
2. How can you protect yourself against phishing scams?

 WebQuest online

To learn more about this topic, visit **PearsonSuccessNet.com**

Investing With Dollars and $ense

Inside, everyone is a millionaire just waiting to happen.
You can tap your potential with basic investments.

Self-Made Success

Look in the mirror, and the face of a future millionaire may be staring back at you. More than 80 percent of millionaires are self-made, first-generation rich. But you have to set your own goals and work toward them.

Pay Yourself First

To get started on your road to wealth, you have to remember one simple rule: Pay yourself first. A good rule of thumb is to set aside 10 to 15 percent of your income. We will talk later about how to achieve this goal, but for the time being, accept the fact. The lifestyle you choose to live now will determine the lifestyle you will be able to have in the future.

Get Help From Interest

Let's assume you have decided to save. The positive news is that your savings will work for you. Banks pay you interest for using your money. Interest rates are expressed as percentages and indicate how much money an account will earn on funds deposited for a full year. Interest is compounded when it is added to your principal and you earn interest on both amounts. In effect, compound interest is interest on interest.

Most first-generation millionaires get rich over a lifetime. Their road to riches has more to do with budgeting, compound interest, and careful investing than salary and inheritances.

Basic Investing

Putting money in a savings account is safe. The only danger to money in a savings account is that the rate of inflation will be greater than the interest rate. Over time, the money in your savings account could lose value—it will buy less. But you will never lose your principal, the amount of money you put in the account.

Investing money is not the same as saving money. Investors take more risk—even possibly losing money—in the hope of getting a higher return on their money.

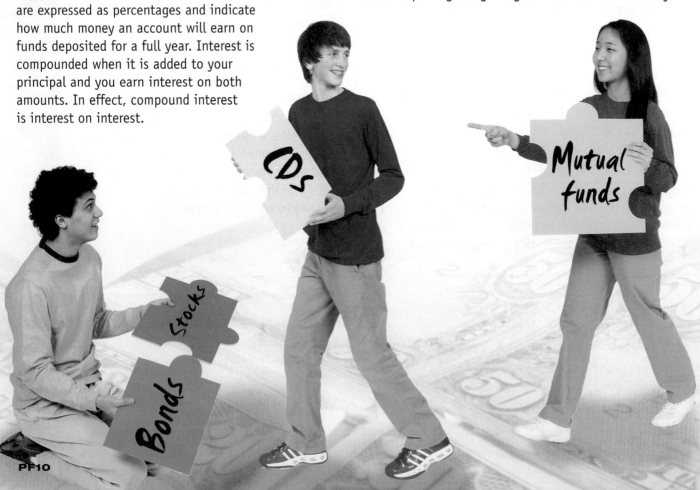

Investing your money can give your dollars a greater opportunity to grow. Bonds, stocks, and mutual funds are among the many investment choices. Of course, with the possibility of greater growth comes the possibility of greater loss. If you invest in a corporate bond, stock, or mutual fund, you risk losing some or all of the money you invested. This risk is offset by the possibility of greater gain, allowing your money to grow at a faster rate than the rate of inflation.

The Name Is Bond

A bond is an IOU issued by a corporation or some level of government. When you buy a bond, you are lending money in return for a guaranteed payout at some later date. The safest bonds to buy are government-issued bonds, because it is unlikely that a government will go bankrupt. You can get U.S. government bonds through your bank, and they can be bought in small denominations.

Tale of Two Search Engines Since 2004, Google's stock has soared to more than $650 a share. Meanwhile, Yahoo! stock has fallen. As much as they try, it is not always possible for investors to find a sure thing.

Price at Closing (in dollars)

- Google
- Yahoo

Date	Google	Yahoo
9/1/04	129.6	33.91
1/3/05	195.62	35.21
5/2/05	277.27	37.2
9/1/05	316.46	33.84
1/3/06	432.66	34.38
5/1/06	371.82	31.59
9/1/06	401.9	25.28
1/3/07	501.5	28.31
5/1/07	497.91	28.7
9/4/07	567.27	26.84
1/2/08	685.19	23.16

SOURCE: Yahoo Finance

Many corporate bonds carry a low-to-moderate risk to investors and take anywhere from 5 to 30 years to mature.

Savings account

Money market

"*Only buy something that you'd be perfectly happy to hold if the (stock) market shut down for 10 years.*"

—Warren Buffett, billionaire investor

Five-Year Rate of Return

The rate of return (profit and loss) on investments changes over time. Historically, stocks have provided investors with the greatest potential for profit. But data also show they're riskier than other types of investments.

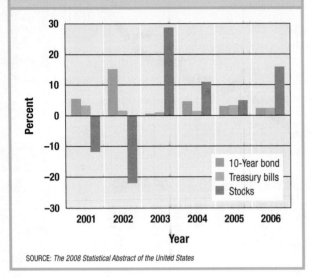

Legend:
- 10-Year bond
- Treasury bills
- Stocks

SOURCE: *The 2008 Statistical Abstract of the United States*

The value of some bonds varies. For example, if you buy a bond when interest rates are 6 percent but you want to sell it before it matures, current interest rates will affect the bond's value. If rates have gone up since you bought the bond, then you will have to discount the price to sell it. Why else would anyone want it, if they could get a higher interest rate elsewhere? If interest rates have gone down, then that 6 percent rate will seem much more inviting. In this case, you could sell the bond for more than you paid for it.

Because the value of bonds is relatively stable, they are a good investment for people who cannot tolerate much risk. Families saving to send children to college may find bonds attractive because they generally earn higher interest than a savings account and aren't likely to fall sharply in value the way stocks can.

Stock Up

Stocks represent ownership in a public company. If you buy stock in a corporation, you become a part owner.

THE RISK PYRAMID

Risk means the danger that an investment will disappoint you. A pyramid is sometimes used to demonstrate the riskiness of various investments. At the top are very risky investments like futures in precious metals. At the bottom, and least risky, are savings accounts, money market funds, and short-term CDs.

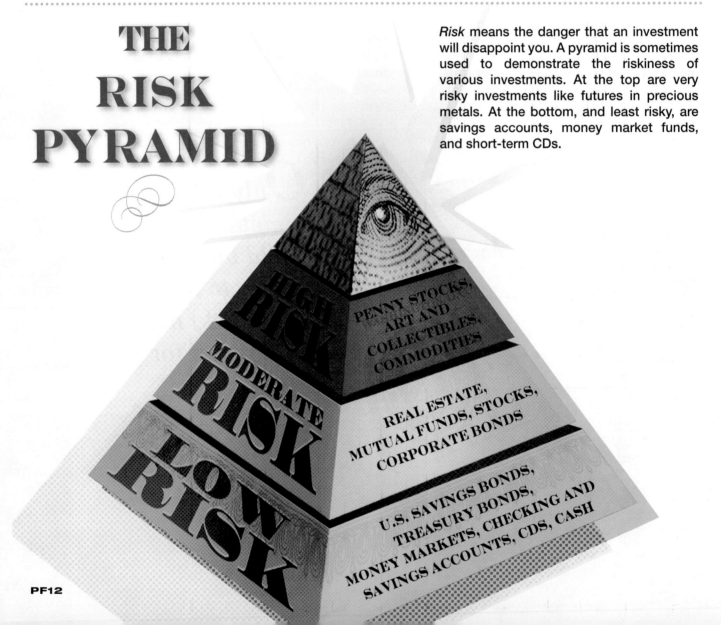

HIGH RISK

MODERATE RISK

LOW RISK

PENNY STOCKS, ART AND COLLECTIBLES, COMMODITIES

REAL ESTATE, MUTUAL FUNDS, STOCKS, CORPORATE BONDS

U.S. SAVINGS BONDS, TREASURY BONDS, MONEY MARKETS, CHECKING AND SAVINGS ACCOUNTS, CDS, CASH

You will earn money if the price of the stock goes up and if you receive dividends, which are a portion of the profits paid to the owners. There are two kinds of stock, preferred and common. Preferred stockholders get a set dividend and are paid from the corporate profits before the common stockholders. Stocks are generally a riskier investment than bonds. Historically, however, stocks have rewarded their owners with higher returns than bonds or savings accounts.

What About Mutual Funds?

A mutual fund is an investment in a company that buys and sells stocks and bonds in other companies. By combining your money with other investors', the managers of the mutual fund can buy a wide variety of stocks and bonds. When you buy a mutual fund, you are buying a part ownership of the stocks or bonds owned by the investment company. The biggest advantage of investing this way is that you instantly have a diversified portfolio. Your risk is spread out. Three kinds of mutual funds have three levels of risk.

▶ Money market funds (not the same as money market accounts) are short-term, low-risk investments. The money you invest is used to make short-term loans to businesses or governments.

▶ Bond funds are investments in bonds. Though riskier than money market funds, they have a higher potential return.

▶ Stock funds are made up of a variety of stocks. Over the long term, they have provided higher returns than either market funds or bond funds.

Mutual fund companies are required by law to register reports and statements with the SEC. You can check up on them through the SEC database at www.sec.gov/edgar. Morningstar and Standard and Poors are two companies that rate mutual funds, stocks, bonds, and other investments.

Investment Strategy

Many first-time investors think the way to earn money is to buy low and sell high. But trying to time the stock market has proven elusive to even the best investor. It's best to use common sense. Dollar cost averaging is one simple investment strategy that rewards the patient investor.

Dollar Cost Averaging

Dollar cost averaging is the strategy of investing on a regular schedule over a period of time. In this way, you capture both the lower and higher prices as prices rise and fall. In the long run, you hope to get a better average price for the purchase or sale of stocks and mutual funds. Dollar cost averaging is an attempt to protect against the ups and downs of the stock market. It is especially useful for common stocks, which can be volatile—that is, the price can swing far above and below the average price.

Other Options

The risk and payout on investments cover a range from the most secure to the really risky. Some people invest in collectibles—fine art, baseball cards, Civil War memorabilia. If the market remains strong, people who can part with what they have bought may earn a lot of money. If no one is interested in your stamp collection, you may end up using it for postage.

What you choose depends on the risk you are willing to accept. You also need to consider the length of your investments and any tax burdens the investment may carry. If your scheme is to count on "sure things" or use tips from the cousin of your neighbor's son-in-law, you are likely to be very disappointed.

The Final Word

Even though the government taxes interest and dividends at the same rate as earned income, the profits from the sale of stocks or property are capital gains. Recently, the taxes on capital gains have been lower than the tax rate on the interest from bonds and savings accounts. As a bonus, interest earned on U.S. government bonds is exempt from state and local taxes. Plan carefully for successful investment.

Are You Ready?

1. What is the difference between saving and investing money?
2. How can dollar cost averaging protect your investments?

To learn more about this topic, visit **PearsonSuccessNet.com**

Building Your Portfolio

An investment portfolio may seem out of your grasp, but learning about them can't come a moment too soon.

Your Assets

An investment portfolio is made up of different investment assets. These include the basics: stocks, bonds, mutual funds, CDs, and a 401(k). A healthy portfolio depends on many things. No portfolios are alike because every investment plan is designed according to individual needs and goals.

Diversify

All investments carry different levels of risk. To protect your investment you need to diversify. In the uncertain world of financial markets, a properly diversified investment portfolio is better equipped to survive the ups and downs of stock prices. If your portfolio consisted only of stocks in companies that made gumballs, its value could take a nosedive if stores stopped ordering gumballs. If your portfolio were properly diversified, only the investments tied to gumball makers would suffer.

Life Stages

Your investment portfolio should change over your lifetime. How it changes will depend on your income and needs. You probably won't need an investment to supplement the money you earn from a full-time job if you're 22 years old and single. By the time you're 40, however, you might be married with children. Then you might need investment income to help

Portfolios: Where Do You Stand?

No government agency provides a standard model for how you should invest your money. Experience suggests a good strategy is focused on a mix of assets that includes stocks, bonds, and cash. The allocations should change as a person ages. This is one widely accepted model of such allocations.*

Legend: Cash, Bonds, Stocks

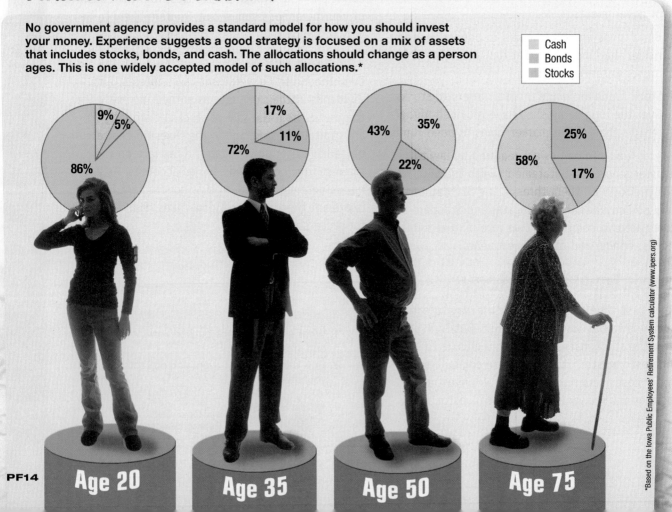

Age 20: 9%, 5%, 86%
Age 35: 17%, 11%, 72%
Age 50: 43%, 35%, 22%
Age 75: 25%, 17%, 58%

PF14

*Based on the Iowa Public Employees' Retirement System calculator (www.ipers.org)

pay for a child's first year at college. Those income-producing investments probably will be more conservative because your needs have changed.

Investments can lose value over the short-term. Over the long term, however, those same investments could recover their initial value and even gain value. That is why it would be unwise for a 75-year-old investor to have the same aggressive investments as a 30-year-old.

Lisa's Story

Lisa at age 25 decided she was ready to invest. Already participating in her company's 401(k), Lisa wanted to take her own investments to the next level: a professionally managed portfolio outside her company.

Lisa wanted to manage her assets on her own. Whom should she choose? Financial planner? Financial consultant? If Lisa's main goal is to get financial advice, she might seek out a certified financial planner (CFP).

Background Check

Lisa can perform a background check on her CFP through the CFP Board of Standards Web site. Financial planners and consultants are required by law to act in the best interest of the client, whereas brokers and brokerage firms earn commissions from their sales. The Central Registration Depository (CRD) database provides background data on brokers. The Financial Industry Regulatory Authority's Broker Check Web site (www.finra.org) provides information from the CRD.

Commissions and Fees

When Lisa narrows down her list, she will find out if the advisers operate on commission, hourly fees, a percentage of assets, or some combination. She will ask for a complete breakdown of the fee structures. A reputable adviser or broker will give her information on their fees, as well as documents outlining the risks of each investment.

How Much Risk?

Because Lisa is just starting out, her financial planner is likely to steer her toward stocks and

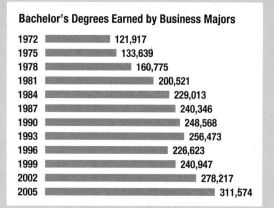

Mind Your Business Managing people's money typically requires training in finance. It is one of the fields contributing to the popularity of majors in business at U.S. colleges. In 2005, twenty-two percent of all bachelor's degrees were in business.

Bachelor's Degrees Earned by Business Majors

Year	Degrees
1972	121,917
1975	133,639
1978	160,775
1981	200,521
1984	229,013
1987	240,346
1990	248,568
1993	256,473
1996	226,623
1999	240,947
2002	278,217
2005	311,574

SOURCE: *The 2008 Statistical Abstract of the United States*

bonds. Lisa wants to limit her risk, sticking to CDs and bonds. But because Lisa is young and single, she should consider taking a higher level of risk for aggressive growth. She knows she also needs money available for an emergency.

Rule of 72

Thanks to the **Rule of 72,** Lisa easily can calculate how long it will take to double her investment at any given interest rate of return. The Rule of 72 is a mathematical shortcut. Investors divide the number 72 by the expected rate of return to estimate the number of years an investment needs to double in value. This assumes that the interest is compounded every year. For example, if Lisa invests $500 in an account that earns a 6 percent return, the account will take 12 years to become $1,000, because 72 ÷ 6 = 12. Her account value will double even if she doesn't invest another penny in it. If Lisa has an investment that earns 10 percent interest, then it will take 7.2 years to double (72 ÷ 10 = 7.2).

Are You Ready?

1. Estimate how much of Lisa's portfolio should consist of stocks.
2. Use the Rule of 72 to find how long it will take $1,500 to double at 4 percent interest.

WebQuest online To learn more about this topic, visit **PearsonSuccessNet.com**

Saving for the Long Haul

*Saving is one habit that pays. The earlier you start,
the bigger the payoff will be.*

Pay Yourself First

You already know about the advantages of making a budget. Spending less than you earn is a critical step to financial freedom. But it's only the beginning.

A Hole in the Budget

Ricky is a recent college graduate with a decent entry-level job. He's developed good financial habits. He got through college without building up a huge credit card debt. He budgets carefully—for rent, food, and car insurance. Only after he has paid all his necessary expenses does Ricky use what's left over to pay for the things he enjoys, such as a weekend trip or a new jacket. This may seem like a good plan until he decides to buy a house, starts a family, loses his job, gets hit with a long-term illness, or retires.

Ricky's habit of living within his budget month to month does not allow for life changes and emergencies. On his list of people to pay, Ricky has left someone out. He has forgotten to pay himself.

Get in the Habit

Paying yourself first simply means making personal savings a regular part of your budget, like rent and food. Everyone has the potential to save, even if it means sacrificing a few wants. Cut out the daily $2.00 for soft drinks at the vending machine, and you've just saved $14 a week. Multiply that by 52, and you've pocketed more than $700 in just one year.

Save money every month by taking a percentage of your monthly income and then paying yourself first. For example, you can have your employer automatically deposit a certain amount into your savings account. People who have trouble saving manage their money in reverse. They spend first, and then save what is left. But what if nothing is left? Then nothing is left to save. Saving doesn't mean you don't get to spend your money. It means you spend it later.

GO FIGURE

$140.6 trillion

The 2008 value of the $24 worth of trinkets that colonists paid to the Manhattoes tribe for Manhattan in 1626, with 8 percent interest compounded annually

TALE OF TWO SAVERS

The age you start saving can make a big difference in the amount you have at retirement. In the case of the two savers shown here, the difference is more than $1 million! Both savers start with $200 and save $200 a month. Both earn 8 percent interest compounded annually. Saver 1 starts at age 18. Saver 2 starts at age 36.

AGE 18

AGE 36

Why Save?

Not many young people think about saving for retirement. Yet when it comes to saving, time is money. There are at least three big benefits to thinking *now* about the day you finally stop working. The biggest benefit is compound interest.

The Magic of Compound Interest

The earlier you start saving, the faster your money will grow. The reason: **compound interest.** This is interest you earn not only on the money you put into an account but also on all the interest you have previously built up. Today's interest earnings will start earning interest tomorrow. The more you save today, the more interest you will gain tomorrow. That savings will add up at a faster rate. For every year you put off saving, you could lose thousands of dollars in the long haul.

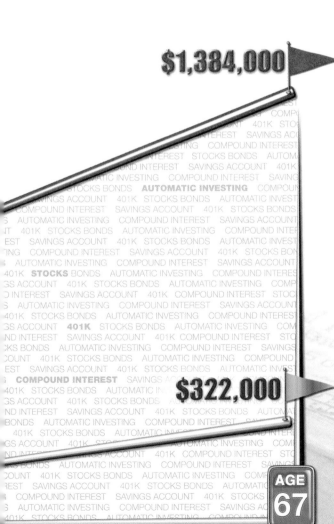

$1,384,000

$322,000

AGE
67

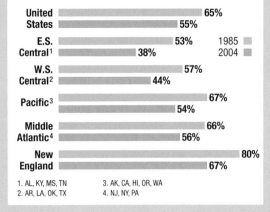

Save Yourselves Economists warned years ago that Americans faced financial burdens not seen by previous generations. Data show that the decline in savings accounts is a national trend.

U.S. Regions With Large Declines in Percentage of Americans With Savings Accounts

Region	1985	2004
United States	65%	55%
E.S. Central[1]	53%	38%
W.S. Central[2]	57%	44%
Pacific[3]	67%	54%
Middle Atlantic[4]	66%	56%
New England	80%	67%

1. AL, KY, MS, TN
2. AR, LA, OK, TX
3. AK, CA, HI, OR, WA
4. NJ, NY, PA

SOURCE: *Savings and Asset Accumulation Among Americans, 25–34,* by Christopher Thornberg and Jon Haveman. October 13, 2006.

Other Benefits

There are also big tax benefits when you stash money away for retirement. If you put funds into an **individual retirement account** (IRA), the money may escape taxation until you retire—or at least until you reach age 59½. That cuts your tax bill now. Even better, when you withdraw your money from a special IRA (called a **Roth IRA**), the money you earn—the appreciation—may not be taxed at all.

Finally, putting money away now allows you to have a cushion in case of emergencies. There are even circumstances in which—despite the government's restrictions—you can dip into a retirement fund to pay for other expenses. For example, you can access some retirement accounts to buy your first house or to cover high medical expenses.

Whether your dream is a comfortable retirement, a nice home, or foreign travel, you're going to need a savings plan to make it come true.

Are You Ready?

1. What are the reasons teens should save?
2. What are three things you can sacrifice to save money?

WebQuest online

To learn more about this topic, visit PearsonSuccessNet.com

Get Personal With Your Savings Plan

You know why you need to save, and save early. But which savings plan is right for you?

Three Savers

You've decided to take a portion of your income every week and put it toward your financial future. Your goal is to achieve financial freedom, meet emergencies, and have a comfortable retirement—maybe even to get rich. But not all paths are equal.

Different "Plans"

Let's look at three young adults: A. J., Amanda, and Tyler. Each earns about the same amount of money. Each decides to take $10 per week and dedicate it to their financial future. A. J. takes his $10 and invests in lottery tickets in the hope of winning a million dollars. Amanda takes her $10 and puts it in a shoebox under her bed. Tyler takes his $10 and puts it in a simple savings account paying 3.6 percent interest.

Different Results

Each keeps this up regularly for 20 years. Each would say, "I'm paying myself first." But see how the results are different: A. J. has paid himself a total of $10,400. He now has $0. Amanda has paid herself a total of $10,400. She now has $10,400. Tyler has paid himself a total of $10,400. He now has $15,392.

The odds of winning a state lottery are something like one in 18 million. So what sounds better to you? A 100 percent chance of increasing your savings by nearly $5,000 . . . or a 99.99999995 percent chance of losing it all? That's a no-brainer. Tyler's savings account is also clearly more profitable than Amanda's shoebox. But even the savings account may not be the best option of all.

Park Your Savings

In making a personal savings plan, the first question you have to ask yourself is: "How much can I save?" You've seen how putting aside even a small amount can build up as long as you do it regularly. The amount you save per week should be one that you can reasonably commit to for a year. The key is doing this even if you cannot afford it. Then pay your other bills as usual.

Savings Account

Usually, saving starts with setting up a basic savings account carrying no monthly fee. But when choosing a place to park your savings, *shop around*. Make sure the bank is FDIC insured. Some banks will charge large fees just for the privilege of having your money. Web sites such as bankrate.com show you the interest different banks currently pay for checking accounts.

CDs

Once you start earning more money, think about moving some cash into a **certificate of deposit,** or CD. Like a savings account, a CD is insured and therefore low risk. But CDs generally offer higher interest than a savings account. The catch is, once you put your money in, you can't take it out for a fixed period of time. Depending on the length of the CD, you would have to part company with your money for as little as three months or as long as five years. There are penalty fees for early withdrawal.

As with savings accounts, you can compare CD rates online. You might even opt for an online bank that offers even higher interest rates than traditional banks.

Money Markets

What if you want higher yield than a regular savings account without tying up your money? You might open a **money market account**. This is a type of savings account with a high yield that allows you to write checks as long as you maintain a high balance in the account.

SAFETY IN NUMBERS

Rainy day fund.
Emergency fund.
Back-up plan.

The name of the game is emergency money to turn to when life throws a curveball. This requires a separate "must-pay" account—just like a bill. Job loss is just one situation that warrants easy-access cash.

Other cases of emergency include illness, car repairs, and appliance repairs. The recommended emergency safety net ranges between three and six months of income. Here are six ways to jump-start your fund.

1 **Funding bill:** Set up an automatic payment into a savings account.

2 **Cash stash:** Relative sent you money? Put a portion toward emergency savings.

3 **Loose change:** Deposit all your coins into a jar. Repeat daily.

4 **Small sacrifices, big savings:** Cut down on impulse buys. Spin that cash toward your fund.

5 **Back to the basics:** Consolidate and resolve outstanding debt.

6 **Uncle Sam's store:** Purchase a U.S. Savings Bond.

(SOURCES: www.bankrate.com, www.marketwatch.com)

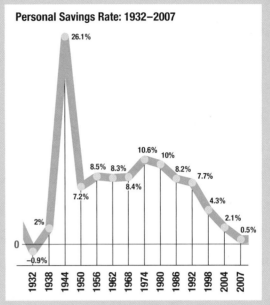

Depressing Savings In 2005, the U.S. government reported that the personal savings rate briefly fell into negative territory for the first time since the Great Depression. Americans spent more than they earned.

Personal Savings Rate: 1932–2007

26.1%
10.6%
10%
8.5% 8.3%
8.2%
7.7%
8.4%
7.2%
4.3%
2%
2.1%
0.5%
0
−0.9%

1932 1938 1944 1950 1956 1962 1968 1974 1980 1986 1992 1998 2004 2007

SOURCE: Bureau of Economic Analysis: National Income and Product Accounts Table (2.1) (May 29, 2008)

Are You Ready?

1. Why is the pay-yourself-first principle a good savings technique?
2. How can you build an emergency fund?

To learn more about this topic, visit **PearsonSuccessNet.com**

Retirement Planning: Me? Now? *Why?*

Believe it or not, it is never too early to start planning for retirement.

Retire in Style

It is never too early to plan for retirement. The longer you wait to save, the less time your money has to work for you. If you have a job now, you're already putting some money away for retirement. The government takes money from your paycheck to save for your future in the form of the FICA tax, or Social Security tax. But experts generally agree that Social Security payments alone will not fund a comfortable retirement.

How Much Will You Need?

How much money will you need in retirement? That depends on your health, your lifestyle, where you live. Everybody has different needs.

Many financial advisers estimate you will need 70 percent of your preretirement income to retire comfortably. By *comfortably*, they mean you will be able to keep up your preretirement lifestyle. Your needs will be lower because you will not have to buy clothes for work or pay for commuting. You also won't have to put as much money into your retirement investments. It is time for them to pay you. No one is average, however. Some people spend more when they first retire because they have more time for travel and entertainment. As they age, they travel less, and those costs go down. But in many cases the cost of healthcare goes up.

Where's the Money?

The first source is Social Security. You might also have a defined pension, a set amount of money paid by your employer based on your wages and length of employment. Defined pensions, however, are disappearing in private industry. The rest of your retirement income depends on you: a 401(k), individual retirement accounts (IRAs), investments, and savings.

Social Security

Each year the Social Security Administration sets the minimum amount you need to earn to receive Social Security benefits. You can begin to collect reduced

Launch Your Plans for Retirement

Statistics say you will live a longer life than your grandparents did. Develop habits now to help you live with the choices you make. When you ride off into the sunset, you want to do it in style.

Solid Financial Planning

benefits at age 62 and full benefits at age 67 for people born after 1959. As the population ages, the point will come when Social Security will pay out more in benefits than it collects each year in payroll taxes. The message here is that you have to prepare to take care of yourself.

401(k)

The law allows you to set aside a portion of your pay before taxes are withheld. Rent, credit cards, and student loans may limit what you can contribute to your 401(k), but the returns are worth the sacrifice. Some employers match every dollar you save up to 3 percent of your salary. Others may choose to contribute 50 cents per dollar you save, up to 6 percent of your salary.

Employers have come to realize that many people do not have a clue how to invest the money in their 401(k) accounts. More and more employers are providing sources of investment advice to help their employees make the most of their money.

Other Accounts

The federal government also encourages you to save for retirement by providing special tax advantages for other retirement accounts.

▶ You can open up a traditional individual retirement account at a bank and contribute $4,000 per year. Depending on your income, this money may be tax deductible. You have to be ready to leave this money alone. Tapping an IRA prior to age 59½ will cost you dual penalties. You will forfeit 10 percent of your interest, plus pay taxes on what you have withdrawn as though it were income. The 10 percent penalty is waived if the money is used for higher education or first-time home ownership.

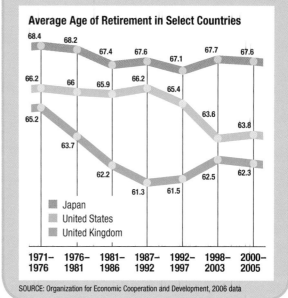

Retiring Nations Although the average age of retirement among American workers has risen in the past decade, it's still about four years less than in Japan. As people live longer, the retirement age is likely to rise even more.

Average Age of Retirement in Select Countries

Japan: 68.4, 68.2, 67.4, 67.6, 67.1, 67.7, 67.6
United States: 66.2, 66, 65.9, 66.2, 65.4, 63.6, 63.8
United Kingdom: 65.2, 63.7, 62.2, 61.3, 61.5, 62.5, 62.3

- Japan
- United States
- United Kingdom

1971–1976, 1976–1981, 1981–1986, 1987–1992, 1992–1997, 1998–2003, 2000–2005

SOURCE: Organization for Economic Cooperation and Development, 2006 data

▶ In a Roth IRA, contributions are taxed before investing, but withdrawals after age 59½ are tax free, meaning you never pay taxes on the interest or dividends that have accumulated over the years. Roth IRA money may be withdrawn for first-time homeowners or higher education on the condition that the account has been open for five years. Early withdrawals will be subject to the 10 percent penalty.

Federal regulations about these kinds of accounts are subject to change by Congress. In recent years, Congress has raised the savings limits to encourage people to save more for retirement.

Are You Ready?

1. What factors influence how much you will need to retire?
2. Describe two ways you can save for retirement.

WebQuest online

To learn more about this topic, visit PearsonSuccessNet.com

Fundamentals of Good Credit

Are you credit worthy? It matters more than you think.

Making the Grade

As a first-time borrower, you may find it tough to get a credit card or a car loan on your own. Without a credit history to check, lenders often will require a cosigner to guarantee the loan will be repaid if you fail to repay. This person could be your parent or another relative with a good credit history.

The rest is up to you. How can you prove to future lenders that you are a good credit risk? Pay your bills on time. Every late or missed payment will end up on your credit report.

Your **credit report** is your financial report card. In addition to your payment history, it includes the details of your bank and credit card accounts. Lenders can see how much debt you already carry. They can also see if you have had any bankruptcies or judgments against you or if you owe back taxes.

National credit reporting agencies create a **FICO score** based on your credit history. The score falls in a range from about 300 to 900. Usually, a score of at least 700 gives you access to reasonable credit. For a fee, you can find out your credit score at MyFico.com.

A bad credit report can sink more than a loan. It also affects your chances of getting insurance, an apartment, a mortgage—even a job. Like lenders, many landlords and employers check credit histories. They see on-time bill paying as an indication

ADVENTURES IN CREDIT

Whether you are judged to be a good credit risk depends on the three Cs.

Good Credit

CAPITAL
What assets you have to back up a loan, like a savings account, property, investments

CHARACTER
Financial history and payment record

CAPACITY
Your expenses, your job, and how long you have had it

of whether you will be a responsible tenant or worker. The **Fair Credit Reporting Act** (FCRA) sets the terms by which credit information about you can be gathered and used.

Protecting Your Credit

If mistakes occur in your credit report or you have made poor credit choices, what can you do?

Check It Out

Free credit reports are available once per year from each national credit-reporting agency: Experian, Transunion, and Equifax. To get a free credit report, go online: www.annualcreditreportonline.com; call (877) 322-8228; or mail: Annual Credit Report Request Service, P.O. Box 105281, Atlanta, GA, 30348.

Review credit reports from all three agencies to check for errors and possible fraud. In some states, consumers who suspect fraud can place a security freeze on their credit file. This action prevents any new accounts from being opened in your name.

If you find an error in your credit report, send a separate letter to each agency where the mistake is found as soon as possible. Include a copy of the credit report with the misinformation highlighted. The credit reporting agency is required by law to investigate with the creditor in question. It should remove from your credit report any mistakes a creditor admits. The FCRA requires creditors to correct errors without lowering your credit rating.

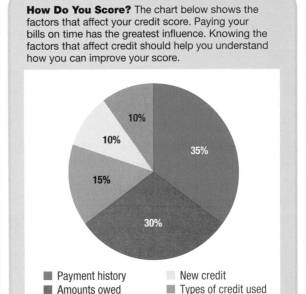

How Do You Score? The chart below shows the factors that affect your credit score. Paying your bills on time has the greatest influence. Knowing the factors that affect credit should help you understand how you can improve your score.

- 35%
- 30%
- 15%
- 10%
- 10%

- ■ Payment history
- ■ Amounts owed
- ■ Length of credit history
- ■ New credit
- ■ Types of credit used

SOURCE: www.myfico.com

Clean It Up

No matter how careful you are, circumstances may get the better of you. The loss of a job or a medical emergency could leave you in a world of financial difficulty. Here are some steps to take if you have trouble paying your bills on time.

Reassess your needs and wants. Be prepared to make hard choices.

▶ Stop using credit until you are out of trouble.

▶ Contact your lenders to negotiate a different payment schedule or interest rate.

▶ Contact nonprofit credit counseling organizations. For a small fee, they can help manage debt and intervene with card issuers. Make sure the service is affiliated with a third party such as the Association of Independent Consumer Credit Counseling Agencies or National Foundation of Credit Counseling.

Are You Ready?

1. What factors affect your credit rating?
2. Why is it important to check your credit report?

To learn more about this topic, visit **PearsonSuccessNet.com**

Ready. Set. *Charge?*

The freedom to charge your purchases comes with fine print, finance charges, and a host of fees. Know your limits.

The Lure of Credit

"Buy now—pay later." This sums up the attraction of **credit**, or deferred payment. Credit comes in many forms, from car loans to mortgages to credit cards.

Credit Convenience

Credit cards make buying easy. With a piece of plastic, you can walk into nearly any store and walk out with merchandise. As for buying online, it would be almost unthinkable without credit cards.

Teens and Credit

Americans under 18 may not have their own credit cards. Still, about one third of all high school students use cards linked to the account of a parent or relative. And when you turn 18, expect a ton of mail from credit card companies eager to issue you your first card. Some may even offer freebies, such as T-shirts or sports gear, just for filling out an application.

Why do they want your business? *Teens spend*. Each year, consumers between the ages of 12 and 19 spend well over $100 billion of their own and their parents' money. Credit card companies want to tap into this spending.

Credit Traps and Tips

Unless you learn how to use credit responsibly, you could find yourself in a deep hole. You won't be there alone. It is estimated a majority of Americans between the ages of 18 and 24 spend nearly 30 percent of their monthly income on debt repayment.

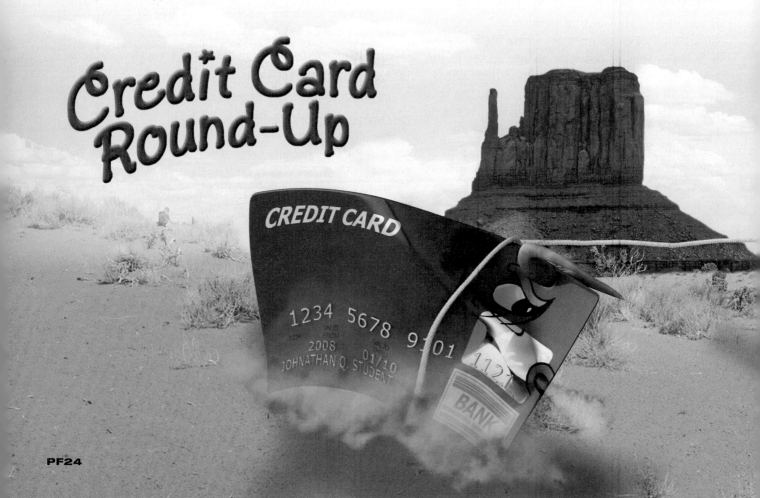

Credit Card Round-Up

CREDIT CARD

1234 5678 9101

2008   01/10

JOHNATHAN Q. STUDENT

BANK

Avoid Those Charges

Ideally, you'll want to pay off your credit card balance in full every month. True, you are *required* to make only a small minimum payment. But look at the table on the right. For every dollar you don't pay this month, you'll pay interest next month. Worse, first-time cardholders without an established credit rating often have a higher-than-normal **annual percentage rate** (APR).

If you pay late or miss a payment entirely, you'll pay a late penalty. The finance charges, which include the APR and any related fees, can quickly add up to more than your initial purchase.

The Cost of Cash

Fees mount up even faster if you use your credit card to get cash. A cash advance carries an up-front fee of 2 percent to 4 percent, plus a higher interest rate than the regular card. The charges start the second the ATM coughs out the cash.

Read the Fine Print

Reading the fine print of a credit card's terms of agreement is extremely important. The **Truth in Lending Act** requires banks to provide complete information on the APR, fees, and surcharges. This information is usually located on the back of a credit card application and monthly statements.

Double the Debt This table shows the cumulative effect of a 19 percent interest rate on a $2,000 credit card debt. A person paying only $40 a month would incur $1,994 in interest charges by the time the loan was paid, in addition to the $2,000 in principal—nearly double the original debt.

Minimum Repayment Schedule on a $2,000 Credit Card Loan at 19 Percent Interest

Monthly minimum payment amount	Number of months to pay	Total interest payment
$40	100	$1,994
$50	64	$1,193
$75	35	$619
$100	25	$424

SOURCE: Government Accounting Office: *College Students and Credit Cards*

Still, banks can change these terms, raising rates and fees when they feel it is necessary. You can opt out of the changes, which will close the account. You can then pay off the balance under the old terms. The time it takes to review these terms could save you headaches and money.

Credit or Debit?

The surest way to avoid the debt trap is to keep credit card use to a minimum. For lower-cost purchases, you are better off using a debit card, a check, or cash. A debit card offers the same convenience as a credit card. Because the money comes straight out of your bank account, there is no interest rate and no risk of going over your limit. The danger of debit cards is they are easy to use. You may lose track of your spending.

For online purchases it's wisest to use a credit card. It offers greater security.

Are You Ready?

1. Give three examples of bank fees.
2. What is the difference between a debit card and a credit card?

To learn more about this topic, visit PearsonSuccessNet.com

Managing Your Debt

Ignore what you owe and erode your credit. Drowning in debt is as bad as it sounds.

Getting Into Debt

Using credit cards or borrowing money is not necessarily bad. You get into trouble when you go overboard.

Types of Loans

Loans come in several forms. Single-payment loans are short-term loans paid off in one lump sum. **Installment loans,** such as home mortgages or auto loans, are repaid at regularly scheduled intervals. Each payment is divided between principal, or the amount borrowed, and interest. (The earlier you are in the life of the loan, the higher the proportion of each payment goes toward interest.) A third kind of debt is revolving credit, where the amount borrowed and paid changes each month. The best example is a credit card.

How Much Is Too Much?

Carrying some debt is not a problem—almost everybody does it. But you need to stay within safe limits. A general rule is that your debt payments, including a mortgage, should not be more than 36 percent of your gross income (income before taxes and deductions). You can estimate your own debt-to-income ratio by dividing the amount of money you owe by the amount of money you earn. If the result is higher than 36 percent, you probably owe too much.

Here are some warning signs:
- ▶ Inability to make minimum payments
- ▶ Relying on credit cards out of necessity and not convenience
- ▶ Borrowing from one credit card to pay another
- ▶ Tapping retirement savings or other investments to pay loans

Take Andy. His entry-level job had an entry-level salary. The debt he ran up in college soared as he depended more and more on "plastic" to cover the basics. Paying just the minimum spared his credit temporarily, but he was racking up high finance charges. Once he started missing payments, creditors began calling.

Credit Counseling

Andy hated to admit it, but he needed help. He tried credit counseling. A credit counseling agency will negotiate on your behalf with the creditors, trying to get you an extension of time and lower interest rates. For a small fee, it will take over your monthly payments.

SOLVENCY STREET

DEBTOR'S WAY

DEBT TO INCOME RATIO UNDER 15%

A HEALTHY EMERGENCY FUND

DISCIPLINED BUDGET

GOOD CREDIT RATING

BILLS PAID ON TIME

BILL COLLECTORS CALLING

MAXED-OUT CREDIT CARDS

NO MONEY TO INVEST

LATE FEES GALORE

CAN'T PAY BILLS ON TIME

Andy checked with the National Foundation for Credit Counseling and the Association of Independent Consumer Credit Counseling Agencies to find a reputable agency. He now writes one check per month to the agency, instead of three to his creditors.

Other Options

If you find yourself in Andy's shoes, consider other options—with caution. You could swallow your pride and ask a relative or friend for a loan. If you go this route, though, make sure you have a written repayment plan and offer to pay interest.

You could also try taking out a loan from a credit union. Credit unions usually offer better terms than banks. You may, however, need a cosigner.

Bankruptcy: The Last Resort

Bankruptcy is truly your last option. Common reasons for bankruptcy are large medical bills, uninsured losses, or high credit card bills. Some of these are unavoidable, but many people get into serious debt because of poor decisions and lack of foresight. Once you declare bankruptcy, it will be harder for you to obtain credit. Nearly every credit application asks: "Have you ever declared bankruptcy?" So take this step only with the help of a lawyer who specializes in bankruptcy and can explain the options and consequences.

Credit Slips Over the past three decades, the number of Americans who filed for bankruptcy has risen more than 300 percent. The 2005 law that changed the rules for bankruptcy appeared to have little effect on the number of Americans who sought protection from their creditors. New cases in 2006 were down only slightly from 2004.

Bankruptcy Petitions Filed in the United States

Year	Petitions
1986	401,575
1988	526,066
1990	660,796
1992	899,840
1994	788,509
1996	989,172
1998	1,379,249
2000	1,240,012
2002	1,466,105
2004	1,599,986
2006	1,453,008

SOURCE: *The 2008 Statistical Abstract of the United States*

One option is known as Chapter 7, or liquidation. You give up your assets in exchange for your debts. The cash value of your assets is paid to the creditors. To reduce fraud and make it harder to declare bankruptcy, the federal government passed the Bankruptcy Abuse Prevention and **Consumer Protection Act** of 2005. Debtors must prove that their income is below their state's median income and complete financial counseling and financial management education. Also, the government randomly audits debtors to check up on the accuracy of the bankruptcy documents.

A second option is known as Chapter 13, or debt adjustment, which involves temporarily suspending foreclosures and collection actions while you create a plan to repay some or all of the debts in three to five years. The amount to be repaid depends on how much you have versus how much you owe. Any form of bankruptcy will make it far more difficult to rebuild a secure financial future.

If you think nobody cares if you're alive, try missing a couple of car payments.

—Earl Wilson, author and newspaper columnist

Are You Ready?

1. Give several reasons why some people get into trouble with debt.
2. Why is bankruptcy a last resort?

 To learn more about this topic, visit **PearsonSuccessNet.com**

Insurance Basics, Part I

As you grow older and acquire more assets, your need for insurance grows as well.

Insuring the Future

You just got ticketed for sailing past a stop sign. You got distracted while you were changing a CD. Your parents are using the word *grounded* a lot—and also the word *insurance*. Sure, you are covered on their policy, but a moving violation could raise their rates and yours.

What Is Insurance?

Insurance is part of a **risk management plan** that will protect you against financial losses. Basically, insurance is a bet between you and your insurer. You are betting that something bad will happen to you, such as illness or a car accident. The company is betting against it.

Types of Insurance

Most adults should have four basic types of insurance coverage. Your age, family situation, and income are some major factors to consider when deciding the type and amount of coverage you should get.

▶ *Auto:* Protects you and other drivers in case of an accident that results in damage and injury. It also protects you in case of theft, vandalism, and natural disasters. Most states require you to have your own auto insurance or to be listed as a driver on someone else's policy.

▶ *Health:* Protects you in case of illness or injury. It also covers the cost of routine medical and preventive care, prescriptions, and in some cases dental care. Even if you're healthy, having health insurance is a good idea.

▶ *Property:* Protects your home or apartment in case of damage or loss of your belongings due to water, fire, or wind. It can cover your liability if someone is injured in your home and sues you for damages. Most policies do not, however, protect you against flood damage. You need to buy that coverage separately.

▶ *Life:* Pays a set amount to your **beneficiary** in case of your death. The beneficiary is the person or entity, such as a charity, that you name as the recipient of the death benefit of your life insurance policy. The two most common types of life insurance are term, or temporary, insurance, and whole life insurance. Rates for term insurance increase over time. The only way to collect from a term policy is to die during the term. Whole life insurance remains in effect for one's entire lifetime at a set rate. It builds cash value. The insured can borrow against the policy.

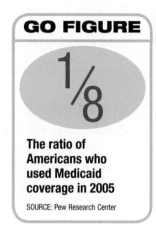

What It Costs

The payment you make to an insurance company is called a premium. The cost of insurance is high and getting higher. So does it pay to buy it? Absolutely. You may never have an accident and file a claim. But if you do, the amount you collect could be many times what you paid in premiums. Even a brief stay in a hospital, for example, can run up a bill of hundreds of thousands of dollars.

In many cases, insurance is not optional. You can't even register a car without proof of auto insurance. Nor can you get a mortgage without homeowner coverage.

Deductibles

Insurance companies spread their risk by collecting premiums from a lot of customers. They also reduce their costs by requiring copays and deductibles. A **deductible** is an amount you have to pay before your coverage kicks in. For example, if your car insurance policy has a $1,000 deductible and you have an accident, you'll have to pay the first $1,000 in damages. The company pays the rest. The higher the deductible, the lower the premium.

Copays

If you have a **copay,** you are responsible for a small portion of the total cost of a service covered by your insurance policy. Your insurance company pays the rest.

Changing Needs

As you get older, acquire more possessions, and expand your family, you have more to replace and more to protect.

Coreen at 18–25

Coreen is finally eligible for employee health benefits. She tells her parents they can remove her from their policy. She finds an apartment and gets rental insurance to protect her possessions from damage or theft. With no dependents, Coreen can probably get by with basic auto, rental and health coverage—for now.

Karen and Bill at 25–54

Coreen's sister Karen and her husband, Bill, have purchased their first home. They are also expecting their second child. With a new home, children, and two cars, Karen and Bill now need a medical policy that covers more checkups for the children.

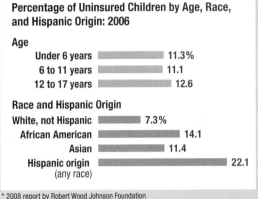

Kid Care More than 9 million children in the United States are not covered by health insurance. According to a 2008 study,* researchers found that uninsured children with serious illnesses are far more likely to have their care delayed or to receive no care. Some programs such as Medicaid and State Children's Health Insurance Program provide aid to about 3.6 million children. The table below shows some background on children without insurance.

Percentage of Uninsured Children by Age, Race, and Hispanic Origin: 2006

Age

Under 6 years	11.3%
6 to 11 years	11.1
12 to 17 years	12.6

Race and Hispanic Origin

White, not Hispanic	7.3%
African American	14.1
Asian	11.4
Hispanic origin (any race)	22.1

* 2008 report by Robert Wood Johnson Foundation

SOURCE: U.S. Census Bureau, Current Population Survey, 2007 Annual Social and Economic Supplement

They also can't risk having to pay for a new car if they have an accident. With lives and assets to protect, this family adds collision insurance to their auto policy and purchases home, mortgage, and life insurance.

Alex and Isabel, over 54

Coreen's parents, Alex and Isabel, decide to revisit their insurance needs. They are less concerned about term or whole life insurance coverage. They are more concerned about the cost of long-term healthcare. Because Alex and Isabel are in their 50s, they can expect to pay more for their coverage, perhaps as much as hundreds of dollars a month. To find the best rates, they will want to get group coverage through an employer or a large organization.

Are You Ready?

1. Why is it important to have insurance?
2. Describe the insurance needs of people at different stages of life.

WebQuest online

To learn more about this topic, visit PearsonSuccessNet.com

Insurance Basics, Part II

People who don't get insurance are betting nothing bad will ever happen to them. Are you willing to take that gamble?

Insurance Is an Investment

Insurance is all about avoiding risk. For you, that means paying now to avoid a gigantic cost later. For the insurance company, it means avoiding people who are likely to cost them a bundle.

Insurers set rates based on **risk factors**, hard statistics that predict whether someone is likely to be a bad risk. Do you plan to become a pilot or take up mountain climbing? That will make you a higher risk than a lawyer who spends leisure time doing crossword puzzles. A smoker must pay higher health insurance premiums than a nonsmoker. In the worst case, a risky lifestyle may make you uninsurable.

Right now, insurance costs are probably not your concern. Most teens are covered for pretty much everything—life, health, property—by a parent or guardian. However, some teens must foot their own auto insurance bill. That's expensive. Statistically, new drivers are high-risk. But if you want wheels, you have no choice.

Health Insurance

No matter how healthy your lifestyle is, you are going to face illness or accident.

Employer Plans

Most kids are covered under parents' health insurance for as long as they're in school—at least up to age 23. Once you enter the working world, it's up to you. If you work for a company that offers health insurance, you can usually choose from a variety of group plans. Some cover you from day one. More often, there is a waiting period. Your share of the premium is deducted from your paycheck each pay period. The higher the deductible, the lower the premium.

The least expensive health insurance plan is generally a **health maintenance organization** (HMO). An HMO allows you to pick a primary care physician, to whom

GO FIGURE

$1,896

The average U.S. auto insurance premium in 2007. Louisiana had the nation's highest average at $2,740. Wisconsin had the lowest with $1,335.

SOURCE: "Most Expensive States for Car Insurance," Insurance.com

5 Tips for Cheaper Auto Insurance

Searching for ways to cut down on the cost of insuring a car doesn't mean you have to skimp on coverage. Even with the best companies, you can take steps that will help lower your bill.

1. Increase your deductible. If you have to file a claim, can you afford to pay a higher deductible? The higher your deductible, the lower your premium.
2. Buy safely. Some cars cost more to insure because they are a favorite target for thieves. Find out which makes and models these are before you buy.
3. Drive carefully. Don't think insurance companies won't notice speeding tickets or accidents. Unsafe driving makes for a big risk and a big bill.
4. Go back to school. Most, if not all, insurers offer discounts for completing a defensive driving course.
5. Install safety and antitheft devices in your car. These will lower your risk profile.

you pay a copay. If you need to see a specialist, your primary doctor will refer you to an in-network doctor. This doctor has agreed to accept the payment level paid by the insurance company.

The Uninsured

Not a full-time student or employee? You are on your own unless you can get private health insurance, which is usually much more expensive than a group policy. Some insurance companies raise premiums or deny coverage for preexisting conditions. If you are denied coverage, you may be eligible for assistance through Medicaid for low-income or disabled persons.

Cut Your Costs

The rising number of claims, plus increasing cases of fraud, have caused insurance premiums to skyrocket. But you can take a number of steps to get the best coverage.

1. **Comparison shop.** Compare the rates of different companies. Check with the Better Business Bureau. And don't forget word of mouth. Don't just ask about premium costs. Ask about customer service as well. Low price is no bargain if an insurer takes forever to service your claim.

2. **Make yourself a better risk.** If you smoke or have speeding tickets, it's going to cost you. Insurers reward behavior that lowers risk. A healthy lifestyle and a good driving record can keep costs in check. Though good grades won't reduce health or life insurance premiums, they might get you a discount.

3. **Cover yourself.** You and your insurer may not always see eye to eye on a claim. It's up to you to provide evidence of loss. Take pictures of that busted headlamp. Keep receipts. That way, you'll be more likely to be covered for everything you've paid.

4. **Know your policy.** Keep your policy updated. Talk to your insurer to make sure you have the coverage you need. Review your coverage before filing a claim. You'll avoid nasty surprises that way.

Climbing Claims Accidents can drive up insurance premiums. The rising costs of car repair and health care cause auto insurance companies to increase their rates. The chart below gives a look at how insurance claims have risen over the past two decades.

Average Claim Payments for Private Passenger Auto Insurance (in dollars)

- Bodily Injury
- Property Damage

Year	Bodily Injury	Property Damage
1997	9517	2183
1998	9437	2240
1999	9646	2294
2000	9807	2393
2001	10,032	2461
2002	10,289	2539
2003	10,510	2590
2004	10,915	2612
2005	11,213	2684
2006	11,847	2801

SOURCE: Insurance Information Institute, 2008 data

Nowadays, you can often buy insurance online. Still, it might pay for you to use a licensed agent. It all depends on your needs.

There are two kinds of insurance agents: captive and independent. Captive agents represent a single insurance company. Independent agents offer policies from many different companies. Both types must be licensed by the state in which they sell.

For most purposes, buying directly with a company or its agents works out just fine. But if you are difficult to insure—for example, if you have a bad driving record—an independent agent might be the way to go. With access to many different companies, the independent agent can help you find a company that can meet your special needs.

A good agent also helps you through the process of filing a claim and acts on your behalf in dealing with the provider.

Are You Ready?

1. Why is insurance an investment?
2. What are some ways you can reduce the cost of insurance?

WebQuest online

To learn more about this topic, visit PearsonSuccessNet.com

Buying a Car

Ready to go for a spin around the car lot? The best car is the one that suits your needs and that you can afford.

A Major Purchase

Like most young people, your first major purchase may be a car. You need to do your homework, and spend some time and effort to get a good deal.

The Costs of Ownership

Step one: determine the car you can afford to buy, insure, and maintain. Consider these issues:

- how much you can put down
- how much you need to borrow
- what your monthly payment will be
- how much your insurance premiums will be
- how much car maintenance, gasoline, parking, and tolls will cost

With no credit history, you may have to search for a bank or credit union to lend you money. To get a vehicle loan, a bank may require you to have a cosigner, a person who is responsible for paying the loan if you default.

New or Used

If you are going to buy a new car, determine the invoice price of the model you want, and then get at least five competitive bids from dealers. Request bids in writing and then try to negotiate. Will the dealer closest to you match the price of the dealer who is less conveniently located? You can use Web sites such as cars.com, yahoo!autos, and myride.com as online resources for researching and getting bids.

ON THE ROAD

You've done your car shopping and driven your ride off the dealer's lot. Now what? Do you know how to change a flat? Do you have an emergency tow-truck number handy? Many service stations and dealership service centers will stick a note on the windshield letting you know when the next servicing is due. Likewise, the state will remind you when you need to renew your registration. Keep your insurance card in the car, and file your car title and insurance policy in a safe place!

POINTS TO REMEMBER

✔ Follow the maintenance schedule for your vehicle in the owner's manual. Don't skimp on oil changes.

✔ Wash your car regularly, and wax it once in a while to keep the car body shiny and free from corrosion.

✔ Treat minor problems early before they become big, expensive problems later.

✔ Use only original parts for repairs.

If you're buying used, get a history of the **vehicle identification number** (VIN) and have a mechanic inspect the car. Online sites also deal with buying used cars. They review online used car classifieds, how to buy a used car from dealers or private sellers, how to negotiate with tough sellers, scams to avoid, and provide a list of questions for you to ask the seller.

New automobiles **depreciate,** or lose value, quickly. A new car loses half its value in the first three years. But buying a new car can make sense if you plan to keep the car a long time. You have to carry collision insurance if you have a car loan. Used cars are less expensive to buy and insure, but maintenance costs will likely be higher.

Leasing

Leasing is primarily used by businesses or by those who don't plan on driving many miles. If you go over the mileage allowed for the term of the lease, generally 12,000 miles per year, you have to pay a substantial fee for each additional mile. If you have a long drive to college or a job, the commute could eat up the mileage limit in no time.

It's Your Money

Consider taking a more experienced person with you when you buy your first car. It pays to have an ally.

Dealing With Dealers

In many cases, salespeople hold the upper hand when it comes to negotiating car prices. You can act to level the buying field and avoid being pressured into spending more than you want or can afford.

▶ *Be prepared.* Know what you want and get bids based on the invoice price.

▶ *Don't be talked into unnecessary options.*

▶ *Don't discuss trade-in* until after you've settled on a sale price. A dealer might want to consider the trade-in vehicle as a reduction in the sticker price. Any trade-in should have nothing to do with the price of the new car.

▶ *Don't be pushed into a quick decision,* no matter what specials are dangled before you.

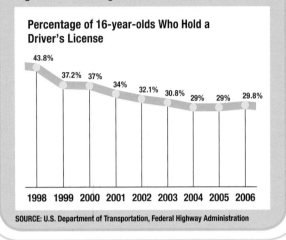

License to Ride Fewer American 16-year-olds are driving now than in 1998. Some possible reasons for the decline are tougher driver's license laws, the students' choice to spend more social time online instead of on the road, and a drop in the number of high schools offering driver's education courses.

Percentage of 16-year-olds Who Hold a Driver's License

43.8% | 37.2% | 37% | 34% | 32.1% | 30.8% | 29% | 29% | 29.8%
1998 1999 2000 2001 2002 2003 2004 2005 2006

SOURCE: U.S. Department of Transportation, Federal Highway Administration

▶ *Get the sale offers in writing.* If a dealer is not willing, walk away.

Warranties

Dealers are required by federal law to post a buyer's guide on the used cars they offer for sale. This guide must specify whether the vehicle is being sold "as is" or with a **warranty** and what percentage of the repair costs the dealer will pay. Most new and some used cars come with a manufacturer's warranty that covers certain repairs for a set period of time or up to a certain mileage limit. Extended warranties increase the amount of time or mileage that repairs will be covered. No warranty covers basic maintenance, like oil changes or new tires.

If you do buy a car and the next day the engine falls out, you're protected by federal and state "lemon laws." First, you should go back to the dealer if you think you've bought a lemon. If you cannot reach an agreement, check the law to see what recourse you have.

Are You Ready?

1. How should you prepare to buy a car?
2. What are some negotiation strategies you can use when buying a car?

To learn more about this topic, visit **PearsonSuccessNet.com**

Renting an Apartment

Home is more than a place to hang your hat. Think twice and act once before unlocking the door to independent living.

Can I Afford It?

You've dreamed of this day of living under your own roof and by your own rules. The first reality check is figuring out what you can afford. A rule of thumb is that your rent and utility payments should not cost more than one week's take-home pay. How can you figure the average monthly cost of utilities? Ask the landlord or the previous tenant.

Plan ahead. Many landlords require the first and last month's rent up front. In addition, you may have to pay a **security deposit**. This money is set aside for repairs of any damage you may do to the apartment beyond normal wear and tear.

KEY QUESTIONS

Finding the right apartment can be hard. Before you sign a lease, get the answers to these questions.

- How long is the term of the lease?
- When is the rent due?
- What are the penalties for paying late?
- Are utilities included in the rent?
- Are there working smoke detectors?
- Is parking available?
- Is the neighborhood safe?
- Is public transportation nearby?
- Are there laundry facilities?
- Are pets allowed?
- How much advance notice is required before moving?
- What happens if you break the lease?
- How are repairs handled?
- Can you make cosmetic changes such as painting or hanging pictures?

Finding the Right Place

Finding the right apartment takes more than a little time, effort, and money. The federal government has stepped in to level the playing field. The federal **Fair Housing Act of 1968** makes it illegal for a landlord to discriminate against a potential tenant because of race, sex, national origin, or religion.

You can make the rental process easier by defining your needs and wants. Usually, to rent an apartment you have to make a commitment of at least six months. If it's located next to the firehouse, it could be home, sleepless home. What if the ideal apartment is beyond your means? That might be the time to consider getting a roommate to share the cost.

Online Web sites are a good place to begin your apartment hunting. You can also look for apartments in the real estate section of a local newspaper. If you're hiring a realtor to search on your behalf, keep in mind they will charge you a fee based on the rental price. So do your homework and check out the Key Questions on this page.

GO FIGURE

4

The number of students that legally can live in a rental unit in Boston

SOURCE: City of Boston Rental Housing Resource Center

Roommates

Can two live more cheaply than one? Often, a two-bedroom apartment is not much more expensive than a one-bedroom place. Plus, you can split the utilities and rent. The sources for finding a roommate are the same as those for finding an apartment—Web sites like roommates.com, newspaper classifieds, and word of mouth. You want someone who has a compatible lifestyle and who can pay his or her share of the bills on time. Your search for the right roommate is just as important as your search for the right place to live.

Furnishings

If you rent an unfurnished apartment, try to avoid major expenses. After you have tapped family and friends, yard sales and thrift shops are potential gold mines. An unfurnished apartment is not only empty, it will probably also be bare, right down to the windows and shower.

Protect Yourself

Learn from others' mistakes. Many apartment complex Web sites are chock-full of comments posted by current or previous tenants. You might even ask a passer-by in the parking lot. To protect yourself from being charged for preexisting conditions, assess and photograph any existing damage before you sign a lease.

The Lease

You, as **tenant** or lessee, and the property owner, as landlord or **lessor,** enter into a contract called the lease or rental agreement. Here are some tips to make it a positive experience.

> ▶ *Be prepared with the documents you will need to provide.* They include proof of income and identity, letters of reference, and a check for any required deposit.

> ▶ *Get the lease in writing!* Never take an apartment on the basis of a handshake with the landlord.

> ▶ *If you don't understand something,* don't sign the lease!

Costs of Living Geography is one factor that will have a major impact on your living expenses. If you live in cities like New York, Boston, or Los Angeles, expenses will be much higher than those in smaller cities or rural areas.

Living Expenses in Select U.S. Metropolitan Areas (monthly, per household)

Metro area	Electricity	Food and beverages	Transpor-tation
Los Angeles, CA	$261	$211	$183
Miami, FL	150	211	190
Chicago, IL	133	200	176
New York, NY	168	211	190
Boston, MA	202	213	176
Houston, TX	185	186	167

SOURCE: Bureau of Labor Statistics (Consumer Price Index), 2007 data

Renter's Insurance

Consider renter's insurance. Maybe your roommate comes fully loaded with a flat-screen television. Should it disappear, you'd be left footing the bill. The benefits can far outweigh the costs.

Rights and Responsibilities

This is your money and your home, and you have rights; for example, the right to privacy. A landlord or maintenance worker is prohibited from entering your apartment without your permission. Renter's rights and responsibilities vary according to location, but most states provide a tenant-landlord bill of rights. Check with your local housing or consumer affairs office for specific information.

Tenants also have responsibilities, such as paying the rent on time and keeping the apartment clean. There may also be quiet hours, a policy imposed on most apartment dwellers. As always, a tenant's rights come with certain responsibilities.

Are You Ready?

1. What are some potential pitfalls in searching for an apartment?
2. What are four things you should do before signing a lease?

 WebQuest online

To learn more about this topic, visit **PearsonSuccessNet.com**

Identity Theft

Keep your personal information personal. Learn how to protect yourself, before somebody else shows up as you.

A Growing Crime

A thief can raid your wallet while you're splashing in the water. A dumpster diver can retrieve old bank statements. Or an innocent-looking e-mail could be a phishing scam to get your personal info. Most people don't realize they are victims of **identity theft** until it's too late. You might not find out until you're denied a student loan because you've missed several car payments—and you don't even own a car.

With your ID, thieves can commit a wide variety of fraud, such as obtaining credit cards or even a mortgage in your name. Worse, if the crook who stole your identity gets arrested for *any* crime, you could get stuck with a criminal record.

In too many cases, the burden of proof is on the victim. According to the Identity Theft Resource Center, it can take 600 hours to repair the damage. Some victims need up to 10 years to fully clear their records. If your identity is stolen, you could face higher insurance costs, credit card fees, and interest rates for loans—or may even have trouble finding a job.

Prime Target: You

Of the more than 255,000 identity theft complaints filed with the U.S. Federal Trade Commission in 2005, about 5 percent were against those under age 18—up from 3 percent in 2003. So congratulations: you are part of the fastest-growing target group for identity thieves.

To download or not to download

After you go through all the trouble of protecting your stuff, did you ever think you might be taking somebody else's stuff illegally?

That's what you're doing if you download software from the Internet or make unauthorized copies of music or movies. It's like cheating on a test. You're taking someone else's hard work without permission.

Just like ID theft, "software piracy" has far-reaching consequences for teens, for teachers and parents, and for software creators and manufacturers. Some of the issues are:

1. Getting files or software secondhand exposes a computer's data and hard drive to viruses and worms that can cause damage.

2. When software is stolen, companies must adjust their budgets to make up those losses, which means software creators may lose their jobs, affecting the families those jobs support.

3. It's very easy to get caught. Internet search engines make it easy for teachers to find the source of plagiarized passages in seconds.

Why are young people so vulnerable? One reason is that most teens have not established credit records that can be monitored. In addition, studies show that teens—

▶ are less likely than adults to check their credit card records

▶ are more likely than adults to frequent the Internet and provide personal information

▶ take greater risks relative to older age groups

▶ often have an "it can't happen to me" attitude

Finally, many Americans do not use their Social Security number until around the age of 15, when they apply for driver permits or first jobs. As a result, identity thefts against them may go unnoticed for years. There have even been cases of babies being the victims of identity theft!

Over half of all personal information thefts take place at universities, experts say. Part of the reason may be that nearly half of all college students have had their grades posted by using a Social Security number. It's within your rights to tell a college administrator not to post or otherwise give out your personal information.

Lower Your Risk

There is no foolproof way to guard your identity, but you can take common-sense steps to protect yourself against fraud.

Be alert online. Think twice before sharing personal information. Social networking sites like Facebook.com and MySpace.com not only post your favorite music and relationship status, but also your addresses, cellphone numbers, and previous employers. This information could be used to create a credit account or take out a loan in your name.

Use passwords. Always use a password to protect your cellphone, laptop, and PDA. Do not store personal information on these electronic devices. Create passwords that contain upper- and lowercase letters, numbers, and special characters such as *!, $, &.*

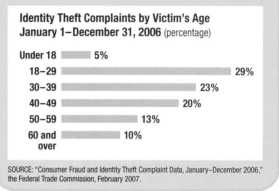

Identity Crisis In 2007, the Federal Trade Commission received more than 800,000 complaints of identity theft, making it the agency's most widely reported consumer crime. Nearly one third of all victims fall in the 18–29 age bracket. One reason for this trend could be that younger people tend to spend more time on the Internet, where identity thieves thrive on credit and banking scams.

Identity Theft Complaints by Victim's Age January 1–December 31, 2006 (percentage)

Age	Percentage
Under 18	5%
18–29	29%
30–39	23%
40–49	20%
50–59	13%
60 and over	10%

SOURCE: "Consumer Fraud and Identity Theft Complaint Data, January–December 2006," the Federal Trade Commission, February 2007.

Check your credit. Check your credit report with a major credit agency like Equifax, Experian, and TransUnion at least once a year. You are entitled to one free report yearly. You can find them online at www.annualcreditreport.com.

Check and shred your statements. Always check your bank and credit card statements for anything unusual. Then dispose of documents containing personal information using a paper shredder. Simply tearing up documents isn't enough to keep thieves from easily reassembling those statements.

Watch your mailbox. If you're too young to have a credit card or don't have one already, you should be suspicious of any unsolicited credit-card offers in the mail addressed to you. For more information on identity theft and what you can do to protect yourself, check out the government's Web site www.ftc.gov/bcp/edu/microsites/idtheft.

Are You Ready?

1. Why are young people especially vulnerable to identity theft?
2. What are some steps you can take to protect yourself?

To learn more about this topic, visit **PearsonSuccessNet.com**

Shopping Online: Be Safe, Not Sorry

It's hard to put a price tag on convenience. But by taking a little care, you can get your money's worth.

Buying Online

If you have ever gone from store to store looking for a hard-to-find item, you will appreciate the ease of shopping online. Who has the item in stock? Who has the lowest price? Free shipping? Quickest delivery? You can get the answers to all of these questions with the click of your mouse. For starters, you can check price comparison sites such as bizrate.com, mysimon.com, or pricegrabber.com.

Read the Reviews

All right, so you can't try on shoes or a shirt online. Online buyers trade that advantage for online customer reviews. A recent study of online buyers shows that 9 out of 10 Americans read reviews posted by other customers online before they make a purchase. You can access detailed customer-driven product reviews for almost any product. Love the product, you can let the world know. Hate it, you can warn others.

E-Buyer Be Aware

Along with its unique benefits, online shopping includes some unique challenges. How do you really know if the online retailer you're dealing with is reputable and your information will be secure? For the most part, you have a higher degree of confidence if there is a brick-and-mortar backup to the online stores. Major retailers devote a lot of resources to ensuring that their customers are satisfied and have secure online shopping.

That does not mean that you should not deal with online-only vendors. See the Five Online Shopping Tips below for advice on making sure the sites you use are secure and reputable.

Five Online Shopping Tips

1. Check out the reviews written by other buyers.

2. Look for a padlock icon in the browser and "https" for security.

3. Check for endorsements from rating agencies, such as the Better Business Bureau (BBB).

Shipping Costs

Credit Card Theft

Better Business Bureau

Fair Credit Billing Act

Federal Trade Commission

BBB

Bidding Online

Comfortable online? The biggest and best deals often exist beyond the big stores. Widely used alternatives are the relatively free local classified, message, and auction sites. These offer shopping alternatives that come with a different set of rules tailored for the online marketplace.

Local appeal can be a major advantage. Online classifieds provide access to backyard buyers and sellers at relatively no cost.

In their attempt to keep you scam- and worry-free, these services encourage buyers to deal locally with folks you can meet in person. The sites also include detailed safety guidelines.

On Internet auctions, buyers can quickly and easily comparison shop for just about anything, from used cars and leather bomber jackets to concert tickets and private jets. In this auction format, shoppers can engage in competitive bidding wars.

4 Steer clear of sellers who offer low prices only to squeeze you on shipping costs.

5 Use a credit card as it offers the best safeguard against fraud, but never e-mail a credit card number, bank account information, password, or PIN number.

Unsecured Sites

Identity Theft

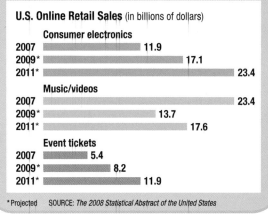

Virtual Sales In 2007, Americans bought more than $20 billion worth of music and video products on the Internet, making them the most popular online purchase. By 2011, however, it is projected that consumer electronics sales will far outpace other products sold online.

U.S. Online Retail Sales (in billions of dollars)

Consumer electronics
2007 — 11.9
2009* — 17.1
2011* — 23.4

Music/videos
2007 — 23.4
2009* — 13.7
2011* — 17.6

Event tickets
2007 — 5.4
2009* — 8.2
2011* — 11.9

*Projected   SOURCE: The 2008 Statistical Abstract of the United States

So how are buyers and sellers protected? Buyers rate the reliability and service provided by sellers, and eBay makes these ratings available to you. However, if you win a bid and do not go through with the purchase, you are stuck with a negative rating for the rest of your eBay life. There are also services that make it possible for you to pay an individual seller using your credit card.

Fighting Fraud

There is a new charge on your credit card bill! But where is the merchandise? You never got it, or even worse, you never ordered it. Many credit card companies will investigate suspected cases of fraud on your behalf, limiting your liability to $50. Also, the Fair Credit Billing Act allows you to withhold payment if you believe someone has stolen your card number.

You have the option of filing complaints with the Federal Trade Commission (FTC) at www.ftc.gov. The FTC offers you advice on how to protect against fraud, identity theft, and questionable business practices. The site guides you step-by-step through the process of filing a consumer complaint.

Are You Ready?

1. What are the advantages of shopping online?
2. What are two possible pitfalls?

To learn more about this topic, visit **PearsonSuccessNet.com**

Paying for College

Learning how to pay for college is an education in itself.

Almost Priceless

It's hard to put a price on a college education. The personal and career rewards last a lifetime. Unfortunately, paying off the costs of a four-year degree can seem almost as long. The hard facts about paying for college are these: in constant dollars, the average cost of **tuition** at public and private universities nearly doubled between 1990 and 2005. For most students, those are pretty scary numbers. Here are a few questions to consider:

▶ What school do you want to attend and why? Examine your goals. Look for the educational resources you need at less-expensive public schools. Private schools generally are more costly but can be more generous with their financial aid.

▶ Does location matter? Tuition costs vary considerably from region to region.

▶ How much debt can you tolerate? If your career goal is to be a freelance artist rather than a brain surgeon, you might want to choose the less-expensive college to cut down on your post-graduation debt.

The thought of paying for college might send you into panic mode. But there is help. It comes in three forms: (a) grants and scholarships; (b) work-study programs; and (c) loans. The idea is to reduce the amount you're going to owe by applying for as many sources of aid as possible. If you're like most students, you will qualify for some type of assistance. The biggest financial aid error is not to apply at all. Many colleges are substituting loans for grants and some are experimenting by waiving tuition for certain income levels altogether.

How will you fund your education?

- Part-time job
- Student loans and parents
- Parents
- Government grants and work-study

FINANCIAL AID TIPS

Apply early: There is a limited amount of aid available, so make sure you get your fair share.

Seek free money: Grants and scholarships need not be repaid. Search for local and government sources of financial aid.

Limit your debt: Finance just what you need.

Use the Web: Several sites have calculators that allow you to estimate your expected family contribution, the amount of your aid awards, and the amount of your loan payments. The College Board has one as well as a search tool for scholarships. The Sallie Mae (www.salliemae.com) site includes a listing of major private lenders.

Types of Lenders

Financial aid comes in many packages. No matter your income, you can qualify for some type of government loan. You might need to supplement it with a loan from your school or a bank.

Federal Government

When it comes to government aid, the Department of Education offers three basic loans: Direct Loans and Stafford Loans for parents or students, and the Parent Loan for Undergraduate Students (PLUS).

For those in financial need, there is the Federal Perkins Loan. These loans have a fixed interest rate and are made available through the college. Students who go on to take teaching jobs in certain areas or who volunteer in the Americorps, Peace Corps, or VISTA programs may be eligible to have their federal loans partially repaid or canceled.

Private Sources

If money from government loans does not cover all your college expenses, private lending sources could fill the gap. Compared to government loans, regular bank loans typically have higher interest rates, fees, and credit requirements. Trade organizations and educational institutions also offer lending aid. Your guidance counselor has more information.

Other Sources

All kinds of students can qualify for financial aid that does not have to be repaid.

A no-strings grant is a no-brainer to consider when applying for financial aid. Available from the federal government, state governments, and higher education institutions, grants are usually awarded according to financial need and tuition rates.

Don't forget the Free Application for Federal Student Aid (FAFSA), available at www.fafsa.ed.gov. All students should complete the FAFSA, even if they believe they will not qualify for aid. There is always a chance that family circumstances will change. You need to complete this form if

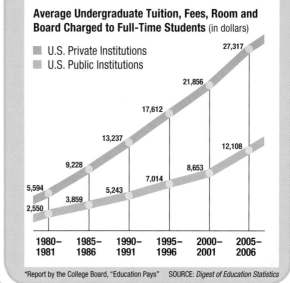

Sticker Shock In recent years, the cost of attending a U.S. four-year-college has risen at twice the inflation rate. A 2007 study,* however, finds that the benefits outweigh the short-term cost. Over a lifetime, a college education increases a worker's earning potential by about $800,000.

Average Undergraduate Tuition, Fees, Room and Board Charged to Full-Time Students (in dollars)

■ U.S. Private Institutions
■ U.S. Public Institutions

U.S. Private Institutions: 5,594 (1980–1981), 9,228 (1985–1986), 13,237 (1990–1991), 17,612 (1995–1996), 21,856 (2000–2001), 27,317 (2005–2006)

U.S. Public Institutions: 2,550 (1980–1981), 3,859 (1985–1986), 5,243 (1990–1991), 7,014 (1995–1996), 8,653 (2000–2001), 12,108 (2005–2006)

*Report by the College Board, "Education Pays"   SOURCE: *Digest of Education Statistics*

you want to be considered for federal aid, such as the Pell Grant and Supplemental Educational Opportunity Grant. These grants are given to students with "exceptional financial need." Find out more by checking out the U.S. Department of Education Web sites, www.federalstudentaid.ed.gov, www.students.gov, your state education agency, or your high school guidance office.

Besides aid from the school itself, scholarships are available from local community and civic groups such as the Kiwanis and Lions Clubs. Some companies also offer scholarships to children of their employees. Work-study programs are a win-win situation for the student, college, and community. This type of aid allows students to earn money to offset their educational expenses.

Are You Ready?

1. Why is it important to complete the FAFSA form?
2. What is the advantage of seeking a federal loan instead of one from a private lender?

WebQuest online   To learn more about this topic, visit **PearsonSuccessNet.com**

Getting a Job

Engineer? Store manager? Teacher? Whatever you want to be, you'll soon have to look for your first real job—and then get it.

Be Prepared!

You may already have had your first job—after school, weekends, or summers. For most of us, finding a full-time job doesn't come until after graduation from high school or college.

Your Resumé

The first step is to prepare a **resumé,** a written summary of your educational and work experience. Think of it as an advertisement to market yourself to an employer.

You might be thinking, "That's fine if I have a lot of experience to list. But this is my first real job." True, but that doesn't mean you don't have qualities employers are interested in. Suppose you worked the same job every summer for three years running. That shows somebody liked you enough to keep hiring you back. Your service in school clubs or volunteer organizations could indicate leadership, planning abilities, and a strong work ethic. Academic honors can count for a lot, too.

Organize your resumé in a neat, readable fashion—no fancy type. Have plenty of copies on hand. (For more tips, see the resumé-writing worksheet available online.)

References

Some employers may ask for references. If you've been applying for colleges, you know the drill. Pick people other than family who can tell potential employers about your character and work ethic: a former boss, a colleague from an internship, a professor or adviser. Be ready with names, home or business addresses, e-mail addresses, and phone numbers.

GO FIGURE

3-5

The average number of careers a U.S. worker will have in a lifetime

SOURCE: Careers in Transition, LLC

Where to Look

There are plenty of good sources of job information out there. Any or all of these can help you land the right job.

The Internet More and more companies are using sites like monster.com and careerbuilder.com to advertise for help.

Newspapers Maybe you don't read the newspaper so much. But a lot of employers do. Find out what day your local newspaper publishes want ads.

Employment Agencies For a fee, the agency can help you connect with a company looking for someone with your skills.

Job/Career Centers High schools and colleges offer career counseling. In addition to helping you find a job, counselors can appraise your resumé at no cost and give you interviewing tips.

Job Fairs Companies get a chance to meet recent graduates—you get a chance to meet possible employers.

Know Where to Look

Where should you start? Some common sources of job information are listed on the previous page. List places that seem most promising. Try to find out something about a company before you apply there. It's all just part of being prepared.

The Interview

That first job interview can be exciting but nerve-wracking. You can prepare for it. Hold a mock interview with family members or friends. Have them ask you possible questions and then critique your responses and your delivery.

Make a Good Impression

The minute you step into a potential employer's office, you are being judged. Don't blow it before you open your mouth. Posture, eye contact, and a firm handshake go a long way to making a positive impression.

Believe it or not, dressing wrong can be a deal-breaker. What works on the beach or in a dance club won't cut it in the office. Even a company that allows "casual" dress on the job doesn't want to see you in tank tops, cutoffs, or flip-flops. Think conservative and professional. That may mean a suit or a dress. Let them tell you you don't have to dress that way—after you get the job.

Turn Off That Cellphone

The person interviewing you may have to interrupt to take a phone call. You do not get the same privilege. Before you step in that office, make sure your cellphone is switched off. Nothing will ruin a good interview faster than a ringing cellphone.

Ask the Right Questions

Where do you see yourself in five years? Why are you the best candidate for this position? Expect to be peppered with questions. Be equally prepared to ask them. Questions like these show you're interested in the job:

▶ What are the company's goals for the next year?

▶ How does this job fit the company's goals?

▶ Describe a typical day here in this department.

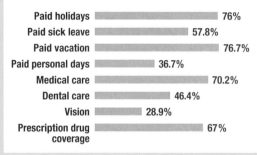

Paid in Full? Not all benefit packages are created equal. For instance, rising medical costs in recent years have forced many private companies to scale back, or even drop, health coverage. The chart below shows that the types of benefits private companies offer can vary greatly.

Average Percentage of U.S. Workers in Private Industry With Access to Select Benefits in 2006

Benefit	Percentage
Paid holidays	76%
Paid sick leave	57.8%
Paid vacation	76.7%
Paid personal days	36.7%
Medical care	70.2%
Dental care	46.4%
Vision	28.9%
Prescription drug coverage	67%

SOURCE: *The 2008 Statistical Abstract of the United States*

> "**You never get a second chance to make a first impression.**"
>
> —Maxim attributed to 20th century Dutch author William Triesthof

Steer clear of questions about pay, benefits, hours, and vacation time. All that will be covered if you are asked back for a second interview.

After the Interview

Follow up with a handwritten or e-mailed thank-you note. This reaffirms your interest and makes a lasting impression. If you're rejected, try not to get discouraged. It's part of the interview process. Remember: rejection can work either way. You're under no obligation to accept the first offer that comes along. Factor in benefits, commuting costs, work environment, and the possibility of career advancement. Look for the best fit for you.

Are You Ready?

1. How should you dress for an interview?
2. What are important things about yourself you should highlight during an interview?

 **WebQuest online**

To learn more about this topic, visit **PearsonSuccessNet.com**

Understanding Your Paycheck

Your pay stub is an important tool in managing your personal finances. Put it to work for you.

What's in a Paycheck?

You've got your first job—and your first paycheck. Attached to your check is a pay stub, also known as an earnings statement, which includes your identification information and the pay period you worked. But there's a lot more to it than that.

It all begins with your wages or salary. Wages refer to hourly pay and can change based on how much time you worked. Salary is monthly or yearly pay, which does not depend on the number of hours worked.

Your pay stub shows your **gross pay,** the total amount of income you earned during the pay period. If you are paid hourly, gross pay should equal the number of hours you worked times your hourly wage. (It will also show if you worked overtime at a higher rate.) If you are on an annual salary, it's your salary divided by the number of pay periods in the year.

You will immediately notice that your net pay—the amount the check is made out for—is far less than your gross pay. Where did the rest of the money go?

Your stub lists all your **payroll withholdings,** the earnings that come out of your check before you get it. Some of these withholdings are voluntary. For example, if you join a company medical or insurance plan, your share of these benefits comes out of your check. Other withholdings, however, go in taxes to the state and federal governments.

Federal and State Deductions

Most workers have federal and state taxes deducted from their earnings. Your employer is also required to pay the federal government a certain percentage of your earnings.

Social Security (FICA) and Medicare taxes are based on a percentage of your earnings. FICA stands for Federal Insurance Contributions Act. It is a U.S. payroll tax on employees and employers to fund programs that provide benefits for retirees, the disabled, and children of deceased workers. Medicare provides hospital insurance benefits.

Federal and state taxes are deducted based on an estimate of how much you will owe in yearly taxes. Most workers are required to fill out the W-4 form when they start a new job. It includes guidelines to help you do the calculations needed to estimate how much will be withheld from each paycheck. The W-4 lets you take certain personal allowances that will lower the amount of tax withheld from your income. For example, you may take an exemption for yourself and your spouse. You also can take an exemption for anyone who is dependent on your income, such as a child. The IRS offers an online withholding calculator (www.irs.gov/individuals) to help you avoid withholding too much or too little income tax.

Pay Check Level of education, skill, and supply and demand are major factors that determine a worker's entry-level pay. Typically, college graduates with technical, medical, or business degrees will command higher salaries.

Average Entry-Level Salaries (2007)

Customer Service Representative	$29,203
Assistant Chef	$31,176
Librarian	$35,684
Mail Carrier	$40,000
Software Developer	$47,088
Biologist	$49,000
Physical Therapist	$52,293
Electrical Engineer	$54,332
Attorney	$57,988
Investment Banker	$58,858
Physician (General Practitioner)	$100,000

SOURCE: Payscale.com

Earnings Statement

Period ending: 00/00/0000
Pay date: 00/00/0000

A **Year-to-date**
(for pay and deductions)
Shows the total amount
withheld for a particular
deduction at any point in the
calendar year.

XYZ Corporation
100 Corporation Crt.
New Town, NY 10000

B **Gross Pay**
The total amount
of income you
earned during
the pay period.

Social Security Number: 999-99-9999
Taxable Marital Status: Single
Exemptions/Allowances:
   Federal: 1
   State: 1
   Local: 1

TOMÁS Q. PUBLIC
123 MAIN STREET
ANYWHERE, USA 12345

C **Leave Time**
Includes vacation
hours or sick hours.
Many employers will
detail how many hours
have been used to
date and how many
hours remain for the
calendar year.

Earnings	rate	hours	this period	year to date
Regular	20.00	40.00	800.00	16,640.00
Overtime	30.00	1.00	30.00	780.00 **A**
Holiday	30.00	8.00	240.00	1,200.00 **A**
B **Gross Pay**			**$ 1,070.00**	18,620.00

Other Benefits and Information	this period	year-to-date
Vac Hrs Left		40.00 **C**
Sick Hrs Left		16.00

Deductions	Statutory		
	H Federal Income Tax	- 235.75	4,351.44
	I Social Security Tax	- 65.10	1,251.67
	J Medicare Tax	- 15.23	272.89
	K NY State Income Tax	- 64.60	1,203.24
	L NYC Income Tax	- 33.86	527.96
	NY SDI Tax	- 1.80	15.20
	Other		
	Medical and Dental	- 35.00	700.00
	401(k)	- 107.00 *	2,140.00 **D**
	Stock Plan	- 15.00	300.00
	Life Insurance	- 5.00	100.00 **E**
	FSA	- 20.00 *	400.00 **F**

Important Notes

YOUR TOTAL NET PAY HAS BEEN AUTOMATICALLY
DEPOSITED INTO CHECKING ACCOUNT XXXX4071.

D **Retirement Plan Contributions**
Contributions to plans such as 401(k)
or 403(b) retirement savings plans.

E **Insurance Deductions**
Deductions for insurance such as health
(medical and dental), and life insurance.

F **Flexible Spending Account**
A pretax benefit offered by some
employers to help workers save for
health- and childcare-related expenses.

Net Pay	$ 598.34 **G**

* **Excluded from federal taxable wages**

Your federal taxable wages this period are $943.00

G **Net Pay**
The amount
of income you
actually take
home.

◀ TEAR HERE

THE ORIGINAL DOCUMENT HAS AN ARTIFICIAL WATERMARK ON THE BACK.   HOLD AT AN ANGLE TO VIEW WHEN CHECKING THE ENDORSEMENT.

H **Federal Tax Amount**
The amount of federal
tax deducted and paid to
the federal government.
It is based on your gross
income, minus any
pretax deductions.

I **Social Security**
The mandatory
6.2 percent tax
imposed on workers
for Social Security
disability insurance
and retirement
benefits.

J **Medicare**
The mandatory 1.45 percent tax
imposed on workers for Medicare.

K **State Tax Amount**
The amount of tax
paid to the state
government.

L **Local Tax Amount**
The local tax is
sometimes applied to
residents of certain
cities, counties, or
school districts.

Are You Ready?

1. What is the difference between gross pay
and net income?
2. What would be the year-to-date Medicare
tax withholding for a worker whose gross
pay was $9,845?

To learn more about
this topic, visit
PearsonSuccessNet.com

Paying Your Taxes

Your country, state, and community want a share of your paycheck. It's a cost of being a responsible citizen.

Taxes and You

Welcome to the workforce! You have joined the ranks of taxpayers. But why do you have to pay taxes anyhow? Governments have expenses. They have to pay salaries for thousands of employees and provide services for millions of citizens. The biggest source of government revenue is taxes. And you are required by law to pay your share.

Don't Mess With the IRS

Among taxes, the federal income tax is top dog. The Internal Revenue Service (IRS), an agency within the Treasury Department, applies federal income tax laws. The agency generates tax forms and collects taxes. The IRS will notice if you don't pay what you owe and impose hefty financial penalties for any misdeeds.

The federal income tax is progressive. People with the highest income have the highest tax rates. The system also includes hundreds of tax breaks for people with special financial burdens, such as people paying for college or starting a business, as well as rewards for actions like donating to charity.

Other Taxes

Most state governments collect income tax, too. States and local communities levy other kinds of taxes, such as sales tax and property tax. Sales taxes vary by state, but they generally involve paying a fixed percentage on most items you buy. Essentials of life—such as food and medicine—are generally exempt from sales tax. Property taxes are based on the value of privately owned homes and land.

Taxes are also collected on income you didn't work for. If Aunt Bessie leaves you money in her will, you have to pay an inheritance tax. If you buy stock and you make a lot of money when you sell it, that's also taxed.

Forms, Forms, Forms

Sometime during the tax season, which runs from January to April 15, you need to fill out and file the appropriate tax forms. Filing is the only way to get a refund, or return of excess taxes paid. Whether you've got a refund coming or not, it's against the law not to file an income tax return.

> **GO FIGURE**
>
> ## $1.236 trillion
>
> **Gross collections from individual U.S. taxpayers in 2006**
>
> SOURCE: Internal Revenue Service

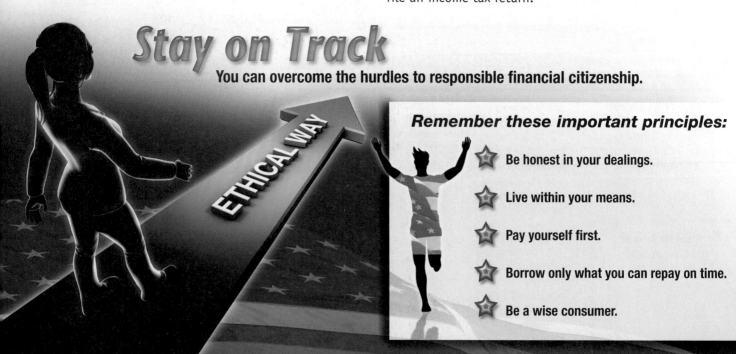

Stay on Track

You can overcome the hurdles to responsible financial citizenship.

ETHICAL WAY

Remember these important principles:

⭐ Be honest in your dealings.

⭐ Live within your means.

⭐ Pay yourself first.

⭐ Borrow only what you can repay on time.

⭐ Be a wise consumer.

The most common federal tax form is the W-2, which reports wages paid to employees and taxes withheld from them. The form also reports FICA taxes to the Social Security Administration. Employers must complete and send out a W-2 to every employee by January 31. Save these documents! Your W-2s must be attached to your tax return when you file.

When you file your income tax return, which is due by April 15, you'll use Form 1040, the Individual Income Tax Return. By filling it out properly, you will learn if you owe more money to the government or if the government owes you money.

State Tax Bites Americans pay federal taxes no matter where they live. State taxes are another matter. Some states, like Florida and Texas, do not impose an income tax. But they assess a sales tax. Alaska residents, who pay no sales or income tax, have the lowest per capita tax rates in the nation.

State Sales Tax Rate: Highs and Lows

Highest Tax Rate	
California	7.25%
Lowest Tax Rate	
Colorado	2.9%
No Sales Tax	
Alaska	New Hampshire
Delaware	Oregon
Montana	

SOURCE: State Sales Tax Rates, January 1, 2008
www.taxadmin.org

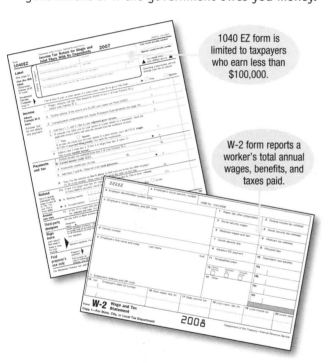

1040 EZ form is limited to taxpayers who earn less than $100,000.

W-2 form reports a worker's total annual wages, benefits, and taxes paid.

To make life easier, the government introduced the Form 1040EZ, which is the simplest tax form. Its use is limited to taxpayers with taxable income below $100,000 who take the standard deduction instead of itemizing deductions, that is, listing them separately. Many unmarried people with no children qualify to use this form.

If you have income other than wages, salaries, and tips, Form 1099 comes into play. It's a statement you receive from payers of interest income, such as banks and savings institutions, that summarizes your interest income for the year.

Make sure you get all the tax deductions the IRS allows. Each form has step-by-step instructions, but they might not answer all your questions. Here are some other places to get advice:

▶ The IRS has a user-friendly Web site, with lots of information. It can be found at www.irs.gov.

▶ Call the IRS at (800) 829-1040. You can talk to a tax specialist or even schedule an appointment for help at IRS service centers. But the closer you get to April 15, the harder it may be to get timely help.

▶ Tax-preparation services and tax accountants will prepare your tax return for you for a fee. Some will file your return for you.

If you prepare your return on paper, you must send it to the IRS Service Center listed in the instruction booklet and at the IRS Web site. There are ways you can prepare and e-file your return online. Filing in this way will get you a faster tax refund. But you usually will have to pay a fee, especially if you use a tax preparation firm.

Are You Ready?

1. Describe the role of a W-2 form when filing your taxes.
2. Why do governments collect taxes?

To learn more about this topic, visit **PearsonSuccessNet.com**

Glossary

annual percentage rate a finance charge, or the cost of credit, expressed as an annual rate
   tasa de porcentaje anual cargo financiero, o costo del crédito, expresado como tasa anual
automatic bill pay an automatic deduction from your bank account on a predetermined date
   pago automático de facturas deducción automática de fondos de una cuenta bancaria en una fecha determinada

bankruptcy a state of being legally released from the obligation to repay some or all debt in exchange for the forced loss of certain assets
   bancarrota condición que consiste en liberarse legalmente de la obligación de pagar parte de una deuda, o la deuda completa, a cambio de la pérdida forzosa de ciertos bienes
beneficiary a person or organization named to receive assets after an individual's death
   beneficiario persona u organización designada a recibir bienes tras la muerte de un individuo

certificate of deposit a savings certificate entitling the bearer to receive interest
   certificado de depósito certificado de ahorros que autoriza al poseedor a recibir intereses
compound interest accumulated interest added back to the principal, so interest is earned on interest
   interés compuesto interés acumulado agregado al capital, de modo que se ganan intereses sobre el interés
consumer protection act an act designed to reduce fraud and make it harder to declare bankruptcy
   acto de protección al consumidor ley designada para disminuir el fraude y dificultar el proceso de declaración de bancarrota
copay a small portion of the total cost of a service covered by your insurance that you are required to pay
   copago porción pequeña, que una persona debe pagar, del costo total de un servicio cubierto por el seguro
credit an agreement to provide goods, services, or money for future payments with interest by a specific date or according to a specific schedule
   crédito acuerdo por medio del cual se proveen bienes, servicios o dinero a cambio de pagos con interés, en una fecha específica futura o según un cronograma de pago específico
credit report a detailed report of an individual's credit history prepared by a credit bureau and used by a lender to determine a loan applicant's creditworthiness
   informe de crédito reporte detallado preparado por la agencia de información crediticia y usado por un prestamista para determinar la solvencia de una persona que solicita un préstamo

deductible an amount you have to pay before your insurance benefits can be applied
   deducible cantidad que se debe pagar antes de beneficiarse de la cobertura del seguro
depreciate to decrease in value
   depreciar disminuir en valor
dollar cost averaging a method of investing a fixed amount in the same type of investment at regular intervals, regardless of price
   promediación de costos método que consiste en realizar regularmente la misma inversión con una cantidad fija de dinero, independientemente del precio

electronic funds transfer the shifting of money from one account to another without the physical movement of cash
   transferencia electrónica de fondos paso de dinero de una cuenta en una institución financiera a otra cuenta, sin necesidad de movilizar dinero en efectivo

Fair Credit Reporting Act a federal law that covers the reporting of debt repayment information, requiring the removal of certain information after seven or ten years, and giving consumers the right to know what is in their credit report, to dispute inaccurate information, and to add a brief statement explaining accurate negative information
   Ley de Informe Justo de Crédito ley federal que cubre el reporte de información sobre la cancelación de deudas, exige la eliminación de cierta información después de siete o diez años y le otorga al consumidor el derecho de acceder a su informe de crédito, cuestionar información errónea y agregar una declaración breve que explique información negativa correcta
Fair Housing Act of 1968 makes it illegal for a landlord to discriminate against a potential tenant because of that person's race, sex, national origin, or religion
   Acta de Equidad en la Vivienda de 1968 ley que establece que es ilegal que el dueño de una propiedad discrimine contra un posible inquilino por su raza, sexo, país de origen o religión
Federal Deposit Insurance Corporation the government agency that insures customer deposits if a bank fails
   Corporación Federal de Seguros de los Depósitos Bancarios organismo gubernamental que asegura los depósitos de los clientes si un banco falla
FICO score a type of credit score that makes up a substantial portion of the credit report that lenders use to assess an applicant's credit risk and whether to extend a loan
   puntaje FICO tipo de puntaje de crédito que representa una porción considerable del informe de crédito que los prestamistas usan para evaluar el riesgo crediticio de un solicitante y si se le debe hacer un préstamo

gross pay wages or salary before deductions for taxes and other purposes
   ingreso neto salario antes de incurrir en deducciones fiscales o de otro tipo

health maintenance organization least expensive insurance plan that allows you to pick a primary care physician who will refer you to in-network doctors
   organización para el mantenimiento de la salud tipo de seguro médico menos costoso que le permite al beneficiario escoger un doctor que lo remite a otros doctores dentro de una red

identity theft the crime of using another person's name, credit or debit card number, Social Security number, or another piece of personal information to commit fraud
   robo de identidad crimen que consiste en usar el nombre de otra persona, su número de tarjeta de crédito o débito, su número del seguro social o cualquier otra información personal con fines fraudulentos
individual retirement account an investment account that provides certain tax advantages to people who set aside money for retirement.
   cuenta personal de jubilación cuenta de inversión que les otorga ciertas ventajas tributarias a quienes ahorran dinero para su jubilación
installment loans loans, divided between principal and interest, that are repaid at regularly scheduled intervals
   préstamos a plazo préstamos, divididos entre capital e interés, que se pagan en intervalos regulares establecidos

lessor landlord
    arrendador dueño de un local o lugar que se ha alquilado

money market account a savings account that offers a competitive rate of interest in exchange for larger-than-normal deposits
    cuenta de alto rendimiento cuenta de ahorros que ofrece una tasa de interés competitiva a cambio de recibir depósitos de grandes sumas

net income an individual's income after deductions, credits, and taxes are factored into gross income
    salario neto ingreso de un individuo después de calcular las deducciones, los créditos y los impuestos que se deben considerar del ingreso bruto

payroll withholdings taxes taken directly out of an individual's wages or other income before he or she receives the funds
    retención en nómina cualquier impuesto que se retiene del pago de un individuo o de otro ingreso antes de que él o ella reciba los fondos

phishing an Internet scam used to gain personal and financial data to commit fraud
    phishing delito cometido a través de Internet que consiste en adquirir información personal y financiera para fines fraudulentos

resumé a document summarizing an individual's employment experience, education, and other information a potential employer needs to know
    currículo documento donde se resume la experiencia profesional, la educación y otra información de un individuo que un empleador puede necesitar

risk factors statistics that predict whether someone is likely to be a bad risk
    factores de riesgo estadísticas que predicen la probabilidad de que alguien sea un riesgo

risk management plan the process of calculating risk and devising methods to minimize or manage loss
    plan de manejo de riesgos proceso que calcula el riesgo y crea métodos para minimizar o manejar pérdidas

Roth IRA an individual retirement plan that bears many similarities to the traditional IRA, but contributions are not tax deductible and qualified distributions are tax free
    IRA Roth plan de jubilación personal que tiene bastantes similitudes con una cuenta personal de jubilación, IRA (por sus siglas en inglés), pero sus contribuciones no son deducibles de impuestos y ciertas distribuciones que califican son libres de impuestos

Rule of 72 a method of finding the number of years required to double your money at a given interest rate; divide 72 by the expected compound return
    Regla de 72 fórmula para calcular el número de años necesarios para duplicar una suma de dinero a cierta tasa de interés; dividir 72 por el rendimiento compuesto

security deposit money given to the landlord by the tenant to cover any damage to the apartment
    depósito de seguridad dinero que un arrendador le entrega a un inquilino para cubrir cualquier daño que se le cause a una propiedad

Social Security a federal government program that provides retirement, survivor's, and disability benefits, funded by a tax on income, which appears on workers' pay stubs as a deduction labeled FICA (for Federal Insurance Contributions Act)
    seguro social programa del gobierno federal que proporciona a los ciudadanos beneficios en caso de jubilación, muerte o incapacitación; se acumula mediante la deducción de impuestos al ingreso y aparece identificado en los talones de pago de los trabajadores como Ley Federal de la Contribución al Seguto Social (FICA, por sus siglas de inglés)

tenant someone who pays rent to use or occupy land, a building, or other property owned by another
    inquilino persona que paga un alquiler para usar u ocupar un terreno, un edificio o cualquier propiedad que le pertenece a otra persona

Truth in Lending Act a federal law that requires financial institutions to disclose specific information about the terms and cost of credit, including the finance charge and the annual percentage rate (APR)
    Ley de Divulgación de los Términos Totales de Crédito ley federal que requiere que las instituciones financieras proporcionen información específica sobre los términos y costos del crédito, incluyendo el cargo financiero y la tasa de porcentaje anual

tuition the charge for instruction, especially at a college or private school
    matrícula cargo por la educación, especialmente en una universidad o una escuela privada

vehicle identification number a unique serial number used by the automotive industry to identify individual motor vehicles
    número de identificación del vehículo serial único que usa la industria automotriz para identificar cada vehículo

warranty a written guarantee from a manufacturer or distributor that specifies the conditions under which the product can be returned, replaced, or repaired
    garantía documento de un fabricante o distribuidor que especifica las condiciones en las cuales un producto se puede devolver, reemplazar o reparar

The United States Economy

This databank gives you information about the economy of the United States, starting with its resources and producers. You will then take a closer look at American workers and consumers.

U.S. Economy by Types of Business

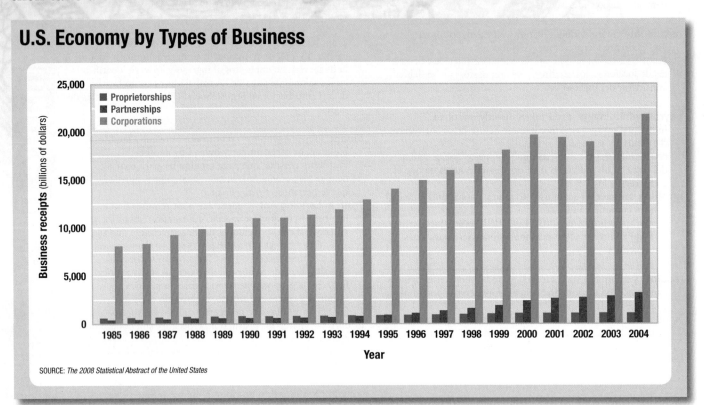

SOURCE: *The 2008 Statistical Abstract of the United States*

Number of Farms

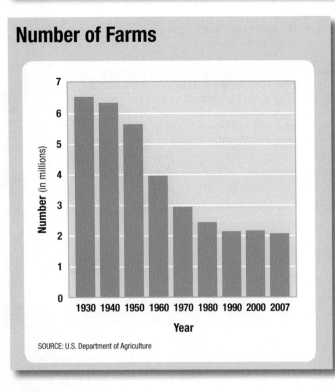

SOURCE: U.S. Department of Agriculture

Size of Farms

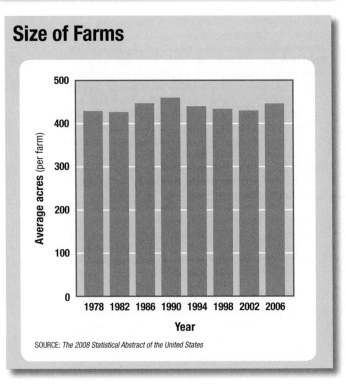

SOURCE: *The 2008 Statistical Abstract of the United States*

United States Economic Activity and Resources

Databank: The United States Economy

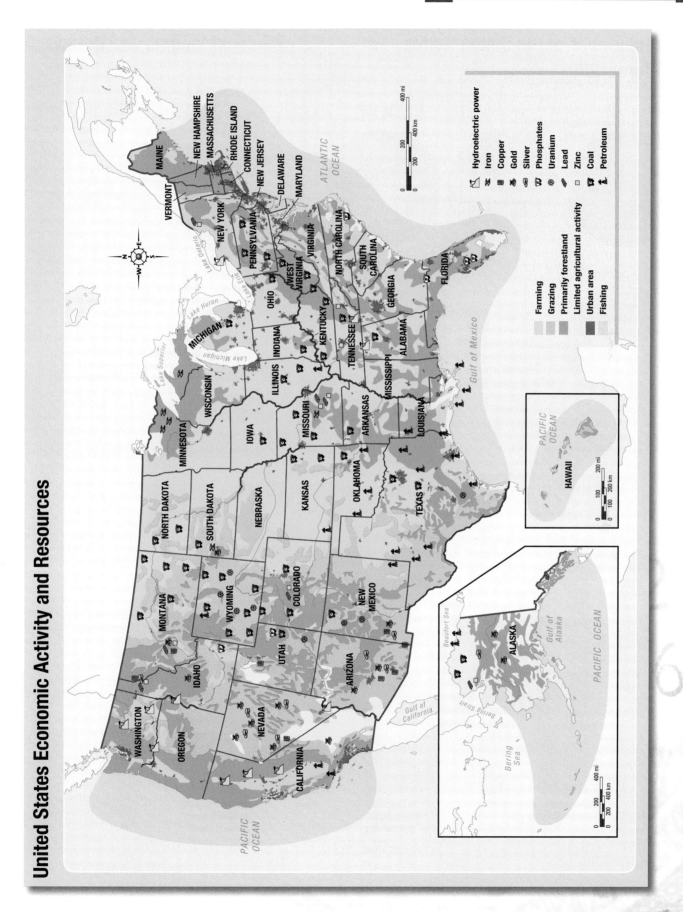

Characteristics of the United States Workforce, 2007

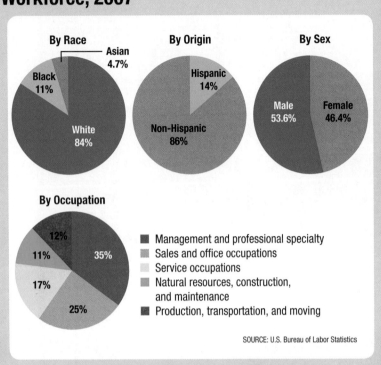

By Race
- Asian 4.7%
- Black 11%
- White 84%

By Origin
- Hispanic 14%
- Non-Hispanic 86%

By Sex
- Male 53.6%
- Female 46.4%

By Occupation
- 35%
- 25%
- 17%
- 11%
- 12%

- Management and professional specialty
- Sales and office occupations
- Service occupations
- Natural resources, construction, and maintenance
- Production, transportation, and moving

SOURCE: U.S. Bureau of Labor Statistics

Personal Income and Outlays

- Income
- Outlays

Dollars (in trillions)

Year: 1990 1993 1996 1999 2001 2004 2007

SOURCE: U.S. Bureau of Economic Analysis

Median Weekly Earnings, by Occupation and Sex, 2007

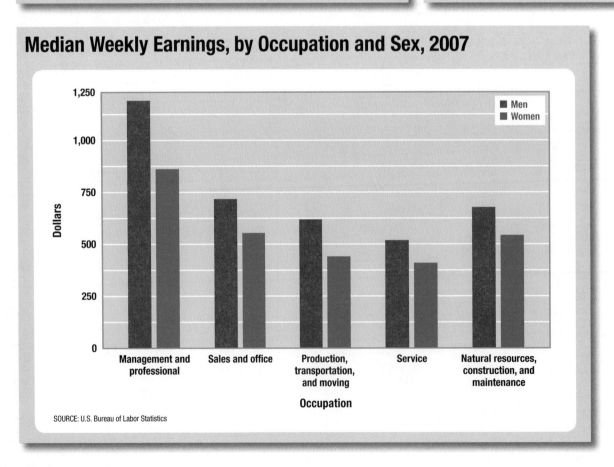

- Men
- Women

Dollars

Occupation: Management and professional, Sales and office, Production, transportation, and moving, Service, Natural resources, construction, and maintenance

SOURCE: U.S. Bureau of Labor Statistics

Fastest-Growing Occupations

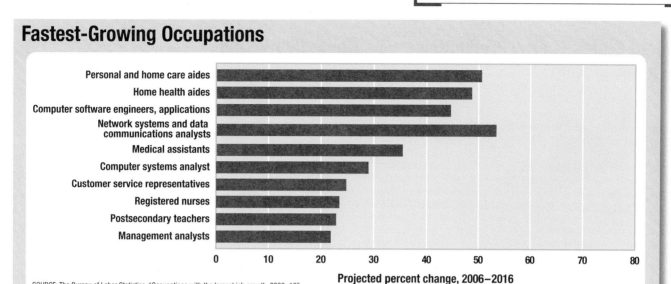

Occupation	Projected percent change, 2006–2016
Personal and home care aides	~51
Home health aides	~49
Computer software engineers, applications	~45
Network systems and data communications analysts	~53
Medical assistants	~35
Computer systems analyst	~29
Customer service representatives	~25
Registered nurses	~23
Postsecondary teachers	~23
Management analysts	~22

SOURCE: The Bureau of Labor Statistics, "Occupations with the largest job growth, 2006–16"

Unemployment Rates, 2007

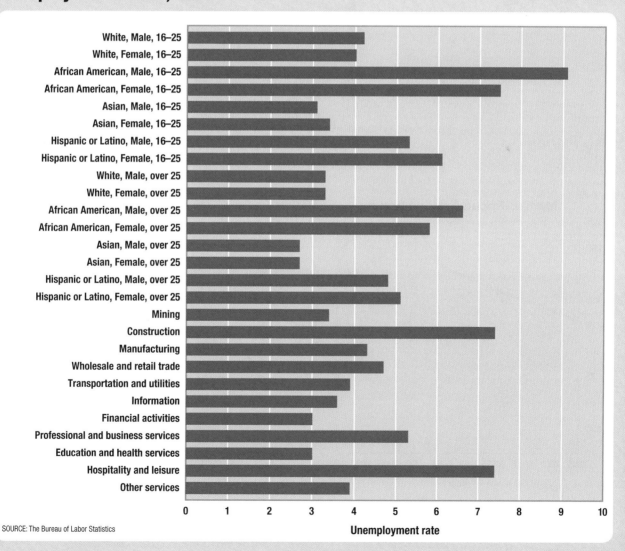

Category	Unemployment rate
White, Male, 16–25	~4.3
White, Female, 16–25	~3.2
African American, Male, 16–25	~9.2
African American, Female, 16–25	~7.3
Asian, Male, 16–25	~2.4
Asian, Female, 16–25	~2.6
Hispanic or Latino, Male, 16–25	~5.2
Hispanic or Latino, Female, 16–25	~6.0
White, Male, over 25	~3.5
White, Female, over 25	~3.4
African American, Male, over 25	~6.4
African American, Female, over 25	~5.6
Asian, Male, over 25	~2.2
Asian, Female, over 25	~2.3
Hispanic or Latino, Male, over 25	~4.8
Hispanic or Latino, Female, over 25	~5.0
Mining	~3.5
Construction	~7.4
Manufacturing	~4.3
Wholesale and retail trade	~4.6
Transportation and utilities	~3.9
Information	~3.7
Financial activities	~3.1
Professional and business services	~5.2
Education and health services	~3.1
Hospitality and leisure	~7.4
Other services	~3.9

SOURCE: The Bureau of Labor Statistics

Databank: The United States Economy

United States Energy Production, by Source, 2006

Coal 27%
Natural gas (dry) 37%
Crude oil 15%
Natural gas (plant liquids) 3%
Nuclear electric power 12%
Hydroelectric power 4%
Biofuels 5%

- ■ Coal
- ■ Natural gas (dry)
- ■ Crude oil
- ■ Natural gas (plant liquids)
- ■ Nuclear electric power
- ■ Hydroelectric power
- ■ Biofuels

SOURCE: U.S. Energy Information Administration

Home Ownership

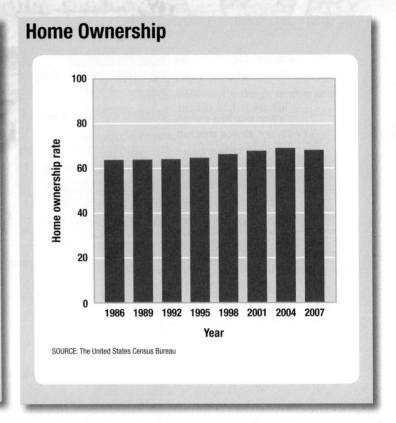

SOURCE: The United States Census Bureau

Housing Prices

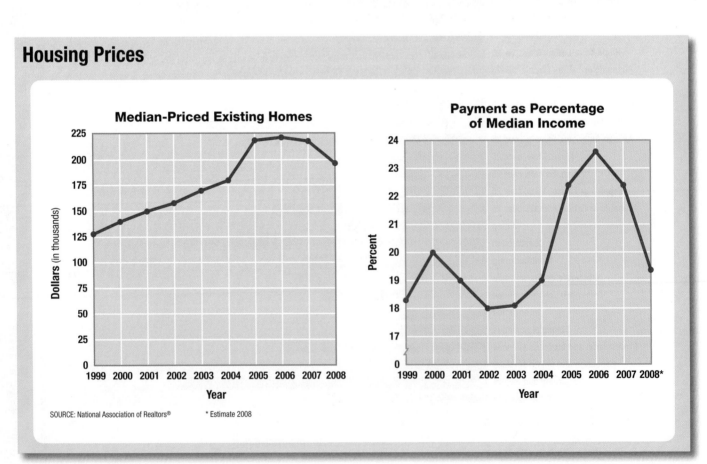

Median-Priced Existing Homes

Payment as Percentage of Median Income

SOURCE: National Association of Realtors®   * Estimate 2008

Per Capita Retail Sales, by Type of Business, 2006

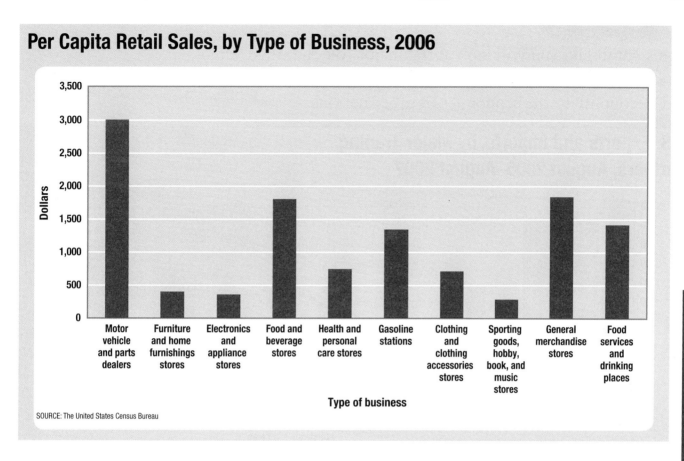

SOURCE: The United States Census Bureau

Selected Personal Consumption Expenditures, 2007

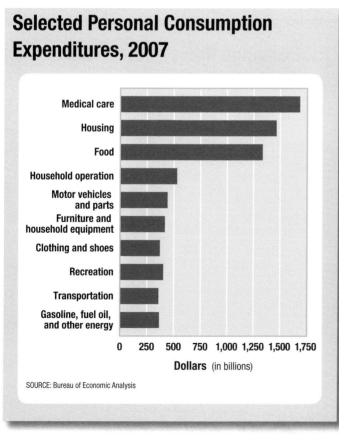

SOURCE: Bureau of Economic Analysis

Consumer Credit Debt

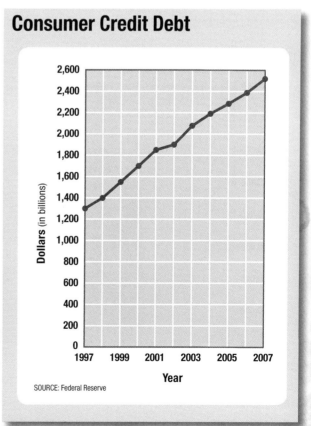

SOURCE: Federal Reserve

Databank: The United States Economy

Databank The World Economy

In this databank, you will look at the major role that the United States plays in world trade. You will also compare the United States economy to the economies of other nations.

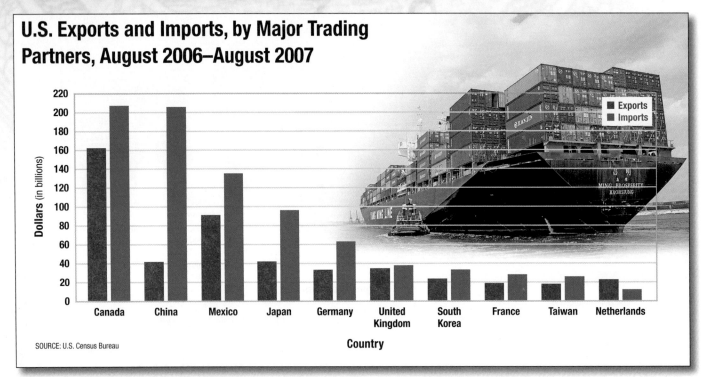

U.S. Exports and Imports, by Major Trading Partners, August 2006–August 2007

Legend: Exports, Imports

Y-axis: Dollars (in billions) — 0, 20, 40, 60, 80, 100, 120, 140, 160, 180, 200, 220

X-axis (Country): Canada, China, Mexico, Japan, Germany, United Kingdom, South Korea, France, Taiwan, Netherlands

SOURCE: U.S. Census Bureau

Major U.S. Exports and Imports, 2006

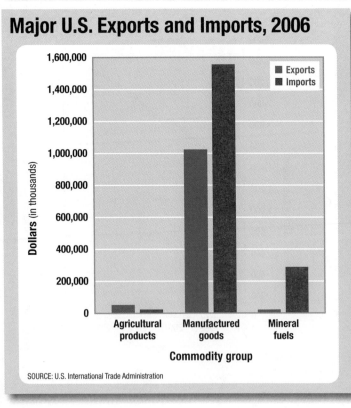

Legend: Exports, Imports

Y-axis: Dollars (in thousands) — 0; 200,000; 400,000; 600,000; 800,000; 1,000,000; 1,200,000; 1,400,000; 1,600,000

X-axis (Commodity group): Agricultural products, Manufactured goods, Mineral fuels

SOURCE: U.S. International Trade Administration

Exchange Rates of the Dollar

Country	1998	2001	2004	2007
Canada $	1.4836	1.5487	1.3017	1.0734
China Yuan	8.3008	8.2770	8.2768	7.6058
European Union €uro	N/A	0.8952	1.2438	1.3711
Japan ¥en	130.99	121.57	108.15	117.76
Mexico Peso	9.152	9.337	11.290	10.928
United Kingdom £	1.6573	1.4396	1.8330	2.0020

SOURCE: U.S. Federal Reserve

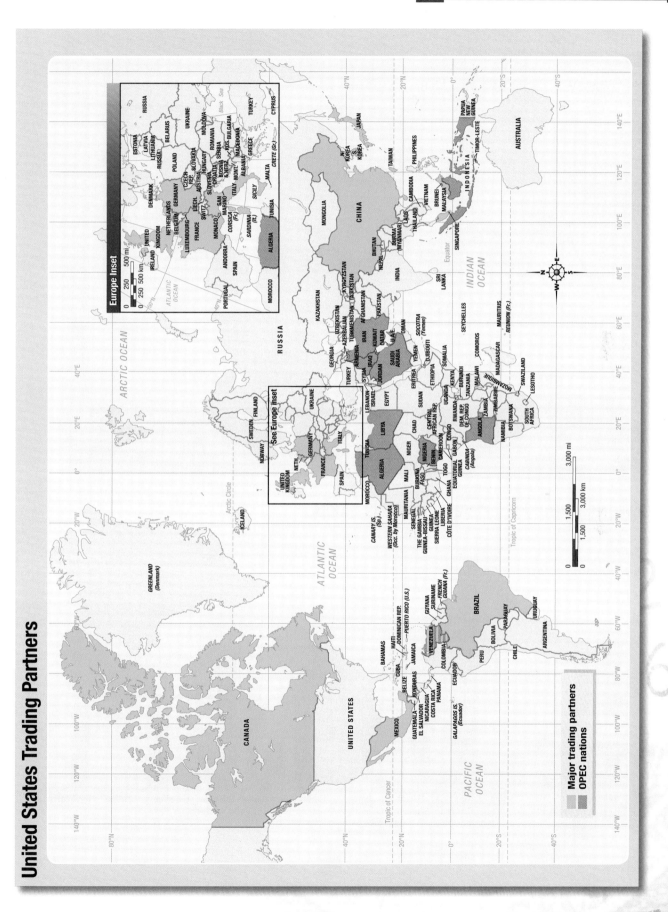

United States Trading Partners

Databank: The World Economy

Europe Inset

RUSSIA
ESTONIA
LATVIA
LITHUANIA
RUSSIA
BELARUS
UKRAINE
MOLDOVA
ROMANIA
BOS.-BULGARIA
MACEDONIA
POLAND
CZECH REP.
SLOVAKIA
HUNGARY
SERBIA
BOSNIA & HERZ.
ALBANIA
GREECE
TURKEY
CYPRUS
Black Sea
CRETE (Gr.)
DENMARK
GERMANY
LIECH.
SWITZ.
SLOVENIA
CROATIA
AUSTRIA
ITALY
MONT.
SAN MARINO
MALTA
SICILY
NETHERLANDS
BELGIUM
KINGDOM
LUXEMBOURG
FRANCE
MONACO
CORSICA (Fr.)
SARDINIA (It.)
TUNISIA
UNITED KINGDOM
IRELAND
ANDORRA
SPAIN
PORTUGAL
MOROCCO
ALGERIA
ATLANTIC OCEAN

0 250 500 mi
0 250 500 km

See Europe inset

GREENLAND (Denmark)
ICELAND
NORWAY
SWEDEN
FINLAND
UNITED KINGDOM
NETH.
GERMANY
FRANCE
SPAIN
ITALY
UKRAINE
TURKEY
LEBANON
ISRAEL
EGYPT

ARCTIC OCEAN
Arctic Circle
RUSSIA
KAZAKHSTAN
MONGOLIA
CHINA
UZBEKISTAN
KYRGYZSTAN
TURKMENISTAN
TAJIKISTAN
AFGHANISTAN
PAKISTAN
GEORGIA
ARMENIA
AZERBAIJAN
IRAN
KUWAIT
QATAR
U.A.E.
OMAN
SYRIA
IRAQ
JORDAN
SAUDI ARABIA
YEMEN
SOCOTRA (Yemen)
BHUTAN
NEPAL
INDIA
SRI LANKA
BURMA (MYANMAR)
LAOS
THAILAND
CAMBODIA
VIETNAM
BRUNEI
MALAYSIA
SINGAPORE
INDONESIA
PHILIPPINES
TAIWAN
JAPAN
N. KOREA
S. KOREA
Equator
INDIAN OCEAN
SEYCHELLES
MAURITIUS
REUNION (Fr.)
COMOROS
MADAGASCAR
MOZAMBIQUE
SWAZILAND
LESOTHO
SOUTH AFRICA
BOTSWANA
NAMIBIA
ANGOLA
ZAMBIA
ZIMBABWE
MALAWI
TANZANIA
BURUNDI
RWANDA
DEM. REP. OF CONGO
CONGO
GABON
CABINDA (Angola)
EQUATORIAL GUINEA
CAMEROON
CENTRAL AFRICAN REP.
UGANDA
KENYA
SOMALIA
ETHIOPIA
ERITREA
DJIBOUTI
SUDAN
CHAD
NIGER
LIBYA
TUNISIA
ALGERIA
MOROCCO
WESTERN SAHARA (Occ. by Morocco)
MALI
MAURITANIA
SENEGAL
CANARY IS. (Sp.)
THE GAMBIA
GUINEA-BISSAU
GUINEA
SIERRA LEONE
LIBERIA
CÔTE D'IVOIRE
GHANA
TOGO
BENIN
NIGERIA
BURKINA FASO
PAPUA NEW GUINEA
TIMOR-LESTE
AUSTRALIA

PACIFIC OCEAN
ATLANTIC OCEAN
CANADA
UNITED STATES
MEXICO
GUATEMALA
EL SALVADOR
NICARAGUA
COSTA RICA
HONDURAS
PANAMA
BELIZE
BAHAMAS
CUBA
HAITI
JAMAICA
DOMINICAN REP.
PUERTO RICO (U.S.)
GALAPAGOS IS. (Ecuador)
COLOMBIA
VENEZUELA
ECUADOR
PERU
BOLIVIA
CHILE
PARAGUAY
BRAZIL
GUYANA
SURINAME
FRENCH GUIANA (Fr.)
URUGUAY
ARGENTINA
Tropic of Cancer
Equator
Tropic of Capricorn

3,000 mi
0 1,500 3,000 km
0 1,500 3,000 mi

Major trading partners
OPEC nations

U.S. Oil Imports, 1973–2007

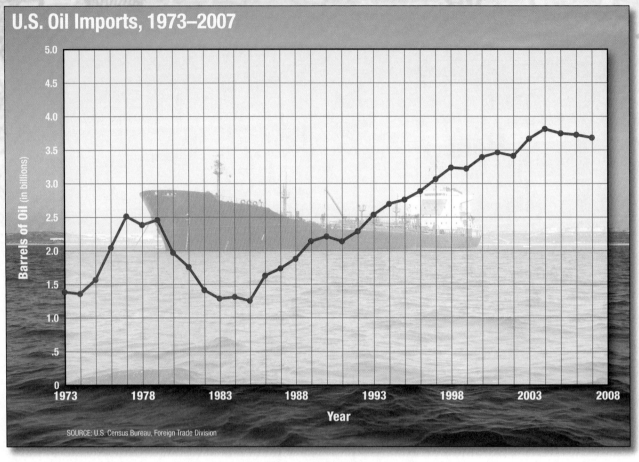

Barrels of Oil (in billions)

Year

SOURCE: U.S. Census Bureau, Foreign Trade Division

Major Agricultural Exports and Imports, 2006

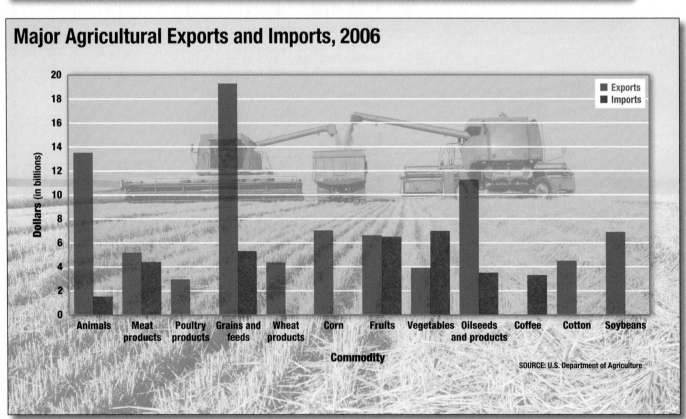

Dollars (in billions)

■ Exports
■ Imports

Animals | Meat products | Poultry products | Grains and feeds | Wheat products | Corn | Fruits | Vegetables | Oilseeds and products | Coffee | Cotton | Soybeans

Commodity

SOURCE: U.S. Department of Agriculture

Health Expenditures as Percent of GDP, 2004

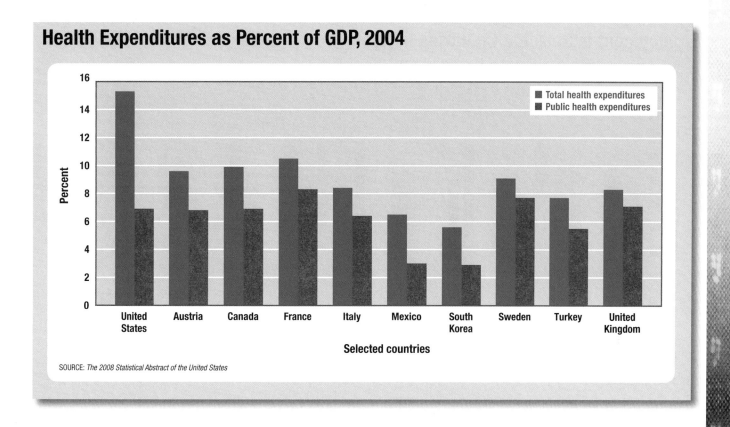

SOURCE: *The 2008 Statistical Abstract of the United States*

Taxes as Percent of GDP, 2006

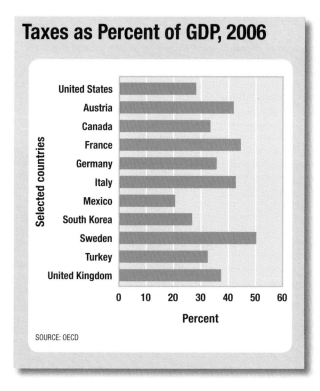

SOURCE: OECD

National Budget Expenditures, 2007

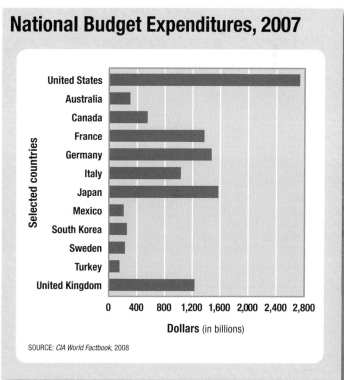

SOURCE: *CIA World Factbook, 2008*

Databank: The World Economy

Employment in Selected Countries by Type

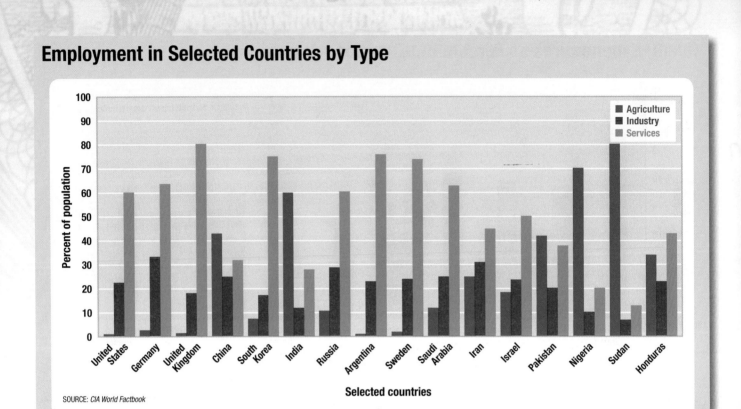

SOURCE: *CIA World Factbook*

GDP Growth of Selected Countries

Country	1997	1998	1999	2000	2001	2002	2003	2004	2005	2006	2007*
United States	8,250	8,695	9,216	9,765	10,076	10,418	10,919	11,679	12,417	13,202	13,860
Germany	2,160	2,184	2,144	1,900	1,891	2,019	2,442	2,751	2,795	2,907	2,833
United Kingdom	1,327	1,425	1,465	1,443	1,435	1,571	1,806	2,132	2,199	2,345	2,147
China	953	1,019	1,083	1,198	1,325	1,454	1,641	1,932	2,234	2,668	7,043
South Korea	516	345	445	512	482	547	608	680	788	888	1,206
India	410	414	450	460	478	508	602	696	806	906	2,965
Russia	405	271	196	260	307	345	431	589	764	987	2,076
Argentina	293	299	284	284	269	102	130	153	183	214	524
Saudi Arabia	165	146	161	188	183	189	215	250	310	310	572
Iran	105	103	105	101	115	116	136	163	190	223	853
Israel	104	104	104	115	114	104	110	117	123	123	185
Nigeria	36	32	35	46	48	47	58	72	99	115	295
Sudan	12	11	11	12	13	15	18	21	28	38	108
Honduras	5	5	5	6	6	7	7	7	8	9	25

Note: Amounts in billions of dollars.
*Estimates for 2007
SOURCE: *CIA World Factbook*, World Bank

Labor Productivity by Country

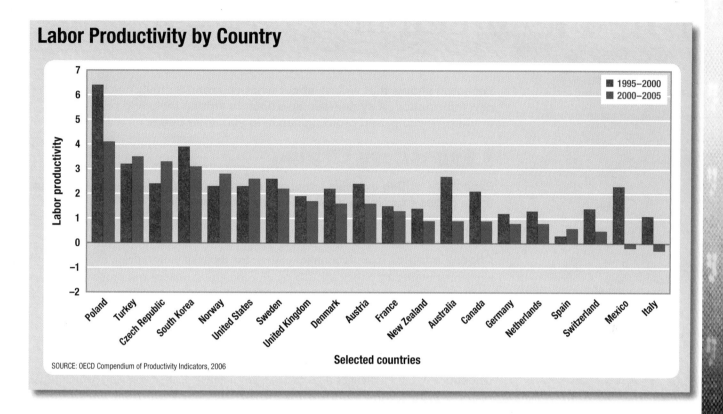

SOURCE: OECD Compendium of Productivity Indicators, 2006

Economic Health of Selected Countries

Country	Infant Mortality (per 1,000 live births)	Life Expect-ancy	Median Age	Literacy (by percent)	Unemploy-ment (by percent)	Internet Users	Cellular Telephone Users
United States	6.37	78	36.6	99	4.6	208 million	233 million
Germany	4.08	78.95	43	99	9.1	38.6 million	84.3 million
United Kingdom	5.01	78.7	39.6	99	5.4	33.534 million	69.657 million
China	22.12	72.88	33.2	90.9	4	162 million	461.1 million
South Korea	6.05	77.23	35.8	97.9	3.2	34.12 million	40.197 million
India	34.61	68.59	24.8	73.4	7.2	60 million	166.1 million
Russia	11.06	65.87	38.2	99.4	5.9	25.689 million	150 million
Argentina	14.29	76.32	29.9	97.2	8.9	8.184 million	31.51 million
Saudi Arabia	12.41	75.88	21.4	78.8	13	4.7 million	19.663 million
Iran	38.12	70.56	25.8	77	11	18 million	13.659 million
Israel	6.75	79.59	29.9	97.1	7.6	1.899 million	8.404 million
Nigeria	95.52	47.44	18.7	68	5.8	8 million	32.322 million
Sudan	91.78	49.11	18.7	61.1	18.7	3.5 million	4.683 million
Honduras	25.21	69.35	19.7	80	27.8	337,300	2.241 million

SOURCE: *CIA World Factbook*, 2008

Databank: The World Economy

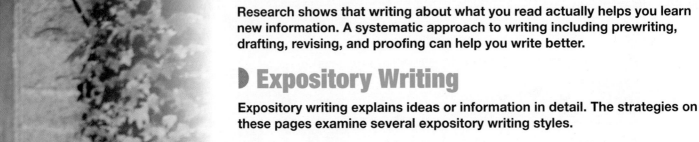

Research shows that writing about what you read actually helps you learn new information. A systematic approach to writing including prewriting, drafting, revising, and proofing can help you write better.

▶ Expository Writing

Expository writing explains ideas or information in detail. The strategies on these pages examine several expository writing styles.

1 Prewriting

Choose a topic. In an economics course, the focus of your writing might be explaining monetary policy, identifying an economic problem and proposing a solution, or examining how incentives affect the choices producers and consumers make.

Ask questions. For process writing, consider the question *how*. For example, "How does fiscal policy affect the economy?"

Question: What challenges does the U.S. government face in choosing which fiscal policy to follow?

Answer: The government faces the following challenges when determining which fiscal policy to follow: figuring out the precise phase of the business cycle, determining the lag between implementation and results, and reconciling various policies with political opponents.

Create a problems/solutions grab bag. With a small group, write on separate slips of paper examples of problems related to each of these challenges: pinpointing the appropriate phase of the business cycle, the time lag before implementation, and political pressures.

Consider audience and purpose. Consider how much your readers know about the problem or process you will address. Explain unfamiliar terms and concepts.

Research the topic. Use library and Internet resources and interviews with local officials or experts if possible. List facts, details, and other information related to your topic. Collect the facts and details you need to write your essay.

Create a graphic organizer. A Venn diagram can help you compare and contrast. For cause-and-effect or problem-solution essays, use a two-column chart. Process writing can be listed as a bulleted list of steps.

Fine-tune your ideas. For a problem-solution essay, decide what you will suggest as a solution. Narrow the scope of your solution to ensure that it is achievable. If others have tried your solution, describe successes or failures.

② Drafting

Match structure to purpose. Typically, problem-solution essays benefit from block organization. This presents the entire problem and proposes a solution. Put process and cause-and-effect essays in sequence order and organize compare/contrast essays by subject or point.

Give background. To discuss fiscal policy, the economy, or trade, first give the reader background. Choose the important facts but don't overwhelm the reader with details. If you need to, return to prewriting to narrow your topic further.

Elaborate for interest and emphasis. Give details about each point in your essay. Add facts that make clear the link between the reasons for decisions made and their consequences.

Identify the topic to → orient readers.	Fiscal policy is an important tool the government uses to stabilize the economy. To avoid a recession, either supply-side or demand-side policies are adopted at different times.
Chronological order → walks readers through the cause-and-effect sequence.	Economist John Maynard Keynes believed the government needed to engage in both approaches to stabilize the economy. By purchasing goods, the government set in motion an economic chain of events that cause economic growth. To provide goods to the government, firms naturally increase output. To increase output, firms have to hire more workers. These workers spend money in other areas of the market. Keynes also believed that the government had to raise taxes to control growth and prevent inflation.
Elaboration supports → the relationship you are highlighting.	By purchasing large quantities of steel, the government increases demand for this product. Steel mills hire new workers to meet this demand. As steelworkers begin to spend their salaries, this increases demand in other sectors of the market.
Connection to today → tells readers why this matters to them.	Today debates over the role of the government in the market are, in part, a debate over how best to implement fiscal policy.

③ Revising

Add transition words. Make cause-and-effect relationships clear with words such as *because, as a result,* and *so*. To compare or contrast policies and processes, use linking words, such as *similarly, both, equally,* or *in contrast, instead,* and *yet*. Use words such as *first, second, next,* and *finally* to help readers follow steps in a process. Look at the examples below. The revised version more clearly shows the order followed by supply-side economics.

First Draft	Revised
Although Keynesian economics was employed for a number of decades in the 20th century, President Reagan followed a supply-side policy during the 1980s.	When President Reagan assumed office, he adopted a supply-side economic policy. A supply-side economist first studies the current tax rate. Second, the economist determines what the appropriate rate should be and advises that tax cuts be made to that level. These tax cuts allow businesses to hire more workers. As a result of more people working, the government's revenue increases.

Remember purpose. Shape your draft so it answers the question or thesis with which you began. Try to anticipate opposing arguments and respond to them. For a process essay, be sure to include all steps. Don't assume readers will make the connections. Always tell readers why they should care about your topic.

Review organization. Confirm that your ideas flow logically. Write and number main points on your draft. Reorganize these points until you are satisfied that the order clearly strengthens your essay.

Revise sentences and words. Vary sentence length to include both short and long sentences. Then scan for vague words, such as *good*. Replace them with specific and vibrant words, such as *effective*.

Conduct a peer review. Ask a peer to read your draft. Is it clear? Can he or she follow your ideas? Revise areas of confusion.

4 Publishing and Presenting

Create an economics manual. Contribute your writing to a class manual on economics.

▶ Research Writing

In a research paper, you gather information about a subject from several different sources. Then, you tie this information together with a single unifying idea and present it to your readers.

1 Prewriting

Choose a topic. Often a teacher will assign your research topic. You may be able to choose your own focus, or you may have the opportunity to completely define your topic.

- **Catalog scan.** Using an online or electronic library catalog, search for topics that interest you. When a title looks promising, find the book on the shelves. Because libraries group research materials by subject, you should find other books on similar subjects nearby that may help you decide on your final topic.
- **Notes review.** Review your class notes. Jot down topics you found interesting. From a lecture on competition you might find a starting point for research into oligopolies.
- **Brainstorming with a group.** As a group, list categories of issues that interest group members. Within each category, take turns adding subtopics.

Analyze the audience. Your audience should strongly influence your research and your paper. How much will readers know about this topic and how much will you have to teach them?

Gather details. Collect the facts and details you need to write your paper. Use nonfiction books or journal articles, newspapers, news magazines, publications by government agencies or advocacy groups, and other resources on issues that interest you.

Organize evidence and ideas. Use notecards or create a computer file on your topic to record information. Start by writing down a possible thesis statement. Then begin reading and taking notes. Write a heading at the top of each notecard to group it under a subtopic. Note a number or title to identify the information source. In the examples below, the number 3 is used. Use the same number for an additional source card or notation containing the bibliographic information you will need.

Information source I.D. number →
3   **Background on Monopolies**

p. 4

"Because of [a] natural tendency toward monopoly, water shipment prices often are higher than they would be if the water transport industries were competitive."

Bibliographic information for source 3 →
Holmes, Thomas J., and James A. Schmitz Jr. "Competition at Work: Railroads vs. Monopoly in the U.S. Shipping Industry." Minneapolis: *Federal Reserve Bank of Minneapolis Quarterly Review*, Spring 2001, vol. 25, No. 1, pp. 3–29.

② Drafting

Fine-tune your thesis. Review your notes to find relationships among ideas. Shape a thesis that the majority of your information supports, then check that it is specific enough to thoroughly address in the time and space allotted.

Plan your organization. Depending on your topic and purpose, you can use various methods to organize your research paper. If you are discussing two items, one approach would be to compare and contrast them. If you are focusing on a complex event or a process, you could use a chronological organization.

Make an outline. Create an outline in which you identify each topic and subtopic in a single phrase. Turn these phrases into sentences and then into the topic sentences of your draft paragraphs. Address a subtopic of your main topic in each body paragraph. Support all your statements with the facts and details you gathered.

An outline helps you structure your information.

Monopolies and Deregulation
Outline

Each body paragraph looks at a part of the whole topic.

I. Introduction
II. What is regulation and what is deregulation?
III. What are the benefits of deregulation?
   A. New firms enter an industry and create greater competition, which lowers prices.
   B. Firms become more efficient.
   C. The government saves money.
IV. What are the risks of deregulation?
   A. Monopolies could form.
   B. Deregulation, coupled with federal antitrust laws, prevents the formation of monopolies.
   C. Prices for consumers increase.
   D. With government controlling markets, prices for consumers are unlikely to fall.
V. Conclusions: Benefits of deregulation outweigh incentives.

The introduction puts the topic in context. The entire paragraph conveys the thesis.

Introduction
In the late 19th and early 20th centuries, the government began to regulate various industries. Toward the end of the 20th century, the government reversed course. It realized that competition without government regulation, lowers prices for customers.

The conclusion recaps key points and leaves readers with a final statement to remember.

Conclusion
When a government regulates an industry, it stifles growth and creates inefficiencies that lead to high prices.

③ Revising

Add detail. Mark points where more details would strengthen your statements. In the following example, notice the added details in the revised version. When adding facts, verify accuracy.

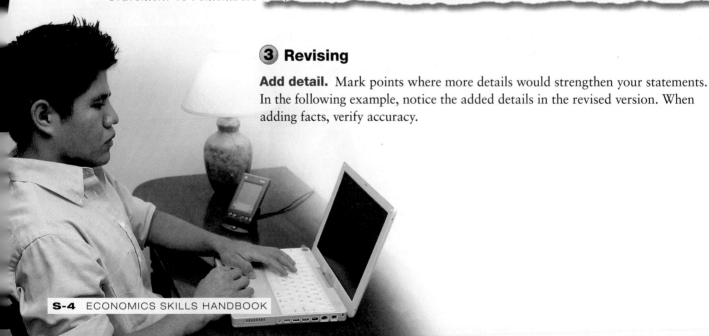

First Draft	Revised
When governments deregulate industries, new companies can enter the field. These new companies have innovative ideas that increase efficiency and lower prices.	In 1978, President Carter deregulated the airline industry. New airlines emerged. This change forced larger airlines into competition, resulting in lower prices for consumers.

Make the connection for readers. Help readers find their way through your ideas. First, check that your body paragraphs and the information within them flow in a logical sequence. If they do not, revise to correct this. Then add transition words to link ideas and paragraphs.

Give credit. Check that you have used your own words or given proper credit to other sources with parenthetical notes, which include the author's last name and the relevant page number from the source. For example, you could cite the notecard here as (Holmes and Schmitz, p. 4).

4 Publishing and Presenting

Plan a conference. Gather a group of classmates and present your research projects.

❱ Persuasive Essay

Persuasive writing supports an opinion or position. This writing style often takes the form of position papers, editorials, blogs, and op-ed pieces. Persuasive essays often argue for or against economic positions such as free trade.

1 Prewriting

Choose a topic. Choose a topic that provokes an argument and has at least two sides. Use these ideas as a guide.

Round-table discussion. Talk with classmates about issues you have studied recently. Outline pro and con positions about these issues.

Textbook flip. Scan the table of contents or flip through the pages of your textbook.

Making connections. Look at blogs, editorials, or Op-Ed pieces in current newspapers. Develop a position on an important issue.

Narrow your topic.
Cover part of the topic. If you find too many pros and cons for a straightforward argument, choose part of the topic.

Use looping. Write for five minutes on the general topic. Circle the most important idea. Then write for five minutes on that idea. Continue looping until the topic is manageable.

Consider your audience. Choose arguments that will appeal to the audience you are writing for and that are likely to persuade them to agree with your views.

Gather evidence. Collect evidence that will help you support your position convincingly.

Identify pros and cons. Use a graphic organizer like the one below to list points on both sides of the issue.

Interview. Speak to people who have firsthand knowledge of your issue.

Research. Investigate the subject to get your facts straight. Read articles about the topic.

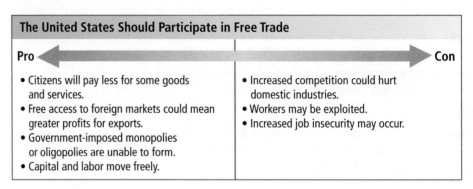

The United States Should Participate in Free Trade

Pro ←——————————————————→ Con

Pro
- Citizens will pay less for some goods and services.
- Free access to foreign markets could mean greater profits for exports.
- Government-imposed monopolies or oligopolies are unable to form.
- Capital and labor move freely.

Con
- Increased competition could hurt domestic industries.
- Workers may be exploited.
- Increased job insecurity may occur.

Because of its many resources and greater comparative advantage in producing goods and services, the United States should participate in free trade.

2 Drafting

State your thesis. Clearly state your position, as in the example to the left:

Acknowledge opposition. State and refute opposing arguments. Use facts and details. Include quotations, statistics, or comparisons to build your case. Include the comments and opinions of community members or officials who were interviewed.

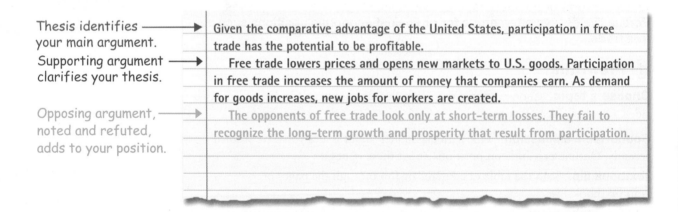

Thesis identifies your main argument.

Given the comparative advantage of the United States, participation in free trade has the potential to be profitable.

Supporting argument clarifies your thesis.

Free trade lowers prices and opens new markets to U.S. goods. Participation in free trade increases the amount of money that companies earn. As demand for goods increases, new jobs for workers are created.

Opposing argument, noted and refuted, adds to your position.

The opponents of free trade look only at short-term losses. They fail to recognize the long-term growth and prosperity that result from participation.

Write a conclusion. Your conclusion should restate the thesis and close with a strong, compelling argument or a brief summary of the three strongest arguments.

3 Revising

Add information. Extra details can generate interest in your topic. For example, add a quotation from a news article that describes the positive impact NAFTA has had on the U.S. beef industry.

Review arguments. Make sure your arguments are logically sound and clearly developed. Evidence is the best way to support your points.

Use transition words. Guide readers through your ideas, using the following words:

- to show contrast: *however, although, despite*
- to point out a reason: *since, because, if*
- to signal conclusion: *therefore, consequently, so, then*

4 Publishing

Persuasive Speech. In addition to position papers, editorials, blogs, and Op-Ed pieces, persuasive essays are also delivered orally. How effective were your efforts to persuade? Report your results and evaluate the effectiveness.

▶ Writing for Assessment

Assessment writing differs from all other writing you do. You have many fewer choices as a writer, and you almost always face a time limit.

1 Prewriting

Choose a topic. Short-answer questions seldom offer a topic choice. For extended response, however, you may have a choice of more than one question.

Examine the question. To choose a question you can answer effectively, analyze what each question is asking. Use key words such as those listed in the chart at right to help you choose topics and respond to short-answer questions in which the topic is given. Notice in the examples below that the key words are underlined:

Key Words	What You Need In an Answer
Explain	• Give a clear, complete account of how something works, or what the causes or effects are of a particular decision or policy.
Compare/Contrast	• Show how two or more things are alike and different.
Define	• Give examples to explain meaning.
Argue, Convince, Support, Persuade	• Take a position on an issue and present strong reasons to support your side of the issue.
Summarize	• Provide the most important elements of a subject.
Evaluate/Judge	• Assign a value or explain an opinion.
Interpret	• Support a thesis with examples from the text.

Short–Answer Question: Why do governments impose <u>taxes</u>?

Extended Response Question: How have taxes <u>been used</u> by governments? Give examples to <u>support your conclusion</u>.

Measure your time. Your goal is to show you've mastered the material. To stay focused on this goal, divide your time: one quarter on prewriting; half on drafting; one quarter on revising. For short-answer questions, determine how much of the overall test time you can spend on each question. Don't spend more than that.

Gather information. Identify and organize the information you need to write your answer. For short-answer questions, this usually involves identifying exactly which facts and details are required.

Use a graphic organizer. For extended responses, divide your topic into subtopics that fit the type of question. Jot down facts and details for each.

② Drafting

Choose an organization that fits the question. With short-answer questions, write one to three complete sentences. Look at the example at left. Extended responses require more elaborate organization. For an extended response on the use of taxes, describe how taxes have been used in a number of ways. For compare/contrast, present similarities first, then differences.

Open and close strongly. Start your answer by restating the question or using its language to state your position. This helps you focus and shows the instructor you understand the question. Finish with a conclusion that restates your position. For short answers, include some language from the question in your response.

Support your ideas. Each paragraph should directly or indirectly support your main idea. Choose facts that build a cohesive argument.

> Governments need the ability to impose taxes to raise revenue. Governments that have been able to raise taxes successfully are able to pay for services for its citizens.

③ Revising

Examine word choice. Replace general words with specific words. Add transitions where these improve clarity.

First Draft	Revised
Taxes play an important role in fiscal policy, international trade, and collecting revenue.	Taxes play a multifaceted role in the American economy. In addition to being a valuable source of revenue for all levels of government, taxes figure prominently in international trade and in the application of fiscal policy.

Check organization. Make sure your introduction includes a main idea and briefly defines each subtopic. Review each paragraph for a single main idea. Check that your conclusion summarizes the information you've presented.

④ Publishing and Presenting

Edit and proof. Check spelling, grammar, and mechanics. Make sure tenses match, subjects agree with verbs, and sentences are not too long. Finally, confirm that you have responded to all the questions you were asked to answer.

▶ Writing Rubric Use this chart, or rubric, to evaluate your writing.

SAT

SCORE OF 6

An essay in this category is outstanding, demonstrating **clear and consistent mastery,** although it may have a few minor errors. A typical essay:

- effectively and insightfully develops a point of view on the issue and demonstrates outstanding critical thinking, using clearly appropriate examples, reasons, and other evidence to support its position
- is well organized and clearly focused, demonstrating clear coherence and smooth progression of ideas
- exhibits skillful use of language, using a varied, accurate, and appropriate vocabulary
- demonstrates meaningful variety in sentence structure
- is free of most errors in grammar, usage, and mechanics

SCORE OF 5

An essay in this category is **effective,** demonstrating **reasonably consistent mastery,** although it will have occasional errors or lapses in quality. A typical essay:

- effectively develops a point of view on the issue and demonstrates strong critical thinking, generally using appropriate examples, reasons, and other evidence to support its position
- is well organized and focused, demonstrating coherence and progression of ideas
- exhibits facility in the use of language, using appropriate vocabulary
- demonstrates variety in sentence structure
- is generally free of most errors in grammar, usage, and mechanics

SCORE OF 4

An essay in this category is **competent,** demonstrating **adequate mastery,** although it will have lapses in quality. A typical essay:

- develops a point of view on the issue and demonstrates competent critical thinking, using adequate examples, reasons, and other evidence to support its position
- is generally organized and focused, demonstrating some coherence and progression of ideas, exhibits adequate but inconsistent facility in the use of language, using generally appropriate vocabulary
- demonstrates some variety in sentence structure
- has some errors in grammar, usage, and mechanics

SCORE OF 3

An essay in this category is **inadequate** but demonstrates **developing mastery** and is marked by one or more of the following weaknesses:

- develops a point of view on the issue, demonstrating some critical thinking, but may do so inconsistently or use inadequate examples, reasons, or other evidence to support its position
- is limited in its organization or focus but may demonstrate some lapses in coherence or progression of ideas
- displays developing facility in the use of language but may use weak vocabulary or inappropriate word choice
- lacks variety or demonstrates problems in sentence structure
- contains an accumulation of errors in grammar, usage, and mechanics

SCORE OF 2

An essay in this category is **seriously limited,** demonstrating little mastery, and is flawed by **one or more** of the following weaknesses:

- develops a point of view on the issue that is vague or seriously limited, demonstrating weak critical thinking, providing inappropriate or insufficient examples, reasons, or other evidence to support its position
- is poorly organized and/or focused or demonstrates serious problems with coherence or progression of ideas
- displays very little facility in the use of language, using very limited vocabulary or incorrect word choice
- demonstrates frequent problems in sentence structure
- contains errors in grammar, usage, and mechanics so serious that meaning is somewhat obscured

SCORE OF 1

An essay in this category is **fundamentally lacking,** demonstrating **very little or no mastery,** and is severely flawed by one or more of the following weaknesses:

- develops no viable point of view on the issue or provides little or no evidence to support its position
- is disorganized or unfocused, resulting in a disjointed or incoherent essay
- displays fundamental errors in vocabulary
- demonstrates severe flaws in sentence structure
- contains pervasive errors in grammar, usage, or mechanics that persistently interfere with meaning

SCORE OF 0

Essays not written on the essay assignment will receive a score of zero.

Social Studies Skills Handbook

▶ Analyze Primary and Secondary Sources

A primary source is information a participant or observer produces during or soon after an event. Primary sources include letters, photographs, memos, and legal documents. A secondary source provides an analysis or interpretation of an event based on primary sources.

Identify the document. Determine when, where, why, and by whom the document was written to decide if the document is a primary or a secondary source.

Find the main idea. A main idea is the most important point in a paragraph or section of text. After identifying the main idea, identify supporting details.

Evaluate the document for point of view and bias. Primary sources give a strong sense of an event but present only a single point of view.

In 1973 Saudi Arabia and several other members of OPEC began an oil embargo, refusing to sell oil to the United States. ▼

Read the excerpt below from the 2003 article "Still Holding Customers over a Barrel." ▼

" Primary Source

The gasoline shortage was acutely [deeply] felt in Chicago last week with drivers waiting sometimes several hours alongside a pump. Several hundred stations, their January allotments depleted, were closed. Many others had...curtailed [cut back] their hours of operation. The Root Brothers service station...was typical. Cars were lined up for blocks, police had to direct traffic and the limit a customer could purchase was set at $5.00....According to Platt's Oilgram Service...the average price a year ago for a gallon of gasoline in the Midwest was 40.9 cents for regular. The range of regular gasoline now runs from 47.9 cents a gallon to 55.9 [cents a gallon]."

—William Farrell, "Oil Is a National Problem, But Seriousness Varies," *The New York Times*, February 3, 1974

" Secondary Source

The Arab embargo has become a symbol of the...chaos and economic troubles endured by the West during the oil shocks of the 1970s....The [long lines] and shortages in America that are now linked in the popular imagination with that period had little to do with the Arab Embargo. Jerry Taylor of the Cato Institute argues, correctly, that the shortages were due chiefly to the... energy policies...adopted by America...In 1971 for example, the Nixon administration imposed price controls...that prevented oil companies from passing on the full cost of imported oil to consumers. That led...to the companies making decisions to reduce their imports...Congress made the situation worse in September 1973 by trying to allocate [distribute] oil to...different parts of the country through bureaucratic fiat....These measures led...to the panic and hoarding..."

—*The Economist*, October 23, 2003

PRACTICE AND APPLY THE SKILL

Use the excerpts above to answer the following questions.

1. What makes one newspaper article a primary source and the other a secondary source?

2. How is the primary source reporter's purpose different from the secondary source writer's?

3. What is the main idea of the secondary source?

▶ Compare Viewpoints

Economists often disagree on economic policies or recommend different responses to the same problem. Comparing viewpoints will help you understand issues and form your own opinions. The excerpts below provide different views on globalization and offshoring, the practice of sending some of a corporation, manufacturing, service operations, or jobs overseas.

Identify the authors. Determine when and where each person was speaking. Identify the intended audience for each speech and the purpose of each.

Determine the author's frame of reference. Consider how each speaker's attitudes, beliefs, frame of reference, values, or social, economic, or political concerns and affiliations, as well as past experiences, might affect his or her viewpoint.

Determine the author's bias. Bias may be revealed in the use of emotionally charged words, strong language, faulty logic, or exaggerated claims. Identify which statements are facts and which are opinions that represent the speaker's viewpoint.

Compare and contrast. Determine how the viewpoints are different. Consider factors that might cause the authors to have different views on the issue.

Diana Farrell, director of McKinsey Global Institute, the economics research division of a global consulting firm for multinational businesses. ▼

"[F]ears of job losses caused by offshoring are greatly exaggerated. New research…shows that the United States will likely lose to offshoring no more than 300,000 jobs each year….Savings from offshoring allow companies to invest in next-generation technologies, creating jobs at home as well as abroad. …Protectionism may save a few jobs…but it will stifle [hold back] innovation and job creation in the longer term. Rather than trying to stop globalization, the goal must be to let it happen, while easing the transition for workers who lose out."

—Diana Farrell in *Economists' Voice,* www.bepress.com, March 2006

Richard Trumka, secretary-treasurer of the AFL-CIO, a federation of labor unions representing more than 10 million U.S. workers. ▼

"Over the past three years, the U.S. has lost 2.6 million manufacturing jobs,…the vast majority…due to offshoring and outsourcing….Everyone talks about retraining, but the problem is that these days, if you're out of work, there's not a job in the area you're trained in and not a job in the area you're retrained in…. Retraining is not the magic solution because there isn't an industry that is safe from the trend anymore that provides the solid jobs needed by the American middle class."

—Richard Trumka, participating in a *Wall Street Journal* Online roundtable on outsourcing, 2004

PRACTICE AND APPLY THE SKILL

Use the excerpts above to answer the following questions.

1. How do you think each person's frame of reference is influenced by his or her viewpoint?

2. How does Farrell's statement that "fears of job losses" are "greatly exaggerated" reflect her point of view?

3. How do the views of Farrell and Trumka about job losses differ?

▶ Drawing Inferences and Conclusions

When people "read between the lines," they are drawing inferences. They have formed their conclusions not from what is stated directly but from what is suggested by other facts.

Summarize information. Identify the main idea to help you understand the text. To find information in a passage that is suggested but unstated, you have to understand what the passage is about.

Apply other facts or prior knowledge. Consider what you know about the topic. Use this knowledge to evaluate the information. A combination of what you already know and what you learn from reading the passage may help you draw inferences.

Decide if the information suggests an unstated fact or conclusion. Combine what you have learned from the text and what you already know to draw inferences and conclusions about the topic.

Read the excerpt from "The Grip of Gas," by University of Chicago economics professor Austan Goolsbee. ▼

In repeated studies of consumer purchases… drivers in the United States consistently rank as the least sensitive to changes in gas prices….The… estimates, based on a [2002] study…predict that if prices rose from $3 per gallon to $4 per gallon and stayed there for a year…purchases of gasoline… would fall only about 5 percent.

Why don't we ratchet down [reduce] more when fuel prices go up? The rule of thumb in economics is that people react to price increases only when they can turn to substitutes. Raise the price of Ford trucks and sales go down because you can buy your truck from Chrysler or GM or Toyota instead. Raise the price of gasoline and what are the alternatives?…

Gasoline purchases are, in fact, the kind of buying affected least by price changes because they are so closely tied up with other things we already own…In the last two decades when gasoline was cheap, Americans switched from cars to minivans and SUVs, seriously reducing their gas mileage. Also, many moved farther from their places of work…As jobs moved…into suburbs, car-pooling became more difficult and public transportation often unavailable….In Europe and Japan, people drive less when the cost of gas goes up because they still can. On average, they live closer to their jobs. About 20% of Europeans walk or ride their bike to work.

…The only hope of changing America's driving habits is a hefty price increase that lasts. …Higher commuting costs…could induce you to buy a smaller car, move closer to work, find a car pool… [F]ew people change their behavior when gas prices spike temporarily…. [M]oral exhortation [urging] doesn't change people's behavior. Prices do…"

—Austan Goolsbee, *Slate Magazine,* September 27, 2005

PRACTICE AND APPLY THE SKILL

Use the magazine article to answer the following questions.

1. What is the main idea or key point this article makes?

2. Based on this article, what can you infer about the demand for gasoline in the United States?

3. Based on this article, what conclusions can you draw about the effect of a gas tax that substantially raises the price of gas? How will American driving habits be affected?

▶ Analyze Political Cartoons

Political cartoons express the cartoonist's opinion on a recent issue or current event. Often the artist's purpose is to influence the opinion of the reader about political leaders, current events, or economic or political issues. To achieve this goal, cartoonists use humor or exaggeration. When analyzing a political cartoon, be sure to examine all words, images, and labels to help you fully understand the artist's intent. Use the following steps to analyze the cartoon below.

Identify the symbols in the cartoon. Decide what each image or symbol represents. Examine the title and any labels or words in the cartoon. Cartoonists often use caricatures, or images of people that exaggerate a physical feature.

Analyze the meaning of the cartoon. Consider how the cartoonist uses the images and symbols in the cartoon to express opinions about people or events.

Draw conclusions about the cartoonist's intent. Identify the opinion or statement the cartoonist is making through this cartoon.

PRACTICE AND APPLY THE SKILL

Use the cartoon to answer the following questions.

1. What do the bulls in the cartoon represent?

2. What does the flower symbolize?

3. What does the cartoon suggest about the cartoonist's view of the economic situation?

▶ Understanding Cause and Effect

Recognizing cause and effect means looking at how one event or action brings about others. One challenge economists face is finding and defining relationships between events.

Identify the central event. Determine the core event or issue that is the subject of the article.

Identify the two parts of a cause-effect relationship. A cause is an event or an action that brings about an effect. Words such as *because, due to,* and *on account of* signal causes. Words such as *so, thus, therefore,* and *as a result* signal effects.

Decide if an event has more than one cause or effect. Most events have more than one cause, and many have more than one effect.

Identify events that are both causes and effects. Causes and effects can form a chain of events. An effect may in turn become the cause of another effect. For example, a sharp decline in new home sales can result in reduced profits for building supply and furniture stores. This in turn may lead to layoffs of workers in factories that produce the goods sold in these stores.

Read the excerpt below from "No Quick Fix on the Downturn." ▼

In the view of many analysts, the economy is now in a downward spiral, with each piece of negative news setting off the next. Falling housing prices have eroded the ability of homeowners to borrow against their property, threatening their ability to spend freely. Concerns about tightening consumer spending have prompted [caused] businesses to slow hiring, limiting wage increases and in turn applying the brakes anew to consumer spending....

...Nouriel Roubini, an economist at...New York University...envisions [sees] foreclosures accelerating this year, and banks counting fresh losses. That could make them less able to lend and further slow economic activity....Federal Reserve chairman, Ben S. Bernanke, zeroed in on the nervousness of bankers as a prime factor slowing the economy.... "Developments have prompted banks to become protective of their liquidity [available funds] and thus to become less willing to provide funding to other market participants."

A recession could pack enormous political consequences. Over the last century, the economy has been in a recession four times in the early part of a presidential election year, according to the National Bureau of Economic Research. In each of those years—1920, 1932, 1960 and 1980—the party of the incumbent president lost the election."

—Peter Goodman and Floyd Norris, *The New York Times,* January 13, 2008

PRACTICE AND APPLY THE SKILL

Use the news article to answer the following questions.

1. Identify the causes and effects in the following statement from the article: "Falling housing prices have eroded the ability of homeowners to borrow against their property, threatening their ability to spend freely."

2. How was the slowdown in consumer spending both a cause and an effect of the economic slowdown?

3. Did the downturn in the economy have a single cause or multiple causes? Explain.

▶ Problem Solving

One difference between successful and unsuccessful business is the ability to solve problems.

Identify the problem. Begin by clearly identifying the problem. Write a statement or question that summarizes the problem you are actually trying to solve.

Gather information and identify options. Collect the facts. Consider the causes of the problem and brainstorm how to solve it. Most problems have more than one solution. Identify as many options as possible.

Consider advantages and disadvantages of each option. Analyze each option by predicting benefits, drawbacks, and possible results.

Choose, implement, and evaluate a solution. Pick the option with the greatest benefits and fewest drawbacks. Once a strategy is in place, look at the results. Decide if the solution works.

Read the excerpt below, which looks at how a popular shoe manufacturer prepared to meet its supply and demand requirements as its business boomed. ▼

From tots walking with their mothers in the mall to the president of the United States captured on camera wearing a pair of black Crocs…the rubbery boat shoe…fueled a business success story….

Crocs now is the country's second-largest footwear manufacturer…."It was the perfect storm: They had the right product, people wanted it, and they were able to produce it in increasing quantities and broaden their focus…," [says Reed Anderson, senior research analyst at D.A. Davidson & Co.].

[CEO Ron Snyder] says Crocs' ascent [rise] has proved manageable because the company laid the groundwork to handle it before it arrived in full force. "Since the beginning, we've always assumed we're a larger company, so we made decisions as a larger company, investing in an infrastructure that was more than we needed at the time," Snyder says.

"Most of the footwear industry works off preorders," Snyder says. "If a particular product isn't selling well, you'll still be building it for late in the season….We take early season orders, then we build more of whatever is popular. Say we have a model that's selling out in our early season," he says. "We'll be making more of that immediately in our local facilities, and we'll get it to the market in a few weeks. If it continues to go, we'll have another larger shipment from China in six or eight weeks….We told our retailers we're going to do our best…to meet demand."

—by Eric Peterson, *Coloradobiz Magazine*, February 2008

PRACTICE AND APPLY THE SKILL

Use the article to answer the following questions.

1. What three conditions led to Crocs' success?

2. What problem could have limited their success?

3. What were the advantages of the option the company chose for solving this problem?

Social Studies Skills Handbook

▶ Decision Making

Decision making in your daily life and in the economy both require a similar approach.

Identify the problem and gather information. Figure out what you are trying to accomplish. Decide what information you need to make an informed decision. Apply what you know and what you can learn about the subject. Look at what others have done.

List and assess alternatives. List and review all possible alternatives. Choose the options with fewest drawbacks or costs and greatest number of benefits.

Identify possible effects and make decisions. Consider all possible outcomes and predict the effects of each option.

Below is an excerpt from an article on Honest Tea, a beverage company started in 1998 by Seth Goldman and Barry Nabeloff. ▼

"For Seth Goldman starting a business was a lot like brewing tea—it all came down to the right blend of ingredients. Goldman took the plunge into the bottled tea business…convinced there was an opportunity in the crowded but fast-growing market for a "less sweet" beverage….But the sweetness profile was not the only thing that set Honest Tea apart. It was the approach Goldman took to business,"…He said…"I knew that what we were going to do would somehow have a social and environmental impact…."

Their challenge…was finding a way to stand out in a market full of bottled teas. Taste was one obvious way to be distinctive….

The program soon evolved on a number of fronts, involving choices about ingredients, packaging and partnerships that expanded the aim of its social and environmental mission. As Goldman learned more about the business, his first aim was to shift the ingredients to organic sources to avoid toxic [poisonous] pesticides and synthetic fertilizers…"Tea…undergoes no rinsing once it is picked," he said. Whatever pesticide residues [remains] are present on the leaf are not washed off until hot water is poured over the dried leaves in a pot or cup of brewed tea."

Organics were the more expensive way to go, Goldman concedes, but the company shaved costs in other areas. It eschewed [avoided] a distinctive shaped glass bottle and went with a cheaper, more generic look…

Another key pillar of the business has been pursuing "fair trade," buying tea from one estate in India, that is certified for its fair labor practices…

[This] adds another dimension [side] to the business by creating a distinct marketing presence…That distinction might be invaluable in a shelf crowded with competitors…"

—by Samuel Fromartz, Reuters News Service, November 15, 2004

PRACTICE AND APPLY THE SKILL

Use the article to answer the following questions.

1. Why did Seth Goldman decide to go into the bottled tea business?
2. What goal drove Goldman's decisions about ingredients, packaging, and partnerships?
3. What costs and benefits did Goldman consider in deciding on the ingredients?

▶ Note Taking and Active Listening

Note taking and active listening are skills that can increase your ability to remember and understand a speech or a lecture.

Identify the main ideas. Once you know the main idea of the overall topic, it becomes easier to identify and record key points.

Take notes selectively. Do not write down every word you hear. Instead summarize key points and the examples or details that support these points.

Practice active listening. Active listening is an important part of the communication process. It requires the listener to participate. Think about what you hear and see. Don't let your mind wander.

Listen for transitions, repetition, and emphasis. Listen for the words or phrases that indicate key points or transition from one point to the next. Frequently repeated statements may be the main points.

Here is an excerpt from a speech entitled "Education and Economic Competitiveness" by Federal Reserve Board Chair Ben Bernanke: ▼

"...The demand for more-educated workers has been increasing rapidly, partly because of the...widespread use of computers and other...information and communication technologies in the workplace...At the start of the 1980s, 22 percent of young adults aged 25 to 29 held a college degree or more; by last year, that fraction had moved up to 28.5 percent. Nevertheless, the supply of educated workers has not kept pace with demand...

The educational challenges our society faces should be considered in the context of three broad trends: the retirement of the baby-boom generation, the... advance of the technological frontier, and the ongoing globalization of economic activity.

As the baby boomers...leave the workforce, their places will be taken by the smaller cohort [group] of workers born in the mid-to-late 1960s and early 1970s.

As a result, the U.S. workforce...will increase more slowly...imply[ing] slower growth of potential output...

Continuing advances in technology also put a premium on education...

Ongoing globalization...will also lead to continuing changes in the...U.S. economy...The world economy is benefiting from...the rising productivity of countries abroad that are...expanding...the educational attainment of their workforces....Our ability to reap the benefits of globalization will depend on the flexibility of our labor force to adapt to changes in job opportunities, in part by investing in...education and training....

If we are to successfully navigate such challenges as the retirement of the baby-boom generation, advancing technology, and increasing globalization, we must work...to maintain the quality of our educational system..."

—Ben S. Bernanke, in a speech to the U.S. Chamber Education and Workforce Summit, Washington, D.C., September 24, 2007

PRACTICE AND APPLY THE SKILL

Use the speech to answer the following questions.

1. What key points are made in the first paragraph?

2. What sentence tells the audience that the speaker will talk about three topics he thinks are important to his main idea?

3. What is the purpose of the final paragraph of this speech?

SOCIAL STUDIES SKILLS HANDBOOK

▶ Think Creatively and Innovate

An innovation is a new idea that improves an existing product or process. Innovators think creatively and take risks to turn their ideas into realities.

Identify what needs improving. Define and make clear what needs to be changed or improved. Keep your goal in mind.

Brainstorm as many ideas as possible. If working with a group, don't criticize the ideas of others. Don't be afraid to suggest ideas that might seem strange or impractical. Innovation often results from an unexpected point of view.

Understand the factors involved. Consider the skills, tools, or methods needed to realize the goal. Identify such factors as costs, materials, competition, consumer behavior, and potential suppliers and markets for product.

Read the excerpt below from "Nike Co-founder Bill Bowerman: His Innovations for Runners Helped Build an Empire." ▼

"

Track coach Bill Bowerman was eating breakfast one morning in 1971 when his wife, Barbara, opened the waffle iron to pour another serving. He constantly looked for ways to help his athletes improve. Then it hit him. If he mixed synthetic rubber, poured it into the back of the waffle iron and let it cool, he could make a better sole for a running shoe.

It took some grunting and wrenching with pliers to get the rubber off, wrote Bowerman…But when he finally did, he'd come up with the first lightweight outsole, the Waffle sole, which revolutionized the running shoe. Today, every athletic shoemaker uses a waffle sole or some variation on everything from running to hiking shoes.

Bowerman…the head track-and-field coach at the University of Oregon in Eugene from 1948 to 1972, was hugely competitive and at the same time fascinated with physiology. In studying the dynamics of running, he saw that the shoes runners used were cumbersome [awkward]. In the late 1950s, he devised a shoe with a heel wedge…One problem: He couldn't find a company to make it….He decided to make the shoes himself. Bowerman tested his designs on his team

members, including Phil Knight…After that, Bowerman would sit in his garage and tinker with the shoe designs, which his team members gladly wore…

In 1964, he and Knight teamed up to found Blue Ribbon Sports Inc. In 1972, the duo started the Nike brand…That year, four of the top seven finishers in the Olympic marathon wore Nikes. The company name was changed to Nike Inc. in 1980.

"Bowerman had a laser focus to solve a problem with an athlete and then move on," said Geoff Hollister, [Nike] marketing manager….Knight, a marketing wiz, was expert at taking Bowerman's solution and making it available to the masses. Bowerman's actions were "all driven by helping us perform better…" Hollister said. This drive led Bowerman to experiment and innovate… Bowerman led by example. He taught his young men and the team at Nike to accept when they were beaten and then pick themselves up again so they could work harder for a better day. He had an insatiable [unstoppable] curiosity and a mind that perceived gaps in the progress of human inventions…"

—by William O'Neil in his 2003 book *Business Leaders & Success*

PRACTICE AND APPLY THE SKILL

Use the excerpt to answer the following questions.

1. What insight led Bowerman to his innovation?
2. What personal experiences and interests helped Bowerman to think creatively about the problem that concerned him?
3. How did Bowerman's position as a coach help him assess the effectiveness of his product?

◗ Give an Effective Presentation

One key to an effective presentation is to combine text, video, audio, and graphics in a multimedia presentation.

Define your topic. In choosing a topic, consider the amount of time you have for the presentation and how difficult the subject is.

Find out what types of media are available for the presentation. Do you have a computer and the software to create a podcast, a PowerPoint presentation, a slide show, a video, audio clips of speeches, or animated graphics?

Make a storyboard or blueprint for the presentation. Create a storyboard by brainstorming ideas. Identify the best way to present each part of the presentation.

Practice your presentation. A trial run gives presenters a chance to check how much time each part of the presentation will take. It also helps identify technical problems and make sure all participants know their roles.

Below is a storyboard for a presentation to aid urban planners in choosing among roadbuilding and other options for alleviating traffic congestion. ▼

1. Run Time 3 mins.	2. 3 mins.	3. 4 mins.
Are More Roads the Answer to States' Traffic Problems? **Introduction** **Highway Congestion:** • More people driving more miles on more roads in urban areas • Increasing number of highways increases vehicle travel, reducing the benefits of building • Looking for alternatives to driving	**Supply and Demand** *Graphs show three supply and demand curves:* • Before road construction • After highway built or expanded • After drivers switch to new roads or move closer to new highway a) b) c) graphs: Travel time vs. Amount of travel	*Video clip of transportation expert talking about whether it is cost effective to build more roads to solve traffic congestion problems*

4. Run Time 3 mins.	5. 4 mins.	6. 5 mins.
What Studies Show • Increased use of cars not due to population growth but to more individual rather than carpool driving • Building roads can attract new traffic to roads, leading to more congestion • New highways could discourage public transit use	**Solutions** • Increase investment in public transit: buses, light rail, metro • Build more Park and Ride lots • Offer incentives to businesses to encourage workers to carpool or commute at different times of day through flextime	**What We Recommend** • Improve or expand existing highways through HOV lanes, increase highway safety, eliminate bottlenecks • Replace aging roads and bridges • Consider more funding for public transit through gas tax

PRACTICE AND APPLY THE SKILL

Use the storyboard to answer the following questions.

1. What issue does the presentation address?

2. How did the presenters narrow or focus the presentation of their topic?

3. How were participants encouraged to stay within the time limits in their presentations?

Social Studies Skills Handbook

▶ Digital Literacy

The Internet is a valuable research tool that provides links to millions of sources of information created by corporations, small businesses, government organizations, and individuals all over the world. E-mails, wikis, and blogs all provide ways for Internet users to share information and express opinions.

Writing an E-mail

Identify the purpose of the e-mail in the subject line. A busy person is more likely to open the e-mail promptly if the subject of the e-mail is stated.

Focus on why you are writing. Include the subject of your e-mail in the first sentence. Make sure the message states why you are writing and what you expect to receive in terms of information or action from the recipient. Keep e-mails short and to the point.

Respect your reader. If you are responding to or following up on an e-mail that is more than a few days old, remind the recipient of why you are writing. Identify yourself clearly if you don't know the person. If you are uncertain about whether your language and tone should be formal or informal, examine the e-mail received from this sender. Take your cues from the sender's level of formality, for example, *Dear Mr. Jones* vs. *Hi Joe.*

Proofread e-mails before sending. Once you have composed your e-mail, use spell checker or other tools to check grammar, punctuation, and spelling. Reread your message before sending it. Remember that e-mail is not private. Think carefully about sending messages that you would not want shared with others. Below is an example of a business e-mail.

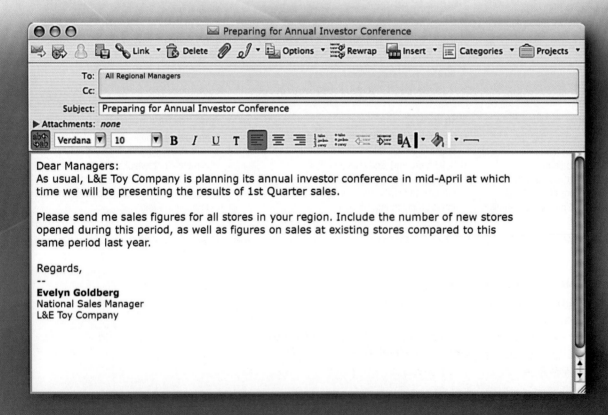

Understanding and Evaluating Wikis

A **wiki** is a Web site that allows users to easily create, edit, and link Web pages to create an online document. One of the most visited wikis is the online encyclopedia **Wikipedia.** Anyone can add or change the articles they find on this Web site. While many Internet users are enthusiastic about sites like Wikipedia, critics question their accuracy. Today corporations and government agencies are creating their own internal wikis. These wikis are almost always password-protected sites only for employees. These wikis allow staff to brainstorm, share knowledge, and update project information.

Identify the sources of the information on the Web site. Look for information on the Web site that tells you who provided this information or presented the data. Consider whether the writer is an expert or has special knowledge of this topic that would make his or her opinion especially worthwhile.

Determine when the article was written. Look for a date that shows when the article was written or last updated. Does the entry reflect changing events or provide current information on this topic?

Verify information by checking other sources. Do not rely on a single source. Compare the information on the wiki with official sources such as government Web sites, medical or legal Web sites sponsored by respected professional organizations, or reliable encyclopedias. Be skeptical and do further research if your sources disagree.

Reading and Assessing Blogs

Blogs are online journals. The word *blog* is short for *weblog*. Most blogs are short posts or entries expressing a single author's opinions. Blogs can be found on everything from politics, finance, economics, and legal issues to health and sports. Most bloggers add a new entry daily or weekly. Most blogs are interactive, providing a space where readers can comment on the opinions or information expressed.

Identify the writer. Look for information up front that gives the name of the author and his or her business or professional affiliation.

Assess the sources the blogger links to. Evaluate the credibility and accuracy of the sources the blogger recommends to readers. Does the blog link to reputable sources?

Identify the writer's bias. Most bloggers do express a point of view. Consider the arguments and evidence the writer presents in support of these opinions. Are positions presented in a balanced way that acknowledges other points of view or is the language clearly one-sided? Scan reader comments to determine whether the blog allows comments by readers with opposing points of view or dissenting opinions.

PRACTICE AND APPLY THE SKILL

Use the information above to answer these questions.

1. How might the language in a business e-mail be different from the language in a personal e-mail sent to friends?
2. What makes wikis useful for projects that require input from many people?
3. What are the advantages and drawbacks of online encyclopedias like Wikipedia?

Math Skills Online

Economics and mathematics are related in many ways.

Economists use mathematics to analyze data and to test and communicate their theories. Your ability to understand economics will depend to some extent on your ability to use and understand mathematics.

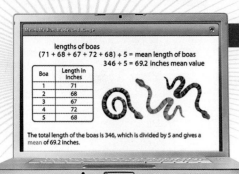

Visual Learning Animations

- Reading and Making Graphs
- Circle Graphs
- Misleading Graphs
- Mean, Median, Mode, and Range
- Line Plots
- Stem and Leaf Plots
- Effects of Outliers
- Appropriate Use of Statistical Measures

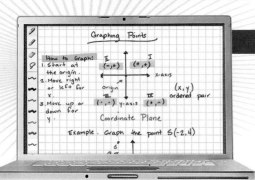

Mathematics Tutorials

- Making a Histogram
- Finding Slope Using Rise/Run
- Graphing Points on the Coordinate Plane
- Finding the Percent of a Number
- Finding Part of a Whole
- Finding Percent Using a Proportion
- Finding Simple Interest
- Finding Compound Interest

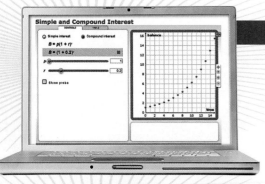

Interactive Math Activities

- Histograms
- Exploring Slope
- Points in the Coordinate Plane
- Percents and Proportions
- Simple and Compound Interest

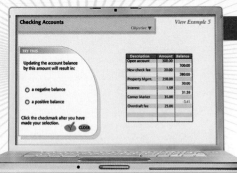

Math Lab

- Using Addition and Subtraction to Balance a Checking Account

You can access help with mathematics at point of use in your Online Student Edition or review these skills at any time.

English and Spanish Glossary

ENGLISH AND SPANISH GLOSSARY

A

absolute advantage (ab′ sə lüt ad van′ tij) the ability to produce a product or service more easily and less expensively than trading partners that use the same resources (p. 435)
ventaja absoluta capacidad para producir un producto o servicio más facilmente y a menor costo, usando los mismos recursos que un socio comerciante

acceptable (ak sep′ tə bəl) recognized as having value (p. 235)
aceptabilidad reconocer como valioso

aggregate demand (ag′ rə git di mand′) the amount of goods and services that will be purchased at all possible price levels (p. 289)
demanda agregada cantidad de bienes y servicios que serán comprados a todos los niveles de precio posibles

aggregate supply (ag′ rə git sə plī′) the total amount of goods and services in the economy available at all possible price levels (p. 289)
oferta agregada cantidad total de bienes y servicios disponibles a todos los niveles de precio posibles

antitrust laws (an ti trust′ lȯz) laws that encourage competition in the marketplace (p. 161)
leyes antimonopolio leyes que promueven la competencia en el mercado

appreciation (ə prē′ shē ā′ shən) a "strengthening," or increase, in the value of a currency (p. 448)
apreciación incremento del valor de una moneda

appropriation bills (ə prō prē ā′ shən bilz) bills that allow a specific amount of spending by the government (p. 378)
leyes de presupuesto leyes que le permiten al gobierno gastar una cantidad específica de dinero

arbitration (är bə trā′ shən) when both sides agree to have a neutral third party listen to both sides and make a decision that is legally binding for both the company and the union (p. 223)
arbitraje situación en la que dos grupos acuerdan tener un tercer grupo neutral que escuche a ambas partes y tome una decisión legal entre una compañía y un sindicato

articles of partnership (är′ tə kəlz əv pärt′ nər ship) a partnership agreement; lists each partner's rights and responsibilities and how the partners will share profits or losses (p. 178)
estatutos de asociación acuerdo de una sociedad que enumera los derechos y responsabilidades de cada socio y cómo éstos se deben dividir las ganancias o las pérdidas

assets (as′ ets) the money and other valuables belonging to an individual or a business (p. 179)
activo dinero y otros valores pertenecientes a un individuo o a una empresa

authoritarian (ə thôr′ ə ter′ ē ən) a type of government that requires everyone to obey and in which citizens have few rights (p. 36)
autoritario tipo de gobierno que requiere obediencia estricta por parte de sus ciudadanos, quienes tienen derechos muy limitados

average cost (av′ ėr ij kȯst) the total cost divided by the quantity produced (p. 110)
costo total promedio costo que se obtiene al dividir el costo total por la cantidad producida

B

balance of payments (bal′ əns əv pā′ məntz) the value of all money exchanged between a country's economy and the rest of the world (p. 451)
balanza de pagos valor de todas las transacciones monetarios entre la economía de un país y la economía del resto del mundo

balance of trade (bal′ əns əv trād) the difference between the value of a country's exports and imports (p. 451)
balanza comercial diferencia entre el valor de las exportaciones y las importaciones de un país

bank (bangk) an institution for receiving, keeping, and lending money (p. 238)
banco institución que recibe, mantiene y presta dinero

bank run (bangk run) a widespread panic in which many people try to redeem their paper money at the same time (p. 241)
pánico bancario situación de pánico general en la cual muchas personas retiran su dinero del banco simultáneamente

barrier to entry (bar′ ē ėr tü en′ trē) any factor that makes it difficult for a new firm to enter a market (p. 147)
barrera comercial cualquier factor que dificulta la entrada de una nueva entidad al mercado

barter (bär′ tėr) the direct exchange of one set of goods or services for another (p. 233)
trueque intercambio directo de bienes o servicios

bear market (bâr mär′ kit) a market in which the prices of most stocks are falling (p. 273)
mercado bajista mercado en el cual los precios de las acciones bajan

benefits (ben′ ə fits) anything besides wages provided to workers, such as paid vacations, retirement plans, and medical insurance (p. 208)
beneficios cualquier cosa, aparte del salario, que se les ofrece a los trabajadores, como vacaciones pagadas, planes de jubilación y seguro médico

a hat	e let	ī ice	ô order	u̇ put	sh she	ə { a in about
ā age	ē equal	o hot	oi oil	ü rule	th thin	e in taken
ä far	ėr term	ō open	ou out	ch child	ᴛʜ then	i in pencil
â care	i it	ȯ saw	u cup	ng long	zh measure	o in lemon
						u in circus

GLOSSARY **R-1**

black market (blak mär´ kit) an illegal market in which goods and services are sold above their legal price (p. 138)
mercado negro mercado ilegal en el cual se venden bienes a un precio más alto que su precio legal

block grants (blok grants) lump sums of money provided to states for poor families (p. 335)
subvención de bloque cantidades de dinero que se les otorga a familias de bajos recursos

blue-collar worker (blü kol´ ər wėr´ kər) someone who performs manual labor, often in a manufacturing job, and who earns an hourly wage (p. 219)
obrero persona que realiza trabajo manual a menudo, éste es un trabajador en el área industrial y recibe un salario por hora

bond (bond) a type of loan that an investor buys from a company or from the government; the seller promises to pay back the investor's money plus a profit later (p. 185)
bono tipo de préstamo que un inversionista compra de una compañía o del gobierno. El vendedor promete devolver en el futuro el dinero del inversionista más intereses

"brain drain" (brān drān) migration of the best-educated people of less developed countries to developed nations (p. 490)
fuga de cerebros emigración de individuos con alta capacitación de países menos desarrollados a países más desarrollados

brokerage firm (brō´ kər ij fėrm) a business that specializes in trading stock (p. 272)
firma de corretaje empresa de corredores de bolsa

budget (buj´ it) a plan that estimates future spending and saving (p. 362)
presupuesto plan que estima los ahorros y gastos a futuro

budget deficit (buj´ it def´ ə sit) when the amount of money spent is more than the amount of money that is collected (p. 389)
déficit presupuestario situación en la cual los gastos son mayores que los ingresos

budget surplus (buj´ it sėr´ pləs) when the amount of money spent is less than the amount of money that is collected (p. 389)
superávit presupuestario situación en la cual los gastos son menores que los ingresos

bull market (bùl mär´ kit) a market in which the prices of most stocks are going up (p. 273)
mercado alcista mercado en el cual el precio de las acciones suben

business association (biz´ nis ə sō´ sē ā´ shən) a group organized to promote the collective business interests of an area or a group of similar businesses (p. 192)
asociación de empresas grupo que promueve los intereses colectivos de un área o grupo de empresas similares

business cycle (biz´ nis sī´ kəl) a period of macroeconomic expansion, or growth, followed by one of contraction, or decline (p. 57)
ciclo económico período de expansión o crecimiento macroeconómico, seguido por una contracción o declive

business franchise (biz´ nis fran´ chīz) a business that pays fees to a parent company in return for the right to sell a product or service (p. 180)
franquicia negocio que paga honorarios a una empresa matriz a cambio del derecho de venta de un producto o servicio

business license (biz´ nis lī´ sens) written permission given by the local government that allows a business to open (p. 174)
licencia comercial permiso escrito emitido por el gobierno para abrir un negocio

business organization (biz´ nis ôr´ gə nə zā´ shən) the ownership structure of a company or firm (p. 172)
negocio estructura propietaria de una compañía o entidad

C

call option (kòl op´ shən) a contract for buying stock at a particular price until a specified future date (p. 272)
opción de compra contrato que permite la compra de acciones a un precio estipulado hasta una fecha determinada

capital (kap´ ə təl) any human-made resource that is used to produce other goods and services (p. 7)
capital cualquier recurso fabricado por el hombre que se usa para producir otros bienes y servicios

capital budget (kap´ ə təl buj´ it) a budget for spending on major long-term projects (p. 363)
presupuesto de capital presupuesto destinado para proyectos de gran importancia

capital deepening (kap´ ə təl dē´ pən ing) the process of increasing the amount of capital per worker (p. 303)
desarrollo de capital proceso en el cual se incrementa la cantidad de capital por trabajador

capital gain (kap´ ə təl gān) the difference between the selling price and the purchase price; it results in a financial gain for the seller (pp. 186, 270)
plusvalía diferencia entre el precio de venta y el precio de compra que resulta en una ganancia financiera para el vendedor

capital loss (kap´ ə təl lòs) the difference between a lower selling price and a higher purchase price that results in a financial loss for the seller (p. 270)
minusvalía diferencia entre un precio de venta más bajo y un precio de compra más alto que resulta en una pérdida financiera para el vendedor

capital market (kap´ ə təl mär´ kit) a market in which money is lent for periods longer than a year (p. 268)
mercado de capitales mercado en el cual se hacen préstamos por períodos de más de un año

cartel (kär tel´) a formal organization of producers that agree to coordinate prices and production (p. 159)
cartel organización de productores que acuerdan la coordinación de precios y producción

cash transfers (kash trans fėrz) direct payments of money by the government to poor, disabled, or retired people (p. 67)
pensión pagos de dinero hechos directamente por el gobierno a las personas de bajos recursos, discapacitadas y a los jubilados

census (sen´ səs) an official count of the population (p. 319)
censo conteo oficial de la población

central bank (sen´ trəl bangk) a bank that can lend to other banks in time of need and regulates overall money supply (p. 241)
banco central banco que puede hacer préstamos a otros bancos en momentos de necesidad y que regula la oferta monetaria total

centrally planned economy (sen´ trəl ē pland i kon´ ə mēz) an economic system in which a group of central planners makes economic plans for the government (p. 35)
economía centralizada sistema económico en el cual un grupo central de planeadores hace los planes económicos para el gobierno

certificate of incorporation (sėr tif´ ə kit əv in kôr´ pə rā´ shən) a license to form a corporation issued by a state government (p. 186)
documento de constitución licencia expedida por el gobierno estatal, que permite formar una corporación

ceteris paribus (kā´ te rēs par´ u bùs) a Latin phrase that means "all other things held constant" (p. 82)
ceteris paribus frase en latín que significa "lo demás permanece constante"

charter (chär´ tər) an official document issued by state governments that gives the right to create a corporation (p. 183)
carta constitucional documento oficial emitido por gobiernos estatales que otorga el derecho de crear una organización

check clearing (chek klir´ ing) the process by which banks record whose account gives up money and whose account receives it (p. 407)
compensación de cheques proceso en el cual un banco lleva un registro de las cuentas que ceden dinero y las cuentas que reciben dinero

circular flow (sėr´ kyə lər flō) a model that shows the process of exchanges between the households and firms (p. 32)
flujo circular modelo que demuestra el proceso de intercambio entre hogares y entidades comerciales

classical economics (klas´ ə kəl ek ə nom´ iks) a school of thought based on the idea that free markets regulate themselves (p. 381)
economía clásica corriente de pensamiento basada en la idea de que los mercados libres se regulan a sí mismos

closely held corporation (klōs´ lē held kôr pə rā´ shən) a corporation that gives stock to only a few people, often members of the same family (p. 184)
sociedad cerrada tipo de empresa que expide acciones a pocas personas, quienes por lo general son familiares

collective bargaining (kə lək´ tiv bär´ gən ing) representatives of labor and management sit down together and try to reach an agreement on something (p. 222)
convenio colectivo de trabajo representantes laborales y administrativos se reúnen para llegar a un acuerdo

collusion (kə lü´ zhən) an illegal agreement among firms to divide the market, set prices, or limit production (p. 158)
colusión acuerdo ilegal entre entidades con el fin de dividir el mercado, ajustar precios o restringir producción

command economy (kə mand´ i kon´ ə mē) another name for a centrally planned economy (p. 36)
economía controlada otro nombre para economía centralizada

commodity (kə mod´ ə tē) a product, such as petroleum or milk, that is considered the same no matter who produces or sells it (p. 147)
bien de consumo producto tal como el petróleo o la leche, que se considera igual independientemente de quién lo produzca o lo venda

commodity money (kə mod´ ə tē mun´ ē) objects that have value in and of themselves and that are also used as money (p. 236)
mercancía objetos que tienen valor por sí mismos y que también se usan como dinero

communism (kom´ yə niz əm) a political and economic system in which the government owns all property and controls all resources (p. 36)
comunismo sistema político en el cual el gobierno posee y controla todos los recursos

comparative advantage (kəm par´ ə tiv ad van´ tij) the ability to produce a product or service at a lower cost and more efficiently than another country (p. 436)
ventaja comparativa habilidad para producir un producto o servicio al costo más bajo y de la manera más eficiente en comparación a otros países

compensation (kom´ pən sā´ shən) payment to an employee for his or her work with the company, including wages and benefits (p. 208)
compensación pago a un empleado por su trabajo en una empresa, incluyendo salario y beneficios

competition (kom pə tish´ ən) the contest between firms or individuals to sell a product or service (p. 33)
competencia contienda entre entidades comerciales o individuos para vender un producto o servicio

a	hat	e	let	ī	ice	ô	order	ù	put	sh	she	⎧ a	in about
ā	age	ē	equal	o	hot	oi	oil	ü	rule	th	thin	⎪ e	in taken
ä	far	ėr	term	ō	open	ou	out	ch	child	ŦH	then	ə ⎨ i	in pencil
â	care	i	it	ȯ	saw	u	cup	ng	long	zh	measure	⎪ o	in lemon
												⎩ u	in circus

complements (kom´ plə mənts) two goods that are bought and used together (p. 86)

   bienes complementarios dos bienes que se compran y se usan conjuntamente

conglomerate (kən glom´ ər it) the business combination that brings together more than three businesses that provide unrelated goods and services (p. 188)

   conglomerado combinación de negocios donde se unen más de tres negocios que producen productos o servicios no relacionados entre sí

consumer cooperative (kən sü´ mėr kō op´ ər ə tiv) a retail outlet owned and operated by consumers that sells merchandise to members at reduced prices (p. 190)

   cooperativa de consumidores agrupación operada por consumidores que ofrece bienes y servicios para sus socios a precios reducidos

consumer price index (kən sü´ mėr prīs in´ deks) a measurement that shows how much the prices of necessary items are changing (p. 323)

   índice de precios al consumidor medida que demuestra cuánto cambian los precios de ciertos productos esenciales

consumer sovereignty (kən sü´ mėr sov´ rən tē) the power of consumers to decide what gets produced (p. 34)

   soberanía del consumidor poder del consumidor para decidir qué se produce

contingent employment (kən tin´ jənt em ploi´ mənt) a temporary or part-time job (p. 205)

   trabajo a destajo trabajo temporal a medio tiempo

continuum (kun tin´ yü um) a range of possibilities with no clear divisions between them (p. 41)

   continuo ámbito de posibilidades sin división claras entre ellas

contraction (kən trak´ shən) a period of economic decline as measured by a decrease in real GDP (p. 294)

   recesión período de declive económico caracterizado por una disminución del PIB

contractionary policy (kən trak´ shə nėr ē pol´ ə sē) a government financial policy used to get the economy to slow down, often through decreased spending or higher taxes (p. 379)

   política de contracción política gubernamental financiera que se usa para disminuir la actividad económica, generalmente por medio de la reducción de gastos o un aumento de los impuestos

cooperative (kō op´ ər ə tiv) a business organization owned and operated by a group of individuals for their mutual benefit (p. 189)

   cooperativa organización comercial que pertenece y es operada por un grupo de individuos para un beneficio común

copyright (kop´ ē rīt) a government license that grants an author exclusive rights to publish and sell creative works (p. 59)

   derechos de autor licencia gubernamental que garantiza los derechos exclusivos a un autor para publicar y vender sus obras

core inflation rate (kôr in flā´ shən rāt) inflation after removing the effects of food and energy prices (p. 324)

   tasa de inflación subyacente inflación que excluye los efectos del precio de la comida y la energía

corporate bond (kôr´ pėr it bond) a bond sold to help raise money to make a business bigger (p. 266)

   bono corporativo bono expedido para ayudar a recaudar dinero para agrandar una corporación

corporate income tax (kôr´ pėr it in´ kum taks) a tax based on the amount of profit a company makes (p. 346)

   impuesto sobre sociedades impuesto que se basa en las ganancias de la compañía

corporation (kôr pə rā´ shən) a business that can be made up of many owners; the law allows it to act like a single person (p. 183)

   corporación negocio que puede tener varios dueños; ley que permite que el negocio funcione como si tuviera un solo dueño

cost/benefit analysis (kôst ben´ ə fit ə nal´ ə sis) a process in which you compare what you will sacrifice and gain by a specific action (p. 13)

   análisis del costo/beneficio proceso de toma de decisiones en el cual se compara el costo y la ganancia de una operación en particular

coupon rate (kü´ pon rāt) the interest rate a bond seller pays a bond buyer (p. 263)

   cupón de interés tasa de interés que un emisor de bonos paga al titular del bono

credit card (kred´ it kärd) a card used to buy goods and services, to be repaid later (p. 248)

   tarjeta de crédito tarjeta usada por el titular para comprar bienes y servicios, que se paga en un futuro

creditor (kred´ ə tėr) a person or institution to whom money is owed (p. 251)

   acreedor persona o institución a la cual se le debe dinero

crowding-out effect (krou´ ding out ə fəkt´) the loss of funds for private investment that are caused by government borrowing (p. 392)

   efecto expulsión pérdida de fondos destinados para inversiones privadas causada por la deuda pública

currency (kėr´ ən sē) coins and paper bills used as money (p. 234)

   moneda monedas y billetes que se usan como dinero

customs duty (kus´ təmz dü´ tē) a tax on goods bought overseas and brought back to the United States (p. 440)

   derechos de aduana impuesto sobre bienes comprados en el exterior que entran a los Estados Unidos

cyclical unemployment (sī´ klə kəl un em ploi´ mənt) when unemployment goes up during recessions and depressions and falls when the economy improves (p. 318)

   desempleo cíclico situación en la cual el desempleo incrementa durante recesiones y depresiones económicas y disminuye al mejorar la economía

D

debit card (deb´ it kärd) a card used to withdraw money from a bank account (p. 250)
tarjeta de débito tarjeta que se usa para retirar dinero de una cuenta bancaria

debt rescheduling (det ri skej´ el ing) an agreement between lending nations and borrowing countries that lengthens the time of debt repayment (p. 475)
renegociación de deudas acuerdo entre naciones acreedoras y naciones deudoras que extiende el plazo de pago

default (di fôlt´) to fail to pay back a loan (p. 242)
mora suspensión del pago de un préstamo

deficit (def´ ə sit) when the amount spent is more than the amount taken in (p. 389)
déficit situación en la cual el gasto de dinero es mayor al ingreso

deflation (di flā´ shən) a general drop in the price level (p. 327)
deflación descenso general de precios

deforestation (dē fôr´ ist ā shən) large-scale destruction of forests (p. 491)
deforestación destrucción forestal masiva

demand (di mand´) the desire to own something and the ability to pay for it (p. 78)
demanda deseo de poseer algo y capacidad para pagar por ello

demand curve (di mand´ kėrv) a graph that shows the same information as a demand schedule (p. 80)
curva de demanda gráfica que muestra la misma información que la gráfica de demanda

demand deposit (di mand´ di poz´ it) money in a checking account that can be paid out "on demand," or at any time (p. 245)
depósito a la vista dinero en una cuenta corriente que se paga "a petición" o en cualquier momento

demand schedule (di mand´ skej´ úl) explains the law of demand in table form (p. 80)
tabla de demanda tabla que explica la ley de la demanda

demand-side economics (di mand sīd ek ə nom´ iks) a school of thought based on the idea that demand for goods drives the economy (p. 383)
economía de demanda corriente de pensamiento basada en la noción de que la demanda de bienes dirige la economía

demographics (dem´ ə graf´ iks) information such as age, race, gender, income level, and occupation of a population (p. 84)
demografía información de edad, raza, género, nivel de ingresos y ocupación en una población

depreciation (di prē´ shē ā´ shən) 1. the loss of the value of capital equipment that results from normal wear and tear (p. 291) 2. a "weakening," or decrease, in the value of a currency (p. 449)
depreciación reducción del valor de los bienes de capital de equipo como resultado del uso

depression (di presh´ ən) a recession that is especially long and severe (p. 294)
depresión recesión económica que se caracteriza por ser larga y grave

deregulate (dē reg´ yə lāt) to remove controls on (p. 242)
liberalizar suprimir el control sobre algo

deregulation (dē reg´ yə lā´ shən) the removal of some government controls over a market (p. 162)
desregulación supresión del control del gobierno sobre la actividad económica

derived demand (di rīvd´ di mand´) demand that depends on the demand for some other service or good (p. 209)
demanda derivada demanda que depende de la demanda de otro bien o servicio

developed nation (di vel´ əp d nā´ shən) a nation with a high average level of well-being (p. 460)
país desarrollado país con un bienestar económico relativamente alto

development (di vel´ əp mənt) the process by which a nation improves the economic, political, and social well-being of its people (p. 460)
desarrollo proceso mediante el cual una nación mejora la situación económica, política y social de su población

differentiation (dif ə rən shē ā´ shən) making a product different from other, similar products (p. 156)
diferenciación hacer que un producto se distinga de otros productos similares

diminishing marginal returns (də min´ ish ing mär´ jə nəl ri tėrnz´) a level of production at which the marginal product of labor decreases as the number of workers increases (p. 106)
rendimiento marginal decreciente nivel de producción en el cual el producto laboral marginal disminuye al incrementar el número de trabajadores

discount rate (dis´ kount rāt) the rate that the Fed charges banks for loans to banks (p. 408)
tasa de descuento interés que cobra la Reserva Federal sobre los préstamos a los bancos

discouraged workers (dis kėr´ ijd wėr´ kėrz) unemployed people who are not actively looking for work because they have been seeking employment for a long time (p. 321)
trabajador desanimado personas desempleadas que han desistido de la búsqueda de trabajo porque han estado buscando por mucho tiempo

a	hat	e	let	ī	ice	ô	order	ú	put	sh	she	ə	a in about
ā	age	ē	equal	o	hot	oi	oil	ü	rule	th	thin		e in taken
ä	far	ėr	term	ō	open	ou	out	ch	child	ᴛʜ	then		i in pencil
â	care	i	it	ȯ	saw	u	cup	ng	long	zh	measure		o in lemon
													u in circus

discretionary spending (dis kresh´ ən ər ē spend ing) spending about which Congress is free to make choices (p. 355)
gastos discrecionales gastos sobre los cuales el Congreso tiene libertad de decisión

disequilibrium (dis ē kwə lib´ rē əm) any price or quantity not at equilibrium; when quantity supplied is not equal to quantity demanded in a market (p. 123)
desequilibrio estado de desigualdad entre precios o cantidades; desigualdad entre la cantidad de oferta y la cantidad de demanda

diversification (də vėr´ sə fə kā´ shən) the strategy of spreading out investments to reduce risk (p. 260)
diversificación estrategia en la que se distribuyen las inversiones para reducir el riesgo

dividend (div´ ə dend) the investor's share of a company's profit (p. 186)
dividendo porción de los beneficios corporativos que les pagan a los accionistas

divisibile (də viz´ ə bil) able to be divided (p. 235)
divisibilidad cualidad de lo que se puede dividir

durable (dùr´ ə bəl) lasting for a long time (p. 234)
duradero que dura o puede durar mucho

durable goods (dùr´ ə bəl gùdz) goods that last a relatively long time (p. 286)
bienes duraderos bienes de consumo cuya durabilidad es relativamente larga

E

easy money policy (ē zē mun´ ē pol ə sē) a monetary policy that increases the money supply (p. 418)
política de dinero fácil política monetaria que incrementa la disponibilidad de dinero

economic growth (ek ə nom´ ik grōth) a steady, long-term rise in real GDP (p. 293)
crecimiento económico aumento constante a largo plazo del PIB real

economic system (ek ə nom´ ik sis´ təm) the structure that a society uses to produce and distribute goods and services (p. 24)
sistema económico estructura de métodos y principios que una sociedad usa para producir y distribuir bienes y servicios

economic transition (ek ə nom´ ik tran zish´ ən) a period of change in which a nation moves from one economic system to another (p. 41)
transición económica período de cambio en el cual una nación pasa de un sistema económico a otro

economics (ek ə nom´ iks) the study of how people seek to satisfy their needs and wants by making choices (p. 4)
economía rama del saber que estudia cómo las personas buscan satisfacer sus necesidades y deseos al tomar decisiones

economies of scale (i kon´ ə mēz əv skāl) factors that cause a producer's average cost per unit to fall as more units are produced (p. 152)
economías de escala factores que hacen que el costo promedio por unidad de un producto disminuya cuando se producen más unidades

efficiency (ə fish´ ən sē) the use of resources in such a way as to maximize the output of goods and services (p. 16)
eficiencia uso de los recursos de manera que se alcance el máximo de producción de bienes y servicios

elasticity of demand (ē las tis´ ə tē əv di mand´) a measure of how consumers respond to price changes (p. 87)
elasticidad de la demanda medida de cómo responden los consumidores a los cambios de precio

elasticity of supply (ē las tis´ ə tē əv sə plī´) a measure of the way a quantity supplied reacts to a change in price (p. 102)
elasticidad de la oferta medida de la forma en que la cantidad ofrecida responde a un cambio de precio

embargo (em bär´ gō) the act of cutting off all trade with another country (p. 440)
embargo suspender todo tipo de comercio con otro país

eminent domain (em´ ə nənt dō män´) the right of a government to take private property for public use (p. 53)
dominio eminente (expropiación) derecho de un gobierno de tomar la propiedad privada de alguien para darle un uso público

enterprise zones (en´ tėr prīz zōnz) areas where companies can locate and not have to pay certain state, local, and federal taxes (p. 334)
zona franca áreas en la que se pueden establecer negocios libres de ciertos impuestos municipales, estatales y federales

entitlement (en tī´ təl mənt) social welfare program that people have a right to if they are eligible (p. 356)
derecho consuetudinario programa de beneficencia social al que las personas tienen "derecho" si cumplen con ciertos requisitos

entrepreneur (än´ trə prə nər´) a person who decides how to combine resources to create goods and services (p. 7)
empresario persona quien decide cómo combinar recursos para crear bienes y servicios

equilibrium (ē kwə lib´ rē əm) the point at which the demand for a product or service is equal to the supply of that product or service (p. 122)
equilibrio punto en el cual la demanda de un producto o servicio es igual a su oferta

equilibrium price (ē kwə lib´ rē əm prīs) the price that both buyers and sellers will accept (p. 122)
precio de equilibrio precio que aceptan tanto el vendedor como el comprador

equilibrium wage (ē kwə lib´ rē əm wāj) the point at which the quantity of labor demanded is equal to the quantity of labor supplied (p. 211)
salario de equilibrio punto en el cual la demanda de trabajadores en el mercado laboral es igual a la disponibilidad de trabajadores

financial aid

estate tax (e stāt taks) a tax on the total value of the money and property of a person who has died (p. 353)
impuesto de sucesión impuesto sobre el valor total del dinero y las propiedades que deja una persona fallecida

excess reserves (ek ses′ ri zėrvz′) reserves that are more than the required amounts (p. 412)
exceso de reservas reservas que sobrepasan la cantidad que se necesita

exchange rate (eks chānj rāt) the value of a nation's currency in relation to a foreign currency (p. 448)
tasa de cambio valor de la moneda de una nación en relación con una moneda extranjera

excise tax (ek′ sīz taks) a tax on certain goods made in this country (pp. 113, 353)
impuesto sobre artículos de uso y consumo impuesto sobre ciertos bienes producidos en un país

expansion (ek span′ shən) a period of economic growth as measured by a rise in real GDP (p. 293)
expansión período de crecimiento económico determinado por un aumento del PIB real

expansionary policy (ek span′ shə nėr ē pol′ ə sē) a government financial policy used to encourage economic growth, often through increased spending or tax cuts (p. 379)
política de expansión política fiscal gubernamental que se usa para estimular el crecimiento económico a través de un aumento del gasto o de una reducción de impuestos

expenditure approach (ek spen′ də chėr ə prōch) a way of calculating GDP in which economists estimate the annual amount spent on four categories of final goods and services (p. 286)
enfoque de gastos manera de calcular el PIB donde los economistas estiman los gastos anuales bajo cuatro categorías de bienes y servicios

export (ek′ sport) goods or services that are sold to another country (p. 434)
exportación bien o servicio que se vende a otro país

externality (ek stėr nal′ i tē) an economic side effect of a good or service; it generates benefits or costs to someone other than the person deciding how much to produce or consume (p. 62)
externalidad efecto económico de un bien o servicio que le genera beneficios o costos a alguien distinto a quien decide cuánto producir o consumir

F

factor market (fak′ tər mär′ kit) an exchange in which firms purchase the factors of production from households (p. 32)
mercado de factores intercambio en el cual hay compañías que compran los factores de producción de las economías domésticas

factor payment (fak′ tər pā′ mənt) the income people receive in return for supplying land, labor, or capital (p. 25)
pago a los factores ingresos que reciben las personas a cambio de proveer tierra, trabajo o capital

factors of production (fak′ tərz ov prə duk′ shən) the resources that are used to make goods and services (p. 7)
factores de producción recursos que se usan para generar bienes y servicios

fad (fad) a product that becomes very popular for a very short period of time (p. 132)
moda pasajera producto que es muy popular por un período breve de tiempo

featherbedding (feᴛʜ′ ėr bed ding) when a labor union agrees to a labor contract that keeps unnecessary workers on a company's payroll (p. 215)
sinecura situación en la que un sindicato acuerda la permanencia de empleados innecesarios en la nómina de una compañía

federal budget (fed′ ėr əl buj′ it) a written document that estimates how much money the federal government will take in and spend in a year (p. 377)
presupuesto federal documento escrito donde se estiman los ingresos y gastos del gobierno federal en un año

federal funds rate (fed′ ėr əl fundz rāt) the interest rate that banks charge one another for loans (p. 408)
tasa de los fondos federales tasa que se cobran entre sí los bancos por el préstamo de sus reservas

Federal Reserve note (fed′ ėr əl ri zėrv′ nōt) the currency we use today in the United States (p. 241)
nota de la Reserva Federal papel moneda que se usa en los Estados Unidos hoy en día

fiat money (fi′ ət mun′ ē) objects that have value because the government has determined that they are an acceptable means to pay debts (p. 237)
dinero fiat objetos que tienen valor sólo porque el gobierno ha determinado que son medios aceptables para pagar deudas

financial aid (fə nan′ shəl ād) assistance in the form of grants and loans to help individuals in a time of need (p. 126)
ayuda económica becas y préstamos disponibles para individuos que necesitan dinero

a	hat	e	let	ī	ice	ô	order	ù	put	sh	she		a	in about
ā	age	ē	equal	o	hot	oi	oil	ü	rule	th	thin		e	in taken
ä	far	ėr	term	ō	open	ou	out	ch	child	ᴛʜ	then	ə	i	in pencil
â	care	i	it	ȯ	saw	u	cup	ng	long	zh	measure		o	in lemon
													u	in circus

financial asset (fə nan´ shəl as´ et) a claim on the property or income of a borrower (p. 259)
activo financiero derecho que tiene una entidad sobre la propiedad o los ingresos de un prestatario

financial intermediary (fə nan´ shəl in´ tèr mē´ dē èr´ ē) an institution that helps channel funds from savers to borrowers (p. 259)
intermediario financiero institución que ayuda a canalizar los fondos de los ahorristas a los prestatarios

financial system (fə nan´ shəl sis´ təm) the network of structures that allows for the transfer of money between savers and borrowers (p. 259)
sistema financiero red de estructuras y mecanismos que permiten la transferencia de dinero entre ahorristas y prestatarios

firm (fèrm) a business that uses resources to produce a product or service for sale (p. 32)
empresa negocio que usa recursos para crear un producto o servicio, que después vende

fiscal policy (fis´ kəl pol´ ə sē) the government's use of spending and taxes to make the economy grow faster or slower (p. 376)
política fiscal uso por parte del gobierno de los gastos y de los impuestos para acelerar o frenar el crecimiento de la economía

fiscal year (fis´ kəl yir) any 12-month period used for budgeting purposes (p. 377)
año fiscal período de doce meses con fines presupuestarios

fixed cost (fikst kòst) costs that stay the same, no matter how much is produced (p. 107)
costo fijo costo que no cambia, independientemente de la cantidad que se produzca

fixed exchange-rate system (fikst eks chānj rāt sis´ təm) a system in which governments try to keep the values of their currencies constant (p. 450)
sistema de tasa cambiaria fija sistema en el cual el gobierno trata de mantener constante el valor de su moneda con respecto a otra moneda

fixed income (fikst in´ kum) income that does not go up even when prices go up (p. 326)
ingreso fijo ingreso que no aumenta aunque los precios suban

flexible exchange-rate system (flek´ sə bəl eks chānj rāt sis´ təm) a system in which changes in the exchange rate are determined by supply and demand (p. 450)
sistema de tasa cambiaria flexible sistema en el cual la tasa de cambio depende de la oferta y la demanda

food stamps (füd stamps) government-issued coupons that people exchange for food (p. 331)
cupones para alimentos cupones que el gobierno distribuye y que se pueden cambiar por alimentos

foreclosure (fòr klō´ zhèr) seizure of property from borrowers who are unable to repay their loans (p. 243)
embargo acción que consiste en tomar la propiedad de prestatarios que no pueden pagar sus préstamos

foreign direct investment (fòr ən də rekt´ in vest´ mənt) when investors start a business in another country (p. 473)
inversión directa extranjera establecimiento de un negocio de inversionistas de otro país

foreign exchange market (fòr ən eks chānj mär´ kit) the market for buying and selling national currencies (p. 449)
mercado de divisas mercado de compra y venta de monedas extranjeras

foreign investment (fòr ən in vest´ mənt) capital that comes from other countries (p. 473)
inversión extranjera capital generado en otros países

foreign portfolio investment (fòr ən pôrt fō´ lē ō in vest´ mənt) when foreign investors buy shares in another country's financial markets (p. 473)
cartera de inversión extranjera compras de acciones que los inversionistas extranjeros hacen en mercados financieros de otro país

fractional reserve banking (frak´ shə nəl ri´ zèrv´ bangk ing) a banking system that keeps only a fraction of funds on hand and lends out the remainder (p. 246)
sistema de reserva fraccionaria sistema bancario en el cual el banco mantiene solamente una fracción de los fondos en reserva y presta el resto de los fondos

free enterprise system (frē en´ tər priz sis´ təm) an economic system in which investment decisions are made by individuals rather than by the government (p. 42)
sistema de libre empresa sistema económico en el cual las decisiones pertinentes a inversiones las toman individuos en vez del gobierno

free market economy (frē mär´ kit i kon´ ə mē) an economic system in which decisions on the three economic questions are based on voluntary exchange (p. 31)
economía de libre mercado sistema económico en el cual las decisiones relacionadas con las tres preguntas económicas clave se basan en el intercambio voluntario en el mercado

free rider (frē rī´ dər) someone who would not be willing to pay for a certain good or service but who would benefit from it anyway if it were provided as a public good (p. 61)
polizón persona que no está dispuesta a pagar por un bien o servicio determinado, pero quien se beneficiaría de él de todos modos si se le ofreciera como beneficio público

free trade (frē trād) the lowering or removal of protective tariffs and other trade barriers between nations (p. 442)
libre comercio disminución o eliminación de las tarifas y otras barreras de comercio entre dos o más naciones

free-trade zone (frē trād zōn) a region where a group of countries agrees to reduce or end trade barriers (p. 444)
zona de libre comercio región en la que un grupo de países acuerda reducir o eliminar las barreras de comercio

frictional unemployment (frik´ shə nəl un´ em ploi´ mənt) unemployment that happens when people must search for a long time to find a job (p. 314)
desempleo friccional tipo de desempleo que ocurre cuando a las personas les toma tiempo encontrar empleo

fringe benefits (frinj ben´ ə fits) anything extra given to workers in addition to their wages, such as paid vacations, retirement plans, and medical insurance (p. 176)
beneficio adicional pago que los empleados reciben además de su sueldo o salario

full employment (fùl em ploi´ mənt) a situation when no cyclical unemployment exists (p. 320)
pleno empleo nivel de empleo alcanzado cuando no hay desempleo cíclico

futures (fyü´ chərz) contracts to buy or sell commodities or financial assets at a particular date in the future at a price specified today (p. 272)
contratos de futuros contratos que establecen la compra o venta de bienes o activos financieros en el futuro a un precio establecido con anticipación

G

general partnership (jen´ ər əl pärt´ nər ship) a partnership in which partners share equally in both responsibility and liability (p. 177)
sociedad colectiva tipo de sociedad en la cual todos los socios asumen la misma cantidad de responsabilidades y obligaciones

gift tax (gift taks) a tax on the money or property that one living person gives to another (p. 353)
impuesto sobre donaciones impuesto sobre el dinero o la propiedad que una persona viva le da a otra

glass ceiling (glas sē´ ling) the belief that women are prevented from rising to a position of leadership in corporations because they are women (p. 213)
techo de cristal idea según la cual se les impide a las mujeres avanzar a la cima de las organizaciones por ser mujeres

globalization (glō´ bə lə zā´ shən) the shift from local to global markets as countries seek foreign trade and investment (p. 316)
globalización cambio de los mercados locales a los mercados globales a medida que países buscan inversión y comercio extranjero

gold standard (gōld stan´ dèrd) a system in which paper money and coins are equal to the value of a certain amount of gold (p. 240)
patrón oro sistema monetario en el cual el papel moneda y las monedas tienen el mismo valor de una cantidad de oro determinada

goods (gùdz) the physical objects that someone buys (p. 5)
bienes objetos físicos que alguien produce

government monopoly (guv´ ərn mənt mə nop´ ə lē) a monopoly created by the government (p. 153)
monopolio gubernamental monopolio creado por el gobierno

grant (grant) a financial award given by a government agency to a private individual or group in order to carry out a specific task (p. 69)
subvención cantidad de dinero que otorga una organización gubernamental a una organización o grupo privados con el fin de utilizarlo en una actividad específica

greenback (grēn´ bak) a paper currency issued by the Union government during the Civil War (p. 239)
greenback dinero creado durante la Guerra Civil estadounidense

grievance (grē´ vəns) a worker complaint (p. 222)
queja formal reclamo de un trabajador

gross domestic product (grōs də mes´ tik prod´ əkt) the total value of all final goods and services produced in a country in a given year (pp. 56, 285)
producto interno bruto valor en dólares de todos los bienes y servicios producidos en un país, en un año específico

gross national product (grōs nash´ ə nəl prod´ əkt) the annual income earned by U.S.-owned firms and people (p. 291)
producto nacional bruto ingreso anual que obtienen las compañías y los habitantes de una nación

guest workers (gest wèr´ kèrz) foreign-born workers who are allowed to live and work in the United States for a set amount of time (p. 206)
trabajadores invitados miembros de la fuerza laboral que vienen de otro país y tienen permiso para vivir y trabajar en Estados Unidos temporalmente

"guns or butter" (gunz ór but´ ər) the idea that a country that produces guns has fewer resources to produce butter (consumer goods), and vice versa (p. 11)
"pan o armas" idea de que un país que decide producir más objetos militares (armas) tiene menos recursos para producir bienes de consumo (pan) y viceversa

H

heavy industry (hev´ ē in´ də strē) the large-scale production of basic products used in other industries (p. 36)
industria pesada producción a gran escala de productos básicos usados en otras industrias

horizontal merger (hôr´ ə zon´ təl mèr´ jər) when a business buys another business that provides the same goods and services (p. 187)
fusión horizontal situación en la que una empresa compra otra empresa que ofrece los mismos bienes o servicios

a	hat	e	let	ī	ice	ô	order	ù	put	sh	she	ə	a in about
ā	age	ē	equal	o	hot	oi	oil	ü	rule	th	thin		e in taken
ä	far	èr	term	ō	open	ou	out	ch	child	ᴛʜ	then		i in pencil
â	care	i	it	ȯ	saw	u	cup	ng	long	zh	measure		o in lemon
													u in circus

household (hous´ hōld) a person or group of people who live together in the same place (p. 32)
  unidad familiar persona o grupo de personas que viven bajo el mismo techo

human capital (hyü´ mən kap´ ə təl) the knowledge and skills a worker gains through education and experience (p. 8)
  capital humano conocimientos y destrezas que un trabajador obtiene a través de la educación y la experiencia

hyperinflation (hī´ pėr in flā´ shən) inflation that is out of control; very high inflation (pp. 324, 390)
  hiperinflación inflación descontrolada; inflación muy alta

I

imperfect competition (im pėr´ fikt kom pə tish´ ən) a market structure in which only a few firms produce the same product (pp. 139, 148)
  competencia imperfecta estructura del mercado en la cual sólo pocas entidades producen el mismo producto

import (im´ pôrt) a good or service brought in from another country for sale (p. 434)
  importación bien o servicio que se trae de otro país para la venta

import quota (im´ pôrt kwō´ tə) a set limit on the amount of a good that can enter a country (p. 440)
  cuota de importación límite establecido de la cantidad de un bien que puede entrar al país

incentive (in sen´ tiv) something that makes a person take a certain action (p. 33)
  incentivo algo que anima a una persona a comportarse de cierta manera

incidence of a tax (in´ sə dəns ov taks) the final burden of a tax (p. 348)
  incidencia fiscal peso final de un impuesto

income (in´ kum) the amount of money a person makes (p. 25)
  ingreso cantidad de dinero que una persona genera

income approach (in´ kum ə prōch) a way of figuring GDP that adds up all the incomes in the economy (p. 286)
  aproximación de ingresos forma de establecer el PIB al sumar todos los ingresos en la economía

income distribution (in´ kum dis´ trə byü´ shən) the way the nation's total income is spread out among its population (p. 331)
  distribución de ingresos forma en que se distribuye el ingreso total de una nación entre la población

income effect (in´ kum ə fekt´) changes in consumption that result from changes in real income (p. 79)
  efecto ingreso cambios en el consumo que ocurren cuando el aumento de un precio hace que el ingreso real disminuya

increasing marginal returns (in krē´ sing mär´ jə nəl ri tėrnz´) a level of production in which the marginal product of labor increases as the number of workers increases (p. 105)
  aumento del ingreso marginal nivel de producción en el cual la productividad marginal aumenta a medida que el número de trabajadores aumenta

individual income tax (in´ də vij´ ü əl in´ kum taks) a tax based on a person's earnings (p. 346)
  impuesto sobre la renta individual impuesto que se basa en los ingresos de una persona

industrialization (in dus´ trē ə liz ā shən) the organization of an economy to manufacture, or make, things (p. 463)
  industrialización organización de una economía con el propósito de fabricar bienes

inelastic (in i las´ tik) describes demand that is not very sensitive to price changes (p. 88)
  demanda inelástica demanda que no es muy sensible a las variaciones de precio

inelastic supply (in i las´ tik sə plī´) when an increase in price has little effect on the supply demanded (p. 102)
  oferta inelástica situación en la que un pequeño aumento del precio tiene un efecto mínimo en la demanda

infant industry (in´ fənt in´ də strē) any industry that is in the early stages of development (p. 442)
  industria en período de arranque industria en etapa temprana de desarrollo

infant mortality rate (in´ fənt môr tal´ ə tē rāt) the number of deaths in the first year of life per 1,000 live births (p. 464)
  tasa de mortalidad infantil número de muertes que ocurren en el primer año de vida por cada 1.000 nacimientos

inferior good (in fir´ ē ər gùd) a good that consumers demand less of when their incomes increase (p. 84)
  bien inferior bien cuya demanda disminuye a medida que el ingreso de los consumidores aumenta

inflation (in flā´ shən) increase in prices over time (p. 207)
  inflación aumento de los precios al transcurrir el tiempo

inflation rate (in flā´ shən rāt) the monthly or yearly percentage rate of change in prices (p. 324)
  tasa de inflación porcentaje de cambio en los precios al transcurrir el tiempo

inflation-indexed bond (in flā´ shən in´ deksd bond) a bond that protects investors against inflation by linking to an inflation index (p. 265)
  bonos indexados por inflación bono que protege al inversionista de la inflación porque se ajusta de acuerdo con un índice de inflación

infrastructure (in´ frə struk´ chər) the basic facilities that are necessary for a society to function and grow (p. 61)
  infraestructura instalaciones básicas que una sociedad necesita para funcionar y desarrollarse

injunction (in jungk´ shən) a court order that prevents some activity (p. 219)
  mandato orden judicial que previene algún tipo de actividad

in-kind benefits (in kīnd ben´ ə fitz) goods and services provided for free or at greatly reduced prices (p. 68)
  beneficios en especies bienes y servicios que se ofrecen de forma gratuita o a un precio considerablemente bajo

innovation (in´ ə vā´ shən) the process of bringing new methods, products, or ideas into use (p. 26)
  innovación proceso que consiste en usar nuevos métodos, productos o ideas

inside lag (in´ sīd lag) the time it takes for monetary policy to go into effect (p. 419)
demora interna tiempo que toma implementar una política monetaria

interdependence (in´ tėr di pen´ dəns) the shared need of countries for resources, goods, services, labor, and knowledge that are supplied by other countries (p. 436)
interdependencia necesidad que comparten los países de obtener recursos, bienes, servicios, mano de obra y conocimiento provenientes de otros países

interest (in´ tėr ist) the price paid for the use of borrowed money (p. 242)
interés precio que se paga por el uso de dinero prestado

interest group (in´ tėr ist grüp) an organization that tries to persuade government officials to act in ways that help its members (p. 52)
grupo de presión organización que intenta persuadir a miembros del gobierno de que actúen de una manera que beneficie a los miembros del grupo

intermediate goods (in tėr mē´ dē it gu̇dz) goods used in the production of final goods (p. 285)
bienes intermedios bienes usados en la producción de bienes finales

internal financing (in tėr´ nəl fə nans´ ing) capital that comes from the savings of the country's citizens (p. 473)
financiamiento interno capital que viene de los ahorros de los ciudadanos de un país

inventory (in´ vən tôr´ ē) the quantity of goods that a firm has on hand (p. 133)
inventario cantidad de bienes que una empresa tiene a su disposición

invest (in vest´) to use assets to earn income or profit (p. 138)
invertir usar activos para obtener ingresos o ganancias

investment (in vest´ mənt) something bought for future financial benefit (p. 258)
inversión compra para beneficio financiero en el futuro

invisible hand (in viz´ ə bəl hand) Adam Smith's idea that competition should regulate the marketplace (p. 33)
mano invisible idea de Adam Smith según la cual la competencia regula el mercado

job security (job si kyu̇r´ ə tē) a guarantee that workers will not lose their jobs (p. 222)
seguridad laboral garantía de que los trabajadores no perderán su trabajo

junk bond (jungk bond) a bond with high risk and, possibly, high yield (p. 266)
bono basura bono que representa un gran riesgo y que podría tener un alto rendimiento

Keynesian economics (kān´ zē ən ek ə nom´ iks) a school of thought that uses demand-side theory as the basis for encouraging economic action (p. 384)
Economía keinesiana escuela que usa la teoría de la demanda como base para provocar acciones gubernamentales económicas

labor (lā´ bėr) the effort people devote to tasks for which they are paid (p. 7)
trabajo esfuerzo dedicado a tareas por las que se recibe compensación económica

labor force (lā´ bėr fôrs) all nonmilitary people who are employed or unemployed (p. 200)
mano de obra toda persona empleada o desempleada que no pertenece a las fuerzas armadas

labor union (lā´ bėr yü nyən) an organization of workers that tries to improve working conditions, wages, and benefits for its members (p. 193)
sindicato organización de trabajadores que busca mejorar las condiciones de trabajo, los salarios y los beneficios laborales de sus miembros

laissez faire (les ā fer´) the idea that government should not get involved in economic matters (p. 39)
liberalismo doctrina que establece que el gobierno no debería intervenir en asuntos económicos

land (land) all natural resources used to produce goods and services (p. 7)
terreno todo recurso natural que se utiliza para producir bienes y servicios

law of comparative advantage (lȯ əv kəm par´ ə tiv ad van´ tij) the idea that a nation is better off when it produces goods and services for which it has a comparative advantage (p. 436)
ley (principio) de la ventaja comparativa principio que reconoce la ventaja que disfruta un país cuando puede producir un bien o servicio a menor costo que otro país

a	hat	e	let	ī	ice	ȯ	order	u̇	put	sh	she	ə {	a	in about
ā	age	ē	equal	o	hot	oi	oil	ü	rule	th	thin		e	in taken
ä	far	ėr	term	ō	open	ou	out	ch	child	ᴛʜ	then		i	in pencil
â	care	i	it	ȯ	saw	u	cup	ng	long	zh	measure		o	in lemon
													u	in circus

law of demand (lȯ əv di mand′) consumers will buy more of a good when its price decreases and less when its price increases (p. 78)
ley de la demanda los consumidores compran más de un bien cuando su precio baja y menos cuando su precio sube

law of increasing costs (lȯ əv in krē′ sing kȯst) an economic principle stating that as production shifts from making one good or service to another, more resources are needed to increase production of the second good or service (p. 17)
ley de los costos crecientes principio económico según el cual al producirse un producto o bien adicional, éste requerirá cantidades cada vez mayores de recursos para aumentar su producción

law of supply (lȯ əv sə plī′) the idea that producers offer more of a good as its price increases and less as its price falls (p. 99)
ley de la oferta los fabricantes proveen más de un bien cuando su precio sube y menos cuando su precio baja

leading indicators (lē′ ding in′ də kā′ tėrz) a set of key economic variables that economists use to predict future trends in a business cycle (p. 299)
indicadores principales conjunto de variables económicas clave que los economistas utilizan para predecir las tendencias futuras del ciclo económico

learning effect (lėr′ ning ə fekt′) the idea that education increases the efficiency of production and results in higher wages (p. 204)
efecto aprendizaje idea que sostiene que la educación incrementa la productividad y por consiguiente genera mayores sueldos

legal equality (lē′ gəl i kwol′ ə tē) the principle that everyone has the same legal rights (p. 51)
igualdad legal principio según el cual todas las personas tienen los mismos derechos legales

less developed countries (les di vel′ əpt kun′ trēz) nations with a low average level of well-being (p. 460)
país en vías de desarrollo nación con un bajo nivel de bienestar material

liable (lī ə bəl) having legal responsibility (p. 175)
responsable que tiene una obligación legal

life expectancy (līf ek spek′ tən sē) the average expected life span of an individual (p. 463)
expectativa de vida promedio de vida anticipado de una persona

limited capital (lim′ ə tid kap′ ə təl) the limit on the amount of money to grow the business (p. 176)
capital limitado límite de dinero que se invierte para la expansion de un negocio

limited liability (lim′ ə tid lī a bil′ ə tē) when investors can lose only the money they have invested (p. 185)
responsabilidad limitada condición en la que los inversionistas sólo pueden perder la plata que han invertido

limited liability corporation (lim′ ə tid lī a bil′ ə tē kȯr′ pə rā′ shən) type of business with limited liability for the owners; it does not pay corporate income tax (p. 186)
corporación de responsabilidad limitada compañía que tiene propietarios con responsabilidad limitada y no paga el impuesto sobre sociedades

limited liability partnership (lim′ ə tid lī a bil′ ə tē pärt′ nər ship) a partnership in which all partners are limited partners (p. 178)
sociedad de responsabilidad limitada sociedad en la que la responsabilidad de los socios está limitada al capital aportado

limited partnership (lim′ ə tid pärt′ nər ship) a partnership in which only one partner is required to have both responsibility and liability (p. 178)
sociedad limitada sociedad en la que solamente se requiere que un socio tenga responsabilidades y obligaciones legales

limited supply (lim′ ə tid sə plī′) not easily available (p. 235)
oferta limitada que no se encuentra con facilidad

liquidity (li kwid′ ə tē) the ability to be used as, or directly converted into, cash (p. 245)
liquidez capacidad para utilizar el dinero o para convertir algo en dinero fácilmente

literacy rate (lit′ ėr ə sē rāt) the percentage of people over age 15 who can read and write (p. 463)
índice de alfabetización porcentaje de la población mayor de 15 años que sabe leer y escribir

Lorenz Curve (lȯr′ ənz kėrv) a graph that shows the distribution of income in the economy (p. 332)
Curva de Lorenz gráfica que muestra la distribución de los ingresos en la economía

M

M1 (em wun) all the money actually in use (p. 245)
M1 todo el dinero en uso

M2 (em tü) includes M1 money plus all other monies, such as money market and savings accounts (p. 245)
M2 incluye el dinero M1 más todos los tipos de dinero restantes, como el dinero en el mercado y en las cuentas de ahorros

macroeconomics (mak′ rō ek ə nom′ iks) the study of economic behavior and decision making in a nation's whole economy (p. 56)
Macroeconomía estudio del comportamiento y la toma de decisiones de toda la economía nacional

malnutrition (mal′ nü trish′ ən) consistently not having enough food to eat (p. 471)
desnutrición nutrición inadecuada continua

mandatory spending (man′ də tȯr′ ē spend ing) spending that Congress is required by existing law to do (p. 355)
gasto obligatorio gasto que el Congreso debe realizar de acuerdo con leyes preexistentes

marginal benefit (mär´ jə nəl ben´ ə fit) the extra benefit of adding one unit (p. 13)
beneficio marginal beneficio adicional que surge al añadirse una unidad

marginal cost (mär´ jə nəl kȯst) the cost of producing one more unit of a good (pp. 13, 109)
costo marginal costo adicional que surge al añadirse una unidad

marginal product of labor (mär´ jə nəl prod´ əkt əv lā´ bər) the change in output from hiring one additional unit of labor (p. 105)
producto marginal del trabajo producción adicional que se obtiene con una unidad adicional de trabajo

marginal revenue (mär´ jə nəl rev´ ə nü) the additional income from selling one more unit of a good (p. 110)
ingreso marginal ingreso recibido al vender una unidad más de producto; en algunos casos similar a precio

market (mär´ kit) a place that allows buyers and sellers to exchange things (p. 30)
mercado lugar donde se le permite a compradores y vendedores intercambiar cosas

market basket (mär´ kit bas´ kit) items that a typical urban consumer might buy, used for tracking the cost of a group of goods from month to month (p. 323)
canasta de mercado artículos que un consumidor urbano típico podría comprar; se usan para hacer un seguimiento del costo de un grupo de bienes mes a mes

market demand schedule (mär´ kit di mand´ skej´ úl) a table that lists the quantity of a good all consumers in a market will buy at each different price (p. 80)
tabla de demanda tabla que muestra la cantidad de un producto determinado que los consumidores de un mercado estarían dispuestos a comprar a diferentes precios

market failure (mär´ kit fā´ lyər) a situation in which the free market, operating on its own, does not distribute resources efficiently (p. 61)
falla del mercado situación en la que el mercado, operando de forma autónoma, asigna recursos ineficientemente

market power (mär´ kit pou´ ər) the ability of a company to control prices and total market output (p. 153)
poder de mercado capacidad de una empresa para influir en los precios y la producción del mercado

market supply schedule (mär´ kit sə plī´ skej´ úl) a chart that lists how much of a good all suppliers will offer at various prices (p. 101)
tabla de oferta tabla que muestra la cantidad de un producto determinado que las empresas proveerán a diferentes precios

maturity (mə chȯr´ ə tē) the time a loan is to be repaid (p. 263)
vencimiento día en que se cumple el plazo dado para el pago de una deuda

means-tested (mēnz test ed´) the practice of giving lower, or no, entitlements to people who have higher incomes (p. 356)
evaluación financiera práctica que consiste en otorgar o no ciertas prestaciones a personas con altos ingresos

mediator (mē´ dē ā tėr) a neutral third party who listens to arguments from both sides and suggests ways an agreement can be reached (p. 223)
mediador tercero neutral que escucha los argumentos de ambos lados y sugiere maneras de llegar a un acuerdo

medium of exchange (mē´ dē əm əv eks chānj´) anything that is used to determine the value during the exchange of goods and services (p. 232)
medio de intercambio estructura que se utiliza para asignar valor a algo durante un intercambio de bienes y servicios

member bank (mem´ bər bangk) a bank that belongs to the Federal Reserve System (p. 241)
banco miembro banco que pertenece al Sistema de la Reserva Federal

merger (mėr jər) when two or more companies join to form a single firm (p. 161)
fusión proceso mediante el cual dos o más compañías que se unen para formar una sola

microeconomics (mī´ krō ek ə nom´ iks) the study of the economic behavior and decision making in small units, such as households and firms (p. 56)
Microeconomía estudio del comportamiento económico de unidades individuales de decisión tales como familias y empresas

minimum wage (min´ ə məm wāj) the minimum price that an employer must pay a worker for an hour of labor (p. 125)
salario mínimo cantidad mínima que un empleador puede pagarle a un empleado por una hora de trabajo

mixed economy (mikst i kon´ ə mē) a market-based economic system in which the government has some involvement (p. 39)
economía mixta sistema económico de mercado en el que el gobierno tiene cierto grado de intervención

monetarism (mun´ i tu riz´ əm) the belief that the money supply is the most important factor in the entire economy (p. 416)
monetarismo doctrina que sostiene que el abastecimiento del dinero en circulación es el factor más importante en la economía

monetary policy (mon´ ə tėr ē pol´ ə sē) the decisions the Fed makes about money and banking (p. 405)
política monetaria decisiones que toma la Reserva Federal en asuntos de dinero y banca

a	hat	e	let	ī	ice	ô	order	ú	put	sh	she	ə	a in about
ā	age	ē	equal	o	hot	oi	oil	ü	rule	th	thin		e in taken
ä	far	ėr	term	ō	open	ou	out	ch	child	ᴛʜ	then		i in pencil
â	care	i	it	ȯ	saw	u	cup	ng	long	zh	measure		o in lemon
													u in circus

money (mun´ ē) anything that serves as a medium of exchange, a unit of account, and a store of value (p. 232)
 dinero todo aquello que sirve como medio de cambio, unidad de cuenta y depósito de valor

money creation (mun´ ē krē ā´ shən) the process of manufacturing currency and putting it into use (p. 410)
 emisión de dinero proceso que crea y pone en circulación billetes y monedas

money market (mun´ ē mär´ kit) a market in which money is lent for periods of one year or less (p. 268)
 mercado monetario o de dinero mercado que ofrece créditos por períodos de un año o menos

money market mutual fund (mun´ ē mär´ kit myü´ chü ə fund) a fund that pools money from small savers to purchase short-term government and corporate securities (p. 245)
 fondos mutuales fondo que reúne el dinero de pequeños ahorristas para comprar instrumentos de crédito a corto plazo emitidos por el gobierno o el sector privado

money multiplier formula (mun´ ē mul´ tə plī´ ėr fôr´ myə lə) the formula economists use to figure out the total amount of new money that can be created and added to the money supply (p. 411)
 fórmula del multiplicador monetario fórmula que utilizan los economistas para calcular la cantidad de dinero que se puede crear y añadir a la oferta monetaria

money supply (mun´ ē sə plī´) all the money available in the United States economy (p. 244)
 oferta monetaria todo el dinero disponible en la economía de los Estados Unidos

monopoly (mə nop´ ə lē) a market which a single seller has control (p. 150)
 monopolio situación de mercado en la que un solo vendedor controla la oferta

mortgage (môr´ gij) a specific type of loan used to buy real estate (p. 242)
 hipoteca tipo de préstamo que se utiliza para comprar bienes inmuebles

multinational corporation (mul´ ti nash´ ə nəl kôr´ pə rā´ shən) a large corporation that operates in more than one country (p. 188)
 compañía multinacional gran empresa que opera en más de un país

multiplier effect (mul´ tə plī´ ėr ə fekt´) the idea that every one dollar change in fiscal policy creates a change greater than one dollar in the national income (p. 384)
 efecto multiplicador concepto según el cual, por cada dólar de cambio en una política fiscal, se producirá un cambio aún mayor en el ingreso nacional

municipal bond (myü nis´ ə pəl bond) a bond issued by state and local government to pay for such things as highways, state buildings, parks, and schools (p. 265)
 bono público bono emitido por gobiernos estatales y locales para financiar obras públicas como carreteras, edificios, parques y escuelas

mutual fund (myü´ chü əl fund) an organization that pools the savings of many individuals and invests it in stocks, bonds, and other financial assets (p. 260)
 fondo de inversión organización que reúne los ahorros de muchos individuos e invierte el dinero en una cartera de acciones, bonos y otros activos financieros

N

national bank (nash´ ə nəl bangk) a bank chartered by the national government (p. 238)
 banco nacional banco regulado por el gobierno federal

national debt (nash´ ə nəl det) the total amount of money the federal government owes to all bondholders (p. 391)
 deuda nacional cantidad total de dinero que el gobierno federal les debe a sus acreedores

national income accounting (nash´ ə nəl in´ kum ə koun´ ting) a system economists use to collect and organize macroeconomic statistics on production, income, investment, and savings (p. 284)
 contabilidad nacional sistema que los economistas utilizan para recopilar y organizar estadísticas macroeconómicas sobre producción, ingresos, inversión y ahorros

need (nēd) something essential for survival such as food, clothing, or medical care (p. 5)
 necesidad algo considerado esencial para sobrevivir como comida, vestimenta y atención médica

net worth (net wėrth) total assets minus total liabilities (p. 408)
 patrimonio neto bienes que posee una persona al deducirse sus deudas

newly industrialized countries (nü´ lē in dus´ trē ə lizd kun´ trēz) less developed countries that have made great progress toward developing their economies (p. 461)
 país recientemente industrializado país no completamente industrializado que ha logrado grandes avances en el desarrollo de su economía

nominal GDP (nom´ ə nəl jē dē pē) GDP measured in current prices (p. 287)
 PBI nominal producto interno bruto medido en dólares a precios actuales

nondurable goods (non´ dùr ə bəl gùdz) goods that last a short period of time, such as food, light bulbs, and sneakers (p. 286)
 bienes perecederos bienes que duran un corto período de tiempo, como comida, bombillas y zapatillas deportivas

nongovernmental organization (non´ guv ėrn men´ təl ôr´ gə nə zā´ shən) an independent group that raises money for development programs (p. 476)
 organización no gubernamental grupo independiente que recauda dinero para programas de desarrollo

nonprice competition (non prīs kom pə tish´ ən) a way to attract customers through style, service, or location, but not a lower price (p. 157)
   competencia sin precios estrategia para atraer consumidores enfocándose en el estilo, el servicio o la ubicación de un bien, sin tener que bajar su precio

nonprofit organization (non prof´ it ôr´ gə nə zā´ shən) an institution that functions much like a business but does not operate for the purpose of generating profit (p. 191)
   organización sin fines de lucro institución que funciona como una empresa, pero no opera con el propósito de generar ganancias

normal good (nôr´ məl gu̇d) a product or good that consumers demand more of when their incomes increase (p. 83)
   bien normal bien que el consumidor demanda más cuando sus ingresos aumentan

O

obsolescence (ob´ sə les´ əns) a situation in which older products and processes become out of date (p. 58)
   obsolescencia situación que ocurre cuando productos o procesos antiguos caen en desuso

offshoring (ȯf´ shôr´ ing) the movement of parts of a company's operations to another country (p. 489)
   deslocalización traslado de las plantas productivas de una empresa a otro país

oligopoly (ol ə gop´ ə lē) a market structure in which a few large firms dominate a market (p. 158)
   oligopolio estructura en la cual unas pocas grandes empresas dominan el mercado

open-market operations (ō´ pən mär´ kit op ə rā´ shənz) the buying and selling of government securities in order to alter the supply of money (p. 414)
   operaciones de mercado abierto compra y venta de valores del Estado para controlar la cantidad de dinero en circulación

operating budget (op´ ə rāt´ ing buj´ it) a budget for day-to-day spending (p. 362)
   presupuesto de operación presupuesto para los gastos diarios

operating cost (op´ ə rāt´ ing kȯst) the cost of operating a facility, such as a factory or a store (p. 111)
   costo de operación costo de operar instalaciones tales como fábricas y tiendas

opportunity cost (op´ ər tü´ nə tē kȯst) the second-best choice, given up as the result of a decision (p. 11)
   costo de oportunidad mejor alternativa que se desechó al tomarse una decisión

outside lag (out´ sīd´ lag) the time it takes for monetary policy to have an effect (p. 420)
   demora externa cantidad de tiempo que demora en surtir efecto una política monetaria

outsourcing (out´ sȯrs ing) sending work to an outside source, in another country, to cut costs (p. 203)
   subcontratación práctica que consiste en contratar a una compañía en otro país para realizar un trabajo, y así para reducir costos

overtime (ō´ vėr tīm) extra money paid to employees for work beyond 40 hours per week or on weekend or holidays (p. 213)
   horas extra dinero adicional que se les paga a los empleados por trabajar más de 40 horas semanales, los fines de semana o los días festivos

P

par value (pär val´ yü) a bond's stated value, to be paid to the bondholder at maturity (p. 263)
   valor nominal valor original de un bono/obligación que debe pagarse a su vencimiento

partnership (pärt´ nər ship) a business that two or more people own (p. 177)
   sociedad negocio que pertenece a dos o más personas

patent (pat´ int) a government license that gives an inventor the exclusive right to produce and sell a product (p. 59)
   patente licencia gubernamental que otorga al inventor de un nuevo producto el derecho exclusivo de producirlo y venderlo

patriotism (pā´ trē ə tiz´ əm) love of one's country (p. 52)
   patriotismo amor por el país propio

peak (pēk) the height of an economic expansion; the point at which real GDP stops rising (p. 294)
   punto máximo máxima expansión económica, cuando el PIB cesa de crecer

per capita GDP (pėr kap´ ə tə jē dē pē) a nation's gross domestic product divided by its population (p. 461)
   PIB per cápita producto interno bruto de un país dividido entre su población

perfect competition (pėr´ fikt kom pə tish´ ən) a market structure in which a large number of firms all produce the same product and no single seller controls supply or prices (p. 146)
   competencia perfecta mercado en el que numerosas empresas producen el mismo producto y ninguna controla la oferta o los precios

a	hat	e	let	ī	ice	ȯ	order	u̇	put	sh	she	ə	a in about
ā	age	ē	equal	o	hot	oi	oil	ü	rule	th	thin		e in taken
ä	far	ėr	term	ō	open	ou	out	ch	child	ŦH	then		i in pencil
â	care	i	it	ȯ	saw	u	cup	ng	long	zh	measure		o in lemon
													u in circus

personal exemption (pėr´ sə nəl eg zemp´ shən) a set amount that taxpayers may subtract from their gross income for themselves, their spouse, and any dependents (p. 350)
deducción personal cantidad fija que el contribuyente puede deducir de su ingreso bruto a cuenta de sí mismo, su cónyuge y otros dependientes

philanthropy (fə lan´ thrə pē) an activity or organization whose purpose is to improve the social or economic welfare of humanity (p. 191)
filantropía actividad u organización cuyo propósito es mejorar el bienestar social y económico de la humanidad

physical capital (fiz´ ə kəl kap´ ə təl) the human-made objects used to create other goods and services (p. 8)
capital físico objetos construidos por el hombre que se utilizan para crear bienes y servicios

population growth rate (pop´ yə lā´ shən grōth rāt) a measure of how fast a country's population increases each year (p. 468)
tasa de crecimiento de la población medida de cuán rápido crece la población de un país cada año

portable (pôr´ tə bel´) easily carried (p. 235)
portátil que se puede cargar fácilmente

portfolio (pôrt fō´ lē ō) a collection of financial assets (p. 260)
portafolio conjunto de activos financieros

poverty rate (pov´ ėr tē rāt) the percentage of people who live in households with income lower than the official poverty threshold (p. 329)
tasa de pobreza porcentaje de personas que viven en hogares con un ingreso por debajo del nivel de pobreza

poverty threshold (pov´ ėr tē thresh´ ōld) an income level below which income is not high enough to support a family or household (pp. 65, 329)
nivel de pobreza ingreso por debajo del nivel necesario para mantener a una familia o un hogar

predatory pricing (pred´ ə tôr´ ē prīs ing) selling a product below cost for a short period of time to drive competitors out of the market (p. 160)
precios depredatorios vender un producto por debajo de su costo por un corto período de tiempo para forzar a los competidores fuera del mercado

price ceiling (prīs sē´ ling) a maximum price that can legally be charged for a good or service (p. 124)
precio tope precio máximo que un vendedor puede cobrar legalmente por un bien o servicio

price discrimination (prīs dis krim ə nā´ shən) a division of consumers into groups based on how much they will pay for a good (p. 153)
discriminación de precios práctica que consiste en dividir a los consumidores en grupos según la cantidad que están dispuestos a pagar por un bien

price fixing (prīs fik´ sing) an agreement among firms to sell at the same or very similar prices (p. 159)
fijación de precios acuerdo entre compañías para cobrar un precio determinado o muy similar

price floor (prīs flôr) the lowest price allowed for certain goods or services (p. 124)
precio mínimo límite inferior al que puede llegar el precio de un bien o servicio

price index (prīs in´ deks) a measurement that shows the average price of a group of goods (p. 323)
índice de precios medida que muestra el cambio del precio promedio de un grupo de bienes estándar

price level (prīs lev´ əl) the average of all prices (p. 289)
nivel de precios promedio de los precios en una economía

price system (prīs sis´təm) the communication between buyers and sellers (p. 135)
sistema de precios comunicación entre compradores y vendedores

primary market (prī´ mer´ ē mär´ kit) a market where newly issued financial assets can be redeemed only by the original holder (p. 268)
mercado primario mercado para vender activos financieros que sólo pueden ser cobrados por el propietario original

prime rate (prīm rāt) the interest rates banks charge their best customers (p. 413)
tipo de interés preferencial tipo de interés que un banco cobra a sus mejores clientes

principal (prin´ sə pəl) the amount of money borrowed (p. 242)
capital cantidad de dinero prestado

private property rights (prī´ vit prop´ ər tē rītz) the principle that people have the right to control their possessions and use them as they wish (p. 51)
derechos de propiedad privada principio según el cual una persona tiene el derecho de controlar y usar sus pertenencias como quiera

private sector (prī´ vit sek´ tər) the part of the economy that involves the transactions of individuals and businesses (p. 61)
sector privado parte de la economía relacionada con los negocios de los individuos y de las compañías

privatization (prī´ vu tiz ā shən) selling government businesses or services to individuals and allowing them to compete in the marketplace (pp. 41, 477)
privatización venta de compañías o servicios operados por el gobierno a inversionistas individuales para que compitan en el mercado

producer cooperative (prə dü´ sər kō op´ ər ə tiv) an agricultural marketing cooperative that helps members sell their products (p. 191)
cooperativa de productores cooperativa agraria que ayuda a sus miembros a vender sus productos

product market (prod´ əkt mär´ kit) an exchange in which households buy goods and services from firms (p. 32)
mercado de productos intercambio comercial en el que una familia compra bienes y servicios de empresas

production possibilities curve (prə duk´ shən pos´ ə bil´ ə tēz kėrv) a graph that shows alternative ways to use an economy's productive resources (p. 14)
curva de posibilidades de producción gráfico que muestra distintas maneras de utilizar los recursos de producción en una economía

production possibilities frontier (prə duk′ shən pos′ ə bil′ ətēz frun tir′) a line on a production possibilities curve that shows the maximum possible output an economy can produce (p. 15)
frontera de posibilidades de producción línea en una curva de posibilidad de producción que indica el límite máximo de lo que puede producir una economía

productive capacity (prə duk′ tiv kə pas′ i tē) the most production possible over time without increasing inflation (p. 383)
capacidad de producción producción máxima que una economía puede sostener por un tiempo sin que aumente la inflación

productivity of labor (prō duk tiv′ ə tē əv lā′ bėr) the amount of goods and services workers can produce in a given time period (p. 210)
productividad cantidad de rendimiento que genera una unidad de trabajo en un período de tiempo determinado

professional labor (prə fesh′ ə nəl lā′ bėr) work that requires advanced skills and education (p. 212)
trabajo profesional trabajo que requiere habilidades y estudios avanzados

professional organization (prə fesh′ ə nəl ôr′ gə nə zā′ shən) a nonprofit organization that works to improve the image, working conditions, and skill levels of people in particular occupations (p. 192)
organización profesional organización sin fines de lucro que busca mejorar la imagen, las condiciones de trabajo y la competencia técnica de individuos que ejercen una determinada profesión

profit (prof′ it) the amount of money a business keeps after all costs of production have been paid (p. 25)
ganancias cantidad de dinero que tiene una compañía al pagar todo sus gastos de producción

profit motive (prof′ it mō′ tiv) the incentive that drives individuals and business owners to improve their material well-being (p. 51)
motivación de ganancia incentivo que conlleva al individuo o compañía a mejorar su bienestar material

progressive tax (prə gres′ iv taks) a tax for which the percentage of income paid in taxes increases as the income increases (p. 346)
impuesto progresivo impuesto cuyo porcentaje aumenta al aumentar el ingreso del contribuyente

property tax (prop′ ėr tē taks) a tax based on real estate and other property (p. 346)
impuesto sobre la propiedad impuesto basado en bienes inmuebles y otros tipos de propiedad

proportional tax (prə pôr′ shə nəl taks) a tax for which the percentage of income paid in taxes remains the same at all income levels (p. 345)
impuesto proporcional impuesto cuyo porcentaje permanece constante en cualquier nivel de ingreso

prospectus (prə spek′ təs) an investment report (p. 260)
prospecto documento que provee información sobre inversiones

protectionism (prə tek′ shə niz′ əm) the use of trade barriers in order to protect domestic industries from foreign competition (p. 441)
proteccionismo uso de barreras comerciales para proteger a las industrias domésticas de los competidores extranjeros

public disclosure laws (pub′ lik dis klō′ zhər lòz) laws that require companies to provide information about their products (p. 54)
ley de divulgación pública ley que exige que una compañía provea información acerca de sus productos o servicios

public good (pub′ lik gùd) a shared good or service for which it would be difficult to make consumers pay individually and to exclude those who did not pay (p. 60)
bien público bien que satisface una necesidad pública o colectiva por lo que resulta ineficiente hacer pagar a los consumidores individualmente

public interest (pub′ lik in′ tər ist) the concerns of society as a whole (p. 54)
interés público preocupaciones de la sociedad en conjunto

public sector (pub′ lik sek′ tər) the portion of the economy that involves the transactions of the government (p. 61)
sector público parte de la economía que tiene que ver con los negocios del gobierno

publicly held corporation (pub′ lik lē held kôr′ pə rā′ shən) a corporation that sells stock on the open market (p. 184)
compañía pública corporación que vende acciones en el mercado abierto

purchasing power (pėr′ chəs ing pou′ ėr) the ability to buy goods and services (p. 323)
poder adquisitivo capacidad para comprar bienes y servicios

put option (pùt op′ shən) a contract for selling stock at a particular price until a specified future date (p. 273)
opción de venta contrato para vender acciones a un determinado precio durante un período de tiempo fijado

a	hat	e	let	ī	ice	ô	order	ù	put	sh	she	a	in about
ā	age	ē	equal	o	hot	oi	oil	ü	rule	th	thin	e	in taken
ä	far	ėr	term	ō	open	ou	out	ch	child	ŦH	then	ə { i	in pencil
â	care	i	it	ò	saw	u	cup	ng	long	zh	measure	o	in lemon
												u	in circus

Q

quantity supplied (kwän´ tə tē sə plīd´) the amount that a
supplier is willing and able to supply at a specific price (p. 99)
cantidad ofrecida cantidad que un proveedor puede y está
dispuesto a ofrecer por un precio específico

quantity theory (kwän´ tə tē thē´ ər ē) the theory that inflation
is caused by having too much money in the economy (p. 324)
teoría de la cantidad teoría que establece que la presencia
de mucho dinero en la economía causa inflación

R

rate of return (rāt əv ri tėrn´) refers to the return stated as a
percentage of the total amount invested (p. 261)
tasa de retorno retorno que se expresa como un porcentaje
del porcentaje original

rationing (rash´ ə ning) a system of allocating scarce goods and
services using criteria other than price (p. 137)
racionamiento sistema de distribución de los bienes y
servicios escasos usando un criterio que no se basa en el
precio

real GDP (rē´ əl jē dē pē) GDP adjusted for price changes
(p. 287)
PIB real PIB ajustado a los cambios de precios

real GDP per capita (rē´ əl jē dē pē pər kap´ ə tə) real GDP
divided by the total population of a country (p. 302)
PIB real per cápita PIB real dividido por la población total
de un país

recession (ri sesh´ ən) long economic contraction (p. 294)
recesión contracción económica prolongada

regional trade organization (rē jə nəl trād ôr gə nə zā´ shən)
an organization that works toward lowering or removing
trade barriers among its members, which are located in the
same region (p. 443)
organización de comercio regional organización cuyo
objetivo es disminuir o acabar con las barreras comerciales
entre sus miembros, que se ubican en la misma region del
mundo

regressive tax (ri gres´ iv taks) a tax for which the percentage
of income paid in taxes decreases as income increases (p. 346)
impuesto regresivo impuesto para el cual el porcentaje
de ingresos que se paga disminuye a medida que el ingreso
aumenta

regulate (reg´ yə lāt) to control or direct (p. 33)
regular controlar o dirigir

regulation (reg´ yə lā´ shən) when a government makes rules
that affect the production of a good or service (p. 113)
regulación intervención del gobierno en un mercado que
afecta la producción de un bien

remittance (ri mit´ ens´) cash payments sent by workers who
have migrated to a new country to family members in their
home country (p. 490)
remesas pagos en efectivo que les envían los trabajadores
inmigrantes a sus familiares en sus países de origen

rent control (rent kə trōl´) a price ceiling placed on rent (p. 124)
control de renta precio tope del alquiler de apartamentos

representative money (rep ri zen´ tə tiv mun´ e) an object that
has value because the holder can exchange it for something
else of value (p. 236)
dinero representativo objeto que tiene valor porque su
dueño lo puede cambiar por otro objeto de valor

required reserve ratio (RRR) (ri kwīrd´ ri zėrv´ rā´ shē ō) the
percentage of deposits banks are required to keep in reserve
(p. 411)
tasa de encaje porcentaje de los depósitos que los bancos
tienen que guardar en reserva

reserve requirements (ri zėrv´ ri kwīr´ məntz) the amount of
funds that banks must hold in reserve (p. 408)
encaje cantidad que los bancos deben mantener en reserva

reserves (ri zėrv´ z) funds that banks keep in accounts with the
Feds, called federal funds (p. 408)
reservas depósitos que un banco tiene en sus cuentas de la
Reserva Federal, llamados depósitos federales

resources (rē´ sôrs´ iz) anything that people use to make things
or do work (p. 5)
recursos cualquier cosa que las personas usan para producir
cosas o trabajar

return (ri tėrn´) the money an investor receives above and
beyond the sum of money initially invested (p. 261)
rendimiento dinero que un inversionista recibe por encima
de la suma de dinero original que invirtió

revenue (rev´ ə nü) the income received by a government from
taxes and other nontax sources (p. 345)
ingreso dinero recibido por un gobierno que proviene de los
impuestos y otras fuentes que no son fiscales

right-to-work law (rīt tü wėrk lȯ) a law against forcing a
worker to join a union (p. 219)
ley de derecho al trabajo ley que establece que no es
obligatorio ser miembro de un sindicato

royalty (roi´ əl tē) share of earning given as payment to the
owner of a patent or copyright (p. 182)
regalía ganancia compartida que se otorga como pago al
dueño de la patente o los derechos de reproducción

S

safety net (sāf´ tē net) a set of programs meant to protect
people who face economic hard times (p. 28)
programas de ayuda social grupo de programas del
gobierno que protegen a las personas con dificultades
económicas

sales tax (sālz taks) a tax based on goods or services that are sold (p. 346)
impuesto a las ventas impuesto sobre los bienes y servicios que se venden

sanction (sangk´ shən) action a nation or group of nations takes in order to punish or put pressure on another nation (p. 440)
sanciones acciones que una nación o un grupo de naciones toma para castigar o presionar a otra nación

saving (sā´ ving) income that is not spent (p. 304)
ahorro ingreso que no se gasta

savings bond (sā vingz bond) a bond issued by the government (p. 262)
bono de ahorro bono de baja denominación ofrecido por el gobierno

saving rate (sā´ ving rāt) the percentage of after-tax income that is not spent (p. 304)
tasa de ahorro porcentaje de los ingresos disponibles que se ahorran

scarcity (skär´ sə tē) the principle that limited amounts of goods and services are available to meet unlimited wants (p. 4)
escasez situación en la que existe una cantidad limitada de bienes y servicios disponibles para satisfacer deseos ilimitados

screening effect (skrēn ing ə fekt´) the idea that a college degree is a signal to employers that a person is intelligent and hardworking (p. 205)
efecto de selección idea según la cual completar estudios universitarios indica que un candidato a un empleo es inteligente y trabaja duro

search costs (sėrch kôsts) the financial and opportunity costs consumers pay when looking for a good or service (p. 132)
costo de búsqueda costos financieros y de oportunidad que los consumidores pagan mientras buscan un bien o servicio

seasonal unemployment (sē´ zən əl un em ploi´ mənt) unemployment that happens when industries shut down for a season (p. 315)
desempleo estacional tipo de desempleo que ocurre cuando las industrias cierran por una estación

secondary market (sek´ən der´ ē mär´ kit) a market where financial assets are allowed to be resold (p. 268)
mercado secundario mercado en el que se pueden revender bienes financieros

sector (sek´ tėr) any one of the three groupings of workers: agricultural, manufacturing/construction, and service (p. 202)
sector cualquiera de las tres agrupaciones de trabajadores: agrícola, manufactura/construcción y servicio

self-interest (self´ in´ tėr est) an individual's own personal gain (p. 33)
interés personal beneficio de una persona

semiskilled labor (sem ī skild´ lā´ bėr) work that requires some training and education (p. 212)
trabajo semicalificado trabajo que requiere algo de entrenamiento y educación

service cooperative (sėr´ vis kō op´ ər ə tiv) a type of cooperative that provides a service rather than a good (p. 190)
cooperativa de servicios tipo de cooperativa que ofrece un servicio en vez de un bien

services (sėr´ vis´ iz) the actions or activities that one person performs for another (p. 5)
servicios acciones o actividades que una persona ejecuta para otra persona

shares (sherz) units of stock in a company (p. 183)
acción unidad del capital de una empresa

shortage (shôr´ tij) a situation in which buyers want more of a good or service than producers are willing to supply at a particular price (pp. 5, 123)
escasez situación en la que las personas quieren un bien o servicio en una cantidad mayor a la que los productores están dispuestos a producir a un precio determinado

skilled labor (skild lā´ bėr) work that requires special skills and training (p. 212)
trabajo calificado trabajo que requiere destrezas y capacitación profesional especializadas

socialism (sō´ shə liz əm) a political and economic system in which the means of production are owned by the state (p. 36)
socialismo sistema económico y político en el que los medios de producción pertenecen al estado

sole proprietorship (sōl prə prī´ ə tər ship) a business that one person (an entrepreneur) owns (p. 172)
empresa unipersonal negocio que le pertenece a un solo individuo (empresario)

special economic zones (spesh´ əl ek ə nom´ ik zōnz) designated regions that operate under different economic laws from the rest of the country in order to attract foreign investment and promote exports (p. 480)
zona económica especial regiones designadas que funcionan bajo leyes económicas diferentes al resto del país para poder atraer inversiones extranjeras y promover las exportaciones

specialization (spesh ə lə zā´ shən) when individuals and businesses do only what they are best at (p. 31)
especialización condición en la que individuos y empresas se concentran en el campo donde son los mejores

a hat	e let	ī ice	ô order	u̇ put	sh she	ə { a in about
ā age	ē equal	o hot	oi oil	ü rule	th thin	e in taken
ä far	ėr term	ō open	ou out	ch child	ᴛʜ then	i in pencil
â care	i it	ȯ saw	u cup	ng long	zh measure	o in lemon
						u in circus

specie (spē´ shē) coined money, usually gold or silver, used to back paper money (p. 236)
metálico dinero en monedas, generalmente de oro o plata, que se usa para respaldar el papel moneda

speculation (spek´ yə lā´ shən) the practice of making high-risk investments with borrowed money, in hopes of getting a big return (p. 274)
especulación práctica que consiste en hacer inversiones de alto riesgo con dinero prestado, con la esperanza de obtener una ganancia alta

stabilization program (stā´ be liz ā shən prō´ gram) an agreement between the borrowing country and the International Monetary Fund in which the LDC agrees to change its economic ways to meet IMF goals (p. 475)
programa de estabilización acuerdo entre una nación deudora y el Fondo Monetario Internacional mediante el cual la nación se compromete a cambiar su política económica para cumplir con los objetivos del FMI

stagflation (stag flā´ shən) a decline in real GDP combined with a rise in the price level (p. 294)
estanflación disminución del PIB real combinado con un aumento de precios

standard of living (stan´ dərd ov liv´ ing) the way of living that is usual for a person, community, or country (p. 26)
nivel de vida calidad de vida habitual de una persona, comunidad o país

start-up costs (stärt up kȯsts) the expenses a new business must pay before it can begin to produce and sell goods (p. 148)
costos de inicio gastos que un negocio nuevo debe hacer antes de que comience a producir y vender bienes

stock (stok) a certificate that signifies ownership in a corporation (p. 183)
acción certificado de propiedad de parte de una corporación

stock exchange (stok eks chānj´) a market where stocks can be bought and sold (p. 269)
bolsa de valores mercado en el cual se compran y venden acciones

stock option (stok op´ shən) contract that gives investors the right to buy or sell stock and other financial assets at a particular price until a specified future date (p. 272)
opción de suscripción de acciones contrato que otorga el derecho a inversionistas de comprar o vender acciones u otro activo financiero a un precio en particular hasta una fecha determinada

stockbroker (stok´ brō kėr) a person who links buyers and sellers of stock (p. 272)
corredor de bolsa persona que conecta a compradores y vendedores de la bolsa

store of value (stȯr əv val´ yü) something that keeps its value if it is stored rather than used (p. 233)
mantenimiento del valor algo que mantiene su valor si se guarda, no cuando se gasta

strike (strīk) the act of stopping work to argue for better pay, benefits, and working conditions (p. 218)
huelga suspensión organizada del trabajo con el objetivo de recibir mejor pago y mejores condiciones de trabajo

structural unemployment (struk´ chėr əl un em ploi´ mənt) unemployment that happens when workers' skills do not match those needed for the jobs available (p. 315)
desempleo estructural desempleo que ocurre cuando las destrezas de los trabajadores no cubren las necesidades de los empleos disponibles

subsidy (sub´ sə dē) a government payment that supports a business or market (pp. 114, 126)
subsidio pago del gobierno que apoya un negocio o mercado

subsistence agriculture (səb sis´ təns ag´ rə kul´ chėr) level of farming in which a person raises only enough food to feed his or her family (p. 466)
agricultura de subsistencia tipo de agricultura en la que una persona sólo cosecha lo necesario para mantenerse a sí mismo y a su familia

substitutes (sub´ stə tütz) goods that are used in place of one another (p. 86)
sustitutos bienes que se usan para reemplazar otros bienes

substitution effect (sub´ stə tü´ shən ə fekt´) the reaction of consumers to an increase in a good's price by consuming less of that good and more of other goods (p. 79)
efecto de sustitución reacción de los consumidores ante el aumento del precio de un bien, que consiste en disminuir el consumo de un producto y aumentar el consumo de otro bien

supply (sə plī´) the amount of goods available (p. 98)
oferta cantidad disponible de bienes

supply schedule (sə plī´ skej´ ul) a chart that shows the quantity of a good offered at each possible market price (p. 100)
tabla de la demanda tabla que muestra la cantidad de un bien que un proveedor ofrecerá a diferentes precios

supply shock (sə plī´ shok) a sudden shortage of a good (p. 137)
shock de la oferta escasez repentina de un bien

supply-side economics (sə plī´ sīd ek ə nom´ iks) a school of thought based on the idea that the supply of goods drives the economy (p. 385)
economía por el lado de la oferta escuela de pensamiento que se basa en la idea de que la oferta de bienes mueve la economía

surplus (sėr pləs) when quantity supplied is more than quantity demanded (p. 124)
superávit condición en la que la oferta es mayor que la demanda

sustainable development (sə stān´ ə bəl di vel´ əp mənt) the goal of meeting current development needs without using up future resources (p. 491)
desarrollo sostenible objetivo que consiste en cubrir las necesidades de desarrollo actuales sin acabar con los recursos que se necesitarán en el futuro

T

tariff (tar´ if) a tax on imported goods (p. 353)
arancel impuesto que se aplica a las importaciones

tax (taks) a required payment to a local, state, or national government (p. 344)
impuesto tributo o pago hecho al gobierno local, estatal o nacional

tax assessor (taks ə ses´ ėr) an official who determines the value of property (p. 368)
tasador especialista que determina el valor de una propiedad

tax base (taks bās) the income, property, good, or service that is subject to a tax (p. 346)
base imponible ingreso propiedad, bien o servicio bajo obligación tributaria

tax credit (taks kred´ it) an amount that taxpayers may subtract from the total amount of their income tax (p. 354)
crédito fiscal cantidad variable que los contribuyentes pueden restar del total de su deuda tributaria

tax deduction (taks di duk´ shən) a variable amount that taxpayers may subtract from their gross income (p. 350)
deducción fiscal cantidad variable que los contribuyentes pueden restar de su ingreso bruto

tax exempt (taks eg zempt´) not required to pay taxes (p. 365)
libre de impuestos exento de pagar impuestos

tax incentive (taks in sen´ tiv) a tax that discourages or encourages types of behavior (p. 353)
incentivo fiscal impuesto que estimula o no fomenta distintas actividades económicas

tax return (taks ri tėrn´) a form used to file income taxes (p. 350)
declaración de impuestos formulario en el cual se reporta un impuesto

taxable income (tak´ sə bəl in´ kum) the earnings on which taxes must be paid; total income minus exemptions and deductions (p. 350)
ingreso imponible entradas sobre las cuales se pagan impuestos; ingreso total menos exenciones y deducciones

technological progress (tek´ nə loj´ ə kəl prog´ res) an increase in efficiency gained by producing more output without using more input (p. 306)
progreso tecnológico incremento en la eficiencia al producir más usando menos recursos

tight money policy (tīt mun´ ē pol´ ə sē) a monetary policy that reduces the money supply (p. 418)
política monetaria restrictiva política monetaria que reduce la oferta de dinero

total cost (tō´ təl kȯst) the sum of fixed costs plus variable costs (p. 108)
costo total suma de costos fijos y costos variables

total revenue (tō´ təl rev´ ə nü) the total amount of money a company receives by selling goods or services (p. 89)
ingreso total cantidad total de dinero que recibe una compañía al vender bienes y servicios

trade association (trād ə sō´ sē ā´ shən) a nonprofit organization that promotes the interests of a particular industry or trade (p. 193)
asociación mercantil organizaciones sin fines de lucro que promueven los intereses de ciertas industrias en particular

trade barrier (trād bar´ ē ėr) something that keeps a foreign product or service out of a country (p. 439)
barreras comerciales medida preventiva que mantiene a un producto o servicio extranjero por fuera del país

trade deficit (trād def´ ə sit) an unfavorable balance of trade that occurs when a country's imports are greater than its exports (p. 451)
déficit comercial balance comercial desfavorable en el cual las importaciones de bienes y servicios de un país son más altas que sus exportaciones

trade surplus (trād sėr pləs) a favorable balance of trade that occurs when a country's exports are greater than its imports (p. 451)
superávit comercial balance favorable en el cual las exportaciones de bienes y servicios de un país son más altas que las importaciones

trade war (trād wôr) a conflict in which a country places tariffs on foreign goods and, in return, finds that tariffs are placed on its own goods (p. 441)
guerra comercial conflicto en el cual un país fija aranceles sobre productos extranjeros y, a cambio, se encuentra con aranceles sobre sus propios productos

trade-off (trād´ ȯf´) the alternatives that we give up when we choose one course of action over another (p. 10)
compensación alternativa que desechamos cuando optamos por una acción en vez de otra

traditional economy (trə dish´ ən nəl i kon´ ə mē) the oldest and simplest economic system in which people do things as they have in the past (p. 29)
economía tradicional sistema económico más antiguo y sencillo en el cual personas actúan de la misma manera que en el pasado

Treasury bills (trəzh´ ər ē bilz) a government bond with a maturity date of 26 weeks or less (p. 391)
Bono del Tesoro documento emitido por el Estado con un vencimiento a 26 semanas o menos

a hat	e let	ī ice	ô order	u̇ put	sh she	ə { a in about
ā age	ē equal	o hot	oi oil	ü rule	th thin	e in taken
ä far	ėr term	ō open	ou out	ch child	ᴛʜ then	i in pencil
â care	i it	ȯ saw	u cup	ng long	zh measure	o in lemon
						u in circus

Treasury bond (trəzh′ ėr ē bond) a government bond issued with a term of 30 years (p. 265)
    Bono del Estado documento emitido por el Estado con un vencimiento de 30 años

Treasury notes (trəzh′ ėr ē nōtz) a government bond with a term of from 2 to 10 years (p. 391)
    Pagarés del Tesoro documento emitido por el Estado con un vencimiento de 2 a 10 años

trough (tròf) the lowest point of an economic contraction; the point at which real GDP stops falling (p. 294)
    punto mínimo punto más bajo en una contracción económica, punto en el que el PIB deja de descender

trust (trust) an illegal grouping of companies that discourages competition (p. 161)
    trust alianza sin fundamento legal entre compañías para evitar la competencia

U

underemployed (un′ dər em ploid′) working at a job which needs far fewer skills than a worker has (p. 320)
    subempleado término que describe a la persona que tiene un empleo para el cual está sobrecalificado

underutilization (un′ dər yü tə lə zā′ shən) the use of fewer resources than an economy is capable of using (p. 16)
    subutilización capacidad no utilizada de los recursos que una economía posee

unemployment rate (un em ploi′ mənt rāt) the percentage of the nation's labor force that is unemployed (p. 319)
    tasa de desempleo porcentaje de la población laboral nacional sin empleo

uniform (yü′ nə fòrm′) looking the same (p. 235)
    uniformidad aparentar ser iguales

unit of account (yü′ nit əv ə kount′) a way to compare the values of goods and services (p. 233)
    unidad de cuenta medida para comparar los valores de bienes y servicios

unitary elasticity (yü′ nə tėr′ ē i las tis′ ə tē) describes demand whose elasticity is exactly equal to 1 (p. 88)
    elasticidad unitaria relación de demanda con un coeficiente igual a 1

United Nations Development Program (yü nī′ tid nā′ shənz di vel′ əp mənt prō′ gram) an international program to control UN development projects (p. 475)
    Programa de las Naciones Unidas para el Desarrollo programa internacional que coordina proyectos para fomentar el desarrollo

unlimited personal liability (un lim′ ə tid pėr′ sə nəl lī ə bil′ ə tē) when the owner of a business is responsible for paying all the money the business owes (p. 175)
    obligación personal ilimitada condición en la cual el dueño de un negocio es responsable por el pago de todo el dinero que el negocio debe

unskilled labor (un skild′ lā′ bėr) work that requires no special skills, education, or training (p. 212)
    trabajo no especializado trabajo que no requiere habilidades, estudios o entrenamiento especializados

V

variable (ver′ ē ə bəl) a factor that can change (p. 100)
    variable factor que puede cambiar

variable cost (ver′ ē ə bəl kòst) a cost that rises or falls depending on the quantity produced (p. 107)
    costo variable costo que aumenta o disminuye cuando la cantidad producida incrementa o disminuye

vertical merger (vėr′ tə kəl mėr′ jər) the combination of businesses involved in the different stages of producing the same good or service (p. 187)
    fusión vertical agrupación de compañías involucradas en distintas fases de la producción de un bien o servicio

voluntary exchange (vol′ ən ter ē eks chānj′) a transfer that someone makes willingly (p. 31)
    intercambio voluntario transferencia que una persona hace por voluntad propia

W

wage discrimination (wāj dis krim ə nā shən) treating a person differently and paying him or her less because of the social group he or she belongs to (p. 212)
    discriminación de salarios tratar a una persona de manera diferente y pagarle menos por su estatus social

wage-price spiral (wāj prīs spī′ rəl) a pattern of higher prices leading to more inflation and then to a round of higher wages, repeated over and over (p. 325)
    espiral salarios-precios patrón de aumento de precios que conlleva a estado de inflación y resulta en aumento de los salarios, que se repite sucesivamente

want (wänt) something that people desire but that is not necessary for survival (p. 5)
    deseo algo que una persona quiere, pero que no es necesario para sobrevivir

welfare (wel′ fâr) government aid to the poor (p. 66)
    asistencia social ayuda que el gobierno presta a los pobres

white-collar worker (whīt kol′ ėr wėr′ kėr) someone who works in a professional or office job and who usually earns a weekly salary (p. 219)
    empleado de oficina persona que desempeña un trabajo de tipo profesional o administrativo y que generalmente gana un salario semanal

withholding (with hōld ing) taking tax payments out of an employee's pay before he or she receives it (p. 350)
    retención porcentaje que se descuenta del salario de un empleado a cuenta del pago de impuestos

work ethic (werk eth´ik) a commitment to the value of work (p. 58)
ética profesional respeto al valor del trabajo
workfare (werk´ fär´) a program requiring work in exchange for government help (p. 335)
workfare programa ofrecido por el gobierno mediante el cual las personas deben trabajar para poder recibir asistencia social

Y

yellow-dog contract (yel´ō dog´ kon´trakt) contract that some employers forced their workers to sign that made the workers promise not to join a union (p. 218)
contrato *yellow dog* contrato que algunos empleados están obligados a firmar que prohíbe su afiliación a un sindicato
yield (yēld) the annual rate of return on a bond if the bond is held until it matures (p. 263)
rendimiento tasa anual de rendimiento que da un bono u obligación a su vencimiento

Z

zoning law (zōn ing lô) law that does not allow people to operate a business in certain areas (p. 175)
reglamento de zonificación ley que no permite que se operen comercios en ciertas áreas designadas

a hat	e let	ī ice	ô order	ù put	sh she	a in about
ā age	ē equal	o hot	oi oil	ü rule	th thin	e in taken
ä far	ėr term	ō open	ou out	ch child	ŦH then	ə i in pencil
â care	i it	ȯ saw	u cup	ng long	zh measure	o in lemon
						u in circus

Index

Note: Entries with a page number followed by a *(c)* denote reference to a chart on that page; those followed by a *(p)* denote a photo; those followed by an *(m)* denote a map; those followed by a *(g)* denote a graph; those preceded by a PF denote reference to the Personal Finance Handbook; entries preceded by DB reference the Databank; entries preceded by S reference the Skills Handbook.

INDEX

education in, 470, 471*c*
environmental protection and, 491
factors of production and, 470–471, 471*c*
financing development in, 472–474, 474*c*
foreign investment and, 473
globalization and, 490–491
health in, 471
human capital and, 490
international organizations and, 474–476
migration and, 489–490
multinational corporations and, 488
natural resources and, 491–492
nutrition in, 471
physical capital of, 470
political factors and, 472–474, 474*c*
population growth rate of, 468–470, 469*g*
lessee, PF35, PF48
lessor, PF35, PF49
Levitt, Steven, 16, 16*p*
liability, 176, 177, 178
licenses, 367
life expectancy, 463, 465, 466
life insurance, 260, PF28, PF29
limited capital, 176
limited liability, 185
limited liability corporation, 186
limited liability partnership, 178, 179
limited partnership, 178
liquidation and liquidity, 245, 261, PF27
literacy and literacy rate, 433, 463, 465, 466
  in developed nations, 470, 471*c*
  in less developed countries, 470, 471*c*
living expenses, PF35
LLC. *See* limited liability corporation
LLP. *See* limited liability partnership
loans, PF26
  banks and, 246–247
  discount rate, 413–414
  education, PF41
  finance companies and, 250
  interest on, 411
local government
  bonds and, 265, 266–267
  education and, 68, 368, 368*c*, 369
  federal aid and, 360–361, 361*p*
  safety nets, 66
  taxes and, 367–369, 368*c*, PF46
location, firms and, 115
Lorenz Curve, 332–333, 332*g*
Louisiana, 361, PF30
luxuries, 88, 91, 353

M

M1, 245, 409
M2, 245, 409
Maathai, Wangari Muta, 483, 483*p*
machine age, 201
macroeconomics, 56, 291–292, 416
Madison, James, 53
malnutrition, 471
Malthus, Thomas, 381
management training, 181
mandatory spending, 355, 356
manufacturing economy, 200, 331
manufacturing sector, 202, 220
marginal
  benefits, 13
  costs, 13, 109, 110
  product of labor, 104*c*, 105, 105*g*
  returns, 104–106, 105*g*
  revenue, 110
market-based economy, 477–478
market basket, 323, 323*c*
market demand schedule, 80, 80*c*
market economy, 124
market entry, 156, 158
market equilibrium, 149
market failures, 62, 63*p*
market power, 153–154, 160
markets, definition of, 30
market structures
  deregulation and, 162
  monopolistic competition, 155–157, 156*c*, 157*p*
  monopoly, 150–154
  oligopoly, 158–159, 158*c*
  perfect competition, 146–149
  regulation and, 160–161, 161*c*, 162–163
market supply schedule, 100*c*, 101, 101*g*
market trends, 200–208, 201*c*, 204*g*
Marshall, Alfred, 45, 45*p*
Marx, Karl, 19, 36
Massachusetts, 236
mathematics, S22
maturity, 263
McGuire, Peter J., 216
means-tested, 356
mediator, 223
Medicaid, 68, 356, 357–358, 380
Medicare, 68, 352, 356*c*, 357–358, 359, PF44
medium of exchange, 232–233
member banks, 241
MERCOSUR, 444, 445*m*
mergers, 161, 187–188, 187*c*
Mexico
  absolute advantage and, 435
  economic success of, 483, 484

globalization and, 487–488
international trade and, 436, 437, 444, 445*m*, 452
as newly industrialized country, 461
as part of G-20, 491
as trading partner, 431
MFN. *See* most-favored-nation status
microeconomics, 56
migration, 489–490
minimum wage, 125, 213, 214*p*
Mississippi, 361
mixed economies
  circular flow model, 40–41, 40*c*
  definition of, 39
  government and, 41–42, 42*c*
  laissez faire, 39–40
MNC. *See* multinational corporations
monetarism, 416
monetary policy, 401, 410–415, 412*c*, 414*c*
  definition of, 405
  financial markets and, 425
  fiscal policy and, 419–421, 422
  function of, 416–418
  inside lag, 419, 422
  outside lag, 420–421, 422
  timing and, 418–421, 418*g*
money
  characteristics of, 234–235
  creation of, 390, 407, 410–412, 412*c*, 414
  exchange rates, 447–451, 448*c*
  flow of, 407
  limited supply of, 235
  require reserve ratio, 411–413
  sources of value of, 236–237
  spending habits, PF2–PF3
  storage of, 245
  transfer services, 250
  uses of, 232–234
  See also commodity money; currency; fiat money; near money; representative money
money market account, PF18, PF49
money market funds, PF13
money market mutual funds, 245, 267, 268
money multiplier formula, 411–412, 415
money supply, 416
  interest rates and, 417
  measuring the, 244–245
  regulation of, 409
monopolistic competition, 155–157, 156*c*, 157*p*
monopoly
  definition of, 150–152, 151*c*
  economies of scale and, 152
  government and, 153
  patents and, 153

real GDP, 287, 288c, 301, 301g, 302
recession, 283, 294, 296–297, 299, 300,
    422
    discount rate and, 413
    inflation and, 327
    unemployment and, 318
Reciprocal Trade Agreements Act (1934),
    442–443
recreation, 365
Red Cross, 476
redistribution programs, 66p
regional trade organization, 443–444,
    486–487
regressive tax, 346
regulation, 113–114, 113g
    competition and, 33
    government, 54–55
    market structures and, 160–161, 161c,
        162–163
    negative effects of, 55
religious groups, 365
remittances, 490
rent control, 124–125, 125g
renter's insurance, PF35
representative money, 236–237
Republican Party, 384
required reserve ratio (RRR), 411–413
research, 306, S2–S5
reserve requirements, 408
reserves, 408. See also excess reserves;
    required reserve ratio
resources
    distribution of, 432–433, 433c
    efficiency and, 26–27
    limited, 5, 9
    profit incentive and, 138
    See also natural resources
resumé, PF42, PF49
Retail Sales, DB5g, PF39
retirement, 356–357, PF17, PF20–PF21. See
    also pension funds; Social Security
return, 261
Reuther, Walter, 218, 218p
revenue, 344, 350c
    local government and, 368–369, 368c
    state government and, 365–367
    See also federal taxes; total revenue
Revolutionary War, 239
revolving credit, PF26
Ricardo, David, 381
right-to-work laws, 219
risk, 260–261, 266, PF15, PF30, PF37,
    PF49
risk management plan, PF28, PF49
risk pyramid, PF12, PF49
Rockefeller, John D., Sr., 187g, 195, 195p,
    201

Romania, 443
Roosevelt, Franklin D., 66, 277, 277p
    bank holiday and, 242
    fiscal policy of, 386
    New Deal and, 384
    Reciprocal Trade Agreements Act and,
        442–443
Roth IRA, PF21, PF49
royalties, 182
RRR. See required reserve ratio
rubrics, S9
Rule of 72, PF15, PF49
Russia, 36, 479
    economic transition in, 478–480, 478p
    globalization and, 487–488
    hyperinflation in, 390

S

safety net, 28, 66–69
safety standards, 214, 214p, 221
salary, PF44
sales tax, 346, 364c, 365, 369, PF46
sanctions, 440
Sarbanes-Oxley Act, 275
Saudi Arabia, 461
saving rate, 304
savings, economic growth and, 304, 304c,
    305
savings account, 245, 257, 260, PF3, PF5,
    PF10–PF11, PF16–PF19
savings and loan associations, 242, 249, 260
Savings Bonds, U.S., 185, 262, 265, 391
savings instruments, PF17
savings rates, PF19
scarcity, 4, 5–6, 23
SCHIP. See State Children's Health
    Insurance Program
scholarships, PF41
scientific research, 306
screening effect, 205
search and arrest warrants, 71
search costs, 132–133
seasonal unemployment, 315
SEC. See Securities and Exchange
    Commission
secondary markets, 268
secondary sources, S10
Second Bank of the United States, 239
securities, 241, 414–415, 414c
Securities and Exchange Commission (SEC),
    266
security deposit, PF34, PF49
self-interest, 33

sellers
    perfect competition and, 147
    price systems and, 135–136
semiskilled labor, 212, 219
Senate, U.S. See Congress, U.S.
September 11th attacks, 275, 300, 319
service cooperatives, 190
service economy, 200, 331
services, 5, 285
    economic systems and, 24–25
    in free market system, 34
    illegal, 287
    taxes on, 346
service sector, 202, 203
severance pay, 206
shareholders, 183–184, 185, 186
shares, 270, 270p
Sherman Antitrust Act (1890), 161, 165
shortage, 130–131, 392–393
    definition of, 5
    prices and, 123, 128
    price systems and, 137–138, 137p
Silent Spring (Carson), 495
silver and silver certificates, 237
simple interest, 248
single-payment loans, PF26
sin taxes, 353, 364c, 365
site permits, 174
Sixteenth Amendment, 71
Sixth Amendment, 68
skilled labor, 212
S&Ls. See savings and loans associations
small businesses, 172, 180–181, 337
smart cards, 251
Smith, Adam, 33, 36, 40, 138, 141, 141p,
    381
Smoot-Hawley Act (1930), 441
social indicators, 463
socialism, 36
Social Security, 67, 68, 221, 352, 359, 380,
    PF20, PF21, PF44, PF45, PF49
    government spending and, 356–357,
        356c
    inflation and, 326
Social Security Act (1935), 318
Social Studies Skills Handbook, S10–S21. See
    also Critical Thinking and Twenty First
    Century Skills
social welfare programs, 356
software piracy, PF36
sole proprietorships, 172–176, 173c, 175p
Sony Corporation, 437
South Africa, 482–483
South America, 444, 445m
Southern Common Market, 444, 445m
Soviet Union, 36–37, 37p, 443. See also
    Russia
space technology, 59

T

INDEX

X

Y

Z

Acknowledgments

Staff Credits

The people who made up the *Pearson Economics* team—representing Bilingual Editorial, Design, Editorial, Editorial Services, Marketing, and Publishing Services—are listed below. Boldface type denotes the core team members.

Scott Baker, Suzanne Biron, **Lynn Burke,** Jennifer Ciccone, Michael DiMaria, **Anne Falzone, Thomas Ferreira, Nancy Gilbert,** Judie Grudin, Tom Guarino, Monduane Harris, **Brian Heyward, Michael Hornbostel,** Paul Hughes, Judie Jozokos, **John Kingston, Kate Koch, Ann Lurie, Marian Manners,** Eve Melnechuk, **Constance McCarty, Michael McLaughlin,** Angelina Mendez, Claudi Mimó, **Xavier Niz, Roger Ochoa, Linda Punskovsky, Maureen Raymond, Jennifer Ribnicky,** Charlene Rimsa, Amanda Seldera, Melissa Shustyk, **Rose Sievers, Frank Tangredi, Kristen Van Etten,** Ana Sofia Villaveces, **Rachel Winter**

Art/Map Credits

Art: Keithley and Associates (all charts/graphs except where noted) with additional design by Sarah Bennett.

Illustrations: Asaf Hanuka/Gerald & Cullen Rapp: all *How the Economy Works* features art with additional design by Sarah Bennett. Marcelo Baez/Shannon Associates: all *Economics & You* features art with additional design by Sarah Bennett. Funnel Inc.: 32, 40 **Personal Finance Illustrations:** Dale Rutter PF 8; Spork PF 12; John Sledd PF 16–17; Shane Rebenschied PF 22–23; Christopher Short PF 24; Nick Dimitriadis PF 26–27; Sean Kane PF 29; Mitch Mortimer PF 42; Ernest Albanese PF 45; John Sledd PF 46.

Maps: GeoNova

Every effort has been made to credit all vendors. Any omissions brought to our attention will be corrected in subsequent printings.

Cover and End Papers: Speakers/©Christopher Gould/Getty Images; **Hi-rise construction:** ©Luis Castaneda Inc./The Image Bank/Getty Images; **Central Park :** ©Mitchell Funk/Getty Images; **Traffic:** ©Kim Steele/Getty Images; **House construction:** ©Lester Lefkowitz/The Image Bank/Getty Images; **Basketball, Cows, Satellite Dish, Piggy Bank, Wood, Pulley, Grass, U.S. Capitol, Water Cooler, Condiments, Conveyor Belt, Dog/cat:** Getty Images; **Stock Board:** ©Mark Segal/Getty Images; **Tractor:** Hemera; **Wind Turbines:** ©Spike Mafford/Getty Images; **Recycle Bin:** ©ThinkStock/SuperStock; **Tomato & Diploma/Books:** Jupiter Royalty Free; **ATM, Sneakers, Coins, Game Controller:** Pearson Curriculum Group: **Spine:** Getty Images

Title page: Bkgrnd Photo Researchers, Inc.; istockphoto.com

Photo Credits
Repeating TOC Images:
Flag, © Joseph Sohm/Visions of America/Corbis; **Money,** istockphoto.com/Emrah Turudu; **Pen,** Gary D. Gold/Creative Eye/MIRA.com; **Keyboard,** istockphoto.com/joaquin ayllon

ii B, Dynamic Graphics; **vi T,** Jupiter Images; **vi B,** istockphoto.com; **xxiii,** ©Danny Kerr; **xxiv L,** Shutterstock, Inc.; **xxiv R,** Shutterstock, Inc.; **xv TM,** Jan Halaska/Photo Researchers, Inc.; **xv TR,** istockphoto.com/Christine Balderas; **xv MR,** istockphoto.com/Jim Jurica; **xv BR,** David Bishop/Phototake; **xx M,** Darren McCollester/Stringer/Getty Images; **xx T,** New York, 2002 Photo by Martin Rowe, Lantern Books; **xxvi,** Shutterstock, Inc.; **xxvii,** Shutterstock, Inc.; **01,** istockphoto.com/Kativ; **02-03,** PhotoEdit; **16,** AP/Wide World Photos; **19,** Corbis; **22-23,** Corbis; **28,** Alamy Images; **31 L,** MARY KAY INC; **33 B,** Cartoon Stock; **37,** Woodfin Camp & Associates; **38,** The Granger Collection; **45,** Getty Images, Inc.; **48-49,** PhotoEdit; **54 R,** Corbis; **59,** AP/Wide World Photos; **63,** istockphoto.com; **71,** Shutterstock, Inc.; **74 M,** www.CartoonStock.com; **74 TR,** Linda McCarthy; **74 BR,** David Bishop/Phototake; **74 BL,** Jan Halaska/Photo Researchers, Inc.; **75,** ©Joe Sohm/The Image Works; **76-77,** Corbis; **84,** Corbis; **85 T,** AP/Wide World Photos; **93,** Shutterstock, Inc.; **96-97,** Getty Images, Inc.; **102,** Corbis; **105,** PhotoEdit; **110,** Getty Images, Inc.; **112 L,** Corbis; **117,** The Granger Collection; **120-121,** eStock Photo; **127,** PhotoEdit; **134,** Shutterstock, Inc.; **137 L,** The Granger Collection; **137 R,** AP/Wide World Photos; **141,** The Granger Collection; **144-145,** Sports Illustrated Picture Sales; **148 L,** Grant Heilman Photography; **148 R,** Alamy Images; **152 L,** The Granger Collection; **161 L,** Corbis; **161 R,** istockphoto.com; **165,** Shutterstock, Inc.; **168 M,** FRANK & ERNEST: © Thaves/Dist. by Newspaper Enterprise Association, Inc.; **168 TR,** Linda McCarthy; **168 BR,** David Bishop/Phototake; **168 BL,** Jan Halaska/Photo Researchers, Inc.; **169,** ©Masterfile; **170-171,** PhotoEdit; **190 T,** SuperStock, Inc.; **190 B,** Redux Pictures; **191,** Getty Images, Inc.; **192,** Atlantic Feature Syndicate; **195,** Corbis; **204,** istockphoto.com; **217 B,** AP/Wide World Photos; **217 T,** Corbis; **218 T,** AP/Wide World Photos; **225,** Corbis; **228 M,** c)The New Yorker Collection 1970 Alan Dunn from cartoonbank.com. All Rights Reserved.; **228 TR,** Linda McCarthy; **228 BR,** David Bishop/Phototake; **228 BL,** Jan Halaska/Photo Researchers, Inc.; **229,** Spencer Platt/Getty Images; **230-231,** Getty Images, Inc.; **234,** PhotoEdit; **236 L,** MIRA/CE; **236 TR,** US Treasury Dept; **236 BR,** Pearson Education Curriculum Group; **237 T,** Cartoonist Group; **238 B,** Pearson Education Curriculum Group; **238 T,** Pearson Education Curriculum Group; **240 R,** Corbis; **250 R,** Getty Images, Inc.; **250 ML,** Pearson Education Curriculum Group; **250 BL,** istockphoto.com; **250 TL,** Pearson Education Curriculum Group; **253,** AP/Wide World Photos; **256-257,** AP/Wide World Photos; **270,** Getty Images, Inc.; **271,** AP/Wide World Photos; **274 T,** Corbis; **274 B TL,** Corbis; **277,** Corbis; **280 M,** Mike Peters/Cartoonist Group; **280 TR,** Linda McCarthy; **280 BR,** David Bishop/Phototake; **280 BL,** Jan Halaska/Photo Researchers, Inc.; **281,** © C. Devan/zefa/Corbis; **282-283,** SuperStock, Inc.; **298,** United Media; **301,** Corbis; **306 T,** AP/Wide World Photos; **309,** ©2009 Dept. of the Treasury Bureau of Engraving and Printing; **312-313,** Getty Images, Inc.; **318 B,** ©2008 The Howroyd Group; **337,** Corbis; **340 M,** www.CartoonStock.com; **340 TR,** Linda McCarthy; **340 BR,** David Bishop/Phototake; **340 BL,** Jan Halaska/Photo Researchers, Inc.; **341,** © Rudy Sulgan/

Corbis; 342-343, SuperStock, Inc.; **352,** AP/Wide World Photos; **357,** Corbis; **361,** Rothco Cartoons; **371,** Corbis; **374-375,** Getty Images, Inc.; **377 B,** King Features Syndicate; **378 BL,** istockphoto.com; **384 T,** Corbis; **384 B,** Corbis; **387 R,** Corbis; **395,** Corbis; **397,** Corbis; **400-401,** Omni-Photo Communications, Inc.; **407,** istockphoto.com; **411,** Corbis; **416 B,** Corbis; **417 T,** PhotoEdit; **422 B,** Cagle Cartoons, Inc.; **425,** Getty Images, Inc.; **428 M,** King Features Syndicate; **428 TR,** Linda McCarthy; **428 BR,** David Bishop/Phototake; **428 BL,** Jan Halaska/Photo Researchers, Inc.; **429,** © Michael Newman/PhotoEdit; **430-431,** SuperStock, Inc.; **437 R,** AP/Wide World Photos; **442 B,** Rothco Cartoons; **448,** Photo Researchers, Inc.; **455,** Corbis; **458-459,** Danita Delimont; **471,** Corbis; **473 T,** ©2009 Bank of Namibia; **473 B,** Corbis; **478,** Rothco Cartoons; **483 B,** Lantern Books; **486 B,** Cartoon Stock; **487,** Art Resource; **488 T,** PhotoEdit; **492,** Cartoon Stock; **492 B,** PhotoEdit; **495,** Corbis; **498 M,** ©Arcadio Esquivel/Cagle Cartooons. All rights reserved.; **498 BL,** Jan Halaska/Photo Researchers, Inc.; **498 TR,** Linda McCarthy; **498 BR,** David Bishop/Phototake; **PF1 BR,** David Bishop/Phototake; **TL,** Gary D. Gold/Creative Eye/MIRA.com; **TM,** Jan Halaska/Photo Researchers, Inc.; **TR,** istockphoto.com/Christine Balderas; **MR,** istockphoto.com/Jim Jurica; **BR,** David Bishop/Phototake; **PF2-3 Bkgrnd,** istockphoto.com/Sheri Bigelow; **PF2 L,** Sylwia Nowik/Shutterstock, Inc.; **PF2 R,** istockphoto.com/ Brandon Laufenberg; **PF3,** istockphoto.com; **PF4 Bkgrnd,** istockphoto.com/Mark Stay; **PF4 L,** Pearson Education Curriculum Group; **PF4-5 Bkgrnd,** Jan Halaska/Photo Researchers, Inc.; **PF4 TL,** Pearson Education Curriculum Group; **PF4 TR,** istockphoto.com/Kelly Cline; **PF4 BR,** istockphoto.com/Filonmar; **PF4 M-1,** Pearson Education Curriculum Group; **PF4 M-2,** istockphoto.com/Mat Barrand; **PF4 M-3,** istockphoto.com/Amanda Rohde; **PF4 B,** istockphoto.com/Marie-France Bélanger; **PF6,** istockphoto. com/Carl Hebert; **PF6-7 Bkgrnd,** Jan Halaska/Photo Researchers, Inc.; **PF8-9 Bkgrnd,** Jan Halaska/ Photo Researchers, Inc.; **PF10-11 Bkgrnd,** Jan Halaska/Photo Researchers, Inc.; **PF10,** Pearson Education Curriculum Group(4); **PF14-15 Bkgrnd,** Jan Halaska/Photo Researchers, Inc.; **PF14,** Pearson Education Curriculum Group (4); **PF16-17 Bkgrnd,** Yurok/Shutterstock, Inc.; **PF16 B,** ©Ron Chapple studios/Dreamtime.com; **PF18 Bkgrnd,** Jan Halaska/Photo Researchers, Inc.; **PF19 M,** Werner H. Muller/Peter Arnold, Inc.; **PF19 T,** istockphoto.com/Nadezda Firsova; **PF19 B,** istockphoto.com/KMITU; **PF20 TM,** Pearson Education Curriculum Group; **PF20 B,** istockphoto.com/Brett Lamb; **PF22-23 TR,** ©2007 Photos.com; **PF22-23 M,** istockphoto.com/Alexander Hafemann; **PF22-23 B,** istockphoto. com/Karim Hesham; **PF22 ML,** Pearson Education Curriculum Group; **PF22 TL,** istockphoto.com/ Alexander Hafemann; **PF22 BR,** istockphoto.com/Tan Kian Khoon; **PF22 BL,** istockphoto.com/Patriek Vandenbussche; **PF23 B,** istockphoto.com/Paul Woodson; **PF24-25,** Angelo Cavalli/Getty Images; **PF25,** Pearson Education Curriculum Group; **PF30,** istockphoto.com/Mark Stay; **PF32 Bkgrnd,** istockphoto.com/egdigital; **PF32 BR,** © Comstock Select/Corbis; **PF32 BL,** Pearson Education Curriculum Group; **PF34 L,** istockphoto.com/Bluestocking; **PF34 R,** © Scott Tysick/Masterfile; **PF34 BL,** Tom McGhee/Jupiter Images; **PF34 M,** ©Geri Engberg/The Image Works; **PF36,** Pearson Education Curriculum Group; **PF38-39,** istockphoto.com/Martina Orlich; **PF38 L,** Pearson Education Curriculum Group; **PF40,** © Masterfile; **PF46 L,** Pearson Education Curriculum Group; **PF40-41 Bkgrnd,** Jan Halaska/Photo Researchers, Inc.; **PF42-43 Bkgrnd,** Jan Halaska/Photo Researchers, Inc.; **PF42 L,** Pearson Education Curriculum Group; **PF44-45 Bkgrnd,** Jan Halaska/Photo Researchers, Inc.; **PF46-47 Bkgrnd,** istockphoto.com/Sheri Bigelow; **PF46,** istockphoto.com; **DB7,** Billy E. Barnes/PhotoEdit; **DB9 T,** istockphoto.com/Scott Leigh; **DB9 B,** © Bill Stormont/Corbis; **S0-S21,** Dynamic Graphics; **S-0,** Neil Overy/Getty Images,Inc; **S-3,** Jupiter Images; **S-4,** © Michael Newman/PhotoEdit; **S-7,** L. Clarke/ CORBIS; **S-8,** © Michael Newman/PhotoEdit; **S-11,** AP/Wide World Photos; **S-12,** © moodboard/ Corbis; **S-13,** © 2006 Jeff Parker, Florida Today, and PoliticalCartoons.com; **S-15,** Tony Robinson/ SHUTTERSTOCK, INC.; **S-17,** Arlene Jean Gee; **S-18,** William Sallaz /Duomo/Corbis; **S-19,** © Masterfile; **S-21 T,** AP/Wide World Photo, **S-22,** Shutterstock, Inc.

Grateful acknowledgment is made to the following for copyrighted material:

The Associated Press
"Pumpkin Growers in Texas Say Demand is Up" by Betsey Blaney from *The Associated Press, October 20, 2008.* "U.S. Says $4 Gas Not Going Away" by H. Josef Hebert from *The Associated Press, June 12, 2008.* Copyright © 2008 The Associated Press. All rights reserved. Used by permission.

Fair Trade Federation
"Fair Trade Myths" from *www.fairtradefederation.org.* Copyright © 2007 Fair Trade Federation. All Rights. The Fair Trade Federation is a trade association of North American businesses and organizations who are fully committed to fair trade.

Frances Collin, Literary Agent
Excerpts from "Silent Spring" by Rachel Carson. Copyright © 1962 by Rachel L Carson. Used by permission of Frances Collin, Trustee. Any electronic copying or distribution of this text is expressly forbidden.

Houghton Mifflin
Excerpts from "Silent Spring" by Rachel Carson. Copyright © 1962 by Rachel L. Carson, renewed 1990 by Roger Christie. Reprinted by permission of Houghton Mifflin Harcourt Publishing Company. All rights reserved.

The New York Times
"On This Day, October 29th, 1929" from *http:www.nytimes.com/learning/general/onthisday/ 991029onthisday_big.html.* All rights reserved. Used by permission and protected by the Copyright Laws of the United States. The printing, copying, redistribution, or retransmission of the Material without express written permission is prohibited.

Note: Every effort has been made to locate the copyright owner of material reproduced on this component. Omissions brought to our attention will be corrected in subsequent editions.